P9-CLH-706

PRAEGER HISTORY OF CIVILIZATION

The Commonwealth Experience

PRAEGER HISTORY OF CIVILIZATION

SABATINO MOSCATI
The World of the Phoenicians

MAURICE ASHLEY
The Golden Century: Europe, 1598–1715

The Commonwealth Experience

NICHOLAS MANSERGH

FREDERICK A. PRAEGER, Publishers
New York · Washington

BOOKS THAT MATTER

Published in the United States of America in 1969
by Frederick A. Praeger, Inc., Publishers
111 Fourth Avenue, New York, N.Y. 10003

Library of Congress Catalog Card Number: 69-10570

PRINTED IN GREAT BRITAIN

To
The Master and Fellows
of
St John's College, Cambridge

'There was a time when we might have stood alone as the United Kingdom of England, Scotland and Ireland. That time has passed. We conquered and peopled Canada, we took possession of the whole of Australia, Van Dieman's Land and New Zealand. We have annexed India to the Crown. There is no going back.

Tu regere imperio populos, Romane, memento.'
JOHN, EARL RUSSELL, 1870

'*Suivez, suivez, Seigneur, le ciel qui vous inspire:*
Votre gloire redouble à mépriser l'empire;
Et vous serez fameux chez la postérité
Moins pour l'avoir conquis que pour l'avoir quitté.'

Maxime to César Auguste
Corneille, *Cinna*

'Our historic Commonwealth which comprises one-fourth of the world's population . . . has the unique quality of embracing nations and peoples from every continent.'

DECLARATION BY COMMONWEALTH PRIME MINISTERS, 12 JANUARY 1951

CONTENTS

LIST OF ILLUSTRATIONS

Between pages 220 and 221

LIST OF MAPS

PREFACE

'Mr Deakin actually contended' wrote John Morley, secretary of state for India, complaining of some remarks made by the Australian prime minister at the Colonial Conference of 1907, 'that India had no right to a place at the conference table, because not self-governing. I dealt faithfully with him on the point. I laugh when I think of a man who blows the imperial trumpet louder than other people, and yet would banish India which is the most stupendous part of the Empire – our best customer among other trifles – into the imperial back-kitchen.'* This book, however, is written on the assumption that not Morley but Deakin had the clearer grasp of essentials – that there was a difference in kind between states that were self-governing and even the greatest of imperial dependencies and that these differences could not be papered over, merely by the nomination by the imperial power of representatives for that dependency. That was also the view, despite India's equivocal position, of Colonial and Imperial Conferences in the past and of Prime Ministers' Meetings in our own time, so much so that, by agreement, admission as of right to such gatherings became the accepted test of independence within the Commonwealth. Or, to put the point in another way, Empire, its government, organisation, administration and ideas is one thing; relations between autonomous polities within a community of states another. Both are deserving of study but it is the second, which in British history superseded the first, that provides the theme of this enquiry.

This book, then, is about the Commonwealth – about its origins, its development, its pattern and concepts of inter-state relations, its experience in peace and war. That Commonwealth was the heir of Empire, and imperial influences bore closely upon its earlier growth. But it developed a life and made a contribution to political thought and relations, not only distinct and distinguishable from those of Empire,

* Lord Morley to Lord Minto, 2 May 1907. India Office Library. MSS.Eur. D.573/2.

but in many respects inherently opposed to them. It is that contribution, broadly conceived, which is studied in this book. The object is not detailed narrative but interpretation and analysis against a chronological background. The approach is historical, but then so in essence was the experience. The Commonwealth was not the product of political abstractions, but of a succession of historical developments.

A work that ranges so widely in time and space must rely greatly on specialist studies by other historians, and I have sought to make clear my indebtedness in this respect in footnotes and in the concluding bibliography. But I have also, at critical phases in Commonwealth evolution, sought to examine or re-examine the first-hand sources of evidence myself. I have quoted freely (though I hope not excessively) from such sources so as to convey something of the sense of occasion or the temper of debate at such times.

I have many acknowledgments to make. In respect of official records I am much indebted for their help and courtesy to the staff of the Public Record Office, and of the Commonwealth and India Office libraries in London; of the Archives of Cape Colony, in Cape Town; of the National Archives of the Republic of South Africa, in Pretoria; of the Indian National Archives, in New Delhi; while with regard to libraries I would like to express my thanks to the staff of the University and Seeley libraries in Cambridge, and also to the staff of the libraries of the University of Cape Town, of Duke University, North Carolina and of the Indian School of International Studies, New Delhi. I have to thank the Trustees of the British Museum for permission to use the papers of Sir Henry Campbell-Bannerman, and Mr C. A. Gladstone for giving me leave to consult the papers of W. E. Gladstone in the British Museum. The late Viscount Bruce of Melbourne showed me the personal records which he kept of meetings between the dominion high commissioners and the secretary of state for dominion affairs during the second world war, but from which I have not felt free to quote directly; Mr John Duncan allowed me to go through the papers of his father, Sir Patrick Duncan; the Indian National Archives, Calcutta, by courtesy of Sarvasri A. N. Sapru, P. N. Sapru and T. N. Sapru, made available to me transcripts from the papers of Sir Tej Bahadur Sapru; the Public Library in Cape Town enabled me to study the papers of J. X. Merriman; the Canadian National Archives in Ottawa, to whom an expression of special appreciation for their arrangements, both for week-end and (for the indefatigable) all-night study, is fitting, gave me permission to examine the papers of Sir Wilfrid Laurier, Sir Robert Borden and William Lyon Mackenzie King (down to 1922). Three extracts from the diary of the Right Hon. Vincent Massey are reprinted from *What's Past is Prologue* by kind permission of Messrs Macmillan. I am indebted to the editors of *The Economist*, *The International Journal*, Toronto, and *The India Quarterly*; to the Duke University Press and to Radio Éireann for permission to make use of material first published by them as articles or, in the last instance, delivered as lectures in the Thomas Davis series. Nor would I wish to leave unrecorded my appreciation of the patience and care with which the University Typewriting Office in Cambridge copied an often difficult manuscript. Finally it is my pleasant duty to acknowledge with gratitude a grant from the Smuts Memorial Fund at Cambridge for research and travel for the production of this book.

My greatest debt is to my wife, who accompanied me on my travels and has not only checked facts and references throughout the book, but has made criticisms, comments and enquiries on every chapter and also many suggestions for additions from her own reading and research which have much enriched the work.

Nicholas Mansergh

St John's College, Cambridge — March 1968

ACKNOWLEDGMENTS

The publishers and the author wish to thank the following for providing illustrations for this volume and for permission to reproduce them:

Radio Times Hulton Picture Library, plates 1, 10, 21, 22, 26–8, 30, 31, 35, 37, 39, 41, 45, 50, 54, 56, 82 and 87; Confederation Life Collection, Toronto, plate 2; Public Archives of Canada, plates 3 and 67; Canadian National Railways, plate 4; Department for Cultural Affairs, Pretoria, plate 6; Rhodes Museum, Hertfordshire, plates 8 and 9; Illustrated London News, plates 11–14, 20, 34, 42, 43, 51, 59, 60 and 115; Anthony Blond Ltd, plate 15; Australian News and Information Bureau, plates 16, 64 and 65; Alexander Turnbull Library, plate 17; John R. Freeman, plate 18; Punch, plates 19 and 23–5; Imperial War Museum, plates 29, 32, 33 and 62; Press Association, plate 36; J. Cashman, plate 38; Beaverbrook Press, plate 40; Keystone Press Agency, plates 44, 58, 85, 92 and 98; India Office Library, plates 46–8; 52, 53, 66 and 71–3; Massers, Malton, plate 49; Oxford University Press (Australia), plate 55; Central Office of Information, plates 61, 81, 91, 93, 97, 106, 107, 111 and 117; Associated Press, plates 63, 75, 77, 88, 89, 94–6, 100–6, 108, 112, 114 and 116; Associated Newspapers, plate 68; United Nations Organisation, plate 69; Pakistan Quarterly, plates 70 and 74; Commonwealth Office Library, plate 76; Fox Photos, plate 78; Times Newspapers, plates 79 and 80; Central Press Photos, plates 83, 84 and 113; United Press International, plates 86 and 99; National Film Board of Canada, plate 90; the High Commissioner for New Zealand, plate 109; Anne Bolt, plate 110; and C. O. Mansergh, plates 5 and 7 from photographs by P. St G. Mansergh.

I

THE FOUNDATION MEMBERS AND THE NATURE OF THEIR ASSOCIATION

'Free States, like all others, may possess dependencies, acquired either by conquest or by colonisation; and our own is the greatest instance of the kind in modern history. It is a most important question how such dependencies ought to be governed.'

JOHN STUART MILL
REPRESENTATIVE GOVERNMENT

Mr Haldane: 'The mother of Parliaments does not coerce her children.'
An Irish member: 'We do not accept that statement.'

HOUSE OF COMMONS DEBATES, 14 MAY 1900,
ON THE COMMONWEALTH
OF AUSTRALIA BILL

CHAPTER 1

THE COMMONWEALTH IN HISTORY

In the gardens at Peshawar, with the Himalayas towering high behind them, there is a statue to a Colonel Makeson of the Bengal Army and commissioner of Peshawar, who in 1853, at the age of forty-six, was murdered by a religious fanatic. 'The defiles of the Khyber and the peaks of the Black Mountains alike witnessed his exploits . . .' begins an inscription, to which is appended a tribute from the governor-general, Lord Dalhousie. 'His value,' it reads, 'as a political servant of the state is known to none better than the governor-general himself, who in difficult and eventful times had cause to mark his great ability, and the admirable prudence, discretion and temper which added tenfold value to the high, soldierly qualities of his public character.' At the southerly tip of another continent in the gardens of Cape Town below Table Mountain there is another statue, not to a soldier of prudence and discretion but to an empire builder not famed for either, one of whose sayings, 'Take all . . . ask afterwards', impressed itself only too well upon the mind of his friend, Dr Jameson. The statue is that of Cecil John Rhodes, in his familiar loose-fitting clothes, with the outstretched hand pointing northward and the inscription below: 'Your hinterland is there'.

On the outposts of an Empire that has passed with others into history, these memorials and many besides for the moment remain. Some are to men little perhaps, but honourably known, and still remembered in the districts where they served; others to men cast in a larger, more controversial mould, whose past actions still press upon the unfolding events of later days. But unremembered or too well remembered, loyal and discreet executors of policies shaped by other hands than theirs, or themselves determining some part of the pattern of history, here were the prototypes of the men who sustained or enlarged the Second British Empire, which was the precursor of the British Commonwealth of Nations. Many more should be added, missionary and bishop, sailor and merchant seaman, administrator and clerk, trader, financier and entrepreneur, pastoralist and settler, and the engineers, military and civil, who planned and developed the lines of communication on which a worldwide empire depended, and who pioneered the railways which, as the young Winston Churchill reflected on his East African travels, provided 'a sure, swift road along which the white man and all that he brings with him . . . may penetrate into the heart of Africa as easily and safely as he may travel from London to Vienna' and without which 'it is only wasting time and money to try to govern, or still more to develop, a great African possession'.[1] And, in a different category, there was the ubiquitous younger son. But for the time being the two commemorated in the gardens at Peshawar and Cape Town will suffice. Dutiful soldier and imperial 'colossus', they were of the essence of nineteenth-century Empire. The Empire which they helped to sustain and enlarge was refashioned into a Commonwealth. Without the one there would not – could not – have been the other. Yet what have they to do with Commonwealth?

One answer, which has at least the attraction of simplicity, is 'nothing'. Yet it invites an equally simple retort. If the soldier-administrator – the two rôles were not infrequently combined – had not been there to discharge his responsibilities on an advancing frontier, the frontier would not have advanced. Had it not advanced, as in fact it did, the area of the subsequent Commonwealth in Asia would have been to that extent diminished. Had Rhodes never looked and journeyed northward, it is at the least unlikely that the later Commonwealth in Africa would have had either the same geographical contour or the same political preoccupations. Both, indeed, it may be thought, would have been less. But the important point is that they would have been different. Even, therefore, at this surface level the answer 'nothing' may not stand.

There is, however, a more fashionable and at first sight more convincing reply. It is set out explicitly in commentaries or by implication in collections – some of them officially inspired – of selected extracts from speeches and documents, usually dating from the middle of the eighteenth century and designed to show that through the British Empire one increasing purpose ran.[2] That purpose was the enlargement of freedom and independence under the British flag, leading onward and upward to a Commonwealth of free nations. Those who did not further it had the misfortune to be on the wrong side of history and might be discounted or even disregarded. Burke and Durham, Elgin and Grey, Campbell-Bannerman, Balfour, Attlee with Indian Independence and Macmillan with the African wind of change, are apt to figure well in such works or anthologies. So (and very justly) do some of the greater Indian administrators who, before and after Thomas Babington Macaulay's famous speech in the House of Commons on 10 July 1833, and in nearly identical terms, hopefully reflected with him that 'the public mind of India may expand under our system till it has outgrown that system; that by good government we may educate our subjects into a capacity for better government; that, having become instructed in European knowledge, they may, in some future age, demand European institutions',[3] and with him imaginatively concluded that should such a day ever come 'it will be the proudest day in English history'. The last of the viceroys, Lord Mountbatten, who was in Delhi in 1947 to satisfy that Indian demand, and did so with a splendid sense of historic occasion, has his niche. But perhaps the most famous of them all, Lord Curzon, the symbol of Empire in its noon-tide splendour, is firmly excluded. He believed in the British Raj, not as a passing stage and necessary preparation, but as a final state and absolute good. The ever watchful guardian of awful responsibilities decreed by providence, he had the soldiers' favourite hymn removed from the Order of Service at the Delhi Durbar of 1902 because of undesirable allusions to the passing of earthly empires. 'Of course,' he wrote, 'all the soldiers think about is a good tune . . . but we cannot possibly have "Onward Christian Soldiers" at the Delhi Service, because there is a verse in it that runs:

> Crowns and thrones may perish,
> Kingdoms rise and wane.'[4]

And as for self-government for India on the white colonial model, that would have meant, in Curzon's opinion, 'ruin to India and treason to our trust'.

Such contrasts are by no means confined to India. While Gladstone is assured of an honoured place in anthologies of Commonwealth, not least by reason of his peroration on Home Rule, and while Lloyd George may slip in, a trifle fortunately, with his speech on the Anglo-Irish Treaty, the voices of statesmen who with Curzon believed in Empire as a British *imperium* over subject peoples are rarely recorded. There are unlikely to be extracts from Disraeli's Crystal Palace speech of June 1872 on imperialism, or from that eloquent passage in the House of Lords on 8 April 1878 in which he spoke of all the communities that were agreed in recognising 'the commanding spirit of these Islands that has formed and fashioned . . . so great a portion of the globe' and exulted in a dominion of very remarkable character, without example known to him in ancient or modern history and more peculiar than any over which a 'Caesar or Charlemagne ever presided.'[5] Neither will there appear Salisbury's caustic allusions to the unfitness of the Irish, Hottentots and even Hindus for self-government,[6] nor any of the utterances of Joseph Chamberlain tinctured with notions of race superiority, nor yet of Balfour's outraged reactions to the restoration of self-government to the Boers. Where is Churchill on the Government of

India Bill? These men may qualify on other occasions but not on these. And as for Cecil John Rhodes, he never qualifies at all! He was, surmised Olive Schreiner, though later she had doubts even about this, too big a man to pass through the gates of hell. And he has assuredly proved too disturbing a figure to allow on to the pages of Commonwealth anthologies. And yet was J. X. Merriman far from the truth when on New Year's Day 1907 he wrote from Stellenbosch to his ageing friend, Goldwin Smith, former Regius Professor of History at Oxford and long since established in Toronto, that if any man could have said, ' "l'Empire, c'est moi", it was Rhodes'.[7] Republican France may repudiate – though even this is questionable – but it certainly does not neglect Louis XIV. Can the Commonwealth neglect the 'Sun-king' of the British Empire in Africa? 'Know ye not that there is a prince and a great man fallen this day in Israel', was the text the archbishop chose for his address at Rhodes's funeral service on 3 April 1902 in Cape Town Cathedral.[8] But Commonwealth historians prefer neither to know nor to inquire if this was so.[9]

There is, despite this selectiveness, much of the truth (though still far from the whole truth) in the progressive view of imperial-commonwealth history. There *was*, wherever British rule was established and accepted, a *Pax Britannica*. There *was* the establishment of the rule of law. On these foundations there *was* a broadening down from precedent to precedent of colonial and later of dominion liberties. A unitary Empire *was* transformed into a Commonwealth of free nations. The men who pierced the shadows of the future to foresee that end, like those who in faith proclaimed that such should be the goal, deserve to have their foresight – or their insight – marked. Historically that is no less than just. But others, some of them more important in their day, had other designs or other visions. If these are not also recorded the outcome will not be history but a distortion of history, the more seductive and not the less corrupting because it appeals to the heart and the mind of a later generation.

Commonwealth history, leaving aside for the moment a precise interpretation of the terms, would no doubt have been a more edifying, as it certainly would have been a less complex affair had all the signposts pointed that way. But they never did. There was at no time an ordered and general progression. If, in politico-constitutional terms in the late nineteenth and early twentieth centuries there were Canada, Australia, New Zealand and at the last even South Africa in respect of its dominant European cultures travelling the well-marked road, there was also Ireland – always Ireland – as it seemed excluded from it. And when there was no longer Ireland, there was Cyprus, and when there was no longer Cyprus there was Rhodesia. And when there is no exception what will that portend? That imperial history has been 'fulfilled' in the terminology of Commonwealth transcendentalists, so lightheartedly adopted by politicians and even historians? Or that with dominant purpose something of life has departed from the Commonwealth?

The selectivity, like the semantics, of many Commonwealth commentaries will find – are finding – their own correctives. But behind them lies something more substantial: the liberal interpretation of Imperial-Commonwealth history. It was by no means an exclusively British phenomenon. In exposition as well as in origin it owed as much to overseas (especially to Canadian) as to British writers. In essence it may be thought to have weathered well the test of time. True, it tended to discount the importance of 'illiberal' imperialist forces as well as words. In terms of subsequent Irish relations with the Commonwealth the question was rarely, if ever, asked whether it was not more important that Joseph Chamberlain should have 'killed' Home Rule, than that Gladstone should have proposed it; or, in terms of South Africa's Commonwealth membership, whether Milner and Chamberlain's predisposition to war in 1899 were not of more lasting consequence than Campbell-Bannerman's restoration of self-government to the Transvaal and the Orange Free State in 1906–7? In the same way there was too much emphasis on the 'idealist' element in liberal solutions. When they were finally adopted, reasons of state, reinforced by the wish of politicians and administrators to be rid of troublesome problems, played a greater part in that decentralisation of British imperial authority which made possible the transformation of Empire into Commonwealth than such interpretations are commonly apt to allow. These are things, however, which may be thought matters of balance rather than of substance. And it is not, indeed, in terms of the broad themes of imperial policy that the liberal interpretation is most likely to be misleading or deficient; it is rather in its failure, from essentially middle ground, to embrace, or indeed wholly to comprehend, those parts of the Commonwealth heritage that derived from imperialism on the one hand and nationalism on the other.

In respect of imperialism the point may be sufficiently illustrated by the posing of a single question. What was the rôle of force in the shaping of Commonwealth? This is something nowadays little weighed by British imperial historians and even less, and most reluctantly, by Commonwealth historians.[10] 'Rome est dessous vos lois par le droit de la guerre' said Corneille's Cinna to Augustus Caesar. But the extent to which this was also true of the British Empire was rarely examined with detachment. Indeed it came to be thought of as something reprehensible and best forgotten. Yet the Roman occupation of a Britain conquered by the legions is accounted beneficial and civilising on the pages of most

English histories and the Norman Conquest accepted as harsh but providential. There was also a period when in its turn British pride in forceful imperial expansion was proclaimed. Sir Richard Cox in his *Hibernia Anglicana: or, the history of Ireland from the conquest thereof to the present time*, published in 1689, commended his work in a dedication as an history 'from the Conquest' for which the Irish people 'is beholden to God'. But the disposition to such sanctimonious reflections departed with the assurance that had first prompted them. Indicative of the inhibitions constraining later historians of empire was Professor A. P. Newton's criticism of Sir John Seeley's 1881 Cambridge lectures on *The Expansion of England*, for the reason that historically they 'dealt in the main with the great wars of the eighteenth century and this gave the false impression that the British Empire has been founded largely by war and conquest, an idea that was unfortunately planted firmly in the public mind, not only in Great Britain, but also in foreign countries.'[11] It may or may not have been unfortunate, but historically what mattered was the extent to which it was true or false.

That is an important question – and not merely in respect of the eighteenth century. It is also a difficult one to answer with finality. It has been remarked that of the territories constituting the Commonwealth at its greatest extent those acquired in war and by conquest greatly exceeded in area and population those peacefully, or comparatively peacefully, occupied or settled, any semblance of balance between the two that might have come into existence disappearing with the loss of the American colonies. This would seem to be substantially true. But is it sufficiently precise? Colonies, after all, were acquired in ways other than settlement or conquest. Some were ceded, others were annexed, others claimed by right of discovery. Nor, as an eminent legal expert, Sir Kenneth Roberts-Wray, has underlined, is the distinction between them, always clear. It is *not* invariably easy to determine conclusively whether for example a colony was acquired by conquest or by cession. Many of the islands in the Caribbean changed hands in the eighteenth century and during and after the Napoleonic wars. Were they acquired by conquest, or by cession under the terms of a peace treaty? Sometimes the one literally preceded the other but it was not always so. A territory might be exchanged as a part of a general settlement. And how, to take an instance posing other queries, was New Zealand acquired? Was it by settlement or by cession or by right of discovery? Certainly there were settlers before there was cession. Their presence was indeed the cause of it. But the Maori chiefs, some five hundred in number, who signed the Treaty of Waitangi on 6 February 1840 and ceded sovereignty to Queen Victoria in return for assurances and protection, were at most entitled to act on behalf of the Maoris on the North Island and – more important – could not be regarded as possessing international personality. The treaty was not, therefore, one of international law and on this ground it has been argued that its terms did not amount to cession to the Crown. British sovereignty over the North Island was, however, proclaimed on 21 May 1840 by virtue of cession under the treaty and on the same day over the South Island, to which the treaty could not be deemed to apply, by right of discovery. New Zealand, while spoken of in general terms as a colony of settlement, was, then, acquired on the British view by cession and right of discovery. On any reckoning it can hardly be placed neatly in a single category. And what of Cape Colony? It was first acquired by the British by conquest in the French revolutionary wars. It was restored to the Dutch by the Treaty of Amiens in 1802 and finally ceded to the British as part of the general peace settlement in 1815. Was it a colony acquired by conquest or by cession? Since it was taken by force in the first instance, in 1795, the most appropriate answer would seem to be by conquest. More intractable problems were raised by the acquisition of Cyprus, a Disraelian addition to Empire, to be discounted by Gladstone as 'a valueless encumbrance', the annexation of which he denounced, with a characteristically involuted oratical flourish, as 'a gross and open breach or rather a gross and manifest breach of the public law of Europe'. In more precise and more prosaic terms, the island was assigned under the terms of the Anglo-Turkish Convention, 1878, by the sultan of Turkey to be occupied and administered by England. There was, however, no transfer of sovereignty. In November 1914, it was annexed by Britain as a result of Turkey's coming into the war on the side of the Central Powers. There was no force employed, the island being already in British occupation. In 1923 the Treaty of Lausanne recognised the 1914 annexation. Was Cyprus then acquired by conquest in 1914, by annexation in 1914 or by cession in 1923? Similar problems arise in many African territories acquired piecemeal, part by settlement, part by annexation, part by treaty and part by cession.[12]

Cumulatively the variety of historical circumstances and subsequent legal interpretations of the manner of acquisition serve as a cautionary reminder of the risks of generalisation about Commonwealth territorial origins, beyond what was self-evidently fundamental and common to them all: namely an outward expansionist pressure from Britain, exploratory, military, commercial, demographic, missionary or some combination of these as the case might be, applying the means best suited to particular circumstances to achieve its ends. But even if the manner of acquisition in each individual instance is accordingly to be thought of as a secondary, or even superficial manifestation of an underlying historical process, it retains its own particular importance.

Indigenous peoples rarely overlooked how it was they came under imperial rule or passed from the dominion of one imperial power to that of another. For them the distinctions between settlement, annexation, cession and conquest, while of terminological indifference, were apt to remain, possibly for generations, matters deep in individual and group consciousness. This was a factor of varying but often of profound significance for Empire and for the shaping of the later Commonwealth and one that is by no means always adequately conveyed in imperial historical writings with their brief, passing allusions to the negotiation of treaties, the establishment of protectorates, forays on the frontier and the native wars which pushed outward the boundaries of Empire. No doubt that is partly because, viewed in the wide context of imperial policy as a whole, these were small affairs. But things looked and are remembered differently on the other side of the hill. There, if and when it came to the final test of force, indigenous peoples had sometimes numbers but rarely weapons. The possession of the maxim gun, as Belloc noted with brutal irony in simple verse, made all the difference. But it made all the difference not only to the outcome of the struggle but to the way in which it was then and later regarded. The possessor of the maxim gun, and his historians, could afford to take a casual view of an episode in colonial history; the victims of it, on the other hand, were more likely to be decimated, dismayed or psychologically overwhelmed in the face of new and unknown instruments of power. Often, indeed, mere knowledge of the existence or evidence of the power of formidable Europeans' weapons of war sufficed to decide the issue with humanity, if without morality. Then there followed cession or protection. Yet if in one sense the end was the same, the importance of the means employed usually remained.

One familiar story may serve to illustrate these points. It is briefly told in the South African volume of the *Cambridge History of the British Empire:*

Though a British protectorate over the Pondoland coast had been proclaimed in 1885, Pondoland itself remained independent for a season; but disturbances on the frontiers and internal anarchy made it an awkward neighbour. For some time there was a question whether it should be annexed to Natal or the Cape, but Rhodes's view prevailed and with the consent of the Pondo chiefs it became Cape territory in 1894.[13]

The *Cambridge History* does not refer to the reason why the Pondo of the eastern Cape consented. To that Mrs S. G. Millin has supplied the answer – and with no lack of telling graphic detail.

Rhodes [she wrote] travelled down to Pondoland in a coach and eight cream-coloured horse, some machine-guns and eight policemen, announced that he proposed to annex Pondoland, and sent for Sigcau [the paramount chief of the eastern Pondos] . . . . He then offered to show Sigcau what would happen to him and his tribe if there was any further unpleasantness, took him to where the machine-guns were trained on a mealie-field, opened fire on the mealies, and brought down the mealie crop.[14]

Sigcau noted the lesson and ceded his country. There was no bloodshed – imperialism on this occasion and in accord with Rhodes's tradition of avoiding force whenever possible achieved its end by demonstration rather than by use of superior power. That had some lasting importance, as may be judged by the testimony of a distinguished South African anthropologist.

The Bantu, noted Professor Monica Hunter, first encountered the European as a conqueror who had defeated him by superior arms. Of necessity he submitted, but impressed by the European's material culture he was anxious to obtain Europeans' goods, and the trade in blankets and guns expanded rapidly. The generation of the Xhosa who had fought the Europeans was slow to forget that the Europeans were enemies and conquerors. But, proceeds Professor Hunter, 'the Fingos who were protected by and became the allies of the British, and later the Pondo, were prepared to make the best of the domination by a stronger power' and turned towards the government 'the attitude of a people towards a superior chief. The personal prefix U is used before government and it is still thought of in remote districts of Pondoland as a person, an old man with a white beard. The people were prepared to be loyal to their new chief but in return expected to receive benefits from him.'[15]

It is also to be remembered that irrespective of the reaction of the indigenous people, submission to force or to the threat of it was by no means always without recompense. It usually brought peace and had, therefore, a reward which they were often the first to recognise. Here the northern plains of India, as well as a tribal area of southern Africa, may supply examples.

The villagers were, to begin with, frightened of the new conquerors [records Prakash Tandon of the first days of British rule in the Punjab], but fear soon gave way to curiosity and then to controversy. . . . Their manners were strange but kindly and considerate, seldom hectoring or bullying. In their dress, manner or speech there was nothing of the rulers, as we were used to, and yet it was soon obvious that there was no authority lacking and that they had a peppery temper.

I think what impressed our elders most, and what they still spoke about when I was young, was that in the past there had been rulers who were virtuous and mindful of the rayats welfare, but never a whole system of government that was bent to the public good, with no apparent personal benefit to its officers. These and many other things at first intrigued the people and later pleased them.[16]

The judgment, it will be noted, was comparative – the Punjab had had much experience of conquest and for a time Punjabis were prepared to count the blessings of peace brought by a just, albeit still alien administration.

In Africa, the lives of Africans from time immemorial had been determined by force and in many cases overshadowed by fear. Africans accepted the arbitrament of the sword – or of the maxim gun. They were long inured to the judgment of arms. Professor Low goes so far as to argue that Rhodes and the British South African Company succeeded Lobengula in the 1890s 'as the paramount authority between the Limpopo and the Zambesi'.

> In two wars – the Ndebele [Matabele] war of 1893 and the Ndebele rebellion of 1896 – the Ndebele were severely defeated and their traditional political authorities destroyed. The royal salute of the Ndebele was the cry 'Bayete, Bayete'. When in 1902 Rhodes was buried in the Matopo Hills in southern Rhodesia, his body was carried to its hilltop tomb by Ndebele warriors crying 'Bayete, Bayete'; Rhodes was given, that is, the Ndebele royal salute. The last paramount chief of the Ndebele was thus, in a very real sense, not Lobengula, but Rhodes; and in the thinking of the Ndebele it seems to have been this white man who, for all that he had done to them, had succeeded by right of conquest (a right the Ndebele themselves fully recognized, for they had often profited from it themselves) to political authority over them.[17]

'Right of conquest' – the very phrase is alien to the idea of Commonwealth. Yet even with the term conquest limited to its precise meaning it is the case that a considerable part of the Empire that preceded Commonwealth came within its confines by virtue of conquest. Nor was this in any way an Asian or an African phenonemon. The Irish, the French-Canadians, the Boers, each in turn and likewise, at one time or another were subdued in war. At the preliminary peace discussions at Pretoria in April 1902, the British commander-in-chief, General Sir Herbert Kitchener, advised the Boers to accept the British flag and then to try to bargain for the best possible terms in respect of self-government. President Steyn of the Orange Free State asked him whether that self-government would be similar to that of the Cape Colony, to which Kitchener replied, 'Yes, precisely so'. President Steyn retorted that the situation in the republics was not analogous to that in the Cape, where the colonists had never lost their freedom. And he is reported to have continued, 'The Afrikanders in the two republics were an independent people. And if that independence were taken away from them they would immediately feel themselves degraded, and a grievance would arise which would necessarily lead to a condition of things similar to that in Ireland. The conditions in Ireland had arisen mainly from the fact that Ireland was a conquered country'.[18] Conquest indeed, with the qualified exception of the hitherto thinly populated colonies of British settlement, was the background for most member states to the free association of Commonwealth. It was not the only background – had it been there would have been no Commonwealth. But that neither alters the fact that the frontiers of Empire were widely extended by force; nor that the maintenance of Empire, in part at least, was conditional upon the existence of force, even if only in reserve. This was most in evidence in the more nationally self-conscious countries within its confines.

On 28 December 1883, Sir William Harcourt warned Gladstone that when full expression was given to Irish opinion with the forthcoming extension of the franchise, almost every seat would go to the Nationalists, and 'there will be declared to the world in larger print what we all know to be the case that we hold Ireland by *force and by force alone* as much as in the days of Cromwell. . . . We never have governed and we never shall govern Ireland by the good will of its people'.[19] And to move to another people and another continent at a later period, *The Times*, commenting upon the argument of the Indian National Congress that because the inhabitants of India were British citizens they were entitled to all the political rights and privileges of Englishmen, observed 'the contention has no more root in history or in law than it has in common sense. We have won India by the sword, and in the last resort, hold it by the sword'. Liberals were taken aback. John Morley at the India Office privately protested to the viceroy, Lord Minto, that it was not so. But for most Liberals, and especially for those who were avowed or unavowed Liberal imperialists, it was not so because it should not be so. In temper they were at one with Morley, when he wrote to Minto, 'Reforms may not save the *Raj*, but if they don't, nothing else will'; and they were far removed from Minto, when he replied, '. . . when you say that "if reforms do not save the *Raj* nothing else will" I am afraid I must utterly disagree. The *Raj* will not disappear in India as long as the British race remains what it is, because we shall fight for the *Raj* as hard as we have ever fought, if it comes to fighting, and we shall win as we have always won'.[20] Liberals were shocked by assertions such as those of Minto and of *The Times* – more shocked, indeed, than many of those forcibly incorporated within the confines of Empire. Yet they hesitated to press the direct question whether, in the last resort India was held by force and await a factual answer, insofar as one could be given. And why? Surely because any affirmative, or partially affirmative answer would have exposed the inconsistency of their liberal with their imperial convictions and so have confronted them with a painful choice between one or the other.

The sanction of force and indeed the element of compulsion are alien to the idea of Commonwealth, but virtually to exclude from the pages of Commonwealth history consideration of the part these factors have played and of the importance at one remove of power in the making of the Commonwealth diminishes, and has diminished, understanding of many of the political and psychological problems that have beset it. The Commonwealth came into being in revulsion against Empire, but historically it could not escape being, among other things, the heir to Empire. It was not alone among the heirs of the privileged and wealthy in sensing that not all of the riches it enjoyed were 'well-gotten'. In the capital of the former metropolitan power it was easy to gloss over or even to forget how dominion was acquired or extended; it was not so easy in Delhi or Dublin, Rangoon or Pretoria, Lusaka or Lagos. Therein lay the principal psychological liability of Empire for Commonwealth.

The bearing of past experiences of conquest and subjection upon the emergence or revival of national sentiment is variable and debatable. At times it is exaggerated to the point of suggesting that colonial nationalisms were derivative and in essence no more than negative reactions to imperial rule. But on any assessment, defeat or experience of subjection – especially when possessing an element of actual or imagined humiliation – were in nearly all cases both corrosive and explosive in their long-term effects. This was something that the imperial power, both its agents at the time and subsequently even its historians, found hard to comprehend. For example how differently, even where there is a sustained and sympathetic attempt at understanding, are the happenings at Jallianwala Bagh in April 1919 set out and interpreted in English and Indian recollections and records. On both sides the actual circumstances and sequence of events – the mounting Indian violence in a traditionally unruly province; British fears of another 1857; the banning of processions and meetings; the gathering despite this of some twenty thousand persons in the public park at Amritsar, surrounded by high walls on three sides; the order to disperse by troops under General Dyer who, conceivably unknowingly, blocked the only exit; the shooting in which, according to the official report of the Hunter Commission of Enquiry, three hundred and seventy-nine were killed; the subsequent imposition of martial law; the public whippings and the order to Indians to crawl past the place where a woman missionary had been assaulted – all these events are generally accepted and in retrospect deemed disastrously, tragically mistaken.[21] Yet to Indians Jallianwala Bagh came to represent something more.

General Dyer, who had no doubt about the rightness of his action and was heard boasting loudly of it later that year by the young Jawaharlal Nehru on the night train from Amritsar to Delhi, was disavowed by the government of India and dismissed from the army. But debates in Parliament showed he had substantial minority Conservative support in the Commons, overwhelming backing in the Lords (a Chamber wielding a malign influence on Anglo-Indian, as on Anglo-Irish, relations at decisive moments), and sufficient sympathy in the country to ensure a presentation to him of nearly thirty thousand pounds. In India however where, as in Ireland after 1916, reactions were delayed, the longer-term impact was at a deep, dangerous and lasting psychological level. The 'frightfulness' of Jallianwala Bagh and the 'Crawling Lane' of Amritsar, attributed by Jawaharlal Nehru in his *Autobiography* to 'a sudden fear' on the part of India's imperial rulers, became 'symbols and bywords'. They were events that were annually commemorated, and when the Congress met again in the Punjab at Lahore in 1929, delegates' minds, so Nehru recalled, 'leapt over that decade and went back to the events of 1919 – Jallianwala Bagh, martial law with all its humiliations. . . .'[22] Nearly thirty years later, in 1965–6, in the period of the Indo-British tension that followed the Indo-Pakistan hostilities of the autumn of 1965, in the press and in periodicals resentful Indian memories of 1919 surfaced once again. All this was part of the legacy of Empire to Commonwealth. It was no more than a part, but none the less it was a burden, not always to be borne as lightly as complacent constitutional commentators, diligently marking progress Report by Report, Act by Act, along the road to independence, were apt to suppose.

In the last stages of the transition from Empire to Commonwealth, that of rapid constitutional advance conceded by the imperial authority uniting with nationalist pressure for independence, liberals and nationalists found their meeting place – but again not necessarily in mutual comprehension. The liberal-nationalist revolutions of nineteenth-century Europe encouraged a facile identification of liberal and nationalist forces; publicists and historians of a liberal cast of mind were apt to assume that overseas nationalists struggling to free themselves from British imperial rule were necessarily also liberal at heart. But historically no such presumption was justified. They might equally well be – and in some cases were – conservative or reactionary. The political outlook and practice of each emergent nationality was determined by its own social system, the homogeneous or heterogeneous composition of its population, its own pattern of interest and security, even the nature of its economy, and might accordingly qualify or not qualify as 'liberal' by some partly artificial external standard. Whether it did so or not had no necessary correlation with its sentiment of nationality. The liberal 'act of faith' in South Africa did not make the Boers liberal; no sensible person, on reflection, could have found social or historical reasons for supposing it would. But English liberal dismay and chagrin remained none the less intense when it did not. When some half a century later African states achieved independence, there was again, despite much experience to the contrary from the past, the confident expectation that the triumph of nationalism would be accompanied by the adoption of liberal democratic processes of law, government and cultural or ethnic relations. When reality in Ghana, Nigeria, Kenya, Tanzania or Malawi belied expectation, there was at first a pronounced predisposition to reject the reality. Yet here was no isolated or transient phenomenon. There was and is a conflict between the creation of a united, self-conscious, purposeful national movement based upon cultural or ethnic unity, deriving inspiration from past cultural or warlike achievement and the bringing into existence of a liberal-democratic society in which individual rights and individual liberties and all the diversity which they imply are fundamental. The conflict is not resolved with the attainment of national independence; it may indeed then enter upon its more acute phase. Its outcome in each case depends upon a variety of factors, the strength of which can be assessed only in relation to each particular situation. This was the complexity for which the liberal interpretation of Commonwealth history most of all failed to allow. It was of significance, because in the last resort it was not liberalism but nationalism that emerged as the dominant factor in the modern Commonwealth. Yet nationalism in its varying manifestations, as much as imperialism, was among the forces that liberalism, with its pronounced, internationalist affinities, was little equipped to comprehend and much disposed to discount.

While nationalism proved to be the most important factor in the later development and subsequent eclipse of the Commonwealth, the actual concept of Commonwealth remained essentially liberal. That explains at once the extent and the limits of its comprehensiveness. The concept of Commonwealth repudiated explicitly the concept of Empire; in fact it was, as has been noted, in no small measure inspired by reaction against it and Rhodes was too much a part of Empire to be acceptable to Commonwealth. The soldier-administrator at Peshawar, it is true, *might* be absorbed into Commonwealth thinking and tradition, as a precursor of Commonwealth as well as a servant of Empire though such indeed was not ordinarily the lot of soldiers more renowned in the story of Empire. Jawaharlal Nehru, while confined in the Ahmadnagar Fort Prison Camp during the second world war, recalled[23] with indignation how the statue of General Nicholson, who was mortally wounded leading his men to the relief of the Indian capital in September

1857, 'with a drawn sword still threatens old Delhi' and, after independence, no doubt with due regard to his views, the menacing figure was duly removed, only the plinth on which the statue rested remaining to recall where it had stood in the gardens beyond the Kashmir Gate. But while the concept of Commonwealth comprehended such nationalist repudiation of the heroic figures symbolic of Empire, it remained unreceptive to though not uninfluenced by the more extreme exponents of nationalism. Eamon de Valera, if at this stage one may further enlarge the gallery of symbolic personalities, was excluded in so far as it was possible from the conventional records of an evolving Commonwealth, as Rhodes was, though for precisely opposite reasons. Neither Rhodes on the one side nor de Valera on the other were, in Commonwealth terms, *reasonable* men; they were both in their very different ways men of purpose or conviction too intense for discussion. Rhodes, advancing across Africa with the railway as his right hand and the telegraph as his mouthpiece, was not prepared to debate whether painting the map of Africa red was a good thing or not. He was concerned to do it. Nor was de Valera, proclaiming the indefeasible rights of the Irish people to national sovereignty outside Empire and Commonwealth, ready to argue why they were rights or what made them indefeasible. He was resolved to assert them. Such men did not fit into the recognised pattern of Commonwealth. They were however the catalysts of changes which bore heavily upon its origins in the one case and upon its later development in the other. For this reason it is not enough to take the short step of including the symbolic soldier-administrator as being among the men who helped to shape the British Commonwealth of Nations; the larger step must needs also be taken of acknowledging that others, and not least the imperialist-adventurer and the ideological nationalist, have also their own significant place in the story.

But who, to continue for the moment to think in terms of personalities, was at the heart of the story? Whose statue might be thought symbolic of it? Hardly one whose contribution was only in the council chamber, for conflict was an essential ingredient in the fashioning of Commonwealth; not a theoretician, for in essence the Commonwealth was not an essay in political theory but in political pragmatism; not an imperialist, for the Commonwealth had roots struck deep in anti-imperialist soil; not a nationalist in a narrower sense, for the Commonwealth, though composed of nations, aspired also in some measure to transcend nationality. Where then is such a representative figure to be found? In Canada, the oldest dominion? Nationally that would seem right. Mackenzie King, perhaps, the man who to his own great satisfaction was prime minister longer than any man in British history? The credentials are also right. Mackenzie King distrusted Empire and imperialists to the very depths of his complex being; he prided himself on being the grandson of a rebel, William Lyon Mackenzie, who could be termed [though by some stretch of historical realities] a nationalist. But if the credentials are right, the man was not; symbolic figures require a touch of imaginative greatness and that was a gift with which Mackenzie King was not endowed. So while recognising that King represents an important, even indispensable, part of the Commonwealth tradition one must look elsewhere. In past years one would have looked with some confidence to South Africa – have pointed perhaps to that statue standing alone on the lawns below the government buildings in Pretoria of General Botha in the uniform of commandant-general of the Boer forces in the South African war, and drawn attention to the six panels round the base depicting successively Botha as a young farmer, as commandant-general of the republican forces with commandos riding into action before him, as prime minister of the Transvaal 1907–10, at the National Convention, on the steps of the Union Buildings in Pretoria as prime minister of South Africa, in the Hall of Mirrors at Versailles with Smuts standing beside him and President Wilson, Lloyd George and Clemenceau seated behind, as a member of the British Empire delegation. Botha had fought bravely against the Empire, he had helped to bring into being a new dominion, he had served as its first prime minister, he had become a statesman of Commonwealth, a champion of decentralisation and liberty as the surest foundations of unity. Or if not to Botha, then to Smuts, his partner alike in war and politics, his heir in domestic politics and in Commonwealth purposes, the only dominion statesman to be a member of the imperial war cabinet of the first world war and to take part in the meetings of Commonwealth prime ministers in the second, the only dominion statesman also to have his statue in Parliament Square, Westminster. Yet however great the appropriateness in an earlier historical context it would seem ironical now to look only towards Pretoria. In these days of multi-racial Commonwealth it seems more fitting to turn one's gaze towards Delhi, to where the River Jumna flows beyond the walls of the Red Fort of the Emperor Shah Jehan and to the place where, some little distance apart, are the memorials of Mahatma Gandhi and Jawaharlal Nehru. Nehru too had known conflict, had experienced long years of imprisonment and emerged as a defender of Commonwealth, the architect of its Asian membership, and finally the most respected of its elder statesmen. Along the walls of the study of his official residence as prime minister hang pictures of him as the young Brahmin, the Cambridge graduate, the barrister, the prisoner, the Congress leader and friend of Gandhi, and the prime minister of India when the appointed day, 'the day appointed by destiny', had come round at last. Liberal, nationalist, internationalist, he was the very archetypal figure of those later days. Surely here history can have no ironic surprises to spring?

But it is time to turn from the personalities of Commonwealth to the history of it. That it is entangled with the history of empire is apparent and that judicious disentanglement is a major task of the historian of Commonwealth may perhaps be allowed. At the very outset the question must be faced: how and when did the Commonwealth story begin? A name may suffice for the starting point to an answer. General Smuts was the first to attribute the term 'British Commonwealth of Nations' to the group of self-governing states within the British Empire on an imperial occasion. But he did not coin the phrase. The credit for that would seem to belong to Lord Rosebery who on a hot and humid afternoon in Adelaide in January 1884 inquired of his Australian audience: 'Does this fact of your being a nation . . . imply separation from the Empire? God forbid! There is no need for any nation, however great, leaving the Empire, because the Empire is a commonwealth of nations.' The phrase was reproduced without capitals by Lord Rosebery's biographer,[24] suggesting, almost certainly correctly, that its author had used it in a purely descriptive sense. It was a description well grounded in English history – had not Lord Rosebery himself made an elegant excursion into Cromwellian studies?[25] – and one to which contemporary relevance had been restored by the urge within Australia towards a federation of states in one Commonwealth, so that for the first time in history, there would be a continent for a nation and a nation for a continent. But its use in a wider imperial setting was inspired by a prophetic sense of things to come.

For this notion of a commonwealth of nations, the closing decades of the nineteenth century were inhospitable years and Lord Rosebery, chief among Liberal-imperialists, might have later entertained reservations about some of the possible implications of the phrase had he thought about it again – of which there is no evidence. But in the reaction against the exuberant, popular, thrustful imperialism of the *fin de siècle*, the description, usually either with limited application or in abbreviated form, gained currency. On 2 May 1900 at a dinner at the National Liberal Club in honour of the Australians visiting London for the enactment of the Commonwealth of Australia Bill, Sir Henry Campbell-Bannerman was reported as saying:

> The proverb ran that there was no rose without a thorn, and there was one thorn in the rose offered by their honoured guests. It lay in the title of 'Australian Commonwealth'. Where could they find a word more exactly indicating the intent and purpose of that great aggregated community of which we are all proud to be citizens, and which included all the dominions of Her Majesty? In that great creation of the energy of our people in the past

and in the present we sought only the welfare and prosperity of all and to make the commonwealth shared by all for the use of all. That was the ideal of our Australian friends, and how could it be better expressed than by the homely native phrase the 'British Commonwealth'? But we had been too late. These enterprising kinsmen of ours from the other end of the world had appropriated the word, and he confessed he owed them a grudge for it.[26]

Radicals, and more especially Fabians, liked the term 'Commonwealth' and were not seemingly discouraged in its use by Australian adoption of it. Mrs Sidney Webb wrote of a socialist Commonwealth in Britain; George Bernard Shaw, as editor of a pamphlet on *Fabianism and the Empire* published in 1900, wrote variously of 'a Commonwealth of the communities flying the British flag', 'the British Commonwealth' and 'a Commonwealth'. In a footnote, which has the air of an afterthought to repair an obvious omission, he dismissed the words 'Empire, Imperial, Imperialist' as 'pure claptrap' used 'by the educated people merely to avoid dictionary quibbles, and by the uneducated people in ignorance of their ancient meaning', and continued, 'What the colonies are driving at is a Commonwealth; and that is what the English citizen means, too, by the Empire when he means anything at all.'[27] But the use of Commonwealth or British Commonwealth in the singular, of which there are a number of examples,[28] was something different from the use of British Commonwealth of Nations in which the singular was balanced by the plural and in which the unit, which alone was implicit in the first, was matched by the national diversity explicitly acknowledged in the second part of the phrase. A unitary Empire transformed into a unitary Commonwealth was a characteristically Fabian purpose; but it was not something to be confused with, nor necessarily in line with, a transformation into a Commonwealth in which the nationalities provided a counterpoise, or more than a counterpoise, to the centre. What mattered was not the use of a word, of which too much is not infrequently made, but the idea behind the usage.

Early in the twentieth century the colonies of settlement came to be known as dominions and often to be spoken of at imperial gatherings as sister-nations. 'The British Empire,' declared Sir Wilfrid Laurier in 1902, was 'a galaxy of independent nations'.[29] This separate nationhood was underlined at successive Colonial and Imperial Conferences. In the capital of Empire their prime ministers assembled, explained their interests and expounded their views. These views were the views of separate states if questionably yet of separate nations, despite Sir Wilfrid Laurier and many others. In replying to messages of congratulation from the governments of Australia and New Zealand on the successful completion of the work of the National Convention for a Union of South Africa, Chief Justice de Villiers, the president of the convention cabled: 'We thank Commonwealth Australia (New Zealand) for its good wishes and sincerely hope the result may strengthen the wider commonwealth of states within the British Empire'.[30] This was a more exact description. The dominions in 1909 are justly spoken of as a Commonwealth of states within the British Empire.

During the first world war a growing sense of national identity on the part of the dominions, stimulated by their individual contributions and sacrifices in a common cause, rendered not untimely the revival of the term British Commonwealth of Nations. The dominions were states that were in the process of becoming nations. There was apparently at the time no sense of conscious debt to Lord Rosebery or to those who had used earlier variants of the Commonwealth designation. Lionel Curtis, the 'prophet' among that group of young men who served with Lord Milner in South Africa and came to be known collectively as the Milner 'Kindergarten' prompted by Professor Hancock[31] recalled how and something of why it came to be revived. More and more, explained Curtis, he had become convinced that the British Empire stood not for Kipling's 'dominion over palm and pine' but for the promotion of the government of men by themselves, and as a result he felt that the term Empire was a misnomer.

> Then hunting about for a good Saxon word to express the kind of state for which it stood, I naturally lit on the word 'Commonwealth'. I developed the theme that while the Greeks had achieved the city-commonwealth, England had made an immense advance in achieving a national commonwealth; but this was by no means the end of the process of development. The next step in the history of mankind must be the creation of an international commonwealth.

Curtis accordingly gave to a work published in 1914 as *The Project of a Commonwealth* the new title *A Commonwealth of Nations*, and these terms came into current use in *The Round Table* which was founded by Curtis and his friends of South African days to promote the cause of imperial federation.

The designation reappeared in a variety of forms in succeeding years. In April 1917 the Imperial War Conference resolved that after the war 'the readjustment of the constitutional relations of the component parts of the Empire . . . should be based upon a full recognition of the dominions as autonomous nations of an imperial Commonwealth'.[32] In speaking to the resolution the prime minister of Canada, Sir Robert Borden, echoed the phrase 'Imperial Commonwealth' and voiced a belief that 'the dominions fully realise the ideal of an Imperial Commonwealth of United Nations'.[33] General Smuts spoke of the dominions as 'equal Nations of the Empire' and their governments as 'equal Governments of the King in the British Commonwealth'. He was at some pains to let it be known that his use of the term in no way implied his conversion to imperial federation. 'The circumstances of the Empire', he said, 'entirely preclude the federal solution . . . and to attempt to run even the common concerns of that group of nations by means of a central parliament and a central executive is to my mind absolutely to court disaster.'[34] But the term British Commonwealth of Nations admitted of a quite different interpretation. Emphasis might be placed as much upon the *Nations* as upon the *Commonwealth*; upon the many comprising the whole, as upon the whole they comprised and this seems to have been the direction of General Smuts' thoughts.

> The British Empire [he said on 15 May 1917, addressing members of both Houses of Parliament at a banquet in his honour] is much more than a state. I think the very expression 'Empire' is misleading, because it makes people think as if we are one single entity, one unity, to which that term 'Empire' can be applied. We are not an Empire. Germany is an empire, so was Rome, and so is India, but we are a system of nations, a community of States and of nations far greater than any empire which has ever existed . . .[35]

Apparently Smuts did not feel that the term British Commonwealth of Nations sufficed to describe so remarkable a political phenomenon as the grouping of Britain and the dominions, for he went on to observe:

> . . . we come to the so called dominions, a number of nations and states almost sovereign, almost independent, who govern themselves . . . and who all belong to this group, to this community of nations, which I prefer to call the British Commonwealth of Nations. Now, you see that no political ideas that we evolved in the past, no nomenclature will apply to this world which is comprised in the British Empire. . . . The man who would discover the real appropriate name for this vast system of entities would be doing a great service not only to this country, but to constitutional theory

But there were others who felt that he had himself given the widest currency to the most appropriate designation and indeed he himself again used the phrase at a meeting of the Imperial War Conference on 12 June 1918.[36] In Article iv of the Anglo-Irish Treaty of 1921 it acquired its official cachet and in the Balfour Report of 1926 the vindication of the ideas it was intended to express. But the notion at the heart of the Curtis Commonwealth concept, of an organic federal unity, which had been expressly repudiated by Smuts, was progressively discounted by these developments. 'Tonight', wrote Lord Harcourt a former secretary of state for the colonies, after Smuts' speech of 15 May 1917, 'was the funeral of *The Round Table*.'[37] In respect of its primary federal purpose, he was not far wrong.

Can it then be said with some assurance that the history of the

British Commonwealth of Nations began in 1917, when it was so named by General Smuts? It would be tempting but disingenuous to give an unqualified affirmative. General Smuts did not say that he was naming something which had just come to birth but rather that he was seeking to identify something which already existed. 'We are not an Empire. What are we?' It was a political fact that prompted the search for an appropriate designation; not the discovery of a designation that originated the political fact. There was, therefore, if this line of reasoning be accepted, a Commonwealth of Nations before it was so described. When can it be said to have come into being? To this the answer may be sought in the extension to territories overseas of traditional British concepts of representative and responsible government, coupled with the existence of a relationship between such states or nations within the framework of one political system.

Here at least there appears to be firm ground. The line of descent in idea and in fact may be clearly traced. It goes back in the first instance to Lord Durham's famous Report on Canada and to the enactment of the British North America Act, bringing to birth the first dominion in 1867. The Report provided the necessary content of political ideas; the Act the successful application on a national or potentially national scale of the more important of these ideas twenty-eight years later. It is true that neither an idea, acceptance of which was by no means easily won, nor an Act, with limited territorial application, created a community of nations. They did however in conjunction bring into existence a form of government in Canada and a developing relationship between Britain and Canada which might, and did, supply a model from which a novel system of inter-state relations might be – and was – fashioned. British statesmen, Australian, New Zealand, South African, Irish, Indian and finally African leaders were in greater or lesser degree conscious of the Anglo-Canadian origins of the Commonwealth. To that extent it is in accord with the historical record and subsequent political understanding to think of the period 1839–67 as the seed time of Commonwealth.

Commonwealth history from that time is not to be thought of as synonymous or coterminous with imperial history. It is a part, a distinct and in some measure distinguishable part of a larger whole. In so far as the concept of Commonwealth derives from British notions of government, it was the more readily accepted and applied in colonies of British settlement overseas. 'The Mother of Parliaments,' as Haldane rightly remarked during the passage of the Commonwealth of Australia Bill, 'does not coerce her children.' But she was for many years to come still prepared to coerce those who were not. Whether it was appropriate therefore or, more important, in accord with British interests that self-government should be extended to phlegmatic and disaffected Calvinist

Boers, to volatile but equally disaffected Roman Catholic Irishmen, to Indians, to Cypriots, to Africans, were matters of extended argument or open conflict of view. Increasingly however argument and conflict were apt to end one way. English historians attributed this to English enlightenment; others chiefly to the pressures of indigenous nationalisms and of changes in the patterns of world trade and power. But as important as any was probably the fact that there had been an experiment in Canada which was deemed successful. There followed other experiments in Australia and New Zealand; they too were deemed successful. There followed yet another experiment in an altogether more intractable and complex situation in South Africa; paradoxical as it was to seem to a later generation it was deemed outstandingly successful. Each experiment was carried out with an awareness, especially on the British side, of earlier experiments. Gladstone, in drafting the first Home Rule Bill, had assembled for him copies of the constitutions of the self-governing colonies, and to judge by his underscoring of phrases in the Preamble and certain sections, notably section 91 on the Powers of Parliament, he paid close attention to the British North America Act, 1867;[38] the architects of the Australian Commonwealth closely studied the same Canadian model before deciding to depart from it in important respects; Campbell-Bannerman, who thought of Canada as 'the greatest triumph' of British imperial statesmanship, and 'of broad liberal views and nobly instructed imagination', when contemplating the restoration of self-government to the Transvaal wrote out in annotated form the lessons to be drawn from Canadian precedents, for South African application.[39] 'The Canadian Constitution,' wrote Smuts to J. X. Merriman (the prime minister of Cape Colony) in January 1908 'supplies some very useful ideas for us in South Africa'; in March Merriman replied setting forth in detail how the way was prepared in Canada for the drafting and subsequent enactment by the Imperial Parliament of the British North America Act 1867, while in October representatives of the South African colonial governments, meeting in National Convention in Durban to devise a form of unification, had circulated to them commentaries upon the working of the Canadian and also of the Australian constitutions.[40] In its turn the South African example influenced British thinking (not least that of the Unionist leader, Austen Chamberlain) favourably towards an Irish dominion settlement, while the status of Ireland in the 1921 treaty was expressly linked to that of Canada, the senior dominion. Something of that story was repeated in respect of non-European peoples. Early in the century Lord Curzon had spoken in spacious Oxonian terms of a place for India at the High Table of the Empire. When in rather more than the fullness of time that place came to be allotted in a Commonwealth which in fact by then constituted the

High Table of Empire, it was again with particular prime ministerial allusion to the success of earlier experiments, most of all in South Africa, that the great departure from an exclusively European Commonwealth was commended to the House of Commons.[41] In politics as in other affairs of men few things succeed like success.

The unfolding pattern meant a Commonwealth by stages. It did not spring into being fully armed like Pallas Athene from the head of Zeus. There was accordingly, if one accepts the years 1839–67 as the starting-point of Commonwealth, an extended period in which in fact, though not in name, Empire and Commonwealth existed side by side. In the nineteenth century there is no doubt that Empire was the predominant partner. To the young Disraeli the colonies of settlement, embryonic dominions, were 'wretched millstones'. To the older and wiser Beaconsfield, the colonial still came a poor second to the Indian connection. Rosebery and Salisbury, would have agreed with this order of priorities though not without some reservations. Chamberlain would not have agreed at all. He was, complained Curzon, 'Colony mad'.[42] He believed that it was the colonies of settlement, the embryonic dominions of the early twentieth century that mattered and in this he was not mistaken. They were, so to speak, in the ascendant; they were first the daughter-nations, then the sister-nations and finally the equal, autonomous dominions of the Balfour Report. They were within the Empire but they were not of it. Even to Hobsonian critics in the aftermath of the South African war and in the full tide of the anti-imperialist reaction, there was little to condemn and much to commend in the association of young, vigorous, democratic overseas societies with Great Britain. By the mere fact of their existence, these societies made at once acceptable and almost predictable (given the character of British political institutions) the emergence of a Commonwealth. If it be asked why it was that no other European empire was transmuted into a Commonwealth, the answer is that all other western empires lacked the necessary popular foundation for commonwealth. Their peoples, with the qualified exceptions of the Spanish in South America and the French in North America, had not migrated in sufficient numbers or over a long enough period of time to form settler communities overseas which would develop in the fullness of time into nations. The British had. They were a seafaring, migrant people. From the sixteenth century overseas migration had been a constant and significant element in their social history. In the century between the end of the Napoleonic and the outbreak of the first world war it reached its phenomenal climax. More than twenty millions sailed from the British Isles in those years to destinations outside Europe and, while thirteen million of them, including the great bulk of the tragic Irish exodus of little short of two millions in the famine and post-famine years of 1846–55, went to the United States, four millions went to Canada and one and a half millions to Australia and New Zealand.[43] In their going lay the exceptional and indispensable legacy of the British Isles to the British Commonwealth, for it was these settlers and their descendants who, impatient of imperial rule yet cherishing notions of imperial partnership, pioneered a road along which a metropolitan power of itself would assuredly never have travelled.

The dichotomy of Empire and Commonwealth was implicit in the later nineteenth and early twentieth century; it became explicit in 1917. Therein lies the significance of General Smuts' essay in semantics. It was outward and audible evidence that an element existed within the British Empire, deriving from empire yet alien to the very concept of it, and that it was gathering political strength. This was the moment of transition. Thereafter the predominance of Empire gave way to the predominance of Commonwealth. The Empire which in its late nineteenth century expansionist phase had seemed the portent of a future in which by natural process of political selection the fittest alone survived in ever declining number and in correspondingly greater territorial magnitude to govern the earth, was already well on the way to becoming the relic of a heady and repented past. The great powers were becoming even greater, the small powers counting for less and less, remarked Lord Salisbury with evident satisfaction at the turn of the century. But seventeen years later as the first world war approached its climacteric, the terrible consequences that might flow from concentration of power in the hands of the few seemed all too evident on the blood-stained battle-fields of Europe. Within the British Empire, the response was a new emphasis on decentralisation and a break down of unitary control. The many were more likely to be restrained and balanced and even just than the one. In place of the politics of power the British Empire in its new guise must set an example to the world of the politics of egalitarian cooperation. That, it seemed in the sanguine post-war years, was the hope of the future and the contribution which a British Commonwealth, and a British Commonwealth alone, might make to the world.

The balance of interest and forces had therefore moved. But the conflict between Empire and Commonwealth was by no means ended. It continued, as it had been before 1917, as essentially a conflict of ideas. The concept of Commonwealth was sharpened by its critics, imperialist mostly at first, unreconciled nationalists later. Evidence of that conflict was reflected in continuing ambiguities of nomenclature, which had their origins in the speeches at the Imperial War Conference, not least in those of General Smuts. When Sir Robert Borden referred to the dominions as 'autonomous nations of an Imperial Commonwealth' the context suggested he was thinking of them as part of a whole. But General Smuts used the term British Commonwealth in direct association with the governments of the dominions as equal governments of the king. Did they then alone comprise a British Commonwealth within a British Empire? Or was their existence, the existence, as Smuts said in his speech of 15 May 1917, of 'the so-called dominions, a number of nations and states almost sovereign, almost independent . . . who all belong to this group, to this community of nations which I prefer to call the British Commonwealth of Nations' within the Empire, the justification for renaming the whole? Phrases could be quoted to support either view. All that was certain was that the existence of the dominions seemed to Smuts, and to others, to outdate the word Empire as a description embracing the British-dominion relationship.

In its limited meaning, the phrase 'British Commonwealth' passed into departmental usage and a paper prepared by the Colonial Office for the Cabinet on *A Common Imperial Policy in Foreign Affairs*[44] in March 1921 referred to the dominions as members of the British Commonwealth. But, again, did they alone comprise it? Certainly such was the reasonable inference, but it was no more than that.

Neither the Anglo-Irish Treaty of 1921 nor even the Balfour Report of 1926 removed these ambiguities. The Balfour Report described the dominions as being 'freely associated as members of the British Commonwealth of Nations' and 'within the British Empire'. L. S. Amery, the theoretician of Empire (the phrase was A. J. P. Taylor's), who was first secretary of state for dominion affairs, later explicitly confirmed that the implication of a self-governing circle of states comprising a Commonwealth within an Empire retaining its structural unity, was deliberate.[45] Though his interpretation carried only ministerial, as distinct from collective conference authority, it remains of weight. The principal objection to it, that is to say to the distinction between Commonwealth and Empire, was that it suggested, especially perhaps to those with little taste for the future extension of the practice of national self-government implicit in the idea of Commonwealth, a clear division between the self-governing territories on the one hand and dependencies on the other, which might in itself prove restricting, whereas by contrast might not 'British Commonwealth of Nations' used as an alternative to 'British Empire' suggest a continuing sense of movement towards an overall Commonwealth goal? Such was the drift of one strand of debate, with the more precise connotation being felt to presume limitation at a time when no non-European people had been admitted to the circle of the self-governing elect, the more comprehensive one implicitly endorsing notions of continuing expansion. But there was another strand. It was maintained, notably in Canada, that to apply or extend the term Commonwealth with or without qualification to territories that were still dependent was a misuse of or abuse of language. In so far as the argument was about words it was of negligible importance: in so far as it was about political intention there was only one answer. The example of the dominions had about it a compulsive attraction for still dependent peoples and if, as Professor Hancock observed on precisely this point, 'Life within the Empire was flowing too vigorously to let itself be congealed in two separate seas',[46] the chief reason was their resolve that the status of dominion should not remain a privilege limited to European settler communities.

The Preamble to the Statute of Westminster 1931, did not significantly clarify the semantic ambiguities. It further and most closely associated the dominions, which were there listed by name, with the British Commonwealth of Nations but equally it neither stated nor necessarily implied that they alone composed it. During the second world war Winston Churchill sought to cut his way out of the verbal thicket with the comprehensive title 'British Commonwealth and Empire'. It had its appeal to all sections of opinion without, however, being satisfactory to any of them or indeed being satisfactory in itself. When the barrier of colour was broken with the admission after the war of Asian self-governing states, the term British Commonwealth of Nations was foreshortened by the discarding, in practice, under pressures of nationalisms that were not British not only (as was logical) of the adjective British, but also, by general consent, of the concluding national counter-balance to Commonwealth. But even then there was neither a new uniformity nor even a new precision. The London Declaration of April 1949 spoke of the government of India having informed 'the other governments of the Commonwealth' of the intention of the Indian people to adopt a republican constitution and also referred to 'the governments of the other countries of the Commonwealth'. There was in these phrases the implication that collectively those countries with their own autonomous governments alone comprised the Commonwealth, though the former legal adviser to the Commonwealth Relations and Colonial Offices has argued that this implication was not strong and that it would be reasonable to interpret the document as if the phrases 'other governments' or 'other countries' were qualified by a phrase such as 'by whom this declaration is made'.[47] Political pronouncements also were less rather than more conclusive. In matters of nomenclature freedom of choice became a matter of principle. 'All constitutional developments in the Commonwealth, the British Commonwealth, or the British Empire – I use the three terms deliberately – have been the subject of consultation between His Majesty's governments, and there has been no agreement to adopt or to exclude the use of any one of these terms . . .' So the British prime minister, Clement Attlee, told the House of Commons in

May 1949, adding the judicious comment that since opinions on this differed 'in different parts of the British Empire and Commonwealth', it was 'better to allow people to use the expression they like best'. This was another way of saying that at that time the Commonwealth meant different things to different people and in different places and that its nature for that reason was likely to elude those seeking for the uniform attitude, which assent to one common appellation would presume.[48] It also suggested the terms were interchangeable. This was not uniformly accepted in the Commonwealth overseas. On the Canadian view, already alluded to, only with the completion of the process of decolonisation would it be correct to apply the term *Commonwealth* to all the territories within this political association. But in general practice by the later 1960s, with the process of decolonisation nearly completed, the Commonwealth had become the accepted and acceptable designation other than in Australia and New Zealand where British Commonwealth of Nations continued to be preferred.

Names are symbols, symbols of aspiration and intention, as well as of political realities. In general it was because this was so that General Smuts attached much importance in 1917 to a new name for a system of states, to which history could furnish no parallel; that traditionalists were reassured in 1926 with the retention of British Empire in the Balfour Report, while reformers rejoiced at the inclusion of the British Commonwealth of Nations; and that the London Declaration of April 1949, by which republican India was enabled to remain a full member, gave the sanction of governments to the shorter designation of Commonwealth without, however, finally discarding older forms. To the historian of the Commonwealth such variations suggest not refinements of little meaning but essentially conflicts of purpose and aspirations which while not always of lasting significance usually indicated the pattern of contemporary thinking, and as such mattered in their day and are of importance as a guide to the likely developments of succeeding days. To those however whose interests are less specialised they may suggest that the Commonwealth, as Hazlitt condescendingly remarked of the universe, if good for nothing else, was at least a fine subject for speculation.

CHAPTER 2

COMMONWEALTH ORIGINS, 1839–67 ENGLISH THINKING AND THE CANADIAN EXPERIMENT

Lord Durham and his Report

'A new era in the colonial policy of nations began with Lord Durham's Report; the imperishable memorial of that nobleman's courage, patriotism and enlightened liberality.' So John Stuart Mill, at once the source and principal interpreter of many of the imperial ideas of Victorian liberalism, wrote in his *Representative Government*[1] of Lord Durham's Report of 1839 upon 'the Affairs of British North America'.[2] The verdict is the more noteworthy in that Mill, subscribing to a widely entertained opinion, discounted Lord Durham's major rôle in the writing of the Report that bears his name, incorrectly (as is now known)[3] attributing the chief part of its composition to two radical colonial reformers, Charles Buller, who had been chosen by Durham to serve as his chief secretary, and Edward Gibbon Wakefield, at the time something of a social outcast, whom Durham also invited to accompany him to Canada. Mill further recalled that 'the honour' of being the earliest champion of the new colonial policy belonged 'unquestionably' to another of the Colonial Reformers, 'Mr Roebuck'.

Later commentators apt, as is their way, to be more enquiring and more critical than near contemporaries such as Mill, have tended to underline what was not original in the content nor wise in the conclusions set down in Lord Durham's Report. Yet while there is much that is just in their observations, particularly in respect of earlier thinking both in the Colonial Office and in Canada on topics and themes developed in the Report, historical perspective neither diminishes the achievement nor lessens appreciation of the impact made by the Report upon British imperial thought and policies. In a century rich in state documents the Durham Report ranks among the foremost, not only for the range and imaginative humanity of its analysis but even more for the clarity of its conclusions. It was these conclusions, owing something to telling oversimplification, that gave to the Report that element of creativeness which even classical state papers do not often possess.

The creative quality of the Durham Report was not limited in its effect to that particular geographical area – the crisis in whose affairs was the occasion of Lord Durham's mission of inquiry – but in time was to extend from the colonies of British North America through the Dominion of Canada to the British Commonwealth of Nations. The memorial Lord Durham left behind him was in that sense not less but greater than John Stuart Mill could know. For more than a century at least no discussion of imperial or Commonwealth constitutions, whether for Australia or South Africa, for India or Ceylon, for Nigeria, Kenya or the West Indies, was complete without a first reference to the seminal contribution of that moody nobleman, with his dramatic good looks and volatile, uncomfortable temperament – a temperament which made Lord Melbourne, his prime minister, well pleased to see him depart for distant places – with his radical opinions, his aristocratic connections and his great wealth, (Creevey called him 'King Jog' because he once remarked that he considered 'forty thousand pounds a year a moderate income – such a one as a man *might job on with*')[4], who by a brief visit of inquiry to British North America had impressed his personality upon the politics of imperial reform as surely as his father-in-law, Earl Grey, by presiding over the passage of the first Reform Bill, had enrolled his name on the page of English domestic history.

British North America was deemed an important, but by no means necessarily the most important, of British overseas possessions in that second British Empire which came into being with the secession of the American colonies. But among the colonies of settlement, as distinct from colonies of conquest or administration such as the West Indies or even India – nominally under the control of the East India Company until the mutiny in 1857 – those in British North America occupied a preeminent position. This was as much by virtue of their geographical position, their extent and their comparatively long established history as by any immediate strategic or economic significance. In a very particular sense they were a test case. First settled by the French in the early sixteenth century, they became British under the terms of the Treaty of Paris in 1763. Some two decades later the St Lawrence and lake region settlements, designated the province of Upper Canada in 1791, became a principal (though by no means the only) refuge of United Empire loyalists – in 1783 some ten thousand had also arrived in the St John's district on the bay of Fundy, mostly military personnel with their wives and children; separating from Nova Scotia they formed in 1784 the province of New Brunswick – men resolved to escape from the claims of republican allegiance. The nationalism of the United States, Professor Lower has observed, 'is founded on violent repulsion from England, that of Canada originally rested on repulsion from the

United States'. But even for the United Empire loyalists and their descendants, the force of example and the draw of environment remained. As the United States advanced in wealth, power and numbers could or would the loyalties of English settlers north of the frontier remain indefinitely unimpaired? And what of the French? In the fullness of time an obelisk was placed on the plains of Abraham just above the ramparts of Quebec, to Wolfe and Montcalm, to the youthful victor and the more seasoned vanquished, in the colonial war which decided that the future of North America should be Anglo-Saxon. *Mortem virtus communem Famam. Historia Monumentum Posteritas Dedit*, reads the Latin inscription with the name of Wolfe inscribed on the left and that of Montcalm on the right. It is a monument rare in commemorative sculpture[5] and one displaying an honourable magnanimity. But the fact remained (as Alexis de Tocqueville and his friend Gustave de Beaumont who sketched it were little disposed to overlook on their visit to Quebec in August 1831)[6] that it was the French who had been defeated. Others might forget; the inhabitants of Quebec did not. Who was to say when and in what circumstances they would seek to turn back the page of history?

By the third decade of the nineteenth century there had been more than one example in the Americas of successful revolt against imperial rule. If British statesmen were shadowed in their imperial thinking by memories of the Stamp Act and the Boston Tea Party, they were stimulated in their international politics by more recent and more exhilarating recollections of George Canning's calling of a New World into being to redress the balance of the Old. Few could doubt that when it came to empires other than their own the British were anti-imperialist. As champions of successful revolution in Latin America they had derived satisfaction not only from their liberal rôle but from the opening up successively of former Spanish and Portuguese colonies to world and – more especially – to British commerce and enterprise. In conjunction, North and South American revolutions strengthened the widely held conviction that as far as the Americas were concerned the days of political Empire were numbered and that being so, wisdom, combined with commercial self-interest, counselled a peaceful parting from settler-subjects.

In 1837 rebellions in Upper and Lower Canada suggested to receptive home opinion that the time of final severance was approaching. As Lord John Russell put it to the House of Commons on 16 January 1838, 'I repeat that I am not prepared to give immediate independence [but] this I will say, that if the time were come at which such an important change might be safely and advantageously made I should by no means be indisposed to give the fourteen hundred thousand of our present fellow-subjects who are living in the provinces of North America a participation in the perfect freedom enjoyed by our mother country.'[7] 'If we are wise,' said the radical, J. A. Roebuck, fearful most of all of the absorption of British North America into the United States – 'a nation that has now dominion from Florida to the lakes of Canada' – 'we shall see and arrange all matters in Canada and in our other North American possessions so as to prepare them for when a separation shall come, as come it must, to be an independent nation.'[8] But while William Lyon Mackenzie's revolt in Upper Canada, provoked by the lack of responsibility of colonial governments to colonial peoples and strongly reinforced by incipient, indigenous radicalism,[9] had certainly sought to advance the cause of Canadian freedom on a United States republican model, that of the eloquent and impassioned Louis-Joseph Papineau in Lower Canada, stirred by particular French-Canadian resentments and backed by underlying separatist or nationalist sentiment, fell into another category.[10] In this second case, animosity was directed not so much against a distant and detached imperial authority as against the proximate and purposeful British settlers. Alexis de Tocqueville and Gustave de Beaumont had already sensed the existence of this deep-seated antipathy on their visit to Quebec in 1831 and had reflected – not without a certain satisfaction – on the prospect of a French rebellion and even, fleetingly, on the possibility of the restoration of a French Empire in North America.[11]

The 1837 rebellions in Upper and Lower Canada while militarily insignificant were politically portentous. But what they portended was not the end of Empire. The rebellion in Upper Canada was insignificant because the loyalty of the great majority of colonists made it so. There *was* antagonism between Crown and colonists but it derived at root from political frustration caused by ill-devised patterns of government and it was the purpose of Lord Durham's mission to end the one by correcting the other. But in respect of Lower Canada where the rebellion, as Lord Durham noted, was the product of a 'conflict of races', no reforms, political or institutional could (as he also recognised) remove causes of conflict which derived from 'the very composition of society'.

> I expected to find a contest between a government and a people: I found two nations warring in the bosom of a single state: I found a struggle not of principles but of races; and I perceived that it would be idle to attempt any amelioration of laws or institutions until we could first succeed in terminating the deadly animosity that now separates the inhabitants of Lower Canada into the hostile divisions of French and English.[12]

He indicated where responsibility for this situation rested with the confident assurance of a nineteenth-century English aristocrat. 'The error,' he wrote, 'to which the present contest must be attributed, is the vain endeavour to preserve a French Canadian nationality in the midst of Anglo-American colonies and states.'[13]

When Durham went to British North America, representative government was the most advanced form of government in British colonies. It ensured in theory and often in practice a tight measure of imperial control. The governor was appointed by the Crown and was responsible to the government of the United Kingdom. In turn he nominated his executive advisers and they were responsible to him. Over against the Executive, thus constituted, stood a Legislature comprised of two Houses, one nominated and the other elected. The Lower House of the Legislature represented (in so far as it was then represented) popular opinion. Members of that House might discuss and debate; and by discussion and debate thus might, and sometimes did, influence executive action. But – and here was the rub – they could not control it. Lord Durham concisely summarised some of the consequences:

> A governor, arriving in a colony in which he almost invariably has had no previous acquaintance with the state of parties or the character of individuals is compelled to throw himself almost entirely upon those whom he finds placed in the position of his official advisers. His first acts must necessarily be performed and his first appointments made at their suggestion. And as these first acts and appointments give a character to his policy, he is generally brought thereby into immediate collision with the other parties in the country and thrown into more complete dependence upon the official party and its friends. Thus, a governor of Lower Canada has almost always been brought into collision with the Assembly, which his advisers regard as their enemy.[14]

What was it, then, that was wrong with a system which produced such consequences? Lord Durham was clear and emphatic in his answer: It was the entire separation of legislative and executive powers – the natural error, as he remarked, of governments desiring to be free of the check of representative institutions.

> It was impossible [he wrote] to observe the great similarity of the constitutions established in all our North American Provinces and the striking tendency of all to terminate in pretty nearly the same result without entertaining a belief that some defect in the form of government and some erroneous principle of administration have been common to all . . . It may fairly be said that the natural state of government in all these colonies is that of collision between the executive and the representative body. In all of them the administration of public affairs is habitually confided to those who do not cooperate harmoniously with the popular branch of the legislature; and the government is constantly proposing measures which the majority of the Assembly reject and refusing its assent to bills which that body has passed.[15]

Such disharmony indicated deviation from sound constitutional principles or practice. No representative body composed of men of experience and standing would be content to act as a mere law-giving and tax-raising assembly while entrusting the direction of policy to an irresponsible clique of officials. In British North America least of all were they likely to acquiesce in so subordinate a rôle when, as Lord Durham noted, they could see men endowed with no greater capacity for the conduct of affairs than at least some among them filling the highest positions of political responsibility in the United States.

Diagnosis of defective principles of government was followed by Lord Durham's enunciation of his sovereign remedy. It was responsible government[16] – a phrase which itself was to become a part of Commonwealth history. Every purpose of popular control, he argued, might be combined with every advantage of vesting the immediate choice of advisers in the Crown, were the colonial governor to be instructed to secure the cooperation of the Assembly in his policy by entrusting its administration to such men as could command the support of a majority there. The authority of the Crown would remain wholly unimpaired but the governor, in Lord Durham's view,[17] should be given to understand that he need count on no aid from home in the event of his having any differences with the Assembly not directly involving relations between the mother country and the colony. This implied a necessary distinction between domestic and imperial affairs. How was this distinction to be drawn? Lord Durham proposed quite simply by the reservation to the imperial government of matters of imperial concern. He identified these concerns as any constitutional amendment of the form of government, the regulation of foreign relations and trade with the mother country, the other British Colonies and foreign nations, and the disposal of public lands. In so doing Durham made clear how 'very few' in his opinion were the imperial interests at stake in day-to-day colonial administration. Indeed, so certain did he feel on this point that he devoted no more than three sentences to his outline of them.[18]

Responsible government later became so widely and unquestionably accepted as the basis of Commonwealth that the force and originality of Lord Durham's proposals in this respect are apt to be underestimated. Yet in the broader imperial as well as in the narrower Canadian context three aspects of them deserve continued emphasis.[19] The first is Lord Durham's determination that British institutions were appropriate and should be developed in British North America. United States' precedents, especially with regard to an elected executive, he considered only to discard as being incompatible with monarchy. Secondly, the British constitutional practice which he desired to see extended to British North America was cabinet government applied, not as in seventeenth-century England, as had been the case hitherto in colonial territories, but as in early nineteenth-century England, with the cabinet responsible to a popularly elected House of Commons. Thirdly, this association between executive and legislature would, he maintained, not only remove the outstanding cause of friction between colonies and the mother country but would further, by giving control over domestic affairs (which ordinarily loom largest on the horizon of most citizens of all states) discourage notions of colonial separation by eliminating what had hitherto been the principal cause of them. This hopeful conclusion, little in accord with the trend of contemporary opinion, may be thought of as being in many respects the most telling feature of the whole Report.

While responsible self-government was the principal recommendation of the Durham Report, it was not the only one of importance. There was a cultural as well as a politico-constitutional cause of discontents. 'Two nations warring in the bosom of a single state' was a phrase which represented something very close to reality. Lord Durham's response to the threat of a cultural conflict, which if it could not be ended might at the least be contained and then diminished, was to recommend union of the provinces of Upper and Lower Canada. It was a recommendation prompted by his faith in the future of the British race. A radical in politics, Durham was conservative and insular in respect of culture. He believed in the great nineteenth-century march of progress; he noted that English people were everywhere in the vanguard of it and he concluded that the destiny of French Canada, not least in the interests of its own people, should lie in gradual absorption in an advancing Anglo-Saxon society. Before he left for Canada Durham, according to Charles Buller, had seen 'what narrow and mischievous spirit lurked at the bottom of all the acts of the French Canadians; and while he was prepared to do the individuals full justice, and justice with mercy, he had made up his mind that no quarter should be shown to the absurd pretensions of race, and that he must . . . aim at making Canada thoroughly British.'[20] 'I entertain,' he wrote in the Report itself, 'no doubts as to the national character which must be given to Lower Canada; it must be that of the British Empire; that of the majority of the population of British America; that of the great race which must, in the lapse of no long period of time, be predominant over the whole North American continent.'[21] Accordingly it should be henceforth 'the first and steady purpose' of the British government to establish 'an English population with English laws and language in this province and to trust its government to none but a decidedly English Legislature.' And accordingly also the project of a federal union, to which Lord Durham himself had first inclined, must needs be discarded in favour of union of the two provinces of Upper and Lower Canada which would ensure in terms of population a clear English predominance in numbers; for only when faced with such numerical preponderance could the French be expected to abandon 'their vain hopes of nationality'.

There is some irony in the contemporary French Canadian esteem for Durham. He was received with awe when he arrived at Quebec. No governor hitherto had come with so great and – be it said – so liberal a political reputation and none assuredly with greater display of magnificence. Quebec's historian writes of the splendours of the festivities and of the quasi-regal reception accorded to one who as high commissioner was deemed to be of even higher status than that of governor-general.[22] His baggage took two days to land; it included his sporting trophies and the horses he was later to race on the plains of Abraham. Finally, on 29 May 1838, clothed in brilliant uniform, wearing the collar of the Bath, Durham himself rode up amid cheering crowds on a white horse from the banks of the St Lawrence to what remained of the Château St Louis after the fire of 23 February 1834.[23] When he left some five months later in the early afternoon of 1 November 1838, accompanied by a military escort and followed by a procession of three thousand citizens, 'the streets' as Buller noted, 'were crowded; the spectators filled every window and every house-top; and though every hat was raised as we passed a deep silence marked the general grief for Lord Durham's departure.'[24] Yet French Canadian regard was by no means wholly misplaced. If Lord Durham thought the future of French Canada lay in absorption in a greater and more progressive Anglo-Saxon whole, he showed also much concern that this should happen equitably, gradually and by natural laws, as he conceived them, of political development. If he was resolved to bring about majority English-speaking rule, he was equally determined not to allow a minority of English settlers in Lower Canada to control the destiny of the French speaking majority.

In respect of union, which was introduced in a form less equitable to the French-speaking minority than Durham had contemplated,[25] Lord Durham was at one with the outlook of his time and the spirit of the old colonial system, while in respect of responsible self-government he was ahead of it. In consequence of this, the latter was extracted by argumentative and frustrating stages, while Union at once commended itself, as responsible government did not, to the home government and was implemented in the Union Act, 1840.[25] The Act was the first and critical step on the road to Canadian federation. And while in the history of the Commonwealth the coming into existence of the first dominion in 1867 of necessity takes pride of place, in Canadian history the order of priority may well be otherwise. It was from union in 1840, however chequered its subsequent development, that thoughts and possibilities of a wider federation stemmed.

Responsible government, by contrast, aroused much contemporary misgiving. There were doubts in particular about its compatibility with Empire. In March 1839 *The Quarterly Review* concluded that the 'new, and to us, incomprehensible system of "colonial connexion" . . . is absolute separation' and asserted that if 'that rank and infectious [Durham] Report does not receive the high, marked, and energetic discountenance and indignation of the Imperial Crown and Parliament, British America is lost.'[26] If this represented an extreme view, not all misgivings were either unreasonable or necessarily misplaced. Adam Smith had observed in *The Wealth of Nations* that to suggest that Great Britain should voluntarily give up all authority over her colonies would be 'to propose such a measure as never was, and never will be, adopted by any nation in the world'. True, any such intention was vigorously repudiated by Lord Durham, whose declared purpose was to consolidate Empire by timely concession and reform, not to hasten its disintegration. But – and here was the crucial issue – might not the concession of self-government in domestic affairs lead to divided authority, with the local government enlarging its powers step by step until it was in fact separate and sovereign? Lord Durham had laid down (in principle) a dividing line reserving matters of imperial concern to the imperial government, but would such an exercise in theoretic definition stand the test of practice? Delicate issues might well arise. 'It may happen', noted Lord John Russell in a dispatch of 11 October 1839 of such a possibility

> . . . that the governor receives at one and the same time instructions from the queen and advice from the executive council totally at variance with each other . . . If he is to obey his instructions from England the parallel of constitutional responsibility entirely fails; if on the other hand he is to follow the advice of his council he is no longer a subordinate officer but an independent sovereign.[27]

The problem was well put, and although long and sensibly evaded it was finally resolved only in terms of independent sovereignty. Britain, in the terminology of Adam Smith, did ultimately and for the most part voluntarily relinquish all authority over her colonies of settlement.

The favourable impact of public opinion and the Commercial Revolution

Lord Durham's Report was doubly fortunate in respect of timing. In the first place by 1839 public opinion in England was predisposed (or resigned) to imperial, over and above domestic, reform;[28] while in the second place the advance towards free trade, culminating in the Repeal of the Corn Laws in 1846 and Navigation Acts in 1849, progressively diminished and finally ended the economic advantages of a centrally controlled and centrally directed imperial system.

The political liberalism of mid-nineteenth century England was compounded, in its imperial context, of reforming zeal and growing indifference. Lord Melbourne, who did not like being pressed into an active reforming rôle, told Queen Victoria that radicals had neither ability, honesty, nor numbers. Of the Colonial Reformers, radicals in domestic politics, the first was as manifestly untrue as the last was obviously correct. They never claimed numbers in the form of wide popular backing for their imperial panaceas but, in respect of ability, not least in publicising their views and pressing home their arguments, they were well equipped to leave a mark upon the thinking of their contemporaries and even more of their successors. Their immediate influence might indeed have been greater but for their eccentricities. Edward Gibbon Wakefield, who went with Durham to Canada twice eloped with an heiress and it was during a three year period of imprisonment in Newgate for abduction that he had made, in his diplomatically if misleadingly entitled *A Letter from Sydney*, his early study of the problems of colonisation. He conceived, ironically enough, the idea of the respectable middle class settler societies of South Australia and New Zealand, and despite an initial setback in the first instance played a critical pioneering rôle in bringing them into existence.[29] William Molesworth, closely associated with him and remembered not least for his assaults upon the Colonial Office, was sent down from Trinity College, Cambridge, after challenging his tutor to a duel. Charles Buller, a more constructive and formidable critic, created in 'Mr Mother Country'[30] the prototype of an insensitive and irresponsible bureaucrat controlling the Empire from a backroom in the Colonial Office, and modelled (but by no means fairly) on Sir James Stephen, under-secretary for the colonies, 1836–47, and subsequently Regius Professor of Modern History at Cambridge. Collectively the Colonial Reformers formulated the ideas, which, like the first draft of a memorandum submitted to a meeting, provided, despite all the criticisms levelled against them, the basis from which subsequent discussion proceeded. That was their great achievement and their lasting contribution to imperial affairs.

The Colonial Office, associated with the War Office until 1854, was a first and favourite target of the Colonial Reformers. Its range of responsibilities was wide and varied and its patronage, both military and civilian, was very considerable, so long as its dual character survived. Moreover, there was so often disturbance, grievance or even conflict in one part or other of the Empire that the office appeared to draw trouble to itself. As the Office 'at war with all the colonies' it was the play of Lord Derby's wit; but to the Colonial Reformers it was itself a source of mischief, not merely the victim of its situation and responsibilities.

In the dark recesses of the Colonial Office [declaimed Molesworth in the debate on Canada in early 1838],[31] in those dens of peculation and plunder – it was there that the real and irresponsible rulers of the millions of inhabitants of our colonies were to be found. Men utterly unknown to fame, but for whom, he trusted, some time or other, a day of reckoning would come, when they would be dragged before the public and punished for their evil deeds. These were the men who, shielded by irresponsibility and hidden from the public gaze, continued the same system of misgovernment under every party which alternatively presided over the destinies of the Empire.

Of course there was much that was exaggerated. Who, in reading Molesworth's diatribes, would think that the affairs of the much-abused Colonial Office were administered by a man whose greatest satisfaction was to have had official responsibility for the emancipation of West Indian slaves and who has good claim to be regarded as the originator of *laissez-faire* in British dealings with colonial governments? In both respects, notes a historian of the Colonial Office,[32] Stephen 'founded traditions which are still at work in the Colonial and Commonwealth Relations Offices – that the welfare of native peoples is paramount and the autonomy of Commonwealth countries is to be continuously championed.' Yet at the time, the greater impact upon the public mind at home and still more in the colonies was made by the appearance – which sufficiently represented reality – of autocracy, remoteness and secretiveness, all of which surrounded the affairs of the Colonial Office. The Colonial Reformers, it is clear, were not voices crying in the wilderness; they were the sharp-tongued, often intolerant spokesmen of sentiments widely, though not universally, entertained by those few who were concerned with the consequences of *laissez faire, laissez aller* in colonial affairs.

The purpose behind the radical reformers' campaigns against the old colonial establishment was constructive at heart and inspired by a faith which few of their fellow-countrymen shared. It was to refashion the system in terms of liberty, which, politically speaking, meant colonial self-government. In itself this was thought desirable, by Stephen within the Colonial Office among others, for were not colonists, like other people, the best judges of their own interests? But the Colonial Reformers went further. They challenged the widespread assumption that colonial freedom to pursue these interests would lead to separation. On the contrary, they argued, it would encourage a close and mutually advantageous association in liberty. The saying 'Emancipate your Colonies', according to Molesworth, meant more at that time than usually appeared. It was used, by some at least, to convey the opinion 'that a country like this would be better without colonies, and even that it would have been better for us if we had never had colonies'. And he proceeded to say to the House of Commons:

> Instead of wishing to separate from our colonies, or to avert the establishment of new ones, I would say distinguish between the evil and the good; remove the evil, but preserve the good; do not 'Emancipate your Colonies', but multiply them, and improve – reform your system of colonial government.[33]

'The experiment of keeping colonies and governing them well', Lord Durham maintained, 'ought to have a trial.' Even if it did, contrary to his own expectation, lead to separation then, at least, there would be the satisfaction of a parting in friendship and with the assurance that 'the British colonies should not be the only countries on the American continent in which the Anglo-Saxon race shall be found unfit to govern itself.'

The cause of the Colonial Reformers was advanced chiefly by circumstance. On 2 February 1848, the first responsible ministry in a British colony was formally instituted, not unfittingly in Nova Scotia, the oldest British colony in the Second Empire. But its formation was the consequence, not of British conversion to the concept of responsible, colonial government in the abstract, but of British appreciation of the relevance of the idea to situations in which they were faced with sustained and mounting pressure of colonial demand for an administration responsive to the opinion of elected representatives. Where Nova Scotia led others followed, but in each instance less because of principle than because of considerations of practical advantage. Yet it was all-important that the idea should have been formulated by Durham in his Report and developed by his reformist friends in argument in advance of the days when colonial demand moved towards its climax. Concessions as a consequence, could, and indeed did, rest upon reasoned conviction.

That conviction at this as at other times was notably assisted by the resigned wisdom – reinforced by niggardliness and verging on indifference – of established statesmen and parties. It was well summed up in a private letter from Lord Grey at the Colonial Office to Lord Elgin in Canada, written on 18 May 1849, in which he observed:

> The main object of our policy ought to be to support the hopes and courage of the Canadians . . . but unfortunately there begins to prevail in the House of Commons and I am sorry to say in the highest quarters, an opinion (which I believe to be utterly erroneous) that we have no interest in preserving our colonies and ought therefore to make no sacrifice for that purpose. Peel, Graham and Gladstone, if they do not avow this opinion as openly as Cobden and his friends, yet betray very clearly that they entertain it, nor do I find

some members of the cabinet free from it, so that I am powerless to do anything which involves expense – it is the existence of this feeling here which is to me by far the most serious cause of apprehension for the future.[34]

In the fastnesses of the Colonial Office, Sir James Stephen, who never visited any colony, entertained much the same notions. 'It remains,' he wrote, 'for the Canadians to cut the last cable which anchors them to us. . . . The same process is in progress in the Australian colonies.' But, it is worth remarking, it was British acquiescence in a Canadian initiative that he contemplated and indeed thought right. Responsibility for any final break must in his view rest with the colonists themselves. Even in respect of the smaller colonies which he described – in a foreshadowing of a more famous Disraelian phrase – as 'wretched burdens', responsibility for which 'in an evil hour we assumed, we have no right to lay down again, unless relieved of the moral obligation by the initiative of the colonists themselves'. Lord Derby, with something of the underlying note of fatalism to be found in Stephen's comments, summed up prevailing opinion well in a debate in the House of Lords in 1854: 'If the North American colonies,' he said, 'increasing in wealth, in population and in importance desire to part from this country, in God's name let us part in terms of peace and friendship.'[35]

This viewpoint was indeed understandable and well-nigh predetermined by the lessons drawn from the apparently conclusive precedent of the American colonies. It was not merely that they had seceded but that in one of the best remembered of historical forecasts Turgot had declared a quarter of a century before the Declaration of Independence that 'colonies are like fruits which cling to the tree only till they ripen' and that accordingly as soon as the American colonies could take care of themselves they would do 'what Carthage did'.

Most of the permanent under-secretaries for the colonies during the early decades of Queen Victoria's reign [wrote Professor D. G. Creighton][36] subscribed to what may be called the pomological view of colonies – the view, that is, that all colonies, like ripe apples, were destined inevitably to drop off the parent tree. They and their contemporaries showed little disposition to arrest the fall. There was scarcely a front-rank statesman in early Victorian England who was not prepared to view the departure of the colonies with cheerfulness decorously mingled with resignation.

The resignation, at least, was comprehensible. If parting was inevitable did not statesmanship demand that this time the parting should be amicable? Why resist the inevitable unravelling of an imperial-colonial relationship? Why not, instead, accede to colonial demands for responsible government as they were advanced and so bring about the withdrawal of imperial authority by stages until responsibility was finally taken over by a successor government not inexperienced in the conduct of affairs?

A widespread presumption about the probable course of events enhanced the probability of its occurrence. Or so at least it has been argued by C. A. Bodelsen, on the ground that the constant talk about the necessity and desirability of separation, by exasperating and wounding colonial loyalties actually brought separation nearer. On the other hand, he has noted – and this at least is hardly open to dispute – that the liberal policy of almost unlimited self-government and the constant yielding to colonial demands, to which the continuance of the connection was chiefly due, was greatly facilitated by the conviction that the connection would not in any case long survive. 'Paradoxically,' Bodelsen concluded,[37] 'the Separatists may thus be said to have contributed their share towards the continued unity of the Empire.'

Political liberalism in colonial affairs, compounded as it was of so many attitudes, considerations and emotions, would hardly have advanced so far or so fast had it not been paralleled by the successful culmination of the campaign for free trade. Britain, the industrial workshop of the world, had thereafter little or no interest in remaining cabined and constricted within the confines of the imperial economic system which she had herself constructed. The world, not the Empire, was or was rapidly becoming her market. Britain (in Professor Hancock's telling phrase),[38] 'the imperial metropolis of a far-flung polity', was becoming, 'the commercial metropolis of a farther-flung economy'. And to the free traders, to Cobden and to Bright, the obliteration of the economic frontier between the Empire and the world was not a matter of accident; it was a fundamental article of faith. The world must be opened to the trade of all nations for by trade came both profit and peace among men.

> For the Second Empire [wrote Professor Creighton in 1938] the meaning of the new industrialism and the new political economy was all too clear. It was not that the English had unselfishly abandoned the urge for empire: it was simply that they had substituted the new, divinely-inspired imperialism for the old, simple-minded, sinful imperialism of the First Empire. They looked beyond the limits of their stunted domination of the world.[39]

Expanding economic interests reinforced by faith in free trade thus demanded the final winding up of the old colonial system, and with the repeal of the Navigation Laws in 1849 it was formally laid to rest.

The free traders, accordingly, far from being hostile to colonial independence tended to favour it, not least as a means of reducing imperial expenditure.

> Hawes [wrote Lord Grey from Howick to Elgin in Canada on 22 August

1849][40] received the other day a letter from Cobden which I think it desirable you should see as there is a good deal of truth in the representation it gives of the state of public opinion here on the subject of the colonies – it is impossible to disguise from oneself that there is a growing impatience as to the amount of expense they occasion and a strong feeling that they ought during peace to pay for their own military expenditure, nor can I deny that there is some justice in this. . . . To proceed as Cobden and his friends would wish would be to abandon the greater part at all events of our colonies which I am old fashioned enough to believe would be a national misfortune, and what is more a misfortune to the civilised world . . .'.

Cobden would certainly have thought such sentiments old fashioned, if not deliberately perverse. But they could also be discounted, as the claims of colonial expenditure could not. For their reduction, a campaign of criticism against the cost of colonies was required and it was pursued in succeeding years.

For the colonies, and especially those in British North America, the transition from the old colonial system to the new free trade era was in some instances painful. One Canadian historian, Professor Creighton, has written of the British adoption of free trade as 'a major catastrophe', followed as it was by profound, if short lived, depression in the North American colonies; he has concluded that the Empire was nearly broken on responsible government and a fiscal revolution carried through in British, not colonial, interests. It was not, he remarks in a telling paradox, the colonies that had separated from Britain, but Britain that had broken away from her own Empire.[41] This, however much it may need qualification (unless indeed the view be taken that the real bonds of Empire were all, or chiefly, economic), focuses attention on the central fact of a British imperial initiative which demanded colonial readjustment in response.

The severance of exclusive trading ties in itself demanded reconsideration of the purposes of Empire. In April 1851 the Editors of *The Edinburgh Review* undertook the task. They noted that in former times colonies were valued as an outlet for manufactures and as sources of supply 'for needful products which we could not obtain, or could not obtain so cheaply or so well, elsewhere'. They were 'the principal and the surest channels for that commerce which we felt to be the life-blood of the nation'. They were bound to the mother country in the bonds of a strict and mutually favouring system of customs duties; 'we compelled them to trade with us exclusively, to take from us exclusively all the articles with which we could supply them; and to send us exclusively all the produce of their soil . . . our colonies were *customers who could not escape us*, and vendors who could sell to us alone.'

But all that was gone, to be replaced by a new system based upon radically different notions. All protective and discriminating tariffs had been removed and Great Britain no longer favoured colonial products and could no longer compel the colonies to favour hers. The colonies had thus become friendly trading communities, nothing more. 'The very object for which we founded, governed, defended and cherished them has been abandoned; why then should we any longer incur the cost of their maintenance?' Why indeed, when this cost had been estimated by Sir William Molesworth to amount to four million pounds a year, nearly equal to the proceeds of income tax which could, were the colonies abandoned, be repealed 'to the infinite relief of our people.'

Was the fiscal argument against Empire conclusive? Certainly there were many ardent free traders who were prepared to think so and in this they had strong support from Goldwin Smith, Regius Professor of History at Oxford. 'The time was,' he observed in retrospect in 1863, 'when the universal prevalence of commercial monopoly made it worth our while to hold colonies in dependence for the sake of commanding their trade. But that time has gone. Trade is everywhere free or becoming free; and this expensive and perilous connection has entirely survived its sole legitimate cause.' This was, characteristically, an extreme statement. But it was not, it will be noted, an anti-colonial expression of view theoretically advanced; it was an argument against political Empire in a free-trade era. The distinction is not without importance. The so-called and now much questioned anti-imperialism of free trade was by no means, even on its own evaluation, necessarily anti-imperialist in absolute terms. An early and formidable critic of liberal interpretations of nineteenth-century imperial history, Professor Creighton, noted on the contrary that 'the heart of the whole movement was Manchester – Manchester, the centre of the new imperialism masquerading in a sober anti-imperialist disguise'.[42] A free trader accordingly might be and usually was anti-imperialist in the particular circumstances of mid-Victorian England because he believed that the essential purposes of Empire might be promoted more effectively when freed from the entanglements of a now outdated political system. In a deeper sense, however, he might be moved by an imperialism as real as that of his predecessors and more 'arrogant' – the term is Professor Creighton's – than that of his late nineteenth-century, territorially expansionist successors. Or to put the point rather differently and more broadly (using terminology which has been given wide circulation by Professor Gallagher and Dr Robinson's frontal assault on traditional concepts of an anti-imperialist mid-Victorian and an imperialist late Victorian period in British history, and to view in one wide perspective the formal Empire over which Britain exercised political control and the informal Empire over which she maintained influence and pursued her interests by means of indirect control in some form or another) it can be persuasively argued, as they have done, that the so-called anti-imperialist and so-called imperialist phases were no more than superficial manifestations of one underlying purpose. The difference, the authors conclude, 'between formal and informal Empire has not been one of fundamental nature but of degree'.[43] The new economic enlightenment, sensible of the advantages to Britain at that time of informal economic control and anxious for Britain to be free of burdensome and expensive direct political responsibility, did not in reality, as it did in outward appearance, necessarily imply departure from – let alone transcendence of – old imperial motivations. On the contrary, the period of its unquestioned predominance coincided – and not fortuitously – with significant extensions of formal and a notable expansion of informal Empire. But despite this apparent paradox the new thinking did predispose British statesmen to contemplate more readily the advantages, both to Britain and to colonies of settlement, of extending measures of self-government that might lead to independence. In the history of the Commonwealth this has lost none of its importance. Without such predisposition on the British side (whatever the motive that inspired it) there would not have been a Commonwealth. Relaxation of metropolitan control at a critical phase in imperial history opened the way to friendly association as against colonial secession on the earlier American model. That the British government in its so-called anti-imperialist phase should continue to acquire new territories in India and Africa was irrelevant in this context. British colonists overseas were at the most only remotely interested in general theories of imperial policy and their application. What concerned them was its direct impact upon the conduct of their affairs. And in that limited context the 'anti-imperialism' of mid-Victorian years marked a break, decisive for a Commonwealth future, with the imperialism of the preceding age.

The argument of Empire was, however, conducted at the time in less abstract terms. *The Edinburgh Review*, in the same article in which it presented the case against retaining our colonies, supplied the counterbalancing arguments *for* Empire. On a point of fact the cost to Great Britain of her colonial Empire, fairly calculated, by 1850 came to two million pounds a year rather than the four million alleged by Molesworth (though admittedly it had been far greater). For the rest, the arguments ran on lines which were to be familiar for a century or more. The colonies, the article noted, did not desire independence and were not therefore unwilling or troublesome dependencies. They might hate the Colonial Office; they did not hate England. England in any case was so bound to them by ties of blood and affection that even if they were independent she would, if need arose, come to their defence. They were countries with expanding populations, possessing most valuable opportunities for commercial enterprise, with whom therefore, on grounds of long-term self-interest alone, the closest ties should be maintained. Their populations were partly or largely British and with growing pressure of numbers at home it was of the greatest importance that the colonies should remain an easy, natural outlet for British overseas migration. Nor should humanitarian considerations be overlooked. There were British obligations to minorities and to peoples of other races in these colonies which it would be dishonourable to discard. In sum therefore, what the situation demanded was not – as purely fiscal considerations might suggest – the abandonment of the colonies but continued rule, exercised with forbearance and justice, leading the colonies forward to the fullest self-government where there was a sufficient infusion of British blood to warrant it. The goal should be the existence and cohesion of a vast dominion 'blest with the . . . most beneficial form of liberty which the world has yet enjoyed'.

With one reservation or qualification this was the language of Commonwealth. What had been modified some seventy years later was the association, common to Lord Durham's *Report*, *The Edinburgh Review* and most nineteenth-century commentaries, of self-government with people of British origin who alone, by reason of history and aptitude in the art of government, were thought qualified to exercise its responsibilities. It was because this opinion was then so widely entertained that the settlement of British peoples overseas was felt to be at once of advantage to Britain, of most significant service to the fulfilment of the continuing purposes of Empire, and a contribution to world peace by extending the areas fitted for the highest recognised form of government. *The Times*, on 4 February 1862, reacting sharply to one more plea from Goldwin Smith in Oxford for the dismemberment of the queen's dominions 'with as little delay as possible', rested its case for Empire not exclusively but most weightily upon the opportunities it afforded and the advantages it offered for continuing British settlement overseas. British settlements abroad, *The Times* argued, were large elements in England's mercantile greatness. Not even the conquest of India had excited more the admiration of foreign nations than the colonisation of Australia.

> Every French traveller [it continued, with mounting enthusiasm] breaks forth into raptures at the prosperity of Melbourne and regrets that the Orleans government did not assert its right to the islands of New Zealand. Yet it is but a few years since colonies of Australia were denounced as failures and philosophers of Mr Smith's school declared that the attempt to renew the experiment of America must end in ruin. Australia has grown up and now

takes our manufactures by millions. The truth is that there is no wiser policy for a country like ours than to take possession of the waste places of the earth, and give our crowded populations the power of settling in them under our own laws, modified, if need be, to suit their particular exigencies.

Economists, though apt to put the case in more sober language, generally reached the same conclusion. With them demography had come to provide a strong, perhaps the strongest argument for Empire. No such generalisation can be made about the 'official mind'. In so far as there was any consensus of opinion on the settled Empire, at the Colonial Office or in Parliament, after the introduction of responsible self-government and the completion of the free trade revolution in British commercial policy, it was along the lines sketched out by Earl Grey (colonial secretary in the critical years 1848–52) in correspondence with Lord John Russell. The first was that Britain had 'no interest whatever in exercising any greater influence in the internal affairs of the colonies than is indispensable either for the purpose of preventing any one colony from adopting measures injurious to another, or to the Empire at large . . .' or for the equitable and impartial administration of colonies whose populations were too ignorant and unenlightened to manage their own affairs. And the second principle, flowing from the abandonment of all restrictive colonial trading policies and of all needless interference in colonial domestic affairs, was that Britain on her side had a right to expect that the colonies should take upon themselves 'a larger proportion than heretofore of the expenses incurred for their advantage'.[44]

The First Dominion and its Constitution

Twenty-eight years elapsed between the Durham Report and the passage of the British North America Act. During that time experience was gained of the working of responsible self-government and some of its little-understood implications were revealed. Of the latter one very important example may suffice. Durham had recommended that the regulation of trade should be reserved to the imperial power. Did this mean imperial control both over colonial trading relations with foreign countries and with Great Britain herself? Lord Durham certainly said so. But had not the position been changed with the coming of free trade? The old imperial tariff arrangements were dismantled. Were the colonies thereafter obliged in all circumstances to adopt and maintain free trade policies? They might require revenue from customs. They might desire to protect infant industries, a legitimate exception approved by Adam Smith. They might even, heretical though the notion might seem in the days of the new economic enlightenment, desire to establish tariffs in their own national interest.

The first question, that in respect of trade with foreign countries, received a partial answer in 1854, when the short-lived Canadian-American Reciprocity trading agreement was concluded. Evidently a self-governing colonial government could negotiate a trading agreement, even if approval by Queen and Parliament was accepted as being necessary for its ratification. But could a colony enjoying self-government further impose tariffs upon goods from other parts of the Empire, from Britain herself, as she wished? The Colonial Office thought not and on two occasions in the early 1850s asserted its opinion. But in 1859 its view was challenged. Alexander Galt, Canadian minister of finance, imposed a first Canadian tariff. It was designed to help home industry, though Galt spoke with deliberate ambiguity of 'incidental protection';[45] by which he meant tariffs levied primarily to produce revenue but also – as the phrase implied – incidentally affording protection. The colonial secretary, the duke of Newcastle, prompted by a memorial from the Sheffield Chamber of Commerce, reacted sharply, expressing in a dispatch of 13 August 1859 to the governor-general mingled reproof and regret at the Canadian action. Galt prepared his reply. In its detailed refutation of the arguments submitted by the Sheffield Chamber of Commerce and of the statistics which buttressed them it was devastating; in respect of the principle at stake it lacked nothing in force and pungency.[46] The relevant passage read:

> The government of Canada acting for its Legislature and people cannot, through those feelings of deference which they owe to the imperial authorities, in any manner waive or diminish the right of the people of Canada to decide for themselves both as to the mode and extent to which taxation shall be imposed. . . . Self-government would be utterly annihilated if the views of the imperial government were to be preferred to those of the people of Canada. It is, therefore, the duty of the present government distinctly to affirm the right of the Canadian Legislature to adjust the taxation of the people in the way they deem best, even if it should unfortunately happen to meet the disapproval of the imperial ministry. Her majesty cannot be advised to disallow such acts, unless her advisers are prepared to assume the administration of the affairs of the colony irrespective of the views of its inhabitants.

For the imperial government the sting was in the tail. They could not 'resume' the government of Canada, or any other colony, against the wishes of a people growing accustomed to the practice of self-government, without assuming virtually unlimited responsibilities and an intolerable burden, for the weight of which continuation of imperial uniformity in tariff policy would afford the most meagre compensation. The debate ended, accordingly, with a notable advance along the road to colonial autonomy.

In British North America itself the two decades following the Durham Report underlined the incompleteness of the union of the two Canadas and the insufficiencies of separate self-governing institutions in the remaining colonies. The Grand Trunk Railway started with government backing in 1854 became, with the opening of the Victoria Bridge across the St Lawrence at Montreal by the prince of Wales in 1860 which marked its formal completion, the longest railway under single management in the world and Canada 'a railway in search of a state'.[47] With the railway, the opening up of the western prairies quickened, and even if it was difficult for east and west to live together politically, it was increasingly deemed impossible for them to develop apart. And to economics was added the powerful argument of defence. Separately the colonies were indefensible, except on the assumption of imperial aid on a scale by no means always likely to be forthcoming, and the United States, or groups within it (as the Fenian raids were to demonstrate in 1866 in the period of the Civil War) was potentially an aggressive or expansionist neighbour, presenting a potential external threat of the kind needed to intensify the efforts of colonists and also of British officials to achieve unity. In all, the combination of economic and political circumstance was such as to invite an experiment in nationhood, and agreement to initiate this great undertaking was reached by the representatives of the provinces in conference at Quebec in 1864. Yet, as so often happens, the approach to the conference and to its goal was devious and not without its surprises.

The first initiative came from the maritimes, when at a conference in Charlottetown, the capital of Prince Edward Island, the possibility of the political union of the three maritime provinces, Nova Scotia, New Brunswick and Prince Edward Island was debated by their leaders. The imperial government inclined favourably to this limited, regional union and later, in the person of the governor-general of Canada, Viscount Monck, played a more active intermediary rôle in enlarging the scope of the original conference and its purpose so as (to quote a letter of Lord Monck's of 9 July 1864 to the lieutenant-governor of Nova Scotia)' to ascertain whether the proposed union may not be made to embrace the whole of the British North American provinces'.[48] The idea, entertained in many quarters, found favour and a larger, more widely representative conference was called to consider it.

The building in which this conference assembled in Quebec, overlooking the great sweep of the St Lawrence River, was originally intended as a post office and had served as a temporary residence for the prince of Wales in 1860 and thereafter as the temporary home for the Canadian legislature, until the Parliament buildings were completed in Ottawa. Each province was represented by men of all parties but the atmosphere at the conference, enriched as it was by a sense of history in the making, was essentially conservative.[49] As to the over-riding intention of the delegates, here there could be no doubt. It was to make in Canada a strong national union. Two years later Lord Monck, writing to the secretary of state for the colonies, Lord Carnarvon, said that he was:

> persuaded both from the internal evidence afforded by the resolutions which they drew up and from intimate personal knowledge of most of the able men who composed the Quebec convention, that their intention was to form out of these provinces a solid and lasting political consolidation with a supreme central authority managing all the general interests of the people of the Union, which would attract to itself the – so to speak – national sentiment and aspiration of the entire people.[50]

The Resolutions[51] which were approved by the conference at Quebec formed the basis of the British North America Act 1867. 'Let us not,' urged Alexander Galt, 'lose sight of the great advantages which Union offers because there may be some small matters which as individuals we may not like.'[52] It was an observation too evidently just to be gainsaid. Yet, as J. A. Macdonald also underlined to the Canadian Parliament when introducing the proposals agreed at Quebec for a federation of all the British North American provinces on 6 February 1865:

> It must be admitted that had we not met in a spirit of conciliation and with an anxious desire to promote this union; if we had not been impressed with the idea contained in the words of the resolution – 'That the best interests and present and future prosperity of British North America would be promoted by a federal union under the Crown of Great Britain' – all our efforts might have proved to be of no avail.

Why were those efforts and so much good will required? The answers lay in the geographical spread and in the cultural variety of European settlement in British North America. The former found its political expression in the regionalism of areas with special community attachments and particularist economic preoccupations. Such regional sentiment was emerging in the as yet sparsely populated prairies lying between the lakes and forests of Upper Canada on the east and the Rockies on the West; it was already self-evident in British Columbia, cut off by the barrier of the mountains from the rest of British North America, and most pronounced in the maritimes along the eastern seaboard, warmly attached to Britain and with a distinctive outlook of their own which made them little enamoured of the idea of absorption in a polity necessarily dominated by the inhabitants of the populous St Lawrence Valley. Theirs happened to have been the initiative but they perhaps more than any others were called upon to make concessions in the interests of federation. Yet while for the maritimes this sense of the prospective submergence of a cherished identity was pronounced, it was tempered, as elsewhere in the English-speaking provinces, by an appreciation of the destiny that might lie before a vast, united and predominantly English-speaking, self-governing dominion of the British Crown in North America. For those of another culture there was no such exciting prospect. Upper and Lower Canada, divided by language and origin, united by the great river which flowed through them, had hitherto been held in a balanced if uneasy union, symbolised by a succession of 'hyphenated' ministries, the best known of which was that of Baldwin-Lafontaine. But now in a federal state that balance was destroyed. There were to be no more such ministries. Lower Canada, Quebec, was no longer one of two but one among many. However securely the religion, the language, the social traditions of the *habitants* might be protected, the fact remained that it was by safeguards alone that the cooperation of the French-speaking minority could be obtained. At the time of confederation and for ninety years thereafter the dominant element in their political thinking was defensive. They were resolved before all else to survive. It was not so much that their situation was about to be changed in political form – but that the realities of it were to be exposed.

Some thirty-six years before Confederation, on 1 September 1831, Alexis de Tocqueville made a record of his impressions of French Canada as he steamed up the St Lawrence to Montreal. They stand the test of time. What was true in the early nineteenth century was still substantially true at the time of the confederation and even in 1967 when the centenary of confederation was celebrated. This was so because there was constancy of purpose. The French Canadians, like all cultural minorities worthy of the name, were resolved to preserve their cultural heritage for themselves and to transmit it to future generations. 'Vous serez ce que vous voulez être, c'est-à-dire maîtres de vous-mêmes . . .' declared the president of the French republic, General de Gaulle, on his dramatic and disconcerting visit to Quebec in July 1967, 'Votre avenir, ce qu'il doit être, un avenir français.'[53] On the longer view and in the deeper sense everything that mattered most to French Canadians was contained in those words – to remain masters of themselves in changing and often unfavourable circumstances and to ensure for Quebec a French future.

De Tocqueville's first exuberant hopes of a restored French Empire in North America soon waned and were replaced by a sobering appraisal of the prospects before the French community in Lower Canada. The instincts of the people, he noted,[54] were against the English, but 'many Canadians belonging to the upper-classes did not seem to us [de

Beaumont, it will be recalled, was travelling with him] animated to the degree we believe [they should be?] by the desire to preserve intact the trace of their origin and to become a people entirely apart.' Several did not seem far from amalgamating with the English, if the latter would adopt the interests of the country.

It is therefore to be feared that with time, and above all with the immigration of the Irish Catholics, the fusion will take place, and it cannot do so except to the detriment of the race, the language and the customs of the French.

However it is certain: 1. Lower Canada (happily for the French race) forms a separate state. Now in Lower Canada the French population is to the English population in the proportion of ten to one. It is compact. . . . 2. The English up to now have always kept apart. . . . 3. In the towns the English and the Canadians form two societies. The English affect great luxury. There are only very limited fortunes among the Canadians. Thence small-town jealousies and vexations. 4. The English have all the foreign trade in their hands and direct all the domestic trade. Thence again, jealousy. . . . 5. Finally, the English show themselves in Canada with all the traits of the national character and the Canadians have retained all the traits of French character. The odds are therefore that Lower Canada will end by becoming a people entirely French. But it will never be a numerous people. They will be a drop of water in the ocean. I am much afraid that . . . fate has in fact decided that North America will be English.'

The notes jotted down by this distinguished French historian and political philosopher express something of the spirit of French Canadian participation in Confederation a generation later. It was a spirit of resignation but by no means of despair. Fate having seemingly decreed that North America would be English it remained for the French Canadians to preserve their own identity as best they might and to ensure their own survival. Federation had self-evident advantages over a union of Upper and Lower Canada in which the will of the majority would prevail. 'In a struggle between two, one a weak and the other a strong party,' observed George Étienne Cartier in the Canadian confederation debates,[55] 'the weaker could not but be overcome; but if three parties were concerned the stronger would not have the same advantage; as when it was seen by the third that there was too much strength on one side, the third would club with the weaker combatant to resist the big fighter.' Cartier added that he did not entertain the slightest apprehension that Lower Canada's rights would be jeopardised by the fact that her representatives would be outnumbered in the Federal Legislature by all the others combined. None the less for French-Canadians the federal constitution must needs be fashioned first and foremost to serve essentially defensive ends.

The constitution of Canada was British in conception and design. It was by no means the first constitution modelled on the principles of government and parliament as practised at Westminster to be transplanted overseas or even to British North America itself. But it was significant that Canadian leaders, with the example of the American system of government constantly before them, should have decided so emphatically in favour of the British. They did not doubt that they should have a Parliament with two Houses, one elective the other nominated, a cabinet by convention collectively responsible to the Lower House, a governor-general at the apex as the representative of the Crown and an independent judiciary. At Quebec the assembled representatives, George Brown explained,[56] were 'earnestly deliberating how we shall best extend the blessings of British institutions'. That preference the French Canadians shared. The British pattern and the monarchical element seemed to offer assurances of constitutional conservatism and stability. Yet what had to be achieved was not the comparatively simple task of adapting British institutions to another continent and another political environment; but the more complicated one of adapting the parliamentary system as it had developed over centuries without a written constitution to the written form which federation demanded. The characteristics of the Canadian constitution were not individually novel; its contribution to political thought and practice lay rather in its successful association of the British parliamentary system with federalism. 'The constitution of Canada,' noted André Siegfried, 'presents no original feature: it partakes at once of the English parliamentary system and of American federalism but there is nothing in any of its provisions to attract attention by reason of its novelty; its chief interest lies rather in the way in which it is applied.'[57] The note is unduly disparaging but the substance of the comment is just.

At the outset the Canadian confederation consisted of Upper and Lower Canada and the maritime provinces of Nova Scotia and New Brunswick. Manitoba joined it in 1870, British Columbia in 1871, Prince Edward Island in 1873, Alberta and Saskatchewan in 1905 and Newfoundland, after a brief, chequered interlude as a dominion on its own, in 1949. The constitutional structure was monarchical with the governor-general filling the rôle of the absent monarch. In the making of this constitutional design – neither their own nor British – United States experience reinforced the claims of loyalty and conservative sentiment. 'By adhering to the monarchical principle,' said J. A. Macdonald 'we avoid one defect inherent in the Constitution of the United States' – namely an elective head of state holding office for a short period of years.[58] And with regard to the actual conduct of affairs the Canadian founding fathers kept as close as circumstances would allow to the British precedents which guided them. 'In the constitution,' to quote Macdonald once more,[59] 'we propose to continue the system of responsible government, which has existed in this province since 1841 and which has long obtained in the mother country. This is a feature of our constitution . . . in which, I think, we avoid one of the great defects in the constitution of the United States.' There the president was in great measure a despot; in Canada ministers would at all times be responsible to the people through Parliament. But there remained the one all important respect in which the circumstances of Canada did not permit of the adoption of the British system. Canada was to be, like the United States but unlike Britain, a federal state, though even here United States' practice was held up as a warning, not as a guide. In the British North America Act all spheres of domestic legislative competency were defined in section 91. To the provinces were assigned sixteen enumerated and exclusive subjects; to the confederation twenty-nine, together with a field for the exercise of concurrent power over agriculture and immigration, with the proviso that in the event of conflict the will of the federal authority would prevail. But while the provinces were given wide powers, including – as was a condition of federation for Quebec – exclusive control over education with specially guaranteed protection for denominational schools, and were sovereign in their own sphere, ultimate residuary authority rested with the federal government. This was the essential element in the Canadian federal system. There were no states, only provinces, and there was no entrenchment of provincial rights in such a way as to give them that higher status. That would have been altogether inconsistent with the resolve of the founding fathers to create a strong central government. As Macdonald put it:

> We have conferred upon them [the provinces] not only specifically and in detail all the powers which are incident to sovereignty, but we have expressly declared that all subjects of general interest not distinctly and exclusively conferred upon the local governments and local legislatures shall be conferred upon the General Government and Legislature. We have thus avoided the great source of weakness which has been the cause of the disruption of the United States.

The purpose of ensuring strong central government was later qualified – only the extent to which this was done remains disputable – by judgments of the judicial committee of the Privy Council in London, which was made the final court of appeal in constitutional cases. In its interpretation of federal and provincial powers notable members of the judicial committee, deliberately and of conviction, adopted at a critical time in the evolution of federation a conservative and limiting view of the extent of the central federal authority, which was deemed by many English-speaking Canadians to be in conflict if not with the letter then certainly with the spirit and intention of the constitution.[60] Yet without discounting the significance of a series of Privy Council judgments, the fact remained that the bias of the constitution towards the centre was too pronounced to be thereby fundamentally changed.

In a true federation the powers of the centre and the constituent units ought to be coordinate, neither subordinate one to the other. It has been questioned whether Canada fulfils this condition and whether therefore she can be regarded as a true federation.[61] If the letter alone counted, this question might be thought deserving of a negative answer. But inevitably this is not so, and in spirit (as indeed in practice) the government of Canada may be thought to be in essence federal. The position of Quebec ensured this for while French Canadians were not satisfied in the longer run with a constitution which placed the province as one among many, all the others being predominantly English-speaking, they would assuredly at no time have been content with a form of government that was not federal at least to the extent of ensuring provincial control over matters closest to the French Canadian heart. Indeed in one respect Quebec was accorded a special (though not a privileged) position in as much as the province was allotted sixty-five seats in the House of Commons, with representation in the rest of Canada to be determined at each decennial census in the same relation to population as existed in Quebec. But while this constitutional provision was valuable by way of protective guarantee, ensuring that Quebec representation could not be reduced other than by constitutional amendment and accordingly not without the approval of the imperial Parliament at Westminster, the population and the economically strategic position of the province made it difficult if not impossible to govern Canada against Quebec, even though it was the case that in other respects the position and powers of the provinces were alike and without distinction. Generally however there is no doubt that the need to safeguard the rights of a cultural minority concentrated in one province, in effect enhanced the status of all and modified in practice the predominance the central government might otherwise have enjoyed. This was the case rather more in respect of the conventions of government than of strict constitutional provision.

Canadian prime ministers (to take one important example), in nominating members of their cabinets, have in practice found it prudent to satisfy the principal regional interests by giving all of them representation in it. This was so well understood forty years after the passing of the British North America Act that William Price sent a memorandum to Sir Robert Borden from Montreal on 2 October 1911, when Borden was engaged in forming his first cabinet, stating '1. It is necessary to have three French Canadian ministers from this province. 2. It is customary that two of the ministers should be chosen from what is known as the Montreal District and one from the Quebec District'.[62] The politically 'customary' in this case, as in many others, reflected the underlying federal nature of Canadian politics and administration. But it existed and found expression within a constitutional framework created by Founding Fathers, most of whom would have preferred union, and all of whom finally agreed to establish a federation, with the balance of power weighted in favour of the centre.

The constitution of the Dominion of Canada was embodied in the British North America Act 1867[63] and subsequent amendments to it. Both the Act itself and the amendments were enacted by Parliament at Westminster. What it had enacted it could alter or repeal. Imperial sovereignty accordingly remained unimpaired. Yet while continuity and ultimate control were thus ensured, the initiative in the framing and in the subsequent amendment of the British North America Act was Canadian. The constitution of the first, as of all later dominions, while modified in certain respects in discussions with the Colonial Office, was essentially home-made. It was however (unlike some of them) the product of agreement between governments without the direct popular sanction of plebiscite or referendum.

Besides its indigenous origin there was another factor of equal significance for the future. The confederation of Canada came into existence through the association of a number of neighbouring but hitherto separate British colonial territories in one political system; that too became part of a later Commonwealth pattern. Once more the initiative was local, not imperial, but the consequences were of more than local importance. The imperial power had its interest in unification both in terms of administrative economy and convenience and of the effective diminution of its own responsibilities. Where for example a number of small colonies were likely to appeal for imperial assistance in times of stress – financial or military as the case might be – a larger and stronger union would be able to rely upon its own resources. In an age dominated by Gladstonian finance and anti-militarist free traders this was a consideration which warmly commended Canadian confederation to the home government – though even that did not suffice to satisfy John Bright. He feared that even with federation there would be perpetual Canadian requests for railways or defence and speaking – as the biographer of John A. Macdonald, the chief architect of confederation, has observed with undisguised distaste – 'with that unctuous mixture of pecuniary considerations and moral values which was so characteristic of his school'[64] he concluded that it would be 'cheaper for us and less demoralising for them – that they should become an independent state, and maintain their own fortresses, fight their own cause, and build up their own future without relying upon us.'[65]

Macdonald, who had talked of 'founding a great British monarchy in connection with the British Empire',[66] voiced a widespread Canadian hope that it would be named the Kingdom of Canada with a viceroy as representative of the Crown. But in the Colonial Office the designation was thought pretentious and opinion in Washington was known to be hostile, and London accordingly demanded a more sober, unprovocative designation. S. L. Tilley, reading from Psalm lxxii, verse 8 – 'He shall have dominion also from sea to sea, and from the river unto the ends of the earth', – is thought to have first pointed to the appropriateness of the title, *Dominion*.[67] And so it was that as the first dominion the Confederation of Canada came into existence, on the first day of July 1867. Lord Carnarvon, the colonial secretary, had sensed much and spoken stirringly in the House of Commons of the significance of the occasion. But the Colonial Office, according to Macdonald, had treated the unification of Canada as if the British North America Act were a private bill uniting two or three parishes, while according to Macdonald's biographer the members of Parliament at Westminster could hardly conceal their 'excruciating boredom' while the measure passed through its necessary stages and when they were at last concluded turned with great relief to a debate on the desirability of introducing modification in the duty on dogs.[68] So, with inspiration and apathy nicely mingled, the first step was taken in the Mother of Parliaments on the road to Commonwealth.

CHAPTER 3

SOUTH AFRICA; RACES AND RICHES, WAR AND UNION

In South Africa it was usual to speak of Britain, Canada, Australia and New Zealand as the foundation members of the British Commonwealth of Nations; elsewhere it was customary to include South Africa itself among their number. Historically the distinction is debatable and in any case of no great importance; conceptually South Africa's place is with the founder-states. At almost every stage in the evolution of the Commonwealth, South Africa was notionally, if not actually, an integral part of it. Canadian confederation was at once preceded and succeeded by abortive attempts at South African federation; and the problems of race and colour, existing with peculiar intensity in the South African colonies, came to be accepted as belonging from the outset to the Commonwealth as a whole. Such problems might no longer exist in more than nominal form in respect of Red Indian survivors in Canada or of the aborigines in Australia; they did exist, but within manageable dimensions, in New Zealand with its indigenous Maori population. But long before a united South Africa became a dominion in 1910, they had their place in the thinking which brought the Commonwealth into existence. It was no chance, it was the logic of history that made first popular reaction against an imperialist war in South Africa and then popular (if in part misguided) enthusiasm for a magnanimous South African settlement the immediate precursors to the recognition by name of a Commonwealth, already thought of as being in embryonic existence.

South African history is too rich and varied to be forced into any particular mould. If the country has its highly significant place in the early history and in formative thinking about the Commonwealth, it has also a place possibly even more important in the history of Empire. This dual rôle derived at root from the composition of its population and the character and resources of its land. The first with its two European cultures and its majority of non-European origin was a challenge at once to humanitarian zeal and to liberal principles; the second with its vast extent and its mineral wealth, a magnet to imperialists, both of the more simple-minded map-painting and of the more sinister Hobsonian capitalist-exploiter variety. The existence of challenges and opportunities made of South Africa a land of divergent and often conflicting purposes, in which the threads of motive and action are unusually difficult to disentangle. British imperial historians have been for the most part predisposed to interpret nineteenth- and early twentieth-century South African history in terms of the safeguarding of imperial strategic interests or of the achievement of imperial economic or political ends, the latter especially too long delayed by confusion of purpose and uncertain resolve; British liberal historians have approached it in terms of European and more particularly of British enlightenment, seeking, in the face of critical settler and obstinately obscurantist Boer opinion, to assert the principles and to introduce by stages the conditions of race equality; South African historians have tended generally to interpret South African history in the context of settler interests, conflicts and territorial expansion, with the English-speaking of them dwelling especially upon the development of self-governing institutions, first in Cape Colony and then in the union, on an acceptable, if limited, Westminster model and the Afrikaners concentrating upon Boer resistance to British imperialism throughout 'A Century of Wrong' – the title chosen by J. C. Smuts[1] for an essay in historical polemics produced at the onset of war, 1899 – which through defeat and near destruction, finally triumphed in the establishment of a South African republic. For a sustained African essay in historical interpretation we have still to wait. It is easy to generalise, to say for example that the imperial factor, as Rhodes called it, has been over or underestimated; to argue that the growth of English institutions or the exclusivist aspirations of Afrikanerdom have been the key factor: to maintain that the course of South African history was determined by the impersonal forces of world capitalism or that the colour question has been its dominant theme. But the study of any extended period is likely to cast doubt upon the validity of such conceptions or preconceptions. There were so many factors which exerted a decisive influence at a particular time but which were in turn superseded not so much by new as by older forces, brought once again by some shift in the seemingly unending struggle for control into a position of power. English writers, complacently recording the downfall and final destruction of the Boer republics early in the century (to take one example) afford ironic and occasionally almost comic warning against any finality of judgment in a field where finality is the one thing that is lacking. The downfall of Kruger's republic presaged not (as they supposed) the end of Krugerism or of republicanism but the triumphant vindication of both in a setting much larger than the Transvaal two generations later. Yet, among all the vicissitudes of South African history in the period, one theme was constant. It was the contact and consequent relationship of European settlers with African peoples, first on a limited scale with the Hottentots at the Cape and then on the eastern frontiers of Cape Province and beyond with a native population to be numbered in its millions, a population which was in large measure subdued but never absorbed, economically, politically or least of all socially into the European controlled provinces or states into which southern Africa was divided.[2] It was this which gave to South Africa its unique place and its unique significance in Commonwealth history.

Jan van Riebeeck landed at the Cape in 1652, during the period of English and French settlement in North America. But the growth of the Dutch settlement was hampered by the restrictive policies of the Dutch East India Company. Its directors were interested not in colonisation but in trade. And in terms of trade the Cape was a refreshment station on the way to the East Indies. Settlement took place – and it was by no means exclusively Dutch. Hollanders and Flemings were reinforced, notably by emigrants from Western Germany, and after the repeal of the Edict of Nantes by Huguenot exiles from France. The Huguenots were few in number and were to lose their separate identity, their language and the original pronunciation of their names but they added nonetheless a distinctive element with a continuing influence in the settler community, as has been testified right down to our own time by the prominence of men of French or part French extraction – Malherbe, du Toit, Olivier, du Plessis, Centlivres, Joubert, Daniel François Malan – in the public and professional life of South Africa. Most remarkable, however, was the number of French names among the early Voortrekkers. Olive Schreiner once contended that it was 'in the French blood which flows in the Boer veins that we have to look for the explanation of great historical movements', on the grounds apparently that the French settlers had 'vivified the torpid mental life of the otherwise Teutonic Boer', stimulated his faculties and 'made his blood course more rapidly in his substantial veins'.[3] It may be, too, that the Huguenots lent something of the sharper edge of French logic to Dutch Calvinist doctrine. Most important for European (as distinct from later British) settlers was the lack of reinforcement from their homelands. There was but little immigration to the Cape from Holland after the end of the seventeenth century with the result that the temper of the Europe of the seventeenth century, the century of the great religious controversies, wars and persecutions, was transplanted to another continent, to be reinterpreted there in terms of frontier conflicts and frontier psychology, and was left untouched by the enlightenment of eighteenth century Europe. Even by the time of the first British occupation, 1795–1803, the sentimental and commercial ties with Holland were no longer supplemented by corresponding social and intellectual contacts. The long isolation of the Boer had already begun. The second and more lasting British occupation from 1806 completed it. The Boers were thereafter no longer colonists under the protective wing of a mother country; they were a people numbering only some twenty-seven thousand souls, out on their own. They were also, for the most part, pastoralists, forever seeking new ground for grazing and moving their cattle with them. In this way they spread themselves thinly over great tracts of land, where they were faced with the harsh alternatives of survival by their own endeavours or destruction as a separate group. They survived; they became a nation – the only European nation in Africa. This was not a matter of choice but of will and of necessity. The former they never lacked and the latter was always before them. They had no other home, no other country. They said so time without number. It happened to be true.

In South Africa there were other settlers; later settlers, British settlers. They came in with the new imperialism – administrators and soldiers, traders, missionaries and farmers. Some of them came on their own initiative; others, notably the 1820 settlers early in the period of British rule, under schemes of officially inspired and planned emigration. They too acquired in the process of time the settler outlook and the frontier mentality. But there was this difference between them and the Boers. The links with their mother country remained strong, secure and binding. They may not have been especially enlightened but they were familiar with the climate of early nineteenth-century opinion; they may not have been markedly humanitarian but they had felt the flowing tide of humanitarian sentiment. While they might not agree or might even sharply disagree with the home government on methods of colonial administration or the treatment of native races they understood something of the motives and forces which shaped home opinion. The Boers did not. James Bryce, writing in the closing years of the century felt that the timing of British annexations was especially unfortunate. Had they happened thirty years earlier no difficulties would have arisen, he thought, over the treatment of natives or slavery because at that time the new philanthropy had not begun to influence English opinion. Had they occurred later then quicker and more frequent ocean communication would not have left room for so much misunderstanding and as a result the errors that contributed to the alienation of the Boers might never have been committed.[4]

Government and treatment of native races in South Africa were not separable things; in the last resort they were one. That was because government there, over and above the ordinary responsibilities of nineteenth-century colonial administration, carried also the extraordinary responsibility of decisions upon the treatment of majority native races. Was this an imperial or a local matter? The home government throughout the greater part of the nineteenth century, despite moments of doubt and contemplated withdrawal, generally believed and asserted that it was an imperial responsibility. Evangelicals and humanitarians were insistent that it should be properly discharged and for the greater part of the century they were able to exert formidable pressure in Parliament. The settlers perforce acquiesced. They were dependent upon imperial protection. But their acquiescence was usually reluctant. They felt they had the knowledge and experience which imperial officials lacked. They knew the Hottentot, the Kaffir, the Bantu; they had daily contact with them. What they would have liked was imperial protection without imperial control. That meant European self-government on liberal Canadian lines, but with a white minority determining the place of the black majority in South African society. It was an end not secured till 1909. Until then there existed an uneasy balance in imperial-colonial relations. The imperial government could not, save at the price of great expenditure of money and effort, govern the colonies against the settlers; the settlers, divided as they continued to be between Boers and British, could not resist the pressure of the imperial factor beyond a certain point. The outcome was an unstable equilibrium of imperial-colonial forces. In South Africa and in South Africa alone among the colonies that were to become dominions, was there continuing conflict between liberal principles of responsible self-government and humanitarian pressure for continuing imperial protection of native races.

The history of nineteenth-century South Africa is its own. But in the context of Commonwealth there are some problems the nature of which must needs be noted. The first is government. In the second period of British rule the governor, appointed by the Crown, was until 1825 in effect an autocratic ruler. But then a new phase began. An advisory council was established, at first composed wholly of officials, but with two non-official members added in 1827. There was a more radical change in 1834 when executive and legislative councils were set up. The members of both, according to the practice of the time, were chosen by the governor. That however did not avoid friction. Settlers on these councils did not cast off their settler outlook or their settler associations. They were not representatives but they were very often representative in their opinions. Having taken the first step, experience (much of it in terms of frustration) underlined the importance of the second. It was taken in 1853. The instrument was the Cape of Good Hope Ordinance. It established representative government. The new Parliament (which met for the first time on Friday 30 June 1854 in the Goede Hoop Banqueting Hall in Cape Town and which passed as its first measure an Act – No. 1 1854 – to secure freedom of speech) was composed of two Houses, with the Upper as well as the Lower Chamber elective – a departure in British imperial history. But in the conditions of South Africa, as important as freedom of speech and more important than the structure of the legislature was the nature of the franchise. It was colour blind. There was a financial qualification, no literacy test and, all-important in the setting, no colour bar. The financial qualification for candidates, as distinct from voters, was high and while Coloured and natives qualified to vote in quite considerable numbers, no non-European was elected a member of the Cape Parliament in all the years of its existence (1854–1910).

Representative government was not responsible government. Members of the Cape Executive Council were not responsible to the colonial legislature but continued to be appointed and dismissed by the governor. That intermediate phase ended in 1872 when self-government on the Canadian model was conferred on Cape Colony. Its timing was due less to a sense of constitutional appropriateness than to a variety of economic, strategic and political considerations. Ostrich farming and the discovery of diamonds at Kimberley heralded a revolution in the economy of Cape Colony and provided a material foundation for self-government, while the opening of the Suez Canal in 1869 reduced its strategic importance to Britain. The prospect of local self-sufficiency, allied to diminishing imperial strategic significance, strongly suggested that the time had come for imperial withdrawal from direct responsibility for the domestic government of the colony. But there was a further factor. It was argued in the Colonial Office that Cape Colony, the oldest and richest of the political communities in South Africa, must become self-governing before there could be consolidation of all of them under one government. As in Canada, self-government was to be a step on the road to unification.

While British settlers first in Cape Colony and then in Natal (which became a Crown colony in 1856 and attained self-government in 1893) advanced along the road to colonial self-government, it was otherwise with the Boers. They did not like British government. It was in the first place alien government. In the second place, both in itself and in many of its actions, it was unfamiliar to the point of incomprehensibility. And thirdly, it brought in its train high-minded evangelicals, whose especial concern was the protection and care of the native peoples but whose principal preoccupation (so it seemed to the Boer farmers) was the disruption of their way of life. Since the seventeenth century they had relied partly upon slave labour and that in itself established a tradition different from any that prevailed in other British colonies of settlement, though not in other British possessions. The social pattern, thus long established, struck deep roots. It was reinforced by Calvinist emphasis upon the Old Testament. Though there were important differences between the three sections into which the Dutch Reformed Church came to be divided, the Boers throughout their history were encouraged by their pastors to liken themselves to the Children of Israel, to the chosen people of God – as was done once again by the moderator of the Nederduits Gereformeerde Church of the Cape in his oration at the state funeral in Pretoria of the assassinated prime minister of South Africa, Hendrik Verwoerd, on 10 September 1966 – a people also seeking their promised land and continually engaged in righteous war against the unbelieving Philistines first to possess and then to preserve it. It was their destiny to survive and to multiply. But, as with the Children of Israel, survival was a hard and bitter struggle – in the nineteenth century a struggle, as it seemed to the Boers, against native hordes thirsting to destroy them, against pestilence, drought and floods, and in later days against the British occupying power.

The new British factor was felt to present a threat more insidious and potentially no less destructive than older and more familiar dangers. For the British with their humanitarian ideals, their evangelical missionary zeal (typified by Dr John Philip of the London Missionary Society) appeared to aim both at confining the Boers within settled colonial frontiers and at placing them on an equality with Coloured and native freemen. Few things, for example, rankled with the Boers more than an ordinance – the nineteenth ordinance – of June 1826 which allowed a slave to give evidence in criminal cases against his master and to purchase his freedom by tendering his appraised value. Then in 1833 slavery was abolished throughout the British Empire. 1 December 1834 was the date that was finally fixed for the emancipation of the 35,742 slaves at the Cape.[5] The Cape of Good Hope Ordinance (No. 1 of 1835) read as follows:

> Enacted by the governor [Sir Benjamin D'Urban] of the Cape of Good Hope with the advice and consent of the Legislative Council thereof, – For giving due effect to the Provisions of an Act of Parliament, passed in the third and fourth years of the reign of His Majesty King William the Fourth entitled 'An Act for the abolition of slavery throughout the British Colonies. . .'. Now therefore, in pursuance of the said Act of Parliament and for carrying the same into effect within the Colony of the Cape of Good Hope be it enacted by the governor of the Cape of Good Hope: with the advice and consent of the Legislative Council thereof . . . upon, from, and after the first day of December 1834 . . .

The Boers resented both the fact and still more the implication of their relations with the natives being determined by an Act of a remote and interfering imperial authority. There was, it is true, compensation for the loss of the slaves, but it was compensation in bonds which depreciated rapidly from their original stated value, so that to resentment at imperial action was added indignation at what appeared to be imperial sharp practice.

The abolition of slavery was not, as has been alleged, the cause nor even the occasion of the Great Trek. The trekkers were in fact by no means the most considerable owners of slaves and the many who came from the eastern border lands of Cape Colony were far more preoccupied with the competitive struggle for land with the Bantu than with any loss of slaves. The frontiersmen of the Cape, indeed, were accustomed to think of six thousand acres as the proper extent of a farm, and while they were comparatively few in number their sense of what was fitting in this respect was more likely to be satisfied in the unsettled north than in the settled Cape. So it was against a growing sense of actual or potential confinement that the abolition of slavery and the circumstances of it, adding significantly to a consciousness of accumulated grievances, was rightly interpreted as evidence that the British government had its own ideas of colonial society and intended to enforce them. It was this which completed the Boer sense of alienation from the British authorities.[6] Many of the Boer farmers, nomadic pastoralists by tradition, in effect decided to recover their freedom to order their own lives and above all to determine the nature of their own relationship with native peoples. Disregarding British attempts to fix the frontier they moved across the line of the northern boundary of Cape Colony where there was least resistance to them, across the Orange and then the Vaal rivers into the lonely and largely untenanted tracts beyond. There were many starting points, many 'Voortrekker-roetes', many destinations and many leaders whose names are still cherished in the folk memory of a people – among them Louis Trichard who left from near Bedford and is buried at Lourenço Marques; A. H. Potgieter from Tarkastad in the eastern Cape, buried at Schoemansdal; J. van Rensburg who reached the valley of the Limpopo, Uys, Maritz, Piet Retief. . . .[7] There were differences among leaders which led on occasion to a fatal parting of the ways, most notably in the case of Piet Retief and his followers, slaughtered by the Zulus in February 1838. And there were famous victories, chief among them that of Andries Pretorius at the Blood River on 16 December of that same year, ever since commemorated. If the Voortrekkers were exiles, their exile was self-appointed and, as their tradition records, they were moved by a sense of destiny to face certain hardships and uncertain perils, sustained in their pilgrimage by the Calvinist faith of their fathers. More than a hundred years later a memorial in dark granite was built on a hill outside Pretoria to commemorate the Trek and there inside, in bas-relief, panels were placed depicting the bearded trekkers with their families, their sheep, their cattle and their household possessions, leaving their homes in Cape Colony, their waggons moving northward or bound together in defensive laager; the disasters, the victories and at last the thanksgiving. There is much depicted there to stir the imagination and to enhance the resolution and fortitude of an isolated people; and even more, to keep alive the racial animosities of trekker times.

The outcome of the Great Trek was the foundation of two Dutch republics in the hinterland of South Africa; the Republiek Oranje-Vrijstaat, or Orange Free State, and the Zuid-Afrikaansche Republiek, or South African Republic of the Transvaal. Both were landlocked. The trekkers hoped for an independent outlet to the sea in the short-lived Republiek Natalia but Zulu power and British intervention denied it to them. In 1843 the Natal republic had perforce to submit to British control of a province, limited in its extent by British understandings with the Zulus and other neighbouring tribes. Great and justly honoured among their own people were the lasting achievements of the trekkers. But while they had travelled far beyond the bounds of British rule they had not finally escaped from dependence on a British power, by which they were still at vital points surrounded.

What action was the British government to take about the trekkers and their republics? Was it to lay claim to their allegiance and the hinterland they had occupied, thus extending imperial responsibilities far to the north? Or was it, in acquiescent dissociation from the trekkers and the consequences of their trek, to allow them to work out their own destiny? Either course, as seen from London, had evident disadvantages, the former because of the expenditure in money and men it would assuredly entail; the latter because the existence of two distinct types of settlement in southern Africa, given especially the known differences between them in respect of native policy, was equally bound to cause embarrassment at the least and might at some stage even constitute a threat to British security at the Cape. The dilemma remained, but not surprisingly reactions to it varied partly in accord with local circumstances and partly with imperial thinking about colonial possessions. The latter, especially by 1850, predisposed the Colonial Office to policies of coexistence. The independence of the South African republic in the Transvaal was accordingly recognised by the Sand River Convention in 1852 and two years later claims to effective control over the Orange Free State were abandoned. Both were deliberate and significant acts of policy. The British decided to pull out of a waste 'fit only for Springbok', and being landlocked, little likely to offer opportunities to foreign nations to disturb the power that controlled the coasts.[8] The principle of reciprocal non-interference between Britain and the republics guided them and this implied among other things – and was understood to imply – freedom on the part of the Boers to apply their own native policies.

Sir George Grey, governor of Cape Colony 1854–61, out of sympathy with Colonial Office views and with a memorable period of office in New Zealand behind him, challenged prevailing opinions. He was not impressed by supposedly conclusive arguments against expansion based on the cost and consequent liability of extending the frontiers of effective British colonial control. He urged on the contrary the need, as he also sensed the opportunity, for the federation of the two British colonies with the Trekker republics and he had at least good reason for believing that the Orange Free State was favourably inclined toward such federation. Against explicit instructions telling him to take no steps without reference to the Colonial Office, Grey continued to do so. He was rebuked by one colonial secretary in 1858 and dismissed by his successor the following year in a dispatch the plainness of whose language left nothing to be desired. 'I can but agree,' wrote the incoming secretary of state of his predecessor's written rebuke 'in its strong terms of disapproval of your conduct, not only in respect of the question of federation . . .'. Sir George Grey did in fact return after a brief interlude to govern the Cape but by then the prospect of federation had departed.

To imperialists later in the century it was the lost opportunities of federation in the 1850s which had left open the way to the conflicts that followed. No words were too strong to condemn the parsimony and lack of imagination shown in London. South Africa, in their view, was one. Geography and economics predetermined it. There was therefore only one question to ask: Who was to control it, Briton or Boer? That, certainly, was political oversimplification on the grand scale. The making of a federation, as is now only too well understood, carries no assurance of its survival or of the avoidance of conflict. Indeed all that may reasonably be said is that the failure to federate in the 1850s probably increased the chances of conflict and accentuated – if only by the passage of time – the problems of future union. The Boers in the republics free from British influence established their own political institutions. Both republics had written constitutions, that of the Orange Free State being rigid, that of the Transvaal very flexible. They were democratic in one respect: the ultimate source of authority was the people. In the Transvaal there was a unicameral legislature, the Volksraad, and an elected president responsible to it. But democracy had its clearly defined colour limit. 'The people desire,' so the relevant section in the Transvaal constitution reads, 'to permit no equal standing [the Dutch word is *gelijkstelling* which is generally but not exactly translated 'equality'][9] between the coloured people and white inhabitants, either in Church or State.' This was a provision sharply at variance with the colour-blind franchise of the near-contemporary Cape of Good Hope Ordinance, and the assertion of two contradictory principles in respect of an issue that was social and economic as much as it was political in its implications and full of perplexities in itself, foreshadowed the dispute and conflict that was to come. For behind the two contrasted constitutional provisions there lay different philosophies of the right relations between men of different colour. They could be practised side by side so long as the Boers continued to live in isolation. But circumstances determined otherwise.

Catastrophe, an Afrikaner historian, F. S. Malan, has remarked, overtook the Dutch republics 'in the form of fabulous riches'. The story of their discovery began in 1866. Erasmus Jacobs, a farmer's son, caught sight of a pebble glittering in the glare of the sun near the banks of the Orange river: he carried it home in his pocket and was playing a family game with the pebble and some ordinary river stones when a neighbour, van Niekerk, arrived. The boy's mother gave it to him, believing it to be only a pebble. Van Niekerk passed it to Jack O'Reilly, a travelling trader, who showed it to Lorenzo Boyes, civil commissioner of Colesberg. He understood the importance of the find and a general examination of the district followed.[10] Other sparkling stones were found near the Orange and Vaal rivers, and then in 1869 there was the romantic discovery by a Griqua shepherd boy of the superb white diamond which later came to be known as the Star of South Africa.

> a tremendous rush ensued . . . ships crews deserted to come up country . . . Everything from a handcart and a chaise to the big Boer wagon joined the trek. A busy line of camps presently formed along the Vaal so that in 1870–1 ten thousand river diggers were ransacking the river soil, shaking it through cradle sieves, far too preoccupied even to notice the advent of newcomers. In moments of inattention fortunes may be lost . . . . A strange brotherhood it was! Like all pioneer encampments, it abounded in colourful characters.[11]

A 'big hole' was dug at Kimberley and the fortunes of Cecil John Rhodes, who later acquired control of it, were laid; and many things besides. Kimberley was in Griqualand West; the Griquas deemed themselves to be under British protection but Griqualand West was disputed territory between the British and the republics. It had now assumed a quite new importance. There were negotiations of a protracted and acrimonious nature, only concluded when President Brand of the Orange Free State came to London in 1876. He agreed that the republics' claim should be abandoned for ninety thousand pounds proferred by way of compensation. Not often has so little been paid for a title to so much.

If the discovery of diamonds at Kimberley imposed strain of one kind, the return of Lord Carnarvon to the Colonial Office in 1874 created tensions of another. Lord Carnarvon, who as earlier remarked had imaginatively and successfully piloted the British North America Act through Parliament in 1867, was neither unmindful of his contribution to that great achievement nor unaware of the possibility of applying some at least of the lessons of Canadian confederation to the very different circumstances of South Africa. But more important, this mild-mannered, erudite but fussy man, who involved Disraeli in many troublesome situations and had earned from him the soubriquet of Twitters, was an imperialist *tout simple*. He believed in Empire and was convinced that if Empire were to be sustained one condition in terms of security and defence was British control of southern Africa. He thought this might best be secured by the once deliberately discarded policy of federation. If the omens were not so favourable as in the 1850s they were at the least not unfavourable. The republics were small and impoverished, the government of President Burgers in the Transvaal being on the verge of bankruptcy; Zulu power was in the ascendant and threatening, and the time – it seemed – was approaching when the Boers in the Transvaal might be faced with the choice of annihilation or annexation. J. A. Froude, historian and adviser to Carnarvon in his South African policy was converted to federation after extensive travels in southern Africa. Carnarvon himself resolved upon action from London with the support of the government of the Cape and the agreement of the republics if both were obtainable; but if not then without them.[12] Neither for the first nor for the last time was British policy in South Africa to be the victim of its own impetuosity.

The colonial secretary's agent was Sir Theophilus Shepstone, secretary for Native Affairs in Natal. He proceeded to Pretoria early in 1877 and was not impressed by what he found there. President Burgers was a man of ideas and some vision but of uncertain following. He wished to preserve the independence of the republic by introducing reforms. The reforms required finance and the Boers, more than most, were reluctant to pay taxes. When Shepstone arrived no salaries were being paid to civil servants and the total resources of the Treasury amounted to twelve shillings and sixpence. He was empowered, by secret instructions, to proclaim the annexation of the Transvaal providing he was satisfied in the first place that it was necessary and in the second that the majority of the inhabitants would approve of it. Shepstone exercised this power on 12 April 1877. President Burgers acquiesced in annexation on condition that he was left free to protest against it in public – Shepstone being shown the terms of the proposed protest and making no objection to them.[13] In January 1879 came the long awaited war against the Zulus, launched by Sir Bartle Frere and approved by the new colonial secretary, Sir Michael Hicks Beach. After an initial British disaster at Isandhlwana[14] there followed, with the arrival of reinforcements, decisive victory at Ulundi on 4 July. Zulu power was destroyed, Zululand broken up and the threat to the Boers removed. They had, accordingly, no longer need for British support. Nor had they received the local autonomy Shepstone had promised. Sir Bartle Frere, it is true, gave renewed assurances of self-government, but General Sir Garnet Wolseley, fresh from his victory over the Zulus, struck another note. 'The Union Jack,' he declared in a burst of soldierly eloquence would fly over Pretoria 'as long as the sun shone and the Vaal flowed down to the sea.' The Boers became increasingly restive. They had, moreover, a particular consideration in mind. Gladstone, in opposition, had denounced annexation; he returned to power in 1880. The Boers thought, not unreasonably, that annexation would be rescinded. The British, both at home and in South Africa, assumed that what had been done could not be undone.

In the event Gladstone pursued an indeterminate middle course. He rejected the policy of federation and recalled Sir Bartle Frere, the man on the spot most closely associated with it. But he gave neither the freedom nor the disannexation he had championed out of office nor yet the long deferred self-government. The Boers revolted. The British under General Sir George Pomeroy Colley were decisively defeated at Majuba Hill on 26 February 1881. Reinforcements however were arriving in Natal; the verdict could be reversed. But was Gladstone, who had condemned annexation, now to fight for it? Or was he to concede independence after conclusive, even humiliating defeat? The dilemma was a painful one. Gladstone decided on peace after defeat. He believed he was acting on principle but the Boers gave little credence to this. They noted simply the consequences of successful revolt and in later years remembered only too well the victory of their arms in what they spoke of as the first war of independence.

The terms of peace were embodied in the Pretoria Convention of 1881. The independence of the Transvaal was recognised, being made subject in the preamble to 'the suzerainty of Her Majesty' and to a British control over foreign policy as expressly stipulated in the text. Three years later the terms of the convention were negotiated afresh and embodied in a new 1884 Convention of London. There was no mention of suzerainty and in respect of relations with foreign countries it was more narrowly stated that the South African Republic should 'conclude no treaty with any state or nation other than the Orange Free State, nor with any native tribe to the eastward or westward of the republic', without the Queen's approval. The British maintained and the Boers repudiated the notion that suzerainty still subsisted. It seems in fact that on the British side there was no deliberate renunciation but a feeling that the term itself had insufficiently precise meaning. 'Whatever suzerainty meant in the Convention of Pretoria,' Lord Derby told the House of Lords on 17 March 1884, 'the condition of things which it implied still remains.' The use of the term had been given up 'because it was not capable of legal definition, and because it seemed to be a word which was likely to lead to misconception and misunderstanding'.[15] But granting that this was the reason for its abandonment the harm was done in that uncertainty was not removed but increased. There were those in later years, eminent jurists among them, notably James Bryce on the British side and Chief Justice de Villiers on the South African, who traced the Anglo-Boer conflicts of the 1890s to the ambiguities consequent upon the omission of that one word 'suzerainty' from the text of the London Convention of 1884, without however any British renunciation of their claim to exercise it. The conception of suzerainty, noted Bryce, was 'purely legal, though somewhat vague, and in practice it served to obscure Britain's obligation to treat the Transvaal with a strict regard to the recognised principles of international law as if it were a great power and regardless of the fact that the Dutch republics were no more than 'petty communities of ranchmen'.[16] Oom Paul Kruger, who as a boy had journeyed northward in the Great Trek, who was elected president of the South African Republic for the first time in 1883, and who least of all men was likely to be unmindful of British expansionist pressures, did not overlook the implications of contrasted interpretations of what might be held to subsist in terms of sovereignty after 1884.

The restored independence of the Transvaal was followed by the discovery and exploitation of new mineral wealth which made of the republic a magnet drawing speculators and adventurers from all over the world and in so doing brought that independence once again into jeopardy. 'The historian of the fall of the South African Republic,' writes Professor J. S. Marais in the opening sentence of *The Fall of Kruger's Republic*, 'must take as his starting point the great gold discoveries of the 1880s in that state.' The wealth of the Witwatersrand led to a sudden chaotic influx of foreigners (or Uitlanders as they were called) many of whom were, and more of whom claimed or aspired to be British subjects. Their numbers, in the absence of any census of population, were a matter of dispute and remain uncertain, but it is likely that within a decade from 1886 the population of the Transvaal was doubled. At a census which was taken in Johannesburg in July 1896, there was a European population of 50,907 of whom 6,205 were Transvaalers and the rest aliens. Of the aliens the largest number, 16,265 came from the United Kingdom, and the next largest, 15,162, also British subjects, from the Cape Colony.[17] As the Uitlanders made their fortunes the president determined that in return they should help to sustain the finances of the republic by the payment of taxes which, while onerous, were by no means incommensurate with their newly-won riches. He was no less resolved that they should not acquire political control of the state. Taxation without representation or with inadequate representation appeared to him a trifling matter by comparison with the safeguarding of the recently regained independence of his people. The 'creators of wealth', as the Uitlanders deemed themselves to be, complained. No doubt there were some who cared about the substance of their complaints but assuredly there were more who, recking little or nothing of the much publicised hardships of Johannesburg financiers, mine-owners or millionaires, saw in them an opportunity for furthering ends on which they had set their heart. Chief among those ends was the unification of South Africa.

In the last decade of the nineteenth century South Africa suffered from a plethora of strong men. At the Cape there was Cecil John Rhodes, forever talking and dreaming about sometimes confused but always spacious imperialist designs, as – seated on his favourite wicker chair – he faced towards the close, overhanging mountains above the stoep of his Cape Town home, Groote Schuur. Against Bismarck's 'blood and iron' Rhodes consciously balanced 'peace and gold'. He possessed a certain largeness of mind and a power of attraction over men as varied in age, in outlook and in background as the elder Hofmeyr, the young Smuts and even Milner at the last. He understood (as most English statesman not least Joseph Chamberlain never did) something of the nature of Afrikaner nationalism. While he believed passionately in the British mission, he was a racialist neither in the older nor yet in the newer sense. He became prime minister of the Cape in 1890 with the support of J. H. Hofmeyr, 'Onze Jan' – a man of stature and wisdom without political intensity and a dislike of final commitment[18] – and the Afrikaner Bond, and he numbered W. P. Schreiner, that early champion of native rights, among his closer friends. He coined the phrase so expressive of the Cape tradition, 'equal rights for all civilised men'. But his insights were not matched by equal patience or balanced judgment. Rhodes thought that mineral wealth as great as that of the Rand lay to the north and he based his hopes of counterbalancing the Transvaal on this conviction. Bechuanaland accordingly was a life-line, his 'Suez Canal to the interior'.[19] But this belief was not well founded and when, faced with deteriorating health – he was thought by his friends never to have been quite the same again after a fall from his horse in 1891 – he understood that this was not so, his mind inclined towards a quicker and more brutal solution. If the South African Republic could not be pressed into union or confederation by economic factors then more forceful means must needs be employed. Rhodes continued to believe in gold; his faith in peace was dimmed. Therein lay the tragedy of a man, to whom ends came to justify means which good judgment alone would have firmly repudiated.

Rhodes dominated the South African scene but in London he had to deal, at the climax of the unfolding South African struggle for power, with one of the strongest administrations and the most formidable colonial secretary in modern British history. Lord Salisbury was prime minister and foreign secretary; his nephew, A. J. Balfour, first lord of the Treasury; Lord Lansdowne was at the War Office and Joseph Chamberlain at the Colonial Office. Chamberlain had travelled far since his early radical-republican days and he knew the issue which had crystallised his latent imperialism. It was Irish Home Rule. The 'killing' of Gladstone's Bill in 1886 was the symbolic gesture. Thereafter he was a Unionist but not a Tory. He thought in terms of a United Kingdom that was strong because it remained united; of an Empire that would be stronger if it became united. The large, elusive themes of imperial federation, imperial defence, imperial *Zollverein* appealed to his restless, thrustful mind. He thought but indifferently of the Colonial Office officials he had inherited and they for their part had their misgivings about the impulsive actions of 'pushful Joe'. For unlike his traditionalist Tory colleagues Chamberlain was not content with policies of imperial *laissez-faire*, *laissez-aller;* he wished to develop imperial estates he deemed undeveloped, to organise imperial power and imperial trade.

He has been [wrote A. G. Gardiner later in a brief, penetrating character sketch] the great disturber of the modern world. He has given it battle-cries and banners – never opiates or anodynes. With him the barometer has always stood at 'stormy'. Long ago, Lord Salisbury hit off his part in politics in one of his happy similis. 'The cabinet,' he said, 'is like an old Dutch weather-clock. When it is going to be fine Lord Hartington appears, and when Mr Joseph Chamberlain is seen you may look out for squalls'.

Joseph Chamberlain did not disturb for the sake of creating disturbance but because he was intent upon the attainment and exercise of power.

The charge [continued A. G. Gardiner] which history will make against Mr Chamberlain is not that he broke with his party but that he broke with his faith. He broke with it because his passion for mastery has been the governing motive of his career. He believed that he could make Toryism the instrument of his purposes. He recreated it and gave it its motive power, and then it used him for its own ends. It found in him the ally it needed. . . .[20]

In 1895 Salisbury offered Chamberlain the Exchequer but he declined, asking for the Colonial Office instead. There was much surprise at his choice, the more so in that as a Liberal Unionist minority leader in a Tory cabinet he might have been expected to buttress a weak political position with a strong traditional office. But this 'modern merchant', as the German chancellor von Bülow called him,[21] sensed better than his aristocratic Tory colleagues the flowing tide of imperialist sentiment and, more substantially, the potential of Empire in a world of changing patterns of power. And last, but by no means least, Joseph Chamberlain never lacked self-confidence.

Rhodes and Chamberlain had one goal in common – the unification of South Africa. But beyond that one large purpose the differences between them were more pronounced than the area of agreement. Chamberlain was intensely 'British' in his approach. To him Crown, flag, nationality had of very necessity to be British. Rhodes entertained more flexible opinions. He was viewed with some suspicion in the Colonial Office because of an earlier contribution to Irish Home Rule funds, assuredly a gift not likely to commend him to the colonial secretary.[22] For Rhodes, winning the confidence of Afrikaners at the Cape and entering into a lasting union with the Afrikaners of the Orange Free State were alike steps in the fulfilment of the wider aims of persuading the Transvaalers of the desirability of cooperation. So long as he was advancing towards that goal he was willing, as Chamberlain was not, to compromise about symbols on the way. Even when he had abandoned hopes of peaceful advance Rhodes expected, in the event of a successful revolt by the Uitlanders in Johannesburg, that the immediate result would be 'an Anglicised and liberalised republic', whereas on the other hand Chamberlain thought in terms of a British colony with the British flag[23] and under the British Crown. Even when Rhodes' emphasis on an emerging South Africanism founded on cooperation between Briton and Boer weakened with growing impatience, it remained something not wholly absent from his thinking. In Chamberlain's mind it was rarely, if ever, present. Rhodes was not a particularly sensitive man but he had not the insensitivity of Chamberlain to the aspirations of another and a smaller people. Then, too, Rhodes disliked and mistrusted the imperial factor; in the all-important years Chamberlain was its physical embodiment.

In the small country town capital founded by the Voortrekker, Andries Pretorius, where the streets were wide enough for an ox-waggon to turn, Oom Paul Kruger presided over the destinies of the Transvaal republic. His greatest asset, the wealth of the Rand, was also his greatest liability. But time, contrary to Rhodes' confident expectation, was not necessarily against him. By October 1894 the railway line to Delagoa Bay was completed, with President Kruger travelling there on a ceremonial first journey to underline the fact that the Transvaal at last had access, independent to British control, to the sea.[24] It could be used for trade and thus reduce dependence upon the Cape railways. It could also be used, and it was used, for the import of arms free from all British control. For Kruger, a patriarchal 'volk' figure of 'gnarled magnificence' – the description was John Buchan's[25] – eccentric, even at times alarming in his personal habits, steeped in his boyhood memories of the Great Trek and ever mindful of annexation and Majuba Hill, was convinced, (not mistakenly) that Rhodes at the Cape was with tacit British support planning to undermine and then to destroy the independence of the Transvaal. He himself, caught in the web of wealth and immigration, franchise and independence, by his own policies provided occasion for intervention.

By 1895 the republic was enjoying unprecedented prosperity due to the gold mines owned and worked by the Uitlanders. The president took the view that he had allowed the Uitlanders to come, but having come of their own free will they must accept what laws and more especially what taxation the republic saw fit to impose. Chamberlain on the other hand, while acknowledging that the republic was free to determine its own immigration policy, was firm in his conclusion that the Uitlanders, once admitted, must be fairly treated. Since they were for the most part British subjects it was the responsibility of the Colonial Office to ensure that this was so. Colonial Office representations however made little apparent impact on the president's actions. The Uitlanders, conscious of injury and encouraged by expressions of British sympathy, plotted to revolt. Chamberlain was made aware of their intentions. He offered no discouragement; on the contrary, he proffered opinions on the most convenient time for a rising.[26] His more general reflections were summarised in a letter to Salisbury dated 26 December 1895. 'I have received private information', he recorded 'that a rising in Johannesburg is imminent and will take place in the next few days. . . . There is nothing to be done but to watch the event which we have done nothing to provoke. If the rising is successful it ought to turn to our advantage.'[27] The rising in Johannesburg did not take place. As revolutionaries, the millionaire mine owners of Johannesburg were tardy and for ever undecided. Relying upon them, it was caustically remarked, was as sensible as backing a carthorse to win the Derby.

There was, then, no rising, but there was a raid.[28] The two were planned to coincide in time, the raiders riding in from Pitsani on the Bechuanaland border in response to an appeal from British subjects in the Transvaal driven to desperate revolt by Boer oppression. But even without the revolt there was still an appeal. It had been composed some time beforehand but was released as the raiders crossed the border. It contained moving allusions to the plight of women and children in

Johannesburg and inspired Alfred Austin, the Poet Laureate, to write:

> There are girls in the gold-reef city,
> There are mothers and children too!
> And they cry, 'Hurry up! for pity!'
> So what can a brave man do?[29]

The girls, the mothers and the children were, however, quite safe when Dr Jameson crossed the border on 31 December 1895, unable any longer to tolerate the perpetual postponements of the Johannesburg rising. He had been stationed there with his force by Rhodes. This had been made possible by the concession, after long negotiations first with the Rosebery and then with the Salisbury administration, of a strip of land on the Transvaal frontier to the Chartered Company to carry the Cape Town-Kimberley line on to Rhodesia. With control went policing rights. Did Chamberlain know of the other purposes for which the territory and the rights that went with it might be used? Did he have foreknowledge of a raid to coincide with a rising? Certainly he denounced Rhodes and the raid in unequivocal terms as 'an act of war or rather filibustering'.[30] Rhodes, ruined by his own impatience and by the rashness of his closest friend, resigned, but Kruger was little impressed. Indeed he did not have great reason to be. To this day, despite a parliamentary inquiry – the Committee of no-Inquiry – which was a model of all that a parliamentary inquiry ought not to be, and despite critical historical investigation, uncertainty and doubt on this point, so closely affecting the honour of the colonial secretary and the integrity of the British government, remain. Was it the case that the colonial secretary, who on his own admission knew all about the rising, knew nothing about the raid? Was he unaware, when the territory around Pitsani was transferred, of the purposes for which it was to be used? Did he not suspect that the timing of the Johannesburg rising was related to the question of armed assistance from across the border? It has indeed been so affirmed but the weight of evidence and probability hardly suffices to sustain the affirmation.[31]

Kruger, moreover, was now strongly placed. Not only had he disposed of the raiders; he had also received commendation from an exalted, albeit a dangerous quarter. It came in the form of a telegram from the Kaiser Wilhelm the Second. The wording was strong but in the circumstances of its drafting the surprise is that it was no stronger. The kaiser presided over a council at which (if Holstein's testimony be accepted)[32] an embarrassed chancellor and state secretary listened to some eccentric proposals for German intervention in the Transvaal. It was suggested that a Colonel Schele, 'a handsome man whose talents were generally considered very mediocre',[33] should disguise himself as a lion hunter and present himself to President Kruger with an offer of his services as chief of staff. More disturbing was the notion, also discussed, that one or two companies of German troops should be diverted from East Africa and proceed via Lourenço Marques to the Transvaal. All that was decided upon was the telegram that has gone down to history as the kaiser's telegram. It was despatched on 3 January 1896 and congratulated President Kruger on repulsing 'the armed bands' which had broken into his country, by his own and his people's energy 'without appealing for the help of friendly powers'.[34] The reaction in England was sharp. The raiders, if not absolved, were deemed misguided and overhasty rather than fundamentally mistaken. And in Anglo-German relations a turning full of danger had been taken.

'Well, it is a little history being made,' said Rhodes in a high-pitched voice, his face all fallen in, as he drove back in his Cape cart from Government House to Groote Schuur, after hearing of the capture of Jameson and his raiders, 'that is all.'[35] But it was by no means all. Between Boer and Briton confidence was gone. And the great issue still remained unresolved. Was it possible for the two Boer republics and the two British colonies to live together independently and also amicably in South Africa? Before the raid a compromise federal solution was conceivable; after the raid there were the sharp alternatives of mistrustful coexistence or war. Events had left Kruger in no mood for conciliatory gestures. He was unrepentant about the treatment of the Uitlanders. New and more oppressive laws were introduced, to be repealed only at the insistence of Chamberlain. The Transvaal armed. War material imported through Delagoa Bay rose in value from £61,903 in 1895 to £121,396 in 1896 to £256,291 in 1897. Forts were constructed at Pretoria and Johannesburg at a cost of over one and a half million pounds.[36] President Kruger, asked what the arms were for, replied on one occasion 'Oh, kaffirs, kaffirs and such like objects'. Yet such evasions (in which the president at all times delighted) are not evidence that the arms were bought for other than defensive purposes. Nor indeed did the British government anticipate Boer aggression. What they feared was that, with increased strength would come increased recalcitrance. Kruger himself was triumphantly re-elected to the presidency in February 1898 by 12764 votes against 3716 and 1943 for his two opponents, Schalk Burger and Commandant-General Joubert, the slogan 'Beware of Rhodes and keep your power dry' being said to have decided many a waverer to support him.[37] There was also strong Boer resentment at the reassertion by Chamberlain in a dispatch of 6 December 1897 of British claims to a suzerainty which in the Boer view had lapsed with the signature of the London Convention in 1884. The Transvaal government proposed international arbitration; the colonial secretary and the high commissioner rejected all such ideas, partly on grounds of principle and prestige and partly because, in Milner's words 'the convention is *such a wretched instrument*, that even an impartial court would be likely to give such an interpretation to it as would render it perfectly worthless to us'.[38] And meanwhile there was the constant, exacerbating pressure of the Uitlanders for what they claimed to be their rights. In Alfred Milner they found a new and most formidable champion.

Milner was a product of Balliol College, Oxford, and among the most distinguished alumni of its greatest age. To his fine classical scholarship he added zeal, method and a capacity for work often attributed to his Germanic background. He came to South Africa as governor of Cape Colony and high commissioner in succession to Lord Rosmead in May 1897 and spent much of his first year in learning Afrikaans. Then he turned his mind to an analysis of the problems of South Africa. He noted that there was full equality in voting rights as between Boers and British in Cape Colony and that there was none in the Transvaal. The contrast exasperated him. He complained of the 'unprogressiveness not to say retrogressiveness of the Transvaal government'. In February 1898 he warned Chamberlain privately that 'There is no way out of the political troubles of South Africa except reform in the Transvaal or war. And at present the chances of reform in the Transvaal are worse than ever.' Kruger had returned to office 'more autocratic and reactionary then ever', and, he continued, '*looking at the question from a purely South African point of view*, I should be inclined to work up to a crisis, not indeed by looking about for causes of complaint or making a fuss about trifles but by steadily and inflexibly pressing for redress of substantial wrongs and injustices. It would not be difficult thus to work up an extremely strong *cumulative case*'.[39] From that conclusion Milner was not to depart. He became progressively less the British high commissioner and more the spokesman of the British in the Cape and in the Transvaal. He urged Chamberlain not to weaken, not to delay the time of final decision. Among the Uitlanders there was a widespread conviction that Kruger would not concede an effective franchise until he had 'looked down the cannon's mouth'. Their opinion was made known in London.[40] A British demand for Uitlander enfranchisement, on this view, would accordingly be met only if backed by the threat of force. On 4 May 1899 Milner, 'risking upon it his reputation and career', sent an official despatch to the secretary of state endorsing Uitlanders complaints and deliberately inflammatory in its phrasing. 'The spectacle of thousands of British subjects kept permanently in the position of helots,' read the most provocative of its sentences, 'constantly chafing under undoubted grievances, and calling vainly to Her Majesty's government for redress, does steadily undermine the influence and reputation of Great Britain and the respect for the British government within its own dominions'.[41] The despatch was not published until 14 June and then one paragraph, emphasising the increasing military strength of the Transvaal, was omitted. In the excitable and emotional atmosphere of late nineteenth-century imperialism, especially in London, the publication of this despatch, even if not in its complete form, stirred up the strong emotional popular reaction that Milner hoped for. Chamberlain was questionably, Milner assuredly, by then convinced of the inevitability of war. And increasingly the atmosphere of impending war spread to Pretoria. The Boers thought the British intended 'to jump the Transvaal'. Sir Robert Ensor believed the cabinet was not affected by popular clamour but he added: 'If the Boers became united by the mistaken conviction that a British government wanted their blood, it was largely because they heard a British public calling for it'.[42]

On 31 May 1899, that is after the 'helots' dispatch had been sent but before it was published, a conference was held at Bloemfontein. President Kruger was there and among his advisers was his youthful state attorney, J. C. Smuts.[43] So too was President Steyn of the Orange Free State. And there also was Sir Alfred Milner. It was not likely even under the most favourable circumstances that the venerable president and the purposeful high commissioner would find each other mutually comprehending; and the circumstances were far from favourable. Milner, described by his friend John Buchan as 'the last man for the task',[44] became more and more impatient. He found Kruger 'very slow'; he 'rambles fearfully', he talked continually of 'my independence', he said a vote for the Uitlanders (because of their numbers) was 'worse than annexation'; he declared it to be 'wholly against God's word to let strangers carry on the administration, seeing that they cannot serve two masters . . .'; and, again, that he was 'not ready to hand over my country to strangers'. 'It is our country that you want,' cried the old president in an emotional climax.[45] Milner unmoved, was prepared to listen no longer. He broke off the conference on 5 June before a telegram from Chamberlain telling him to let Kruger talk himself out, had reached him. There were no reforms of the kind he deemed sufficient, so he urged war. The cabinet approved an ultimatum. But it was not delivered. It was anticipated by an ultimatum from the Boers on 9 October 1899.

The war that followed could have only one outcome – the defeat of the Boers and the British annexation of the two republics. It happened, annexation preceding final defeat, with the Orange Free State being annexed in May and the Transvaal in September 1900. Nor was such annexation to be temporary: 'If we are victors,' declared Chamberlain, '. . . the territories of these republics must be finally incorporated in Her Majesty's dominions.' This implied unconditional surrender. Milner, easily convinced of the impossibility of conciliating (in his own words) 'panoplied hatred, insensate ambitions, invincible ignorance' was insistent that it should be so. And peace, albeit with qualifications, was made on that basis at Vereeniging on 31 May 1902. Thus by force of arms the extent of the future Commonwealth was significantly enlarged.

The war established British supremacy in South Africa. It does not follow from this alone that the war was fought to establish it. In 1900, George Bernard Shaw surmised: 'Whether the electorate shares President Kruger's political ideas or believes them to be as outdated as his theology, it probably suspects that if the government had been as earnest in its efforts to stave off war as in its efforts to stave off Old Age Pensions, there would have been no war.'[46] This was less than the truth. The question which preoccupied the government was not whether to stave off but whether to precipitate war. In fact they did precipitate war by adopting a posture of menace, deliberately intended to force the pace and the issue. Certainly there were other factors in the situation, from the manipulations of financiers to the still insufficiently analysed ambitions of the Boers, but they do not alter the fact that the purpose of British government policy – including in the term government, high commissioner, colonial secretary and the cabinet acting with collective responsibility – was to secure undivided British control over southern Africa by any necessary means. Milner expounded that purpose more clearly than any other and the war, accordingly, has been called by Professor Le May 'Sir Alfred Milner's War'.[47] Certainly Milner had his 'grand design' in which quick and decisive military victory in a limited war – 'an Austerlitz in the veld' – would open the way for 'a gigantic exercise in physical and social engineering' intended to ensure for the foreseeable future British supremacy in South Africa. He was too the most influential of British proconsuls in the decisive years. Yet on the other hand neither a theoretician's formulation of aims nor the undoubted reality of Milner's influence warrant any such token attribution of final responsibility. Milner was not colonial secretary; still less was he a member of the cabinet which in the last resort determined British policy in South Africa. The members of the cabinet were neither the victims of circumstances nor under the domination of Milnerism. They were acting – notably the colonial secretary despite his occasional recorded misgivings – in conformity with their own views and in accord with a vocal section of public opinion in sanctioning policies which led, as they were intended to lead, to the establishment of British supremacy.

It was not, therefore, in this context Milner's war; it was a war embarked upon for reasons of state which whether subsequently thought sufficient or insufficient convinced those responsible for British policy in South Africa at the time of the need to act.

The conduct of the war was not unrelated to its purposes. It was a war to end disputed supremacy in South Africa by destroying the Boer republics as separate political entities. 'You want to take away my independence' Kruger had complained to Milner at Bloemfontein. That was so. Divided sovereignty in South Africa was deemed too dangerous to be allowed to continue. That meant a war to establish a single sovereignty. In turn that meant, in fact and possibly of necessity, insistence upon a policy of unconditional surrender. And unconditional surrender meant, short of the quick victory that Milner understood to be near-essential for the fulfilment of his aims, protracted, inconclusive campaigning across the vast spaces of southern Africa and with it, what Milner so greatly deplored, a blunting of the fine edge of resolution.

The prolongation of war meant other things besides. It meant most of all the sanction of successive commanders-in-chief of measures which cast long shadows down future years: indiscriminate or nearly indiscriminate burning of farms ostensibly in order to preserve law and order in the Orange Free State – 'what fool in his folly,' commented Lionel Curtis,[48] 'taught us we could prevent men from brigandage by making them homeless?' – the rounding up of women and children in concentration camps in which more than twenty thousand died of epidemics or disease, as well as threatened deportations first of large numbers of Boers – Fiji and Madagascar were in Kitchener's mind as their possible destinations provided that, in the latter case the French were agreeable – and when the cabinet rejected the policy, then selective deportation of wives, Kitchener taking the view, which once again the cabinet firmly rejected, that they were the more implacable and therefore responsible for prolonging the war. On the other hand, it is also to be recorded, as a matter of historical consequence, that the war itself was conducted with a chivalry that left behind it feelings among fighting men of mutual esteem and respect.

Peace was imposed but not without conditions. It could hardly have been otherwise. The Boers were skilful negotiators, they knew what mattered to them most and moreover they found the military arm, in the person of Lord Kitchener, more conciliatory than the civilian. The terms of peace accordingly proved more tolerant and more tolerable than had been anticipated. But the decision to make peace was nevertheless painfully reached by the Boer leaders.

It was in May 1902 near Vereeniging in a large tent pitched by command of Kitchener that the sixty representatives of the two republics discussed the issue of peace or continued war.[49] It had already been made clear to them that the British, however adaptable on lesser matters, were not prepared to negotiate on the basis of continuing Boer independence. The debate opened with an account of declining Boer fortunes, of shortages of horses and food in many though not in all areas, of the necessary abandonment of hope of foreign aid or of a rising in the Cape. 'There will be no general rising in the Cape'[50] despite much sympathy, reported Smuts. Many commanders voiced their great anxiety about the women and children and the casualty roll in the concentration camps.

Have we not now [asked Acting State President Burger][51] arrived at that stage when we should pray: 'Thy will be done?'. . . We have already effected supernatural things at which the world stands amazed. Shall we now allow a people who have sacrificed even women and children, to be exterminated?. . . We were proud and despised the enemy, and is it not perhaps God's will to humble us and cast down the pride in us by allowing us to be oppressed by the English people?. . . Our people do not deserve to be annihilated.

A more considerable figure, Commandant-General Botha, dwelt upon that self-same thought:

It has been said we must fight to the bitter end, but no one tells us what that bitter end is. Is it where everyone lies in his grave or is banished? In my opinion we must not consider the time when everyone lies in his grave as the 'bitter end'. If we do so, and act upon that view, we become the cause of the death of our people. Is the bitter end not here, where the people have struggled till they can struggle no more?. . . If we wish to negotiate, now is the time. If the Lord God wills it, then, however bitter, we must come to terms.[52]

General Smuts was in agreement with him. There was one thing that could not be sacrificed even for independence. That was the Afrikaner people. For their sake, for the sake of its women and children, must peace be made. But not all shared that opinion. There was also heard the voice of the romantic, unrealistic, militant nationalist.

The war is a matter of faith [declared Chief Commandant de Wet]. If I had not been able to do so in faith, I would never have taken up arms. Let us again renew our covenant with God. . . . The entire war has been a miracle. . . . I cannot see into the future, but this I know, that behind me it is light. What lies before me I do not know. There it is dark, but we must go on trusting God, and then, when victory comes, we shall not be proud.[53]

The realists won the day, but the voice of the romantic remained to trouble the thoughts and divide the minds of later generations.

Some among the Boers who made peace at Vereeniging were later to be numbered among the chief architects of the Commonwealth. Their insight was applauded and the road they had travelled viewed mostly in comfortable Commonwealth retrospect. Yet it was as important that they and their people had known defeat as that they – or rather some among them – should have been reconciled to Empire within a broadening Commonwealth concept. And history records that the impress of that defeat and the resolve that it should be undone was more enduring than that of subsequent and magnanimous reconciliation. In September 1905 J. X. Merriman, reflecting in Cape Town with some asperity about the events of the recent past, in a letter to Goldwin Smith deplored, among other things, evidence of continuing British fears of the Dutch 'and the terrible things they may do'. He remarked upon the fact that since defeat the Boers had shown great dignity and self-control, and concluded with the sobering and in the event well-justified warning that the Boer 'is a good man at a waiting game'.[54] On this occasion, however, he did not have long to wait.

The Treaty of Vereeniging decided the vexed question of sovereignty in South Africa. By compulsion of arms the Boer republics had been brought under the British flag and for the first time since the Great Trek all Europeans in South Africa owed allegiance to one ruler. It was this which opened the way to the unification of South Africa; but it did not of itself bring it about. There remained after the treaty the four separate political entities, Cape Colony and Natal enjoying responsible self-government, the Transvaal and the Orange River Colony the status only of Crown colonies. Divided by war, unequal in political standing, by whom and by what means were they to be associated in one larger whole?[55] For most Englishmen and for not a few Afrikaners the imperial statesman whose name was most closely linked with the unification of South Africa was the Liberal, Sir Henry Campbell-Bannerman, who succeeded Balfour as prime minister in December 1905. Campbell-Bannerman had condemned the wartime concentration camps as 'methods of barbarism', and his courageous denunciation of them especially in the face of divided opinions in the party about future South African policy, was thought by Botha to have left the door open for Anglo-Boer reconciliation after the war. On 7 February 1906, Campbell-Bannerman had a talk with General Smuts on the basis of a memorandum Smuts had brought with him to London about the future of the former Boer republics, which in the opinion of Smuts 'settled the future of South Africa'. On the following day, Campbell-Bannerman made a speech to the cabinet which Lloyd George was to describe as 'the most dramatic, the most important ten minutes' speech ever delivered in our time'[56] and which persuaded his colleagues to agree collectively to the prompt concession, without any intermediate period of representative institutions as had been contemplated by the Unionists, of responsible government on the basis of a new constitution to the defeated Dutch republics. This was against the weight of Colonial Office opinion and the judgment of Lord Selborne, who had succeeded Milner as high commissioner and who believed that the Boers, far from being predisposed towards reconciliation, were biding their time, but it had the vigorous backing of the under-secretary of state, Winston Churchill.

Responsible government was restored to the Transvaal on 6 December 1906, and to the Orange River colony, thereafter known once more as the Orange Free State, on 5 June, 1907, in both instances by Letters Patents, thereby avoiding the judgment of the House of Lords. It was as well for the application of Liberal policy that such a device could be employed, for the restoration of self-government to the Transvaal was described in the Commons by the Unionist leader A. J. Balfour as 'the most reckless experiment ever tried in the development of a great colonial policy'[57] and the great Unionist majority in the Lords had already shown themselves to be in no mood to defer in any matter to the opinion of the Liberal majority in the lower House. As for the decision to restore self-government itself, while certainly a bold political step, it was neither rash nor little considered, as opposition denunciations of it sought to suggest, nor for that matter so dramatic as Smuts' later comments upon his conversation with Campbell-Bannerman might lead one to suppose. Rather did it follow naturally from the strand of Liberal thinking, best represented by Campbell-Bannerman himself, about South Africa during and after the war.[58] The principle which guided Liberal policy was reconciliation with the Boers, made possible, despite all that had taken place, by a timely concession of political autonomy within the British Empire.

Neither the prime minister, nor, as the files abundantly testify, the Colonial Office, were unmindful of the implications of the decision taken in February 1906 to restore self-government forthwith to the former republics. It was not a leap-in-the-dark; it was a calculated risk, or, as Campbell-Bannerman's biographer wrote, 'an act of faith'.[59] More than forty years later General Smuts remembered it, and the man who was chiefly responsible for it, in an address delivered in the Senate House at Cambridge. '. . . I would specially mention', he said, 'one whose name should never be forgotten . . . Campbell-Bannerman, the statesman who wrote the word *Reconciliation* over . . . that African scene, and thus rendered an immortal service to the British Empire, aye, to the cause of man everywhere.'[60] Of course, even such an act of faith could not obliterate all the memories of war. Grass may grow quickly over a battlefield but it grows slowly over burnt homesteads and civilian concentration camps. And, even responsible government within the

Empire could not compensate in most Afrikaner minds for loss of republican independence but at least it contributed, more than any other action conceivable in the circumstances could have done, to further Anglo-Boer reconciliation.

Liberal policy in 1906–7 did not bring about the union of South Africa but it made its advancement possible, psychologically by helping to reconcile the Boers to existence within the Empire and technically by placing the four South African colonies on an equal footing in negotiation about future relations between them. But the nature of their relationship was something that after the South African war could be determined only in South Africa. The 'imperial factor' had to be and was firmly excluded. That was a condition of Afrikaner support for union. Accordingly, as earlier in Canada and Australia, the constitution was fashioned in debate and protracted conference by representatives of the four self-governing colonies. It was 'home-made'. This meant that the preconceptions and preoccupations of those who made it, and not those of the imperial government, determined its character. Those preoccupations were many and varied but through them all ran the consistent purpose of the Transvaal to create a strong, unitary state.

The wealth of the Transvaal constituted the occasion for war and was a condition of unification. Of necessity therefore the views of the Transvaal weighed heavily, even conclusively, in respect of the nature of a united South African state. The Transvaal government, with General Botha as its first prime minister, increasingly favoured strong and stable government. For this there were many reasons, some of them subsequently overmuch discounted. One such was the continuing antagonism of the great financial interests to the Boers and the deeply ingrained mistrust of the Boers for the financiers and mineowners, the Uitlanders of other days and more recently the instigators and beneficiaries of indentured Chinese immigrant labour on the Rand. In December 1906 General Smuts, expatiating once more on a subject which had loomed large in a memorandum he had brought with him to London and shown to British ministers in February that year, wrote to Merriman saying that the South African idea 'is waging a mortal war with organised money power which is corrupting politics and tampering with men's souls all over South Africa . . .'. The existence of this power and its influence was a reason for favouring 'federation or rather (if possible) unification. Believe me, as long as we stand divided and separated in South Africa the money power will beat us in the Transvaal government and as a consequence over the rest of South Africa. I know the practical difficulties, which will be well-nigh insurmountable.'[61]

The phrasing verges on the melodramatic but despite some historians' doubts the sentiments were almost certainly authentic. Fear of financiers was supplemented by another and again possibly insufficiently regarded but more familiar factor. While Downing Street desired to discard its South African responsibilities, South Africans – English and Afrikaners in this at one – wished to discard Downing Street.

The one aim for us [Smuts told Merriman in 1906] is South African self-rule. But it sounds almost like a mockery at present – what with the malevolence of Conservative governments and the stupidity of Liberals. However we can but do our duty, knowing that the events of the last seven or eight years have stirred and set free forces in South Africa which are quite beyond the control of Downing Street or any other street or lane in London.

And in passionate climax, associating imperial with financial influences, he declared that he would rather suffer defeat in the cause of a united and free South Africa 'than triumph with the satanic hacks of a Milner or a Rhodes'. Clearly the more firmly united the South African colonies, the greater would be the measure of their effective independence from both. 'My own position,' wrote Smuts more temperately in August 1907 'is that federation or rather unification is a good and wise ideal; it is the only alternative to Downing Street which is a most baneful factor.'[62]

There remained – most important of all in terms of political as distinct from economic or administrative considerations – the place of non-Europeans in South Africa. The stronger the central government, the greater would be its control over native policy. Unified administration might result in the magnanimity that derives from assured authority, as many Liberals in England wished to believe, or, alternatively, in policies of repression which concentration of power would make practicable. What alone was certain was that while a federal government might preserve diversities, a unitary government predicated pressure towards uniformity and a concentration of European power and authority at the centre.

There was a press campaign against federation in which many have sensed the hand of Smuts. Certainly he was strongly opposed to a federal solution but then so were others, President M. T. Steyn of the Orange Free State among them. 'Surely,' the president wrote to Merriman on 30 January 1907, 'Australia ought to be an object lesson to us not to federate in haste', and he continued, 'Our duty I take it is to see we are not jockeyed into some or other ready-made federation scheme.'[63] Merriman himself probed more deeply. The paraphernalia of four separate governments, judiciaries and administrations was, he pointed out to Goldwin Smith in a letter later that year,[64] absurdly expensive. Yet some of the difficulties in the way of unification were very great – 'the local jealousies – the terrible native question which is always with us and to which we have added the Asiatic trouble.' How was the franchise to be determined in a unified state? The franchise at the Cape, without distinction of colour but with a high educational qualification, had 'on the whole . . . worked well'. 'Our natives have increased both in wealth and in habits of industry and civilisation. They have given little or no trouble. . . . I must confess that viewed merely as a safety valve I regard the franchise as having served its purpose.' But none of the other colonies approached to this system. 'In the two Boer states they have refused the native civil rights – in Natal the whole system has been designed to keep him in a state of barbarism.' In any negotiations Merriman correctly surmised 'they will attempt to get us to abandon our franchise'. The best course, he thought, would be to adopt a franchise with a real educational test which would 'shut out all but the native who was fit to exercise the rights of a citizen, while not denying to any man the privileges of citizenship on the ground of accident of colour.' But he feared, again correctly, that this would be impossible and speculated about the possibility of retaining the Cape franchise, while allowing a differential franchise elsewhere. Was this possible? Were there precedents? The New Zealand practice was not altogether applicable. There was, it was true, separate representation for Maoris, but on the New Zealand basis that would mean in time the swamping of the white electorate in South Africa. 'There is this difference,' he concluded, '. . . in New Zealand the Maoris are the idle classes, the Europeans industrious. In the Cape the natives are the workers growing in riches as a result of their industry' and accordingly qualifying in increasing numbers for the franchise as time went on. There was, in sum, no solution in respect of the native question that was politically practicable and morally acceptable for the whole of a united South Africa. In that context questions of a unitary or a federal state were matters self-evidently only of degree.

The constitution of the Union of South Africa was shaped in successive conventions held at Durban, Cape Town and Bloemfontein in 1908–9.[65] The governments of the four colonies, Cape Colony, Natal, the Orange Free State and the Transvaal were represented as equals, but among equals the position of the Transvaal with its able and hard-working delegation and its expert advisers drawn from the ranks of Lord Milner's young men remained in all respects pre-eminent. That delegation, Smuts not least among them, presented the case for union as against federation with a logic, force and a persistence which their possible opponents altogether lacked.

The aim of the architects of union was the fusing of the two European races and thereby, to quote General Smuts, 'the remaking of South Africa . . . on a higher plane of political and national life.' The unitary form of government, subject to whatever safeguards were agreed, as advocated by the Transvaal delegation, was accepted partly because of obvious economic advantages and a general desire for efficient administration but chiefly because it was thought the more likely to weld white South Africa 'into one compact nationality inspired by one common pervading spirit', and, be it added, applying one consistent and coherent native policy. It meant – and despite some superficial concessions to the provinces was understood by the powerful Transvaal delegation to the convention to mean – strong centralised government with ultimate authority resting in the union Parliament. It meant also (as federation might not have done) that if the experiment of fusion failed then the majority white community would be well placed to control the government of the country should it so desire. The Canadian federal precedent which had ensured the safeguarding of French Canadian rights was considered but deemed inappropriate, partly because of very different financial, trading and transport problems and still more because the European peoples were geographically interspersed in South Africa as they were not in Canada. But it is also the case that the counterbalancing advantages of a federal system were insufficiently weighed because of the indolence and ineptitude of the political leaders up in English-speaking Natal, the one province which had a clear interest in federation rather than union on almost every political and cultural ground. The case for federation went almost by default. 'I could always in the last resort,' wrote Patrick Duncan, 'ask opponents in Natal whether under unification they thought their affairs would be more inefficiently managed than they are now and none of them could truthfully say that their worst apprehension went as far as that.'[66] In the sequel, union was in fact approved in Natal, alone of the four provinces, by popular referendum. Positively this illustrated more than anything else the impressive degree of confidence that prevailed in the principle of one white South African state at that time.

The Boers feared and the natives hoped that after the war the British government would insist on extending the application of Cape native policy to the northern provinces. In the event the fears of the Boers proved unfounded and the hopes of the natives were belied. There were two principal reasons for this. In the first place the thinking of the imperial government was dominated by what was called 'the Racial Question', by which was meant relations between the two European peoples in South Africa. And it was dominated for the very good reason that these white communities alone could at that time provide men locally, who could assume responsibility for the government of Southern Africa. Though not without its difficulties it was possible to think of the administration of the defeated republics with the co-operation of the defeated Boers, but was it possible to think of their administration *against* the Boers? The second and more concrete point to be noted is that the Liberal governments were bound by the concession their Conservative predecessors had approved in respect of native policy by Article 8 of the Treaty of Vereeniging. That article read: 'The question of granting the franchise to natives will not be decided until after the introduction of self-government.' This was an explicit undertaking not to admit any native to the franchise in the Transvaal or the Orange River Colony while Britain had direct control over their domestic policies. Together with the other terms of peace, Article 8 was submitted to the high commissioner, the Colonial Office, the colonial secretary and the cabinet. In the Colonial Office, it was noted that 'it did not seem possible to debar the native, if duly qualified, from having the franchise under representative government and suggested that the franchise should be granted before representative government was instituted but 'so limited as to secure the just predominance of the white race as in Cape Colony'. The official principally concerned, F. Graham, minuted, 'The native franchise is I think the only point worth hesitating about. As [the clause] stands the native will never have the franchise. No responsible government will give it to him.'[67] But neither the high commissioner, the colonial secretary nor the cabinet appear to have hesitated. Why should they? They had fought the war to ensure British supremacy, not to establish native rights. Later Milner conceded that acquiescence in Article 8 was a mistake. He added that he believed 'as strongly as ever that we got off the right lines when we threw over Mr Rhodes' principle of "equal rights for every civilized man".'[68]

The Colonial Office files later abound in statements of what in these circumstances an imperial government could *not* do. It could not go back on Article 8 of the treaty. It could not interpret that Article narrowly, applying it only to the natives because, as a Committee of Enquiry under the chairmanship of Sir Joseph West-Ridgeway reported, the Boers had in good faith interpreted it as applying to all non-European inhabitants. The secretary of state, Lord Elgin, who thought it quite evident that 'the time must come when there will be danger of a collision between the white and coloured races unless the relations between them are fair and equitable',[69] anxiously considered what steps might be open to the imperial government. But when the steps 'open to us to secure the just interests of the natives' were reviewed one by one, the objections to each seemed well-nigh insurmountable. The secretary of state himself conceded that the terms of surrender 'absolutely preclude' representation of natives as in Cape Colony, and he felt obliged to infer that it also excluded representation of Coloured people. He weighed the possibility of making reservations in the grant of the constitution but noted that there would obviously be difficulty in framing any provision and that quite certainly any such provision would be objected to. The root of the problem was to reconcile the humanitarian aims of the Liberal government towards the non-European with their policy of generosity towards the defeated Boers in the form of restoring self-government to them. But there was in fact no way in which the imperial government could ensure improvement in the lot of the non-Europeans consistent both with the terms of Article 8 of the treaty and with their policy of self-government for the Europeans.

While nothing could be done before the restoration of self-government in respect of native rights, nothing could be done after because there was self-government. The debate in South Africa leading to union made it abundantly clear that either there was union with at most existing electoral laws in each colony, which meant an absolute political colour bar in the inland provinces and a nearly absolute political colour bar in Natal, or negotiations for union broke down. The Cape was no more prepared to sacrifice its liberal franchise than the Transvaal or the Orange Free State were prepared to extend it to their own territories. There were individuals, W. P. Schreiner notable among them, who foresaw many of the consequences of compromise and protested at acquiescence in illiberal northern practices. They enjoyed, however, only qualified support within the Cape and lacked any solid backing elsewhere. On a tour of the Transvaal after the convention had published its Report, Louis Botha had in fact great difficulty in preventing resolutions being passed for the removal of the Cape native franchise. 'All parties,' he wrote to Merriman on 17 March 1909,

> object most strongly to the provisions retaining in the Cape colony the native franchise for the Central Parliament . . . no other point has given me so much trouble as this and I must confess that it was all I could do to prevent mandates to amend this clause. I can assure you that a very great number of people in the Transvaal, English as well as Dutch, are quite prepared to wreck the union on this question.[70]

This was something not to be lightly discounted. Union without the Transvaal was at once unthinkable and impracticable. And so the solution was a compromise, with each province retaining its existing electoral laws. Self-evidently the issue was suspended, not concluded. Self-evidently too the balance of power would rest with the north. It was the Cape franchise which needed to be safeguarded and which was in fact entrenched in the constitution of the union – the South Africa Act 1909 – so that it might be amended only by a two-thirds majority of both Houses of the South African Parliament sitting together.

There was much debate before this electoral compromise was

reached. It touched on matters of deep import for the future of South Africa and the Commonwealth; it illuminated some lasting questions inseparable from the political association of different races but the most enduring impression that emerges from later reading of it is the sense of bafflement. Smuts at all times was ready to give sophisticated expression to acquiescent agnosticism. Thus in 1906 he wrote to Merriman of the natives:

> I do not believe in politics for them. Perhaps at bottom I do not believe in politics at all as a means for the attainment of the highest ends; but certainly so far as the natives are concerned politics will to my mind only have an unsettling influence. I would therefore not give them the franchise. . . . When I consider the political future of the natives in South Africa I must say that I look into shadows and darkness; and then I feel inclined to shift the intolerable burden of solving that sphinx problem to the ampler shoulders and stronger brains of the future. Sufficient unto the day. . . ![71]

And two years later he returned to the same theme:

> On the question of the native franchise my mind is full of Cimmerian darkness and I incline very strongly to leaving that matter over for the Union Parliament. I also feel pretty certain that a native franchise imported into the constitution would make union impossible of acceptance by the people. Let us therefore adhere to the comfortable gospel of *laissez-faire*. To us union means more than the native question. . .'.[72]

So potentially explosive an issue could not even then be put to rest quite so easily as that, as Smuts himself had reason to know. In June 1908 J. A. Hobson, writing on behalf of The New Reform Club Political Committee (a radical group in London), enquired of him how he thought the coming unification of South Africa would affect the position of the natives. In his reply Smuts argued once again that the only sound policy at that stage was to avoid any attempt at a comprehensive solution. Public opinion on the subject of the natives was in a chaotic state and, that being so, any solution would be a poor compromise which would probably prejudice a fairer and more statesman-like settlement later. He also gave renewed warning of the graver danger that any constitution which conferred the franchise on natives would not be ratified. Then he proceeded:

> My view is that the different franchise laws of the several colonies ought to be left undisturbed . . . and that the question of a uniform franchise law be gone into only after the union has been brought about. You will then avoid the dangers I have referred to; and you will in the union Parliament, representing as it will all that is best in the whole of South Africa, have a far more powerful and efficient instrument for the solution of the question along

> broad and statesmanlike lines than you will have in the union convention. . . . The political status of the natives is no doubt a very important matter, but vastly more important to me is the union of South Africa, which if not carried now will probably remain in abeyance until another deluge has swept over South Africa.

In that last sentence lay the crucial issue. Smuts had his order of priorities; at the head of it was union and that was understandable. But did he really believe, as he also wrote, that the right course for a British statesman concerned with the future of the natives was to 'trust the people of South Africa in this matter and commit the government of the whole of British South Africa [including the Basutoland, Bechuanaland and Swaziland protectorates] unreservedly to their charge' on the ground that it would best bring home to the South Africans 'their solemn duties in the matter'?[73]

Smuts sent to Merriman a copy of his reply to Hobson. On the practical and immediate issue both Hobson and Merriman were at one with Smuts. Hobson conceded that a uniform federal franchise appeared impracticable,[74] though pointing out with some emphasis that there was a pronounced objection on the part of the Liberals to any idea of handing over the protectorates to South Africa. Merriman commented, 'I entirely agree with you that it would be quite impossible to dream of any general native franchise at the present time. If it were adopted at the convention it would unquestionably lead to the rejection of the constitution in the majority of the states.'[75] The Cape would not abandon its non-European franchise in the interests of uniformity any more than the northern provinces would adopt it. The one sensible compromise was therefore agreement to continue existing and contrasted electoral practices. But looking to the future Merriman was not at one with Smuts. He was attracted by the idea of native territories governed as provinces with the natives allowed 'large privileges in local government' as in the Transkei. But the practical difficulties in the way of its general application appeared too formidable. So he was driven back reluctantly to the idea of a 'civilisation' franchise. The numbers of the natives 'constitute, and always will remain, our greatest menace'. There were four and a half million of them 'in different stages of progress but they are all progressing'.

> To me personally [Merriman continued] the idea of a native franchise is repellent but I am convinced that it is a safety-valve and the best safety-valve, and that so far from its leading to any immediate danger it will be generations before the European political supremacy will be menaced, while it does undoubtedly not only safeguard the rights of the inferior race but also gives them a content which puts an end to the unrest that any unrepresented population always will have.

Behind these debates and compromise solutions lay the fact that the war, by bringing under one allegiance communities which differed so profoundly on race relations, had at once sharply accentuated an existing problem and brought it within the frontiers of an Empire soon to become a Commonwealth. And the problem thus accentuated was one to which men in office had no solution to offer. Even the most clear-sighted among them looked also 'into the shadows and darkness'. 'The great African group' of which Lord Crewe spoke with so much satisfaction (when piloting the South Africa Act through the House of Lords) as joining the great American and the great Pacific group and bringing the self-governing Empire into something like its final form,[76] brought with it unsolved, first into the circle of the dominions, and then of the Commonwealth, one of the most difficult and disruptive of all human issues. The dilemma of the imperial government was plain. They could not at one and the same time pursue a liberal and a humanitarian policy in South Africa and so perforce they consoled themselves with thoughts of the entrenchment of the colour-blind franchise at the Cape, continuing imperial responsibility for the high commission territories and the magnanimity that might come with union and with the assurance of strength. Milner had advised Asquith, prime minister when union was enacted, as long ago as November 1897:

> You have, therefore, this singular situation, that you might indeed unite Dutch and English by protecting the black man, but you would unite them against yourself and your policy of protection.
>
> There is the whole *crux* of the South African position . . . You say and say truly that self-government is the basis of our colonial policy and the keystone of colonial loyalty. That principle, fearlessly and unflinchingly applied, would make South Africa as loyal as Canada – but what would be the price? The abandonment of the black races, to whom you have promised protection . . .'.[77]

Reluctantly that price in part was paid. What Ramsay MacDonald called the 'imperial standard' in dealing with native peoples was not maintained. This was no casual decision. It was taken to avoid the final alienation of the Boers, already embittered by their 'century of wrong'. It is widely assumed today that there was a practicable and preferable alternative policy open to the British government ensuring a measure of political rights for Africans. This may be so but it was not apparent to any British statesman with experience of government at the time. And the time was five years before the outbreak of the first world war.

CHAPTER 4

THE PACIFIC COLONIES; SELF-GOVERNMENT AND CONSOLIDATION

From the Cape to Australia – from political discord, the conflict of races . . . and the perpetual interference of the imperial government, to a country where politics are but differences of opinion, where the hand of the imperial government is never felt, where the people are busy with their own affairs . . . where everyone seems occupied, and everyone at least moderately contented – the change is great indeed.

So wrote James Anthony Froude on arriving at Adelaide from Cape Town in 1885. And to what did he attribute so vast a difference?

One is a free colony, the other is a conquered country. One is a natural and healthy branch from the parent oak, left to grow as nature prompts it [the other] a branch . . . withering from the point where it joins the trunk. . . . It is pleasant to turn from shadow to sunshine . . . to a country . . . where the closest acquaintance only brings out more distinctly how happy, how healthy English life can be in this far off dependency.[1]

The colourful contrasts may be somewhat discounted but assuredly Froude struck the right chord in writing of 'a branch from a parent oak' and English life in the far Pacific.

In the history of the Commonwealth there were two member states that were exceptional, they were Australia and New Zealand. They were, and are, exceptional in that they are British. Canada it is true had a population predominantly British in extraction until the second half of the twentieth century. But recognition in respect of language and of provincial rights of the existence of another, a French, culture was a condition of confederation. In South Africa the majority of the population was non-European and of the European minority, the majority was non-British. Of subsequent members, the Irish Free State, with the six plantation counties of Ulster excluded from it, lacked any substantial British settler element, though for historical reasons it also had two official languages; while Asian, African, West Indian and Mediterranean additions were of other races, cultures or civilisations. So it was that Australia and New Zealand, while constituting a fundamental element and the strongest cohesive force in the limited European Commonwealth which existed between 1917 when the designation Commonwealth was first used in formal conference, and 1947 when India, Pakistan and Ceylon became dominions, lacked counterpart or potential reinforcement. In the nature of things an expanding Commonwealth would include no more such British member states. The conditions for that did not and would never exist despite imperialist illusions entertained from time to time about close British settlement in climatically congenial areas in Africa and also (James Bryce would have added) because of missed opportunities of British sovereignty and settlement in southern South America.[2]

The distinctive Australian-New Zealand contribution to the Commonwealth is accordingly to be traced to the fact that they were projections of England (or more precisely of Britain) overseas; they were, in the phraseology of Dilke exactly applied, parts of Greater Britain. In Melbourne Froude found

> the Victorians and Victorian society . . . it was English life over again. . . . All was the same – dress, manners, talk, appearance. . . . I could not help asking myself what, after all, is the meaning of uniting the colonies more closely to ourselves. They are closely united; they are ourselves; and can separate only in the sense that parents and children separate, or brothers and sisters . . .[3]

If ever there was to be a *British* Commonwealth in the strict sense of the term it would have consisted of Great Britain, Australia and New Zealand. And it is further questionable if without the existence of these two Pacific dominions there would ever have been the diluted British Commonwealth of history.

The unique position of the Pacific colonies that became dominions largely predetermined their rôle in Commonwealth history. In difficult and vexing questions of racial and cultural policies, Australia had nothing and New Zealand – despite the unusually good relationship established between European majority and Maori minority – only a limited amount to offer by way of experience that was fruitful in other and more complex Commonwealth contexts. Nor did either dominion, by reason of the origin of the great majority of its population, possess that inner sensitivity to the problems implicit in the reconciliation of indigenous, national aspirations with Commonwealth membership; problems with which Canada, South Africa and – with particular intensity – the Irish Free State were so much preoccupied in an earlier and India in a later phase of Commonwealth history. So it was that Australia and New Zealand stood, paradoxically, at the very heart of and at the same time somewhat apart from the main stream of Commonwealth development, consciously British in their reaction to non-British nationalist movements and notably conservative in their response to those Commonwealth developments in the inter-war years which are now seen to have been a condition of its post-second world war expansion. But (and partly by reason of the very fact that they were little troubled by problems of national or cultural diversity) Australia and New Zealand were unusually well placed to make contributions in different fields, most notably in defence and security. To their peoples, whatever their differences on lesser matters with Britain, there remained – at least until the middle years of the twentieth century – one King, one Cause, one Flag. The common origin of the great majority also made it easier for them to enrich Commonwealth experience in other important respects. The colonists, 'despite their pretensions to being *enfants terribles*', had a respect for the traditional forms of English colonial government but, so M. André Siegfried noted,[4] they advanced beneath them to patterns of political or social democracy more egalitarian in spirit and for the most part in practice than were to be found elsewhere in the Empire. In New Zealand, 'the chosen land of the most daring experiments', this was most in evidence in matters of social policy, where the New Zealanders (so Siegfried also observed early in the century), uninterested in the theory of socialism 'have without doubt pushed the application of it further than any other people'.[5] In Australia, more radical than New Zealand in the temper of its citizens but less progressive in its social legislation (partly because of the restrictive influence after 1901 of its federal constitution) it was chiefly in the allied fields of law and government that new precedents were established and radical, popular practices applied.

From the time of its discovery by Captain Cook in 1770 and the arrival of Governor Phillip in Botany Bay eighteen years later, one problem had loomed large in Australian history – settlement. Who was to populate the newly found continent – unexplored, unknown, untenanted except for black aborigines who were few in number and backward in their customs, a continent without trace of earlier civilisation or previous migration, seeming to one visitor to bear not the slightest resemblance to the outside world: It was 'so primitive, so lacking in greenness, so silent, so old', with an 'appearance of exhaustion and weariness in the land itself. . . '.[6] Was Britain alone to people this continent in the southern seas? The answer was in the affirmative. At one time that most notable of the pioneers of planned British settlement, Edward Gibbon Wakefield, contemplated emigration from 'those numerous overpopulated countries' by which the colonies 'are, as it were, surrounded', from the islands of the Pacific to the mainland of Asia and including 'the poorest class of Hindoos' and the Chinese 'by far the most industrious and skilful of Asiatics'.[7] But to that and all other such suggestions the response of the colonists was emphatic and consistent. Australia was to be kept white. The first Act passed by the Parliament of the Commonwealth of Australia in 1901 was to reaffirm on the new federal basis the sanctity of that white Australian policy. In so far, therefore, as the continent is populated, it has been more than ninety per cent peopled by immigrants from the British Isles. This is to be attributed in some measure to planning on the British side but chiefly to the power of attraction of economic and social opportunity in temperate climatic conditions in new countries under the British flag – though in respect of the last it is worth recalling, without endorsing, Dilke's opinion that 'under separation we should, perhaps, find the colonies better emigration-fields for our surplus population than they are at present. Many of our emigrants who flock to the United States are attracted by the idea that they are going to become citizens of a new nation instead of dependents upon an old one'. With the separation of Australia from England a portion of these 'sentimentalists', he thought, might be diverted to that continent.[8]

The first British settlers were in no position to decide their own destination. They were some seven hundred convicts brought out by Governor Phillip in 1788 as the result of a government decision that Australia should take the place of the independent American colonies as a convict settlement to which criminals might be transported. This continuation in another continent of the policy of penal colonisation did not pass unchallenged. The philosophical Radicals, with Jeremy Bentham as their spokesman, condemned it as vicious. But it lasted well into the nineteenth century. The number of transported convicts, reckoned to be just under two thousand in 1825, rose fairly consistently thereafter to over four thousand in 1833. Against this the number of free immigrants was only a matter of hundreds until the late 1820s when the total rose to some two thousand a year.[9] Radical opinion strongly pressed for organised migration of free settlers to Australia on a scale sufficient to outnumber the convicts and submerge the character of the earlier settlement.[10] From Newgate prison Wakefield produced his blue-print,[11] his chief concern being to ensure orderly and balanced settlement. Colonial development, he thought, depended upon the maintenance of a right relation between capital and labour, since the one was dependent upon the other. In order to ensure such a balance he recommended first that unoccupied land in the colonies should be sold and the funds thus obtained be used to finance immigration on the scale required and second that the sale of waste land should be controlled in such a way as to ensure a reasonable balance between people and territory. 'As a wise man eats just as much as will keep him in the best health, but no more: so a wise government would grant just enough land to enable the people to exert their utmost capacity for doubling themselves, but no more.'[12] He urged that the government should fix a price for waste land high enough to ensure that land already occupied should be reasonably exploited and valued before new land was settled. The application of this vicinity-maximising or dispersion-preventing principle would, so Wakefield thought, bring about that degree of concentration in settlement at which he aimed. It was also (if incidentally) a principle favouring middle-class rather than working-class occupation of new land since capital was a condition of the acquisition of it.

Earlier experience was not encouraging in respect of planned emigration; attempts to organise it after the Napoleonic wars had been unusually disappointing in their results. Thus in 1823, at a time when the government was actively engaged in promoting emigration overseas, fifteen thousand British people went to British territories under government-sponsored schemes, while unorganised private emigration accounted for some sixteen thousand. None the less, the settlement of South Australia, founded in 1834, between the established colonies of New South Wales and Van Diemen's Land, provided after some vicissitudes substantial practical vindication for Wakefield's ideas. Nor was it his only contribution to British settlement in the Pacific. With Molesworth, Wakefield was also responsible in 1839 for the formation of the New Zealand Company, the initial enterprise of which was claimed (though questionably) to have been decisive in stirring a hesitating and uncertain government to forestall the French and to proclaim the islands a British colony a year later.[13] By the later 1830s total British emigration to Australasia had climbed to some fifteen thousand a year with a temporary peak of nearly thirty-three thousand in 1841.[14] If not assured, their British future was at least beginning to take shape.

In New Zealand the impression of Wakefield upon the pattern of colonisation was even more pronounced than in South Australia. He had deplored the fact that these Pacific territories should have been so long regarded 'as fit only for the residence of convicts, labourers, mechanics and desperate or needy men'. The Greek colonies, he emphasised, contained a mixture of all classes of society; he claimed that it was for that reason that they had risen to wealth and eminence much earlier than they would otherwise have done and their example ought therefore to be followed. In accordance with such preconceptions, a cross-section of British Victorian society lacking only in its extremes of wealth and poverty was transplanted to New Zealand. Settlement there – solid, bourgeois and respectable[15] – faithfully reflected the aspirations of its promoters. The purposes behind the planning were given succinct expression in one sentence of a report of the directors of the New Zealand Company, 1847, which read:

> The aim of this company is not confined to mere emigration but is . . . to transplant English society with its various gradations in due proportions, carrying out our laws, customs, associations, habits, manners, feeling – everything of England, in short, but the soil.[16]

One consequence implicit in this composition of New Zealand society was the strongest possible attachment on the part of the settlers to their mother country. Another was a measure of cultural and intellectual dependence upon Britain, which proved a source of recurrent frustration to New Zealand's intelligentsia in later times.

The accidents of history and of geology contributed much in the case of New Zealand and more in the case of Australia to determining the character and pace of settlement. In both instances, for most of their history, up to 97 per cent of these settlements remained British. That was the fundamental factor. But there were others, one of which has already been noted.

> Australia had a bad start [wrote the Liberal, F. W. Eggleston]. It started as a gaol, and those who started it appeared to plan it for that purpose and for nothing else. Though I do not think that this 'birth-mark' left any criminal taint in the community, the deficiencies of the original plan caused extraordinary difficulties which lasted for generations.

Professor Shaw agreed that socially the convict settlements did Australia no great harm while economically they greatly helped Australian development. Transportation had provided a labour force which, if less efficient than free workers, was far better than no workers at all.[17] Then in the middle years of the century the exodus from Ireland after the famine brought many, mostly embittered, emigrants to Australia to reinforce the settlers both convict and free and to swell the existing Irish population, estimated in 1837 (if Catholics and Irish be near equated) at close on twenty-two thousand. A Young Irelander of the 1840s, Charles Gavan Duffy, became prime minister of Victoria and was knighted. Succeeding generations had a spokesmen in Archbishop Mannix, who expressed in public utterances over a long period of years as well as in private practices – he posted his letters with stamps bearing the monarch's head upside-down – something of the transplanted, transmuted, but by no means wholly extinguished nationalism of his country of origin. More important in terms of settlement however were the motley crowd of hardy adventurers brought to the continent by news of discoveries of gold, first in the Bathurst district and elsewhere in New South Wales and subsequently in Victoria, Queensland, Western Australia and the South Island of New Zealand.

The excitement of the first discoveries of mineral wealth in Australia was as intense as it was later to be at Kimberley or on the Rand. Some of them were made by chance, others by intuitive reasoning. Notable among the latter, and giving in fullest measure the dramatic quality which in some degree belonged to them all, was Hargraves's strike in the Bathurst district. Hargraves, an Australian who migrated to California, disclaimed all pretensions to scientific knowledge. But he became convinced, by comparing in his own mind what he saw before him in California with what he had seen in Australia eighteen years earlier, that there was gold in Australia. In the light of that conviction he returned to Sydney and journeyed on horseback to the remembered site. Memory had served him well and the resemblance of the formation was beyond doubt. He dug a panful of earth, and sure enough there was gold in it. In his excitement he exclaimed to his guide, 'This is a memorable day in the history of New South Wales. I shall be a baronet, you will be knighted, and my old horse will be stuffed, put into a glass-case, and sent to the British Museum.'[18] The first alone was true; and it was enough. In succeeding years there were to be even more memorable days in the history of Victoria.

It is quite impossible for me [wrote Lieutenant-Governor Latrobe to Earl Grey at the Colonial Office][19] to describe to your lordship the effect which these discoveries have had upon the whole community, and the influence which their consequences exercise at this time upon the position and prospects of everyone, high and low. The discoveries early in the year in the Bathurst district of New South Wales unsettled the public mind of the labouring classes of all the Australian colonies. . . The discoveries within our bounds [Victorian] . . . exercise a far wider influence upon our excitable population. . . Within the last three weeks the towns of Melbourne and Geelong and their large suburbs have been in appearance almost emptied of many classes of their male inhabitants . . . cottages are deserted, houses to let, business is at a stand-still and even schools are closed. In some of the suburbs not a man is left. . . .

From other countries and all continents men came to Australia to join in the search for gold. The pattern of its society, its thinking, the pace of economic development – all were profoundly affected. Nor was New Zealand left out. While no such rich or widely publicised discoveries were made there, gold was found in Otago in 1861, turning Dunedin almost overnight from a quiet country town into a rough and – for the older inhabitants – frightening mining centre. But it also brought new population to stimulate economic development and to confirm European numerical preponderance over the Maoris.[20]

The fever of the gold rushes passed but the social and economic consequences of them remained. As it became apparent that as much – possibly more – money might be made out of gold miners than out of gold mines, the camps of pioneering days gave way to mining settlements, with their stores, services and sense of community and these, in turn, to townships. The wealth of the gold fields percolated through the townships to the cities and served as a magnet drawing new population from across the seas. The 'image' – if the terminology of mid-twentieth century political scientists may be retrospectively applied to the Pacific colonies of the mid-nineteenth – of young, adventurous, even if improvident communities where hand-in-hand went hardship and opportunity, destitution and riches spectacularly won, an image which owed so much at the outset to the drama of the gold rushes, continued thereafter to draw to the far south young men who felt the flavour of life in England was long since spent.

The overriding importance of increasing population, despite the accretions from the gold rushes, continued to be a constant preoccupation of the British settlements in the Pacific, throughout the colonial and the succeeding dominion phase in their history. In the later Victorian age there were confident prognostications from Seeley, Dilke and others about the expansion of the British people overseas until the population of Greater Britain would equal or surpass that of the mother country herself. There were sanguine forecasts in Australia also but there prognostication however confident was more apt to be balanced by a present sense of realities. And not the least significant among those realities was the existing pattern of widely scattered seaboard settlements round the coast of a continent, and of a tremendous hinterland which except for isolated mining or other centres remained largely uninhabited and partly unexplored. 'Don't let us be mistaken,' warned Sir Henry Parkes in 1890 in presenting his arguments for the federation of Australia, '. . . population is the one great basis for the growth of nations either here or anywhere else. . . .'[21] And in relation to size and resources adequate population in Australia was woefully lacking.

Questions of population also occupied the minds of settlers in New Zealand though not for quite the same reasons. Australia was a continent; New Zealand an island, or rather islands – even if in Auckland and Wellington men preferred to speak of the mainland with an island to the south. But while the islands were thinly populated in relation to resources there was not so much a problem of empty spaces to be filled as a concern on the part of the settlers that a native population (one, moreover, among the most advanced and adaptable of all the indigenous peoples in the Empire) should be matched and ultimately outdistanced in numbers. New Zealand, like South Africa but unlike Australia, had a native question. If it was, by comparison with that of southern Africa, modest in its dimensions, this by no means necessarily implied it was susceptible of an easy, straightforward solution. In New

Zealand there also loomed large familiar questions of land and franchise policies in which Colonial Office views of an 'imperial standard' by no means always coincided with settler interests or settler opinion.

Neither the Australian nor the New Zealand colonists were the pioneers in the advance from representative to responsible colonial government. That trail was blazed in North America. But, conditioned by not dissimilar circumstances in terms of environment and political heritage, it is not surprising that they were stirred by emotions and aspirations similar to those entertained by their Canadian contemporaries. In 1852 Lord Salisbury heard a din of indignation against Downing Street from 'bishop to pot-boy', from the Cape to New Zealand. Each colony had its own individual causes of complaint but there were also the common sources of friction which Lord Durham had diagnosed, chief among them being the alienation of an executive, appointed by a governor, from a representative assembly to which it was not responsible. Where there was no indigenous people with rights or interests to be safeguarded and where there was a sufficient settler population to sustain the responsibilities of self-government, there were also thought to be no continuing imperial interests or considerations of policy sufficient to warrant withholding the concession of self-government or incurring the odium which would almost inevitably result from so doing. Accordingly responsible self-government on the Canadian model was granted to the Australian colonies from the middle years of the century onwards as they became sufficiently populated. It was also granted to New Zealand, but there – because of the existence of a substantial indigenous population with interests to be safeguarded – it could not be conceded without reservations. It was with reluctance that the British government had decided to annex New Zealand in 1839 and a deciding factor had been concern to protect the rights of the Maoris from settlers who had come hitherto chiefly from Australia but whose numbers were about to be increased by migration organised by the New Zealand Company. A policy of protection implied limitation in respect of powers of settler self-government.

In 1846 representative institutions were conceded to New Zealand on the basis not only of a General Assembly with an elected House but also of provincial councils, each with an elected House of Representatives. The governor, Sir George Grey, felt misgivings at the prospect of control by some twelve thousand colonists over 'the well-armed, proud and independent' Maoris,[22] especially in the provincial assemblies, and as a result the constitution was not brought into force. In 1852, however, pressure by the New Canterbury settlers led by an Anglo-Irishman, John Robert Godley – who protested that he would rather be governed 'by a Nero on the spot than by a board of angels in London' on the ground that if the worst came to the worst Nero's head could be cut off whereas the board would remain beyond reach – hastened the enactment of a New Zealand Constitution Act. The Act established a General Assembly, consisting of two Houses, together with six provincial councils (which survived until 1876) for dealing with provincial affairs. This was government on a grand scale! But in respect of representation a key question remained. Who was to be entitled to vote? The Maoris at that time still outnumbered the settlers. They had been guaranteed 'all the rights and privileges of British subjects' in the 1840 Treaty of Waitangi. Was exclusion from the vote consistent with such assurances? In one sense the question was at that time theoretical rather than practical. The majority of the Maoris, living on their own land, apart from the new settlers, were not yet adapted to European political practices. But the issue of principle remained. It was met by a franchise based on a low property qualification, with the Maoris disfranchised in practice by reason of their system of land tenure. Their system was communal and individual Maoris consequently failed to qualify for the vote. But the question could not rest there.

When the first New Zealand Parliament met on 24 May 1854 (Queen Victoria's birthday) in Auckland, the first capital – some of the Otago members had taken two months to travel there – members declined to conduct business until a ministry responsible to Parliament was appointed.[23] The principal ulterior purpose behind this demand was to establish settler control over the disposal of Crown Lands. Parliament was first prorogued and then dissolved, a further election taking place in 1855; it having by this time become apparent that there was no reasonable alternative, a responsible ministry was appointed the following year. But the extent of its responsibility in one all-important particular remained in dispute. The governor, Colonel Thomas Gore Browne (who succeeded Grey in the same year), had pronounced views on the responsibilities of his office and without the specific authority in his own or his predecessors' Instructions, took steps to reserve control of native affairs to the Crown, which meant in practice largely to the governor. He did so in the belief that 'the interests of the two races were antagonistic', and that such a division of responsibility was a matter of principle because it would be wrong in such circumstances to subject one race to the other.[24] In practice this diarchical arrangement proved unworkable. The settlers were intent upon securing free sale of land, which meant individualisation of land-holding in the Maori communal areas. Despite the opposition of the governor and of the imperial government they managed to force the issue. They also underestimated the Maoris and wars followed. The Maoris were defeated but the settlers learned by painful experience the merits of compromise.

In respect of representation, the long-term outcome of the Maori wars was the special allocation of four seats to the Maoris on a basis of adult suffrage, with a view to the ultimate standardisation and merging of electorates. Like so many devices intended to serve a temporary purpose, this special representation for Maoris has continued down to the present day. If anomalous in principle, it has proved workable in practice. It has meant in turn over-representation and under-representation in relation to Maori population though not, in the second case, in relation to Maori registered voters.[25] From the time of the first European settlement until 1900 the Maori population steadily declined but since then it has risen consistently and in recent years at a rate faster than the European. While it would be over-sanguine, especially in view of increasing Maori urbanisation, to think of the problems of race relations in New Zealand as belonging only to the past, none the less through a chequered history and a reliance upon pragmatic solutions in social as well as political life, a spirit of inter-racial community has developed which is generally in accord with the later professed principles of the Commonwealth.

There are two further aspects of New Zealand development which have a place in the context of Commonwealth history. The first is of Australasian, the second of more widespread interest. From the early years of settlement Australian and New Zealand colonists thought in terms of exclusive British predominance in the Pacific. England, commented André Siegfried, 'remains in the eyes of Australasians the pre-eminent nation, the chosen worker of any civilising mission. The colonials, an integral part of the superior race, work by its side.' A sure instinct had warned them from the very first that it was necessary for them to remain as far as possible, 'alone and without troublesome neighbours in the South Pacific'. In this way the programme 'Australasia for the Australasians' developed into 'Oceania for the Anglo-Saxons'.[26] M. Siegfried wrote with something less than enthusiasm of the colonial jingoism that might be called Australasian imperialism – understandably so since the French, after all, were by no means the least of the European powers the colonists wished to exclude. But he was right in the importance he attached to it. The Colonial Office also had good reason to feel its force and good cause to seek to restrain its impetuosities.

In the last three decades of the nineteenth century New Zealand's imperial, or imperialist, aspirations in the Pacific received their strongest expression and have had, in Professor Angus Ross, their historian. Even before New Zealand became a British colony, the New Zealand Company had thought of New Zealand as 'the Britain of the south' with an imperial destiny of its own. With steady consistency of purpose, successive New Zealand prime ministers sought first to secure the annexation and government of the Pacific Islands or, failing that, to ensure that control over them did not pass into the hands of foreign imperial powers. On 17 October 1873 Sir Julius Vogel, the prime minister of New Zealand, prepared a memorandum for the Colonial Office which conveys in graphic phrases something of the outlook of New Zealanders and the purposes which they had in mind. The memorandum urged that 'a policy or line of conduct should be decided on, not alone in connection with one or two clusters of islands, but applicable to all Polynesia', with a view to Britain taking up 'the work of reducing to civilisation the fertile islands of the Pacific'. New Zealand would gladly cooperate in the task:

> Ministers venture to urge that Great Britain . . . may with justice be proud of having reproduced herself in the 'Great Britain of the south' as New Zealand has aptly been called . . . but there is a lesson which New Zealand teaches, and that is that local efforts to maintain peaceful relations with an uncivilised race are far more successful than those directed by a distant power. It may be worth consideration whether, if Polynesia is not to be abandoned to foreign nations, it would not be well to entrust to New Zealand, which possesses so much experience in dealing with the government of a mixed race, the task of aiding in extending the British sway to the islands of the Pacific . . . the Parliament of New Zealand would cordially entertain proposals which had for their object to give to the colony the opportunity of assisting Great Britain in the great national work of extending the British dominion throughout the unappropriated islands of the South Pacific.[27]

The British government, however, was unreceptive. They had other interests and other priorities, chief among them being relations with the European powers. In the critical years between 1880 and 1886 Gladstone was much more concerned to reach some tolerable understanding with Germany on colonial questions than to satisfy the New Zealand ambitions – strongly backed though these were throughout the period by the Australian colonies. Vogel was written off in the Colonial Office as 'an imperial busybody', while Germany and France by agreement extended their colonial empires to the Pacific. In practice as well as in theory foreign policy remained in the last resort the preserve of the imperial power. New Zealanders and Australians might lament lost opportunities of Anglo-Saxon hegemony in the Pacific but having failed to persuade London to act in accordance with their aspirations they were without remedy – except for the no doubt wry satisfaction, afforded in 1919 to the prime minister of New Zealand, Mr Massey, of telling the House of Representatives in Wellington how right New Zealand leaders had been in urging that Samoa should have been annexed either by Britain or New Zealand and not allowed to pass into German hands.[28]

Of more lasting consequence than her imperial aspirations were New Zealand's social reforms. The Liberal Party, dominant in New Zealand politics in the late nineteenth and early twentieth century, had affinities with the new Birmingham School, inasmuch as the chief trends in its thinking were imperial development and expansion on the one hand and domestic social reform on the other. Manhood suffrage on a property or residential qualification, introduced in 1889, was followed in 1893 by votes for women, conceded for the first time in British history. This in its turn was followed, during the Liberal Party's long tenure of office (which lasted from 1891 to 1912), by pioneering legislation in education which created a national system of primary schooling, free, compulsory and secular for all children under thirteen. In 1894 was enacted legislation on industrial conciliation and arbitration, described as being at once the most novel of the labour measures and one of the most decisive in moulding New Zealand society.[29] Between 1896 and 1901 there was introduced a whole code of labour legislation, including the regulation of working hours, factory inspection and non-contributory pensions.

To what causes are these pioneering social reforms to be attributed? Chief among them would seem to have been the patterns and ethics of New Zealand society. Unlike Australia, New Zealand was populated – save only at the extremes of wealth and poverty – by 'a virtual slice' of nineteenth-century English society, by people who had gone out 'not in despair but in hope.'[30] The government was in a particular sense the government chosen by and representative of the people. It was too close and familiar to inspire the mistrust that comes with remoteness and there were accordingly few psychological reservations on the part of the people about the extension of its powers – on the contrary, it was felt to be the duty of the state to promote the happiness of the people and to better their lot. The most effective way in which it could do so was by social legislation; government was considered to 'be benign'.[31] There was no deep cleavage of view about the theoretical limits of its responsibilities; there was rather a constant clamour for state action. The New Zealanders were not a race of theoreticians; their approach to such matters was direct and practical. They thought in terms of their own welfare and, in more exalted moments, of a mission to humanity and of their destiny 'to show the old world the paths of social progress'. 'A people can advertise itself, just as a merchant or a manufacturer can,' noted M. Siegfried. And he added that the New Zealanders, well aware of this fact, had not chosen the worst means 'for, since the passing of such measures as those for compulsory arbitration and woman suffrage, everybody has heard of the little antipodean colony of whose very existence people were once scarcely aware.'[32]

There were men, two in particular, as well as measures to be remembered in New Zealand's reformist years. The first was Richard Seddon, 'King Dick', prime minister from 1893 to 1906. With his 'burly frame and a chest like Vulcan's', his 'cheery laugh' and his 'crushing hand-grip' (as James Bryce found it) went an approach correspondingly robust and practical. Of humble origins, his friends said he never read a socialist book, his enemies that he never read a book. This however was not true. In the House of Representatives he relied on Erskine May's *Parliamentary Procedure* and he was also once observed by a colleague reading a history of pirates in the Spanish Main. While James Bryce thought him wanting in learning and eloquence he acknowledged that he had force and drive. It was well observed of him, commented Bryce, that he 'never could estimate the precise value of comparatives and superlatives and seemed to the last to imagine that strong language was the only language befitting a strong man.' Yet Bryce also remarked upon his adroitness as a parliamentary leader and his closeness to the people. 'His audiences, especially in the provinces,' noted Pember Reeves, of Seddon's semi-regal progresses through his dominions, 'welcomed both the visits and the oratory. They liked to hear their own views, feelings and wishes . . . given back to them in language not too far removed from their own. They liked the comforting official statistics, the patriotic platitudes, the inevitable reference to "God's own country" . . .'.[33]

William Pember Reeves, minister of education, justice and labour 1891 to 1896 (when he went to London as New Zealand's Agent-General), and Seddon's principal lieutenant, provided a counterpart. Reeves, well remembered as the author of *The Long White Cloud*, a most readable general history of New Zealand, supplied the intellectual force behind its social legislation in this great period of reform. Siegfried described Reeves's socialism as experimental and practical, noted his rooted distrust of financiers and capitalists and admired him as one possessing a power of logical analysis peculiarly associated with Frenchmen.[34] Not altogether surprisingly perhaps Reeves ended his days far from New Zealand, becoming a prominent member of the Fabian Society and third director of the London School of Economics and Political Science.[35] Yet the reforms he had helped to shape remained and they fixed upon New Zealand the image of an egalitarian society desiring to become still more egalitarian and one which in so doing gave Empire and Commonwealth a pattern of social legislation from which all – including Britain herself – could learn; and which many, including countries in South Asia in later years, sought at least in part to adapt to their own, and often very different, circumstances.

The development of a distinct political identity in New Zealand has about it a certain air of paradox. It might be supposed that New Zealand's dreams of Anglo-Saxon hegemony in the Pacific, combined with the common British origins of New Zealand and Australian settlers, would bring British colonists throughout the Pacific into one political community. But on the shorter term at any rate it was not to be. New Zealand cherished the idea of Empire, but for New Zealanders Empire meant most of all close and continuing association not with neighbouring Australian colonies but with the mother country. Many New Zealanders became ardent advocates of imperial federation. But it was federation on that larger and not on a limited Pacific scale to which they aspired. For them it was an all-embracing imperial system or nothing.

The case for Australasian federation, buttressed as it was by not unimpressive arguments of political, economic and even strategic advantage, did not go by default. On the contrary it was considered and deliberately rejected by New Zealanders. The arguments against it were conveniently summarised by Captain W. R. Russell, a New Zealand delegate at the Australasian Federation Conference in Melbourne in 1890. He argued first that New Zealanders living under different climatic conditions, colonised in an entirely different manner, having had 'a very much rougher time than the colonies of Australia', were likely to develop a very complete individuality – a distinct national type. They had no wish to be submerged in a greater Australasia where their population of seven hundred thousand would be heavily outnumbered. Nor was he much impressed by the strategic argument. A federal army might involve New Zealanders in expenses they were not prepared to meet while its value in the event of a sudden assault upon the islands was questionable: the issue might well be decided before news of the attack ever reached Australia. There were also likely to be differences of interest and of opinion on trading policy. Would New Zealand be wise, would she be prepared, to join irrevocably in a customs union which might bring about more protection than already existed? There was also the question of native administration. The New Zealand delegate argued that it was bound to be one of the most important questions in New Zealand politics for many years to come. Were responsibility for that question to be handed over to a federal Parliament – 'to an elective body, mostly Australians, that cares nothing and knows nothing about native administration, and the members of which have dealt with native races in a much more summary manner than we have ventured to deal with ours in New Zealand' – it might well provoke renewed and disastrous conflict between settlers and Maoris in the islands.[36]

The outcome of the debate was that New Zealand was left free to join in the contemplated federation, but in fact it did not opt to do so. Nor would Sir Charles Dilke have been surprised. Englishmen, he learned on his Pacific travels, were 'given over to a singular delusion as to the connection of New Zealand and Australia'. They were apt to think the comprehensive designation Australasia appropriate and meaningful. But Dilke was made aware only of the separateness and the indifference of the one to the other.

> The only reference to New Zealand [he recalled] except in the foreign news that I ever found in an Australian paper, was a congratulatory paragraph on the great amount of the New Zealand debt; the only allusion to Australia that I detected in the Wellington *Independent* was in a glance at the future of the colony, in which the editor predicted the advent of a time when New Zealand would be a naval nation and her fleet engaged in bombarding Melbourne or levying contributions upon Sidney.[37]

While federation did not come to New Zealand at all, it came only after long delay and protracted discussion to the Australian colonies. For this a number of explanations have been offered. The main centres of population were geographically widely dispersed along the seaboard, the settlers themselves were of varying social backgrounds, most of them had become accustomed to domestic self-government over a comparatively long period of time – in New South Wales and Tasmania since 1855, in South Australia since 1856, in Victoria and Queensland since 1859 – and they were apt to feel that what had been so comparatively long enjoyed should not be lightly abandoned. Vested interests had been entrenched with the passage of time and there were fears, as in the case of New Zealand, on the part of the less densely populated states, that their interests should be subordinated or even altogether overlooked in a federation inevitably dominated by New South Wales and Victoria. For all these reasons debates about the possibility of federation, which was pursued intermittently from the middle of the century and of which Dilke heard much in the 1880s, were apt to concentrate upon its negative implications in respect of the status and authority of the individual colonies. Mr (later Sir Edmund) Barton, a delegate from New South Wales to the Federal Convention at Adelaide in 1897, even then felt obliged to remind his audience that the purpose of federation was not to diminish but

> to enlarge the powers of self-government of the people of Australia. . . . That is a proposition which, from the many discussions that have taken place in public in various parts of the colonies, appears to have been lost sight of. The idea of surrender seems to have occupied a large place in the minds of the people. Federation really adds to the powers of self-government, a fact which seems to have been put aside and left out of consideration.[38]

While explanation is required as to why progress towards federation was so slow – given in particular the homogeneity of the colonial populations – it is also necessary to consider why in the last decade of the century the idea of 'a nation for a continent and a continent for a nation' suddenly gathered momentum. The most evident environmental change had come with the intrusion of European powers other than Britain into the Pacific in the 1880s. It was a change much resented by the colonists but one in which Britain acquiesced, as evidenced most notably in the case of New Guinea (where unauthorised annexation by the Queensland government was repudiated by the colonial secretary in order to allow of a mature consideration which in turn – and incidentally – gave Germany time to organise an expedition and in 1884 to proclaim north-eastern New Guinea a German colony). With the arrival of newer European imperialisms, dreams of undisputed Anglo-Saxon hegemony in the south-west Pacific dissolved. The Australian colonies, hitherto free from all experience or even serious risk of war, now had a challenge (however remote it might appear) to their continuing security. It was time for them to consolidate their strength and resources.

Sir Henry Parkes, who championed the cause of federation over so many years, deployed arguments of this kind forcefully at the Australian Conference in Melbourne in 1890. He said that he had no doubt whatever in his mind that if there had been a central government in Australia in 1883 New Guinea would have been annexed to Australia. This was almost certainly untrue. Alfred Deakin, as prime minister of the Commonwealth of Australia, was unable (much to his annoyance) to exercise any effective influence over British negotiations with France in 1904–6 leading to the Anglo-French condominium over the New Hebrides. But that did not necessarily lessen the impact of Parkes's contention. He also played more generally upon Australian anxieties in saying: 'Those great armed powers of Europe which are shut in from the sea are not only wanting more earth for their multitudes to live upon, but are wanting the earth which fronts the ocean in any part of the world. . .'. Again, however questionable as a matter of political fact, this was an interpetation of European expansionist aims which led on naturally to the conclusion that Australia 'ought to be mistress of the southern seas'.[39] Such, in Parkes's view, was indeed Australia's destiny. But that destiny was one of the two great objects 'which can only be properly attained, properly promoted, by a federal government'. The other was the increase of national and individual wealth. Parkes produced figures purporting to show that the average private wealth per inhabitant in Australasia exceeded and in many cases far exceeded that in Austria, Germany, France, the United Kingdom and even the United States. 'There is not one so wealthy as we. . .'. That wealth had been used to establish systems of education, to construct means of communication and to make 'such progress as has excited the admiration of the best of other countries'. Further advance and development was conditional upon arrangements, management and regulations that a single national authority alone could make. The grandest purpose of all, however, was the making of a united people who would appear before the world as one and form a federal dominion for ever part 'of one beneficent Empire'.[40] Throughout the language was sanguine, even grandiose and to many Australians must have had a flavour of irony in the economic crisis that followed. But in a new country these were the days for expansive reflections and while historians are apt – not unreasonably – to discount the emotional, as against strategic, economic or political factors, in this case it may be that Sir Henry Parkes was wiser than they. Oratory, noted Alfred Deakin who employed it with great effect, was not likely to make 'hard-boiled inter-colonial politicians fall weeping on each other's shoulders amid universal protestations of indissoluble federal brotherhood'. No doubt – but without the use of oratory would the federal idea have passed from its parliamentary to its successful popular phase?[41]

The final stages of the federation movement in Australia may be briefly recorded. A conference of all the colonies was held in 1883 at the instigation of Sir Henry Parkes and a Federal Council, experimental in character and advisory in function, was then established. It enjoyed, however, neither popularity nor unanimous state support since, apart from New Zealand, New South Wales from the first refused to be represented at its deliberations and South Australia later withdrew from them. There followed, among important landmarks, the Melbourne Conference on Australasian federation in 1890 and in the succeeding year a further conference at Sydney at which the draft of a Commonwealth Bill was produced. The purposes of the draft bill were publicised through the organisation of the Federation Leagues and by 1895 it was agreed, with the approval of the several colonial governments and Parliaments, to hold a convention in Adelaide in 1897 to prepare a further and final draft Bill. The convention was duly held in March of that year; it went to work, so Joseph Chamberlain later informed the House of Commons, 'in that business-like spirit which we flatter ourselves distinguishes British proceedings throughout the world'.[42] The convention produced a draft which after submission to the respective colonial Parliaments and redrafting in the light of their suggested amendments finally emerged after further discussion in Melbourne and Sydney as the Commonwealth of Australia Bill.

Federation in Australia was not, however, to be the outcome (as it had been in Canada) of inter-governmental debate alone. It was to carry also the sanction of the people. From the outset it had been accepted among the representatives of the several colonial governments that ratification by popular referendum was a necessary precondition of the final adoption of any measure upon which they might agree. And in fact there was not one but two referenda, the proposed measure not securing on the first occasion the prescribed minimal majority of eighty thousand in New South Wales. In the second referendum, in which the electorates of New South Wales, Victoria, South Australia, Queensland and Tasmania took part – but not Western Australia which of its own choice stood apart – there was a vote of 377,000 for the Bill and 141,500 against. Accordingly it was submitted to Westminster not only with colonial parliamentary but also with colonial popular sanction for legislative enactment.

There was, it has been remarked,[43] no Damascus Road miracle about Australia's conversion to federation and this is certainly true. One reason was the toughness of the bargaining and the manoeuvring for position among the states' representatives, so illuminatingly and often entertainingly described in Alfred Deakin's *The Federal Story*, and in his biographer's analysis of Deakin's rôle, especially in Victorian politics, where he was 'the very symbol of the federal cause'.[44] But while the advance was slow it also carried with it an impressive air of a growing conviction on the part of governments, parliaments and peoples alike. There was faith that federation was the right way, the ideal course.

> A federal constitution [Deakin had declaimed in 1898] is the last and final product of political intellect and constructive ingenuity; it represents the highest development of self-government among peoples scattered over a large area. . . . I venture to submit that among all the federal constitutions of the world you will look in vain for one as broad in its popular base, as liberal in its working principles, as generous in its aim as this measure.

There were many Australians who were convinced these things were so.

The procedures by which federalism was adopted in Australia showed some significant contrasts with those employed in bringing the Canadian confederation into existence. Such differences were by no means fortuitous. The cultural homogeneity of the Australian population, coupled with its social composition, favoured a predominantly radical approach to questions of politics which found expression in this instance in the insistence that, unlike Canada, there should be approval by the people for the new federation and its constitution. It was even reflected in some measure in the title 'Commonwealth' with its republican overtones, as against a dominion with its imperial associations. It also accounted at least in part for the less conservative character of the Australian constitution in which once again reliance was placed – as it had not been in Canada – upon the people for the final resolution of contentious issues. But there were also, of course, other influences.

Canada was the neighbour of a great and (as it seemed in the 1860s) potentially aggressive power; Australia, despite the recently established French and German colonies, remained still virtually isolated in the southern seas. Where the fathers of Canadian confederation had been deeply influenced by American experience, which had impressed them with the dangers of divided authority that derived from strongly entrenched states' rights, the Australians entertained no such misgivings, in fact were altogether otherwise predisposed; the Canadian confederation, with its bias towards the centre, being generally regarded as an example not to be followed. 'I am quite sure,' remarked a South Australian delegate at the Adelaide Convention, 'that no one who has studied the question of a federal form of government will contend that the essence of federalism in the strict sense of the term is to be found in Canada.' But a federation in the strictest sense of the term was what the majority of Australians looked for because that would bring into being, not a Commonwealth with subordinate states, but a Commonwealth and states which would be equal and coordinate in their powers. Not Canada but the United States must be, as Deakin observed, their source of inspiration. The constitution of the Commonwealth of Australia accordingly gave to the federal parliament only powers over matters listed and defined in the constitution. Residual powers were left not with the centre, as in Canada, but with the states. 'I hold it,' said Richard O'Connor at the convention at Adelaide in 1897, 'to be a basic principle of this federation that we should take no powers from the states which they could better exercise themselves, and that we should place no power in the federation which is not absolutely necessary for carrying out its purposes.' This was in essence the principle that was applied. And, as Joseph Chamberlain explained to the House of Commons when introducing the Commonwealth of Australia Bill on 14 May 1900, the result was that whereas in Canada the underlying purpose of the constitution was 'substantially to amalgamate the provinces into one dominion, the constitution of Australia created a federation for distinctly definite and limited objects of a number of independent states, and state rights have throughout been jealously preserved'.[45]

The constitution of the Commonwealth of Australia is embodied in the Commonwealth of Australia Act passed by the British Parliament in 1900 and having effect from 1 January 1901. The bill was drafted, amended and, as has been noted, finally approved both by governments and people in Australia before its final submission for legislative enactment in London. There was no discussion preliminary to or in the course of drafting such as had taken place between the Canadian leaders and the colonial secretary before the enactment of the British North American Act 1867. This did not however mean that Joseph Chamberlain acquiesced in the view that his rôle as colonial secretary was limited to piloting a measure agreed and approved by Australians through the House of Commons. On the contrary, he asserted that while 'the bill has been prepared without reference to us' it should none the less receive in the imperial Parliament 'the fullest consideration and even the fullest discussion'.[46] If need be Chamberlain was prepared and felt entitled to propose and urge any amendments he thought desirable on grounds of general imperial interest; and in fact in respect of appeals to the judicial committee of the Privy Council he did so, even if only with very qualified success. But he also reminded the House of the realities of the situation. There was a limit beyond which the imperial government could not prudently go.

> We have got [said Chamberlain] to a point in our relations with our self-governing colonies in which I think we recognise, once for all, that these relations depend entirely upon their free will and absolute consent. The links between us and them at the present time are very slender. Almost a touch might snap them. But, slender as they are, and slight as they are, although we wish, although I hope, that they will become stronger, still if they are felt irksome by any one of our great colonies, we shall not attempt to force them to wear them.[47]

It was a significant and statesmanlike admission. It meant that by the turn of the century the British government recognised, even in respect of matters of admitted imperial importance such as appeals to the judicial committee of the Privy Council, that it could and should proceed to secure what it deemed to be imperial interests only by discussion and through exchanges of view.

The preamble to the Commonwealth of Australia Constitution Act[48] recorded that the people of New South Wales, Victoria, South Australia, Queensland and Tasmania had 'agreed to unite in one indissoluble Federal Commonwealth under the Crown of the United Kingdom of Great Britain and Ireland' and under the constitution established by the Act. The first eight Articles of the Act dealt with matters of formal importance – the citation of the Act, the succession to the Throne, the binding character of Acts made by the Parliament of the Commonwealth, the meaning of the term 'Commonwealth' and of the term 'the States' and the admission of Western Australia as an original state on the result of a referendum held before the Act came into force. The constitution of the Commonwealth of Australia was set out in section 9. While the Act itself could be amended only by the imperial Parliament, the constitution as embodied in section 9 prescribed the means whereby it might itself be amended by the Australian Parliament and people. This distinction between constitution and the Act in which it was embodied, together with the provisions for the indigenous amendment of the constitution, represented a notable departure from Canadian precedent. It had, moreover, its counterpart in a corresponding difference in respect of judicial interpretation. Under the British North America Act, it will be recalled, final judicial interpretation of the Act was vested in the judicial committee of the Privy Council. The Australians, however, desired the interpretation of their constitution to be vested in the Australian high court. To this there were objections from the imperial government which gave rise to protracted argument. Chamberlain was insistent upon the importance of preserving intact the ultimate authority of the judicial committee of the Privy Council, the Australians little disposed to make the concession this would have required of them. A compromise was proposed which was much to the satisfaction of the Australian delegates in London, the chief among them being Deakin, who told Dilke when its terms were first communicated to him: 'This is all we want and if we get this we shall secure a great victory.'[49] The compromise which was suggested and adopted did not exclude appeals to the judicial committee in principle but vested ultimate authority, in respect of the allowance of them, in the high court of Australia. Section 74 of the constitution, as finally agreed and embodying the compromise laid it down that:

> no appeal shall be permitted to the Queen in Council from a decision of the high court upon any question, howsoever arising, as to the limits *inter se* of the constitutional powers of the Commonwealth and those of any state or states, or as to the limits *inter se* of the constitutional powers of any two or more states, unless the high court shall certify that the question is one which ought to be determined by Her Majesty in Council.

The high court has in fact used the power of decision conferred upon it by section 74, as the Australians intended and Chamberlain feared. A certificate giving leave to appeal to the judicial committee has been granted in one case only and legislation has been passed by the Commonwealth Parliament to ensure that appeals from the supreme courts of the states in respect of *inter se* questions should lie to the high court only.[50] These were matters of more than strictly legal significance. They reflected something of the outlook of the architects of Australian federation. They cherished Empire as much as Chamberlain but their notions of Empire did not coincide with his. Already they were thinking in terms of equality under the Crown. Australians, remarked Deakin, would be proud to fight and if need be to die for Queen and Country, but he had never heard of anyone prepared to die for the judicial committee of the Privy Council. Chamberlain's notions of its significance as a link of Empire he discounted as high-flown and exaggerated. More positively the Australians were clear that they wished federal-state relations to be interpreted by an indigenous court familiar with Australian law and practice. While therefore the right of the judical committee to hear appeals from the Australian high court was preserved in principle, the interpretation of Commonwealth-states rights was effectively vested in practice in the high court which alone could grant leave to appeal to the judicial committee. This was a case in which Australians were able to profit from Canadian experience by not following Canadian example.

There were other interesting and in some cases ingenious innovations in the Australian constituion. As in Canada, Parliament consisted of a governor-general as representative of the Crown and two Houses, a Senate and a House of Representatives. But while forms coincided, neither attitudes nor composition nor the balance of power was by any means identical. There was a pronounced coolness on the part of Australians towards the office of governor-general. To Alfred Deakin the title of governor-general appeared 'to be little better than a glittering and gaudy toy', while to John Cockburn, another Founding Father, the governor-general's highest function was 'to be a dummy'.[51] Not only was Australian language about the office altogether less respectful than Canadian but there was also a corresponding Australian desire to limit in practice the discretionary authority of the holder. Professor Crisp has commented that the history of the governor-generalship in the first fifty-four years of the Australian federation was a history 'of gradual but constant encroachment upon the initially very restricted personal initiative and discretion of its incumbents'. And he added that in becoming 'ever more innocuous and politically unobtrusive' the governor-generalship had provided 'an ever more satisfactory keystone to the constitutional arch'.[52] Furthermore, in respect of actual status, the designation was somewhat misleading. There was no official hierarchical relationship between the governor-general and the governors of the several states. On the contrary, the governors continued to be appointed by the Crown and to serve as symbols of the separate and coequal identity of the states with the Commonwealth, precedence however being yielded to the governor-general at dignified functions.[53]

The composition of the two Houses of the Australian Federal Parliament and the relationship between them underlined more notably the difference in purpose of the Australian and the Canadian Founding Fathers. The Australian Senate consisted originally of six, and subsequently of ten, senators from each state. They are elected for six years by the people of the states voting on the same franchise qualification as for the Federal Lower House, the House of Representatives, but with each state voting not in separate consituencies as for the Lower House but as one electorate. So far as possible the members of the Lower House were to be double those of the Senate, the relation between them being in certain circumstances of practical importance. The purpose of these arrangements was to ensure that the Senate should serve as the guardian of states' rights and in particular as the protector of the less populous states which, it will be noted, had equal representation with those of greater numerical resources. On paper this was a Senate very different from its nominated Canadian counterpart, with a specific function to fulfil and popular sanction behind it. In practice however the contrast has not been so pronounced. The large constituencies for Senate elections coupled with the tightness of Australian party organisation (particularly on the left) and the rigours of Australian federal politics generally have combined to ensure party predominance in the Upper as in the Lower House.

The democratic outlook of the Australian constitution-makers, again by contrast with the Canadian, as well as their ingenuity was well illustrated in the devices adopted for resolving differences between the two Houses of the Federal Parliament and for amendment of the constitution. Under section 57 of the constitution the rejection by the Senate of a measure passed by the House of Representatives on two occasions with an interval of three months between them in the same or the next session of Parliament entitled the government to advise a double dissolution, that is to say a dissolution both of the House of Representatives and Senate, and if after the subsequent election the Senate should again and for a third time reject the same measure, there was to be a joint sitting of both Houses at which the will of the majority would prevail. Such a double dissolution has in fact taken place on two occasions (in 1913 and in 1951) but in both cases the government was returned with control of both Houses so that no joint sitting was required after the election.

In the critically important field of constitutional amendment there was likewise reliance upon appeals to the people. Under section 128, a proposed amendment to the constitution had to be passed by an absolute majority in each House of the Federal Parliament and then submitted to the electors. If there was a difference between the two Houses, an amendment passed by an absolute majority on two occasions by one House and twice rejected by the other might also be submitted to the people in a referendum. In the referendum, approval of the proposed amendment required a double majority, that is to say a majority of the electors in the Commonwealth as a whole and also a majority in a majority of states. If the amendment affected a particular state then additionally there had to be a majority in the state (or states) concerned. These majorities were not readily obtained. Of the twenty-one proposals for amendment of the constitution submitted to referenda in the first sixty years of federation, only four were carried. This was the more significant in that many of the amendments proposed, for example by the Labour government immediately following the end of the second world war, were designed to extend federal powers in order to help reconstruction and ensure uniformity and improvement in social services as a whole. Even in times of high political emotion the conservatism of the electors remained pronounced. One example may suffice. In 1951, during the period of the Korean war, in which Australian forces were engaged, the Menzies government dissolved the Communist Party and seized its property. Their action was challenged in the courts and on appeal, the high court (which had been stigmatised in slogans painted on the walls above the Yarra the night before judgment was delivered as a 'capitalist stronghold' and was hailed the evening after in hastily amended letters as the 'guardian of the people's rights') declared the legislation *ultra vires*. The government responded by proposing a constitutional amendment to validate their action. It secured the necessary approval of both Houses and was duly submitted to the people but was narrowly defeated in the country as a whole and also failed to secure the support of a majority in a majority of states.

In so far as there has been enlargement of federal powers it has been mainly by judicial interpretation. For the rest the strong bias towards states' rights evident in the constitution as enacted remains, with only such matters as are expressly listed in the schedule to the constitution as vested in federal authority falling within its competence and everything not expressly so attributed remaining with the states.

> If any country and its government were to be selected [wrote James Bryce] as showing the course which a self-governing people pursues free from all external influences and little trammelled by intellectual influences descending from the past, Australia would be that country. It is the newest of all the democracies. It is that which has travelled farthest and fastest along the road which leads to the unlimited rule of the multitude.[54]

Bryce, who could hardly imagine a representative system of government in and through which the masses could more swiftly and completely exert their sovereignty, viewed the prospect with some misgivings. He reminded his Australian readers of the maxim that nations must not presume too far upon their hereditary virtue and he thought it might be said of the Australian system of government what Macaulay said 'not quite correctly, of the United States government. It is "all sail and no ballast".'[55] But Bryce (like other and later commentators) underestimated the ballast of a people's conservatism behind the sometimes brash expression of radical sentiments.

CHAPTER 5

'THE BUSINESS MAY SEEM PROSAIC'; CO-OPERATION BY CONFERENCE, 1887–1911

'Prodigious greatness' – such were the terms in which Sir John Seeley wrote of England in the widely read and highly influential published version of his Cambridge lectures of the spring of 1881 on *The Expansion of England*.[1] 'We seem,' he reflected, in one of the most quoted (if more questionable) of his sentences, 'as it were, to have conquered and peopled half the world in a fit of absence of mind.'[2] It was the peopling, not the conquest, that appeared to him of first importance. The 'English Exodus' had been 'the greatest English event of the eighteenth and nineteenth centuries'.[3] It had brought into being a Greater Britain comprising mother country and colonies of settlement. The growth of that Greater Britain was 'an event of enormous magnitude'.[4] Yet associated with Greater Britain were colonies not of settlement but of conquest, India chief among them, not united to Britain by blood – the strongest of ties – and in that and most other respects on quite a different footing. They were by no means necessarily a source of strength – not even the greatest among them. 'It may be fairly questioned,' observed Seeley, 'whether the possession of India does or ever can increase our power or our security, while there is no doubt that it vastly increases our dangers and responsibilities.'[5]

While Seeley marvelled at the greatness of the British Empire he was also somewhat fearful. His fears were not of declining dominion – on the contrary he rightly sensed that it would be yet further extended – but of corrupting influences. 'Bigness,' he warned, 'is not necessarily greatness; if by remaining in the second rank of magnitude we can hold the first rank morally and intellectually, let us sacrifice mere material magnitude.'[6] Others, he recognised, were more confidently expansionist and he suspected they were less wise. It offended him to hear 'our Empire described in the language of Oriental bombast';[7] and for the 'bombastic' school of imperialists 'lost in wonder and ecstasy at its immense dimensions',[8] advocating the maintenance of Empire as a point of honour or sentiment, preoccupied with notions of further expansion regardless of its purpose, Seeley had contempt mingled with some concern. The Empire, which took over the rule of unassimilable races, he admonished them, was weakening its health, perhaps fatally weakening it. Had not Empires in the past declined into nothing more than 'a mere mechanical union of alien nationalities'?[9] Indeed, once a state advanced beyond the limits of nationality its power became precarious and artificial and that, Seeley believed, was the condition of most empires and 'the condition for example of our own Empire in India'. The subcontinent rested heavily upon his mind. 'India is really an Empire and an Oriental Empire'; withdrawal would be 'the most inexcusable of all conceivable crimes' but none the less retention carried its own risks and weighty responsibilities. Might not the possession of India also prove corrupting, 'drag us down, or infect us at home with Oriental notions or methods of government?'[10] Seeley, without dismissing the possibility, discounted it. India was not attached to Britain as the Roman Empire had been to Rome and the foundations of English liberty might accordingly remain secure. Moreover, while the connection with India especially gave cause for some sobering reflections, Seeley entertained few doubts on this or other grounds about the destiny of the British Empire. History, he felt, when studied and rightly interpreted, could be seen to have marked out for Britain a place in the first rank of states with Russia and the United States, and in a higher rank than the states of the European continent.[11] The important practical question was, how was this place to be attained and retained? It was a question that had begun to preoccupy the minds of many of his contemporaries.

Neither Britain's resources nor her manpower were concentrated as were those of her continental rivals of the future. Might not this alone exclude the prospect of equal greatness? Seeley thought not. Why? His assurance in this regard derived neither from the extent of the Empire nor even from contemporary indications of reviving imperial sentiment. Disraeli, that harbinger of a new imperialism, in his speech at the Crystal Palace nine years earlier, had poured scorn on the opinions of Liberal 'statesmen of the highest character, writers of the most distinguished ability' who had 'proved to all of us that we have lost money by our colonies' and had shown 'with precise, with mathematical demonstration, that there never was a jewel in the Crown of England that was so truly costly as the possession of India', had gone on to appeal directly to consideration of power, prestige and pride of nationality.[12] With these later day Disraelian imperialist sentiments Seeley sympathised only in part for, as we have seen, he was not among the growing number who were carried away by the romantic notions of grandeur, which the queen's assumption of the title of Empress of India – 'theatrical bombast and folly' Gladstone termed it[13] – supremely symbolised. 'When we enquire into the greater Britain of the future', Seeley insisted firmly, 'we ought to think much more of our colonial than of our Indian Empire'. It ought to be thought of more because it was not only a part but the condition of the greatness of the future. The population of the colonies, Seeley predicted confidently and more sensibly than many of his contemporaries, would greatly expand. 'In not much more than half a century', he wrote,[14] 'the Englishmen beyond the sea – supposing the Empire to hold together – will be equal in number to the Englishmen at home, and the total will be much more than a hundred millions'. But in essence his argument rested not upon uncertain prognostication of numbers, but upon the actual existence of British settler states in North America, in the Pacific, in southern Africa and, Seeley added, in conformity with contemporary opinion, in the West Indies. What was required, in his view, was to build upon the foundation which they, and they alone, provided and to organise a United States of Britain to take its place in the future, coequal in power, status and extent with the United States of America and with Russia. The contemplated means were federal and the goal an imperial federation.

Sir John Seeley was thinking of the future in the light of the past. Others with more direct responsibility for the formulation of political aims inclined, though not always for the same reason, towards a similar conclusion. They noted that the balance of power in Europe had been decisively changed by the German victories of 1870–1, that in consequence of them, the German Empire had emerged as the most formidable military power in the world and most important, that a new, more active and more dangerous era in great power rivalries had opened. In this situation there was self-evident need to look more closely at Britain's resources in relation to her world wide obligations and to consider afresh her ability to discharge them on the basis of existing imperial organisation – or lack of it.

The many wars in which Britain had been engaged since 1815 had, with the exception of the Crimean, all been 'small wars' and most of them the 'small wars' of Empire. The waging of them was costly and the advantages gained usually debatable at a time when it was becoming a constant concern of Whig-Liberal administrations (in the main) to limit and if possible to diminish military expenditure. This concern was understandable. In 1846–7 the total cost of the army and navy accounted for roughly 73 per cent of the national expenditure (excluding debt services) and one third of the total cost of the army was spent upon colonial garrisons. Partly because of traditional mistrust of a standing army at home and partly because of contemporary thinking on colonial defence 'as if the defence of each separate part of the Empire was a problem entirely self-contained',[15] many of these garrisons were apt to be more fully manned than would otherwise have been required. With colonial self-government a new concept was introduced, well-expressed in the phrase 'self-government begets self-defence'. This was a favourite theme of Gladstone, whose argument spelled out was that self-government was a condition of self-reliance and self-reliance in its turn a condition of self-defence, neither of which could grow so long as colonists were taught that 'come what would, they would be defended by a power thousands of miles away'.[16] In 1862 the House of Commons, after considering the report of a parliamentary committee known from the name of its chairman, Arthur Mills, as the Mills Committee, enunciated the principles that should determine the allocation of defence responsibility between Great Britain and her colonies in a resolution which read:

> That this House (while fully recognising the claims of all portions of the British Empire to imperial aid in their protection against perils arising from the consequences of imperial policy) is of the opinion that colonies exercising the rights of self-government ought to undertake the main responsibility of providing for their own internal order and security and ought to assist in their own external defence.

The moral was driven home for the colonists by the subsequent withdrawal of British garrisons from Canada, the Australian colonies, New Zealand and (partially and temporarily as it proved) from southern Africa. But restatement of principles was not accompanied by a parallel redefinition, for practical purposes, of future imperial-colonial responsibilities for defence expenditure or contributions and in his Crystal Palace speech Disraeli drew attention to this omission. Self-government should have been conceded in the first instance, he argued, as part of a great policy of imperial consolidation. It ought to have been accompanied by an imperial tariff and 'by a military code which should have precisely defined the means and the responsibilities by which the colonies should be defended, and by which, if necessary, this country should call for aid from the colonies themselves'.[17] But instead the principal – indeed to many the all-sufficient justification for 'the recall of the legions' – had been the economies thereby effected and the appeasement of anti-imperialists.[18]

The assumption made by the critics of imperial expenditure on colonial defence (shared, it would seem, by the great majority of their fellow countrymen) was that the colonies, incapable of defending themselves, could be thought of only in terms of financial or military obligation, rarely, if ever, of contribution. As Dilke put it in 1868, in a passage remarkable for its insight into the pattern of the future even if it was mistaken in its forecast:

> It is not likely, however, nowadays, that our colonists would for any long

stretch of time engage to aid us in our purely European wars. Australia would scarcely feel herself deeply interested in the guarantee of Luxembourg, nor Canada in the affairs of Servia. The fact that we in Britain paid our share—or rather nearly the whole cost—of the Maori wars would be no argument to an Australian but only an additional proof to him of our extraordinary folly. We have been educated into a habit of paying with complacency other people's bills – not so the Australian settler.[19]

Yet in 1878 Disraeli gave dramatic cause for reconsideration, if not in respect of colonial at least in respect of possible imperial reinforcement of British resources in a European theatre, by moving Indian troops into the Mediterranean to strengthen the garrison at Malta at a time when Anglo-Russian tensions over the terms of the Treaty of San Stefano neared breaking point – and by so doing incidentally inspiring a parody of what Sir Henry Lucy described as the 'popular music-hall doggerel' of the day:[20]

We don't want to fight;
But, by jingo, if we do,
We'll stay at home and sing our songs
And send the mild Hindoo

Already the Russian war scare had led, with prompting from the colonial secretary, Lord Carnarvon, to the appointment of an interdepartmental defence committee. As a result of its reports and recommendations a Royal Commission under the chairmanship of Lord Carnarvon (whose interest in defence continued unabated despite his resignation from the government on its policy towards Russia) was set up in the following year to enquire into 'the defence of British possessions and commerce abroad'. The appointment of colonial representatives was considered but not effected. Some famous colonial personalities, however, testified before it, including Sir Henry Parkes from New South Wales and Sir John A. Macdonald from Canada, who believed that no common system of defence could be established and that it was better to trust to a loyal and patriotic response under the stimulus of crisis than to grants of men or money in times of peace. Gladstone's return to office in 1880, after impassioned Midlothian denunciations of jingoism and of the financial profligacy of Disraeli's administration in the pursuit of 'false phantoms of glory',[21] gave cause for doubt about the Commission's continued existence. But the need for it was accepted by the new government, albeit reluctantly, and it was enabled to complete its work. The outcome was the first systematic survey of British imperial defence in the nineteenth century and one that was made not in the old pecuniary but in the new power context. Recommendations for future organisation were set out in three Reports, none of which was published in full. The emphasis was upon the sea communications of Empire, the conditions of their security and the contributions the colonies might make, chiefly by way of harbour facilities and coaling stations. The Commission allowed that the cost of the navy must for the time being fall upon imperial funds but noted that the capacity of the colonies to share in imperial defence would continually increase and the relative apportionment of burdens, as between the mother country and her colonies, would accordingly require to be adjusted in time. Of broader significance was the fact that new alignments in world power had shifted British defence interests from problems of the local security of particular colonies or outposts to those of imperial defence and strategy conceived as a whole, with each individual colony or territory having a rôle to play and a contribution to make.[22]

Changes in the patterns and practices of international trade were no less significant than the shifts in the balance of world power. So long as England's industrial supremacy remained, all she wanted was access to the markets of the world. Free trade and peace were her self-interested, but none-the-less enlightened, objectives. The Manchester School had believed that in time others would follow along the same liberal, progressive road but after 1870 most European states, with Germany in the lead, far from continuing the advance towards the free trade goal, reversed course and from behind protective tariffs began to compete with Britain in world markets. Germany became fully protectionist in 1879, Russia increased her tariff in 1881 and 1882, France and Austria-Hungary in 1882 and Italy in 1888. When France and Germany entered the colonial field in Africa and Asia they surrounded their new possessions with tariff walls; evidently they believed there was a connection between sovereignty and economics, between colonies and trade. Did not this suggest that some reconsideration of accepted economic notions in Britain might also be due or even overdue? The depression of the 1880s and evidence of Britain's declining share of world trade strengthened the case for critical reappraisal, not least of the rôle of the Empire overseas in the British trading system. One characteristically English reaction was the foundation of the Fair Trade League in 1881 favouring imperial preferences and – more important – tariff retaliation against foreign countries (always apt to be suspected of not trading 'fair'), with a view to reducing imports of food from protectionist foreign states and increasing supplies from the colonies on a long term, developing basis.[23] Nothing, however, came – or perhaps could have come – of these proposals, which were before their time and in conception near-impracticable.

Superimposed upon military and commercial factors were the less tangible considerations of the inter-relation between Empire and national power and prestige. Was Empire the foundation of British greatness? Gladstone thought not, spacious though he recognised that Empire to be.

There is no precedent [he declared in the opening speech of his Midlothian campaign, on 25 November 1879] in human history for a formation like the British Empire. A small island at one extremity of the globe peoples the whole earth with its colonies. Not satisfied with that, it goes among the ancient races of Asia and subjects two hundred and forty millions of men to its rule. Along with all this it disseminates over the world a commerce such as no imagination ever conceived in former times and such as no poet ever painted. And all this had to do with the strength that lies within the narrow limits of these shores. Not a strength that I disparage; on the contrary, I wish to dissipate if I can the idle dreams of those who are always telling you that the strength of England depends, sometimes they say upon its prestige, sometimes they say upon extending its Empire, or upon what it possesses beyond these shores. Rely upon it the strength of Great Britain and Ireland is within the United Kingdom.[24]

But in England this view was increasingly challenged while on the continent many writers, principally (though not only) German, failed, so A. J. P. Taylor has written, 'to grasp the truth about the British Empire – that it had come into being as the result of British commercial enterprise and industrial success; and they asserted the reverse, that the prosperity and wealth of Great Britain were due to the existence of her Empire.'[25] Yet while their arguments remained questionable they possessed superficial force and they were heavily underscored with popular emotional overtones. Even Bismarck, who late in life told the Reichstag that he had never been a 'colonial man', found it advantageous to let colonialist currents fill his diplomatic sails. Was Britain alone, the possessor of the greatest of European Empires, to stand aside aloof and detached, to discount its Empire's potential and to allow her colonies and possessions, unorganised and little regarded, to drift away into independence as casual sentiment suggested or circumstances decided on the complacent assumption that greatness resided not in Empire but in its own small island state? The answer – in the last quarter of the century as distinct from its middle period – was an increasingly emphatic and often a strident negative. The 'pomological theory' of colonies[26] was discarded and homely analogies from the orchard were superseded by harsher parallels from Darwinian concepts of the survival of the fittest. No longer ripeness but greatness was all!

The Imperial Federation League which was founded in 1884 reflected the new thinking. It numbered some distinguished figures including Joseph Chamberlain and W. E. Forster among its converts but it was important historically not because its aims were fulfilled but because the gradual realisation that they were impossible of fulfilment exposed the fundamental misapprehension about the aspirations and interests of the self-governing colonies – as entertained or interpreted by the colonists themselves – which had brought the League into existence and in so doing helped to focus the minds of British statesmen, albeit in many cases reluctantly, upon more limited but realisable ends. The misapprehension (which Seeley, himself associated with the league for several years, shared) derived from a belief that the British people at home and in the overseas colonies would, or should, form not several states but one state or even nation. In an address to the Philosophical Institution of Edinburgh on 5 November 1875, W. E. Forster suggested, as conditions of the imperial federal union of the future, that all the self-governing communities of the Empire should agree in paying allegiance to one monarch, in preserving a common nationality, and 'not only in maintaining a mutual alliance in all relations with foreign powers but in apportioning among themselves the obligations imposed by such alliance'. Forster understood that the comprehensive character of his last condition was likely to provoke colonial objections but he argued that the very essence of a continuance of the imperial connection was 'a common patriotism; the feeling throughout all the different communities that, notwithstanding the seas that roll between them, they are yet one nation; and that all their inhabitants are fellow-countrymen'.[27] But therein, concisely stated, lay the fundamental federal misconception. Englishmen overseas though somewhat divided in mind were for the most part preoccupied not with building up a common nationality or a single state but with the development of the distinct and separate political identities of their own territories, on the basis not of one but of several states or nations. In so far as they were moved by deliberate intention, that intention was antagonistic to the aims of the federalists. This was something that federalists, carried along with the rising tide of imperial sentiment, were slow to perceive and reluctant to acknowledge. Their propaganda did, however, serve a constructive purpose but not the purpose it was intended to serve; not for the first time did the championing of an impossible cause concentrate attention upon what was possible. In itself this was no mean achievement but it is important that it should be recognised for what it was. The idea of federation, once actively publicised and promoted, acted as a catalyst stirring into action over the years the forces that were predestined to provide the alternative to it.

The chief purpose of the Imperial Federation League was to ensure effective reorganisation of Empire under continuing control of London. If the early federationists forgot or ignored India that was because, as an Indian writer has observed, 'she was quiet and securely in hand'.[28] It was the colonies of settlement – enjoying responsible self-government and advancing towards a state of autonomy that might lead by easy stages to sovereign independence – which gave point to the slogan 'federate or disintegrate' and on which federationists' attention was accordingly focused. It had been alleged by the same Indian writer that their concept of a federal Empire to be confined in practice to colonies of European settlement was for this reason 'frankly racial'. In as much as the purpose of federation was – in the words of James Anthony Froude – to 'reunite the scattered fragments of the same nation', this was true. But would it not be truer to say that it was this immediate purpose of the federationists – namely, to retain these 'scattered fragments' within an Empire to which they seemed by no means securely attached – which gave to their propaganda its racial tone rather than the existence of a sense of racial exclusiveness which inspired their aim? The balance is not easy to strike; but there is no doubt that the majority of federationists were profoundly influenced by a particular example – the reunification of the majority of the German people in one state – which certainly had its cultural and racial overtones.

The advocates of imperial federation were apt to think more spaciously than those actually holding responsibility for the conduct of imperial affairs. At the first Colonial Conference, held in London in 1887, the year of Queen Victoria's Golden Jubilee celebrations, the prime minister, Lord Salisbury, was at some pains to make clear that imperial federation with its 'grand aspirations' was a matter 'for the future rather than for the present'. The Empire, which 'yields to none – it is, perhaps, superior to all – in its greatness' had about it one peculiarity which distinguished it from other empires – 'a want of continuity; it is separated into parts by large stretches of ocean; and what we are here for today is to see how far we must acquiesce in the conditions which that separation causes, how far we can obliterate them by agreement and by organisation.' The geographical factor meant that the British Empire could not emulate the German Empire in conducting all its imperial affairs from one centre and Lord Salisbury was sceptical as to whether it would ever be possible for it to do so. There were however other prospects before it. He hoped that they might 'present to the world the spectacle of a vast Empire, founded not upon force and upon subjection, but upon hearty sympathy, and a resolute cooperation in attaining those high objects of human endeavour which are open to an Empire like this'. But such cooperation was conditional upon agreement among themselves and could rest only upon continued self-reliance and self-determination in respect of domestic policies. So much indeed was already implicit in the imperial-colonial relationship and in turn it predicated the nature of the Conference's conclusions. 'The decisions of this Conference,' Lord Salisbury remarked, 'may not be, for the moment, of vital importance; the business may seem prosaic, and may not issue in any great results at the moment. But we are all sensible that this meeting is the beginning of a state of things which is to have great results in the future.'[29]

Some eighty years have passed since Lord Salisbury spoke of the deliberations of the first Colonial Conference in these deflationary terms. On two points – superficially unrelated but in fact closely associated – he may be seen from this vantage point in time to have shown considerable foresight. The Colonial Conference of 1887 did mark the beginning of a state of things which had great results, not despite but largely because of the prosaic nature of its business. A long succession of imperialists was to express disappointment at the pedestrian character of the proceedings, the limited aims, the meagre results first of colonial then of imperial conferences, and in more recent times of Commonwealth Prime Ministers' Meetings. Yet had those imperial or Commonwealth gatherings concentrated their attention, as imperialists wished, on grand designs and spacious purposes then it may be remarked with some assurance that there would have been no later Commonwealth of Nations.

The prime minister had reason for supposing that the proceedings of the first Colonial Conference would be prosaic. There was debate on the arrangments for the naval defence of the Australian colonies; discussion on postal and telegraphic communications in general and a resolution in favour of a trans-Pacific cable in particular. Other questions that were considered related to the Pacific islands, to the adoption by the colonies of parallel legislation to that proposed in the United Kingdom regarding merchandise, marks and patents. There was a report from Canada on the Canadian Pacific Railway as a new Empire route important alike in its naval, military and political implications. All these were matters of moment to men concerned with practical affairs; they were hardly of a kind to excite the emotions of the multitude or to satisfy the aspirations of the new imperialists. But the latter were not left altogether comfortless.

A conference, even if it had been a rather casual gathering composed of public men from the colonies who happened to be in London for the Jubilee celebrations and one to which colonial premiers were not as such specially invited – though three in fact attended – had, after all, been held. Nor did it pass unremarked that while Lord Salisbury discounted possibilities of imperial federation he spoke in more qualified terms of other lessons that might be drawn from German experience.

First he reminded members of the Conference that there had been a *Zollverein*, or customs union, and also a *Kriegsverein*, or a union for military purposes, before the German Empire came into existence. Then he argued that so far as the British Empire was concerned, the former, the *Zollverein*, though not to be dismissed as impractical by reason of the Empire's geographical dispersal had for the time being to be put 'in the distant and shadowy portion of our task' while the latter, the *Kriegsverein*, or union for purposes of mutual defence, which Lord Salisbury assured them was 'the real and most important business upon which you will be engaged', was to be regarded as a question for immediate and explicit consideration. It was also a matter of common interest. It was not only Britain but the colonies too who might be threatened by the changing patterns of world power and by the enormous increase in the means of communication. 'The English colonies,' Lord Salisbury observed in thinly veiled admonition, 'comprise some of the fairest and most desirable portions of the earth's surface. The desire for foreign and colonial possessions is increasing among the nations of Europe.' Not only a sense of obligation to the mother country but considerations of self-interest should prompt colonial governments and peoples to assist Great Britain in discharging the obligations of imperial defence. The colonies for their part were not unresponsive though neither could they be called uncritically acquiescent. From Cape Colony, J. H. Hofmeyr proposed a 2 per cent *ad valorem* tax on all imports, the revenue deriving from it to be expended on imperial naval defence. This was at once unacceptable and deemed impracticable, though in principle it approximated to British ideas of colonial contributions to the upkeep of the Royal Navy. The terms of agreement about Australasian naval defence, concluded at the 1887 Colonial Conference after two years of negotiations, introduced a more realistic note. The Australian colonies and New Zealand were to pay a contribution of £126,000 per annum towards the support of an auxiliary squadron of ships which would reinforce the ships of the Royal Navy in Australasian waters, and which it was specifically agreed should not be reduced in number. Under Australian pressure the Admiralty reluctantly conceded that the ships should not be employed outside Australasian waters without the consent of Australasian governments.[30] The principle of contribution though not of unrestricted contribution was thus introduced.

In 1894 a further conference met in Ottawa at the invitation of the Canadian government. In Canada but not in Britain it has been regarded as being in the strict sense a Colonial Conference. Its proceedings (which did not include defence) were again prosaic. The record of them fills some four hundred pages[31] and there was a new departure in the passing of resolutions. Questions that were discussed included once again the Pacific cable project, and proposals for a fast line of steamships across the Pacific, particularly between Australia and New Zealand; ranging more widely were resolutions in favour of imperial legislation to enable the colonies to enter into agreements of commercial reciprocity with one another and recommending, in principle, imperial trade preferences between Great Britain and the colonies. It was however further resolved that the colonies should proceed to make arrangements between themselves about trading preferences until such time as Britain, free trade discarded, was able to participate in them. Herein was foreshadowed one of the great imperial debates of succeeding years.

The Colonial Conference of 1897 which met in London at the time of Queen Victoria's Diamond Jubilee celebrations was unquestionably in the true line of succession. It was called by Joseph Chamberlain and attended in addition by the prime minister of Canada and the premiers of New South Wales, Victoria, New Zealand, Queensland, Cape Colony, South Australia, Newfoundland, Tasmania, Western Australia and Natal, all of whom were received as honoured guests at celebrations which, in their ordered magnificence and in the variety of the people's participation in them, marked the heady apogee of Empire.[32] At the Conference Chamberlain expressed his opinion that there was a real necessity for some better machinery of consultation between the self-governing colonies and the mother country. He remarked:

> . . . it has sometimes struck me – I offer it now merely as a personal suggestion – that it might be feasible to create a great council of the Empire to which the colonies would send representative plenipotentiaries – not mere delegates who were unable to speak in their name without further reference to their respective governments but persons who by their position in the colonies, by their representative character and by their close touch with colonial feeling, would be able, upon all subjects submitted to them, to give really effective and valuable advice. If such a council were to be created it would at once assume an immense importance and it is perfectly evident that it might develop into something still greater. It might slowly grow to that federal council to which we must always look forward as our ultimate ideal.[33]

The principal colonial representatives were however either critical or reserved and the Conference contented itself with a resolution (carried with two dissentients, one of them being Richard Seddon) stating that the existing political relations between the United Kingdom and the self-governing colonies were 'generally satisfactory'. But notwithstanding this resolution, there was a feeling that some preparatory step should be taken in the direction of giving the colonies a voice in the control and direction of imperial interests[34] – but only within the accepted framework of colonial self-government. Chamberlain's proposals transgressed this proviso. He was of course right in thinking that any council the members of which could commit their countries to certain imperial policies without reference to their own governments would assume immense importance; where he was mistaken was in supposing that the majority of the self-governing colonies would be prepared to impair in this way the responsibility of individual governments to individual parliaments.

The colonial secretary pressed the colonial premiers more urgently in respect of defence. He reminded them of the military review they had seen as part of the Jubilee celebrations and he told them that later in the week they would see at Spithead 'an astounding representation' of naval strength, by which alone a colonial Empire could be bound together. 'You are aware', he said to them, 'that that representation – great, magnificent, unparalleled as it will be – is nevertheless only a part of the naval forces in the Empire spread in every part of the globe.' This 'gigantic navy' and the military forces of the United Kingdom were maintained at heavy cost. But they were not maintained exclusively for the benefit of the United Kingdom or the defence of home interests. They were maintained still more as a necessity of Empire, for the maintenance and protection of imperial trade and of imperial interests all over the world. Every war, great or small, in which the United Kingdom had been engaged during Queen Victoria's reign had, so Chamberlain alleged, 'at the bottom a colonial interest, the interest that is to say either of a colony or of a great dependency like India. That is absolutely true, and is likely to be true to the end of the chapter.' If it was the case that Chamberlain was attributing the root cause of the greatest of these wars, the Crimean, to the Indian interest, he was relying greatly upon his gift for overstatement. At any rate the colonial premiers listened, but they responded only in modest measure. Cape Colony offered an unconditional contribution to the Royal Navy but the Australian colonies contented themselves with the renewal of their earlier contribution, which was still restricted to the protection of Australasian interests in Australasian waters. As for Canada, explained Sir Wilfrid Laurier, the question of a contribution, now that it had become a practical one, would no doubt be considered but, he proceeded, in reply to Australian criticism of Canadian inaction, the Canadian position was different from the Australian in that Canada was an inaccessible country.[35]

There was however a more noteworthy reponse in circumstances which Chamberlain cannot have altogether relished. At the outbreak of the South African war, the colonial secretary saw little reason to doubt War Office forecasts of an early, victorious conclusion to hostilities. How sanguine they were may be judged by the prospect held out to the young Winston Churchill by the British commander-in-chief, Sir Redvers Buller, on the troopship that carried them both to South Africa in the late autumn of 1899, who opined that they should be in time for one final engagement before Pretoria.[36] But there was no 'promenade to Pretoria'. As the war dragged on, contingents came from the Australian and New Zealand colonies and also from Canada where participation in an imperial war (although placed on a voluntary basis) still remained a source of much controversy between English and French-speaking Canadians. The colonial contributions were significant. Instead of English defence of colonial interests there was colonial re-inforcement of England in a war in which the colonies had little or no interest. For nineteenth-century thinking about the colonies of settlement as defence liabilities, there was thereby ushered in a new phase in which they were earning the right to be thought of as military assets. Yet British feelings about colonial assistance in South Africa were inevitably mixed. It was heartening that this help should have been forthcoming; it was disturbing that it should have been required. Rudyard Kipling (whose reputation was never quite the same again after the war) sought to drive home the moral in *The Islanders*, written in 1902 in passionate advocacy of conscription which alone, he believed, could give to Britain the measure of military self-sufficiency she required and which South African experience had shown to be lacking.

> And ye vaunted your fathomless power and ye flaunted
>   your iron pride,
> Ere ye fawned on the younger nations for the men who
>   could shoot and ride!
> Then ye returned to your trinkets; then ye contented
>   your souls
> With the flannelled fools at the wicket or the muddied
>   oafs in the goals.

The Colonial Conference of 1902 was the third conference to meet at a time of Royal celebrations, in this case the coronation of King Edward VII. The sobering experiences of the South African war rested heavily upon it. Gone was the exuberant imperialism of earlier years. 'I feel,' said Chamberlain, 'that . . . it would be a fatal mistake to transform the spontaneous enthusiasm which has been so readily shown throughout the Empire into anything in the nature of an obligation which might be at this time unwillingly assumed. . .'. Accordingly, a new emphasis upon the weight of British responsibilities was counterbalanced by a greater British sensitivity as to the nature of the colonial connection and enhanced appreciation of its value. 'We do require your assistance,' Chamberlain told the Conference, 'in the administration of the vast

Empire which is yours as well as ours. The weary Titan staggers under the too vast orb of its fate. We have borne the burden for many years. We think it is time that our children should assist us to support it. . .'.[37] Here were echoes not of great powers ever becoming greater but of Matthew Arnold and his weary Titan –

> Staggering on to her goal;
> Bearing on shoulders immense,
> Atlanteän, the load,
> Wellnigh not to be borne,
> Of the too vast orb of her fate.[38]

And there followed an appeal – more insistent than in 1897 – for organised colonial contributions for defence. As international dangers had multiplied so had expenditure on armaments increased. They involved a cost per head of the United Kingdom of twenty-nine shillings and threepence per annum on naval and military defence whereas in Canada the comparable expenditure was only two shillings per head; in New South Wales three shillings and fivepence; in Victoria three shillings and threepence; in New Zealand three shillings and fourpence and in the Cape and Natal somewhere between two and three shillings per head of the white population. 'Now, no one,' said Chamberlain, 'I think, will pretend that that is a fair distribution of the burdens of Empire. No one will believe that the United Kingdom can, for all time, make this inordinate sacrifice.'[39] The Admiralty rubbed in the lesson with a memorandum showing a breakdown of the figures in respect of naval expenditure. They told even more strikingly the same statistical story. Per head of the population in the United Kingdom such expenditure amounted to fifteen shillings and one penny, in New South Wales to eightpence-halfpenny, in Victoria to nearly one shilling, in New Zealand to sixpence-halfpenny, in the Cape of Good Hope to one shilling and a penny-farthing and in Natal four shillings and fivepence-threefarthings per head of the white population, and in Canada nil.[40] Was such a disparity warranted? When the colonies 'were young and poor', the colonial secretary conceded, they had clearly been incapable of providing large sums for their defence, but now that they were rich and powerful, growing every day 'by leaps and bounds', with their material prosperity promising to rival that of the United Kingdom itself, it was inconsistent with their position and their dignity that they should leave the mother country to bear the whole or almost the whole of the expense. Nor was it wise. 'Justification of union,' argued Chamberlain, 'is that a bundle is stronger than the sticks which compose it, but if the whole strain is to be thrown on one stick, there is very little advantage in any attempt to put them into a bundle.'[41]

A constructive proposal for spreading the strain – and incidentally a display of the colonial initiative for which Chamberlain had hoped – came from Richard Seddon, the prime minister of New Zealand. It was not novel but it was not on that ground the less welcome. It contemplated the creation of a joint colonial and imperial reserve force. The colonial secretary underlined the need for such a reserve at the conference table. He acknowledged with appreciation the assistance of colonial forces in South Africa. But what, he felt obliged to ask, had it amounted to? In the case of Canada one thousand men out of a population of five million. What the situation had demanded was something like ten thousand to twenty thousand men, already trained and in being as a reserve force, in each of the colonies according to its population and resources. But the provision and organisation of such forces were matters for the self-governing colonies themselves to decide. Regrettably it had been made plain to him that, other than New Zealand, in the existing conditions of public opinion in the colonies it would not be practicable to bring any such scheme into effect. 'That being the fact,' concluded Chamberlain severely, 'I am bound to say that in my opinion public opinion in these colonies must be very backward. I think it will have to progress, and that it cannot in the natural course of things but progress, especially as the dangers which lie all round you are better appreciated.'

On the naval side the colonies were only a little more forth-coming. The Admiralty underlined in a memorandum which they prepared for the Conference, the importance of command of the sea, supporting their argument with a wealth of historical illustration ranging from Salamis and Actium to Lepanto, Chesapeake Bay, the Peninsular war, the expedition to the Crimea and the South African war, the last three being used as examples of great military enterprises which could have been carried out only by a power supreme at sea. To maintain such supremacy the Admiralty asked for colonial contributions to naval strength, not in the form of local navies but of subsidies to the Royal Navy. The reason for this was their conversion to the newer orthodoxy of Admiral Mahan which demanded concentration of naval power at the decisive point and, as a necessary consequence, centralised control. The first lord, Lord Selborne, drew the particular attention of the colonial prime ministers to the elimination from the Admiralty memorandum of any allusion to the word 'defence', on the ground that the term suggested an outdated and heretical approach to contemporary strategic requirements. The colonial response was varied. Cape Colony and Natal offered unconditional contributions of fifty thousand and thirty-five thousand pounds respectively. For New Zealand, Seddon vigorously repudiated the notion of a separate navy and disliked the idea of a fixed contribution but finally agreed to a payment of forty thousand pounds a year, later increased to one hundred thousand pounds a year. Laurier excused Canadians from all contribution on the ground of heavy expenditure on domestic development and especially on transcontinental railroads – a point on which he had some exchanges with Chamberlain – while for Australia Sir Edmund Barton, after placing on record the existence of strong popular support for a local navy in the Commonwealth,[42] agreed upon an increase in the Australian contribution to the Royal Navy from one hundred and twenty-six thousand pounds a year – the figure determined under the Naval Agreement negotiated in 1887 – to two hundred thousand pounds a year, which was one hundred thousand pounds a year less than the Admiralty had asked for, the short fall being justified, as with Canada, on the ground of heavy expenditure at home on railways. Even so, Barton's action came in for heavy criticism in the federal Parliament. This was chiefly because successful Admiralty insistence upon the need for undivided responsibility so as to allow for concentration of forces should need arise, meant that Admiralty control of the ships in the Australian squadron was not limited, as heretofore, by the need for consultation with the Australian government about their employment outside Australian territorial waters. Even though not ready to undertake the responsibility of a separate navy, most Australians were not prepared to discard earlier notions of the value of local defence. Despite vigorous criticism, however, in Parliament and the press the subsidy was approved and continued to be paid, though with steadily diminishing conviction of its appropriateness, until the Naval Agreement of 1909.

The nature of British-colonial differences on defence responsibilities in 1902 was variable and at times elusive. They had a socio-economic content in Australia and most notably in Canada, where as Laurier emphasised there was a small population developing a huge territory – the precise opposite of the position in the United Kingdom – and fixed military contributions were likely in consequence to impose a quite disproportionate burden. But the root source from which such differences stemmed was clear. It was not economic or strategic but political; the colonies were instinctively averse to any development which might impose a limit to the growth of their autonomy and an imperial military force might do precisely this. The colonies had decided the extent and the nature of their contribution to the South African war and they wished to decide the extent and nature of their contributions to future and possibly greater wars. This was true of all except New Zealand but of none was it more true than of Canada. Canada's business, said Sir Wilfrid Laurier in 1900, was Canada's business. 'I claim for Canada this, that in future, Canada shall be at liberty to act or not act, to interfere or not interfere, to do just as she pleases, and that she shall reserve to herself the right to judge whether or not there is cause for her to act.'[43] Did that mean no cooperation on imperial issues? Clearly not; the South African war even if recruitment had been on a voluntary basis had shown as much. But it had also shown that Canadian co-operation and the nature of it would be conditional upon the approval of and determined by the Canadian government.

The insistence of colonial governments and especially that of Canada upon their powers of decision was at least in part defensive. Before he left for the 1902 Colonial Conference, Sir Wilfrid Laurier remarked that there was 'a school in England and in Canada, . . . which wants to bring Canada into the vortex of militarism which is now the curse and the blight of Europe.'[44] What might be the effects in Canada if it were even partially successful in securing identification of Canadian with British imperial interests? Chamberlain himself was warned in a letter from Canada that should Laurier agree to a Canadian financial contribution for imperial defence, there would be a cry of 'Tribute' from Quebec and, added the correspondent, 'We do not want a French Ireland in Canada between us and the sea'.[45] It had already become apparent before 1902 that the future rôle of the colonies in imperial defence would have to be thought of, not on traditional lines, but in conformity with their status and aspirations as self-governing political entities. In 1902 colonial concepts were formulated chiefly by negative responses to imperial propositions. In respect of military forces they were final. But no parallel categoric responses were, or could be, made in respect of naval forces. The new strategic orthodoxy, coupled with self-evident dominion dependence upon the Royal Navy, saw to that. So it was that in the naval sphere the 1902 Colonial Conference marked less an ending than the opening of a new phase in imperial-colonial relations.

While the initiative in respect of the political and defence organisation of the Empire was taken by the United Kingdom, in respect of trade it lay with the colonies. For this there was good reason. The colonies enjoyed a freedom of manoeuvre which the mother country did not possess. Their approach was pragmatic, that of the United Kingdom rigid. They were free trade or protectionist as suited their particular needs at a particular moment; Great Britain remained, despite some misgivings, a country doctrinally committed to free trade. As a necessary consequence proposals for tariff reform came not from London but from the colonies. While the elder Hofmeyr's 1887 proposal for an imperial customs tariff with the revenue from it to be devoted to the general defence of the Empire came to nothing, a new departure was made between 1894 and 1897, with the Canadian government deciding to give British goods tariff preferences, which amounted at first to 25 per cent and were subsequently increased to $33\frac{1}{3}$ per cent. They were preferences voluntarily accorded by Canada on British taxable goods imported into the dominion. The Canadian initiative was followed by other colonial governments. But it was not requited. Might the British government not be persuaded to do so?

At successive Colonial Conferences the British government had been categoric in its assertions that it desired to increase the volume of Empire trade, which amounted to about one-third of Great Britain's total trade. But, in the first instance at least, it was not in terms of imperial preference that British statesmen were thinking. Their thoughts ran on a more ambitious scale and in a different direction. What was uppermost in their minds, and most notably in the thoughts of the secretary of state for the colonies, was a customs union, or *Zollverein*, on the German model. Free trade within the Empire was a first object. That, were it feasible, would bring substantial benefits in its train. It would, so Chamberlain told the Colonial Conference in 1902, 'enormously increase our inter-imperial trade . . . it would hasten the development of our colonies . . . it would fill up the spare places in your lands with an active, intelligent and industrious, and above all a British population . . . it would make the mother country entirely independent of foreign food and raw material.'[46] But there was no acceptance of the argument or its implications in the colonies. Why? Professor Hancock has summarised the reasons in two brief sentences. For them Chamberlain's *Zollverein* was impossible because 'it meant tariff assimilation with Great Britain and a surrender of tariff personality. Tariff personality was an essential element in self-government.'[47] Even with the concessions that Chamberlain was prepared to make, an imperial customs union meant centralised direction; that meant loss of fiscal autonomy and might well mean more besides. Association within a free trade area with one of the most industrially advanced societies in the world would imperil the future of growing colonial industries. The advantages in terms of an assured market for raw materials and primary products were accordingly likely to be offset, or more than offset, by diminished prospects of industrial development. And thinking in politico-economic terms, as did colonial leaders almost without exception, that meant in turn a readiness to postpone or even abandon hopes of building up a balanced economy within their own frontiers. The sacrifice was not to be contemplated and they held (and again almost without exception) – to quote Professor Hancock once more – 'to the national system of political economy'.[48]

For the British government, for Chamberlain personally, imperial preference – the cause for which he sacrificed the later part of his political career – was a second-best. But for the colonies with Canada in the lead, it was their first choice. They too wished to increase imperial trade and imperial preference might well enable them to do so in a manner consistent with their national economic aspirations. Preferences were at once compatible with policies of protection at home and with special trading relations with the Empire overseas. In fact as it appeared to colonial statesmen preferences presented only one major problem: a free trading Britain could not participate in an imperial preferential system. The practical choice before the colonies, therefore, was preferences without requital for Britain or no preferences. For the most part the colonies chose the first course. Increasingly they applied pressure, at times beyond the limits of what was conventional, upon successive British governments. Their persuasive efforts yielded no fruit for more than thirty years but this was not because the issue went by default in British domestic policies; on the contrary, the problem was fully ventilated.

During the South African war the chancellor of the Exchequer, Sir Michael Hicks Beach, imposed duty of a shilling a quarter on imported corn as a temporary war-time fiscal measure. It was proposed that this duty should be retained after the war but that the colonies should then be allowed to import free. Before he left on a tour of South Africa, Chamberlain understood that agreement had been reached on such a basis by all the members of the cabinet except C. T. Ritchie, Hicks Beach's successor at the Exchequer. While the colonial secretary was away however the cabinet, much influenced by Ritchie, an out and out free trader, decided that the duty should be altogether repealed. With that decision there disappeared the last chance of introducing some qualified form of preference without major assault upon the citadel of free trade.[49]

On his return Chamberlain resigned from the cabinet in order to be free to campaign for imperial preference and the more senior and ardent free traders resigned to contest it, leaving Arthur James Balfour, as prime minister, to try out the possibility of avoiding a final party split on fiscal issues with the insubstantial but characteristically ingenious suggestion that tariffs be imposed, but only as retaliatory measures against unfair foreign competition. The idea served a purpose – that of prolonging Balfour's period of office – but it satisfied neither the out and out free traders nor the imperial trade reformers.[50] And in the statistical confusion of the nation-wide debate upon the fiscal issue that followed one thing emerged clear beyond dispute. The English working man was not prepared to risk the chance, and free traders assured him it was a certainty, of dearer food in the supposed interests of imperial unity and greatness.

In the broader setting of imperial organisation, colonial backing for imperial preference as against Empire free trade showed that, as in defence and politics, the colonies were in fact resolved to establish and confirm their several and separate identities and not to allow them to be submerged in a greater imperial whole. The protagonists of imperial integration were thus confronted by the champions of nascent dominion nationalism – Chamberlain by Laurier, the spokesman of Canada's 'everlasting no'; as one shrewd observer, Richard Jebb, noted,[51] by the time of the Colonial Conference of 1902 the forces of patriotic nationalism were triumphing over the forces of imperial loyalty. Jebb did not think that the unity of the Empire would be thereby impaired; rather that in the future it would of necessity rest upon the foundation of colonial nationalism. Chamberlain, it is clear, was by no means so certain. 'His ideal is an independent Canada and he is certainly not an imperialist in our sense,' Chamberlain remarked of Laurier on 25 August 1902, in a letter to his son, Austen.[52] It was true; and it was the imperialism of Laurier that was destined to survive.

In succeeding years changes in name serve to illustrate the developing character of imperial relations. In 1902 the desirability of altering the name 'Colonial Conference' to 'Imperial Council' was referred to governments for consideration. In 1905 the colonial secretary, Alfred Lyttelton, formally suggested in a dispatch to colonial governors that the title Colonial Conferences' which 'imperfectly expresses the facts' should be discarded and replaced by 'Imperial Council'. The Canadian government objected strongly. They pointed out that the change in name would be interpreted 'as marking a step distinctly in advance of the position hitherto attained in the discussion of the relations between the mother country and the colonies', the term 'Council', with its implication of a formal assemblage possessing an advisory and deliberative character, suggesting to them, in conjunction with the word 'Imperial', a permanent institution which might eventually encroach upon dominion autonomy; 'Conference', a neutral term, implied no more than an unconventional gathering for informal discussions.[53] In the light of these objections (and as the Canadian government itself proposed) the adjective was retained, the noun discarded, and after 1907 the Colonial Conference was re-named not 'Imperial Council' but 'Imperial Conference'.

It was the changing nature and purpose of the Conferences that were responsible for the change in their designation. Gone was the indeterminate character of the 1887 gathering and in its place was a Conference with a defined composition and an established status. In 1907 the designation 'dominion' supplanted the older title of colony in the Conference record for the first time and it was dominion governments which were to be represented at future Conferences. It was decided also that the re-named Imperial Conference should meet every four years and that at its meetings 'questions of common interest may be discussed and considered as between His Majesty's government and His governments of the self-governing dominions beyond the seas. The prime minister of the United Kingdom will be *ex officio* president, and the prime ministers of the self-governing dominions *ex officio* members of the Conference.'[54] The colonial secretary was also to be an *ex officio* member. There was debate about the organisation of the Conference. Was it right that its work should be organised by the Colonial Office? Was it in accord with the principles of dominion autonomy? Was it likely to ensure due and proper attention to the affairs of the dominions? Alfred Deakin, for one, thought not. He came prepared for controversy, an entry in his diary after his first visit reading, so his biographer tells us: 'Informal meeting at C.O. – Battle with Elgin [secretary of state] and C.O. begins'.[55] 'Affable Alfred's' affability, indeed, never extended to the Colonial Office. In 1887 he had complained of its 'natural *vis inertiae*' and in 1907 he followed this up with an allegation that it was not fitted to conduct relations with self-governing dominions nor to organise Colonial Conferences. Although he said he would have preferred, if he could thereby have accomplished his object, to handle the subject without 'brushing the dust off a butterfly's wings', he did in fact launch a major frontal assault upon the department.

The Colonial Office, so Deakin argued, was no more than a department of the British government, and one moreover associated with past days of colonial subordination. The manners of its officials, he alleged, were apt to be casual, while dominion representations were met with an understanding neither of the real causes from which they sprang nor of precise dominion intentions. 'Our responsible and representative governments are dealt with as you deal with a well-meaning governor or well-intentioned nominee council.' He complained about 'an attitude of mind'. The Colonial Office had about it

> a certain impenetrability; a certain remoteness, perhaps geographically justified; a certain weariness of people much pressed with affairs, and greatly overburdened, whose natural desire is to say 'Kindly postpone this; do not press that; do not trouble us; what does it matter? we have enough to do already; you are a self-governing community, why not manage to carry on without worrying us?'[56]

Deakin's conviction that the Colonial Office was ill-fitted to deal with dominion affairs led him to conclude that a new department was required which would be genuinely representative of all the governments attending the Imperial Conference and serve as a Conference secretariat. It would be in the strict sense an imperial body. But other dominion leaders, notably Laurier (whatever their private reflections about the Colonial Office), had not the least wish to see it replaced for these purposes by a new and nominally imperial body with uncertain powers and uncertain responsibilities. Their reasons were not far to seek.

In an earlier discussion, General Botha had remarked that the root objection to the adoption of the word 'Council' was that it might make an infraction upon the rights of responsible government in the various self-governing colonies. 'On this point,' he said, 'I am conservative.'[57] But might not an imperial or Conference secretariat carry the same threat? In logic the case for the secretariat was strong. Why should responsibility for arranging and organising the business of Imperial Conferences be vested in the hands of officials in a government department responsible to one government alone? Was not the logical alternative a body with shared responsibility to all governments, British and dominion? But on the other hand, in practice might not such diffused responsibility in fact lead, possibly by slow stages, to the emergence of a quasi-autonomous administrative authority? The secretary of state, Lord Elgin, feared this might be so. He said it would be very difficult, for that reason, for His Majesty's government to agree to the establishment of a body with independent status. 'In the self-governing colonies, as with us,' he continued, 'I need scarcely remind the members of the Conference [that] the basis of all British government is the responsibility of ministers to their Parliaments: not only, as here, our responsibility to the British Parliament, but your responsibility to your Parliaments.' That responsibility could not and should not be impaired. Sir Wilfrid Laurier was even more disturbed. The notion of a Council had been happily disposed of but there now appeared the possibility of a surviving secretariat. Laurier enquired about its functions. Would members of the secretariat give independent advice? What reports would they make? What would they do during the four or five years between conferences, all on their own? He had no doubt of the answers. Of necessity such a body would always be inclined to act independently. He was convinced that it should not be brought into being and he was altogether of the view of Lord Elgin that, on the principle of responsible government, no one should give advice of any kind except a man who was directly responsible through Parliament to the people.[58]

Such misgivings were not universally entertained. The New Zealanders did not share them. On the contrary, neither for the first nor for the last time they had put down at the head of their proposals resolutions about an Imperial Council and secretariat for discussion at the Conference. If they did not endorse what Deakin said, they sympathised with his general aims. The most British and the most distant of the dominions was, neither then nor later, fearful of measures of centralisation such as might ensure more speedy and effective attention to imperial needs.

The upshot of debate was in one respect strange and in another significant. The Colonial Office felt obliged to bring into nominal existence not an imperial but a conference secretariat, and one was duly created, theoretically separate from, but in respect of personnel wholly a part of the Colonial Office itself. This secretariat had no distinct existence and served no purpose – not even that of appeasing Deakin; a phantom suspended in a void, in due course it vanished almost as though it had never been. The reorganisation of the Colonial Office as from 1 December 1907 into three departments, the first of which – the dominions department – was to be responsible for relations with the overseas dominions was, however, another matter. While to outward appearance the change was not great – and to dominion reformers correspondingly disappointing – administratively it marked the beginning of a new phase. One day the dominions department, under another name, was to absorb the parent Colonial Office.[59] When that day came it marked the completion in terms of administrative responsibilities – as 1907 marked the first administrative recognition in London – of the transformation of Empire into Commonwealth. It was recognition accorded under Australian pressure and however short it fell of Deakin's original purpose it was his achievement. 'An eloquent, or at least a fluent, smart sort of fellow', wrote John Morley disparagingly of him, and added, echoing the views of the Colonial Office – 'Laurier is excellent, but Deakin is intolerable'. One reason for it was Deakin's aggressiveness, another, however, was his persistence in pursuit of his aims. He was not in fact a man easily to be deflected from his purpose or cajoled by compliments. If there was something a little ironic in Sir Wilfrid Laurier's graceful acquiescence, against earlier inclination, in the conferment of a knighthood at the Jubilee Conference in 1897, there was something altogether characteristic in Alfred Deakin's consistent declining of honours, even to the point of twice refusing an honorary degree from the University of Oxford. 'Perhaps you will excuse my saying,' wrote the vice-chancellor in studied rebuke on the first occasion, 'that we have only once before had this degree refused.'[60]

The pattern of emerging Commonwealth was also to be traced in Conference deliberations on trade and defence. In 1907 the debate on preferences was renewed and once more was protracted. Pressures upon the United Kingdom government to modify traditional trading policies were so considerable, especially from Deakin (who spoke far more than anyone else at the Conference and who by reason of some of his public utterances was accused of intervening in British politics), that General Botha thought it worth while to remark that Britain also was a self-governing state. But essentially the position remained unchanged and the Conference of 1907 had no option but to reaffirm the resolution of 1902, which had stated that the conference favoured reciprocal preferences 'with the exception of His Majesty's government, who was unable to give its assent, so far as the United Kingdom was concerned, to a reaffirmation of the Resolutions in so far as they imply that it is necessary or expedient to alter the fiscal system of the United Kingdom'.[61] Whatever else might be the case, it was apparent by 1907 that the developing relationship between Great Britain and the dominions would not in the near future be strengthened by an imperial preferential trading system.

In defence, as distinct from trade, there were indications of new thinking and of closer British-dominion accord. The Committee of Imperial Defence, first formed in 1902 as a consequence of the national searchings of heart over the South African war and formally created by a Treasury minute dated 4 May 1904, played an important part in bringing it about. The committee, an advisory body to be summoned by the prime minister, normally included the heads of the service departments and of the Treasury, the Foreign, Colonial and India Offices, in a membership which was not precisely defined. It had a permanent secretariat, but since the committee was itself only a consultative body the secretariat was without specified administrative or executive functions.[62] It was however not only vested with the responsibility of preserving a record of proceedings and decisions but with collecting and co-ordinating for the use of the committee 'information bearing on the wide problems of imperial defence and to prepare any memoranda or other documents which may be required. . . '. The services of both committee and secretariat were at the disposal of the national organisations within the Empire for the working out of their defence policies but it was for dominion governments to decide how much use to make of them. There was no obligation. The committee, though concerned with the defence of the Empire, was neither in composition nor constitution an imperial but only a United Kingdom body and was rightly named (as L.S. Amery noted) a Committee of Imperial Defence, not an Imperial Committee of Defence.[63] In 1903 Sir Frederick Borden, the Canadian minister of militia, attended both sessions of the committee while in London for other reasons. Formal agreement was recorded at the 1907 Colonial Conference both to the effect that the dominions might refer to the committee any local questions in regard to which expert assistance was thought desirable and that a representative of a dominion might be summoned to attend as a member of the committee during the discussion of questions raised at its request. But as Lord Hankey (first appointed as naval assistant secretary to the Committee of Imperial Defence in 1907) later recalled, no immediate opportunity occurred for translating this resolution into effect. The dominions referred no question to the committee and nominated no representative to attend.

At the 1907 Colonial Conference the secretary of state for war, J. B. Haldane, restated the principles of imperial cooperation in defence in terms that took due account of dominion susceptibilities. On the level of practical cooperation he spoke of plans for the interchange of General Staff officers between Britain and the dominions and of a corresponding broadening of the basis of the recently created General Staff – 'a purely advisory organisation of which command is not a function' – so as to provide for the association and liaison of dominion forces with it. 'The beginning,' he proceeded cautiously, 'of course, would have to be very modest.' But most important would be agreement upon aims broadly conceived. ' . . . we know that this thing must be founded simply upon the attaining of a common purpose, the fulfilment of a common end. It cannot be by the imposing of restrictions or by rigid plans which might not suit the idiosyncrasies of particular countries.'[64] This was an approach well calculated to win dominion acceptance.

The Conference had before it a series of papers on the possibility of assimilating war organisations throughout the Empire, on patterns and provision of equipment and stores for colonial forces, and – always allowing for the particular circumstances of individual colonies – on the need for agreement upon measures that would make common action effective if and when it was desired. In the paper prepared by the General Staff and submitted by the prime minister, it was accepted as a first and fundamental principle that the maintenance of the Empire rested primarily upon supremacy at sea. The second great principle which (it was stated) should govern the military organisation of the Empire was that each portion of it should as far as possible maintain sufficient troops for its own self-defence. And the third principle was 'the great one' of mutual support in time of emergency. Changes in the pattern of warfare were underlined and the new dangers and the new responsibilities which they brought with them outlined.

Since the last Conference, the paper argued, there had been a great conflict between two nations powerful on land and sea and that conflict, [the Russo-Japanese war] . . . had taught us lessons, tactical and strategic, ashore and afloat. [But] . . . the one great lesson which stands out clear and well-defined, admitting neither argument nor disclaimer, is that the nation of which the naval and military authorities are in a position to make their preparations for emergency on a definite plan and with a full knowledge of the strength and organisation of the forces which they will be able to put in the field at the critical moment, starts with an incalculable advantage over an opponent who does not enjoy the same position. War is in the present day becoming more and more an exact science.[65]

The mother country, it was affirmed, was seeking to live up to these principles. It was for the dominions to consider them and to contribute what they might to imperial resources.

But it is not to be supposed that imperial defence problems could be disposed of merely by drawing lessons from the experiences of others or the enunciation of mutually satisfying principles. There were the often vexing questions of their application. In 1907 there was unanimous support for the establishment of a General Staff for the Empire, working on a basis of co-operation and having as its principal tasks the surveying of the defence of the Empire as a whole, and for the bringing about of the uniformity in weapons and training that would make possible effective cooperation in a great war. But at the same time the dominions declined to enter into advance military commitments, as a necessary part of their resolve to retain in their own hands decision as to the nature and extent of their participation in a war; nor were they strongly pressed to do so, partly because it was recognised to be inadvisable but equally because the British government (and not least the Colonial Office) entertained an indifferent, even at times a contemptuous view of possible dominion military contributions in a war waged by the professional armies of Europe.

In respect of naval policies the position was rather different and the outcome of the 1907 Conference correspondingly less clear-cut. In the Memorandum already referred to which Lord Selborne, as first lord of the Admiralty, had submitted to the 1902 Conference, the doctrine of naval concentration had received classic statement:

> The sea [the memorandum read] is all one, and the British Navy therefore must be all one; and its solitary task in war must be to seek out the ships of the enemy, wherever they are to be found, and destroy them. At whatever spot, in whatever sea, these ships are found and destroyed, there the whole Empire will be simultaneously defended in its territory, its trade and its interests. If, on the contrary, the idea should unfortunately prevail that the problem is one of local defence, and that each part of the Empire can be content to have its allotment of ships for the purpose of the separate protection of an individual spot, the only possible result would be that an enemy who had discarded this heresy and combined his fleets will attack in detail and destroy those separated British squadrons which, united, could have defied defeat.[66]

A strategic doctrine asserting unequivocably the need for unified control of naval forces was bound at all times to possess some unpalatable political implications for the dominions. In naval as in military matters dominion governments (with the one exception of New Zealand) felt a strong and continuing interest in the development of local defence, with local dominion navies providing an essential element in it. Was there not here then a conflict between a strategic and the national principle? And if the navy were to be under unified control, did not that mean determination of policy by a single authority? And would not that single authority inevitably be the imperial authority? Was any purpose then to be served by the development of autonomous dominion navies? In the event of Anglo-German naval war, what happened in the North Sea was likely to be conclusive. If the Royal Navy were defeated in a major engagement there, what resistance could dominion navies in distant waters offer to a victorious German High Seas fleet? If, therefore, the Admiralty principle were applied in practice and the logic of the strategic situation accepted, would it not mean that the appropriate dominion contributions – in whatever form they were made – would be for the strengthening or maintenance of the Royal Navy? Successive British governments, as has been noted, certainly inclined to this view. Strategically it may well have been the correct view. On the other hand, it inevitably meant a delay or even the indefinite postponement of the creation or expansion of separate dominion navies. Could some compromise be reached here? This was not merely a matter of imperial-dominion relations; it was a matter of vigorous domestic dominion controversies and of dominion self-esteem. The peoples of the dominions could derive but little emotional satisfaction from contributing to the building of a dreadnought or a battleship they might never see. They desired to have their own ships under their own control, cruising in their own waters and based on their own ports. 'They want,' as the first lord of the Admiralty, Winston Churchill observed with insight and understanding, 'to have something they can see, and touch, and take pride in, with feelings of ownership and control. Those feelings, although unrecognised by military truth, are natural. They are real facts which will govern events.'[67]

In 1909 the British government were brought face to face with the realities of German naval competition. It was not merely that Germany was building 'all big-gun' ships at a faster rate than Britain – four to two in 1908 and with a further four to follow – but that German construction was more rapid. It seemed, despite continued superiority in total numbers, that British naval supremacy was being rapidly eroded. Both cabinet and people were alarmed. There was a cry for acceleration in the building – 'We want eight, And we won't wait' in the words of a music hall refrain. The apprehension spread to the dominions. There was evident need for consultation which was met in supplementary Imperial (Defence) Conference in 1909.[68] The temper of the Conference held against so threatening a background was realistic; so too was the approach of the Admiralty. They showed a readiness to yield some ground in the face of dominion objections – most forcibly stated over the years by the Australians – to the subsidy principle and themselves advanced alternative proposals on the basis of the coming into existence of supporting but separate dominion navies. The memorandum they submitted first restated the contention that 'the greatest output of strength for a given expenditure is obtained by the maintenance of a single navy with the concomitant unity of training and unity of command' and that 'the maximum of power would be gained if all parts of the Empire contributed, according to their needs and resources, to the maintenance of the British Navy', but this proposition was followed by a second which, recognising the desire of some dominions to create their own local navies, argued that on this premise the aim should be the formation of a distinct fleet unit capable of being used in its component parts in time of war. This second proposal contemplated dominion responsibility for the maintenance of a certain naval strength, each in its own sphere of interest 'thus relieving the imperial fleet of direct responsibility in distant seas'. Were the principle to be adopted, then there would in the future be a United Kingdom fleet unit in the East Indies and China (with the aid of the New Zealand contribution), an Australian squadron in the South Pacific, and a Canadian squadron in the eastern Pacific, each squadron being capable of action individually not only in defence of coasts but also of trade routes, and the three in conjunction forming a far eastern fleet.

Neither Admiralty proposition was acceptable to Canada. They rejected the idea of subsidy, and as Laurier later explained to the Canadian House of Commons, Canada's double seaboard rendered the provision of one fleet unit for the time being impracticable. He proposed in the Navy Bill he introduced in 1910 that Canada should make a start with cruisers and destroyers, part of which were to be stationed on the Atlantic seaboard and part on the Pacific, the double seaboard being vital to the Canadian position. There was however some closer approximation of Admiralty and Australian views. It was given formal expression in a Naval Agreement by which the British government undertook to keep in the Indian and Pacific Oceans double the force of the Australian fleet unit. For Australia this seemed to promise reinsurance in respect of regional security and also a direct incentive to increase her naval strength. But in fact the agreement was never fully implemented, the British government seeing small reason for overmuch preoccupation with Pacific security in view of the Anglo-Japanese alliance and the Anglo-Russian Convention, 1907. Nonetheless the 1909 Conference led on to the creation of the Royal Australian Navy.[69]

At the next, and full, Imperial Conference in 1911, preoccupation with the threat of impending war in Europe was responsible for a dramatic departure from precedent in the Conference Proceedings. At specially convened sessions of the Committee of Imperial Defence, reinforced in its membership by the prime ministers of the dominions, Sir Edward Grey, the secretary of state for Foreign Affairs, gave an exposition of British foreign policy as seen against the circumstances and realities of the struggle for power in Europe. At the conclusion of the Conference Asquith remarked that this was an event in itself in that it was the first time that the dominions had been admitted into the innermost parts of the imperial household. 'What in the old classical phrase were called *arcana Imperii* had been laid bare to you without any kind of reservation or qualification.'[70] This was however not quite the case. Sir Edward Grey was choosing his words carefully when he said that 'we are not committed by any entanglement that ties our hands. Our hands are free, and I have nothing to disclose to our being bound to any alliances which is not known to all at the present time.' The Anglo-French and Anglo-Russian staff talks were not alliances or commitments of this kind and Lloyd George recalled that the fact of these talks having taken place was not disclosed to dominion prime ministers any more than it had been to most members of the British cabinet.[71] But in making this qualification, Lloyd George also remarked upon the range and candour in other respects of the foreign secretary's review. It was not of course presented merely to satisfy a natural dominion interest. Dominion governments were far removed from Europe; they might understandably underestimate the dangers that threatened to engulf the continent and Britain herself; they might the better appreciate the gravity of the German naval challenge to British sea power if the facts and their implications were authoritatively expounded to them and might finally be moved to contribute more to collective imperial resources. All the evidence suggests that the impression in fact made upon the dominion prime ministers by the foreign secretary's disclosures was marked. General Botha, breakfasting with Lloyd George a few days later, told him he was going back to South Africa apprehensive of war with Germany and that should it come he would invade German south-west Africa at the head of forty thousand men.

On the naval side the agreement of 1909 was followed in 1911 by a further Anglo-dominion understanding to the effect that, while the armed forces of Canada and Australia would be exclusively under the control of their respective governments, training and discipline in their navies would be generally uniform with the training and discipline of the Royal Navy. Furthermore there would be inter-changeability of officers and men. It would be for each dominion to place its naval service at the disposal of the imperial government in time of war and in that event the dominion ships would form an integral part of the British fleet and would remain under the control of the British Admiralty during the continuance of the war.[72] The Canadian government furthermore enquired in what form temporary and immediate aid might best be given by Canada, receiving the reply that 'such aid should include the provision of a certain number of the largest and strongest ships of war which science could build or money supply'. Robert Borden (who succeeded Sir Wilfrid Laurier as prime minister on the defeat of the Liberals in the elections of November 1911) introduced a Navy Bill on 5 December 1912 to authorise a Canadian contribution of some thirty-five million dollars for the construction of three battleships for the Royal Navy.[73] The Bill passed the Commons but was rejected by the Senate with its continuing Liberal majority, and as a result Canadian naval strength at the outset of war amounted to no more than two cruisers, which were at once transferred to Admiralty control. New Zealand however contributed one battleship and offered another should need arise. In so doing it earned high commendation from the first lord of the Admiralty.

> In giving a splendid ship to strengthen the British Navy at this decisive point [Churchill told the House of Commons in March 1914] . . . according to the best principles of naval strategy, the dominion of New Zealand have provided in the most effective way alike for their own and for the common security. No greater insight into political and strategical points has ever been shown by a community hitherto unversed in military matters.[74]

Before the Imperial Conference of 1911 assembled, Asquith had a paper specially prepared by the Committee of Imperial Defence setting out the various ways in which greater and more effective dominion participation in imperial defence might be secured. In it the principal aim of the United Kingdom was stated to be the creation of administrative machinery which would ensure that at the moment of the outbreak of war the measures decided upon would be taken without delay. The position of the dominions, however, introduced an element of uncertainty. While it was possible for the Committee of Imperial Defence to discuss the construction of machinery for enforcing measures agreed to in the United Kingdom, in India and in the Crown colonies, the co-operation of the dominions could be obtained only by consultation. It was thought most likely to be forthcoming if permanent, in place of occasional, representation of the dominions on the Committee of Imperial Defence could be secured. But there was here a difficulty later to become familiar. Permanent dominion representatives were likely to lose touch with their home governments and peoples; members of dominion cabinets, on the other hand, while in a position of responsibility, were unlikely to be able to attend meetings with the desired regularity. The answer, it was therefore thought, might best be found in the constitution of a dominion defence committee in each dominion, keeping in the closest touch through its secretariat with the Committee of Imperial Defence in London. From the discussion of these proposals at the Imperial Conference certain conclusions emerged: that one or more representatives appointed by the respective governments of the dominions should be invited to attend meetings of the Committee of Imperial Defence when questions of naval and military defence affecting the oversea dominions were under consideration, and secondly an acceptance in principle of the idea of establishing defence committees in each dominion, subject to separate dominion decision in practice. The resolutions were not published because of reservations about publication entertained by some dominion representatives, notably Sir Wilfrid Laurier. But in the later opinion of Lord Hankey, if any single episode can be selected as bearing more than any other on the stupendous effort of cooperation which the dominions made in the Great War it was those quiet discussions in the friendly atmosphere of Disraeli's old room at 2 Whitehall Gardens (the offices of the C.I.D.) which led to these understandings about cooperation through co-ordination of war plans.[75]

It was not to be supposed however that even on the eve of the first world war the dominion prime ministers were chiefly preoccupied with high matters of defence or still less of foreign policy. In respect of the latter at least they were present to understand but not to determine. Responsibility for foreign policy, Asquith told the 1911 Imperial Conference, could never be shared. This was an overstatement which perhaps concealed his own doubts; but at that time at least it was not shared. Apart from defence, it was about detailed questions of imperial cooperation in its political, social or economic aspects that dominion prime ministers and governments – as private papers and official records make clear – were chiefly preoccupied. For the most part then, the proceedings of the Conferences of 1907 and 1911 continued to be prosaic. The matters to be considered were selected on the principle laid down by Elgin in a dispatch of 4 January 1907 and reaffirmed by Lewis Harcourt, as secretary of state, on 20 January 1911, that preference should be given to subjects proposed by the dominions and that subjects should have precedence according to the number of dominions proposing them, regard being had to the intrinsic importance of the subjects and the possibility of arriving at a definite result by discussion. The topics that qualified were important and varied but for the most part unexciting. They included the position of British Indians in the dominions, naturalisation, enforcement of arbitration awards, uniformity of laws, weights and measures, merchant shipping and navigation laws, currency and coinage, income tax and death duties, treaties and commercial relations, wireless telegraphy, land settlement – this was in 1907 with a paper for consideration submitted by Rider Haggard – emigration, an all-red mail route and penny post.[76] Some of these matters were easily settled or disposed of, others required detailed and technical enquiry. But one way or the other it was important for people in the dominions or in Britain that so far as possible they should be considered and that action should be taken on them.

More enlivening debate in 1911, as in 1907, was prompted by a variety of proposals of Australian or New Zealand origin for the formal strengthening of the ties of Empire by administrative reorganisation or federal reconstitution. Harcourt considered in advance with Asquith what concessions might be made and the outcome of their deliberations was submitted in a paper to their cabinet colleagues. With regard to renewed pressure for the reform of the Colonial Office, prime minister and colonial secretary came to the conclusion that the least that could be conceded was 'a bifurcation of the Office below the secretary of state' (i.e. the creation of two permanent under-secretaries – one for dominions and one for Crown colonies) and 'the addition to the secretariat of the Imperial Conference of a standing committee which will include the high commissioners or other representatives of the dominions'. The arguments in favour of departmental bifurcation were thought to be 'of a purely sentimental nature' but not for that reason to be neglected.

Ministers of the younger 'Dominions' [the paper proceeded] appear to feel some degradation in any association with the Crown colonies, some of which were almost autonomous before the discovery of Australia or the civilisation of South Africa. The demand for dissociation from the other possessions of the Crown is in the nature rather of social precedence than administrative efficiency.

The secretary of state conjectured that the dominion prime ministers would reject the offer of 'bifurcation' if they understood the arguments against it. In domestic terms it would create undesirable administrative dualism and result in the conduct of affairs by permanent officials who would not have knowledge both of dominions and Crown colonies. From the dominion point of view the loss would be equally considerable.

It appears almost certain [wrote the colonial secretary in a passage of imperial prognostication strange for a Liberal statesman] that in a future not very remote the dominions in temperate zones will desire to acquire for themselves 'hothouses' for consumable luxuries and other purposes. It may not be unreasonable to contemplate the ultimate absorption of the West Indies by Canada; of the Pacific Islands by Australia and New Zealand; of Rhodesia and the native protectorates (even of Nyasaland) by South Africa. But if the complete bifurcation of the Colonial Office is to be effected at once, these dominions will be divorced far more completely than at present from any knowledge of, or interest in, or indirect influence over, their neighbouring Crown colonies than they would be under a homogeneous Colonial Office with a single permanent under-secretary, possessing the daily knowledge of and control over the administration of both branches.'

The Paper also gave (and in these cases, surely deservedly) short shrift to proposals that the prime minister should take over control of the dominions, leaving the Colonial Office to deal only with Crown colonies, and to the suggestion that if bifurcation took place the secretary of state should in future be styled secretary of state for 'the dominions, Crown colonies and protectorates' – a 'cumbrous and rather ludicrous title'.[77] In the event Harcourt was not pressed to adopt it, not even sufficiently strongly to give effect to the changes he himself was prepared to make. In 1911 there was no confrontation on such matters and the Colonial Office emerged from the Conference without suffering even bifurcation!

There were other suggestions not alluded to in the secretary of state's Paper. The Australian government proposed that the judicial functions exercised by the Judicial Committee of the Privy Council in respect of the dominions should be vested in an Imperial Appeal Court, so as to ensure effective representation from overseas. The New Zealand government suggested that, in the interests of the governments of the United Kingdom and of the oversea dominions alike, there should be an interchange of selected officers of the respective Civil Services with a view to a widening of knowledge of questions affecting Britain and the dominions. Neither proposal was accepted in the form in which it was submitted chiefly because of the practical difficulties involved.[78]

Altogether more far-reaching was the resolution submitted by the prime minister of New Zealand, Sir Joseph Ward. Seemingly unmindful of the significance of the exchanges of 1905 about Council or Conference, he proposed in 1911 the creation of an Imperial Council of State. This proposal was alluded to in the secretary of state's cabinet Paper. Harcourt was confident it would not commend itself to the Conference. 'I know,' he wrote, 'that it will be opposed by General Botha and it is certain to secure the vehement hostility of Sir Wilfrid Laurier. . .'. He was right. By way of the longest and possibly the most confusing speech ever recorded at such a gathering Ward submitted his resolution. The following exchanges sufficiently indicate the reaction of his conference colleagues to it:

Sir Joseph Ward: .... My opinion is that there ought to be established an Imperial Council or an Imperial Parliament of Defence, in the interests. ...
Sir Wilfrid Laurier: There is a difference between a council and a parliament. What do you propose, a parliament or a council? I want a proper definition of what you mean, because you have proposed neither so far.
Sir Joseph Ward: I prefer to call it a Parliament of Defence.
Sir Wilfrid Laurier: Very well.
The President (Mr Asquith): That is a very different proposition to the one in your Resolution. Your Resolution is 'An Imperial Council of State' – nothing about defence – 'advisory to the Imperial Government'. It is limited, as I understand the Resolution, to giving advice.
Sir Wilfrid Laurier: When it is started it is to be a parliament; who is going to elect that parliament?
......
Sir Joseph Ward: I would point out that the resolution is 'with representatives from all the self-governing parts of the Empire.
Sir Wilfrid Laurier: But you say 'Council'. Is it a council, or is it a parliament? It is important that we should know exactly what is the proposal.
Sir Joseph Ward: I prefer to call it a parliament.
Sir Wilfrid Laurier: Very good, then; now we understand what you mean.
Sir Joseph Ward: I prefer to call it a parliament, although I admit there is a good deal in the name.
Sir Wilfrid Laurier: There is everything in the name.[79]

Sir Joseph Ward's proposals, conciliar or parliamentary (the exact origins of which remain somewhat obscure),[80] had no chance of adoption and no one put the reasons more clearly than General Botha, an inflexible champion of imperial decentralisation.

If any real authority [he argued] is to be vested in such an imperial council, I feel convinced that the self-governing powers of the various parts of the Empire must necessarily be encroached upon, and that would be a proposition which I am certain no Parliament in any part of the Empire will entertain for one moment.

If no real authority is to be given to such a council, I fear very much that it would only become a meddlesome body which will continually endeavour to interfere with the domestic concerns of the various parts of the Empire, and cause nothing but unpleasantness and friction'.[81]

No parliament in any part of the Empire was likely when it came to the point to entertain the thought of conciliar derogation from its authority – in that General Botha had put his finger on what to parliamentarians was the essential issue; and so long as parliamentarians decided the forms and methods of cooperation within the Commonwealth there would not be a council or any other central authority such as might impair the responsibility of their own cabinets to their own parliaments.

More significant than the defeat of particular and ill-digested proposals for centralisation was the newer force of dominion nationalism gathering strength and insistent upon continuing decentralisation of imperial authority. Laurier and Botha were its spokesmen. 'Laurier and I have renewed our friendship,' Botha told Smuts in a letter of 15 June 1911. 'He and I agree about everything.' And he proceeded: 'The Conference work is going quite well. We have destroyed root and branch the proposal for an Imperial Council of State or Parliament, and we have succeeded in keeping the Conference as a round table affair.'[82] The balance of power within the self-governing Empire had perceptibly shifted with the addition of a united South Africa to the number of the dominions.

It would however be a misconception to conclude a review of dominion/British relations on the eve of the first world war in terms of negation. The first and most important fact about them was that they existed and subsisted on the basis of cooperation in peace and also (in Hankey's opinion, which was almost certainly correct despite some Anglo-Canadian exchanges in 1911), in the event of any major war after the Conference in 1907 on the principle 'United we stand: divided we fall'.[83] The second was that over a wide range of subjects they were conducted on terms of equality. 'In the early Victorian era,' Asquith reminded the Conference in 1911, 'there were two rough-and-ready solutions for what was regarded with some impatience, by the British statesmen of that day as the "colonial problem". The one was centralisation. . . . The other was disintegration.' But after seventy years' experience, he continued, neither view commanded the slightest support at home or overseas.

> We were saved from their adoption – some people would say by the favour of Providence – or (to adopt a more flattering hypothesis) by the political instinct of our race. And just in proportion as centralisation was seen to be increasingly absurd, so has disintegration been felt to be increasingly impossible. Whether in this United Kingdom, or in any one of the great communities which you represent, we each of us are, and we each of us intend to remain, master in our own household. (Hear, hear.) This is, here at home and throughout the dominions, the life-blood of our policy. It is the *articulus stantis aut cadentis Imperii.*'

This was warmly received by dominion prime ministers – even if not all of them may have shared Asquith's liking for classical quotation.[84]

On 1 August 1912 there was a discussion at the Committee of Imperial Defence which may serve at once by way of epilogue and pointer to the future. The new prime minister of Canada, R. L. Borden, accompanied by two of his ministers, was present and showed himself as interested in foreign policy as in defence. He reminded British ministers that south of the Canadian border people had a direct and immediate voice in the government of their country, including all matters of foreign policy, while north of it foreign policy remained reserved to a distant imperial power. Borden allowed that the contrast had not as yet impressed itself strongly upon the imagination of the Canadian people but he had no doubt that it would begin to do so in the very early future as the country advanced in wealth, population and resources and more especially 'as it advances in its conception of what a national spirit demands'. His colleague, C. J. Doherty, put the point concretely. As the Canadian government was willing that the dominion should take a larger share in contributing in one form or another to imperial defence, then some means should be found by which it could be given a voice in the direction of the foreign policy of the Empire. The difficulties were well known. What was required was examination of them as evidence that there was not only a recognition of the principle that the dominions ought to have a voice in foreign policy, but further, an intention that they should be given one.[85] Within a year of Asquith's dictum about responsibility for foreign policy as something that could never be shared, representatives of the senior dominion were discussing the sharing of it.[86]

II

THE BRITISH COMMONWEALTH OF NATIONS, 1914–47

'Then if we are to continue as nations and to grow as nations and govern ourselves as nations the great question arises: How are we to keep this Empire together?'

GENERAL SMUTS AT THE IMPERIAL
WAR CONFERENCE, 1917

'The British Empire is . . . the most hopeful experiment in human organisation which the world has yet seen. It is not so much that it combines men of many races, tongues, traditions and creeds in one system of government. Other Empires have done that, but the British Empire differs from all in one essential respect. It is based not on force but on goodwill and a common understanding. Liberty is its binding principle.'

THE RIGHT HON. DAVID LLOYD GEORGE
AT THE IMPERIAL CONFERENCE, 1921

'We cannot consent to any abandonment, however informal, of the principle of allegiance to the King, upon which the whole fabric of the Empire and every constitution within it are based. It is fatal to that principle that your delegates to the Conference should be there as the representatives of an independent and sovereign state. While you insist on claiming that, conference between us is impossible.'

THE RIGHT HON. DAVID LLOYD GEORGE
TO EAMON DE VALERA, 17 SEPTEMBER 1921.

'The Conference made clear, without doubt, that the predominant ideal and purpose of the British Commonwealth was peace, and that all efforts would continue to be directed to the end of securing world appeasement and peace.'

THE RIGHT HON. J. A. LYONS, IN THE AUSTRALIAN
HOUSE OF REPRESENTATIVES, 24 AUGUST 1937

It is true we have not, sitting in London continuously, an invisible Imperial War Cabinet or Council. But we have, what is much more important, though invisible, a continuing Conference of the Cabinets of the Commonwealth.

THE RIGHT HON. W. L. MACKENZIE KING
11 MAY 1944

CHAPTER 6

THE CATALYST OF WAR

If Joseph Chamberlain, in Curzon's already quoted phrase, was 'colony-mad', that was not an affliction widespread among British politicians of his generation. For the most part, in colonial affairs they heeded Talleyrand's advice – 'pas trop de zèle' – instinctively and without effort. Another but a misleading impression, it is true, is apt to be conveyed by overmuch reading of Seeley, Froude and Dilke or even of Goldwin Smith and Hobson and still more of composite volumes such as *The Empire and the Century*[1] with its contributions from no less than fifty hands and prefaced with a poem of Rudyard Kipling's reminding readers of *The Heritage*:

> Our fathers in a wondrous age,
>   Ere yet the Earth was small,
> Ensured to us an heritage,
>   And doubted not at all
> That we, the children of their heart,
>   Which then did beat so high,
> In later time should play like part
>   For our posterity.
>
> A thousand years they steadfast built,
>   To 'vantage us and ours,
> The Walls that were a world's despair,
>   The sea-constraining Towers:

The British public had its moments of Kiplingesque exaltation: British politicians however experienced them comparatively rarely. But in neither instance was it aroused by or extended to the dominions. They were (with the partial exception of South Africa) too ordinary, too British, too sensible to be romanticised. Even the set speeches with which Colonial and Imperial Conferences opened and closed rarely took wing, though in their own way they may be as inimical to balanced understanding as eulogistic appreciations of the prospects and purposes of Empire. Students of the Commonwealth are indeed well advised on general grounds to eschew them as staple reading diet. They are, moreover, unusually unreliable in one respect, namely as a guide to British preoccupations. From 1907 a British prime minister presided over such Conferences by virtue of his office. This was designed to enhance their status and it was successful in doing so. But in so far as it may suggest that dominion affairs were becoming a major interest of British prime ministers or cabinets, it is misleading. Apart from great occasions, it was not prime ministers but colonial secretaries who were responsible *inter alia* for relations with the dominions. What manner of men were they? That is the important personal question. The calibre of Joseph Chamberlain was as evident to critics as to friends but who were the men who followed him at the Colonial Office? Were they men of political stature, close to the heart of the British electorate and to the springs of power? The answer is a qualified but revealing negative.

From September 1903 to December 1905 Alfred Lyttelton was colonial secretary. The Colonial Office was the only cabinet post he ever held. He was not a dominating figure. 'In the world of shadows,' he wrote to Milner, 'I was called your political chief. But in the world of realities you must know that I always thought of you as mine . . .'[4] It is true that others succumbed no less to the power of Milner's personality but in the case of Lyttelton the record of his period at the Colonial Office reinforces the impression of a secretary of state with authentic interest in colonial development but of secondary force politically and otherwise. Lyttelton's successor was the ninth Earl of Elgin. He had been viceroy of India but his had not been a momentous viceroyalty. During the tenure of Lansdowne and Elgin – 'these two acquiescent, unimaginative men' – the viceroyalty, in the opinion of Dr Gopal, 'reached its lowest ebb' in the nineteenth century and he notes especially of Elgin that he had no firm views and was happy to leave the power of decision to Whitehall.[3] Elgin's period at the Colonial Office is clouded by recollections of its close. Asquith, on succeeding Campbell-Bannerman in April 1908, decided to dispense with Elgin's services. He neglected, however, to tell Elgin. News of his impending dismissal appeared in *The Daily Chronicle*, but Elgin's first intimation was a letter from the new prime minister, which remarked on the need for advancing younger men, but made no acknowledgment of Lord Elgin's past services and, by way of adding insult to injury, concluded with the query: 'What about a marquessate?'[4] The incident fairly reflected Asquith's lack of tact and Elgin's lack of political weight. Departmentally, it has been persuasively argued, Elgin was an altogether more considerable figure than has hitherto been supposed.[5] His comments on the Colonial Office files certainly show a man of experience and sound judgment, with a firm grasp of the essentials of British-dominion relations. They also suggest a man of conservative temper conscientiously trying to remember that he was a member of a Liberal administration.

Elgin was succeeded at the Colonial Office by Lord Crewe, who was much esteemed for his skill in the easing of party differences and in inter-party negotiation. Unlike his predecessor, he had, in consequence a distinct and recognised political rôle. But this was counterbalanced, in respect of his tenure of the Colonial Office, by the lack of any marked interest in imperial affairs, Crewe being concerned most of all that they should run smoothly. He was followed in 1910 by Lewis Harcourt, later Viscount Harcourt, who held office till the first wartime coalition, 1915. As a young man, and under the soubriquet of 'Loulou', he had acquired, through his father, Sir William Harcourt, the most intimate knowledge of the intrigues and dissensions that finally destroyed Lord Rosebery's shortlived administration.[6] Departmental evidence suggests that in respect of routine administration Lewis Harcourt may have been under-estimated as colonial secretary. On the other hand the cabinet paper 6 prepared for the 1911 Imperial Conference, and already alluded to, contemplating as not unreasonable the ultimate absorption of the West Indies by Canada, and of Rhodesia, the Protectorates and even Nyasaland by South Africa, would seem to indicate a lack of realistic appreciation of the problems and patterns of the future. Certainly in relation to the towering personalities of Asquith's prewar administration, Lewis Harcourt was an altogether minor force.

In sum, Chamberlain's successors at the Colonial Office down to the outbreak of the first world war were conscientious and in many respects enlightened men, none of whom, with the possible exception of Crewe, exercised a major influence in cabinet or in the country. Nor were any of them, including Crewe, of a calibre to have probed the major issues of colonial policy in depth. They responded to dominion pressures, usually with understanding and often with wisdom, albeit of a negative kind, but the intitiative in the development and progressive redefinitions of British dominion relations rested increasingly (as was perhaps inevitable) overseas.

The record invites the further question: Why were colonial secretaries after Joseph Chamberlain, as indeed before him, for the most part men of secondary political significance? The answer would seem to be two-fold. Generally speaking, younger men of political capacity and ambition did not seek the office. In this, it is true, as in so many other matters Winston Churchill was an exception. In 1908 he asked Asquith for it, setting out his qualifications in a letter which hardly could be said to have erred on the side of modesty and suggesting that the government would have much to gain 'from a spirited yet not improvident administration of an imperial department'.[7] Asquith appointed him instead to the

Board of Trade. The second part of the answer is not unrelated to the first. Men of ambition did not generally opt for the Colonial Office because the affairs with which it dealt, including final responsibility for the administration of Crown colonies as well as for relations with the dominions, were not deemed to be of first importance either to the British electorate or in themselves. The former was hardly open to dispute; the latter more questionable. It was alleged, not only overseas, that the British public and parliament, by their comparative neglect and want of interest in the growth of the self-governing dominions, showed a lack of political perspective. One illustration may suffice. Sir Henry Parkes' proposals for the federation of Australia were laid before the premiers of the other Australian colonies at the same time as the kaiser paid a dramatic visit to the Turkish sultan. In the British press the first passed virtually unnoticed while the second attracted much attention. *The Pall Mall Gazette* complained on 4 November 1889 of the fact that the two chief organs of

> a government which professes above all things to be imperialist should devote columns of criticism this morning to the chances and changes in eastern Europe, but have not a word to say of the new departure taken at the Antipodes. Decidedly, Europe is too much with us. . . . The future of eastern Europe is no concern of ours; but the future of Australia is of enormous concern in every way both in itself – as a greater England – and for its bearing on the Empire as a whole.

Yet statesmen, journals and the public showed themselves far more interested in the German emperor's phrases and the sultan's smiles than 'in watching the development of a policy which, conceived in the fertile brain of Sir Henry Parkes, may be destined to mould the future of the whole British Empire'.[8] The implications of these comments were just in so far as they suggested that readers of British newspapers were as much predisposed to the playing-up of the importance of moves in European politics as they were to the discounting of the possible significance of imperial developments. One reason was clear – relations between Britain and the dominions were good and good relations were not – and are not – news. Another was the attitudes of governments and their advisers. 'What is curious,' wrote John Morley from the India Office to the viceroy, Lord Minto, at the time of the Colonial Conference 1907, 'is that India – the most astonishing part of the Empire – is never mentioned, and people are very much obliged to you and me for keeping it under an extinguisher.'[9] The less the information or news, the less was likely to be the trouble!

Colonial leaders, apt to assume that their sense of priorities ought to be shared in London, were resentful when they found this was not so even in the Colonial Office itself. Deakin's assault upon the Office in 1907 was given edge by his conviction that its staff had got their priorities – in this case imperial priorities – wrong. And away from the Office, colonial interests were lightly regarded and colonial representatives were thought of in many influential circles as men to be humoured and entertained but not to be taken over-seriously. John Morley, in his correspondence with the viceroy made no secret of his anxiety for the day when Britain's colonial guests would have come and gone.

At this moment [he wrote on 12 April to Minto, who had served as governor-general of Canada from 1898 to 1904] people are going to be bored out of their lives (the boredom is already felt) by our colonial kinsfolk, of whom you know something. Your Canadians are excellent, but some of the others are uncommonly rough diamonds. The feasting is to be on a terrific scale, and we shall listen to any amount of swagger on one side and insincere platitude on the other. Yet the Empire is a wonderful thing for all that.

By 26 April Morley feared: 'The Colonial Conference is becoming the greatest bore that was ever known.' And by 24 May he was telling the viceroy – who had reminded him that 'these rising nations are the young life-blood of the Empire', like 'all young things full of conceit and full of confidence, but . . . young and strong' – that while he was not out of sympathy with them, the fact remained that 'our young colonial kinsfolk are apt to be frightful bores, and if you had been condemned to eat twenty meals day after day in their company, and to hear Deakin yarn away by the hour, I believe you would have been as heartily glad to see their backs as I am.'[10] The most recent biographer of Asquith, Roy Jenkins,[11] did not even allude to the Imperial Conference of 1911. The list of papers circulated to the cabinet in the years before the first world war and the prime minister's daily accounts to the king of cabinet proceedings both serve to show how rarely the cabinet attention was occupied with dominion (including South African) affairs or problems.[12] Nor is it suggested or to be supposed that the cabinet sense of priorities was in this respect misconceived. Domestic politics and the possible approach of a European war dominated cabinet thinking. At the Colonial Conference in 1897 Chamberlain had sought to persuade colonial premiers to think in terms of larger colonial contributions to imperial defence with the argument that every war in which Britain had been engaged since the queen's accession had had 'at the bottom' a colonial interest and by the inference that this would continue to be so.[13] By the close of the first decade of the new century no such contention could be advanced at such a gathering with even a semblance of conviction. As European tensions intensified, great power colonial rivalries eased. With the signature of the Anglo-Russian Entente in 1907 it became probable, and with the Bosnian crisis of 1908–9 it became certain, that any major war would be fought by the great powers of Europe in Europe and with a European *casus belli*. Was it not then at once right and inevitable that Britain's external preoccupations should be overwhelmingly European at this time and, as a necessary consequence, that imperial, including dominion, affairs should be relegated to the background, except in so far as the Empire had a rôle to play in a European war?

While it is important not to overestimate the place of the dominions in British thinking and still less in the determining of British attitudes or the shaping of British policies before the first world war, it is also important not to discount or disregard it. The dominions – even collectively – were not a great but they were a growing factor, influencing certain aspects of British policy. It was true (to recall Asquith's candid comment) that responsibility for foreign policy was not shared before 1914. Equally however the dominions were not without opportunities for making their views known and thereby exerting pressure from within. In the later nineteenth century questions of foreign or defence policy directly affecting the interests of colonial governments were accepted in practice as being matters for some degree of consultation between the colonial government or governments concerned and the imperial government. Indeed in one instance the practice provoked the indignation of Bismarck. The year was 1884 and the occasion German enquiries about the protection of German traders at Angra Pequeña; enquiries which were soon to be formulated as claims for the occupation of what was later known as German south-west Africa. Procrastinating tactics were adopted by the Foreign Office, and the foreign secretary, Lord Granville, explained an inordinate delay in replying to German enquiries by asserting that in such a matter the British government could not act 'except in agreement with the government of the colony, which has an independent Ministry and Parliament'. On this Bismarck commented: 'That is untrue, and does not concern us; if it were true, we should have to maintain a legation with these British colonial governments.' When the German ambassador conveyed the chancellor's mounting dissatisfaction to the foreign secretary, Granville explained once again that this had happened 'owing to the independent position of our colonies, which we cannot get over with the best will in the world'.[14] Cape representations about possible German occupation of south-west Africa had their parallel, over an extended period of time, in the more strident though no more effective pressure of Australian and New Zealand colonies for the exclusion of foreigners and the establishment of Anglo-Saxon hegemony in the Pacific. In all cases colonial views were subordinated in the last resort to the demands of European diplomacy, but the expression of them was not denied nor did they pass unconsidered.

In fact Bismarck, in his allusion to legations to be accredited to colonial governments, may be thought to have hit upon an underlying truth. As representative government was a step on the road to responsible government, so expression of opinion on matters of foreign policy – albeit only those of limited local interest – was likewise a first and often (as the Australians found) a frustrating step on the road to participation in the determination of such issues and ultimately to full and separate control of foreign policy.

There was good reason for this. In constitutional terms control of foreign and defence policies was reserved to the imperial government. But in terms of political realities the situation had changed from one in which the colonies relied upon British protection to one in which dominion assistance was still a small but an increasingly significant factor in Britain's plans for imperial defence. By 1914 the dominions were not suppliants seeking favours; they were states with military and naval contributions to offer. Those contributions remained conditional in form, even if it could be (as it was) assumed that, in Lord Hankey's cautious words, 'it was unlikely that any dominion would not offer to co-operate'[15] in the event of war. Indeed it was only on such an assumption that the agreement reached in 1911 – by which on the outbreak of war dominion fleets were to be placed by dominion governments under the control of the imperial government, and to form 'part of the imperial fleet and to remain under the control of the Admiralty . . . and be liable to be sent anywhere during the continuance of the war' – had meaning. It was an assumption, too, which underlay the discussions in the same year about the nature of military cooperation which had taken place; the planning to make it effective through dominion association with the Committee of Imperial Defence; the creation of dominion defence committees and the preparation in all the dominions of war Defence Schemes in the form of 'War Books' on the British model. None of these things was sufficiently advanced – Hankey felt one more Imperial Conference was required to bring them past the experimental stage[16] – but there had been progress in planning for coordination in war efforts that in 1907, and still more in 1902, would have seemed remarkable. Politically its effect was twofold: to draw the dominions closer to Britain and at the same time – since the implementation of plans and the measure of dominion cooperation remained a matter for the determination of their several governments – to make the British government increasingly sensitive to dominion views.

The changing nature of British-dominion relations did not pass altogether unnoticed in the European chancelleries. The German ambassador in London, Prince von Lichnowsky, told the German chancellor in 1914 that the possibility of the tightening of the Anglo-

French *Entente* and of its transformation into a definitive military alliance of the kind which both the French and the Russian governments would have welcomed and which the German government feared, might be discounted on a number of grounds, one of them being that the dominions would not approve of it. The source of his information was the Foreign Office, where it was pointed out to him that 'most continental critics forgot entirely that not England alone, but also the entire British world Empire had a word to say in military and naval matters, and that the British cabinet had to pay much consideration to the wishes and needs of the dominions.' The German ambassador did not himself question the correctness of this Foreign Office view but confined himself to the comment that further use might be made of it.[17]

When war came on 4 August 1914 it was not the diversity but the unity of the Empire that was apparent. King George V declared war on behalf of the whole Empire on the advice of the cabinet of the United Kingdom. In theory, therefore, on this issue of supreme national moment the status of the dominions remained subordinate. But in practice this was only partially so since, as foreshadowed, the dominions (unlike India or the Crown colonies) determined the extent of their own participation. This qualification implicit in self-government was important. It meant that practice was continuing to make inroads upon theory. Those inroads were to be driven deeper in the course of the war, though from the outset and throughout within the context of an impressive unity. Immediately on the outbreak of war there was coordination on the basis of pre-war planning, with dominion navies placed at once under Admiralty control and dominion expeditionary forces recruited, trained and sent overseas, with their officers to serve under British supreme command and strategic direction. Outside the continent of Africa the war proved, as widely forecast, to be one of naval and military concentration, with the outcome to be determined in the North Sea and the continent of Europe including its near-east borderlands.[18] This concentration increased the closeness of Anglo-dominion cooperation and the sense of solidarity in a common cause.

Great Britain and the overseas dominions fought in the first as in the second world war from first to last. The challenge and the sacrifices of war sharpened their sense of separate identities and strengthened their feelings of nationality. The war memorials to be found throughout the length and breadth of the dominions; the Room of Remembrance in the Peace Tower high over the Parliament buildings in Ottawa with its record, on which few can look unmoved, of Canadian contributions to victory on the Western Front 1914–18; the Anzac memorial at Port Said, visited by countless Australians and New Zealanders until destroyed by the Egyptians in 1956; the memorial to the million dead of the British Empire on a pillar in the shadows of an aisle in the Cathedral of Notre Dame in Paris; all bear witness to the losses of the dominions on battlefields thousands of miles from home. These losses have been set out statistically, though not altogether precisely as citizens of the dominions or of the United Kingdom by no means invariably served in their own national units. But with such qualifications in mind, the record shows that of the 6,704,416 men – 22·11 per cent of the adult male population – who enlisted in the British Isles, 704,803 lost their lives; of the 458,218 Canadians who served overseas, 56,639 lost their lives; of the 331,814 Australians who served overseas 59,330 lost their lives; of the 112,223 New Zealanders who served overseas 16,711 lost their lives; of the estimated 76,184 South Africans who served outside South Africa 7,121 lost their lives. The dominion forces that served overseas, or in the case of South Africa outside South Africa, accounted for 13·48 per cent of the male population of Canada; 13·43 per cent of the male European population of Australia; 19·35 per cent of the European male population of New Zealand and 11·12 per cent of the European male population of South Africa. There were contingents from Newfoundland among colonies of settlement, and combatant troops from West and East Africa and other parts of the colonial Empire. There was also, in a category all its own, the Indian Army in the ranks of which there enlisted nearly one and a half million volunteers, of whom over 62,000 lost their lives.[19] And while the cause was common, each dominion had memories of its own – the Australians and New Zealanders of the landings at Gallipoli, the Canadians of Passchendaele and Vimy Ridge, the South Africans of the early seizure of German South-West and later of the more protracted gentlemanly campaigning of General Smuts against the Germans under General von Lettow Vörbeck in East Africa. These were harsh and heroic experiences that served at once to strengthen the bonds of nationhood and to enrich each national treasure-house of memories.

Within the dominions, war was at once a unifying and dividing force. In 1914 dominion governments and parliaments were at one in their support – majority support in the case of South Africa – for active participation in the war. In New Zealand and Australia this was at no time in doubt or question – the temper of the two dominions being well expressed in the pledge of Andrew Fisher, prime minister of Australia from 17 September 1914 till 27 October 1915 when he was succeeded by W. M. Hughes, that Australia would support Britain 'to the last man and the last shilling'. In Canada the German invasion of Belgium was deemed to have been decisive in enlisting French-Canadian sympathy for the Allied cause and thus ensuring a unanimous vote in the House of Commons for the government's war measures, while in

South Africa the government, of which the former commandant-general of the Boer forces in the South African war, Botha, was head, sent a cabled message to London announcing its willingness 'to employ the defence force of the Union for the performance of the duties entrusted to the imperial troops in South Africa' and so to release these troops for service elsewhere.[20] The British government, in accepting the offer, enquired further whether the South African government would desire and feel themselves able to seize strategic areas in German South-West Africa and in so doing to perform 'a great and urgent imperial service'. The Union government answered, as Botha had forecast to Lloyd George in 1911, in the affirmative. In so doing they divided Afrikaner opinion.

South Africa's participation in the war was approved by a large majority in the House of Assembly. But what mattered was less the size of the majority than the intensity of the feelings of the minority. They were expressed constitutionally by General Hertzog. He acquiesced in the fact that South Africa was legally at war because of the king's declaration on behalf of the whole Empire but urged that the Union's belligerency should be passive. Some among his fellow Afrikaners felt however that South Africa's involvement in an Empire's war demanded forceful protest, while many others (especially in the Orange Free State, who did not themselves necessarily feel impelled to take so grave a step) nevertheless were understanding of those who did so. Their sympathies were heightened to the point of open antagonism to the government firstly by the shooting, on 15 September 1914, of General de la Rey after nightfall while on his way to the western Transvaal to urge opposition to the government's attack on German South-West Africa, accidentally – though this was far from universally credited – by a police patrol; and secondly, on the night of 8 December by the death of General Beyers, who was in command of the Union defence forces at the outbreak of war but who, after seeming acquiescence, openly led the protest against the invasion of south-west Africa, left Pretoria and was drowned when his horse was shot under him while he was trying to escape across the Vaal river. The rebels were crushed and General Botha took personal command of the Union forces in a successful campaign in South-West Africa, but the rebellion (though militarily of no great significance), and the personal tragedies associated with it, added to the burden of memories which shadowed all attempts at the final reconciliation of a united Afrikanerdom with the British Commonwealth. The events of 1914, as interpreted by General Hertzog, meant that South Africa enjoyed a free constitution but had an unfree government – one that acted at the behest of imperial authority. So long as that situation continued, so long in his view and in that of the Nationalist party he had founded in 1912 and now led, would there be cause for dissension among Afrikaners. As Botha and Smuts moved towards the achievement of their destinies as Commonwealth statesmen there remained – drawing sustenance from unhappy circumstances and nurtured by General Hertzog's hand – the conviction that responsibility for the division of Afrikanerdom was to be attributed not to those who had rebelled against the participation in an Empire's war but rather to those who had sought first reconciliation with that Empire and then involved South Africa in an imperial war. In so doing they had shown themselves, so nationalists alleged, to be 'lackeys of imperialism' and 'traitors' to the Afrikaner people.

In the dominions other than South Africa the strain of long extended war with its heavy casualties produced severe political strains. Notable among them were the conscription crises of 1916–8. Conscription was enforced in Britain for the first time under the National Service Act of January 1916. That example was followed in New Zealand. Opinion in Australia however was deeply divided, there being strong objections to it, voiced by many spokesmen of unorganised labour as well as by the organised unions and also by the Irish-Australians with Archbishop Mannix as their spokesman. The issue was submitted to the electorate in a referendum in September 1916, in which conscription was rejected by a narrow majority. Of the Australian soldiers in France 72,000 voted for and 59,000 voted against conscription.[21] A second referendum produced no different result.

In Canada the conscription crisis of 1917 revealed not social but cultural division. While there had been agreement from the outset among English- and French-speaking Canadians about participation in the war, the emphasis was different. This was reflected in the utterances of the political leaders of the Liberal and Conservative parties even at the outbreak of war when Sir Robert Borden gave unquestioned and immediate backing to the mother country while Sir Wilfrid Laurier, in full accord on the major issue, underlined once again that it was for 'the Canadian people, the Canadian parliament and the Canadian government alone to decide'.[22] In June 1917 Borden introduced a Conscription Act into the Canadian Parliament. Laurier opposed it. He believed that conscription would do more harm than good, that it would divide the country on cultural grounds and that it would hand over Quebec to the extremists. The Liberal party split. Some supported Laurier, others the prime minister's efforts to form a union government pledged to conscription as part of an all-out war effort. There followed a general election in December 1917, fought in an atmosphere of high emotion, which strained national unity almost to breaking point. The outcome was a clear verdict in favour of conscription, the Union government securing 153 seats against 82 for the Opposition Liberals. Yet no less than sixty of the Opposition members were returned by Quebec constituencies. The dominion had divided along its line of cultural cleavage and as a result the confederation was subjected to a test which was thought by many to threaten its survival. There was then 'introduced into Canadian life', Professor Lower has commented, 'a degree of bitterness that surely has seldom been equalled in countries calling themselves nations'.[23] Conscription was enacted but not vigorously enforced in Quebec, where even qualified attempts to do so resulted in resistance or riots. The objection of French-speaking Canada to conscription was passionate and sincere; the grievance of English-speaking Canada authentic. Of the four hundred thousand Canadian soldiers overseas in 1917 it was estimated that less than thirty thousand were French Canadians.[24]

The position of dominion governments in the earlier years of the first world war was not altogether enviable. Their countries were at war, their forces were fighting in distant theatres of operations, they were responsible for their recruitment and their equipment, they determined as they thought best the extent and the manner of their country's participation in the war including the use of its manpower and resources, but they had control neither of the higher direction of the war itself nor of the policies that might determine its duration and its ending. If on their part there was acceptance of necessary and practical limits of their authority in respect of the command and higher direction of the war, there was marked and increasing restiveness at the lack of consultation or even of information from London on the part of Canada, Australia and New Zealand. Early in 1915 it prompted Sir Robert Borden to go to London in the hope of securing fuller knowledge of events and policies, while in October of the same year Andrew Fisher resigned his prime ministership in order to serve as Australian high commissioner in London with the same object in mind.

Borden's visit to London, while serving some immediate purposes, effected no lasting improvement in respect of consultation. On 1 November 1915 he found it necessary to cable the Canadian high commissioner in London, Sir George Perley, asking him to tell the colonial secretary, Andrew Bonar Law, that the Canadian government would appreciate fuller and more exact information from time to time respecting the conduct of the war and proposed military operations

... AS TO WHICH LITTLE OR NO INFORMATION VOUCHSAFED. WE THOROUGHLY REALISE NECESSITY CENTRAL CONTROL OF EMPIRE ARMIES BUT GOVERNMENTS OF OVERSEAS DOMINIONS HAVE LARGE RESPONSIBILITIES TO THEIR PEOPLE FOR CONDUCT OF WAR, AND WE DEEM OURSELVES ENTITLED TO FULLER INFORMATION AND TO CONSULTATION RESPECTING GENERAL POLICY IN WAR OPERATIONS.

When the high commissioner conveyed the message to Bonar Law, the colonial secretary explained that while the British government had been only too delighted to put the Canadian prime minister in possession of all the information available to the cabinet when Sir Robert Borden had been in London, it was much more difficult to keep in touch with him once he was back in his own country. In principle Bonar Law allowed that the Canadian government was entitled to be consulted and to have some share in the direction of a war effort in which Canada was playing so big a part. But, he continued:

> I am, however, not able to see any way in which this could be practically done. I wish, therefore, that you would communicate my view to Sir Robert Borden, telling him how gladly we would do it if it is practicable and at the same time I should like you to repeat to him what I said to you – that if no scheme is practicable then it is very undesirable that the question should be raised.[25]

Borden commented with some asperity and more justice that the colonial secretary's letter was not especially illuminating and had left the matter precisely where it was before he had raised it. He then proceeded to restate the grounds of his complaint:

> During the past four months since my return from Great Britain, the Canadian government (except for an occasional telegram from you or Sir Max Aitken) have had just what information could be gleaned from the daily press and no more. As to consultation, plans of campaign have been made and unmade, measures adopted and apparently abandoned and generally speaking steps of the most important and even vital character have been taken, postponed or rejected without the slightest consultation with the authorities of this dominion.
>
> It can hardly be expected that we shall put 400,000 or 500,000 men in the field and willingly accept the position of having no more voice and receiving no more consideration than if we were toy automata. Any person cherishing such an expectation harbours an unfortunate and even dangerous delusion. Is this war being waged by the United Kingdom alone or is it a war waged by the whole Empire? If I am correct in supposing that the second hypothesis must be accepted then why do the statesmen of the British Isles arrogate to themselves solely the methods by which it shall be carried on in the various spheres of warlike activity and the steps which shall be taken to assure victory and a lasting peace?
>
> It is for them to suggest the method and not for us. If there is no available method and if we are expected to continue in the role of automata the whole situation must be reconsidered.[26]

In 1916 a more formidable dominion controversialist, in the person of W. H. Hughes, set out for London. On his way he called at Ottawa and reached an understanding with Sir Robert Borden about dominion aims which was of first importance. Once in London Hughes showed that he was no respecter of persons in high positions, least of all of Asquith, and had no inhibiting sensitivity about proclaiming publicly his views about what was needed for the effective direction of the Empire's war. He was invited to attend a session of the war cabinet and was placed at the prime minister's right hand. The two principal matters that came up for discussion, although indirectly affecting the dominions, were within the exclusive jurisdiction of Britain. Hughes, so he recalled, spoke on them 'as I would have done had the problems arisen before the Commonwealth cabinet' and supported the minority on each occasion. He reflected later that

> Mr Asquith was not so enamoured of the reception of what no doubt appeared to him as a most courteous gesture towards the dominions as to make him eager to issue regular invitations and thus crystallise into an institution that which he could only regard as a most unfortunate experiment. . . . So other invitations came along – at spacious intervals intended to make it clear that one must regard what he had done as an act of courtesy rather than an established practice. The dominion representative attended when he was invited. When he was not, he just hung around or went through the country making speeches.[27]

The second was Hughes's practice. But when due allowance is made for the forthright tactics of this passionate and pugnacious controversialist, the fact remains that dominion leaders were far from satisfied with the overall direction of war policy and more particularly in respect of their own participation in it; they were interested not in the occasional courtesies but in formal acknowledgment of what they deemed to be their due share of responsibility. The attendance of an individual prime minister at a cabinet meeting was an arrangement welcome so far as it went but it satisfied neither the Australian nor general dominion demand for continuing participation in the direction of an imperial war. As the Report of the Imperial War Conference 1917 later recorded, the feeling continued to grow that 'in view of the ever-increasing part played by the dominions in the war . . . it was necessary that their governments should not only be informed as fully as was possible of the situation, but that, as far as was practicable they should participate, on a basis of complete equality, in the deliberations which determined the main outlines of imperial policy'. How was this feeling to be satisfied? Lloyd George in his first speech to the House of Commons as prime minister on 19 December 1916 (acting, it would seem, on Milner's advice) took the first significant step by announcing that the dominions were to be invited to meet at an Imperial Conference in the Spring of 1917.[28]

The Conference, which met in March that year, was a successor Conference to the Imperial Conference of 1911, and it has gone down to history as the Imperial War Conference. The Conference had little to do with the conduct of the war. Its proceedings are remembered chiefly because of one debate on the future constitution of the Empire. It took place in the light of a new departure in the conduct of British-dominion relations for which L. S. Amery has claimed the credit. When, on 19 December 1916, he heard Lloyd George's announcement in the House about the forthcoming Imperial Conference the thought occurred to him, why should not the representatives from the dominions be asked 'to join the war cabinet itself and so assert their full equality and their right to be at the heart of things in deciding the conduct of the war?'[29] In cabinet, Milner gave his influential backing, the idea was adopted and Lloyd George invited dominion governments to take part in 'a series of special and continuous meetings of the war cabinet in order to consider urgent questions affecting the prosecution of the war. . . .'[30] There was accordingly to be an imperial war cabinet – the name was of Hankey's devising[31] – in addition to an Imperial War Conference. It was arranged that they should sit on alternate days, the prime minister presiding over the cabinet, the colonial secretary over the Conference. Responsibilities were to be divided so that the Conference would be left with its traditional rôle of reviewing imperial relations, while the imperial war cabinet was to be concerned with the conduct of the war and the defining of peace aims in their imperial aspects.

The imperial war cabinet met for the first time on 20 March 1917 and was served by the cabinet secretariat established by Lloyd George on his accession to office in December 1916.[32] The original intention had been to confine its membership to dominion prime ministers, allowing them to bring ministerial colleagues only on occasion and as required, but this aim was not realised. There was a coalition government in New Zealand with W. F. Massey as prime minister and Sir Joseph Ward as his principal partner-colleague – a sort of political Siamese twins, Hankey termed them. Ward insisted upon coequality of status with Massey in the imperial war cabinet as the price of continued coalition in New Zealand. Concession followed, and with concession to New Zealand there had of necessity to be concessions to the other dominions. In addition to the dominions India was represented by the secretary of state assisted by three assessors, two of them Indians the maharajah of Bikaner and Sir S. P. Sinha nominated by the secretary of state and present in recognition of India's outstanding services in the war. The imperial war cabinet thus became not the compact body Lloyd George had originally contemplated but a comparatively large gathering. As a result, to avoid the British ministers being outnumbered the prime minister felt compelled to increase the British war cabinet from five to eight among whom, however, from June 1917 was General Smuts, a member of the South African Parliament. Moreover (so Hankey recalled) Lloyd George, while deciding that 'the whole caboodle' of dominion ministers must be asked, 'was very bored'.[33] More important, the size of the imperial war cabinet led to the delegation both in 1917 and 1918 of much of its business to subcommittees. The most important of these was the subcommittee of prime ministers set up in June 1918 while the imperial war cabinet was meeting for its second session to consider the critical situation on the Western Front. It met between 21 June and 16 August.[34]

The imperial war cabinet captured the imagination of governments and of most of those preoccupied with problems of imperial relations. Sir Robert Borden – hitherto so critical of lack of information and consultation with the dominions on major issues of policy – sensed its potentially far-reaching implications. Addressing the Empire Parliamentary Association in 1917 while the imperial war cabinet was still in session, he observed that for the first time in the Empire's history there were sitting in London two cabinets, both properly constituted and both exercising well-defined powers. The prime minister of the United Kingdom presided over each of them. One was designated the war cabinet; the other the imperial war cabinet, and each had its distinct sphere of responsibility and jurisdiction. Borden noted especially that in the imperial war cabinet prime ministers and other representatives of dominions met with the prime minister and ministers of the United Kingdom cabinet as equals. Ministers of six nations sat around the council board, all of them responsible to their respective Parliaments and to the people of the countries which they represented. Each dominion, Borden felt, had its voice upon questions of common concern and of the highest importance as the deliberations proceeded; and each preserved unimpaired its perfect autonomy, its self-government and the responsibility of its own ministers to their own electorate.[35] Lloyd George was no less enthusiastic. He told the House of Commons on 17 May 1917 that members of the imperial war cabinet were unanimous that the new procedure had been of such service that it ought not to be allowed to fall into desuetude. He had himself proposed at the concluding session that meetings of an imperial war cabinet should be held annually and that the cabinet should consist of the prime minister of each of the dominions (or some specially accredited alternate possessed of equal authority) and of a representative of the Indian people to be appointed by the government of India. This proposal, generally approved, opened the way for further meetings of the imperial war cabinet in 1918. Lloyd George also laid some emphasis on the fact that dominion leaders, through their membership of the imperial war cabinet, would be able 'to obtain full information about all aspects of imperial affairs and to determine by consultation together the policy of the Empire in its most vital aspects, without infringing in any degree the autonomy which its parts at present enjoy'.[36]

There is little doubt that many of those most closely associated with the work of the imperial war cabinet thought of it (particularly after its second session in 1918) as an innovation that had grown out of the necessities of war but one which in some form would survive the immediate occasion of its coming into being. It was the full and formal imperial war cabinet that attracted the attention of the public but the sub-committee of prime ministers constituted in 1918, though technically subordinate to the larger body and reporting to them when time allowed, were compelled by force of circumstances to take decisions 'every time they met' on matters that 'would brook no delay'. Had the war continued, the trend towards a concentration of authority in the prime ministers' hands might have continued.[37] But in any case there were institutional problems deriving from the very nature of the cabinet (or its sub-committees) apt to be overlooked or discounted by some enthusiastic contemporaries.

One characteristic of the imperial war cabinet was that in the established meaning of the term it was not a cabinet at all. The ministers who composed it were neither collectively responsible to nor members of a single Parliament, and accordingly two of the classic conventions of cabinet government were not observed. Amery, a principal architect and eulogist of the imperial war cabinet, while conceding that it had no collective responsibility to a single representative body argued at the time that a substitute for this might be found in its distributed responsibility to a number of Parliaments. He also later recalled, and with approval, Sir Robert Borden's 'apt phrase' – 'a cabinet of governments rather than of ministers'. In so far (he wrote) as the imperial war cabinet 'worked as a single body of colleagues all concerned with the same end and each contributing to the best of his individual judgement, it deserved the title of cabinet as fully as any cabinet that I have ever attended'.[38] Meriting and being however are by no means always the same thing.

Amery thought of the innovation of the imperial war cabinet not as an end in itself but as the hopeful starting point for further imperial consolidation in purpose and action. From the premise that 'the imperial cabinet is undoubtedly a real cabinet' he proceeded, in a memorandum[39] of some eighteen pages dated June 1918, which was circulated to dominion prime ministers among others, to argue in favour of a continuing imperial cabinet that was small so that it might be personal and intimate; that was responsible; and that was continuous. Yet only the first of these conditions could be satisfied without posing fundamental questions about the nature both of the cabinet and of imperial relations. If there were to be an imperial cabinet that was responsible, to whom and for what was it to be responsible? Amery, it would seem from his memorandum, contemplated the disentangling of imperial from United Kingdom interests with responsibility for the former lying to all the parliaments of the Empire. He conceived that the principle of equality of status and responsibility as between Britain and the dominions really postulated that a department, such as the Foreign Office and its various agencies abroad, serving imperial purposes should be jointly controlled and financed by a contribution shared between Britain and the dominions, with the shadowy figure of an imperial minister of finance to deal with the consequential problems of imperial financial cooperation. And as for continuity in session, that was possible only if dominion prime ministers or their representatives were to remain more or less permanently in London. If they did so, what authority would they carry with their colleagues at home? How closely in touch would they remain with dominion public opinion? Amery suggested, at least as a part answer, that the imperial cabinet system should have as a necessary complement something in the nature of a sounding-board; some arena in which policy could be openly expounded and discussed and so reach the press and public of the Empire. 'The Imperial Conference,' he noted hopefully, 'expanded into a Conference of Parliaments, would exactly fill this need.' Dominion experiences of war presaged developments in quite other directions but historically it is interesting – even ironic – to recall how the appearance and to some extent the reality of concentration of power in the imperial war cabinet encouraged thoughts of the possibilities of developing post-war centralisation of Empire.

However Amery's spacious reflections be regarded, the problem that inspired them was real enough. The dominions at the Imperial War Conference and cabinet were moving towards a measure of control in war and foreign policy. How was this in fact to be exercised? Was there to be an area of joint British-dominion responsibility? Austen Chamberlain, reflecting on this, as a result of some observations of W. M. Hughes at a meeting of the imperial war cabinet in July 1918, felt the matter was essentially one not for Britain but for the dominions to resolve. He did not question the perfect justice of the dominions' claim to be regarded as sister nations in free and willing cooperation with the United Kingdom but he did wonder how this cooperation was to be carried on.

Even in war-time [he noted] when the most momentous issues arise from day to day and have to be rapidly decided, it is not possible for the prime ministers of the sister nations to be present at our deliberations for more than a few weeks in the year. In peace time they may find that their own electorates and Parliaments become impatient even of such short absences. How then can touch best be maintained during that large portion of the year when the personal presence of all the prime ministers in London is not possible, and how can the dominion governments be given their due influence in the decisions of the Empire's policy?

If and when there were dominion representatives in London, an imperial cabinet might meet weekly or as often as required, whether in war or in peace.

The real problem [he continued] I think is how these dominion representatives are to be chosen and how it can be secured that they shall possess the mind and confidence of the government which they represent sufficiently to be of real assistance in council, or in other words, under what circumstances and in what measure a dominion government would be content that such a representative should take decisions in its name.[40]

Austen Chamberlain posed with cogency and precision the question to which dominion statesmen were unable to find an answer that was acceptable and satisfying to them. So long as that was so, notions of joint control and joint responsibility, exercised through an imperial war cabinet or otherwise, fell to the ground. The remarkable thing is how slow many British and some dominion statesmen were to become reconciled to these facts of imperial political life.

The opportunities and the perplexities inherent in a changing dominion/United Kingdom relationship alike became apparent when victory was won. Lloyd George's original invitation to the dominion prime ministers to come to London for an Imperial War Conference and to take part in the meetings of an enlarged war cabinet had referred not only to urgent questions affecting the prosecution of the war but also to the possible conditions of peace. Both were in fact discussed during the sessions of the imperial war cabinet in 1917 and again in August 1918. Later that year the collapse of the Central Powers necessitated an urgent summons to the dominion prime ministers (other than W. M. Hughes of Australia who with commendable foresight had remained) to return to London so as to take part in discussions about peace terms at meetings of the imperial war cabinet, which began what proved to be its last session on 20 November. Already there had been indications, notably from Hughes, of dominion concern about the rôle in peace-making that might or might not be allotted to their representatives. Thus on 29 October 1918 Sir Robert Borden sent a secret, private and personal message to Lloyd George saying that there was need of serious consideration on the question of the representation of the dominions in the peace negotiations.

> The press and people of this country [he observed] take it for granted that Canada will be represented at the Peace Conference. I appreciate possible difficulties as to representation of the dominions but I hope you will keep in mind that certainly a very unfortunate impression would be created and possibly a dangerous feeling might be aroused if these difficulties are not overcome by some solution which will meet the national spirit of the Canadian people. We discussed the subject today in Council and I found among my colleagues a striking insistence which doubtless is indicative of the general opinion entertained in this country. In a word they feel that new conditions must be met by new precedents.[41]

Lloyd George was receptive and sympathetic to dominion representations and there was discussion about them in the imperial war cabinet proceeding on the initial assumption that only five places could be secured for the British Empire at the Peace Conference. If that assumption proved correct, it meant the adoption in some form or another of a panel system under which representation of the British Empire at the Peace Conference would be selected from day to day from a panel made up of representatives of the United Kingdom and the dominions. This was bound to be a constricting arrangement for both. Accordingly, the members of the imperial war cabinet agreed that they should press not only for a British Empire representation of five according to the panel system but also for separate representation for each dominion similar to that accorded to smaller Allied powers. These proposals were discussed with the principal Allied powers; though received with initial coolness they were finally accepted. As a result the dominions and India secured dual representation, first, as occasion required, on the British Empire panel, and then separately as belligerent powers with special interests entitled to send two plenipotentiary delegates to Paris. In the first capacity Britain and the dominions formed the British Empire Delegation which was regarded as an extension of the imperial war cabinet, meeting in Paris for the particular purpose of agreeing a common policy on the terms of peace, and as such was served by Sir Maurice Hankey as secretary and by the secretariat of the war cabinet reinforced by dominion personnel. In the second capacity each dominion decided upon its own representation.

What were the implications of dual dominion representation, and how effective did it prove? Dr Loring Christie, the legal adviser to the Canadian prime minister, essayed an answer in a Memorandum summarising the development of the status of Canada as an international person at the Paris Peace Conference. He felt that the dominions gained by their dual status. As members of the British Empire delegation they received the confidential papers of the Conference such as the minutes of the Council of Ten and the Council of Five, denied to other smaller powers, and as a result were able in their own individual capacities to watch and check the proceedings more effectively. The dominions also secured through membership of the British Empire delegation a more significant rôle on committees and commissions than would have otherwise been the case. Dominion ministers were, for example, nominated to and acted for the British Empire on the principal inter-Allied commissions of the Peace Conference, and all the dominion prime ministers took part in the Council of Ten when the disposition of the German colonies was being discussed and decided. Since the Peace Treaty was largely drafted by commissions of the Peace Conference in the first instance, dominion representation on them was correspondingly important. Moreover, as Christie recorded: 'Every Commission report, every aspect, every section of the Conditions of Peace was first considered in meetings of the British Empire delegation (whose personnel was the same as that of the imperial war cabinet) before the assent of the British Empire was given'. In view of this, in view of the attendance of dominion prime ministers from time to time at the Council of Ten and of the prime minister of Canada's participation on a number of occasions in the work of the Council of Four and the Council of Five, Christie concluded that the dominions' participation in the making of peace has been very substantial.[42] If a longer retrospect suggests an altogether more sceptical opinion it is nevertheless worth recording that on the British side Amery reached much the same conclusion as Christie. The dominions, Amery thought, by virtue of their membership of the British Empire Delegation and their association in it with the representatives of one of the 'Big Four' were able to exercise a continuous influence on the negotiations and were 'in a quite different position from the ordinary run of secondary powers whose delegates hung about, picking up such stray crumbs of information about their own fate as might be vouchsafed to them'.[43]

The influence of Australia, New Zealand and South Africa was certainly significant in respect of the disposition of the former German colonies and the extension of the Mandates' system to the Pacific and Africa. They were all interested parties. Australia at the outset pressed vigorously for the outright annexation of the former German possessions in the Pacific and, after protracted disputation, W. M. Hughes yielded reluctantly, in the face of 'overwhelming odds', on the understanding that the 'C' class mandate granted would be 'the equivalent of a 999 years' lease as compared with freehold'. For reasons of security there could never be an open door to Asiatic immigration. 'There should be,' asserted Hughes later, 'a barred and closed door with Australia as the guardian of the door.'[44] South Africa was equally resolved to secure – and obtained – comparable control over south-west Africa. From the dominions the evidence of a revival or stirring of the expansionist spirit was as pronounced as that of the enlightenment that might be thought implicit in notions of intra-imperial equality founded in national freedom. In so far as the latter found expression at Versailles it was through the voice of General Smuts, the second delegate for South Africa, who used all his gifts of persuasion and his personal prestige in a vain endeavour to modify the harshness of the peace terms imposed upon the defeated enemy.[45]

The form of status accorded to the dominions at the Peace Conference carried one possible theoretic liability. When the treaty came to be signed the dominion plenipotentiaries appended their signatures, 'for Canada', 'for Australia', as the case might be, under the signatures of the plenipotentiaries from the United Kingdom, who signed for the British Empire as a whole. While on the one hand therefore it might be asserted that the dominion signatures represented recognition of the dominions as international persons, it could be argued on the other hand that they were formal or even superfluous.[46] This was an ambiguity some at least of the dominions were resolved in due course to remove. In the meantime they had established their individual right whether or not to accede to the treaty and had simultaneously secured (again not without some misgiving on the part of other powers) membership and representation in the Assembly and Council of the new League of Nations in all respects the same as that of other members. Technically they became members of the League as signatories of the treaty and no distinction was made in this respect between them and other signatory members. The dominions, Christie cautiously concluded in his memorandum 'have asserted a sovereign status of some sort and have for some purposes entered the family of nations. There were at Paris, and will be, anomalies . . . '. That was certainly true; but whatever the anomalies about the status of the dominions in the present, it was clear after 1919 that each was moving towards the goal of separate sovereignty, internationally recognised.

In the one debate of lasting moment at the Imperial War Conference 1917 the dominion representatives had considered the future of imperial relations. The language was for the most part hopeful but not complacent. They gloried in the nationhood of the dominions. They spoke constantly of equality. 'I believe,' said Sir Robert Borden, 'that the dominions fully realise the ideal of an imperial Commonwealth of United Nations . . . '. They were really bound together by the tie of common allegiance, by like institutions and ideals of democracy, and by like purposes.

We are [said General Smuts] the only group of nations that has ever successfully existed. People talk about a league of nations and international government, but the only successful experiment in international government that has ever been made is the British Empire, founded on principles which appeal to the highest political ideals of mankind.

But this was not sufficiently recognised in the constitution of the Empire. General Smuts proceeded:

> Too much, if I may say so of the old ideas still clings to the new organism which is growing. I think that although in practice there is great freedom, yet in actual theory the status of the dominions is of a subject character. Whatever we may say, and whatever we may think, we are subject Provinces of Great Britain. That is the actual theory of the constitution. . . .

It was a theory that in his view could not and should not survive. The young nations were growing into great powers; they would require readjustment of relations on a basis of equality and such readjustment was not the appointed task of the Imperial War Conference of 1917. The Conference approved a Resolution (Resolution 9) recommending that this should be the chief responsibility of the first Imperial Conference to assemble after the end of the war.[47] But by the time that Conference met in 1921 something of the warm glow of common conviction had departed from dominion representatives, while the British government had reason to be more preoccupied with the opening of negotiations for a dominion settlement in Ireland than with a review of relations with existing dominions. Yet the purpose of the 1917 Resolution was not forgotten. General Smuts saw to that. He was not politically in a position to remain passive. He was under constant Nationalist fire in South Africa about his own and his country's subservience to British policy. He did not, comments his biographer, have the option of leaving the question of imperial constitutional relations alone. 'Both his personal history and his political circumstances compelled him to formulate a doctrine, to promulgate a code.'

In 1921, Smuts drafted a memorandum entitled, *The Constitution of the British Commonwealth*[48] and intended to serve as a basis for the discussion of questions which might come before the Constitutional Conference, recommended by the Imperial War Conference 1917. But the memorandum was not, in fact, circulated to the Imperial Conference 1921, because Smuts wished first to prepare the ground for it in discussion and the proposed Constitutional Conference did not take place. It was not, therefore, an official Conference Paper, though actually it was something more. It was a telling personal appraisal of the direction in which the Commonwealth should advance, consistent with past development, present position and its own political nature. The language of the memorandum was urgent and its conclusions in some respects remarkable, even if regarded as no more than essays in political prognostication. But its chief interest lies in the light it throws upon the nature of the debate on Commonwealth and Empire, provoked by the cataclysmic experiences of war.

At the outset the tone of Smuts's memorandum was cautionary. 'Delay in the settlement of dominion status is fraught with grave dangers. . . . The national temperature of all young countries has been raised by the event of the great war'. Unless dominion status was settled soon, in a way that would satisfy the legitimate aspirations of 'these young nations, we must look', he argued, 'for separatist movements in the Commonwealth. Such movements already exist, notably in South Africa, but potentially in several other dominions also.' The only way to deal with them was 'to forestall them and to make them unnecessary by the most generous satisfaction of the dominion sense of nationhood and statehood. The warning against always being too late with a proper solution, of which Ireland is an example to the whole Commonwealth, is one which we can ignore only at our own peril.' The root of the problem lay in the conflict between law and usage.

In principle Smuts conceded that the existence of dominion equality was to be inferred from dominion signatures to the peace treaties in 1919 and their membership of the League of Nations. But that equality did not exist in law. Law, therefore, ought to be brought into harmony with practice. It was true that as things stood, any attempt of the Parliament of the United Kingdom to legislate for a dominion would be unconstitutional and revolutionary. But clearly it was legal. Could, enquired Smuts, action in conformity with existing law be then regarded as 'revolutionary'? Therein lay the paradox. A simple solution would be to end the legislative sovereignty of Parliament at Westminster in respect of the dominions. Smuts did not favour it. It would be a negative step; it was better to leave such theoretic sovereignty alone as 'a sort of symbolic reminder of the historic unity of the Commonwealth'. The positive and constructive course would be to assure the legislative sovereignty of dominion Parliaments and to give them the power, which they did not possess, of legislating with extra-territorial effect. All dominions should have the power to amend their own constitutions. The Colonial Laws Validity Act, 1865, which laid down that any dominion legislation in conflict with British statute law was to the extent of such repugnancy null and void, should be repealed. Given the necessary authority, particularly to amend their own constitutions in every case, the dominions could decide for themselves whether or not for example they should abolish appeals to the judicial committee of the Privy Council in cases where appeals were still admitted.

Smuts then turned to the field of foreign affairs. Here too he detected continuing anomalies. The dominions had acquired international status and received international recognition in 1919 but practice had not been correspondingly changed. In effect the Foreign Office still continued to control the relations between the dominions and foreign countries. There was in fact little consultation between the British and dominion governments in such matters beyond the sending of occasional summaries of the international situation. True there had been important advances. The dominions could now advise the king to appoint dominion ministers to foreign countries. It was also now recognised by convention that the dominions could not be bound by treaties they had not signed. But practice was unsettled and foreigners were confused. They found it

> difficult to grasp the difference between legal theory and constitutional practice in the Empire and to see how the law of the constitution is moulded and finally abrogated by the practice of the constitution, and how, without a change of the law, a British colony becomes in constitutional fact an independent state. These abstruse matters might be cleared up in some formal way which would show the true nature of dominion status as distinct from legal archaisms.

How should it be done? Here too Smuts had his proposals. They were remarkable chiefly for the measure of continuing centralisation which he was ready to contemplate.

Dominion governments, Smuts suggested, should become coordinate governments of the king with full equality of status. This would mean 1. that they should

> cease to be placed under the Colonial Office or any other British Department, 2. that the Dominion government should have direct access to the king who will act on their advice without the interposition of the British government or a secretary of state, 3. that the governor-general should become viceroy simply and solely and only represent the sovereign in his dominion executive and not also the British government.

The second – direct dominion access to the sovereign – was all important to Smuts. In his view it would represent the crucial step from which all else would follow. It would necessarily have to be laid down that the king in his conduct as a dominion sovereign would act only on the advice of his dominion government. Since the king in practice resided in England this would mean the residence in England of a dominion minister of the Crown with direct access to the sovereign. But (argued Smuts) this should not be allowed to impair the intimate relations keeping British and dominion governments in close touch. Machinery would be needed; without it there was the risk they would drift apart. This machinery should comprise three organs of conference for consultation about the policies and common concerns of the Commonwealth. One was to be a 'Commonwealth Congress, or Imperial Conference', held every four years. It was to include not only cabinet ministers but also representatives of Parliamentary oppositions. The second was to be a prime ministers' Meeting, or Conference, in place of the imperial cabinet, which should meet every two years 'to review the foreign and defence or other common policies of the Commonwealth as a whole'. Finally there would be a smaller body, a dominions' Committee, consisting of the prime ministers or their deputies and providing a continuing organisation to ensure continuous consultation. This Committee would be served by a Commonwealth secretariat.

Smuts concluded his analysis with a recommendation that the imperial cabinet should draft a general scheme of future Commonwealth constitutional relations; that the scheme should take the form of resolutions to be submitted to a Constitutional Conference and that these resolutions should provide for legislation by the Parliament at Westminster 1. giving power of constitutional amendment to the dominions, 2. extending their legislative jurisdiction beyond their territorial limits, and 3. abrogating the Colonial Laws Validity Act. There should be further a declaration of rights, as had been suggested by H. Duncan Hall in *The British Commonwealth of Nations*, providing that 1. the British Parliament had no constitutional right of legislation in respect of the dominions, 2. that the Royal Veto was in the same constitutional position in the dominions as in the United Kingdom, 3. that the dominions had direct access to the sovereign without the intervention of any British secretary of state, and 4. that the international status and rights of diplomatic representation of the dominions were unquestioned. Finally Smuts proposed that a new name should mark 'this epoch-making departure'. It should be the British Commonwealth of Nations, for what was no longer an empire but a society of free and equal states. He also thought that there should be some great symbol to mark the equal status of the dominions and their entry among the nations of the world and that the most appropriate might be the adoption, in the case of each dominion, of a distinctive national flag.

The immediate importance of General Smuts's memorandum was less than might have been supposed. There were three reasons for this. The first, already mentioned, was its lack of official status. That meant it was not formally laid before an Imperial Conference nor formally debated. But more substantially, the theme of the memorandum was unacceptable to majority opinion at the Imperial Conference, 1921 and knowledge of its content, if anything hardened opposition to any attempt to reduce the Commonwealth to writing or to the formulation of what Hughes discounted as a 'flamboyant declaration of rights'. Thirdly – and technically and tactically important – the Imperial Conference 1921 was not the constitutional Conference contemplated in

Resolution 9 of the Imperial War Conference of 1917. On this point Lloyd George was explicit in issuing invitations to it. Was it part of its responsibility then to prepare for such a Conference? This was a matter that was left to the Conference to decide and it could do so if it seemed desirable, or even necessary, to consider afresh the purposes a constitutional conference might serve. 'It may be that I am very dense', remarked W. M. Hughes, 'but I am totally at a loss to understand what it is this Constitutional Conference proposes to do. Is it that the dominions are seeking new powers, or are desirous of using the powers they already have, or is the Conference to draw up a declaration of rights, to set down in black and white the relations between Britain and the dominions? What is this Conference to do? What is the reason for calling it together?'[49] Hughes thought there was none that justified its assembling. Massey from New Zealand agreed with him. So long as there was a partnership of nations it appeared to Massey to matter little whether it was called a family of nations, a Commonwealth of Nations, or anything else. Nor did the words that might be placed upon paper to define that relationship matter much more. The strength of the Empire rested upon the patriotic sentiments of the British people, by which the New Zealand prime minister meant not only Anglo-Saxons or Europeans but 'the British people right through the Empire, including the native races. You cannot go beyond sentiment.'[50] Arthur Meighen, who represented Canada and was chiefly preoccupied with discouraging the further extension in time of the Anglo-Japanese alliance, was more inclined to sympathise with such Australasian opinions than any Canadian prime minister of the century. Opposition, reinforced by indifference, sufficed accordingly to ensure the inclusion of a sentence in the Resolutions at the end of the Conference saying that in view of developments since 1917 no advantage was to be gained by holding a Constitutional Conference. While retrospectively therefore it may seem a foregone conclusion that the status of the dominions and their relations with Great Britain should be reviewed and, so far as was possible, defined in terms of convention and of law, this was by no means self-evident even as late as 1921. It was not Hughes, who was well pleased to be able to report to his fellow countrymen on his return that he had soldered up the constitutional tinkers in their own tin can, but Smuts who had reason to feel frustrated when the Imperial Conference dispersed.

Against short-term disregard, however, must be placed long-term reality. General Smuts's memorandum was closer to that reality than any known contemporary document. It expressed succinctly the problems and the possibilities of the British Commonwealth of Nations as it emerged from the first world war. It had an appreciation, which time proved to be well founded, of the dangers particularly of disregard of nascent dominion nationalisms. In itself it proved a programme for the future. 'Smuts's memorandum of June 1921' claims his biographer[51], 'contained by anticipation the Balfour Declaration of 1926 and the entire constitutional achievement from then until the Statute of Westminster of 1931 . . .'. Essentially it was a sanguine document. It was infused by a sense of the possibilities before the Commonwealth. 'The tents have been struck, and the great caravan of humanity is once more on the march.' So Smuts had said in 1918 and he at least had no doubt that the Commonwealth was in the vanguard. His greatest misconception, as may be seen from this vantage point in time, lay in his implicit assumption about British imperial power. The British Empire, he told his colleagues later at the Imperial Conference, 'emerged from the war quite the greatest power in the world, and it is only unwisdom or unsound policy that could rob her of that great position'.[51] It was an assumption which did not qualify the politico-psychological arguments for dominion equality with Britain but one which never the less encouraged facile disregard of the possible politico-strategic price of the progressive decentralisation of imperial authority.

CHAPTER 7

IRELAND: THE DOMINION SETTLEMENT

'I need not enlarge to you on the importance of the Irish question for the Empire as a whole.' Smuts to Lloyd George, June 1921.

The Irish question in the form in which it had dominated the politics of late Victorian England passed into history with the signing of the Anglo-Irish Treaty in the early morning of 6 December 1921. It had a threefold importance in its concluding phases. In English politics the Irish settlement was a principal cause of the break up of Lloyd George's Coalition government and of the subsequent return to traditional party alignments at Westminster. In Irish history it represented the substantial but not the complete failure of English attempts to rule Ireland which had lasted some seven hundred years, the incompleteness deriving from the continuing inclusion of the six plantation counties of the north-east within the United Kingdom. Finally, the Irish question was a landmark in the history of the British Commonwealth of Nations because dominion status was conferred by the treaty for the first time on a country which was not in origin a colony of settlement and had not progressed by stages towards that politico-constitutional relationship with Britain. It is the last alone that has its place in Commonwealth history. But how and why it attained that place, against logic and historical probability, is not to be understood without consideration first of English and then of Irish political attitudes.[1]

The Liberal approach to the solution of Anglo-Irish relations was in full accord with the classical doctrines of mid-nineteenth century Liberal imperialism adapted to a situation that had no close parallel historically or geographically in the British Empire. The essence of the doctrine was consolidation, in this case of union, by timely concession and consequent enlistment of indigenous, national opinion in its support. In 1882 Gladstone himself had attempted – vainly as it proved – to persuade Queen Victoria of the wisdom of pursuing such policies in Ireland by drawing her attention to their earlier success, in the face of much gloomy foreboding, in Canada. By a comparable concession of autonomy Ireland also, he urged, might be reconciled to Britain and to the

Empire.[2] The correctness of his conclusion remains a matter of historical speculation. There were three attempts, the first two by Gladstone himself, to apply such traditional Liberal remedies, in the form of Home Rule, to Ireland. All of them failed. The first Home Rule Bill was defeated by a narrow majority in the House of Commons in 1886; the second passed the House of Commons but was rejected by an overwhelming majority by the House of Lords in 1894; the third, introduced in April 1912, was placed on the Statute Book together with an Act suspending its operation until after the end of the war and coupled with an assurance of amendment in respect of the Ulster counties. Suspended and to be amended, the Act served most of all to discredit the Irishmen who had followed first Charles Stewart Parnell and then John Redmond in the constitutional parliamentary movement. John Redmond, so it would appear from some of his letters,[3] thought it not impossible that he might be cast in the rôle of an Irish Botha, and by 1912 many Liberals, elated by the success of their South African policies, shared his hope that it might be so. But the events of 1914 ensured that there would be no Irish Botha.

The defeat of Home Rule stemmed from roots growing deep in English domestic politics. After 1886 it was not the parties of reform, whether Liberal or Labour, but the Unionist, or Conservative, party that was the major force in English politics. In the eighty years that have since elapsed that party has been in office either on its own, or in coalitions in which it has been the dominant partner, for close on sixty. In the shorter period between the introduction of the first Home Rule Bill and the Anglo-Irish settlement, the balance between Unionists and Liberals was somewhat in favour of the Liberals in terms of time, but in the decisive years in Anglo-Irish history, 1886 and 1920–1, the Unionists and their allies possessed a parliamentary majority, while in the prewar struggle over the third Home Rule Bill they were sufficiently strong to frustrate Liberal purposes. This fact of Unionist dominance – especially at critical moments – needs re-statement if only because historical interest is apt to be drawn disproportionately to Liberal or Labour administrations. This is not surprising. It is more exciting to read or write about change and reform than about conservation. Yet it can be misleading, as it has been in the historiography of Anglo-Irish relations. If classical Liberal notions were never applied to Ireland, Unionist policy was fully tested.

At this point it is well to look more closely at the common Liberal assumption that it was more important that Gladstone should have proposed a Home Rule Bill in 1886 than that Joseph Chamberlain should have killed it. Is the assumption well founded? Might it not be argued that the rejection of Home Rule by the Radicals in association with Tories and dissident Whigs was the event that was crucial in its consequences for the next half century? It had meant in the first place that the establishment, in terms of the traditional landed interest and propertied classes, was reinforced by radical lower middle-class and working-class votes, which were important and at times possibly decisive electorally. But it had also a further, long-term significance. The cause that united left with right, deriving from common opposition to Home Rule, was maintenance of the union. Their association accordingly brought into existence a party generally pragmatic in its outlook but of political necessity rigid and ideological on the issue which had brought it into being.

'Jack Cade' may have vanished, as Professor Thornton[4] has remarked of the archetypal radical-unionist Joseph Chamberlain, 'behind orchid and eyeglass, taking his Radicalism with him'. But his Unionism always retained its pristine importance. The Conservative Party became the Unionist Party and the change of name symbolised a modification, at the least, in character. Adaptable as the party might be in its response to changing interests in other fields, implicit in its very being was one unchanging element – support for the union. In this respect it was a party depriving itself, from 1886 to 1921, of its customary freedom of political manoeuvre. Its attitude to Ireland could not change in response to changing circumstances (as, for example, it was to do a generation later – with dramatic consequences – in respect of Africa) because of the manner in which Home Rule was defeated in 1886. Unionism was a party dogma and was in effect written into its constitution. And it was this party, tied to dogma in this one particular, that with the aid of its in-built majority in the House of Lords negatively or positively determined British policies in Ireland between 1886 and 1905; and which, down to 1921, was generally able to call up sufficient reserves of establishment influence or electoral strength to block all but the most resolute of Liberal reformers, in a period in which Liberal reformers were not generally remarkable for their resolution on Irish issues.

Was Unionist policy towards Ireland in these years then a study in political negation? The answer is qualified. Its unchanging premise was a negation – no Home Rule – from which there derived certainly a broad but by no means necessarily a detailed conclusion. Herein lay the area of debate and discussion within the party. Home Rule rejected, what was to replace it? Coercion? Or conversion? In essence those were the alternatives. Four-fifths of the Irish electorate supported Home Rule. Home Rule was not to be conceded. Were the Irish then to be coerced in perpetuity into acceptance, or at the least acquiescence in union? Or was there some other way by which they might be persuaded to abandon the Home Rule dead end? The second, it is not to be doubted, was the hope of all except a die-hard (but possibly realistic) minority. Arthur James Balfour supplied the necessary conceptual foundation for it. 'He is,' noted Sir Henry Lucy[5] when Balfour first made some mark in the House of Commons in 1880, 'a pleasing specimen of the highest form of the culture and good breeding which stand to the credit of Cambridge University.' But he was also something more – 'a pretty speaker, with a neat turn for saying nasty things',[6] and as Sir Henry had occasion to note in 1890, in him was to be 'recognised the most perfect living example of the mailed hand under the velvet glove'.[7]

Balfour's analysis of the Irish question possessed a broad imperial interest. In his opinion what went at the time by the comprehensive name of Parnellism was a superficial and dangerously misconceived political expression of ills which were real. Those ills were social and economic. They were endemic in the Irish social system, especially the land system. They were deep-seated, hard to alleviate, but given persistence, time and above all a sense of common British party purpose, not beyond remedy. Such political consensus, in the Balfourian exegesis, should be forthcoming if only by reason of British self-interest, or to be more precise of the interests of the British propertied classes. For while the outward manifestations of Parnellism were political, its inward dangers were in equal measure social. The exploitation of agrarian distress for political purposes had resulted in an assault upon the rights of property in Ireland where they were most vulnerable and Balfour, like Salisbury and many others besides and before him, argued that the undermining of property rights in one part of the United Kingdom would by necessary consequence open the way to their impairment in others. On this reasoning, which (it will be noted) had little force or application in respect of distant colonies, the right course was to remedy Irish grievances, relieve Irish social distress, foster industries and the welfare of the Irish people and so not merely maintain, but strengthen through new contentment, the union and incidentally, but significantly, re-insure the rights of property throughout the United Kingdom. The phrase was 'killing Home Rule with kindness'. The kindness, however, on the Unionist premise, was a pre-condition of the killing. But therein lay – as Balfour was to find – a familiar and inexorable dilemma. The moment of reform is always difficult, sometimes dangerous, for an autocratic régime. Hitherto (Balfour had said at the outset of his chief secretaryship in 1887) English governments had 'either been all for repression or all for reform. I am for both: repression as stern as Cromwell; reform as thorough as Mr Parnell or anyone else can desire.'[8] He sought, in other words, to avert the risks associated with reform by 'resolution' in government. The price however was that the resolution counterbalanced or outbalanced the psychological effects of reforms. 'Bloody Balfour', 'the man of Mitchelstown', was not associated in the Irish mind with 'kindness'. That was a handicap for the chief secretary and, more important, for the policy he propounded, which was never overcome.

Balfour, however, did not stand alone. There were twenty years of Unionist rule between 1886 and 1905, broken only by a three-year interlude of uncertain Liberal administration. In the chief secretary's office, A. J. Balfour was followed by his brother, Gerald (who first applied the phrase 'killing with kindness' to Home Rule) and then by George Wyndham – an attractive, gifted personality and a romantic Tory, of whom it was said that Sir Walter Scott was 'his only outpost in the modern world'.[9] Yet, for all his gifts Wyndham lacked one thing, as important to politicians as Napoleon deemed it to be for generals – luck.[10]

He came to office resolved to settle the land question. It is not much of an exaggeration to say he settled it. The foundation provided by a Land Conference under Lord Dunraven's chairmanship was used to frame an Act that encouraged landlords to sell and tenants to buy, the inducement for both being provided by a substantial Exchequer grant. Wyndham however was not content to think of the Land Act as an end. It was a means – a means, as his biographer has written, 'of euthanasia for Home Rule'.[11] There was an element (or possibly a double element according to the point of view) of illusion here. Even Liberals, by no means convinced of the reality of Irish nationalism, argued that if nationalism derived from social oppression, where was the assurance that it would end with it? And if Irish nationalism was in itself not a derivative but an absolute, then there was no possible foundation for the notions Wyndham entertained.

Wyndham himself soon had reason for doubt. He had appointed, as happened on a number of occasions in Irish administration under the union, an eminent imperial administrator, Sir Antony MacDonnell (lieutenant-governor of the United Provinces who was, however, also an Irishman and a Catholic with Home Rule sympathies) under-secretary at the Irish Office. Balfour's keen political nostrils scented the whiff of danger. But Wyndham, less perspicacious and relaxing abroad after the passage of the Land Act, inadvertently overlooked the extent (of which he was, albeit a little casually, informed)[12] of the under-secretary's commitment to a modest programme of political and administrative devolution for Ireland. There were first indignant rumblings and then angry protests from within the Unionist Party at this supposed official commitment to some small loosening of the sacred bonds of union. MacDonnell survived the storm but Wyndham resigned. In effect the Unionist experiment in killing Home Rule with kindness was ended. It had had its successes, notably the 1903 Land Act, on the road to final failure. Far from being killed, Home Rule was showing every sign of re-invigoration. Nor was it a question of Home Rule alone; it was self-evidently the larger question of Irish nationalism. Salisbury, Balfour, George Wyndham, all alike had denied the reality of its existence. That was an article of their Unionist faith. How much longer could the party subscribe to it?

Out of office from December 1905 until the formation of the first wartime coalition in 1915, the Unionist Party moved (though not so rapidly as is retrospectively apt to be supposed) towards an extreme position, or perhaps more accurately towards an extreme attitude, for it could be argued that Unionist insistence upon the union and nothing but the union was in itself the extreme fundamentalist position. But at least – so long as Balfour was leader of the party – it spoke the language of reason and not of violence. There could be no compromise about the union, but were there not ways in which concessions might be made to Irish sentiment consistent with that fundamental purpose? Indications were not lacking that this was a possibility, which had all the appearance of a last chance and which was about to be more seriously weighed. No one can read English Unionist discussion about future Irish policy at this time without sensing behind the polemics a mood of deepening perplexity.

In 1906 there appeared F. S. Oliver's *Life of Alexander Hamilton*. It enjoyed great success – except with historians; it had far-reaching influence. Its theme, in biographical form, was the making of the American federation. Oliver believed with George Washington that 'influence is not government' and the moral he drew from the early experience of the United States was the need for authority to ensure the triumph of centripetal over centrifugal forces. Some years later he sought to apply the lessons to the British Isles. In 1910 he published a series of letters under the title *Federalism and Home Rule*, the argument of which was that while 'the union of the United Kingdom is a great thing, and to impair that would be to lose all', that union was not necessarily inconsistent with federalism or even conceivably – certain conditions being fulfilled – with Home Rule. In further pamphlets, *The Alternative to Civil War* (1913) and *What Federalism is Not* (1914) Oliver elaborated his views. In so far as federalism or Home Rule were consistent with devolution of authority, as distinct from division, he was prepared to favour them. He believed that a delegation of powers from Westminster to the four national units in the British Isles on a permanent basis would at once preserve the union and might be made a part of a larger plan for the federation of the whole of the British Empire, the 'grand federal idea' on which Oliver and his colleagues in *The Round Table* had set their sights. It was all a dream. Irishmen were even more opposed to the federation of the British Isles than Canadians and South Africans were to the federation of Empire. But in each case the reason was the same. They were aware that such a federation would not lead, and was not intended to lead, to recognition of their several and separate political identities, but to their merging with and ultimate submergence in a larger whole. At root therefore, behind the forms, the phrases and the idealism of the Round Tablers, the gulf between imperialism and nationalism lay unbridged. Oliver's conception of Home Rule was limited to a delegation of power to all four national units in the British Isles, leaving unimpaired 'the union of these Islands', which as he wrote and as Stephen Gwynn[13] who later edited his letters noted, was to men of his views 'by its nature, sacramental'. In that context federalism implied, not as Oliver suggested 'a new departure' for Unionism, but superficial rearrangement of the forms of union to make it more palatable to Irish nationalists.

In 1913, in the same year in which Oliver wrote of federalism, A. J. Balfour, now dispossessed of the leadership of the party by Andrew Bonar Law, reflected, also in pamphlet form, upon *Nationality and Home Rule*. His approach was closer to political realities. He conceded that there was an Irish problem. He argued that it lay neither in the existing parliamentary system nor in the existing financial system, both of which indeed he claimed were more favourable to Ireland than to Britain. The land system was reformed, the administrative system was being reformed. Where then was the justification for Home Rule?

> It lies in the fact [noted Balfour] that the Irish Nationalist Party claim that Ireland, *on the ground of a separate nationality*, possesses inherent rights which cannot be satisfied by the fairest and fullest share of the parliamentary institutions of the United Kingdom. What satisfies Scotland cannot satisfy them, and ought not to satisfy them. It would be treason to Ireland.

Balfour then proceeded to probe the foundations of Irish nationality and concluded that neither in respect of Irish institutions nor of Irish culture nor of Irish descent or civilisation was there sufficient ground for the separate nationalism implicit in Home Rule. The explanation for that was to be found 'in the tragic coincidences of Irish history'. In them, Irish nationalism originated and from them it derived its anti-British tradition. How should British statesmen respond? To Balfour there were only two alternatives. The first was maintenance of the union and the keeping of Ireland in full political communion with England and Scotland. The second was to give her complete autonomy. That was 'a counsel of despair'. Yet, Balfour noted, it was apparently suited to the disease. It gave nationalist Ireland what it professed to desire. In that respect it was at least a solution of the Irish nationalist problem. But what of Home Rule? It offered the middle course but it solved no problem whatsoever. Financially, administratively and constitutionally, he argued, it was at once indefensible and unworkable. His own answer was time, time in which to give the measures enacted by the Unionist administration a chance to have their remedial and beneficial effects. And to those who argued that 'Irish patriotism, in its exclusive and more or less hostile form, is destined to be eternal', he replied that they should think in logic not of Home Rule but of separation.

By 1913 Balfour possessed influence but no longer enjoyed power within the party. That rested in the improbable hands of Bonar Law, a pugnacious pessimist elected to the leadership because he was known to be politically a first-class fighting man. On the ground that the curbing of the powers of the House of Lords by the Parliament Act of 1911 had upset the balance of the constitution, Bonar Law felt warranted in urging the party of 'law and order' to take all steps to resist Home Rule. The Liberal government was, he declaimed at Blenheim on 27 July 1912, 'a Revolutionary Committee' which had seized by fraud upon despotic power. The Unionists accordingly would no longer be restrained by the bonds which would influence their action in any ordinary political struggle. They would use whatever means seemed most likely to be effective. Under Bonar Law's leadership the English Unionist Party committed themselves, even to the point of threatened violence, to the support of the Ulster Unionist cause. Yet Ulster was not an end in itself to the majority of English Unionists, even if Bonar Law's own position on this point (possibly by reason of his Ulster descent) remained personal and distinctive.[14] It was a means to an end and that end was the preservation of the union and thereby of the integrity of the Empire. The imperial interest thus reinforced, in a way that has been insufficiently recognised, domestic opposition to Home Rule. It moved imperial administrators, soldiers, and even statesmen not otherwise interested in Irish affairs to action. Many of them had at most qualified faith in democratic processes.

Lord Milner provided the outstanding example. By temperament and by reason of his pro-consular experiences in South Africa he had nothing but contempt for the British parliamentary system. He felt 'only loathing for the way things were done in England, in the political sphere' and despised English politics. He hated the pressure of parliamentary necessities, he disdained the whims of a 'rotten public opinion', and if in South Africa he had made sacrifices they were not 'for this effete and dislocated Body Politic'. In the supposed interests of Empire and without regard for British parliamentary tradition, Milner (as

A. M. Gollin in his *Proconsul in Politics* first made plain) used his remarkable administrative gifts for the organisation of opposition to Home Rule in Great Britain, chiefly through the Union Defence League, securing by 1914 close on two million signatures for the British covenant. He also sought, and apparently succeeded, in securing substantial financial backing for measures which he was only too ready to contemplate but from which even the Ulster leadership under Sir Edward Carson and James Craig shrank. Of all the Unionist leaders Milner 'was the least anxious to seek a compromise solution to the Ulster problem'.[15] As for the English Unionist leaders, Milner himself noted that they preferred to talk rather than to enter into any definite plan for ridding themselves, by other than constitutional means, of the 'horrible nightmare' of a Home Rule into acceptance of which Ulster might have to be coerced. If these leaders are remembered for the great lengths to which they went, there were even greater being urged upon them.

In the last phase of Unionist opposition to Home Rule, poised as it was on the brink of violence, there were at least three identifiable elements in Unionism. There were first the Irish Unionists (whose attitudes and assumptions by no means always coincided with those of their English allies) themselves subdivided between the Ulster and southern Unionists; secondly there was the main body of English Unionists who thought of Home Rule chiefly as an issue in domestic politics; and finally there were the imperialists, accustomed to autocratic rule, some though not all of them with Milner on the extreme right, little interested in Anglo-Irish politics for their own sake but thinking of the unity of the British Isles as an essential condition of the unity and therefore of the greatness of the British Empire. Bound together by one supreme and testing issue, this was the formidable combination before which Liberals weakened and the cause of Irish constitutional nationalism succumbed.

For Unionism the Easter Rising, 1916, was the moment of truth. Unionists had declined to credit the authenticity of Irish nationalism. That was not for them a matter of political opinion but something that had become in effect close to an article of political faith. The rising, immediately for some but in the longer run for almost all, destroyed the conviction on which it rested. Irish nationalism came to be recognised for what it was. In time this introduced a new element of realism. Arthur Balfour had already argued, as we have seen, that there was no halfway house between union and separation. In that important respect at least he was at one with Sinn Féin. The two extremes were agreed in discounting the possibility of a *via media* if in nothing else. After 1916, Home Rule discarded and discredited, they were left face to face. The outcome, almost inevitably, was violent. Not until 1921 was the Unionist dilemma resolved – with the abandonment of union. Henceforward, British Conservative (no longer Unionist) statesmen, freed from their ideological burden, returned to pragmatic paths and for the most part showed a steady resolve, as Baldwin remarked in the 1930s, that there should not be another Ireland in India or anywhere else. If it be true that Unionist fundamentalism, lending countenance to threats and preparations for armed resistance in Ulster to Home Rule in the years before the first world war, bore a heavy – possibly a decisive – responsibility for creating a situation in which a violent resolution of the Irish question became probable, it has also to be remarked that with the qualified exception of Cyprus the party still dominant in English political life till the early 1960s was not again immobilised by credal conviction on a national issue on 'the wrong side of history'. That was one part of the legacy of the Irish question to Empire and Commonwealth. There were others.

While British and more especially Unionist attitudes to Irish self-government were not merely distinguishable but at significant periods sharply contrasted with their response to demands for colonial or dominion self-government, so too the Irish claims were couched – even by constitutional nationalists – in terms different from those commonly used in the colonies or dominions of European settlement. These differences suggested that while the Irish enjoyed less freedom they were likely, despite the modesty of their immediate claims, in the long run to demand more than their colonial contemporaries. Even their constitutional leaders talked not of concessions to be granted but of rights to be acknowledged. They deemed themselves to be the spokesmen not of colonists but of an ancient people. They referred to the Irish race and to the Irish nation. No man, said Parnell in words later inscribed around the plinth of his statue in O'Connell Street, can fix a boundary to the march of a nation. In moments of foreboding, British statesmen of all parties feared that this might be precisely true.

While Home Rule was championed by one of the great English parties as a means of strengthening the union by timely but carefully circumscribed concession, no British party or statesman advocated colonial or dominion status for Ireland. Nor did the members of the Irish Parliamentary Party, with the qualified exception of John Redmond, ordinarily think along such lines – despite their pointed references in the debates on the Commonwealth of Australia and South Africa Bills, to the liberties still denied to Irishmen but to be extended to Australians and South Africans; Tim Healy on the former occasion not missing the opportunity of taunting 'the Right Hon. Gentleman, the colonial secretary' with an enquiry as to why it was that he 'and all his friends, who took so large a part in endeavouring to defeat the [second] Home Rule Bill, do not think it necessary upon this occasion to move any of the Amendments which they considered were so absolutely vital seven years ago', and with a suggestion that it might be because an Irishman was not to 'be trusted with Home Rule unless he has first been transported'.[16] At a fundamental level however both British and Irish leaders could neither overlook nor discount the differences between Ireland and the dominions. The Irish were not, even if some of their leaders were, of settler stock; they felt rather as Europeans and, even the constitutionalists among them, were mindful of the revolutionary, nationalist currents that filled their sails. Those revolutionary forces were anti-British and in the main anti-monarchical even before they became dogmatically republican. For those reasons alone the goal of British settler communities overseas could hardly be the goal of Irish nationalism. Yet the question seemingly remained at least debatable until 1916 whether despite such identifiable and natural differences the Irish might not be reconciled to partnership within the Empire on the basis of responsible government. After all, in immediate purposes and broad objectives there was much in common between Ireland and the dominions and it might be the course of wisdom not to seek to probe the secrets of a more or less remote future. In Canada, Australia, New Zealand and in English-speaking South Africa the colonists had sought domestic self-government in the first instance: they had then pressed for its bounds to be extended into areas of government hitherto reserved to the imperial authority; and ultimately they were to seek its reinterpretation and redefinition in terms of national autonomy. It is true that although, so to speak, they wanted more, they did not aspire to something different. But neither, it may be (such certainly was the Gladstonian-Asquithian presumption), did the Irish before 1916. The Parnellite claim was not for separation here and now but for the restoration of an Irish Parliament with adequate political and fiscal authority (including a right to levy tariffs), and with the passage of time and under Redmond's leadership that demand was not enlarged but diminished. No dominion in 1912 would have tolerated limitations upon its powers of domestic self-government of the kind embodied in the Third Home Rule Bill and yet the bill was warmly welcomed in spirit by the Irish constitutional party leadership. Furthermore, the aim of Sinn Féin, founded by Arthur Griffith in repudiation of constitutional methods and in the disillusioned temper of Irish politics that followed the fall of Parnell, while revolutionary in the sense that it involved the rejection of the authority of the British parliament – an authority in Griffith's view without legal foundation, having been 'usurped' in 1800 – was also conservative and traditionalist in its professed purpose of substituting for the single crown of the United Kingdom an Anglo-

Irish dual monarchy on the Austro-Hungarian model of 1867.[17] This was something which despite its continental and revolutionary – as distinct from Commonwealth evolutionary – conceptual origins would hardly have chilled the blood of that staunch and very British conservative Canadian, Sir John A. Macdonald, with his dreams of a vast kingdom in North America associated forever with the British Crown.

It is however quite wrong to suppose the Irish at any time before 1921 rejected dominion status. They were not offered it. The British parties were united in excluding them from it. The division between the parties was on Home Rule – something altogether more limited. But in 1914, when the hour of final frustration for the Irish Parliamentary party had struck, popular revulsion against the humiliating ineffectiveness of constitutional methods opened the way psychologically for the revival of a revolutionary nationalism relying upon physical force and a blood sacrifice to win independence. It received its classic expression in Pádraic Pearse's graveside oration for O'Donovan Rossa, the venerable Fenian, at Glasnevin in 1915:

> Life springs from death: and from the graves of patriot men and women spring living nations. The defenders of this realm have worked well in secret and in the open. They think that they have pacified Ireland. They think that they have purchased half of us and intimidated the other half. They think that they have foreseen everything, think that they have provided against everything; but the fools, the fools, the fools! – they have left us our Fenian dead, and while Ireland holds these graves, Ireland unfree shall never be at peace.[18]

Here was the spirit that was behind the Easter Rising and that inspired the Proclamation of the republic, in the name of God and of the dead generations'. The executions that followed, 'few but corroding' in Churchill's words,[19] served in time only to harden the temper and extend the area of revolt. They also changed the nature of the political debate. It was no longer, except in form, about the concession by Britain of Home Rule to Ireland, but about the relationship nationalist Ireland might be prepared or compelled to accept with Britain and the Empire.

At the Sinn Féin Árd-fheis, 1917, Arthur Griffith's concept of a dual monarchy was discarded, an incidental casualty, so to speak, of deepening Anglo-Irish antagonism, and a new constitution was adopted, stating that Sinn Féin aimed at securing 'the international recognition of Ireland as an independent Irish republic' and that, having achieved that status, 'the Irish people may by referendum choose their own form of government'. But all the emphasis was on republican achievement, not on the ultimate (and soon largely to be forgotten) libertarian goal. It was for a republic that the martyrs of 1916 had died; it was, in Fintan

Lalor's phrase, 'the banner that floats nearest to the sky'. It was under this banner that the Irish revolt gathered momentum.

In the post-war general election, the results of which were declared on 28 December 1918, Sinn Féin republican candidates captured seventy-three seats; the Unionists twenty-six (chiefly in their north-eastern strongholds), and the constitutional nationalists a miserable remnant of six. Twenty-four of the thirty-two counties of Ireland had returned none but republican members. The republican majority convened an Assembly of Ireland (*Dáil Éireann*), to be composed of all elected members and to act as an independent Constituent Assembly of the Irish nation. At its first meeting on 21 January 1919 the establishment of the Irish republic was ratified, the independence of Ireland declared and the elected representatives of the Irish people alone vested with authority to make laws binding on the people.[20] Further, and in accord with Griffith's programme, Sinn Féin administration was established, technically at least responsible to the *Dáil*, which during the succeeding years of guerilla warfare operated side by side with the disintegrating machinery of British controlled government from Dublin Castle. Behind the conflict of arms there existed a conflict of ideas, no longer only in the form of political abstractions but clothed now in partial reality.

The ideological conflict, susceptible in itself of no easy solution, developed immediately in passionate intensity, partly because of the nature of the Anglo-Irish conflict 1919–21, but at a deeper level – because with 1916 the spirit of compromise departed from Anglo-Irish relations. W. B. Yeats had clothed a moment of history, weighty with consequence, in poetic immortality:

'O but we talked at large before
The sixteen men were shot,
But who can talk of give and take,
What should be and what not
While those dead men are loitering there
To stir the boiling pot?'

More prosaically but altogether realistically an Australian historian later wrote of the 'dreadful tyranny of the dead' that hung thereafter over Irishmen who thought of or engaged in negotiation with England. But even this was not the whole truth. Behind 1916 lay a revolutionary tradition which had claimed many martyrs down the centuries. The 'tyranny' (if that remains *le mot juste*) was of more than the dead of 1916; it was also of those who had died before them creating and confirming a tradition which itself, as Pearse's words by the graveside of O'Donovan Rossa themselves signified, inspired the Easter Rising. When the time came for negotiation with England, the Irish approach was conditioned immediately by memories of 1916 but in historic perspective by this tradition to which Easter 1916 provided an actual and a symbolic climax.[21]

Had dominion status and membership of the British Commonwealth of Nations, conceived and developed elsewhere in terms of compromise, anything to offer against a background and in a situation such as this? The Irish had risen in revolt not to establish an Irish republic at some distant date but to secure recognition for a polity already claimed to be in existence – the republic, in the Irish view (first stated in 1916 and re-stated in the Declaration of Dáil Éireann in January 1919) deriving *de jure* existence from the indefeasible national right of the people to determine a nation's destiny. This was a concept which by its nature did not admit of compromise. It was also a concept altogether alien to the Commonwealth tradition, with its notion of ultimate authority residing in the Crown in Parliament and to be delegated only by legislative enactment or Order in Council. The surprising thing remains not that a dominion status settlement in Ireland proved to be a source of controversy but that one was ever made. The surprise is the greater because of the British reaction to armed protest in Ireland. It was not in favour of concessions on dominion, let alone on national lines. What the Unionists had disputed in the face of constitutional pressure before the war, the Coalition government, Unionist-dominated, seemed equally prepared, between 1919–21, to deny to physical force.

Under the Government of Ireland Act 1920, Ireland was partitioned. The north-eastern counties, where before 1914 the Unionist majority had enrolled in an Ulster Volunteer Force to resist Home Rule for all-Ireland, accepted the regional Home Rule – embodied in the Act as a means whereby they might order their affairs apart from the rest of Ireland and united with Great Britain. Elsewhere in Ireland Home Rule and partition were uncompromisingly repudiated. Force was met with force. Winston Churchill recorded that by the end of 1920 there were two alternatives before the Coalition government; 'war with the utmost violence or peace with the utmost patience'.[22] With the Black and Tans and the Auxiliary Police, to outward appearance, Lloyd George had adopted the former. But where was it intended to lead? And against whom was the violence directed? The answer to the first question was implicit in the official response to the second. Force was directed against Sinn Féin, designated as an illegal and unrepresentative terrorist organisation. Its illegality under British proclamation was indisputable but even in a British context its unrepresentative character seemed questionable. Sinn Féin candidates had swept the twenty-six counties in the general election of 1918. They had assembled to legislate for Ireland as *Dáil Eireann* in January 1919. The *Dáil* was banned, its members proscribed. But could that be given as evidence that they did not represent popular opinion? Such indeed was the theory. Force was being employed, in Lloyd George's phrase, against 'a small nest of assassins'. It was a theory that allowed rational justification for acquiescence in the supposed insistence of Unionists within the Coalition government that the union should be maintained at all costs. It was one which also provided rather flimsy moral cover for a policy of authorised reprisals. It was a 'murder gang' that was to be rounded up. 'We have murder by the throat', declared Lloyd George at the Guildhall Banquet in November 1920. The British government would not rest, boasted Sir Hamar Greenwood, chief secretary for Ireland, 'till we have knocked the last revolver from the last assassin's hand'. With King George v, as with many of his subjects, this language carried no great conviction. When (also in November 1920) Greenwood assured the king's private secretary that 'everywhere the move is upward towards improvement', the king felt obliged to question the correctness of his diagnosis and to complain of his oversanguine representation of the course of events.[23] In succeeding months public opinion in Britain and in the dominions overseas showed signs of increasing dismay. 'If the British Commonwealth can only be preserved by such means', declared the Round Table,[24] 'it would become a negation of the principle for which it has stood. In the early summer of 1921 Lloyd George, under pressure, abruptly changed course. He abandoned almost overnight the policy of violence and substituted one of negotiation. 'No British government in modern times,' commented Winston Churchill, 'has ever appeared to make so complete and sudden a reversal of policy.'[25] In May the whole power of the state and all the influence of the Coalition were being used to 'hunt down the murder gang'; in June the goal was a 'lasting reconciliation with the Irish people'. That reversal was symbolised in an invitation of 24 June from Lloyd George to Eamon de Valera, described in a face-saving formula as 'the chosen leader of the great majority in Southern Ireland', to a conference in London. From this initiative there followed a truce dating from noon on 11 July.

On the British side the basis of negotiation was dominion status for Ireland. Lloyd George made that clear from the outset in official pronouncements, in speech and – with carefully contrived dramatic effects – at his first meeting with de Valera. It was in the cabinet room at 10 Downing Street on 14 July 1921. Lloyd George's secretary had never seen him so excited as he was just before the meeting. He had a big map of the British Empire hung up on the wall, 'with its great blotches of red all over it', and his secretary commented to him that he was 'bringing up all his guns!' When prime minister and 'chosen leader' met, Lloyd George, with studied deliberation, pointed to the chairs around the table at which dominion leaders sat at the Imperial Conference – there was Meighen's, representative of English and French Canadians united in one dominion; there was Massey's from New Zealand; there was Australia's Billy Hughes; there was Smuts', with the general symbolising in person the reconciliation of Boer and Briton in a sisterhood of free nations. Then Lloyd George looked long and fixedly at the remaining chair. De Valera knew he was expected to ask for whom it was reserved. He declined to do so. So Lloyd George was left to tell him it was for Ireland. 'All we ask you to do,' he said, 'is to take your place in this sisterhood of free nations.' It was an open and (it may be thought) a handsome invitation. If however the Irish did not accept it, if they persisted in thoughts of a republic rather than a dominion, then Lloyd George, reminding de Valera of the troops that would soon be coming home from Mesopotamia and the 'trouble-spots' of Empire, looked anxiously to the dreadful consequences that would follow.[26] In its bare essentials, then, Lloyd George's offer was dominion status, with Irish rejection of it meaning renewed warfare on an intensified scale. From this position Lloyd George never departed in the course of his subsequent correspondence with de Valera or in the protracted negotiations in London which culminated in the signature of the treaty in the early hours of 6 December 1921.

Under the terms of the treaty, Ireland became a dominion. In a document of many ambiguities there was at least no ambiguity on that point. The first Article stated that Ireland should have the same constitutional status in the community of Nations known as the British Empire as the Dominion of Canada, the Commonwealth of Australia, the Dominion of New Zealand and the Union of South Africa. The second and third Articles of the treaty defined the Irish position more closely by saying that her relation to the imperial Parliament and government should be that of the Dominion of Canada, and that the governor-general should be appointed in like manner as Canadian governors-general. The fourth Article prescribing the terms of the Oath, which Lord Birkenhead (regrettably enough) may *not* have described as 'the greatest piece of prevarication in history', made particular reference to Irish membership of the group of nations forming the British Commonwealth of Nations, the description thereby acquiring official documentary status for the first time. But while the provisions of the treaty left no room for doubt about the fact that the Irish Free State was to be a dominion, they invited two larger questions – why dominion status for Ireland? and what in fact was a dominion?

Why was dominion status extended to Ireland? There is a simple answer. It was imposed by the British. Certainly from the outset of the negotiations dominion status was (with qualifications) the favoured

British solution. On 20 July Lloyd George expressed his hope that 'the Irish people may find as worthy and as complete an expression of their political and spiritual ideals within the Empire as any of the numerous and varied nations united in allegiance to His Majesty s Throne'.[27] It is true that the dominion status which he then contemplated was a qualified dominion status. It permitted, among other things, no protective tariffs. De Valera rightly commented that 'the principle of the pact' was not 'easy to determine'. But it was not unqualified dominion status that de Valera sought. It was not dominion status at all. Accordingly the removal in subsequent negotiation of the more important of the limitations, including those on Irish fiscal autonomy, in no way altered the fact that it was the solution favoured by the British. It was finally accepted by the Irish Plenipotentiaries in London following upon an ultimatum – the word was Churchill's – and on pain of a resumption of immediate and terrible war – the phrase was de Valera's. Is the simple answer then a sufficient one, namely that dominion status was indeed imposed by the British? Not really; it is misleading in so far as such a view implies that dominion status was altogether objectionable to the Irish and altogether acceptable to the British. It was neither.

The problem central to the whole issue was indicated in Lloyd George's question to de Valera at the climax of their exchanges by correspondence seeking to find an agreed basis of negotiations – how might the association of Ireland with the community of nations known as the British Empire best be reconciled with Irish national aspirations? The answer, in the Irish view, was not by dominion status. On this, so far as existing knowledge goes, the *Dáil* cabinet in the summer of 1921 were unanimous. Their demand was for a republic, externally associated if need be, and by way of reasonable concession, with the British Commonwealth. And it was with suggestions to the same end that they sought to counter British proposals for dominion status. In respect of form the two ideas were incompatible. Republican status implicit in external association was inconsistent with dominion status. In one sense this was all-important. Lloyd George and de Valera, however much they might differ on lesser matters, agreed on what was fundamental. For both men it was the symbols of sovereignty that signified most. But their agreement ended there; Lloyd George never failing, during the long correspondence that preceded the negotiations, in his insistence that the monarchical symbolism of the Crown must be the essential feature of any settlement, and de Valera resolved that the republic should not be sacrificed. It is true that de Valera did not phrase it in quite that way. What he said was that Ireland's right to choose for herself 'the path she shall take to realise her own destiny must be accepted as indefeasible'. But the meaning was clear. The exercise of that right at the time meant in fact a republic. In this conflict the British view prevailed, or was imposed, with dominion status. It was the Crown not the republic that was embodied in the treaty and later, in a form as diluted as its draftsmen could devise, in the constitution of the Irish Free State. This presence of the Crown in the constitution, with its necessary corollary of an Oath of Allegiance, was a distinguishing feature common to all dominions of dominion status. Inevitably it was this feature that attracted attention and resentment in nationalist Ireland. It symbolised the nature of the settlement. Whether it was in fact the most important feature of the settlement is a matter on which Irishmen were, and long remained, deeply divided.

There was in any case more to dominion status than the symbolism of the monarchy. There was the expanding, though still debatable, area of freedom. At the Imperial Conference held in the summer of 1921, dominion statesmen, who showed themselves much concerned to ensure a peaceful settlement of the Irish question, debated (as has already been noted) the present extent and possible future enlargement of their autonomy. They were well aware, and were reminded by W. M. Hughes, that while they had entered the first world war as British colonies, they ended it as separate signatories to the peace treaties at Versailles and as foundation members of the new international organisation, the League of Nations. Two among them, Canada and South Africa, were seeking to secure for themselves a wider independence in international affairs so that they might, for example, assume international obligations or not assume them, as their own parliaments and governments saw fit, enter treaties or not enter into them as their own governments decided and generally to be in no way obliged to follow British foreign policies. It is true that the growing practice of equality was still counterbalanced by a surviving theory of subordination. But might not theory under dominion pressure increased, as it would be, by the coming into existence of an Irish dominion, soon be brought in line with practice? It is true also that there was the fear, strongly voiced by President de Valera and by Erskine Childers, lest in the case of Ireland geographical propinquity would mean a diminution of dominion powers. But, against that, would the overseas dominions readily acquiesce in any such curtailment? In sum, however these things might be regarded, was there not at least a prospect that, in terms of independence, Irish national aspirations might be reconciled with membership of the community of nations known as the British Commonwealth through dominion status? Certainly it did not concede republican symbolism, but it did provide at least a good deal of the substance of what Sinn Féin had been fighting for. There were accordingly assets in respect of power and practice to offset liabilities in respect of constitutional form. With dominion status Ireland at least would pass altogether beyond the constricting limits of Home Rule.

If the argument be accepted that dominion status was not without advantages to the Irish, it was assuredly not without objection for the British. Moreover, what was especially attractive about it to the Irish side, namely the prospect of expanding freedom, was precisely what was most objectionable about it to critics of the Irish settlement on the British side. If Lloyd George's approach to dominion status for Ireland was unusually devious there was at least a reason for it. He remained the Liberal leader of a Coalition cabinet dependent on the support of a great Unionist majority for survival in office. This majority may not have been made up (as was alleged after the 1918 election and widely publicised by J. M. Keynes) of a lot of hard-faced men who looked as if they had done well out of the war, but at any rate it was made up of men for the most part hostile and in some few cases almost pathologically hostile to the idea of a self-governing Ireland. They talked about Lloyd George as 'the great little man who had won the war' but in matters on which emotion ran high he was not a free agent. He was the prisoner of the Coalition, a prisoner who more than once, so Tom Jones has recorded, thought of escape by resignation.[28] It was not Lloyd George but his defeated and much condemned predecessor Asquith who first among British statesmen, in 1919, formally proposed dominion status for Ireland. The proposal was received by Unionists with a storm of protest. That was partly because of the intensity of their campaign against the former Liberal leader but chiefly because of what they feared would be the consequences. Bonar Law, leader of the Unionist Party in the Coalition and well remembered for his pre-war assault on the third Home Rule Bill, gave one telling reason for this. The connection of the dominions with the Empire, he warned the House of Commons in 1920, depended upon themselves. If they 'chose tomorrow,' he said, 'to say "We will no longer make a part of the British Empire" we would not try to force them'.[29] Dominion status for Ireland therefore might and probably would mean first secession then an independent republic. The very idea of dominion status must accordingly be resisted root and branch. Until the summer of 1921 Lloyd George gave every appearance of doing so. Further dominion status proposals from Asquith elicited from him the comment 'was ever such lunacy proposed by anybody?' That was in October 1920. In July 1921 however he warmly commended a dominion status settlement to de Valera. This time the suggestion had come (immediately at least) not from a British but from a Commonwealth source.

On 13 June 1921 General Smuts, in England for the Imperial

Conference, lunched with King George V at Windsor Castle. He found the king 'anxiously preoccupied'[30] about the speech he was shortly to deliver at the opening of the Northern Ireland Parliament. No draft had been submitted to the King by the Irish Office though reputedly 'a blood-thirsty document' had been composed. General Smuts suggested something altogether different. He prepared a draft of which he sent one copy to the king and another with a covering letter to Lloyd George. In the letter he spoke of the Irish situation as 'an unmeasured calamity' and 'a negation of all the principles of government which we have professed as the basis of Empire, and it must more and more tend to poison both our Empire relations and our foreign relations'. He suggested that the king's speech in Belfast should contain a promise of dominion status for Ireland, a promise which he felt sure would have the support of the dominion prime ministers then gathering in London. But, he warned 'such a declaration would not be a mere kite, but would have to be adopted by you as your policy . . . '. Lloyd George, who alone could advise the king, was not prepared to adopt it and the promise was not made. But the king's speech contained an anxious and moving plea for peace and understanding and it was shortly thereafter that negotiations were opened. Nor is it to be doubted that General Smuts had given new point and urgency to the idea of dominion status for Ireland. Indeed, in a little more than a month after his conversation with the king, Lloyd George formally submitted proposals for an Irish settlement on a dominion basis. And even if that offer was hedged about with reservations and qualifications, as indeed it was, from the British point of view the offer was decisive. It was one to which the majority of the Coalition's supporters were instinctively opposed. Their hearts had been with the prime minister when he denounced dominion status as insanity; against him when he recommended it as a basis of settlement. Yet in England there was one thing greatly in its favour.

Dominion status was an experiment that had been tried elsewhere and had succeeded. The union of the English and French in the dominion of Canada continued to be thought of as a major triumph of English statesmanship overseas, whilst fresh in the minds of Lloyd George, Austen Chamberlain and Winston Churchill was the success of the policy of trust and reconciliation which brought into being the Union of South Africa. Austen Chamberlain, leader of the Unionist party at the time (because of Bonar Law's temporary withdrawal through illness), said explicitly in defence of an Irish dominion settlement, that it was the success of Liberal policies in South Africa in bringing a South African dominion into existence which more than anything else persuaded him to break with his party's and his family's tradition.[31] In England it is always much easier to take a revolutionary step if it can be said at the same time 'we have travelled this road before'. But in Ireland the advance was to be by untrodden ways.

That might not have mattered quite so much but for one thing. Dominion status lacked precision being traditionally conceived of not as something possessing final form at any given point in time but as something in process of continuing development. In negotiation this was an undoubted liability. Uncertainties implicit in the status served greatly to accentuate mistrust and suspicion, the British coming to regard President de Valera as 'a visionary' likely to see mountains where they saw only molehills, while the Irish thought of Lloyd George as a master of political dexterity – not to say duplicity – who used the liberal-imperial vocabulary of Gladstone to further the purposes of Castlereagh. Yet at root the problem was more than personal. It was not easy to state concisely and with precision especially at that juncture in time, what dominion status for Ireland would involve.

In the House of Commons debate on the Treaty, Lloyd George asked himself, 'what does dominion status mean?' But he did not answer it. He talked instead, and by no means unreasonably, of the dangers of definition, of limiting development by too many finalities, of introducing rigidities alien to British constitutional thinking. He was prepared to say what dominion status did not mean. But not what it did. The treaty itself was no more helpful. It defined dominion status by analogy, that is, by saying that the status of the Irish Free State would be that of the other dominions, which it listed by name, and more particularly that of Canada. The British prime minister was prepared to go no further. Nor were the dominions themselves well placed to do so. When the Irish tried, as some of them did, to look at dominion status through the eyes of the dominions, there were unhelpful obscurities in what they could discern.

In one sense it was very timely that the dominions should be debating their own status at an Imperial Conference in the summer of 1921. But the debate, for a prospective but highly sceptical partner, was hardly sufficiently conclusive. There was General Smuts seeking to have dominion status more clearly defined. Certainly he repudiated Empire and championed Commonwealth. But it was part of his argument that the dominions, while they enjoyed a large measure of equality in practice, were subordinate to the United Kingdom in law and constitutional form. Smuts might want the theory brought into line with practice. But the majority did not. Chief among them was the Australian prime minister, W. M. Hughes. He contended forthrightly that there was no need to define imperial relations. 'The difference between the status of the dominions now and twenty-five years ago', he said, 'is very great. We were colonies, we became dominions. We have been accorded the status of nations. . . . What greater advance is conceivable? What remains to us? We are like so many Alexanders. What other worlds have we to conquer?'[32] The Irish leaders, had they had the opportunity, could have told him of the other worlds they wished to conquer. But would dominion status enable them to do so? At that crucial moment in the summer of 1921 when it was first formally proposed for Ireland, and even more in the *Dáil* debates on the treaty some six months later, it was hard, if only because of this still unresolved dominion debate, for the Irish or indeed for anyone else to answer that question, for in order to do so it was necessary first to forecast how dominion relations would develop – and how difficult that was can be imagined by asking, for instance, now, what relations between the countries composing the European Common Market are likely to be in the year 2000.

It is now known that the tide of dominion nationalism was flowing too strongly to be checked. 'The fact of Canadian and South African independence,' said Michael Collins in the treaty debate in the *Dáil* 'is something real and solid, and will grow in reality and force as time goes on.' That certainly proved to be true. He was right too in saying: 'We have got rid of the word "Empire". For the first time in an official document the former empire is styled "The Community of Nations known as the British Empire".'[33] Kevin O'Higgins, who like most supporters of the treaty did not believe that dominion status was the fulfilment of Ireland's destiny, hoped none the less that what remained would be won by agreement and by peaceful political evolution. That too proved substantially true. Dominion status, despite the fears of some of its critics and (perhaps even more important) despite the forms with which it was still enshrouded, conferred a substantial measure of freedom and opened the way for complete independence. This might have been more generally recognized at the time but for one thing. Kevin O'Higgins put his finger on it when he said that the most objectionable aspect of the treaty was the threat of force that had been used to influence Ireland to a decision to enter what he called 'this miniature league of nations'. He went on: 'It has been called a league of free nations. I admit in practice it is so; but it is unwise and unstatesmanlike to attempt to bind any such league by any ties other than pure voluntary ties. . . . I quite admit in the case of Ireland the tie is not voluntary . . . the status is not equal.'[34] Ireland was forced into a free association. That contradiction, that handicap, laid upon dominion status when Lloyd George foreclosed debate on 5 December 1921 with an ultimatum, clung to it like an old man of the sea, shaken off only when dominion status itself was discarded.

Many particular objections to dominion status were raised in the treaty debate – objections to the subordination that it might mean in respect of the Crown or its representative, the governor-general, or the armed forces or the judiciary. But in fact such limitations upon Irish (or for that matter upon dominion) sovereignty did not survive very long. At the first Imperial Conference at which the Irish played an active part, in 1926, the actual process of redefining Commonwealth relations was begun. In 1931, with the enactment of the statute of Westminster, what remained of the old colonial Empire had been pulled asunder and the Irish minister for External Affairs, Patrick McGilligan, had reason for claiming in the *Dáil* that the Irish had played a large part in doing it. In that sense dominion status gave freedom to achieve freedom. It may not have been the goal but it had opened the way to the goal. The road to the goal was, however, slow and winding and young men brought up in time of revolutionary change generally prefer to travel by faster ways.

But, probing a little further, as the historian should, the problem central to the debate in 1921 appears in another light. How might the association of Ireland with the community of nations known as the British Empire best be reconciled with Irish national aspirations? Canadians and Australians had advanced with satisfaction from colonial to dominion status. This was the road along which they wished to travel. They felt it was a road along which it was natural they should travel. They were countries of settlement. In Ireland there were counties of settlement – in the north-east. In the dominion their inclusion was the natural, their exclusion the illogical thing. For the rest, Ireland was not a country of settlement. It was one of the historic nations of Europe. It was not extra-European but European national symbolism to which it aspired. The republic, not dominion status, was the goal. The point was put with characteristic forthrightness by Austin Stack in the treaty debate. Assuming that under the treaty Ireland would enjoy 'full Canadian powers', 'I for one,' he declared, 'cannot accept from England full Canadian powers, three-quarter Canadian powers, or half Canadian powers. I stand for what is Ireland's right, full independence and nothing short of it.'[35] What was natural and appropriate for the existing dominions would in effect be unnatural and inappropriate at any rate for a partitioned Ireland. The countries that were dominions in 1921 might seek independence, but Ireland was seeking something more as well – independence and recognition of a separate national identity. Dominion status at that time might lead to the one without necessarily including the other. And to that extent dominion status was conceived, and well conceived, but for another situation. And in so far as the British believed that by conceding dominion status to Ireland she would become a dominion psychologically as well as constitutionally they were mistaken.

And at this point one comes back to a simple but basic fact: dominion status in 1921 was not compatible with republican status. Allegiance to the Crown was then an essential feature of it. That allegiance had to be expressed in the form of an oath. That oath was embodied in the treaty; it was embodied in the constitution and it could not be removed (because of a fundamental status given to the provisions of the treaty by the Constitution Act) without denouncing the treaty and dominion status of which the oath, at British insistence, was an integral part. It was because this was so that de Valera said in the treaty debate: 'I am against the treaty, because it does not do the fundamental thing and bring us peace.' And again he protested: 'I am against this treaty because it does not reconcile Irish national aspirations with association with the British government . . . I am against this treaty because it will not end the centuries of conflict between the two nations of Great Britain and Ireland.' And why? Because the treaty did not recognise, as de Valera claimed external association would have done, the separate, distinct existence of a republic. On the contrary, it gave away republican independence by bringing Ireland as a dominion within the British Empire and more precisely, as he said, by according recognition to the king as the source of executive authority in Ireland. 'Does this Assembly,' he asked, 'think the Irish people have changed so much within the past year or two that they now want . . . to choose the person of the British monarch, whose forces they have been fighting against . . . as their monarch?'[36] And so against the substance (in part still prospective) of freedom there had to be placed the abandonment of the symbolism which expressed national aspirations and the acceptance of another. The distinction between dominion status and external association was sharp rather than broad and that helps to explain why the division that ensued was deep and lasting. There are times when constitutional forms express the things that for many men matter most and this was one of them.

It was because this was so that the debate on dominion status in Ireland – it sounds paradoxical but is nevertheless true – enlarged the experience of the British Commonwealth of Nations and had an interest far beyond its frontiers. The question posed in 1921 might be rephrased to read: How may national, republican aspirations best be reconciled with a monarchical, imperial or commonwealth status system? The suggested answer on the Irish side was external association, something that would possess the substance of dominion states but replace its monarchical with republican forms. In 1921 that solution was deemed impossible of consideration, as politically it then was, by the British negotiators. India, a historic nation of another continent, later posed the same problem, coupled with an explicit wish to remain a member-state of the Commonwealth as a republic. Profiting by Irish experience with which many leading members of the Indian constituent assembly were fully familiar, the problem of republican India's relations with the Commonwealth was resolved in 1949; the formula by which India acknowledged the king as Head of the Commonwealth being virtually identical with the formula proposed by President de Valera for the same purpose in Document No. 2 in 1922. The Commonwealth henceforward allowed complete constitutional as well as political equality, its member states being monarchical or republican as they themselves desired. But by the time the Commonwealth had found the answer the Irish had lost interest in the question.

CHAPTER 8

STATUS SEEKING AND TARIFF REFORM, 1921–36

Two fundamental questions of dominion status remained unresolved after the Imperial Conference 1921. The first, discarded but not disposed of by the Conference, was the necessity or otherwise of redefining British-dominion relations in terms that would bring law into line with conventional practice on a basis of equality, or near-equality. The second, entangled with the first but distinguishable from it, was the international status of the dominions. The answers to both questions were sought and found in the decade 1921–31 against a pattern of imperial relations determined for the most part in distant pre-war years. The nature of that pattern conditioned both the dominion demand for change and the formulae and statutory forms in which it was ultimately effected. The structure of the British imperial system, as it emerged from the first world war, is accordingly the appropriate starting-point for an enquiry into the reasons for, and the manner of its subsequent transformation. There was an imperial, as well as dominion – nationalist, premise to the Commonwealth conclusion.

The outline of the system was clear.[1] The king in Parliament was sovereign throughout the Empire. In theory he could act, and Parliament at Westminster could legislate, for the whole Empire. Laws extending to the dominions, it is true, were no longer enacted by the imperial Parliament, but the legal competence of that Parliament to do so was in no way impaired. The constitutions of all the dominions, including that of the Irish Free State enacted in 1922, were embodied in British Acts of Parliament and in the view of British and dominion governments, other than that of the Irish Free State, derived authority from them. By way of logical counterpart to this overriding British legislative competence went continuing British control over colonial and dominion legislation. In every case the assent of the sovereign's representative, the governor-general, was essential to the valid enactment of dominion legislation. In theory at least it was not to be thought of as necessarily forthcoming, since the governor-general in each dominion remained entitled either to withhold such assent or to reserve a bill for the signification of the sovereign's pleasure by Order in Council. Furthermore, even when the assent of the governor-general had been given, it lay within the discretionary authority of the Crown to disallow a dominion Act. It is true, once again, that these powers were deemed obsolescent or even obsolete in practice, but dominion objection to their theoretic survival persisted. There were other relics of imperial control which if also obsolescent were evidently not yet altogether obsolete. There was the Colonial Laws Validity Act, 1865, which *inter alia* declared that any Colonial Legislation which conflicted with any of the provisions of a British Act of Parliament was to the extent of such repugnancy null and void and which, in so doing, expressly maintained the subordination of the former colonial legislatures to the Parliament of the United Kingdom. This subordination was by no means hypothetical. It was a matter of law and as *Nadan's case* was to demonstrate in 1926, the law had to be interpreted and should occasion arise, applied. In practice the Colonial Laws Validity Act also imposed limits upon dominion freedom of legislative action in respect of appeals to the judicial committee of the Privy Council, the conferment of honours and the determination of the national flag – though in the last instance the Irish Free State exceptionally was enabled to make its own unfettered choice – all being matters on which enactments by the Parliament at Westminster possessed overriding authority.

Subordination in law was paralleled by subordination in constitutional practice. The governor-general in a dominion was the representative of the Crown. But he was also the agent of the British government through whom formal communications were conveyed to dominion governments and from whom their communications to the Colonial Office were received. A governor-general, furthermore, furnished the home government with reports upon the political situation in a dominion, and should he feel so disposed or should occasion demand it, he was free to seek advice about the action he should take from the Colonial Office. In practice there was a strongly established convention that such advice should be sought only when matters of imperial interest were at stake, but it was the governor-general who remained the judge of what constituted such an interest. The dominions, other than New Zealand, disliked and had come to mistrust the duality implicit in the governor-general's rôle and sought to divest him of his politico-administrative responsibilities as an agent of the British government and so to leave him as a royally representative figure, fulfilling only the political and social duties performed by the sovereign in Great Britain. There was also the question of appointment. It had become established practice by 1921 that the government of a dominion should be consulted informally in advance about the appointment of a governor-general, so as to ensure at least that the nominee of the imperial government would not be unwelcome to them. But the initiative still rested with London. It was a reinsurance to dominion governments to have thus acquired something approaching an informal veto but it was not tantamount to possessing the right to advise. It was this on which their sights were set.

Externally it was not doubted that the first world war had brought about a significant advance in the international status of the dominions but the nature and extent of this advance remained debatable. The dominions were recognised as being completely self-governing within their own frontiers, they recruited and controlled their own armed forces, they had been brought into consultation on imperial foreign policy and they had received qualified international recognition in the making of peace and in membership of the League of Nations. But, the question remained, were they sovereign states? This was a question that could be (and was) debated in terms of international law. But it was also one to be considered in terms of international practice and it was this in which the dominions were the more immediately interested. What was their position in respect of the treaty-making power? Were they entitled to separate representation at international conferences? How was their membership of the League of Nations to be interpreted? India, also, was a member and was evidently not a sovereign state.

In 1919 the prime minister of Canada had obtained a signed Declaration from President Wilson, Clemenceau and Lloyd George stating that

> upon the true construction of the first and second paragraphs of Article 4 [of the League of Nations covenant] representatives of the self-governing dominions of the British Empire may be selected or named as members of the [League of Nations] Council.

This was intended to provide and was generally taken to represent international recognition of the dominions as separate political communities – a status which was also implicitly acknowledged in the assimilation of their position to that of all other League members in the International Labour Organisation and by the grant to them of the rank of distinct states, under the statute of the Permanent Court of International Justice in 1920.[2] But (other perhaps than by reasonable inference) such recognition registered no explicit advance in respect of sovereignty. Nor did it carry, as the Canadian government was to learn to its chagrin, any necessary consequences in respect of separate representation at international conferences. That was conditional upon the invitation or form of invitation issued by the Powers summoning the conference and the Powers in these years, the United States no less than the United Kingdom, were apt to be unmindful of dominion susceptibilities, interests and newly acquired status. The dominion response, New Zealand always excepted, was apt to be pained remonstrance and a patient resolve to establish dominion international identities in practice. Separate diplomatic representation in foreign capitals was one way in which this dominion purpose could be furthered, and in 1920 the Canadian government made the necessary arrangements for the appointment of a Canadian minister plenipotentiary to Washington. For a number of reasons (not the least of them being that no Canadian of sufficient wealth and appropriate qualifications was prepared to expend his resources on a diplomatic enterprise upon which the Canadian government saw fit to embark but not to provide for financially) the post was not filled until 1926 and in the meantime the Irish Free State had taken over the Canadian diplomatic pioneering rôle with the appointment of an Irish minister to Washington in 1924.[3]

Treaty-making proved a testing ground of status. Until 1919 dominion participation had been confined to consultation in respect of treaties in which their interests were likely to be involved, except – and it was an important exception – in the case of commercial treaties. Here the precedent established in the negotiation of the United States-Canadian Reciprocity Treaty 1854 was accepted, with the result that such treaties might be negotiated by and for any colonies that desired them even though the resulting agreement remained British in respect of formal ratification. The position was comprehensively defined in 1894, when in response to submissions from the colonial governments represented at the Conference then meeting in Ottawa, the secretary of state laid down certain principles which were in essence sustained till 1919. The colonies, Lord Ripon noted,[4] did not desire treaty-making power and it would not be possible to give it to them since that would result in the destruction of imperial unity. But separate treaties could be made with colonial co-operation for colonies that desired them, a condition of their negotiation however being that concessions from foreign states detrimental to the interests of other parts of the Empire should not be accepted and that concessions to foreign states should be extended to all other powers entitled by treaty to most-favoured-nation treatment and *gratis* to all other parts of the Empire. The application of these principles was variously tested before 1914 but always within the agreed framework of a single imperial treaty-making authority.

How much was changed in theory by the procedures adopted in the signing of the peace treaties in 1919? The United Kingdom delegates, it will be recalled, then signed for the Empire as a whole. In so far as their signatures were to be regarded as possessing overriding authority, it could reasonably be contended that while there had been concessions to dominion sentiment in practice, the principle of a single imperial treaty-making authority remained unimpaired. Sir Robert Borden would have preferred a different procedure, with the United Kingdom signatures limited to Britain and the dependent Empire and dominion signatures separately for each dominion, so as to signify the existence of separate dominion treaty-making powers. But all that he obtained was the deferment of United Kingdom ratification of the peace treaty, pending approval by dominion parliaments.[5] This was a concession which was significant in an imperial context without, once again, being conclusive internationally. There was, accordingly, carried over into the 1920s an unresolved British-dominion debate about the nature of dominion treaty-making power, behind which lay the larger theoretic questions of international status and more immediate practical issues of the making and control of imperial foreign policy.

In 1911 Asquith had declared that responsibility for foreign policy could never be shared. During the war years it was shared. But did dominion participation in the making of foreign policy in the imperial war cabinet mean that there had come into being a system of joint British-dominion responsibility for the making of imperial foreign policy? The procedures adopted for the negotiation of the peace treaties and for the signature of the Treaty of Versailles suggested (with certain qualifications) that such was the case. Furthermore, the notion of such joint responsibility survived the disappearance of the imperial war cabinet. So much was apparent from the argument of the Colonial Office paper on *A Common Imperial Policy in Foreign Affairs*[6] submitted to the cabinet in March 1921, preparatory to the Imperial Conference of that year. The paper noted the changes that had taken place during the war. 'Before the Great War,' it recalled, 'the direction of foreign policy was in theory and in practice vested in His Majesty's government.' Apart from occasional consultation on particular issues

> the general foreign policy of the Empire, while in fact largely influenced by consideration for the known policies and interests of the dominions and India, was still shaped and controlled by ministers whose only direct responsibility was to the Parliament of the United Kingdom.
>
> The sudden outbreak of the Great War revealed the anomaly of this state of affairs. Effective consultation during the critical days of the negotiations in which His Majesty's Government strove to avert the catastrophe was impossible and was not attempted. . . . It was clearly recognised from the very outset that such a situation could not be allowed to recur.

But how was this to be done? The Colonial Office felt that the answer was to be found in the Empire's experiences in the making of peace. The negotiations and the Treaty of Versailles were 'a landmark of the greatest significance in the constitutional development of the British Commonwealth', but of far greater practical importance, was the fact that through the British Empire delegation 'effect was given to the views and wishes of every member of the British Commonwealth as a single co-ordinated imperial policy'. With the break up of the British Empire delegation, however, 'the control of the ever changing field of foreign policy has almost entirely relapsed into the hands of the United Kingdom'. In 1920 the imperial cabinet had not met; the international situation could not be left to itself and while the dominions had been kept informed far more fully than before the war they had not had any appreciable share in shaping the policy pursued, 'though that policy may have involved consequences of the greatest moment for the whole future of the Empire'. The conclusion to be drawn, argued the Colonial Office memorandum, was not that unity of policy had become less necessary but rather that the more complete the equality of status, the less tolerable was a state of affairs 'in which one member of the group should exercise exclusive control over a policy which may involve the most vital interests and even the existence of the others'. The outstanding need was, therefore, for unity in policy, and the chief practical problem to devise a satisfactory means by ministerial representation in London, improved communications, or in some other way, by which the acknowledged difficulties of continuity of discussion might be overcome.

At the Imperial Conference, Lloyd George lent his support to ideas of unity through joint control. 'There was a time when Downing Street controlled the Empire', he told the dominion delegations at the Imperial Conference; 'today the Empire is in charge of Downing Street'. Six months later in the debate on the Anglo-Irish Treaty he was more specific. A million men had come from the dominions to help the mother land in the hour of danger. But although they had come, their governments had had no share in the making of policies that had brought Britain into the war. They should not in the future be placed in the dilemma of supporting Britain in a policy that they might or might not have approved, or of deserting her in time of trouble. Therefore there must be consultation before the event. That was right; that was just; that was advantageous. There must be one instrument of policy and in the circumstances that instrument could only be the Foreign Office. But the dominions claimed a voice in the determination of future policy and that claim, Lloyd George recalled, had been gladly conceded. At the Imperial Conference general decisions were arrived at with 'the common consent of the whole Empire'. Then, warming to his theme, the British Prime Minister moved on to his eloquent climax:

> The sole control of Britain over foreign policy is now vested in the Empire as a whole. That is a new fact. . . . The advantage to us is that joint control means joint responsibility, and when the burden of Empire has become so vast it is well that we should have the shoulders of these young giants under the burden to help us along. It introduces a broader and a calmer view into foreign policy. It restrains rash ministers and it will stimulate timorous ones. It widens the prospect.[7]

These were stirring thoughts. They invited, however, certain questions. Was not joint responsibility a mirage unless there was effective joint control? Was there effective joint control? If so, by what means was it exercised? Perhaps such questions would have been thought unreasonable, or unseasonable, at the time. Yet some nine months later Lloyd George himself, in an episode that has gone down in Commonwealth history as the Chanak incident, lent to these questions new point and dramatic urgency. The occasion was the repudiation by the young Turks, under Mustapha Kemal in 1922, of the near eastern treaty settlement. They rose up in arms and drove the Greeks headlong from Asia Minor. By early September that year the British were left at Chanak and on the Straits as the principal defenders of Constantinople against the onrush of the victorious Turkish advance. In this situation of military exposure and political peril Lloyd George decided to appeal to the dominions. On 15 September he sent a dispatch to their several prime ministers, asking whether dominion governments wished to be associated with the British stand in defence of the Straits and of the peace settlement and whether they would wish to be represented by a contingent. Even the announcement of dominion armed support, the message urged, would of itself exercise a most favourable influence on the situation and might help to prevent actual hostilities. The dispatch was followed by a statement to the Press disclosing that an appeal had been made to the dominions for contingents in defence of interests for which they had already made enormous sacrifices and 'of soil which is hallowed by immortal memories of the Anzacs'.

The response to the British prime minister's appeal was varied. New Zealand replied affirmatively and at once. The Australian reply was reassuring. So much, however, could not be said of the rejoinder from the new prime minister of Canada, William Lyon Mackenzie King. On Saturday 16 September 1922 King was in his constituency, North York, and the first he heard of the British appeal was an enquiry by a newspaper reporter about the response Canada proposed to give to it. Later he learned that the dispatch itself had in any case reached his office in Ottawa several hours after the Canadian newspapers had printed the public announcement from London. Nor had there been any information, still less the joint consultation which might have been thought of as a pre-condition of joint responsibility. The dispatch was the first and only intimation which the Canadian government had received, so King later told the Canadian House of Commons, from the British government about the impending crisis in the near east. It was all, King suspected (and throughout his life he was much given to such suspicions), an imperialist device to test out 'centralisation versus autonomy as regards European wars'. With this uppermost in his mind he decided on his reply. It had the merits of simplicity, democratic impeccability and complete impregnability. Parliament, he said, should decide. Parliament was not sitting. It would have, should circumstances demand it, to be summoned. That would take time – a circumstance as satisfying to Mackenzie King as it was frustrating to Lloyd George. There were further attempts at persuasion from London and a later protest from the Canadian Conservative leader, Arthur Meighen that the Canadian reply should have said 'Ready, aye ready; we stand by you', but Mackenzie King not only remained firm but if anything stiffened in negation. He did not stand alone; General Smuts was with him.[8] Nor was Australian opinion unanimously on the other side – Chanak was a party issue – and the government privately protested at the brusqueness of Lloyd George's appeal. Yet Chanak became a landmark in Commonwealth history, because Mackenzie King made it so.

In the immediately succeeding years there were two interpretations of the Chanak incident. The first was that it was a warning against thinking of joint responsibility without ensuring full, prior joint consultation. On this line it was argued that the Canadian prime minister was affronted because he had been neither informed nor consulted about British policy in advance. Had he been so, the argument proceeded, then the incident itself, in the form in which it actually arose, could not have occurred. Furthermore, was it not possible that, had the Canadian prime minister and his cabinet colleagues been in full possession of the facts and the dangers of the situation in the near east, they would have proved more co-operative? What was required therefore, above all, was effective machinery. But was this the correct interpretation? What had Mackenzie King in fact said? He had told the Canadian Parliament that it was neither right nor proper 'for any individual or for any group of individuals to take any step which in any way might limit the rights of Parliament in a matter which is of such great concern to all the people of our country'.[9] He was, in fact, asserting the supremacy of Parliament. On that principle he took his stand. He might have done otherwise. He might have complained, as did the Australian government, at the failure to consult or at the breakdown of all semblance of joint responsibility for the making of policy but he did neither. The reason was clear. Had such been his chief grounds for complaint then the remedy would indeed have been more effective machinery to ensure that joint responsibility became a reality. But Mackenzie King did not want joint responsibility; he felt it was a device to commit the dominions to British policies. He wanted something quite different – the disentangling of dominion from British policies. He wanted separate dominion policies, not joint imperial policies, howsoever arrived at. There was no better means of advancing his aim than by appeal to the sovereignty of Parliament. He stood then upon a rock of principle. From that rock he was not to be moved either by the cajolings of imperialists or in subsequent years by the plight of the League of Nations. King was under no misapprehensions about the wider implications of his stand. The principle he had enunciated was one that could be (and was to be) applied as effectively against international as against imperial commitments or obligations.

In retrospect the aims of Canadian policy are apt to appear deceptively clear-cut. At the time there was confusion about them, certainly in London – a confusion more pardonable perhaps than Canadian historians are apt to allow. As a result of experience during the war the British government were convinced that the dominions, Canada included, wished to participate in the making of foreign policy. This was true, broadly speaking, in respect of Australia and New Zealand and also, though with certain qualifications, of South Africa, so long as General Smuts remained in office. But in respect of Canada under Mackenzie King's Liberal administration it was a conviction well calculated to foster misunderstanding. The Canadian government desired control of foreign policy, of Canadian foreign policy, but far from being anxious to participate in the making of a common imperial or Commonwealth policy, it was anxious at all costs to be dissociated from it. For Canada the road to equality was deemed to lead not through equal participation in the making of one policy but in the separate control of several policies. Canadian emphasis was therefore consistently upon the plural 'policies' and against the singular 'policy' for the British Commonwealth of Nations, upon separateness and against the unity advocated in the Colonial Office Cabinet paper of 1921. It was this that successive British governments found difficult to grasp, despite Mackenzie King's explanations and aggrieved remonstrances.

Chanak was followed by the Canadian-United States Halibut Fisheries Treaty 1923, the Lausanne Treaty 1924, and the Locarno Pact 1925, all of which raised points of principle and two of which were the cause of Anglo-Canadian disputation. The first, the Halibut Fisheries Treaty, was negotiated by the Canadian minister of fisheries with the United States representatives, and Mackenzie King advised the British government that since the proposed treaty was of concern solely to Canada and the United States and did not affect any particular imperial interest,

Canadian origins

1 Lord Durham, by Sir Thomas Lawrence

2 The fathers of Canadian confederation in London, 1866. Seated at the far end of the table (left to right) are Sir Alexander Galt, Sir Charles Tupper (under the Queen's portrait), John A. Macdonald and Georges Cartier. Leonard Tilley sits in the left-hand corner holding a book. Lord Monck, the Governor-General, is the bearded figure standing in front

3 The Parliament Building in Ottawa. A photograph taken during the construction of the Centre Block, *c.* 1865

Railways laid in a period of expansion, settlement and development

4 Northern Railway of Canada. No. 1, 'Lady Elgin'

5 Queensland Central Railway. A viaduct built *c.* 1890

6 The first train in Pretoria, 1 January 1893

7 Rhodesia's outlet to the sea. The laying of the line from Beira to Salisbury, $52\frac{1}{2}$ miles from Fontesvilla on the Portuguese border, as photographed by the surveyor, P. St G. Mansergh, *c.* 1897

Personalities in Southern Africa

8 Lobengula, the last King of the Matabele, who on 30 October 1888, in return for £1,200 a year, 1,000 rifles, 100,000 cartridges and a steamboat on the Zambesi, assigned all mineral rights within his territories to emissaries of Cecil John Rhodes

9 Cecil John Rhodes at his camp in the Matopo Hills, from which in 1896 he rode out unarmed with two or three companions to persuade the Matabele, who had risen in rebellion, to make peace. By his own wish, Rhodes was buried in these hills

10 Oom Paul Kruger, the last President of the Transvaal Republic (1883–1901)

South Africa. War and peace

11 and 12 Colonial contributions to the war. 11 The Canadian contingent passing up Adderley Street, Cape Town, and 12 the S.S. *Moravian* leaving Woolloomooloo Bay, Sydney, with troops for South Africa from New South Wales

13 The British commander-in-chief, Sir Redvers Buller's transport waggons crossing the veldt. An artist's impressions in the high imperial style, sketched in 1900, as hopes of early British victory faded

14 Sir Henry Campbell-Bannerman, Liberal Prime Minister, December 1905–April 1908, of whom it was said by General Smuts that he 'wrote the word *Reconciliation* over that . . . African scene, and thus rendered an immortal service to the British Empire, aye, to the cause of man everywhere'

15 The Boer negotiators and signatories to the Peace of Vereeniging, 31 May 1902. General Christian de Wet (top left), F. W. Reitz (top right), Generals de la Rey and Lucas Meyer (bottom left), General Smuts, General Botha and Schalk Burger (bottom right, from the left) and the British High Commissioner, Sir Alfred (later Lord) Milner (centre)

Early days in the Pacific Colonies

16 The Founding of Australia, by Algernon Talmage, R.A., depicting the scene when the British flag was unfurled at Sydney Cove on 26 January 1788. Captain Arthur Phillip, first Governor of the Colony of New South Wales, and officers and guard of marines, are shown about to drink the health of King George III

17 Emigrants landing at Lyttelton, New Zealand, *c.* 1850

18 Washing gold by tubs and cradles at Waitahuna, Otago, where the first discoveries were made in 1861. The gold rushes brought not only wealth but much needed, if sometimes lawless, immigrants to Australia and New Zealand

SWAIN SC

THE IMPERIAL DISPENSARY.

THE KANGAROO. "I'VE GOT A SORT OF—ER—FEELING OF OPPRESSION. MY DOCTOR AT HOME GAVE ME THAT PRESCRIPTION!"

MR. CH-MB-RL-N (*Colonial Chemist and Druggist according to the British Pharmacopœia*). "'ABOLITION OF APPEAL TO PRIVY COUNCIL'—OF COURSE, I *COULD* MAKE IT UP FOR YOU, BUT I THINK I CAN GIVE YOU SOMETHING THAT WILL EXACTLY SUIT YOUR CONSTITUTION!"

19 The Imperial Dispensary, a cartoon from *Punch*, 23 May 1900

20 The inauguration of the Commonwealth of Australia, 1 January 1901. Sydney Post Office illuminated. The first Governor-General was the Earl of Hopetoun

Colonial and Imperial conferences, 1887-1911

21 The Colonial Conference, 1887, with Lord Salisbury presiding

22 The Colonial Conference, 1897. Front, left to right, R. Seddon (New Zealand), Sir Wilfrid Laurier (Canada), Joseph Chamberlain, Secretary of State for the Colonies and Chairman, G. H. Reid (New South Wales), and Sir Gordon Sprigg (Cape Colony). Immediately behind, Sir E. N. C. Braddon (Tasmania), Sir G. Turner (Victoria) and Sir W. Whiteway (Newfoundland)

THE INCOMPLETE ANGLER.

John Bull. "I DON'T SEEM TO BE DOING SO WELL AS I DID."
Joe. "WELL, IF YOU WANT TO GET THE BETTER OF THOSE FOREIGN CHAPS, YOU MUST CHOOSE YOUR FLY TO SUIT THE FISH—AS *THEY* DO!!"

23 The Incomplete Angler, a cartoon from *Punch*, 25 September 1897. The conference in 1897 marked the opening phase of the campaign for tariff reform and imperial preference

SPITHEAD. JUNE 26.

British Lion (*taking the Young Lions out to see the Great Naval Review*). "LOR' LOVE YER, MY LADS, THIS IS THE PROUDEST MOMENT OF MY LIFE!"

24 Spithead Review, 26 June 1897, a cartoon from *Punch*

25 A New Year's Greeting, a cartoon from *Punch*, 4 January 1899. Postal and telegraphic communications were important to a scattered Empire and early Colonial Conferences were concerned to make them quicker and cheaper

A NEW YEAR'S GREETING.

26 The Colonial Conference, 1907, over which the Secretary of State for the Colonies, the Earl of Elgin, presided. Front row, seated left to right, H. H. Asquith, Sir Joseph Ward, Sir Wilfrid Laurier, Lord Elgin, Alfred Deakin, R. F. Moor (Natal), D. Lloyd George. Second row (first and third from left), W. S. Churchill, Under-Secretary of State for the Colonies, and General Botha; and Dr Jameson, Prime Minister of Cape Colony 1904–8, but better remembered as a Raider (third from right)

27 The Imperial Conference, 1911, over which the Prime Minister, H. H. Asquith, presided. Front row, left to right, Sir Joseph Ward, Sir Wilfrid Laurier, Asquith, Andrew Fisher. Behind, Sir E. P. Morris (Newfoundland) and General Botha. Laurier and Botha were the key figures. 'He and I agree about everything', wrote Botha

War and peace

28 The cruiser *New Zealand* launched in 1911 and presented by the New Zealand government to the Royal Navy. 'In giving a splendid ship to strengthen the British Navy at a decisive point, wherever that point may be . . .', said the First Lord of the Admiralty, Winston Churchill, 'the Dominion of New Zealand have provided in the most effective way alike for their own and for the common security.' Canada and Australia, however, preferred to develop their own separate navies

29 King George V with New Zealand troops on the Western Front

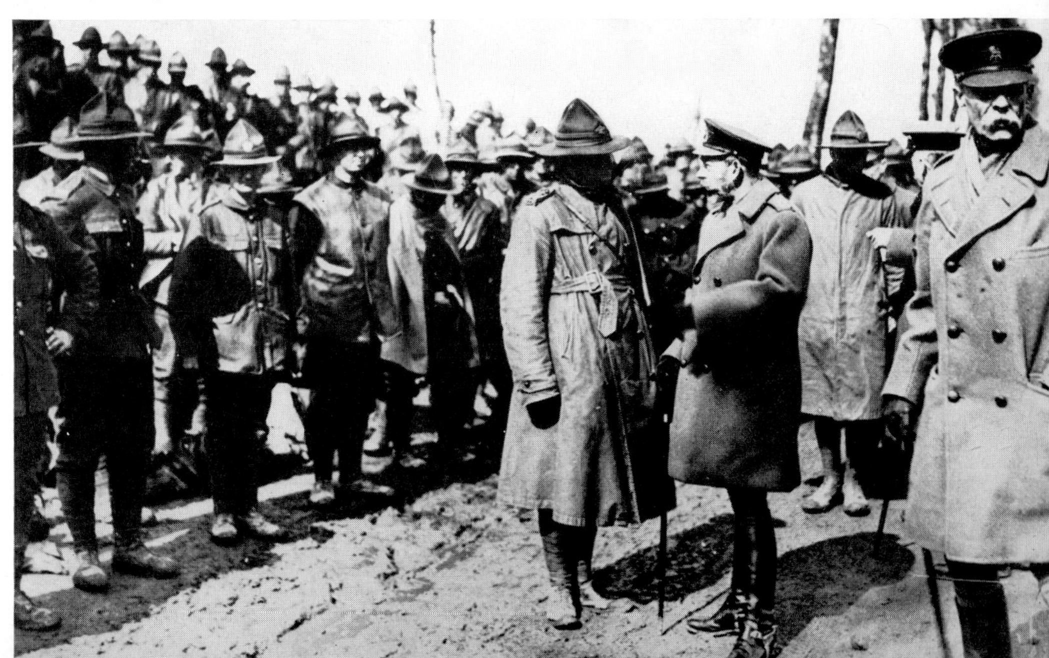

30 General Botha directing operations during the campaign in South West Africa, 1915. The German forces surrendered on 9 July 1915

31 Gallipoli. Australian and New Zealand troops landing at Anzac Cove, Dardanelles, 25 April 1915

32 Canadians in the front line trenches at Ypres, 1916

33 The Imperial War Cabinet and Conference, 1917. Front row, left to right, A. Henderson, Lord Milner, Lord Curzon, A. Bonar Law, D. Lloyd George, Sir R. Borden, W. F. Massey, General Smuts. Second row, Sir S. P. Sinha, Maharajah of Bikanir, Sir J. Meston, Austen Chamberlain, Lord R. Cecil, Walter Long, Sir J. Ward, Sir G. Perley, R. Rogers, Mr Hazen. Back row, Captain L. S. Amery, Lord Jellicoe, Sir E. Carson, Lord Derby, Sir F. Maurice, Sir M. Hankey, Sir H. Lambert, Lt-Col L. Storr

34 The British Empire delegation to the Peace Conference in Paris at Lloyd George's house in the rue Nitot

35 The Imperial Conference, 1921. Lloyd George and Arthur Meighen, followed by General Smuts and W. F. Massey with W. M. Hughes behind, coming down to the garden of No. 10 Downing Street

Ireland from the Easter Rising, 1916, to the Dominion Settlement, 1921

36 The General Post Office in Dublin, from which the Republic was proclaimed on Easter Day 1916, as photographed from Nelson's Column after the Rising

37 Éamon de Valéra, who was invited as 'the chosen leader of the great majority in Southern Ireland' to London in July 1921, for talks on Irish settlement with Lloyd George

38 Arthur Griffith and de Valéra leaving the Mansion House, Dublin, July 1921

39 The Irish delegation to the Treaty negotiations in London. Left to right, seated, Arthur Griffith (Chairman of the delegation), E. J. Duggan, Michael Collins and Robert Barton. Standing, Erskine Childers (Secretary), Gavan Duffy and John Chartres (second Secretary)

40 T. M. Healy, the first Governor-General, and W. T. Cosgrave, the first President of the Executive Council of the Irish Free State

The defining of the Commonwealth

41 The Imperial Conference, 1926. Front, left to right, W. T. Cosgrave, General Hertzog, W. L. Mackenzie King, Stanley Baldwin, S. M. Bruce, J. G. Coates and W. S. Monroe (Newfoundland). Behind, the Maharajah of Burdwan, Lord Birkenhead, Winston Churchill and Lord Balfour

42 The Imperial Conference, 1930, with Ramsay MacDonald in the centre, R. B. Bennett, G. W. Forbes and Patrick McGilligan to his right, and J. H. Scullin and General Hertzog to his left. The Secretary of State for Dominion Affairs, J. H. Thomas, is behind MacDonald, and the Secretary of State for the Colonies, Lord Passfield, is behind Forbes

43 The Imperial Economic Conference, 1932. A picture taken outside the Parliament Buildings in Ottawa, with R. B. Bennett in the centre and Stanley Baldwin, J. G. Coates and S. T. O'Kelly on his right, and S. M. Bruce and N. C. Havenga on his left

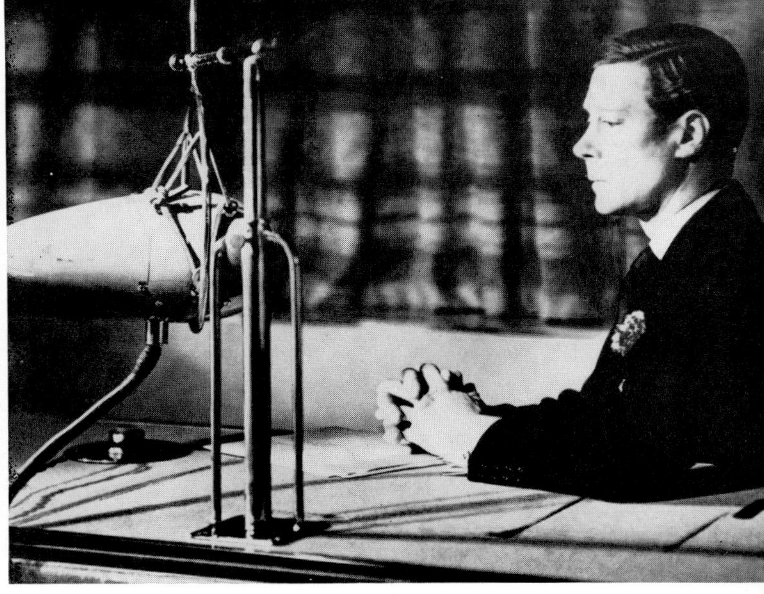

44 The abdication of Edward VIII in December 1936 was a matter of concern to all the self-governing members of the British Commonwealth, because of their direct relationship with the Crown since the passage of the Statute of Westminster, 1931

India. The British Raj: the penultimate phase

45 The Delhi Durbar, 1903. The procession approaches the Red fort on 1 January, with the King's Representative, the Duke of Connaught, and the Viceroy, Lord Curzon, riding on State elephants

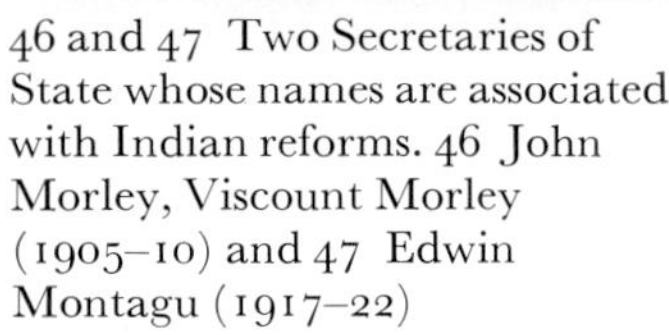

46 and 47 Two Secretaries of State whose names are associated with Indian reforms. 46 John Morley, Viscount Morley (1905–10) and 47 Edwin Montagu (1917–22)

48 and 49 Two Viceroys. 48 The 4th Earl of Minto, Governor-General of Canada 1898–1904, and Viceroy 1905–10. 49 Lord Irwin (1926–31) as 'Viceroy in Procession' with his son Richard Wood and the son of the Maharajah of Bharatpur as train bearers

50 Civil disobedience campaign. M. K. Gandhi on his way to the salt mines to protest against the salt monopoly, *c.* 1930

51 The Round Table Conference, 1931. The concluding session with the Prime Minister, J. Ramsay MacDonald, addressing the conference, with the Secretary of State, Sir Samuel Hoare, on his right and the Indian poetess Mrs Sarojini Naidu with Gandhi to his left

52 The Imperial Secretariat and the Council Chamber, New Delhi, designed by Sir Herbert Baker, with the Viceroy's House, designed by Sir Edwin Lutyens, in the centre. The buildings were only completed during Lord Irwin's Viceroyalty. Looking down from the hills on the ruins of older Delhis, Georges Clemenceau remarked: 'They will make the finest ruins of them all.'

53 The Viceroy's summer residence at Simla. It was here that pre-partition and pre-independence conferences were held, the British Raj cherishing the idea that the cool air of the hills was itself conducive to compromise

Representatives of the King in the Dominions

54, 55 and 56 Three Governors-General. 54 General the Lord Byng of Vimy, Governor-General of Canada 1921 to October 1926. His political marksmanship was less sure. 55 Mr Justice Isaacs, who became Chief Justice of the Commonwealth of Australia in 1930 and, as Sir Isaac Isaacs, served as the first native-born Governor-General, 1931–6. 56 John Buchan, in an appropriately romantic climax to his own life-story, as Lord Tweedsmuir and Governor-General of Canada, 1935–40

The Commonwealth on the eve of the Second World War

57 The Imperial Conference, 1937. Neville Chamberlain is in the centre with W. L. Mackenzie King and M. J. Savage on his right and J. A. Lyons and General J. B. M. Hertzog on his left. The youthful Secretary of State for Dominion Affairs, Malcolm MacDonald, is immediately behind Chamberlain

58 The Taoiseach, Mr de Valéra, with Mr S. McEntee, Minister for Finance, and Mr John Dulanty, Irish High Commissioner in London, to his right and Dr Ryan, Minister for Agriculture, and Mr Sean Lemass, Minister for Industry and Commerce, to his left, in London (January 1938) for talks which resulted in an Anglo-Irish Agreement ending the economic war and restoring the Treaty Ports to Irish sovereignty

59 The Canadian Prime Minister and the President of the United States, opening the Thousand Islands bridge over the St Lawrence, 1938. Mackenzie King attached great importance to Canada's developing relationship with the U.S.

60 Munich. A send-off for Neville Chamberlain from members of his Cabinet, with the High Commissioner for Canada, Vincent Massey, on the extreme right. New Zealand apart, the dominions favoured appeasement

The Second World War and the United Nations

61 The Battle of Libya. Australians storming a German strong-point

62 Canadian troops manning East Coast defences and visited by Mackenzie King on his first wartime visit to Britain in 1941

63 The British surrender at Singapore, February 1942. The Japanese Commander, Lt.-Gen. Tomoyuki Yamashita, is facing the camera and the British Commander, General Percival, is in the right foreground

64 United States sailors and marines welcomed by enthusiastic crowds in Brisbane. 'Australia looks to America, free of any pangs as to our traditional links with the United Kingdom', declared the Prime Minister, John Curtin, in January 1942

65 Men of 'India's martial races'. The Commander-in-Chief, General Sir Claude Auchinleck, inspecting Indian troops

66 General Douglas MacArthur, Commander-in-Chief, Allied Forces in the South-West Pacific, with the Australian Prime Minister, John Curtin, on his right and the Governor-General, the Earl of Gowrie, V.C., on his left, and wearing the insignia of the G.C.B. with which he has been invested by the Governor-General

67 The Quebec Conference, 1943. Mackenzie King, President Roosevelt and Winston Churchill with their Service advisers on the terrace of the Citadel at Quebec

69 Field Marshal Smuts in his role as world statesman, addressing the United Nations Conference at San Francisco, 1945

68 The Prime Ministers' Meeting, 1944. Seated, left to right, C. R. Attlee, Peter Fraser, W. L. Mackenzie King, Churchill, John Curtin, General Smuts and Anthony Eden. Behind, Lord Woolton, Oliver Lyttelton, Sir John Anderson, Ernest Bevin and Herbert Morrison

India: the transfer of power

70 The Cripps Mission, March–April 1942. Sir Stafford Cripps with Mohammed Ali Jinnah, the architect of Pakistan

71 The Cabinet Mission, March–May 1946. Lord Pethick-Lawrence, the Secretary of State for India, with Gandhi, 18 April 1946

72 and 73 Indian leaders. 72 Pandit Jawaharlal Nehru with Jinnah, May 1946. Their ways were soon to part. 73 The strong man of the Congress, Sardar Vallabhbhai Patel, with its Muslim President, Maulana A. K. Azad. At the last they came to differ, the Sardar opting for independence even at the price of partition, the Maulana for unity even at the price of a delayed transfer of power

74 The Viceroy with the leaders of the Congress and the League at a historic conference on 2 June 1947 in the Viceroy's house at which he communicated to them the British plan to transfer power to two new dominions, India and Pakistan, in August. Nehru, Patel, Acharya, J. B. Kripalani (the Congress President) and Sardar Baldev Singh, as spokesman of the Sikhs, are on Mountbatten's right, and on his left, Jinnah, Liaquat Ali Khan and Abdur Rab Nishtar. Behind, Sir Eric Miéville and Lord Ismay

76 Prime Ministers' Meeting, 1948, the first attended by Asian leaders. Left to right, Sir Godfrey Huggins (Southern Rhodesia), D. S. Senanayake (Ceylon), Liaquat Ali Khan (Pakistan), Dr H. V. Evatt (Australia), King George VI, C. R. Attlee, N. A. Robertson (Canada), E. H. Louw (South Africa), Peter Fraser (New Zealand), and Jawaharlal Nehru (India)

77 Prime Ministers' Meeting, April 1949, which agreed to India's republican membership of the Commonwealth. The two principal architects of the settlement, Attlee and Nehru

75 One consequence of partition; a train crowded with Muslim refugees fleeing for safety to Pakistan. It is believed that the total migration both ways following partition amounted to more than 12 million, and that more than half a million of all communities perished in the blood bath in the Punjab

The Commonwealth in the cold war years

78 The Prime Ministers' Meeting, 1951. Left to right, Dr T. F. Dönges (Minister of the Interior, South Africa), Sir Godfrey Huggins (Southern Rhodesia), C. R. Attlee, Louis St Laurent (Canada), D. S. Senanayake (Ceylon), Robert Menzies (Australia), S. G. Holland (New Zealand), and Nehru (India)

79 The Prime Ministers' Meeting, 1953. Left to right, Senanayake, Nehru, Holland, St Laurent, Churchill, Menzies, Malan, Mohammad Ali, Sir Godfrey Huggins

80 Menzies and Churchill at the Prime Ministers' Meeting, 1955, the last over which Sir Winston Churchill presided

81 Before the Suez Crisis. The Prime Ministers' Meeting, 1956. Left to right, S. R. W. D. Bandaranaike (Ceylon), Nehru, Holland, St Laurent, Sir Anthony Eden, Menzies, J. G. Strijdom (South Africa), Chaudhri Mohamad Ali, and Viscount Malvern (Central African Federation)

82 After the Suez Crisis. A convoy trapped in the canal near El Qantara, 66 km. south of Port Said

The background to independence, its achievement and outcome

83 Independence by international agreement, after years of strife for Cyprus. Sir Hugh Foot signing the Proclamation flanked by the Greek- and Turkish-Cypriot leaders, Archbishop Makarios and Dr Kutchuk, on 16 August 1960, with the representative of the Greek government, Mr George Christopoulos, on the extreme left and the representative of the Turkish government, Mr V. Turel, on the right

84 Independence in Tanganyika. Julius Nyerere handing over the torch to be lit on Mount Kilimanjaro on Independence Day, 9 December 1961, to 2nd Lt Nyirenda, the first Tanganyikan to pass out of Sandhurst

85 Kenya. Mau Mau suspects closely guarded behind barbed wire after Mau Mau raids in the Uplands, north of Nairobi. The revolt (1952–9) was anti-European, but whether it is to be described in terms of social protest or a national rising remains debatable

86 Independence Day in Kenya. Jomo Kenyatta, the new Prime Minister, detained during the Mau Mau emergency, at the celebrations on 12 December 1963, with the Duke of Edinburgh

87 and 88 The West Indies. 87 The federation that failed. The final meeting of the British Caribbean Federation Conference on 23 February 1956. The Federation came into existence on 3 January 1958, and was dissolved in May 1962. In the same year Jamaica and Trinidad and Tobago became independent member states. The second picture (88) shows Mr Norman Manley and Sir Alexander Bustamente signing the Report on Jamaican Independence

89 Conference on the Federation of Malaysia, July 1963. Harold Macmillan with the Prime Minister of Malaya, Tunku Abdul Rahman, on his right and the Colonial Secretary, Duncan Sandys, and the Prime Minister of Singapore, Lee Kuan Yew, on his left. Singapore seceded from the Federation in August 1965, to become a separate member state of the Commonwealth

Commonwealth co-operation in development, defence and government

90 The Colombo Plan. Market day at Mayurakshi, India, with 'the Canada Dam' contributed by the Canadian Government under the Colombo Plan in the background

91 Colombo Plan and other overseas students in north-west England on a special food production course. Methods used to reclaim land for cultivation are being explained to them

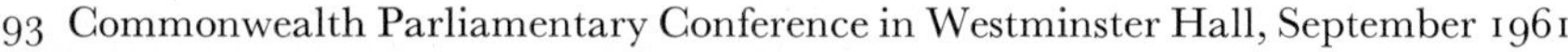

92 Commonwealth service chiefs at Camberley, 1961, with Admiral of the Fleet Earl Mountbatten of Burma, Chief of the U.K. Defence Staff, in the centre

93 Commonwealth Parliamentary Conference in Westminster Hall, September 1961

The wind of change in Africa

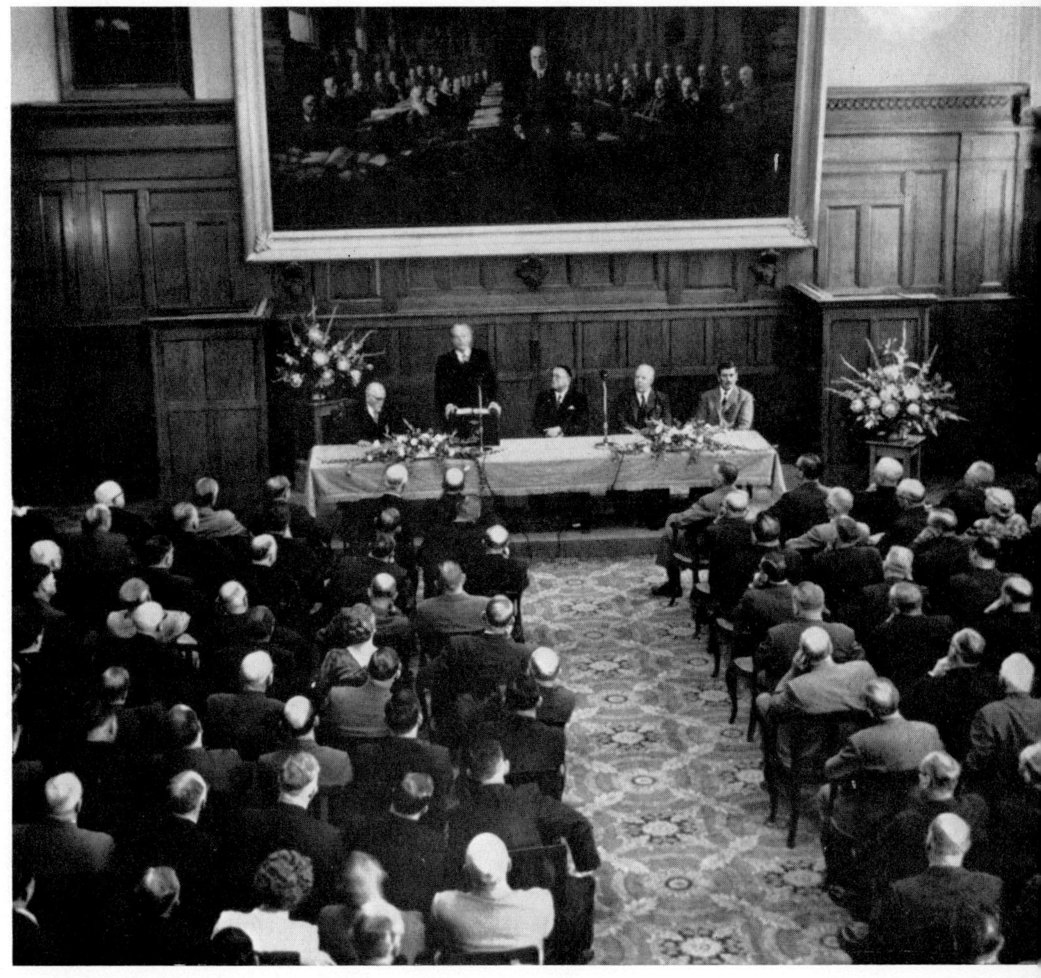

94 Harold Macmillan addressing the two Houses of the South African Parliament on 22 March 1961, on the wind of change, which he had felt on his African travels

95 Traditional Africa. Mr Macmillan greeted by warriors in Swaziland, one of the three British High Commission Territories in Southern Africa

96 South African racial tension. 30,000 Africans march on Cape Town, 30 March 1960, to demand the release of their leaders. Ten days earlier 67 Africans were killed and about 80 wounded at Sharpeville while holding a demonstration of protest against the pass laws

97, 98 and 99 The Prime Ministers' Meeting, 1961, and the secession of South Africa.
97 Mr Macmillan with Pandit Nehru. 98 The Prime Minister of the Union of South Africa, Dr Hendrik Verwoerd (with Dr Eric Louw on his right) leaves the Commonwealth conference for the last time. 99 The Queen with the Commonwealth leaders. Left to right, Sir Abubakar Tafawa Balewa, Dr Nkrumah, John Diefenbaker, Jawaharlal Nehru, Field Marshal Ayub Khan, Queen Elizabeth II, Sir Roy Welensky, Mrs Sirimavo Bandaranaike, Harold Macmillan, Robert Menzies, Archbishop Makarios, Keith Holyoake, Tunku Abdul Rahman

100 Dr Julius Nyerere, President of Tanganyika, in his capital, Dar-es-Salaam, at the annual conference of the ruling Tanganyika African National Union in January 1963, after announcing that a special committee would be set up to examine the country's constitution and to advise on the amendments necessary to put a one-party system of government into effect. Vice-President Kawawa is in the centre, and Home Affairs Minister O. Kambona on the right

The Rhodesian question and unsettlement in Africa

101 Sir Roy Welensky, Prime Minister of the Federation of Rhodesia and Nyasaland, with R. A. Butler, who as Minister for Central African Affairs, 1962–3, carried immediate responsibility for British disengagement from the Federation after 10 years of its existence

102 Dr Hastings Banda, Prime Minister of Nyasaland, addresses a mass rally in Blantyre on 1 January 1964 held to mark the dissolution of the Central African Federation. A coffin symbolising the death of the Federation was ceremonially burnt during the rally

103 The Colonial Secretary, Duncan Sandys, with Kenneth Kaunda at the end of a conference which decided that Northern Rhodesia should become independent on 25 October 1964, as the Republic of Zambia

104 Southern Rhodesian aftermath. After a breakdown of talks in London, the British Prime Minister, Harold Wilson, flew to Salisbury in an unavailing attempt to avert a Rhodesian declaration of independence. He is seen here with the Commonwealth Secretary, Arthur Bottomley, and Rhodesian African leaders, including Joshua Nkomo (with his arm in a sling), at Government House, Salisbury, on 27 October 1965

105 The first postage stamps issued by the Rhodesian regime to mark U.D.I.

106 Rhodesian independence unilaterally proclaimed. The Rhodesian Prime Minister, Ian Smith, signing the proclamation, watched by members of his cabinet, on 11 November 1965

107 The Commonwealth Heads of Government Meeting in Lagos on Rhodesia, January 1966. Harold Wilson with Sir Abubakar Tafawa Balewa, Prime Minister of the Federation of Nigeria and chairman of the conference

108 A military coup d'état in Nigeria, within days of the ending of the Commonwealth Conference, hailed by university students at Lagos, 18 January 1966. The Federal Prime Minister was murdered. Soon afterwards Dr Nkrumah's regime in Ghana was likewise overthrown by an army revolt

Britain and the Common Market

109 and 110 Commonwealth primary produce, exports of which were likely to be affected most adversely by British membership of the European Common Market. 109 New Zealand lamb, the picture being of sheep on the Glentanner Station, Canterbury; and (110) West Indian sugar-cane, here shown being loaded by hand on to a truck

111 Commonwealth Finance and Trade Ministers at a meeting of the Commonwealth Economic Consultative Council in Accra in September 1961 expressed 'grave apprehension and concern' at the United Kingdom decision to apply for membership of the European Economic Community

112 The end of the debate. President de Gaulle says 'non' on 14 January 1963

The contemporary Commonwealth

113 Queen Elizabeth II with the representatives of the Commonwealth in London for a meeting of Prime Ministers and Heads of State, July 1964. Left to right, Dr Eric Williams (Trinidad and Tobago), Mr S. Kyprianou (Cyprus), Dr Hastings Banda (Malawi), Dr Albert Margai (Sierra Leone), Sir Abubakar Tafawa Balewa (Nigeria), Tunku Abdul Rahman (Malaysia), Mr Jomo Kenyatta (Kenya), Mr Lester Pearson (Canada), Dr Milton Obote (Uganda), President Julius Nyerere (Tanganyika), Mr D. B. Sangster (Jamaica), Sir Robert Menzies (Australia), Dr Nkrumah (Ghana), Mr T. T. Krishnamachari (India), Mrs S. R. D. Bandaranaike (Ceylon), Sir Alec Douglas-Home, Mr K. J. Holyoake (New Zealand) and President Ayub Khan (Pakistan)

114 'All the way with L.B.J.' Australia's Prime Minister, Harold Holt, with President Johnson at the President's Camp David mountain retreat, 17 June 1967. They were allies in the war in Vietnam

115 and 116 Canada's centenary celebrations. 115 Balloons and a huge birthday cake about to be cut by Queen Elizabeth II on Parliament Hill, Ottawa, on 1 July 1967. 116 *'Vive le Québec libre!'* President de Gaulle on his arrival at Wolfe's Cove with the Quebec Premier, Daniel Johnson, on his right and the Governor-General, Roland Michener, on his left on 23 July 1967. The President by his encouragement of French-Canadian separatism won acclaim in Quebec and provoked protest in Ottawa

117 The contemporary Commonwealth with representatives of twenty-five nations in conference at Lancaster House, London

the signature of the Canadian minister would suffice. This meant the deliberate by-passing of the British ambassador, to test and establish a Canadian right to make and sign a treaty of particular concern without the intervention of United Kingdom government authority. The British government acquiesced with, and the British ambassador without, grace and the treaty was signed in a tense atmosphere in Washington on 2 March 1923.[10] Mackenzie King had reason to be satisfied for he had established a precedent by which he set much store, namely that a Canadian minister acting alone might sign a treaty and that treaty might be subsequently ratified by the king, acting on the advice of the Canadian government. It was a precedent important for all dominion governments and one vindicated by the Imperial Conference 1923. It opened the way in a vital respect to separate dominion control over foreign relations. As such it was duly remembered. Thirty years later, on 2 March 1953, a commemorative ceremony was held on Parliament Hill in Ottawa in the presence of the American ambassador and the prime minister, Louis St Laurent, with television cameras duly recording the scene. One thing only was missing – a halibut.

The limits, however, as well as the extent of the Halibut Treaty precedent are to be noted. The treaty was a commercial treaty, and the dominions' right to negotiate their own commercial treaties was comparatively long-established. It is true that there had been a significant procedural departure from precedent since hitherto at each stage nominal British control had remained in the appointment of dominion negotiators by the king on the advice of the British government, in the formal signature of the treaty by a British representative and finally in ratification by the king acting on the advice of the British government, and all had been dispensed with. But what of the other side of the coin? Hitherto the British government had also possessed the right to conclude treaties for the whole Empire, including the dominions, without dominion participation in negotiation or ratification. Did that right subsist? Or had treaties affecting the whole Empire henceforward to be concluded by the British government on behalf of the United Kingdom and the dependent Empire and also by the dominions severally on their own behalf? What was at issue here, at root, was whether for treaty-making, and by necessary inference, for diplomatic purposes, the British Empire was or was not to be thought of as a unit. This was the crucial question and it was debated, once again in an Anglo-Canadian context, most notably in respect of the negotiation and conclusion of the peace treaties with Turkey.

The precedents of Versailles were all-important for the dominions as a point of departure in post-war peace-making procedures. But they were not all-sufficient. Neither the British government nor those of the dominions could decide alone upon the nature and composition of the British presence at an international conference. Other states also had opinions. They raised objections to dominion representation at the conference called at Lausanne to conclude peace between the allied Powers and Turkey. The British government acquiesced and the Versailles precedent of a British Empire delegation was thus discarded. Dominion governments were duly informed of the position in this respect and also of the general lines of British policy. They were further informed that in due course they would be asked to sign the subsequent treaty. The Canadian government thereupon raised certain questions of principle, about which they were in fact concerned, but from which the British government inferred Canadian disappointment at not being invited to the conference. They were seemingly encouraged in their belief by communications from General Lord Byng, the governor-general of Canada.[11] But in fact the Canadian government did not wish to be represented and were much relieved when the British government had first apologetically explained that their representation was impracticable. 'Thank God we weren't [invited]' was apparently the sentiment of all the members.[12] What Mackenzie King was concerned to do was to exact the highest possible price in terms of status from the non-invitation. In particular he had no intention of agreeing to sign, on behalf of Canada, a treaty about which he had not been consulted, in the negotiations for which Canada had not been represented and in which the dominion had no immediate interest. The consequence, as it appeared to him, of such non-participation was non-commitment. He was careful to distinguish between the Canadian position at Lausanne and as it had been at Versailles. At Versailles, Canada had immediate and direct interest. In such circumstances, so Mackenzie King recorded in a note reprinted by his biographer,[13] Canada should be represented with full powers, it should sign the treaty, Parliament should be given an opportunity to approve it, and assent to ratify it should be given by the governor-general in council. But where interest was not immediate or direct, as at Lausanne, then Canada did not need to be represented, and if not represented should not be expected to sign, and if not signing should be left to approve or not to become a party to any such treaty on the merits of the case, with assent to ratification conditional on approval. On these premises Canada, not being represented at Lausanne, should not be asked to sign nor Parliament be required to approve nor the governor-general to ratify the subsequent treaty.

The Canadian prime minister's exposition of the rôle and responsibilities of a dominion in treaty-making was approved in the detailed Resolutions of the Imperial Conference 1923 on treaty-making, it being laid down *inter alia* that, in respect of treaties negotiated at international conferences, 'the existing practice of signature by plenipotentiaries on behalf of all the governments of the Empire represented at the conference should be continued.' Practical affairs, however, are apt to be more complicated than logical analysis may suggest and not all eventualities were covered by the Resolution. In the particular case of the Turkish Treaty, Canada, not being represented at the Lausanne Conference, was under no obligation to sign the resulting treaty. But, and here was the rub, she remained technically at war with Turkey, unless and until she did so. The Canadian position had to be further refined. It was necessary after all to sign and ratify the treaty in order to end the war, though in so doing Mackenzie King was at pains to circumscribe narrowly the degree of responsibility incurred. It was one thing, he argued, to sign a treaty to end a state of war; another to enter thereby into actual or moral obligations for the future. King made it clear that Canada, unrepresented at the conference, was assuming no obligations of either kind.

The debates on treaty-making derive their significance from their bearing upon the international status of the dominions on the one hand and the extent of dominion responsibility for imperial international commitments on the other. King was concerned at once to enhance Canada's international status and to limit her obligations. On both counts he objected to dominion commitment, by treaty or otherwise, to the fulfilment of obligations entered into by Britain alone and he sensed that such would be the consequence in practice of any acceptance of ideas of a common imperial foreign policy.

> A common foreign policy [warned his closest adviser, Dr O. D. Skelton, in 1923[14]] . . . offers a maximum of responsibility and a minimum of control. It commits a dominion in advance to an endorsement of courses of action of which it knows little and of which it may not approve, or in which it may have little direct concern. The real way in which the dominions may extend their power is the way in which such extension has come in the past – by reserving for their own peoples and their own parliaments the ultimate decision as to their course of action.

The argument was logical, the conclusion convincing, and in fact guided the course of Canadian policy. It is to be noted however that the extension of dominion freedom of action inevitably curtailed the range of Britain's imperial authority. If ultimately the dominions were to determine individually their own external policies in all respects, then Britain's ability to speak for the Empire as a whole would be conditional upon prior consultation with the dominions and their agreement in each individual case that she should do so. Mackenzie King understood that in critical international issues this represented a major practical problem of politics. He allowed specifically, in the notes already alluded to, that in high political treaties affecting peace and war, the Empire would act as one, though the extent of obligation imposed upon its self-governing members would be a matter of arrangement to be determined by each of them in the light of the merits of the issues at stake. But it was the direction that immediately mattered and it was not to be supposed that London would acquiesce in such a reinterpretation of imperial-international obligations without first testing the ground.

The Imperial Conference 1923 provided the occasion. The principal protagonists were Curzon as foreign secretary and Mackenzie King. King thought of Curzon as the archetype of the superior, overbearing, centralising imperialist, while Curzon found King 'obstinate, tiresome and stupid'[15], though he had reason also to note his remarkable persistence. As the major issues of the conference were reviewed one by one – foreign affairs, trade, defence – King considered what was said and analysed what was written lest inferences be drawn or precedents established by which common policies and centralised control might unobtrusively gain acceptance. Among British historians it has been widely assumed that Mackenzie King was tilting at windmills. But fuller evidence makes it clear that this was not altogether so. Whitehall, it may be allowed, was not in the hands of conspiratorial imperialists as King was only too apt to suppose, but there was a determination, deriving from an assessment of British interests, to preserve the diplomatic unity of the Empire so long as the price in terms of imperial relations was not too high. It was believed that the means existed to promote this end. The Imperial Conference was conceived to be a qualified albeit obviously second best peacetime substitute for the imperial war cabinet and as such it was thought the Conference could formulate at least the broad outlines of policy for the whole Empire. On that assumption there was the machinery and, it was hoped, there was also sufficient common will to ensure agreement on a single imperial foreign policy. But King was far from being interested in improved machinery: he was profoundly, indeed passionately, opposed to the end that machinery was intended to serve. He felt that in peace and also in war it was not for any central body, however composed, but for each autonomous government of the Commonwealth to determine its own course of action. His views passed neither unnoted nor unchallenged. One entry in his diary records how

> Lord Derby . . . rather tried to force my hand in the matter of how far the dominions might be expected to go with respect to the Empire being attacked at any point. I felt obliged to interrupt him and to point out that Canada's co-operation could not be taken for granted. I stated that had war arisen last year against the Turks it is extremely doubtful if Canada would have supplied any troops.

It was an unpleasant and somewhat trying experience. . . . However, it constitutes to my mind the most important of all the statements made at the present Conference.[16]

At the end, after rather more than the familiar flurry of last minute consultation and revision of drafts, Mackenzie King succeeded in securing the addition of a paragraph in the section of the Report on foreign relations, which stated that the Conference was a Conference of representatives of the several governments of the Empire, that its views or conclusions on foreign policy were necessarily subject to the action of the governments and Parliaments of the various portions of the Empire and that it hoped the results of its deliberations would meet with their approval. These words, in the opinion of King's biographer of this period, Professor MacGregor Dawson, signified the departure of the imperial cabinet from the scene, and at the same time let it be inferred that the earlier imperial Conference, with its non-committal conversations, had quietly resumed its place.[17] This gave to King the substance of what he wanted.

How important was the outcome of the Imperial Conference 1923, in the broader imperial setting? Professor Dawson has argued that it was this Conference and not its successor in 1926 that was decisive, on the ground that the 1923 Conference marked the point at which the Empire reversed the centralising tendencies of the war and post-war years and moved towards a more stable condition based on the nationalism and independence of the dominions.[18] On this argument change was initiated in 1923, confirmed in 1926. It is an argument to be accepted only with qualification. The 1923 Conference opened the road to a recasting of imperial relations in terms of a dominion autonomy extending to foreign, over and above domestic, policy but it did not ensure that there would be the necessary consensus of opinion to enable that road to be travelled in united company. That necessary measure of agreement remained to be achieved and its achievement was not to be lightly assumed.

The 1923 Imperial Conference certainly reflected the coming of a new spirit into Commonwealth relations. King was mainly responsible but it is well to remember that behind King stood Skelton, the biographer of Laurier, who was to become the chief artificier of a Canadian diplomatic service. No one who worked with him, thought Vincent Massey, could fail to recognise that he was anti-British. Lord Lothian more penetratingly observed in 1940 that relations with his Canadian colleagues in Washington would be better if 'Skelton did not regard co-operation with anyone as a confession of inferiority', while Professor Soward retrospectively, and after studying the official records, concluded that Skelton was essentially North American 'determined not to become involved in European power politics, hostile to the centralisation of Commonwealth policies in Downing Street . . . '.[19] Those attitudes were shared by General Hertzog, the spokesman of renascent Afrikaner nationalism, who was to succeed Smuts as prime minister in 1924, and by the Irish administration of W. T. Cosgrave, which was resolved furthermore with the easing of its domestic problems, to seize each opportunity that offered to assert the international personality of the Irish Free State. In 1923 the Irish Free State, in the face of British discouragement, became the first dominion to establish a permanent delegate to the League: in 1924, the year in which it accredited a minister to Washington, it also registered the treaty, despite British objection, as an international agreement with the League. Clearly the forces pressing for change were gathering momentum.

In November 1924 L. S. Amery was appointed colonial secretary in Stanley Baldwin's first administration. He made it a condition of his acceptance of office that at long last the Colonial Office should be broken up into its component parts and a separate department created responsible for relations with the dominions.[20] In 1925 this division took place and Amery became the first secretary of state for dominion affairs, though in fact he continued to combine this new office with that of secretary of state for the colonies throughout his tenure. Amery had his own views of the pattern of dominion development and he was not predisposed to notions of separate dominion responsibility for foreign policy. In 1917 he had contemplated consolidation of the self-governing empire on the basis of establishing permanent machinery for the making of common imperial policies, and in 1921 he had responded to Smuts' proposal for a declaration of dominion rights with the suggestion that they should 'of course, include an affirmation not only of the complete independence and equality of the several partners, but also the indissoluble unity of all of them under King and Crown.'[21] But while Amery thought in terms of common loyalty, common policies and common action, he appreciated that such aims might be furthered by timely concessions to dominion sentiment more effectively than by grudging acquiescence in their demands. The all-important thing for him was the preservation of the unity of the Empire in a period of transition and while he was a man of tenaciously held ideas, his approach to Commonwealth issues was in the pragmatic Colonial Office tradition.

The negotiation and ratification of the Locarno Treaty in 1925 underlined the Commonwealth lessons that were to be drawn from Chanak and Lausanne. In this instance there was no search for a common imperial initiative in Europe because the co-ordination of separate policies through consultation between widely scattered governments appeared to present too many practical difficulties. It was impossible, said Sir Austen Chamberlain in the debate on the Locarno Treaty, to wait on the dominions.

> . . . the affairs of the world do not stand still . . . I could not go, as the representative of His Majesty's government, to meeting after meeting of the League of Nations, to conference after conference with the representatives of foreign countries, and say, 'Great Britain is without a policy. We have not yet been able to meet all the governments of the Empire, and we can do nothing.' That might be possible for an Empire wholly removed from Europe, which existed in a different hemisphere. It was not possible for an Empire the heart of which lies in Europe . . . and where every peril to the peace of Europe jeopardised the peace of this country.

Accordingly the Locarno Treaty was signed by the United Kingdom government alone, with a proviso in Article 9 to the effect that 'the present treaty shall impose no obligation upon any of the British dominions, or upon India, unless the government of such dominion or of India signified its acceptance thereof.' None in fact did so. Their reasons were given at a meeting of the inter-imperial relations committee of the Imperial Conference 1926. For Canada Ernest Lapointe, minister of Justice, noted in a prepared statement that the treaty involved additional obligations in a European field which, though of interest to Canada, was not 'our primary concern', while Mackenzie King added that the fact that the United States had not assumed any obligations in European affairs placed the Canadian government in a somewhat difficult position. General Hertzog was equally clear that South Africa should not enter 'more deeply into matters concerning Europe and Great Britain, unless cause were shown'. The Irish Free State in reserving its position in effect adopted the same attitude, and the New Zealand prime minister concurred, saying that New Zealand was very much concerned about becoming 'responsible for obligations to which she might find it difficult to give effect'. Stanley Bruce who 'felt very keenly that there should be common action' from the dominions underwriting the Locarno Treaty, received support from Newfoundland alone.[22] But it is important to note that the countervailing majority dominion view did not indicate dissent from the policy of the British government, but merely the conviction that the treaty was the responsibility of the British government. Nor did it mean that the dominions would necessarily dissociate themselves from consequences which might arise from the British signature of the treaty; on the contrary comments offered by dominion leaders at the 1926 Imperial Conference suggested that for the most part they would be predisposed to support Britain in resisting any challenge to the security system established at Locarno especially, Lapointe carefully noted, as it applied to frontiers in Western Europe only.

The changing pattern of Commonwealth international relations, important in itself, was furthermore a manifestation of deeper forces at work. It was not Mackenzie King and his insistence upon the supremacy of Parliament and the consequent logical necessity of separate foreign policies within the Commonwealth who required a new exposition of the nature of Commonwealth relations, it was the nationalists throughout the dominions, in Canada certainly, but more particularly in South Africa and in the Irish Free State. When General Hertzog came to office in 1924 he made, so one of his biographers has told us,[23] a 'meticulous study' of the minutes and documents of all the Imperial Conferences up to that time, as well as various memoranda including that drafted by Smuts in 1921. His first speech as prime minister was on the theme of 'South Africa first' and South Africa's Commonwealth membership was implicitly made conditional upon national self-interest.

General Hertzog's immediate aim was to advance South Africa's Commonwealth standing by securing international recognition of her independent status, and he was correspondingly the more sensitive to any failure on the part of foreign countries to recognise South Africa's separate international identity. When Amery wrote to tell Hertzog of the impending separation of the dominions from the Colonial Office, he sought also to give him some reassurance on this count.

> I think the real answer you seek [wrote Amery] lies in action which will enable foreign countries to grasp the essential, peculiar character of the British Commonwealth. But of course the fact that the nations of the British Commonwealth came into being through evolution has prevented their existence impressing itself upon the outside world and it will take a little time before foreign governments will remember at international conferences that all H.M.G.'s will be entitled to be present and are each entitled to the individual courtesies due to sovereign states.

But Hertzog was not prepared to give time. He wanted recognition here and now. He came to the Imperial Conference in 1926 thinking in terms of a public assertion of dominion sovereignty on the basis of the full equality of the dominions with Britain within the Commonwealth and resolved, if these ends were not obtained, to return home and set 'the Veldt on fire' with a demand for republican independence.

The balance of forces within the Commonwealth, together with her standing as the senior dominion combined to place Canada in the position of near-arbiter. South Africa and the Irish Free State, though not in agreement about means were insistent upon redefinition of relations in terms of equality. Australia and New Zealand were dubious of the wisdom of any such dialectical exercise, so Canada was left to fill her traditional mediatory role. The Canadian attitude however was the outcome less of her central position or of any theoretic preconception than of experience and circumstance, and it was these which persuaded the Canadian government, in the person of Mackenzie King, Ernest Lapointe and their advisers, to come down on the side of redefinition. Before the Canadian prime minister came to London for the Imperial Conference he had had cause to reflect that those forms, which W. M. Hughes had dismissed in 1921 as a few figments, might represent realities.

The 1925 Canadian general election had given no party a majority. Arthur Meighen and the Conservatives had swept English-speaking Canada, King himself being defeated, but the Liberals were enabled to remain in office so long as they enjoyed the support of the Progressives from the prairies. In this treacherous political situation news broke of a customs scandal of distressing dimensions. A motion of censure was tabled in the House of Commons. On defeat, though not on the censure motion itself, King asked the governor-general for a dissolution. The governor-general declined on the ground that Meighen could form an alternative government. Meighen was invited to do so, formed his government and then in melodramatic circumstances was defeated in the House. Meighen asked for a dissolution and the governor-general acceded to his request. Mackenzie King campaigned on the constitutional issue. Did not the refusal of a dissolution to him in the first instance imply subordination of status? Would it be in accord with convention for the king to refuse a request for dissolution in similar circumstances by a British prime minister? He contended that the answer to the first question was in the affirmative and to the second in the negative, since no request for a dissolution had been denied in Britain for a hundred years. He enlisted the weighty support of Professor A. B. Keith, who believed the refusal of the dissolution to King to be a challenge to 'the doctrine of equality in status of the dominions and the United Kingdom and has relegated Canada decisively to the colonial status which we believed she had outgrown'. The Colonial Office however had not been consulted by the governor-general and Amery refused to express any opinion. Indeed, it is apparent from a letter from General Byng to King George V that the governor-general had acted on his own initiative and judgment.[24] But that did not qualify the fact that his judgment might have been mistaken or that his action might have carried with it the suggestion of the discretionary authority enjoyed by nineteenth- rather than twentieth-century British monarchs or colonial governors.

The King-Byng controversy was not the only experience stiffening Mackenzie King's resolve to insist upon equality of status. In 1926 the supreme court of Alberta dismissed appeals from a petitioner named Nadan against convictions by a police magistrate for carrying unbonded liquor in unlicensed transport on his way from Alberta to Montana. Nadan thereupon appealed to the judicial committee of the Privy Council. His appeal (subsequently dismissed) was allowed on the ground that Canadian legislation – Section 1025 of the Criminal Code of Canada – purporting to abolish Appeals in criminal cases was *ultra vires*, because it conflicted with nineteenth-century enactments of the British Parliament allowing appeals to Her Majesty in Council in all cases.[25] The Colonial Laws Validity Act remained on the Statute Book. That Act provided, it will be recalled, that any Act of a colonial legislature conflicting with an Act of the British Parliament was to the extent of such conflict null and void. Was not the judgment conclusive proof of continuing Canadian subordination?

While the Canadian prime minister came to London in 1926 with substantial reason to seek for the removal of remaining elements of subordination in British-dominion relations, his approach was different from that of Hertzog and, while rather closer, still quite distinct from that of the Irish Free State representatives. The status seekers were of one mind in seeking to enhance their countries' status, but not about the means by which this should be done. The Irish listed the elements of continuing subordination with a view to their systematic elimination; the South Africans desired first and foremost a definitive declaration; while King, anxious to secure full equality and autonomy for Canada, was so opposed temperamentally to such abstract definition that he remained dubious of the advantages of it, especially in view of the almost certainly acrimonious debate to which the attempt would give rise.[26] His first inclination therefore was to avoid any such discussion and to concentrate upon particular reforms which would achieve the ends he had in mind. At the head of his list was the complete separation between the office of governor-general as representative of the Crown and as an agency of the British government. Such separation, earlier advocated by Smuts among others, would ensure on the one hand that a governor-general would henceforward fill the rôle of constitutional monarch alone and on the other, the development at the inter-governmental level, of the system of high commissioners representing their respective governments in other Commonwealth capitals. His proposals in fact commended themselves to the Conference, but in so far as King was sanguine enough to think that particular reforms of this kind might satisfy South African demands without the need for any formal declaration he was mistaken. It is true that neither Australia nor New Zealand desired a declaration and that at the outset Amery was not only averse to one, but further contended that such an unprecedented attempt to define the undefinable was beyond the authority of an Imperial Conference.[27] The South Africans, however, were not to be deflected.

The committee on inter-imperial relations set up by the Imperial Conference and comprising the prime ministers and principal delegates of the dominions held its first session on 3 October 1926. Lord Balfour, as chairman, opened the proceedings with a statement on imperial relations. Before 1914, he observed (rather questionably), the British Empire

> seemed to alien observers the frailest of structures. A state which (so far as its western elements were concerned) consisted in the main of six self-governing communities, bound together by no central authority, not competent to enlist a single recruit or impose a single shilling of taxation, might look well painted on the map but as a fighting machine is surely negligible.

But the war had refuted 'this plausible conjecture'. It had, however, also left the Empire unexplained and undefined. The peace brought not enlightenment but, if anything, added to the obscurities. Yet the general character of the Empire was easy to define. It might be conveniently divided, thought Lord Balfour, into elements of three different kinds: 1. Britain and the self-governing dominions, 2. India, 3. the dependencies of the self-governing states including mandated territories as well as colonies. Only the first was the particular business of the committee. They were concerned with the problems raised by 'the most novel and yet most characteristic peculiarity of the British Empire', namely the co-existence within its unity of six (or seven including Newfoundland) autonomous communities. 'The statement of fact,' Balfour proceeded, 'though very simple, is barely intelligible to foreigners and no doubt among ourselves has given rise to some secondary difficulties'. Their task was to enlighten the world outside and remove these 'secondary difficulties'.

Were they 'secondary'? Clearly General Hertzog did not think so. He followed closely upon Balfour with an address that set the tone of the committee discussions and settled the character of its Report. Hertzog made plain that he could speak for South Africa alone but he claimed that it would 'be monstrous, and certainly disastrous', if the freedom of one dominion were dependent upon the will of others. 'The dominions are all free and equal in status but no one has the right to claim, and I hope no one will claim, that the exercise of the rights and privileges inherent in that freedom and equal status shall be standardised for all with mechanical monotony. That would be the death of organic development within the Empire, a stagnation leading to decay'. As for South Africa it was 'imperatively necessary' that the nature of dominion relations should not remain uncertain either in the world or in the Commonwealth itself. Since 1921 there had been no longer any question as to the character or degree of dominion independence. The British government had assured the dominions that they were 'independent states', 'equal in status' and 'separately entitled to international recognition as independent states'. But the facts thus acknowledged had been neither publicised nor proclaimed. They should have been. 'We are not a secret society', and quoting very extensively from General Smuts' 1921 memorandum, Hertzog advanced to the conclusion that the nature of dominion status should be authoritatively declared to the world. Smuts had warned against the danger of always being too late. 'Much ill-feeling and unpleasantness would have been avoided if effect had been given to his advice at the time.' But it was still not too late and Hertzog ended with the anxious appeal: 'I implore that what should have been done in 1921, shall now no longer be delayed.' By his plea, he ensured it should not.[28]

General Hertzog was not only determined upon a declaration, but he had arrived in England with a first draft. He was invited to submit it to the committee and he did so. It spoke of the prime ministers of the United Kingdom and of the dominions recognising that they were respectively the representatives of independent states, equal in status and separately entitled to international recognition, with governments and parliaments independent of one another, united through a common bond of loyalty to the king and freely associated as members of the Commonwealth of Nations, and acknowledging that any surviving forms of inequality or subordination were conditional solely upon the voluntary agreement of the associated state concerned, and deeming it desirable that the constitutional relation between Britain and the dominions should be made known and recognised by all other states. The drafting was rather ponderous and may perhaps in part explain the somewhat critical comments of Kevin O'Higgins, who, while allowing that Hertzog was 'a very decent and likeable kind of man', also complained that he talked 'a lot and none too clearly'.[29] But in any event Hertzog's draft retains its importance as the basis of subsequent detailed discussion. The nationalist initiative therefore, in respect of a declaration, came from South Africa and it achieved its purpose. But there were other initiatives both Canadian, in respect of the office of governor-general and of improved intra-imperial consultation especially through the appointment of high commissioners both in London and in dominion capitals – it was 'an anomaly and an absurdity', alleged Mackenzie King, that the British government should have no representative in Canada – and Irish, in respect of particular surviving inequalities which the Irish delegation listed in a memorandum and all of which they wished to see removed. Not least among Irish preoccupations were appeals to the judicial committee of the Privy Council which the Irish delegation urged should be dealt with upon 'principles of equality'.

It is, an Irish submission on this subject contended, in strict accord with such principles that an appeal should lie to the judicial committee from the courts of any state in the Commonwealth which desires the continuance of such appeals but it would be 'a violation of such principles to deny the right of a state which desires that finality on judicial questions should be reached within its own areas to determine that such shall be the case'.[30] The Irish achieved in this as in most other matters their particular purposes. They were concerned to dismantle piece by piece what remained of the British Imperial structure, Kevin O'Higgins commenting (in discussion on Hertzog's proposals) that a declaration would be of little value if contradicted by the facts. But the Irish delegation having repudiated external association in 1921, and having embraced, as members of the pro-treaty party, dominion status as a means rather than an end, would seem to have thought on the longer term of filling the void left by the republic with an Anglo-Irish dual monarchy on early Sinn Féin lines. This may have added to the emphasis which they placed upon the importance of direct and equal Irish access to the Crown.

There were many succeeding drafts and suggestions, in the course of which Amery reintroduced the term British Empire, while the Irish rejected 'Common bond of allegiance' and the South Africans 'common citizenship of the Empire'. Ultimately the committee, (over which Lord Balfour 'somewhat deaf, occasionally somnolent' but 'with intellectual powers unimpaired by the years', presided 'with a smile like moonlight on a tombstone',) produced the Report, which bears his name.[31] It is a document to be considered as a whole, with particular attention to but without undue emphasis upon that section of it which was italicised because of a typist's misunderstanding – or so Amery records, though if so it may be thought the typist had a better sense of history than the assembled prime ministers – and which described the relations of the United Kingdom and the dominions in phrases, as well known as any in British constitutional history.[32]

The Balfour Report stated that the committee on Inter-imperial relations were of the opinion that nothing would be gained by attempting to lay down a constitution for the whole Empire but that there was in it one important element which from a constitutional viewpoint had reached full development. This element was composed of the United Kingdom and the overseas dominions. Their position and mutual relations might therefore be 'readily defined'. 'They are autonomous communities within the British Empire, equal in status, in no way subordinate one to another in any aspect of their domestic or external affairs, though united by a common allegiance to the Crown, and freely associated as members of the British Commonwealth of Nations.' In this sentence four important characteristics of membership of the British Commonwealth, which comprised the United Kingdom as well as the dominions, were identified. The dominions were 1. autonomous communities 2. within the British Empire 3. freely associated as members of the British Commonwealth of Nations 4. united by a common allegiance to the Crown. There was deliberate variety in phrasing, which enabled New Zealanders to place most emphasis on their being within the British Empire and South African nationalists, by contrast, on 'autonomous' communities. But it was of secondary importance. So too were the questions of interpretation that arose about the meaning of 'freely associated' – did it or did it not imply that a dominion was free to dissociate if it so desired? – and 'common allegiance' – was it or was it not to a common Crown? Henceforward these were questions that could be debated at least within an accepted context. That is what made the 1926 Report so significant. And in identifying the things deemed to be of fundamental importance in a new and experimental inter-state relationship it helped to shape the pattern of future development.

The setting in which the 1926 italicised definition was placed was written by Lord Balfour, resting on his bed, on sheets of a loose-leaf notebook he always used for his original drafts.[33] It observed that a foreigner attempting to understand the true character of the British Empire by the aid of this formula 'would be tempted to think that it was devised rather to make mutual interference impossible than to make mutual co-operation easy.'[34] But the foreigner, it need hardly be said, would be mistaken. The rapid evolution of the dominions, the Report continued, demanded an adjustment to changing conditions. 'The tendency towards equality of status was both right and inevitable.' 'Geographical and other conditions' made federation 'impossible' and the only alternative was autonomy. Every dominion in 1926 was in fact if not always in form master of its own destiny and subject to no compulsion whatever. But the British Empire 'is not founded upon negations'. It depended upon positive ideals. Free institutions were its life blood. Free co-operation was its instrument. And 'while each dominion is now and must always remain the sole judge of the nature and extent of its co-operation no common cause will, in our opinion, be thereby imperilled'. Equality of status, the Report continued, was thus the root-principle governing inter-imperial relations, not, be it noted, either common allegiance or free association. But principles of equality did not extend to function. Diplomacy and defence required more flexible machinery and for a long time the United Kingdom would remain the predominant partner. This was certainly true. It was also a distinction which imperialists emphasised, nationalists discounted. It existed markedly in the transitional period and it made relations psychologically difficult in the years before the second world war.[35] Equality in principle is not easy to reconcile with continuing dependence in practice.

The Balfour Report was 'first and foremost, finely accurate description'. It described, noted Professor Hancock, 'not merely the form but the motion of a community'.[36] Professor Wheare, in his authoritative study on *The Statute of Westminister and Dominion Status*, observed that the importance of the Balfour Report was underestimated in 1926 and in consequence that of the Statute of Westminster overestimated in 1931, because the full implications of the definitions included in the former were not realised until the attempt was made to translate some of them into strict law five years later[37] – or to put the matter rather differently, the Balfour Report had made explicit the principles on which the British Commonwealth rested and what remained to be done thereafter was the important but lesser task of giving them effect where necessary in law. Since equality was the 'root-principle', this involved first the removal of inequalities. They included the power of reservation whether obligatory or discretionary, the power of disallowance, the sections of the Colonial Laws Validity Act of 1865 which declared that 'an act of Parliament or any provision thereof shall be said to extend to any colony when it is made applicable to such colony by the express words or necessary intendment of such Act . . .' and that such colonial legislation (Section 2) as was repugnant to any provisions of an act of the imperial Parliament 'shall be to the extent of such repugnancy . . . void and inoperative'. Even if it was at the time of enactment 'an enabling Act, not a restrictive or disabling Act', [38] its provisions were clearly inconsistent with equality of status. There were also limitations on the power of dominions to enact extra-territorial legislation, implying inequality and causing practical inconvenience. All these were matters on which detailed and expert inquiry was necessary. It was carried out in 1929–30 by the Conference on the Operation of Dominion Legislation and Merchant Shipping Legislation[39] and the Imperial Conference 1930[40]. Where appropriate their recommendations were embodied in the Statute of Westminster.

The Imperial Conference 1926, in enunciating the root-principle of equality had itself either reinterpreted certain of the conventions of intra-Commonwealth relations or made recommendations to ensure the full application of this principle. Thus the Conference tendered advice to the effect that a small amendment be made in the king's title to take account of the status of the Irish Free State. This amendment contemplated the substitution of a comma for an 'and' between Great Britain and Ireland, so that the title would read, 'George v, by the Grace of God, of Great Britain, Ireland and the British Dominions beyond the Seas King, Defender of the Faith, Emperor of India'. King George v acquiesced with reluctance in this modification, for in such matters, we are told, he disliked change.[41] In respect of the office of governor-general the Conference recommended that the governor-general in a dominion should no longer act in any way as the representative or agent of the United Kingdom government and should in all essential respects hold the same position in relation to the administration of public affairs as the king in the United Kingdom. This general redefinition of function satisfied Mackenzie King, mindful of his controversy with General Byng about the discretionary authority of governors-general, while judiciously refraining from comment upon the exercise of the royal prerogative or the king's position. The Imperial Conference 1930 carried this reinterpretation of the rôle and functions of governors-general to its logical conclusion by stating that 'the parties interested in the appointment of a governor-general of a dominion are His Majesty the King, whose representative he is, and the dominion concerned . . . The ministers who tender and are responsible for such advice are His Majesty's ministers in the dominion concerned.'[42] The prime minister of Australia, J. H. Scullin, in the exercise of this exclusive dominion responsibility and to the embarrassment of Sidney Webb, improbably esconced as Lord Passfield at the Colonial Office, overbore King George v's wishes in 1929 in pressing and ultimately obtaining, despite every objection which it occurred to the sovereign to advance, the appointment of Sir Isaac Isaacs as the first Australian-born governor-general of Australia.[43]

Equality in the relationship of the dominions and the United Kingdom to the Crown was most significantly recognised by according to them an equal responsibility in determining the succession to it.

> In as much as the Crown is the symbol of the free association of the members of the British Commonwealth of Nations, and as they are united by a common allegiance to the Crown, it would be in accord with the established constitutional position of all the members of the Commonwealth in relation to one another that any alteration in the law touching the Succession to the Throne or the Royal Style and Titles shall hereafter require the assent as well of the Parliaments of all the dominions as of the Parliament of the United Kingdom.[44]

This definition of dominion responsibilities in respect of the royal succession set out in 1929 was reproduced in the preamble to the Statute of Westminster. Amery entertained misgivings lest it should lead to a dominion relationship to the monarchy that amounted to no more than a purely personal union. General Hertzog on the other hand, and for precisely the same reason, was well contented until General Smuts argued that the new relationship precluded secession without agreement.

Hertzog responded by moving an amendment in the House of Assembly adopting the Report of the 1929 Conference subject to the condition that the relevant section should not be taken as 'derogating from the right of any member of the British Commonwealth of Nations to withdraw therefrom'. This was duly noted by the Imperial Conference 1930.

The Preamble of the Statute of Westminster 1931[45] set out by way of historical record the conventions already agreed in respect of status and of succession to the Crown, and further declared that in accordance with the established constitutional position no law made by the Parliament of the United Kingdom 'shall extend to any of the said dominions otherwise than at the request and with the consent of that dominion'. The Act itself restated this fundamental principle so that, as a matter of law, the Parliament of the United Kingdom was thereafter precluded from legislating for a dominion without the request and consent of its government or Parliament. The Act also, by way of counterpart, clarified the powers of dominion Parliaments in accordance with the principles of the 1926 Imperial Conference by giving them authority to legislate on matters of dominion concern, hitherto within the competence of the imperial Parliament, to repeal legislation on such matters and to legislate with extra-territorial effect.

In conformity with the principles embodied in the Act it was at the request of some of the dominions that some continuing restrictions were placed upon their powers. At Canada's request, section 7 expressly excluded the British North America Acts 1867–1930 from the operation of the statute; at the request of the Pacific dominions section 8, likewise, excluded the constitutions of Australia and New Zealand; section 10, inserted again at the request of the dominion governments concerned, stipulated that the statute should not apply to New Zealand, Australia, and Newfoundland (whose dominion status was shortly to lapse), unless and until it was adopted by their respective Parliaments. More generally, it may be said that South Africa and the Irish Free State accepted the statute without reservation, though neither altogether relished the notion of an Act of the British Parliament as the charter of their freedom, that Canada adopted it subject to the reservation in respect of its constitution, but that neither Australia or New Zealand did so, not wishing to exercise the powers the statute proposed to confer upon them. These varied reactions throw much light upon the outlook and balance of opinion in the British Commonwealth at that time.[46]

It was not till 1942 and 1947 that the Statute of Westminster was adopted in Australia and New Zealand respectively. The reasons for the delay, ended because of practical inconveniences experienced in wartime, were those elaborated by Menzies in Canberra in 1937. 'I think that the business of devising the Balfour Declaration in 1926, and the business of devising and drafting the preamble of the Statute of Westminster . . . were both open to grave criticism.' The 1926 declaration was 'a grave disservice'; the 1926–31 process 'a misguided attempt' to reduce to written terms something which 'was a matter of the spirit and not of the letter'. W. M. Hughes, five years later, spoke of the 1926 Report as a 'wonderful document'.

> It took stock of everything. Nothing escaped it . . . Every prime minister went away perfectly satisfied – Mr Bruce because it altered nothing that affected Australia, Mr Mackenzie King because it taught Lord Byng where he got off, and General Hertzog because he was able to assure the burghers that the king of England was no longer the king of South Africa, although it was true that the king of South Africa was also king of England.[47]

But to Hughes it was all a mistaken attempt to appease the unappeasable. These Australian views were to some extent reflected or shared by section of Conservative opinion in Britain, *The Times*, dismissing the statute as a piece of 'mere pedantry', for which there was and could be no enthusiasm, but about which also there need be no great apprehension.

The attitude of the Canadian government to the Act was very different and advantage was immediately taken of its enactment to abolish Canadian appeals to the judicial committee of the Privy Council in criminal cases. In South Africa the statute had important political repercussions and constitutional implications. For nationalists its substance was more satisfying than its origin. They deemed the assertion of a South African, as distinct from a United Kingdom source as hitherto, for the fundamental law of the Union to be a condition of equality within the Commonwealth. Accordingly they concluded that the substance of the Statute of Westminister should be enacted by the South African Parliament as a South African law so as to give its provisions indigenous authority. This could not be done without risk of complications, chief among them being the possibility that the entrenched clauses of the South Africa Act 1909 safeguarding existing voting rights in the Cape and equality of the English and Dutch languages, might no longer, should the South African Parliament so decide, be excluded from amendment by simple majority vote. Hertzog and Smuts, in requesting the enactment of the Statute of Westminster, had placed on record that their request was made on the understanding that the Act would not derogate from the entrenched clauses of the South Africa Act. Their statement however, if morally binding, was certainly not legally binding and the bearing of the Statute of Westminster upon the entrenched clauses of the South Africa Act remained legally untested and was to be the crucial question in a major constitutional crisis some twenty years later. Subsequent agreement between the two generals, resulting in a coalition and then in a fusion government, made possible the enactment of the Status of the Union Act in 1934.[48] Section 2 indicated its principal purpose. 'The Parliament of the Union shall be the sovereign legislative power in and over the Union.' As a corollary the position of the king as king of South Africa was emphasised and by implication there was enunciated the doctrine of a divisible crown. In all this Afrikaner legalism was seeking to find a way by which a separatist policy could – if or when occasion arose – be legally carried through.

The Irish reaction was rather different, but of a comparable complexity. At the Conferences of 1929–30 and in the drafting of the Statute of Westminster, the Irish played a very active part. Patrick McGilligan, the Irish delegate to the 1930 Conference, declared in July 1931 that with the passage of the Statute of Westminster the imperial system 'which it took centuries to build' was finally demolished. In its place there was a Commonwealth of Nations. It was not an Empire. It was an association of free and equal nations. And the Irish Free State was one among them. But *was it* free? McGilligan's political opponents were by no means convinced. The government had secured right of direct access to the king. They had secured a separate, Irish Great Seal for the separate ratification of treaties. But were these the things that really mattered? What of the treaty, that treaty imposed under threat 'of immediate and terrible war?' What about the hated Oath of Allegiance? What about the governor-general residing in the old vice-regal lodge and symbolising the presence of the Crown in the constitution? What about Irish neutrality with the Treaty Ports in British hands? What about the right of seccession itself? All these questions were asked; they were the coin of contemporary political controversy. And at least some of them were soon to be put to the test.

With republican nationalism once more in the ascendant de Valera was brought to power early in 1932 and one consequence was that the period of Irish refashioning of the Commonwealth ended before it had really begun.

The passage of the Statute of Westminster had brought out some of the ambiguities in the Treaty Settlement 1921. The first article of the treaty had declared that the Irish Free State should have the same constitutional status as the Dominion of Canada, the Commonwealth of Australia, the Dominion of New Zealand and the Union of South Africa, and the third Article had more particularly defined Irish status by reference to that of Canada, the oldest dominion. The treaty as a whole was vested with the force of fundamental law, both the Constituent Act and the constitution declaring that if any provision of the constitution, or any amendment thereof, or any law made thereunder, was in any respect repugnant to any provision of the treaty, it was to the extent of such repugnancy 'absolutely void and inoperative'. But was there not and had there not always been the possibility of conflict here? Canadian status was not fixed; it was changing, it was developing fast. Was it not the case that under the earlier provisions of the treaty, Irish status should likewise develop and advance? But what if such advances were in conflict with other provisions of the treaty? Was Irish status then to be regarded to that extent as frozen and immutable? English die-hard opinion took this view and sought to except the Irish Free State from the Statute of Westminster on that ground. President Cosgrave objected; the Irish Free State was not excepted. When de Valera came to office, he announced his intention of removing the Oath of Allegiance from the constitution. It was mandatory under the treaty – though President de Valera voiced his doubts even about that. But was it mandatory under the Statute of Westminster? President de Valera, it is true, did not pose this question; after all the statute was a British enactment. He deployed instead arguments grounded in national right. He told J. H. Thomas, the secretary of state for the dominions, on 22 March 1932, that the constitution was the people's constitution; that the government had an absolute right to modify it as the people desired. The people had declared their will. There was no ambiguity about their resolve to remove the oath. It was an intolerable burden and a relic of medievalism. It was the cause of all the dissension in Ireland since the treaty. It made friendly relations with Britain impossible. It was a test unparalleled in treaty relationships between states, and it had been imposed under threat of immediate and terrible war.[49] It had to go and it was clear it was going, whatever the British government or Irish lawyers might say.

Was President de Valera, in his assault upon the oath, challenging the sanctity of the treaty settlement as a whole? J. H. Thomas, after some increasingly acrimonious exchanges in which the area in dispute was widened both constitutionally and economically by the Irish government's decision to retain Irish land annuity payments, was convinced that this was so. He maintained that the oath was mandatory under the treaty, that it was an integral part of the 1921 settlement and that the treaty as a whole was an agreement 'which can only be altered by consent'. President de Valera remained unmoved. 'Whether the oath was', he wrote on 5 April 1932, 'or was not an integral part of the treaty made ten years ago is not now the issue. The real issue is that the oath is an intolerable burden to the people of this state and they have declared in the most formal manner that they desire its instant removal.' They desired the removal of other things besides and their wishes were met. Following the abolition of the oath in 1933, there came a series of constitutional amendments culminating in the abolition of the office of the governor-general, the keystone as it were of the dominion constitutional arch, in 1936. The constitution of 1922 in consequence became a thing of shreds and patches and whatever validity the treaty continued to possess in contractual terms it had lost in law since the Removal of the Oath Act 1933 deleted the 'repugnancy clause' from the constitution.

Had the Irish acted unconstitutionally? There were two answers, conflicting and paradoxical to this question. The Irish courts, basing themselves on the constitution of 1922 and the fundamental authority it gave to the provisions of the treaty, as late as 1934 maintained that the Irish government were acting *ultra vires* in their constitutional reforms because no power had been conferred upon them by which they were entitled to repeal the repugnancy clause in the constitution. But the judicial committee of the Privy Council concluded otherwise in a judgment delivered a year later. They argued that the effect of the enactment of the Statute of Westminster was to remove the fetter that lay upon the Irish Free State legislature and that accordingly the *Oireachtas* had become free to pass legislation repugnant to imperial legislation – in which the treaty had also been embodied – and that they had in fact done so. In other words, in British law, though not in Irish, de Valera's revolution was not in a legal sense a revolution at all. He had done in the constitutional field what under British law he was entitled to do after 1931. It was J. H. Thomas who on this point had had the ground cut away from under his feet.[50]

The abdication of King Edward VIII in 1936 was the first major test of the new constitutional arrangements. All the self-governing members of the Commonwealth were concerned with the succession to the Crown. In the early stages of the crisis however, Baldwin alone advised the king as his 'counsellor and friend'. The king was the first to suggest that there should be consultation with dominion governments – on the question of a possible morganatic marriage with Mrs Simpson. Consultation followed, but between governments, and not (as might have been expected) between the king and his governors-general.[51] Dominion governments were united in opposition to marriage in any guise. The Australian prime minister, J. A. Lyons, spoke of 'widespread condemnation' if Mrs Simpson became queen and of a morganatic marriage as 'running counter to the best traditions of the monarchy'.[52] Mackenzie King said that Canada would not approve whether Mrs Simpson became queen or not; General Hertzog that abdication would be a lesser evil than marriage. 'The one would be a great shock, the other a permanent wound.' The king abdicated. Because Australia and New Zealand had not adopted the Statute of Westminster, the Abdication Act merely records their assent thereto. Canada requested and consented to its enactment. The South African government maintained no legislation was necessary in the union, whereupon King George VI succeeded under the relevant provisions of the Status of the Union Act on the signature of the Instrument of Abdication by King Edward VIII on December 10. This interpretation of the constitutional position served further to underline the separate position of the king as king of South Africa. The Irish Free State took the opportunity of removing all reference to the Crown in the constitution and of enacting the External Relations Act which specifically defined the functions that might be discharged by the Crown at the discretion of the Executive Council of the Irish Free State. This took two days, so that between 10–12 December there were, as Professor Wheare has noted, two kings in the Commonwealth.[53] This is a matter of interest to constitutional historians but of incidental importance. What was important and impressive was the measure of agreement among Commonwealth governments throughout the crisis. Because Baldwin's opinion that the Crown was the 'last link of Empire that is left' was widely endorsed, all who were anxious to preserve its unity exercised their responsibility with due regard to the magnitude of the issues at stake.

Yet the Commonwealth was more than a constitutional experiment; it was, in so far as it was anything, an historic association of peoples and governments. Their interests whether separate or held in common were manifold, and at the climax of the constitutional changes in the relations between Britain and the dominions in 1931, peoples and governments alike were preoccupied with the reality of twentieth-century international economics in their harshest manifestation.

The dominions valued their tariff personalities as they valued their political personalities. But in terms of trade there had been no centralised Empire since the commercial revolution of the mid-nineteenth century. There was no question, therefore, in the inter-war years of dominion preoccupation with the dismantling of a imperial trading system. It had long since been dismantled – by the imperial power itself. There was no possibility, as Joseph Chamberlain had learned to his disappointment, of reestablishing a unitary trading system within the Empire. But while Empire free trade was beyond the bounds of practical politics a reciprocal imperial preferential system remained for many years precariously poised on the margin of them. There was one condition of its realisation, as Imperial Conference after Imperial Conference recognised, and that was a British retreat from her free trade principles. She received preferences from protectionist dominions, she gave nothing in return. Would she be prepared in any circumstances to abandon traditional trading doctrine or dogma?

The first world war fostered an upsurge of imperial economic sentiment. The emphasis was on economic defence, on the economic siege, but the goal was imperial self-sufficiency. The most extravagant hopes were entertained by a committee under the chairmanship of Lord Balfour of Burleigh appointed in 1917 to enquire into British commercial and economic policy after the war. It recommended that all new United Kingdom duties should be made preferential in favour of the Empire. The Imperial War Conference endorsed the recommendation. But once victory was achieved and the economic strains of wartime relaxed, enthusiasm for economic, as for political, integration waned and the goal of imperial preference seemed almost as remote as ever. But not quite. The Conservative Party was in the ascendant and among the Conservatives there were many converts to the cause. In 1923, abruptly and evidently without full consideration, the new Conservative leader Stanley Baldwin, in order, so Amery alleged, 'to dish Lloyd George', announced that he would fight the forthcoming election on the platform of preference. He was defeated. It was not an encouraging experience. But perceptibly the party, and perhaps also the country, were moving away from earlier, often uncritical, faith in free trade.

It was not, however, slowly maturing conviction but a world economic crisis that finally brought about the change. As world markets collapsed Empire statesmen sought refuge within imperial frontiers. Certainly there was the attraction of an idea but it was desperate necessity that impelled them to action. On 4 February 1932 the British government introduced the Import Duties Bill. By allowing the imposition of tariffs the enactment of the bill later that year opened the way to imperial preference. Neville Chamberlain, with the process of political decentralisation that had culminated in the Statute of Westminster in mind and with his father's frustrated campaign to inspire him, spoke of renewed endeavours to promote imperial trade as 'an attempt to bring the Empire together again'.[54] An Imperial Economic Conference assembled in Ottawa under the zealous and enthusiastic chairmanship of R. B. Bennett. He hailed the Conference as unique among all other assemblies of history. 'Faced with the need for unselfish and concerted action,' he said, 'the prospects of achievement were never more certain'. But behind the Ottawa Conference lay the shadow of falling prices, the ruin of countless primary producers in the dominions, among them the wheat growers of the Canadian prairies, New Zealand dairy farmers, and wool growers in Australia, faced with a fall of no less than 50 per cent between 1928 and 1931 in the export value of their wool. In such circumstances it is not surprising that the exhilaration which undoubtedly prevailed in Ottawa appeared to some as having an air not of natural spontaneity but of the enforced gaiety of a septuagenarian wedding.

At Ottawa the cry was for more trade within the Empire. Yet the welfare of the Empire was tied in with world trade. 'Anything tending to check the foreign exports in the United Kingdom', said Baldwin, 'must lessen the purchasing power of her people and so damage the market on which the dominions so largely depend.' The spokesman of an exporting manufacturing country could say no less. But Britain was prepared to continue to allow free entry of dominion primary produce. This was 'the greatest boon' that Britain was able to offer to the dominions. Since the enactment of the Import Duties Act it was an exclusive privilege, its value enhanced by the raising of tariffs against foreign competitors. This tariff barrier was reinforced in some instances by quantitative restrictions on a quota basis. In return British manufactured goods secured increased preferences in dominion markets. But the advantages that accrued both to Britain and to the dominions were secured chiefly by raising trade barriers against the foreigner. Imperial protectionists welcomed this and R. B. Bennett spoke of the 'new and greater Empire' which was coming into being. But Liberals whose aim was the gradual freeing of world trade were affronted. Mackenzie King on 17 October 1932 professed himself dismayed at the great 'protectionist wall' which was being arranged around the frontiers of Empire, making trade with the rest of the world increasingly difficult. The protagonists of preference discounted the idea that they were engaged in economic warfare with the rest of the world. They were concerned to develop Empire resources and claimed that they were moved as much by an ideal as by necessity. Their economics were defensive, the economics of siege, and they neither intended nor desired to engage in economic warfare with foreign countries.

There was much hard bargaining in Ottawa. The outcome of it was not an agreement but a multiplicity of agreements. Their range, variety and detail makes difficult any general assessment of the results of the Conference. In the immediately succeeding years statistics show an increase in Empire trade. But was this wholly due to Ottawa? Between 1932 and 1938 Canadian exports to the United Kingdom increased sharply. But they increased equally sharply to the United States where there were no preferential arrangements. In themselves these figures by no means discount the value of the Ottawa agreements to Canada. Those agreements ensured the vitally important United Kingdom market for Canadian wheat. But a larger question remains as to whether the Ottawa agreements modified or even changed the direction of Canadian trade. Mackenzie King and Bennett were in agreement about the importance of keeping open to Canada and holding 'the most valuable market this dominion has ever known', but King at least was not content with concentration upon the British market alone. He was anxious to broaden the basis of Canada's export trade. Multilateralism was a distant objective but negotiating with the United States to restore trade to its former level led first to bilateral and then to triangular United Kingdom, United States, Canadian commercial agreements in 1938, the United Kingdom and Canada sacrificing advantages in their own markets and receiving corresponding compensation in United States markets. As a result by 1938, six years after Ottawa, 'the greatest triangular exchange of commodities in the world' had been frozen into patterns of reciprocal advantage by three commercial treaties, to two of which Canada was a signatory.[55] Australian experience ran roughly parallel with Canadian. It was, as Professor Hancock has observed,[56] that imperial preference was good but not enough. Britain's own agricultural protectionism, Japan's value as a market for wool (Japan took 13.2 per cent of Australia's wool exports in 1928–9, 20 per cent in 1932–4), as a good customer by bilateral standards and her expansionist policies, despite the disturbing element of the dumping of cheap textiles, had both to be taken into account. Imperial trade was only a part of Australia's general interests – an important part but still only a part, as is statistically shown with some 60 per cent of Australia's exports going to Empire countries in 1936. In 1937 Menzies pointed out that 'we are reaching a point in economic history when a rigid insistence upon the fullest measures of Empire preference may prevent the British countries from taking their proper part in a great movement of world appeasement through the revival of trade.' The same point was put more precisely when it was remarked that wool was too big a thing to be imperial in its trade outlets.

What was true of Canada and Australia and the other dominions was even more true in the case of Britain. It was essential for a great manufacturing nation dependent upon export markets to retain and develop the foreign markets for her goods. She could not afford to be cabined and confined within a constricting Commonwealth framework. Yet the figures suggest that the Ottawa agreements somewhat improved the position of the dominions in the British market and of British goods in dominion markets. Between 1929 and 1936 British imports from the Empire amounted to 29.4 per cent of total imports in the first year; 35.3 per cent in 1932 and 39.1 per cent in 1936. The percentage for 1932, the year of the Ottawa Conference, did not reflect the results of that conference. There was, therefore, a trend towards larger British imports from the Empire before the Ottawa Conference. The figures show that in respect of imports it was confirmed and developed after the Conference. But might not some of that development have taken place in any case? Analysis has revealed that at least some items in dominion export lists to Britain which enjoyed no preference showed a more marked increase immediately after the Ottawa Conference than those which had the benefit of preference. In sum, the very complexity and variety of the Ottawa agreements induces a certain caution in judgment upon their consequences. The least that can be said is that at Ottawa the possibilities of increased Empire trade were examined and that as a result of the Ottawa Conference they were given opportunities for development more favourable than they would otherwise have enjoyed. But already in the 1930s the sufficiency of Commonwealth trade – especially for Britain – and its growth-potential, even under favourable stimuli, were becoming suspect. It was valuable but it was not enough, and even more important it was not likely to become enough. Despite superficial appearances, the dominions in their trading as in their international policies were perforce looking increasingly outwards.

CHAPTER 9

INDIA: AN UNCERTAIN GOAL

The dominions whose status was defined in the Balfour Report and whose names were listed in section 1 of the Statute of Westminster were predominantly European in respect of their population and wholly European in respect of their government. There were minorities of non-European origin in Australia, in Canada and in New Zealand; there was a large non-European majority in the Union of South Africa. But neither minorities nor majority were in a position to exert a decisive influence upon government. In Canada and even in South Africa it was the cultural tensions between peoples of European stock that hitherto had exercised a formative influence upon national policy, and possibly for that reason it was in the past by no means unknown, however much discountenanced by Canadian scholars, for the term 'race' to be applied to relations between English and French-speaking Canadians, while on the lips of South African politicians the terms 'race' and 'racial', until recent times, customarily referred to relations between British and Afrikaners.[1] That they did not warrant such a description if the term 'race' were to be precisely defined was in a sense beside the point; it was terminology that in South Africa at least was felt to have both traditional justification and an inner appropriateness, since the term 'cultural' seemed (and to a fast diminishing number may still seem) an anodynous description of the painful intensities of Anglo-Afrikaner antipathies at critical moments in their common history. Multi-racial membership of the Commonwealth in the strict sense, meaning the self-governing membership of states inhabited by peoples of different racial origin, dates only from 1947. For that reason in March 1954 the prime minister of Pakistan, Mohammad Ali, spoke of 1947 as a year in Commonwealth history in true line of succession from 1867 and 1926 and as important as either. It was from the British North America Act that the conception of dominion self-government derived; from the definition of dominion status in the Balfour Report that the contemporary Commonwealth might be dated; and while in the prime minister's opinion the pace of constitutional evolution thereafter had been 'slow, painfully slow',[2]

South Asia had attained self-government; and multi-racial Commonwealth membership thereupon became a political reality eighty years after the Dominion of Canada had come into being.

The association between self-government and Commonwealth membership, to which Mohammad Ali referred had proved to be the historical precondition of the enlarged Commonwealth, but on the British side at least it was by no means always assumed that this would be so. Radical imperialists like Joseph Chamberlain, the great proconsuls Curzon, Cromer, Milner, had alike emphasised excellence in the art of government as the outstanding contribution by Britain to the Empire overseas. By government, however, they meant orderly and impartial administration of non-European dependent territories, not the government of them by their own peoples. That British settlers in Canada or Australia or New Zealand should believe that they inherited the traditions, and were therefore entitled to practise the art of responsible self-government, was a matter for acquiescence or welcome according to the viewpoint, but assuredly one neither for surprise nor for concern. It was a rather different matter when other Europeans, non-British in extraction, claimed corresponding rights. Neither Afrikaners nor Irish were considered well fitted to exercise them, the former largely because they were too paternalist in their notions of government as well as hostile to the British connection, the latter also on that second ground and because they were deemed politically too volatile. As for representative institutions and responsible self-government for non-Europeans, that for long seemed altogether inconceivable to the traditional British imperial ruling class. To a later age preoccupied with problems of race there seemed a simple explanation – racial prejudice. But this explanation is insufficient. The government of Empire in its higher reaches was as aristocratic as it was autocratic – this it was that gave point to James Mill's jibe, later to be quoted with relish by J. A. Hobson,[3] about imperial administration being a vast system of outdoor relief for the upper classes – but the great majority of its peoples, including all its non-European peoples – the 'lower races' – were not thought of as qualified to govern themselves on Darwinian notions of fitness rather than racial preconceptions, though indeed the two often merged. Curzon, noted Dr Gopal,[4] had no racial prejudice. But he proceeds – 'this was a mental blindness and not an ethical virtue. A man who was not really aware even of the lower orders in Britain could not be expected to register the full significance of the problem of race relations in India.' It was not tolerance but insensitivity that precluded discrimination on Curzon's part. Curzon as viceroy stood in lonely preeminence, but his insensitivity was shared for precisely that reason by many lesser men who on lesser heights but in corresponding isolation sustained the administration of Empire.

The outlook of the rulers, acclaiming at once the supreme virtues of the British system of government and refusing to extend its benefits to subject peoples, produced an Indian paradox. It was the Indian National Congress which from the day of its first session in Bombay in 1885 demanded the extension of British parliamentary institutions to India, while the British exponents of what Joseph Chamberlain once described as 'the best form of government', continued to express doubts about the wisdom of acceding to the Congress demand. Thus the oblique introduction of the representative principle in India in 1892 and its further extension in the Morley-Minto reforms of 1909 were widely regarded in Britain, and not only by conservative opinion, as a 'sop to impossible ambitions'. 'The notion', said Lord Kimberley, a former Liberal secretary of state for India in 1890, 'of a Parliamentary representation of so vast a country almost as large as Europe containing so large a number of different races is one of the wildest imaginations that ever entered the minds of men.'[5] 'We are no advocates of representative government for India in the western sense of the term'; wrote the viceroy, Lord Minto to Morley at the India Office in March 1907, 'it could never be akin to the instincts of the many races composing the population of the Indian Empire. It would be a western importation uncongenial to eastern tastes.' In reply Morley concurred in the repudiation of 'the intention or desire to attempt the transplantation of any European form of representative government to Indian soil' and two years later reassured the House of Lords by saying that he thought it neither desirable nor possible nor even conceivable that English political institutions should be extended to India.[6] 'If I were attempting to set up a Parliamentary system in India,' he told the House of Lords[7] in speaking of the reforms jointly associated with his name and that of the viceroy, 'or if it could be said that this chapter of reforms led directly or necessarily up to the establishment of a Parliamentary system in India, I, for one, would have nothing at all to do with it.' For the foreseeable future 'a Parliamentary system in India is not the goal to which I for one moment would aspire'. Not even with war and all the changes it brought did this note of scepticism disappear. The Simon Commission, wholly British in its membership, in a Report published in 1929 exuded the depressing sort of wisdom that springs from doubt and misgivings.

> The British Parliamentary system . . . has been fitted like a well-worn garment to the figure of the wearer, but it does not follow that it will suit everybody. . . . British parliamentarianism in India is a translation, and in even the best translations the essential meaning is apt to be lost.[8]

But while in common with others before and after them the commission talked somewhat spaciously of forms of democratic government other than the British – the American presidential system, because of the strong, stable executive it was thought to provide and the Swiss, with non-party administration, were apt to be the most favoured alternatives – it remained doubtful whether the British rulers of India, or indeed Indians trained under the British system, would have been qualified to apply them. What is certain is that the British system was what self-conscious Indian opinion wanted and it was also the system which by a gesture of faith rather than by reasoned conviction was proclaimed in 1917 to be the goal of British policy in India.

The ambivalence in British attitudes to the future government of India was implicit in the nature of British rule. The *Raj* was strangely compounded of splendid assurance and inner uncertainties. The assurance came the more easily to the men on the spot, to the soldiers and the administrators, the governors and the viceroys of British India. They occupied the seats of power; they determined how it should be exercised; they were the heirs of Empire and in 1903 and 1911 (a trifle self-consciously perhaps) they organised Durbars in Delhi with a king-emperor in the second case making spectacular entry in person into the Red Fort so as to underline imperial succession from the Mughal rulers who preceded them; they were aware that behind them, sustaining their authority, were not only the indigenous instruments of power, but also, should the need arise, the resources of a world-wide Empire. Yet behind the sometimes formal and occasionally glittering façade of absolutism there remained the reality of divided responsibility. The British rulers of India were subject to control. It was remote control, that of the secretary of state for India in London, of the cabinet (of which he was a member) and of the Parliament, to which that cabinet was responsible. Autocracy was thus subject to democracy. That subjection was in practice intermittent and apt on occasion to be irritating rather than effective. It could hardly, indeed, have been otherwise. Yet subjection there was and in principle and practice alike its ultimate reality was asserted and reasserted.

The form of Indian government and of imperial control over it was determined when the Mutiny sounded the death-knell of East India Company rule in India. 'India,' it was stated succinctly in the Government of India Act 1858, 'shall be governed by and in the name of Her Majesty, and all rights in relation to any territories which might have been exercised by the said Company if this Act had not been passed shall and may be exercised by and in the name of Her Majesty. . .'[9] In addition the governor-general was invested by Royal Proclamation with the more resounding designation of viceroy, as was deemed appropriate for a representative who was at once to exercise the august responsibilities of government in India and to serve as counterpart to the new secretary of state for India responsible to cabinet and Parliament, not as the colonial secretary for a multiplicity of dependent territories but for an Empire as it had been and as it was soon to be known again. The viceroy was to be assisted in the discharge of his Indian duties by an Executive and Legislative Council, composed in the first instance of officials, but to the number of which was added in 1861 not less than six or more than twelve unofficial members, for the discussion of legislative proposals.[10] These reforms somewhat broadened the basis of government but since the Legislative Council were limited to discussion, with members debarred from the asking of questions or the moving of resolutions, and the viceroy retained the power to overrule his Executive Council, there was no effective restraint on vice-regal authority in India. The checks upon it existed not in India but in London, and for their efficacy in practice much depended upon the personalities of viceroys and secretaries of state and the relations between them.

There were some parallels but as many contrasts between Indian and Irish administration. Under the union, the highest executive officers in Ireland were the lord lieutenant and the chief secretary, but while it was customary for one or other of them to sit in cabinet, it was by no means uniformly the chief secretary who did so and Balfour was of the opinion that the real headship of the Irish government belonged to the minister who happened to be both in the cabinet and the House of Commons.[11] But in the case of India distance alone precluded any such alternation. The secretary of state, by virtue of his office, was securely entrenched in the cabinet, the viceroy resident in India for his period of office. There was, accordingly, clearer demarcation than in contemporary Ireland of status and function. The secretary of state had no executive duties to discharge in Calcutta or Delhi, as had the chief secretary in Dublin, while the viceroy far away had few opportunities of influencing the cabinet in the event of disagreement with the secretary of state. More generally the different responsibilities discharged by viceroy and secretary of state, and the sharply contrasted worlds in which they moved, fostered not personal rivalries but a sense of common participation in an historic undertaking. As communications with the east improved with the laying of the overland cable to India in 1868, the opening of the Suez Canal in 1869 and the completion of a British submarine cable in 1870, the possible direct influence in practice of the secretary of state over government in India increased.[12] But in principle there was no change. In contrast again with the continuing administrative confusion in Ireland from the time of union, the relationship between secretary of state and viceroy had been defined at the outset and was as need arose subsequently restated. Thus the secretary of state in a dispatch of 24 November 1870 to the government in India noted that the risk of serious embarrassment would become much greater than hitherto it has been found to be, if a clear understanding were not maintained as to one great principle which from the beginning has underlaid the whole system. That principle is, that the final control and direction of the affairs of India rest with the home government, and not with the authorities appointed and established by the Crown, under Parliamentary enactment, in India itself.

The government established in India is (from the nature of the case) subordinate to the imperial government at home. And no government can be subordinate unless it is within the power of the superior government to order what is to be done or left undone, and to enforce on its officers, through the ordinary and constitutional means, obedience to its directions as to the use which they are to make of official position and power in furtherance of the policy which has been finally decided upon by the advisers of the Crown.[13]

This subordination which the secretary of state re-emphasised could be, and was, irksome to viceroys, not least, as may well be imagined, to Lord Curzon:

I have been thinking [wrote Curzon to the secretary of state, Lord George Hamilton, in May 1902] over the experience of the last 3½ years. . . . It seems to me to establish conclusively a desire upon the part of your advisers in the India Office to thwart and hamper me in the work which I am endeavouring to undertake here . . . I will ask you to try and put yourself in my position. Here I am working away the whole day long and a considerable part of the night, in the discharge of what I believe to be a serious and solemn duty. I am conducting the task in exile, in complete isolation from all friends or advisers, surrounded by forces and combinations against which it often requires great courage to struggle, habitually harassed, constantly weary, and often in physical distress and pain. If, in addition to all these anxieties, against which I am capable of holding up my head, I am also to be perpetually nagged and impeded and misunderstood by the India Council at home, I say plainly that I would sooner give up the task.

Hamilton replied with tolerant understanding.

The very magnitude of the work which the viceroy can do [he wrote] makes control of any kind the more obnoxious to him. . . . But, after all, is the viceroy's position in this respect more trying than that of the other public servants and ministers of the British Empire? Look at the prime minister in this country, or the head of any one of the great departments of state who has to represent that department in the House of Commons. Take the position either of Salisbury, Balfour, Beach, or Chamberlain: they are subjected to a different form of check and interference far more annoying, and far more effective, than any to which a viceroy can be subject. Take the great men who have preceded you in your office: Warren Hastings, Cornwallis, Wellesley, Hardinge, and Dalhousie – they all had to carry on their work under the same conditions which you find irritating and dilatory, and I think I may fairly say that not one of those distinguished predecessors had as easy a colleague to deal with in this country as myself.[14]

Yet might Curzon not have retorted that the checks upon colleagues in London were the outcome of personal debate and discussion and that, as a matter of fact, his distinguished predecessors in India had been ridden on a looser rein?

There was more at issue in these exchanges than particular situation or personality. Behind them lay the question of final control. Curzon, in his dispatch, had challenged established tradition in expressing the view that 'the keys of India are not in England, nor in the House of Commons. They are in the office desk of every young Civilian in this country.'[15] He was, however, mistaken and it was important at the time and for the future that he was mistaken. It became the practice in subsequent years for reforms in Indian government to be known by the hyphenated names of secretary of state and viceroy – Morley-Minto in 1909, Montagu-Chelmsford in 1919 – the secretary of state's name coming first, in accord with appropriate constitutional usage. And usage in this case coincided with political reality. The keys of India were in the House of Commons in so far as they were in British hands at all. The secretary of state was necessarily responsive to the mood of the House and the House itself was responsive to the mood of the people. In the critical twentieth-century years both House and people were notably more disposed to change than were the viceroy, his advisers and the British administration in India and their disposition, intermittently or even negatively voiced, had greater influence than the government of India's aversion to it.

In the perspective of history the determining of policy assumes its decisive importance, but what was apt to loom larger in the eyes of contemporaries was the outlook and impact at the personal level of imperial government and administration in India. What manner of men were responsible for the administration of this vast eastern autocracy? The answer, in respect of all the higher reaches of administration, was Englishmen – carefully prepared, rigorously selected by public examination and, as a body of men, of higher calibre than administrators in any other part of the Empire. But they were nonetheless for most of the period for the most part Englishmen. The queen's proclamation announcing the new order in 1858 had specifically admitted all, irrespective of race or creed, who were suitably qualified to offices in the administration. But in practice there was a wide gap, much resented by politically self-conscious Indians, between intention and fulfilment. That gap created, among other things, what was known as 'the service question'. Entry into the Indian civil service was by competitive examination. But the syllabus for that examination was based on the English school curriculum and the examination itself was held in England. Both inevitably discouraged Indian candidates whether Moslem or Hindu.

For the latter there was additional discouragement in as much as Hindus travelling overseas were automatically deprived of their caste and obliged to seek readmission to it on return. In 1878, furthermore, the age of examination was reduced from twenty-two to nineteen – at which age Indian candidates had not had the teaching to enable them to compete with much hope of success against the products of English schools. In India there arose a demand for 'simultaneous examinations' in Britain and in India so as to relieve Indian candidates at least of the necessity to travel to Britain. It was accepted in principle in 1893, and a bill was introduced and passed in the House of Commons to give effect to it. But even this modest ameliorative measure was not acted upon until 1919. Truly was it remarked that Englishmen in the east acquired an oriental insensitivity to time.

The composition of the Indian administration was one question – a political question with racial overtones – the outlook of the administrators another. In so far as it was reflected in their idealised concept of their rôle, that outlook owed its distinctive quality to the historiography of the Empires of the ancient world as reinterpreted in the ancient English universities and transmitted by them to those who taught at Haileybury and other English public schools. The virtues these administrators prized were courage, independence, manliness, fair play and the even-handed justice enjoined upon rulers in the last words of David, king of Israel:

> He that ruleth over men must be just,
> Ruling in the fear of God.
> And he shall be as the light of the morning
> when the sun riseth,
> Even a morning without clouds.

With these idealised concepts went a Virgilian bias in favour of the solid virtues of the countryman and against the unstable urban intelligentsia, combined with a reliance for their own part upon character, good sense and good judgment rather than ideas. The more lasting achievements of British administration – the introduction of a unified system of law and justice, with a code of civil and criminal procedure such as India had not hitherto known, the organisation of administration, in the districts, the provinces and at the centre of British India – are themselves indicative of the outlook of the administrators and of the immensity of their achievement. Their memorialist has written a record of the men of the I.C.S. in two volumes carrying the appropriately Platonic subtitles of *The Founders* and *The Guardians*. But the work as a whole carries the title, *The Men who Ruled India*.[16] They were rulers who came from outside and ruled from above. The barriers that existed in practice against Indian recruitment heightened their isolation in their homes, their clubs, the residencies of governors and the palaces of viceroys. They were insulated largely in self-protection against the ideas of those whom they ruled, but with time and detachment, movements of opinion at home also ceased to have much impact upon them.

James Bryce, when he visited India in November 1888, returned somewhat disappointed with the civil service. He recognised the quality of the men in the higher posts and noted that they were intelligent, very hard-working, with apparently a high sense of public duty and a desire to promote the welfare of the people of India. But he proceeded,

> they seem rather wanting in imagination and sympathy, less inspired by the extraordinary and unprecedented phenomena of the country than might have been expected, with little intellectual initiative; too conventionally English in their ways of life and thoughts to rise to the position. . . . They are more out of the stream of the world's thought and movement than one was prepared to find.[17]

Fifteen years later Lord Curzon, confessedly in a mood of frustration, made sharper comment.

> How often have I not pointed out to you [he wrote to the secretary of state] that there are neither originality, nor ideas or imagination in the Indian Civil Service, that they think the present the best, and that change or improvement or reform . . . sends a cold shiver down their spine.[18]

This was unjust but it contained an underlying truth. If and when change was to come to India, the impetus from the British side would be from the House of Commons and from sections of public opinion at home, emphatically not from the general body of British administrators or soldiers in India. They were as little welcoming to the ideas of the Liberal, Edwin Montagu, at the close of the first world war, as they were to the cautious reformism of the Conservative, Lord Irwin, a decade later, while of their reception of Sir Stafford Cripps in 1942 it may be remarked that it was as correct as it was constrained. Ironically enough the greatest achievement of these men who were so averse to change was to provide the conditions without which change might have led to chaos. In this respect their work was without parallel in the British or in any other western European empire.

On the longer view and in a wider context there was a deeper ambivalence about British attitudes to change in India. There was on the one hand the firmly established tradition that British rule in India had a fixed term and purpose. The Mills among thinkers and Thomas Munro, Mountstuart Elphinstone, Sir Henry Lawrence and many others subscribed to it. They spoke, with Macaulay, of 'the proudest day' in British history when the British rulers of India, having equipped the peoples of India to govern themselves, would withdraw, their task accomplished. Nor was it chance that these sentiments of early thinkers and administrators were much favoured for quotation by those whose responsibility it was to transfer power in 1947. But it is not to be supposed for a moment that this view was universally or consistently entertained in the intervening years. For the greater part of what K. M. Panikkar wrote of as 'the Augustan age of European Empire in Asia',[19] which he dated from 1840 to 1914, most of the British rulers of India were more disposed to think of the present hour of greatness than of some future day of abdication as the 'proudest moment'. The British Empire in India was, in Curzon's view, 'the miracle of the world' and 'the biggest thing that the English are doing anywhere'.[20] Why should he, why should men who worked under or after him, hasten the day of its eclipse? 'No one,' wrote Curzon's successor, Lord Minto, in 1907,[21] 'believes more firmly than we do that the safety and welfare of India depend on the permanence of British administration. . . .' To a sense of mission in the conscientious discharge of a great task laid upon Britain by Providence there was allied the more realistic calculation, as Curzon phrased it, 'as long as we rule India, we are the greatest power in the world. If we lose it, we shall drop straight away to a third-rate Power.' This, indeed, was part and parcel of the thinking of Empire; these very words were to be echoed by Winston Churchill in the 1930s when he was campaigning violently against plans of the predominantly Conservative national administration to bring into being a self-governing Indian federation. Who, sharing Curzon's opinion, would deliberately bring forward the hour of departure and so precipitate the British decline from greatness? And for those who questioned mission and *real politik* judgment alike, there were still doubts and uncertainties. The subcontinent was not only vast; its destiny was obscure. Even Roman history could provide no satisfying parallel to British rule in India, nor all history point a way by which it might reach its supposedly natural term. Macaulay, it will be remembered, had found it difficult to form any conjecture as to the fate reserved for a state which resembled no other, and acknowledged that the laws which regulated its growth and decay were unknown. His successors a century later rarely claimed to have been able to define them. If change, therefore, there had to be, as even Curzon allowed, what direction should it take? There was one answer, and one answer only, that had a reassuringly familiar ring to those brought up in the British political tradition. It was that the peoples of India should advance by way of representative to responsible government and finally to dominion status. But however right the familiar answer may have appeared to a growing body of British parliamentary and public opinion at home and to the majority of politically self-conscious Indians, it seemed for long inapplicable in such unfamiliar surroundings to the British rulers of India. In its Commonwealth setting the last half century of the British Raj in India is in one part the story of how these rulers of India and those associated with them in the India Office – where unlike in the Colonial and Dominion Offices the Durham Report was not likely at any time to have been recommended reading for new recruits – were at last persuaded (though even then with qualifications) that the familiar road, even in an unfamiliar setting, was the one to travel, if only because no other was sufficiently known to them.

The strangeness and complexities of the setting are not in question. In the cities and the countryside of twentieth-century India, contrasts between great wealth and abject poverty, splendour and misery, self-sacrificing integrity and degrading corruption might find a parallel, not in the twentieth- but in the eighteenth-century western world where, as Balzac remarked 'l'incessant concubinage du Luxe et de la Misère, du Vice et de l'Honnêté' were of the essence of life in pre-revolutionary France. Politically India was no less evidently divided between the provinces of British India and the Indian princely states which comprised well over a third of the territory of the subcontinent and one quarter of its population. At the deeper level of religion and culture it was divided into several communities, there being at the time of the 1931 census some 239 million Hindus, 78 million Muslims, 4 million Sikhs and 6 million Christians in the subcontinent. So long as the alien imperial power remained, the positions of classes, provinces, princes and communities were fixed from above. They might seek for advantage here or betterment there but their appeal was to a final and absolute authority. Once the endurance of that authority appeared in doubt then there was bound to open (as there did) a struggle for succession or survival.

The claims of the Indian National Congress for the succession appeared to its own members, and indeed to many outside, to be virtually conclusive. 'Congress alone,' Gandhi told the Round Table Conference in London in 1931, 'claims to represent the whole of India . . .'[22] and to it, and to it alone, should power be transferred. That claim was disputed by the princes – British officers in Indian dress the Mahatma termed them – and first disquieted and ultimately alienated the great majority of the Muslims. The reason was clear. The Congress not only demanded independence from the British but looked forward to an independent India, democratically governed by a people exercising their will through representative institutions. In a land in which community commanded a first allegiance, such institutions were bound to place ultimate power in the hands of the majority community. Unrestricted exercise of that power, which electoral arithmetic thus conferred, might be mitigated by constitutional devices of one kind or another, but no amount of constitutional ingenuity could alter the balance of numbers or deprive the majority of the final authority which numbers conferred upon it. For this reason there existed, below the superficial complications of the Indian political scene, an underlying simplicity which left none of the parties concerned with the succession of power – the princes, the Congress, the Muslim League, the British – with much ground for manoeuvre.

The princes, from the greatest among them in Travancore, Hyderabad, Kashmir and the Rajput states, down to the smallest rajahs exercising sway over some few thousand acres, were dependent for survival against the rising tides of nationalism, democracy and a hostile Congress, upon their association by treaties with the Paramount Power. They were insistent, therefore, upon the sanctity of those treaties, from which they derived the essential reassurance for their continued status and privileges. Down to 1947 the princes could count upon sympathetic understanding from an imperial power grateful for their loyalty in time of war and well content to see these islands of stability (not to say reaction) standing seemingly secure, as bulwarks against the assaults of popular and left-wing nationalist revolution. The Muslims, it is true, as the second largest community in India, enjoyed a somewhat wider freedom of action. Nonetheless the Muslim leaders, from Sayyid Ahmad in the last quarter of the nineteenth century, to the Aga Khan early in the twentieth century, to Mohammed Ali Jinnah in the inter-war years, were compelled, sooner rather than later, in each case to concern themselves with the question of what would be the position of this large and therefore potentially disruptive minority community in an India from which the British *Raj* had withdrawn. There were two possible answers. The first was submergence of the smaller community in a national movement before independence and thereafter in a nation-state in which inevitably the majority community, the Hindus, would play the dominant part. Such merging, or submerging, of community interest implied first, confidence in the goodwill and sense of justice of the majority and secondly, acceptance of a national before a communal allegiance. There were periods of Muslim-Hindu *rapprochement*, most notably the so-called Lucknow Pact of 1916, when it seemed as if the first condition was to be fulfilled. But the periods of such understanding proved intermittent and in each case they were followed by a more prolonged and more intense expression of mistrust and finally of open antagonism. However these movements in opinion are to be interpreted historically, the Muslim leadership had little choice in the end. Once there was insufficiency of trust, the minority had to seek safeguards. They did so in 1906–7 and they secured them in the Morley-Minto reforms of 1909, with communal electoral rolls and voting weighted in their favour. Subsequently the aim of the Muslim leadership was defensive, holding the British to the concessions they had made and seeking in the inter-war years to strengthen still further their position against the day of majority rule. Step by step they advanced from a position of special voting rights to insistence upon a federal as against a unitary state, from a federation with a strong centre to a federation with a weak centre and finally to partition.

The Indian National Congress for its part had every reason to press the simple claim of majority rule in a unitary state. The Congress High Command demanded representative institutions on the British model without distinction of class or creed, a unitary form of government with a cabinet responsible to an elected lower House and ultimately an independent India in which the fragmentation of princely states and divergent communities, would be erased from the political map. The nature of their demand presupposed their hostility to the princes and British backing for them and while, in 1916, they accepted electoral discrimination in favour of the Muslims, their later demand as formulated, notably in the draft constitution prepared in 1929 under the chairmanship of Motilal Nehru, was for a unitary state with minimal minority concessions. Therein lay the natural interest of the Congress, and it might reasonably be argued that they could not in the circumstances think or act otherwise. But the hard question that lay before its leadership in the critical years was the extent to which they should or should not modify their aims in the interests of national unity.

British purposes in India, down to the outbreak of the second world war, were to all outward appearances the least narrowly circumscribed. The initiative in respect of enunciation of policy rested in their hands. They were well placed, especially in view of the always latent and ultimately open conflict for the succession to power, to hasten or retard the time of their withdrawal. It was widely credited by the Congress that the British government used this freedom of action to strengthen the position of the princes against democratic India and to entrench Muslim minority against Hindu majority, on the well-established imperial principle of divide and rule. The first is hardly open to dispute; the second, while less easy to determine, is certainly true to the extent that the allegation can be supported by reference to particular policies or actions, the more important of which were the partition of Bengal and the concession of separate electorates and of weightage to the Muslims in the Morley-Minto reforms. Both raised issues which in changing situations down to 1947 retained their essential character and significance.

The first partition of Bengal was the work of Lord Curzon, who, industrious as always, had stated in 1902, his intention of 'looking into the question of political boundaries generally' and on so doing found those of Bengal 'antiquated, illogical and productive of inefficiency'.[23] 'I should like to fix the boundaries for the next generation' he told Sir Alexander Godley. The purpose of the Bengal partition was twofold. The first, an administrative object, was to free the governor-general from responsibility for the government of the province, which had been considered too large by Lord Dalhousie in 1853 and which in his opinion had placed upon the governor-general 'a burden which in its present mass is more than mortal man can fitly bear'. The second was political, at least in its effects, namely to create a new province of East Bengal including all districts in which the Muslims were in a majority. This meant the creation of a Muslim majority province out of an area where the Muslims had hitherto been in a permanent minority. The Muslims were not unitedly in favour, many of the landed classes especially being opposed to the partition of the province, and the Hindus were violent in their denunciation. Thousands of articles were written and speeches made against it. Lord Curzon read them. He did not find in them 'one single line of argument, there is nothing but rhetoric and declamation'. The partition was effected in 1905. It was undone at the Delhi Durbar in 1911. But its consequences were great. It served as a sharp stimulus both to Indian nationalism[24] and to Muslim separatism. Neither, and most certainly not the former, was part of the viceroy's intention. His opinion, expressed in a dispatch to the secretary of state in November 1900, was that 'the Congress is tottering to its fall, and one of my great ambitions while in India is to assist it to a peaceful demise.'[25] But the Congress, despite its division between constitutional moderates and extremists, emerged from the viceroyalty, not weakened but strengthened.

One important cause of the revival of the Congress was the resentment at a partition which was thought to indicate a deliberate British policy of building up Muslim minority consciousness as a counterweight to nascent Indian nationalism. That suspicion was heightened by the concession in the Morley-Minto reforms of weightage and special electorates to the Muslims. In the inter-war years it was all pervasive in the Congress ranks, drawing sustenance from these past experiences and present force from the supposed bias of many British administrators in favour of Muslims as against Hindus. Supposition, however, even with an air of probability about it, is not tantamount to conclusive historical evidence. But politically it can be, and in this case almost certainly was, of first importance. It presumed a deliberate British purpose, not of early withdrawal, but of the extension of the period of

British rule by the accentuation of India's domestic divisions. Such an interpretation of British governmental policy in so far as it rested upon an equation of the actions and words of particular British leaders at varying times with settled governmental policy over an extended period of time, was clearly an oversimplification and systematic analysis of the evidence only now becoming available is needed before any final historical judgment can be essayed. One point, however, may be noted here, in respect of the British political background. There was no consensus in British opinion about India. On the contrary at the critical time informed opinion in Britain was much exercised and divided about British policy in India. Nor could it be determined in isolation. No British government could pursue for long a policy in India inconsistent with the general pattern of British imperial policy and of a kind not generally acceptable at home. The more important limiting factors upon British freedom of action in India in the inter-war years were, therefore, compounded of Indian nationalist pressures and the reaction of public and parliamentary opinion at home to those pressures. In India the second was apt to be unduly discounted.

It was against this pattern of varied Indian and British interests that the advance to responsible government and dominion status proceeded. The Morley-Minto reforms had increased Indian representation in the legislative councils at the centre and in the provinces and in so doing had served to heighten the Congress demand for a crossing of the line that divided representation from responsibility. But the British government had remained uncommitted about ultimate purposes, and when challenged about them Morley (as earlier noted) had taken refuge in philosophic agnosticism. The first commitment was that given by the secretary of state for India, Edwin Montagu, in 1917 when on behalf of the government he declared that responsible government was the goal of British rule in India. Once the goal was proclaimed the debate henceforward became one of form and timetable, not of purpose. Both were important. The form of government was bound to touch closely on majority-minority relations as well as on the future rôle of the princes, while in respect of time there was not likely to be any departure from the tradition of imperial powers doing too little too late. But far more important was the self-imposed limitation upon British freedom of action. After 1917 they were formally committed to responsible government for India. That implied an Indian constitution on the dominion model. The Indian nationalist leaders were quick to grasp the significance of the weapon which the British cabinet, only half-comprehendingly, had placed in their hands. A promise had been made and the Indians were resolved that Britain should be kept to it. Adolf Hitler addressing the German chiefs-of-staff in the Reich Chancellery in

November 1937 put this aspect of the situation in a nutshell when he remarked that Britain's half-measures in India 'had given to the Indians the opportunity of using later on as a weapon against Britain the non-fulfilment of her promises regarding a constitution'.

The Montagu declaration was made in the third year of the first world war, after the collapse of tzarist Russia and before the entry of the United States, when German fortunes were once more in the ascendant and when the presence of dominion statesmen and Indian representatives in London for the meetings of the Imperial War Conference and cabinet served as a constant reminder of the critical importance of wartime aid from the Empire overseas. Was it not at once right and reasonable, in view of the massive Indian contribution to imperial forces, to seek to conciliate rising national sentiment with assurances of greater Indian participation in the government of the subcontinent? And was it not natural in the circumstances to think of that greater association developing on a dominion pattern, all the more so in view of the great advances in dominion reputation during the war? The answers to both questions, as authorised by members of the war cabinet, were in the affirmative. But it was left to their successors to formulate practical policies on the basis of this broad definition of aims. It was not an easy assignment.

The language of the Montagu declaration was the language of the Durham Report and, at one remove, of dominion status. But what were its actual implications? The war cabinet was too preoccupied to ponder them. But one day they had to be faced. First to be considered was the question of area. The Montagu declaration spoke of India, not of British India. The distinction was not without importance. The gradual development of self-governing institutions, to quote the words of the declaration, 'with a view to the progressive realisation of responsible government in India as an integral part of the British Empire',[26] was to be the goal of British rule. Since India meant the whole of the subcontinent, this in turn meant the inclusion of the Indian states, and since the representative element was altogether lacking in the government of the great majority of them, it implied of necessity slower advance towards the goal than conditions in British India of itself might have been felt to justify. In the context of international and even of British Commonwealth relations any alternative was probably impracticable, as indeed the constitutional advisers to the viceroy concluded in 1929[27] when reviewing this among other related questions, while in domestic terms any distinction in respect of the goals for British and princely India would have been interpreted, and not unreasonably, as a classic example of an imperial essay in the tactics of 'divide and rule'. But the price of common advance was the familiar one of the more backward slowing down the more forward.

There were larger issues. Responsible government implied dominion status but was not synonymous with it. The Government of India Act 1919, giving effect to the Montagu-Chelmsford reform programme, established a diarchical system of government in the provinces of British India, with control of selected subjects transferred to Indian ministers responsible to Indian elected legislatures and, at the centre, an Assembly and a Council of State, both with a majority of elected members though neither having power of control over the viceroy and his executive, together with a Chamber of Princes as a consultative body. These reforms were intended to be steps (albeit more modest than Indian opinion hoped for) along the road to responsible government. But they had no bearing upon status. They served indeed to underline the fact that India's status in the Commonwealth and internationally had outstripped her government. At home there would be no question about India's continuing dependence: abroad she wore at least the trappings of autonomy. India was represented with the dominions at the Imperial War Conference 1917 and in the imperial war cabinet; she was a signatory to the Treaty of Versailles and a founder-member of the League of Nations. It is true that her representatives were nominated by the secretary of state but, it could be argued, this in itself could not diminish the status accorded externally to the country. And on any reckoning India's international personality had developed further than her domestic self-government. Yet it was responsible government, not dominion status, that was the proclaimed goal of British rule. Was it conceivable then that the status of a dominion might be accorded to India without, or in anticipation of, the acquisition and practice of responsible government? Technically it was not impossible, as subsequent developments in the Commonwealth were to demonstrate, but politically it was precluded if only because the British *Raj*, startled by the pace of the advances in dominion status, was concerned to delay rather than to hasten the date of the coming into existence of an Indian dominion and, therefore, predisposed to insist upon responsible government as a pre-condition of it.

In April 1929 the viceroy, Lord Irwin, asked his advisers for a note on 1. dominion status showing what it would mean in practice as applied to India, 2. how far the British government had ever given any undertaking to work up to it and 3. how far Indian opinion had demanded it.[28] The questions and the answers to them reflected the ambiguities of British policies subsequent to the Montagu declaration and the difficulties of the British position as seen from Delhi. Both stemmed from a single source. In 1917 responsible government, while carrying a dominion implication, had been of itself reassuring. It had a fixed and static meaning. Dominion status, however, had not. The decade that followed the Montagu declaration witnessed the transformation of the old system of British-dominion relations, with its assurance of British predominance, into the new Balfourian association with equality as its fundamental doctrine. Not surprisingly, the advisers to the *Raj* sought reassurance in the fact that it was responsible government that had been specifically promised to India in 1917. It was also what had been reaffirmed in the Montagu-Chelmsford Report and in expositions of it by the viceroy, Lord Chelmsford, and the secretary of state, Edwin Montagu. The duke of Connaught, however, at the inauguration of the new Council of State and Legislative Assembly on 9 February 1921 had delivered a message from the king-emperor referring to the 'beginnings of *Swaraj* within my Empire' and to the 'widest scope and ample opportunity for progress to the liberty which my other dominions enjoy' – a phrase open to more than one interpretation – but then Lord Reading, as viceroy, once more retreated to safer ground in speaking of 'the high destiny' which awaited India as a partner in the British Empire. The first Labour secretary of state, Lord Ollivier, was predictably more forthright, saying in 1924 that His Majesty's government had themselves the same ultimate aim as the Indian *Swaraj* party, namely, 'a responsible Indian dominion government'. In substance this was reiterated by Stanley Baldwin on 24 May 1927 when he spoke of India 'in the fullness of time' being in 'equal partnership with the dominions'. While these later statements were indicative of the trend of British thinking, they were not tantamount to formal commitments. Some of them understandably were seized upon by the Congress, despite contrary and controversial interpretation by the Home Member, Sir Malcolm Hailey, on behalf of the government of India, in 1924[29] as evidence that responsible government necessarily implied dominion status.

The Indian National Congress, unlike Sinn Féin, positively embraced the idea of a dominion goal. In 1906 it adopted as its objective 'the attainment of a system of government for India similar to that enjoyed by the self-governing dominions of the British Empire'. In 1916 the Congress and the Muslim League jointly proposed that India should 'be lifted from the position of dependency to that of an equal partner in the Empire with the self-governing dominions'. In 1924 the alternatives for India were spoken of by Gandhi as *Swaraj* within the Empire on terms of equality or outside if the British government made that necessary. The first recommendation of the All-Parties Conference 1928, under the chairmanship of Motilal Nehru, based on article 1 of the Anglo-Irish Treaty read:

India shall have the same constitutional status in the comity of nations known as the British Empire as the Dominion of Canada, the Commonwealth of Australia, the Dominion of New Zealand, the Union of South Africa and the Irish Free State, with a Parliament having powers to make laws for the peace, order and good government of India, and an executive responsible to that Parliament, and shall be styled and known as the Commonwealth of India.

It was, and was intended to be, an article which firmly associated responsible government with dominion status. Motilal Nehru did not regard dominion status as a final goal; he declared in favour of 'Complete Independence', but not against full dominion status 'as full as any dominion possesses it today'.[20]

The viceroy's constitutional advisers noted in 1929 that while the Indian demand for the same status as the dominions remained constant, this status changed and so altered the nature of the demand. It was this which had prompted an attitude of greater caution on the part of the British government. There were said to be two particular grounds for it – the first the content of the 1926 Balfour Report on Inter-Imperial Relations and the second the Indian claim that dominion status after that date carried with it the power to secede. But disturbing in some of its aspects though the prospect of dominion status in its redefined and developing manifestations might appear to the British *Raj* in Delhi, there were also counter-balancing and more reassuring considerations. There was the distinction which the Balfour Report had drawn between status and function which might, so it was suggested to the viceroy by his advisers, enable a relationship to be established between Britain and an Indian dominion which would concede equality of status but permit of a continuing functional inequality in its turn leaving open the way for a continuing British exercise of responsibility in special fields. More important still was the obverse of the Congress insistence upon dominion status as a necessary corollary of responsible self-government – namely British insistence upon responsible self-government as a necessary corollary and precondition of dominion status.

The argument entered upon its most highly controversial phase with the Report of the Simon Commission. The all-British membership of the commission appointed to review the working of the diarchical system of government set up under the Government of India Act 1919, and boycotted by Indian leaders and parties during their enquiries, became so sensitive to the manifold difficulties of adapting a system of responsible government to India that they avoided all reference to a dominion status goal in their Report. In the face of Indian indignation the Viceroy, Lord Irwin, repaired the omission[31] on 31 October 1929 in categorical terms, by saying that it was implicit in the declaration of

1917 that the attainment of dominion status must be regarded as the natural issue of Indian constitutional progress. But despite the public controversies that prompted and surrounded his action, including sharp right-wing protests in Britain at his dominion status assurances, did it really represent a new departure? Was it conceivable that the British government could have stood firm on the letter of responsible government and rejected the dominion status spirit implicit in it?

The Home Department had prepared their memorandum of June 1929 on dominion status for the viceroy before he made his statement. The argument of the memorandum was to the effect that in practical terms the significance of the distinction between responsible government and dominion status was of little importance. The relevant passage read as follows:

> . . . are the implications of dominion status now so wide that the imperial government could not feel itself able honestly to assert that dominion status is the goal of its policy equally with responsible government? The answer might seem to be in the negative, since the implications of dominion status need to be considered conjointly with the implications of responsible government. In each case whether the goal of Parliament be responsible government or whether it be dominion status, the problem is essentially the same, namely the extent to which government in India can be released from external control. In neither case can the consummation of the policy be reached by a stroke of the pen. The reality of dominion status cannot be obtained until the goal of responsible government has first been reached. If we assume for the moment that the immense obstacles in the path of full responsible government have been successfully removed, that the entire executive and legislative authority in India has been made to accord with the will of Indian electorates, and the Parliament has ceased to be responsible even that there shall be a government in India, it would seem to follow that the imperial government, even if it so wished, might then be unable to deny to India a status equal to that of the other autonomous units of the Empire, which also reached dominion status through the same channel of responsible government. If there be anything in this argument, the difficulty of accepting dominion status as the goal of British policy may be little, if at all, greater than the difficulty involved when responsible government was adopted as the declared policy of Parliament; and the connection between the two may be found to be so intimate that the final consummation of full responsible government may automatically involve the realisation of dominion status.

In the 1930s the correctness of this analysis was underlined. The British government, assailed at every stage in the country and in the House of Commons by the diehards, proceeded by way of Round Table Conferences in London in 1930–1, through a Parliamentary Select Committee, to the Government of India Act 1935, condemned with Churchillian gusto as 'a monstrous monument of sham* built by the pygmies'. The advance was towards responsible government in British India, and an all-India federation comprising British India and the princely states with no suggestion that the coming into being of the federation should be conditional upon responsible or even representative government in the states.

The Government of India Act 1935, in all its length and complexity was a major state document. In the fullness of time it was to serve a larger purpose, as a means whereby a transfer of power might be effected with speed and in constitutional order. But in its immediate objectives it was only partially successful. It suffered from one considerable and one fundamental disadvantage. The Preamble, describing the Act as one 'to make further provision for the government of India' contained no reference to dominion status nor did the Act itself make any provision for its attainment. But the fundamental liability lay in the fact that the Bill was drafted and debated in London. The constitutions of other dominions had been home-made. Mahatma Gandhi was insistent that the constitution of a free India should follow that precedent. Since the Government of India Act did not do so, he had no use for it and declined, despite encouragement from Pandit Nehru, to read its provisions. In such circumstances it was not surprising that the Act failed to win the confidence or to appeal to the sentiments of nationalist leaders whether in the Congress or the League. It was in fact a highly conservative document. The federation of India which it contemplated was not to come into existence until two-thirds of the princes had agreed that it should do so, and then, if and when they had done so, the position of the princes was to be strongly entrenched within the federation. A calculation made for the viceroy in 1937 indicated that should the minimal number of princes accede there would be a Federal Lower House of 346 members and that on the basis of the provincial election returns, the Congress, despite its impressive showing in them, was not likely to secure more than a hundred seats in it. 'A Congress strength of 100 in a House of 346,' commented the secretary of state on receiving this assessment, 'is not unduly alarming . . . '.[32] As objectionable to Congress sentiment as the electoral system with its inbuilt checks and

* Churchill insisted that this and not 'shame' was the word he had used. The following exchange about it took place in the House on 11 February 1935:

Mr Foot: The Right Hon. Gentleman broadcast the other day, and he told the people of this country . . . that we had erected 'a monstrous monument of shame built by the pygmies'.

Mr Churchill: Not 'shame' but 'sham'.

Mr Foot: I was quoting from *The Listener*.

Mr Churchill: I am quoting from the speaker.

balances, was the extent and range of the reserve powers vested in the viceroy and the provincial governors. Nor were they alone in this. Jinnah spoke of the Act as consisting of 98 per cent safeguards.

The federal provisions of the 1935 Act never came into force, because a sufficient number of the princes did not accede to the proposed federation. Provincial elections under the Act were, however, held in 1937. They demonstrated the formidable organisation and popular backing for the Congress and were followed, after protracted exchanges between the Congress leaders and the viceroy about the exercise of the governors' reserve powers, by the formation of Congress ministries in the Congress-majority provinces. With their formation a new page in Indian history had opened.

In terms of responsible government, dominion status and partition, the decade 1937–47 had a unity of its own. At its opening the British government had conceded an extension of the area of responsible government while reserving their position on dominion status and reposing their faith in federation; the Congress and the League were preparing efficiently in the first case, inefficiently in the second[33] to exploit the political possibilities of mass electorates; and the Congress made ready to repudiate the dominion status-Commonwealth goal in favour of *Purna Swaraj*, or complete independence. At the close of the decade responsible government was a reality; federation had died without ever coming to life and India was divided, no longer between British India and the Indian states but between Pakistan and Hindustan; and dominion status, mistrusted by more conservative British opinion because of its capacity for development and by the Indian National Congress – which over the years had paid too much attention to the weighty volumes in which Professor A. B. Keith with unrivalled learning expounded the still continuing inequalities in the status of the dominions[34] and too little to what Mackenzie King was actually doing – because it was thought to fall too far short of independence, came into its own at last as the one means by which power might be effectively and speedily transferred. Upon the principal participants there was thus exerted at a time of imperial retreat, domestic division and national revolution, the pull of Commonwealth experience with a persistence that few of them recognised and posterity is unlikely to credit.

CHAPTER 10

APPEASEMENT AND WAR: THE COMMONWEALTH RÔLE

We accepted in this motherland [Winston Churchill told the House of Commons in the debate on the Statute of Westminster in November 1931] the view of those who wish to state the imperial obligation and imperial ties at their minimum; we abandoned the whole apparatus of sovereignty and constitutional law to which our ancestors, and even the later Victorians, had attached the greatest importance. Remembering that, and remembering the atmosphere of those days, not long gone, and the spirit of those days, I cannot think that we were wrong, and I do not think that we are wrong now. I feel that we are bound, where the great self-governing dominions of the Crown are concerned, boldly to grasp the larger hope. . . .[1]

In isolation these words might suggest that on the British side the whole process of redefinition had been an act of faith. Faith there was certainly and it was the more easily sustained in years when the prospect of world war appeared remote or, to the more ardent believers in the League, nonexistent. It was powerfully reinforced by an idealised concept of Commonwealth, to which much contemporary writing, not least Lionel Curtis's *Civitas Dei*, bears heady witness, as well as by cooler appraisal which saw in the new relationship an escape from imperialism by way of an experiment in free and equal association between nations. Did not this last, alone, provide sufficient cause to proceed with magnanimity, courage and vision?

Had there been some practicable alternative to Commonwealth, in the form of imperial federation or other centralising system, there might have been no very assured British, as distinct from dominion, answer.

I had misgivings [said Churchill speaking of 1926] that we were needlessly obliterating old, famous landmarks and signposts, which although archaic, have a historic importance and value. I remember that that great statesman, the late Lord Balfour, with whom I talked this matter over very often, answered me, and to some extent reassured me, by saying, 'I do not believe in wooden guns.' I thought that a very pregnant remark. He saw no advantage in preserving an assertion of rights and powers on which, in practice, we should not find it possible effectively to base ourselves. I still repose faith in the calm, lambent wisdom of that great man in his later years.[2]

But had the guns not been wooden, Churchill might well not have been so easily reconciled. Those who thought of the twentieth century as the age of democratic progress and of the common man in all his natural goodness regarded the dismantling of Empire with facile optimism, while those who feared the century was likely to be dominated by wars on the greatest scale were troubled about the looseness of Commonwealth ties and the consequent undermining, as it seemed to them, of British power. Governments, and especially British governments, in the 1930s were compelled by unfolding dangers to ask themselves, and others, what dominion status, as redefined between 1926 and 1931, implied in terms of the Commonwealth willingness and capacity to wage war. The framers of the Balfour Report had expressed their belief that no common cause would suffer as a result of the full autonomy of the dominions in external as in domestic affairs. In the 1930s that conviction was put to an earlier and more severe test than they can have foreseen.

As the threat of war re-emerged, certain fundamental considerations about the rôle of the dominions were bound to occupy the mind of any British government. Dominion advances in status in the 1920s and early 1930s, while not the by-product of a sense of security, were more widely and more readily acceptable in many circles because of the supposed safeguard against war offered by the League of Nations. Once that safeguard began to appear inadequate, official (and unofficial) opinion in London began to realise for the first time the new element of uncertainty in British planning and thinking introduced by separate dominion responsibility in external policy. This realisation was accompanied by a new appreciation of the variety of dominion interests and of the factors that were likely to influence their policies. Canadian preoccupation with national unity; South Africa's concern to keep European warfare out of the continent of Africa; Australia's anxieties about a two-ocean war and sense of exposure to attacks from her near-north; Irish resentment at continued British occupation of the Treaty ports, not merely on the grounds of infringement of national sovereignty but as a limitation in practice upon Irish freedom of action – all of these were factors to be taken into account. It was not enough for the government of the United Kingdom to seek in general terms, and as a United Kingdom interest, to give substance and effective being to the new concept of equal dominion partnership within a Commonwealth of Nations, but it had further to reckon with the fact that henceforward unity of Commonwealth policies, even in face of grave dangers, could no longer be assumed but had in each instance patiently to be worked for. There were questions of critical importance to be asked. Under what circumstances could the United Kingdom count on dominion, or majority dominion, backing in war? Was it, to be more specific, certain that the dominions would fight in a war for the enforcement of the authority of the League of Nations, or in a war for the maintenance of the peace treaties which so many of their leaders had condemned and continued to denounce, or in a war for the safety and survival of the Empire? These were questions the answers to which were open, or partially open, in the early 1930s and they were only to be made explicit by a process of actual confrontation. Later commentators, so mindful of pre-war errors in judgment, are apt to overlook the questions and consequently to ignore the achievement. A substantially united Commonwealth entered the war in 1939 and emerged victorious from it in 1945.

The testing phase for the Commonwealth internationally opened in 1931, the year of the Japanese attack upon Manchuria. The moment for the attack was well chosen. There was confusion and disorder in China and preoccupation with the application of near-desperate remedies to prop up collapsing markets in the British Commonwealth and the United States. Of the dominions, Australia and New Zealand were regionally the most concerned. Other countries, far from the Pacific, thought the time had come to enforce the authority of the League, but even after Japanese naval action against Shanghai, the attitude of the Australian government remained reserved. Public opinion was said to regard military action as 'unthinkable' and the Australian government, mindful of the 'vulnerability of our empty north' and Australia's almost exclusive reliance on the Royal Navy, waited on Britain and on the United States. In Canada, also, caution was the keynote. The government was prepared to accept the conclusions of the League but felt that it was not for a small power to give strong, positive direction. In the debate at Geneva on the Lytton Report on events in Manchuria, the Canadian delegate, owing to the absence of adequate instructions from home, was said (it may be thought with commendable prudence in the light of a later incident) to have spoken 'strongly on both sides of the question'. South Africa and the Irish Free State were more forthcoming. But they were also further away. In sum, the outcome of the Manchurian incident served to underline the difficulty of concerted action in the far east without active United States participation, and to drive home the lesson that the writ of a non-universal League could not, and did not, run in the Pacific. What of the Mediterranean?

In September, 1935, Mussolini resolved to invade Abyssinia 'with Geneva, without Geneva or against Geneva'. This time there was no occasion for procrastinating enquiry into what had taken place. On 7 October 1935 Italy was branded as an aggressor by the League of Nations. All the dominions endorsed the declaration. It was shortly followed by a speech at Geneva by the British foreign secretary, Sir

Samuel Hoare, indicating in most forthright terms British support for the League and for sanctions. How far were the dominions themselves prepared to go? The autumn election in Canada returned Mackenzie King to office. His government issued a statement saying that the absence of three of the Great Powers from the League, its failure to secure disarmament and the unwillingness of members to enforce sanctions in the case of countries distant from Euope had increased the difficulty of assuming obligations in advance. Canada accordingly 'did not recognise any commitment to adopt military sanctions and only Parliament could decide upon them'. On 2 November 1935 the Canadian delegate, Walter Riddell, misinterpreting his inadequate instructions and carried away by his own zeal, proposed the addition of sanctions on petroleum, coal and iron and steel against Italy. In Rome these sanctions were branded as 'the Canadian proposals'. In Ottawa Mackenzie King read his Monday morning newspaper 'with amazement' while in Quebec the reaction was sharp and unfavourable. In due course Riddell was disowned in a statement issued by Ernest Lapointe, the minister of justice, the leading French-Canadian member in the cabinet and Mackenzie King's life-long political ally, while the Canadian prime minister was away in Washington. Canadian repudiation did not imply opposition to sanctions of this kind but that Canada did not wish to take the initiative. 'It was only from the fame of leadership that the government backed with such rapid steps' a Canadian diplomatic historian has written.[4] But Mackenzie King had been genuinely alarmed. 'What a calamitous act was that of Riddell's at Geneva!' he wrote to Vincent Massey. 'Had we not made clear that it was Riddell speaking for himself . . . Canada might for all time have come to be credited with having set Europe aflame. . . '.[5] Later he went so far as to tell the House of Commons that but for his rapid retreat from the Canadian delegate's imprudent initiative, 'the whole of Europe might have been aflame today'.[6] The lesson drawn in Ottawa was that of the need for cautious reserve as dangers in Europe and the far east intensified.

From South Africa, the Irish Free State and New Zealand there was vigorous and continuing support for the League and for sanctions against Italy. South African policy was firmly grounded upon South African interests. At Geneva the Union's eloquent spokesman, C. te Water, spoke of the danger to the adventuring nations, of the black peoples of Africa, who never forgave and never forgot an injury, and to 'our own white civilisation' through the spread of European ambitions to Africa by force. The New Zealand Labour government zealously supported the League and sanctions. Their ideal was social security within and international security overseas. In the Irish Free State the imposition of sanctions against Italy was materially of no importance but psychologically of controversial moment because sanctions, even if only nominal in their effect, by a Catholic country against the homeland of the Papacy, disturbed the minds of many of its people. Nor was the fact that their imposition meant close cooperation with Britain at Geneva calculated to afford psychological compensation. On the contrary, stung by opposition taunts on this score, de Valera was moved to retort: 'If your worst enemy is going to heaven the same way as you are, you don't for that reason turn around and go in the opposite direction'. But it was also apparent that any such Anglo-Irish co-operation in international affairs was possible only under the umbrella of the League. The cover it could offer never looked reassuring again after December 1935 when the British stand for sanctions collapsed amid the indignities of the Hoare-Laval Pact. At one blow, faith in Great Power leadership and in the League itself was gravely undermined. 'Where are the Great Powers leading us, who have not the faith to persevere?' enquired te Water, when later sanctions were lifted.[7] Others asked the same question and received no reassuring answer.

The reactions of the dominions to the failure of the League in Abyssinia were, broadly speaking, twofold – greater reliance on imperial defence, coupled with a policy of appeasement. In the circumstances both were prudent, even if the second was not heroic. Without a League resolutely supported by the majority of Great Powers there was a risk that attempts on the part of the British Commonwealth alone or in association with France to maintain peace on the basis of the European *status quo* might overtax their combined resources or fail to enlist their combined effort. The first counselled a careful assessment of military resources, the second a restrained approach, especially where the aggression was in some way qualified or capable of an exculpatory, as well as a censorious, interpretation.

The first (and, as it subsequently came to be regarded, the critical) step in the Nazi career of aggression, the militarisation of the Rhineland in March 1936, elicited no forthright condemnation from Britain or from the dominions, partly because it was susceptible of varying interpretations. Their governments did not support the French, still less the Polish view, that this open defiance of the Versailles Treaty and of the freely-negotiated Locarno Pact should be resisted by force. Lord Halifax later recalled defensively, but correctly, that 'there was no section of Britain public opinion that would not have been directly opposed to such action in 1936. To go to war with Germany for walking into their own backyard . . . at a time moreover when you were actually discussing with them the dates and conditions of their right to resume occupation, was not the sort of thing people could understand'.[8] If it were not understood in Britain there was no prospect of its being understood in distant dominions. General Smuts for his part expressed unqualified appreciation of Britain's restraint. 'We are tremendously proud,' he said,[9] 'of the way she has stood in the breach.' The tribute was perhaps the more appreciated because totally unmerited, the one thing that the British government had declined to do being to stand 'in the breach' with their French ally.

There were three landmarks in the shaping of Commonwealth policies between 1936 and the outbreak of war. The first was the Imperial Conference 1937, the second the Czech crisis of September 1938 and the third the Anglo-French guarantee to Poland in March 1939. The Imperial Conference meeting in late May-early June 1937, devoted seven sessions to the discussion of foreign affairs. The principal preoccupation of delegations was the formulation of their respective responses to the failure of the League and, arising from it, of their attitudes henceforward to collective security. Fear of being committed by obligation to an ineffective and discredited international organisation was predominant. The covenant, argued Hertzog, had been dealt so heavy a blow that the sanctions provisions (Articles 10 and 16) – which anyway had come to be regarded as part of the Treaty of Versailles and as a means by which those who wanted to keep what they had got might be enabled to do so – would have to be looked upon as non-existent. The League itself, he proceeded, would have to be reduced to something that corresponded with the realities of the situation, namely to a moral force rather than one to be relied upon by small countries in the case of aggression, because any such reliance would be 'like relying on a piece of wood which had already proved rotten and which broke every time a strain fell on it'. Chamberlain and, it need hardly be said, Mackenzie King, warmly concurred. It was impossible, argued King, to restore Abyssinia or redress the wrong that had been commited and any further attempts to do so might hasten the risk of a conflagration in Europe. It was necessary to avoid such a calamity. Nor with the substance of the League's authority gone, could King see any merit in clinging to the form. It would serve only to enhance the risk that Canada might become embroiled in a League war. 'In Canada', he told his colleagues, 'the people had been much disillusioned by what happened at the League. In Canada the people were saying that membership of the League constituted a real risk of their becoming involved in war'. For his part 'he did not want to base Canadian policy on the League of Nations. If the covenant remained as at present, that meant supporting collective security which he did not believe in'. He was prepared to base Canadian policies on the ideals but not on the principles of the League. Hertzog specifically agreed and Bruce's general assent reflected most clearly

Australian concern lest the Japanese situation should be reopened. Only New Zealand challenged these general assumptions, Savage declaring that he could not subscribe to anything which had the appearance of destroying the League of Nations. As long as the gun was unloaded, he said with the Canadian delegation clearly in view, there were those who were willing 'to support the League but the moment the gun was loaded they would not have anything to do with it'. The majority of the delegations, however, were not to be moved and in the closing stages of the Conference Mackenzie King showed himself furthermore concerned about possible commitments to the Empire over and above the League. In Canada, he said, there was 'a great dread lest the country should be committed at the Imperial Conference to some obligation arising out of the European situation'. It must accordingly be made clear that the Conference was not laying down a policy, only reflecting a consensus of opinion with the right of individual parliaments to decide fully recognised.[10]

The published Report of the Conference reflected the balance of opinion, as expressed in these private exchanges of view, and duly underlined the predominant dominion desire for dissociation from European problems and freedom from European commitments. New Zealand's unsupported advocacy of continued and unqualified support for the League was consigned to a footnote, while the consensus of remaining opinion was expressed in non-committal phrases about the basing of policies on the aims and ideas of the League. Resolved at all costs that their countries should not enter into nor accept obligations to a moribund institution, British and dominion representatives expressed their faith in the settlement of differences 'by methods of co-operation, joint enquiry and conciliation'. They declined to be drawn into ideological divisions and, while themselves firmly attached to the principles of democracy, registered their view that differences between political creeds should be no obstacle to friendly relations. Behind the easy, complacent phrases, it is true, there were certainly misgivings. But the hopes of the great majority of the Commonwealth leaders, whether from the United Kingdom or the dominions, were in favour of 'international appeasement' both in political relations and in trade. The aim of the Conference was best summed up by General Hertzog, who concluded that 'in the attainment of this high object of world appeasement . . . the mission of the Commonwealth stands clearly defined'.

One thing at least was made clear beyond all question by the Imperial Conference, namely, that a united Commonwealth would not fight or run the risk of being involved in a war to uphold or enforce the authority of the League of Nations. By 1937, in other words, collective security on a League basis was a non-starter in the Commonwealth. That narrowed the field and it became at once more important, and more difficult in consequence of it, for Great Britain to ensure that the conditions of dominion cooperation in wartime were fulfilled. What were they? They were summed up in the word 'appeasement' which the Imperial Conference had accepted as describing the approach which offered the best chance of preserving world peace. The conclusion (except for New Zealand) was common but it derived from varied premises. This is frequently overlooked. Even in foreign policy the overseas dominions were thought of at the time, and apt to be written of later, as a category or species of state with shared outlook and shared interests. This was far from being the case, as even a brief résumé of dominion preoccupations will serve to illustrate.

In 1931–2 Australia recognised that the writ of the League did not run in the Pacific and it caused little surprise in Australia when some three years later it was found not to run in the Mediterranean either. There were Australian fears of a head-on clash between the Royal Navy and the Italian Navy, because damage to the Royal Navy might, among other things, alter the balance of power in the Pacific. When Italy's adventure in East Africa was followed within a year by German reoccupation of the Rhineland, the vulnerability of Australia, should Britain be heavily engaged in the west, was brought home. In the Abyssinian crisis, noted a contemporary,[11] for the first time the faith of the Australian public in British naval supremacy was severely shaken. The Australian government's reaction was to increase defence expenditure, with the Labour opposition demanding first priority for air defence, and diplomatically, so far as lay within Australia's influence, to limit the geographical extent of war. With these aims and considerations in mind the Australian government would seem never to have entertained misgivings about the wisdom of seeking to appease Italy and detaching her from Germany. At all costs, in their view, must the Mediterranean lifeline be kept open. Nor did the Australian government favour an agreement with the Soviet Union, because Japanese membership of the anti-Comintern pact meant that Russian participation in war was likely to extend that war to the Pacific. Towards Japan, Australian policy was variable, but in the last years of peace it moved perceptibly towards appeasement, as evidenced by the export to Japan of scrap metal from Port Kembla. Towards Germany, however, Australia's attitude was more robust and there was no doubt at any time of Australia's solidarity with Britain in the event of her being forced into war by the European dictators.

In Canada, Mackenzie King walked delicately. After the Imperial Conference he visited Berlin and gave to Hitler (who appears to have listened courteously though he may not have been greatly interested) a lucid résumé of recent developments in Commonwealth relations. He delivered, to judge by his own record, which alone would seem to have survived,[12] a warning that if the time

> ever came when any part of the Empire felt that the freedom which we all enjoyed was being impaired through any act of aggression on the part of a foreign country, it would be seen that all would join together to protect the freedom which we were determined should not be imperilled.

And while, like so many visitors to the German chancellor at that time, King concluded that Hitler was at once patriotic and essentially pacific, he grasped that expansion of some sort in eastern Europe was in Hitler's mind. At home the Canadian government strengthened national defences, while the prime minister continued to emphasise that Canada was not committed to any particular course of action. Only Parliament could decide what Canada would do in the event of a world war. This dismayed the protagonists of Empire, the protagonists of the League and the protagonists of Canadian neutrality. Against each in turn he deployed the same argument. He could not commit Canada to a war in which the Empire was engaged, or to a war sanctioned by the League, or to neutrality, because each and all would deprive Parliament of its rightful freedom of choice. His policy was directed towards two ends – preservation of Canadian unity and the strengthening of ties with the United States. The second was notably advanced when on August 18 1938, President Roosevelt visited Canada and said at Kingston: 'The Dominion of Canada is part of the sisterhood of the British Empire. I give to you assurance that the people of the United States will not stand idly by if domination of Canadian soil is threatened by any other Empire'.[13] Both considerations – of national unity and closer association with a still isolationist United States – led Mackenzie King to detach Canada more and more from day-to-day issues in Europe, and both seemingly served to strengthen the argument in favour of appeasement. Before Canada went to war King felt he had to convince all Canadians from Quebec to Vancouver that there was no honourable alternative. He even hoped that with time he might be in a position to persuade the United States likewise.

Unity, unattainable but long sought, was also the goal in the Union of South Africa. The Fusion government, with Hertzog as prime minister and Smuts as deputy prime minister, was founded upon an agreement to differ on controversial and still unresolved politico-constitutional questions, notably secession and neutrality. In foreign policy, the Fusion government could remain united only in inaction once the unifying bond of the League was fraying. The formula was 'South Africa first'; the test, how it was to be interpreted. General Hetzog attributed most of the evils of the time to the iniquitous Treaty of Versailles – the 'monster treaty' which, in his view, had murdered its own offspring, the League, and which by provoking German attempts to remedy the injustices it had inflicted upon them, was the main cause of the threat to European peace. The next war, he prophesied, not once but many times, would be 'the child of Versailles'. Responsibility for Hitler's aggressive actions was to be attributed not so much to Hitler as to the peace treaties and the actions of the victorious allies, who had been responsible for imposing them in 1919 and upholding them since. 'If war did come because England continued to associate with France,' he said at the Imperial Conference in 1937,[14] 'in a policy in respect of central and eastern Europe calculated to threaten Germany's existence through unwillingness to set right the injustices from the Treaty of Versailles, South Africa cannot be expected to take part in the war. . .'. Smuts was in no strong position, even if he had so wished, to dissent from his prime minister's general opinion for had he not himself protested at the time and subsequently at the vindictiveness of some of the provisions of the Versailles Treaty? More positively it is clear that he agreed with Hertzog on the more particular point that South African interests did not demand South African participation in a war to defend the post-war territorial settlement in eastern Europe. Where he differed was in thinking and later in saying, that if England were attacked or threatened South Africa would fight. In the actual circumstances of the time, the survival of the Fusion experiment thus became conditional upon either a policy of appeasement or, in the event of war, upon a *casus belli* which Hertzog and Smuts were agreed in regarding either as involving or not involving South African interests.

As the Czech crisis neared its climax in the late summer of 1938, the British government were aware that the three larger dominions favoured a policy of appeasement, that the Irish Free State was edging towards neutrality and that in New Zealand alone was the wisdom of concession seriously questioned. In the critical month of September the dominion high commissioners in London, Vincent Massey (Canada), Stanley Bruce (Australia), te Water (South Africa), J. W. Dulanty (Irish Free State) – New Zealand's representative W. J. Jordan remained throughout in Geneva – individually or collectively pressed their point of view upon the secretary of state for the dominions affairs, Malcolm MacDonald, upon the foreign secretary, upon the prime minister himself when opportunity offered, and by no means least upon the editor of *The Times*, Geoffrey Dawson. A few extracts from the entries in the diary of the Canadian high commissioner, Vincent Massey,[15] suffice to indicate dominion feelings in the interval between Neville Chamberlain's second visit to Hitler at Godesberg on 22–3 September when, in his words to the House of Commons, he 'bitterly reproached the chancellor for his failure to respond in any way to the efforts which had been made to secure peace', and Munich – the period, that is to say when it seemed that even Chamberlain's patience might also be exhausted.

September 24th. A meeting with the H.C.'s and Malcolm MacDonald at the Col. Office. All four of the H.C.'s (Jordan of N.Z. is at Geneva) take a view on the basic issue rather different from MacDonald's emphasis. We are all prepared to pay a higher price for peace than he. The difference is because the dominions are removed further away from Europe, not because our sense of honour is less acute. Bruce . . . feels very strongly that the German proposals can't be allowed to be a *casus belli* and says so on behalf of his Govt. Te Water and Dulanty speak with great vehemence as well . . .

September 25th. Greatly perturbed at the mood of the morning papers on the crisis. Extreme condemnation of German proposals given to Chamberlain. . . . Little or no appeal to calm judgment. . . . I had an hour's talk with Geoffrey Dawson at his house and he and I agreed that something must be done. I suggested that he see Halifax and also get Bruce who having been prime minister had special influence among the H.C.'s in such matters – to do all he could. . . . Bruce delivered to Chamberlain a helpful message on behalf of his government – which is a record. I wish mine would act!

September 26th. 10.30 meeting of H.C.'s with MacD. at the Col. Office. Things look worse and worse. All four H.C.'s – N.Z. is still absent – feel that the German proposals should not be allowed to wreck peace . . .

September 27th. . . . A talk with Te Water at my house in evening – then a H.C.'s meeting at Dom. Office with Malcolm MacD. – then after the officials had retired we talked until 2 a.m. on the general subj. of dominion opinion on the present issue. We all made it clear for ourselves (and some spoke for their governments) that there might be a dangerous reaction in the dominions to a decision to plunge the Empire into war on the issue of how Hitler was to take possession of territory already ceded to him in principle . . . surely the world can't be plunged into the horrors of universal war for a difference of opinion over a few miles of territory or a few days one way or the other in a time-table! That thank God is I believe Chamberlain's view and that of his cabinet. . . .

It was indeed. In view of the strong official and personal pressures from the dominions in favour of the appeasement of Hitler in the Czech crisis of September 1938, and the generally enthusiastic dominion response to the Agreement, it has been alleged that the dominions had a direct responsibility for Munich. But this is not substantiated by the facts. It is true that the dominion governments both wanted and welcomed the avoidance of war on the Sudeten question at almost any price. When the Australian government was challenged in the House of Representatives with having done nothing effective, Menzies replied: 'We kept in touch with the British prime minister. We said: "This is a great work you are doing. . . We are completely behind what you are doing to avoid war".'[16] But it was Chamberlain who was doing the work, the Australian and other dominion governments who were behind him. It could hardly have been otherwise. None of the dominions had either treaty obligations or commitments in Europe. Had the British government contemplated a course other than the appeasement of Hitler at this time, then indeed they would have been confronted by strong dominion opposition and would have necessarily had to face the prospect of a war with a divided Commonwealth behind them. In such circumstances Ireland would have been neutral and South Africa non-belligerent, since Smuts and Hertzog had signed a compact early in September 1938, agreeing that in the event of war South Africa's interests demanded non-belligerency. For Smuts this was an unwelcome conclusion and his enthusiasm on 30 September for Chamberlain – 'a great champion has appeared in the lists, God bless him' – reflected his relief at escape from a painful predicament. There would have been New Zealand, Australian and Canadian cooperation, but in the case of Australia and Canada there would have been, at the very least, strong minority reservations about the *casus belli*. 'The probability of having to meet Parliament with Europe at war was a nightmare,' Mackenzie King told Malcolm MacDonald on 1 October 1938, but he was prepared to advocate Canadian participation. Had the British government, therefore, contemplated resolute rejection of Hitler's demands and had that policy led to war, then they would have been confronted with the failure of their long-term aim to preserve substantial Commonwealth unity. This the Munich settlement averted. If war came later and after the western powers had made sacrifices even if principally at the expense of another, in the interests of peace, then, as J. A. Lyons, the prime minister of Australia, said 'at least our hands are clean'. The phrase in the circumstances has its irony. But 'clean hands', meaning hands free from the stain of responsibility for starting a war, were, it is not to be doubted, a condition of Commonwealth unity in war. Had the Czechs at all times stood firm on principle and declared that they would rather go down fighting than discuss with allies or enemies the unity and integrity of their country, then other aspects of the situation would have been driven home and nationalist opinion in the Commonwealth been shaken in some of its preconceptions. But there was little evidence of such a hard, uncompromising stand.

British apologists for Munich and especially members of Chamberlain's cabinet have in their memoirs attached much importance to the influence of the dominions on British policy at that time.[17] Dominion pressures, Lord Templewood (Sir Samuel Hoare) recalled later, were a major consideration in the shaping of United Kingdom policy and he noted that had war come in September 1938 'we should have started with a broken Commonwealth front'. The critics of Munich, complained Lord Halifax, either 'did not know or greatly care that there was grave doubt whether the Commonwealth would be at one in supporting the United Kingdom in a policy of active intervention on behalf of Czechoslovakia in 1938. . .'.[18] The first point, Lord Templewood's, was substantially true in the negative sense already indicated, namely of discouraging ideas of resolute resistance to Hitler's demands at the risk of war; the second, Lord Halifax's, erred if anything on the side of understatement. There was more than doubt, there was certainty that a united Commonwealth would not have entered a war to preserve the integrity of Czechoslovakia. In general terms, and well in advance of the Munich crisis, the more nationalist dominions had made it clear that they would not consider a war to uphold the territorial provisions of the Versailles Treaty in central Europe justified and more particularly, at the 1937 Imperial Conference, General Hertzog had indicated that he was not prepared to see South Africa engaged in any war to preserve the territorial integrity of Czechoslovakia. Emphasis was placed upon reports of Commonwealth concern lest Britain should accept commitments that might involve the Empire in war by the British ambassador in Paris in conversation with the French prime minister and foreign minister on 20 July 1938, and account was also taken of dominion attitudes in a memorandum expounding British policy which was handed to the State Department in Washington on 7 September 1938 by the British Chargé d'Affaires, who further commented that it was 'becoming clear that the dominions were isolationist and there would be no sense in fighting a war which would break the British Empire while trying to secure the safety of the United Kingdom'.[19] This did not accurately reflect the position of the dominions but it was correct as far as immediate prospects went. When it was written, moreover, the British government were not aware of the Hertzog-Smuts compact formally committing both leaders and their principal lieutenants to a policy of non-belligerency for South Africa in the event of war on the Sudeten issue.

Apart from discouragement of war on the Czech issue at the official inter-governmental level, dominion official or unofficial representatives sought to exercise and doubtless exercised at one remove a seemingly significant but necessarily indeterminate influence upon British public opinion. Two of the dominion high commissioners, Vincent Massey of Canada and S. M. Bruce of Australia, were in close touch with Geoffrey Dawson, the editor of *The Times*, a paper which gave full coverage to dominion news and to dominion views. Dawson was also a member of *The Round Table* and while the influence of *The Round Table* in Britain at this time is not to be overestimated, nonetheless, supplied with material by overseas groups, it reflected dominion opinion on foreign policy more accurately and more fully than any other periodical, and both editorially and regionally strongly supported appeasement. Yet it is a long step from saying that, officially or unofficially, the dominions influenced or urged Britain to pursue a policy of appeasement, to stating that they were responsible for it. In order to demonstrate this it would need to be shown (as D. C. Watt who has explored this theme allows) that Neville Chamberlain at the formative stage of a policy which he made peculiarly his own was moved to adopt it as a result of Commonwealth considerations and in response to dominion pressures. On the evidence so far available this would seem to lie in the borderland between speculation and proven historical fact. No sufficient evidence has been adduced to show that this was so and probabilities would seem to indicate that it was not.

On the larger issue of dominion policies in the Munich crisis it is worth noting that the range of options open to their governments, about which so many, often facile judgments have been made, was narrower than is often credited. They could, as they did, press for the concessions that would avert war, or they could acquiesce in British policy. They could not honourably or realistically urge Britain to take steps that might involve an unprepared country with a virtually undefended capital in a war in which most people supposed, with Stanley Baldwin, that the bomber would always get through. Conceding this limitation in realistic choice, the general verdict is that of the courses open to the dominions they took the wrong one. Here a *caveat* may be entered. What was 'wrong' in a European context was not necessarily 'wrong' in a Commonwealth context. But for that extra year, reflected Mackenzie King in 1943, 'there would have been divided counsels everywhere'. All the evidence suggests this was precisely true.

The policy of appeasement perished with Hitler's midnight march on Prague in March 1939. This time no nationalist or racial chords of sympathy were struck. It was not Germans who were being reunited with their own *volk*, but Czechs who were to be subjected to German rule. Nor could the occupation of Czechoslovakia be explained away in terms of rectification of the injustices of Versailles. For dominion as for British statesmen, the fruits of appeasement had now a bitter taste, and while not allowing that the policy had been initially misconceived, they were now prepared for its abandonment. The initiative was British and the change of course in British policy was signalled dramatically by the unilateral Anglo-French guarantee given to Poland on 31 March 1939. Churchill wrote later that history might 'be scoured and ransacked to find a parallel to this sudden and complete reversal of five or six years' policy of easy-going placatory appeasement, and its transformation almost overnight into a readiness to accept an obviously imminent war on far worse conditions and on the greatest scale', while nearer the time, on 6 April 1939, Smuts recorded his astonishment in a letter. 'Chamberlain's Polish guarantee', he wrote, 'has simply made us gasp – from the Commonwealth point of view. I cannot see the dominions following Great Britain in this sort of imperial policy the dangers of which to the Commonwealth are obvious. We still remember Lloyd George's Chanak[20] escapade...'. But his early reaction was soon qualified. The need that was felt by the British government to take new, near-desperate steps to halt aggression came also – and it is a remarkable fact – to be accepted by dominion governments, who had neither been consulted nor forewarned of the British break with appeasement. A new Commonwealth consensus on resistance – in which Hertzog, however, did not share – following close upon the old Commonwealth consensus on appeasement, may reasonably be thought to indicate a capacity, on the part of Commonwealth countries, to think and react alike. And in the last resort such consensus of British and dominion views on great and critical issues was the only basis, on which the Commonwealth could endure in those testing days.

While there was community in sentiment, there was no community in commitment. In September 1939 the dominions had no external military or political treaty obligations or understandings. None of them were parties to the Anglo-French guarantees to Rumania, Greece or Poland, nor to the Anglo-Polish Treaty. Their hands were free. In 1914, they went to war because the United Kingdom was at war. In 1939, the decision rested upon them individually. They had full freedom of choice. How they exercised that freedom gave new insight into the meaning of, and the deeper realities that lay behind, the constitutional developments of the inter-war years.

The Federal Parliament was sitting in Canberra on 3 September 1939, but the prime minister, R. G. Menzies, without consulting it, declared in a broadcast, 'Britain is at war, therefore Australia is at war'. There was one king, one flag, one cause. The New Zealand response was similar without being identical, the New Zealand declaration of war being later submitted to and confirmed by Parliament. New Zealand's prime minister coined a sentence which came to symbolise the sentiments of an island people. 'Where Britain goes, we go,' said Savage, 'where she stands, we stand.' The New Zealand government thought in fact that Britain might have stood a little earlier, but there was no recrimination, only a phrase at the end of the message to London noting that the stand had been taken 'not a moment too soon'. In Canada it was otherwise. Mackenzie King had never departed from his conviction that Parliament should decide. And when the day came,

Parliament decided. The British declaration was made on 3 September. The Canadian Parliament assembled on 7 September. The prime minister told the House of Commons that he wished to make it perfectly clear that Parliament and no other authority had to decide the question of peace or war. No one would be able to allege that Canada was being dragged into an imperialist war. Six days separated the United Kingdom and Canadian declarations and during the interval, since Canada was not listed as belligerent, supplies from the United States poured over the Canadian border. The test of King's policy came in the vote of 9 September. Fewer than five members opposed Canadian participation and so, in accordance with the rules of procedure, Canda went to war without a division in the House. The attainment of so great a measure of unity, in support of participation in war in a culturally divided country bordering on a great republic committed to neutrality, must surely rank as one of the outstanding achievements of Commonwealth statesmanship.

There was no unity in South Africa. The cabinet divided on the issue of peace or war with the prime minister, General Hertzog, supported by five ministers recommending the former, and the deputy prime minister, General Smuts, with the backing of seven of his colleagues advocating the latter. Perforce the issue was left for Parliament to decide. Hertzog moved a neutrality motion in the House of Assembly, Smuts an amendment to it, proposing participation without the dispatch of troops overseas. The course of debate was fluctuating, the outcome almost to the last uncertain. There were two speeches that were thought to have swayed opinion – in each case contrary to the speaker's intention. The first was General Hertzog's overstatement of a case, which rested essentially upon the interpretation of the concept of 'South Africa first', by the introduction of a provocative and essentially irrelevant *apologia* for Hitler. The second was overstatement on the other side by Heaton Nicholls,[21] an English-speaking member from Natal, who argued that the South African Parliament had no power of decision, since all South Africans owed allegiance to the king and the king being at war, his subjects *ipso facto* were at war. The impact of this second speech which, as its author himself candidly recalled, 'fell on the House like a bomb', and was the more damaging in as much as it came from an English-speaking source, was at least qualified by an immediately succeeding contribution from B. K. Long, another English-speaking member, who argued that there was no limit to South African freedom under the Statute of Westminster. When the speeches were ended, the tellers recorded eighty votes for General Smuts' amendment, sixty-five for General Hertzog's original motion. But the tension was not yet finally resolved. Hertzog advised the governor-general, Sir Patrick Duncan, to dissolve Parliament and to hold an early general election. The governor-general declined, on the ground of an election having been held as recently as May 1938 at which the issues in debate had been before the electorate, and also because of the risk of violence and of the known ability of Smuts to form an alternative government. This was the first occasion in Commonwealth history in which a governor-general had set out in a memorandum his reasons for refusing a dissolution to an outgoing prime minister. Smuts accordingly formed an administration which, reinforced in its electoral support in the 1943 wartime election, survived till 1948. But its constitution made clear not only that the Fusion experiment had ended but that with Hertzog's departure and his subsequent political eclipse the way had been opened for the electoral triumph in 1948 of the more extreme, or Purified Nationalists as they were known, under the leadership of Dr Malan.

The Balfour Report had confidently asserted that no common cause would suffer as a result of separate dominion control of foreign policies. In September 1939 its faith was justified. It is true that Eire, as the Irish Free State was now known, decided upon neutrality but by then Eire was on any reckoning a dominion with a difference and in the view of its own government not a dominion at all. For the rest the dominions by their own decisions had reached conclusions that had brought them into war by the side of Britain and France. They were belligerent from first to last and for one year it was not Britain, it was the Commonwealth, that stood alone. That year was perhaps not so much Britain's as the Commonwealth's finest hour.

The contribution of the Commonwealth to the victory of the United Nations is part of the history of the second world war, but some facts may be recalled to serve as a reminder of the place of war in Commonwealth experience. In 1939 Canada became the headquarters of the British Commonwealth Air Training plan by which the countries of the Commonwealth, including Britain, were enabled to train their airmen under favourable Canadian conditions and secure from enemy air attack. By early 1944 more than eighty-six thousand air crew cadets had been trained in this way. There was a smaller but similar scheme in Rhodesia and many other such examples of sharing military, naval and other facilities or resources to the advantage of a common cause. Nor was there at any time any weakening in Commonwealth purpose. In the dark days that followed the fall of France, messages were received from all dominion prime ministers endorsing Britain's decision to fight on and pledging their support in men and materials. There was, too, in that summer of destiny evidence of a growing co-operation between a belligerent Commonwealth and a non-belligerent United States with a United Kingdom – United States destroyers-bases deal and a Canadian-

United States defence agreement signed at Ogdensburg. During the year when the Commonwealth stood alone, Canadian divisions manned the shores of Britain against invasion; Australian, New Zealand and Indian troops fought a second time to protect the middle eastern artery of imperial communications, while the South African forces played their part in the East African campaigns which freed Abyssinia from Fascist rule before joining the other Commonwealth forces in North Africa. The irruption of the Japanese into south-east Asia and their threatened invasion of Australia led to the withdrawal of the Australian forces from the middle east, first to protect their own homeland and then, with the Japanese threat to it ended by the United States naval victories at Midway and in the Coral Sea, to take part in bitter fighting across the south-western Pacific. The Australian demand for a voice in the higher direction of the Pacific War was met, in part at least, with the creation of a Pacific War Council in 1941, with headquarters first in London and then jointly in London and Washington. Dominion participation in 'mutual aid' agreements with the United States on the model of the original United States-United Kingdom agreement drew them economically as well as militarily into the orbit of United States' influence and power. Their often first-hand knowledge of the vast resources the United States could deploy under pressure of war made its own enduring impact. But inevitably most deeply graven upon the minds and memories of Commonwealth peoples were their own experiences of war from September 1939 in the west, till its final ending in August 1945 in the east. Statistically the number and casualties of Commonwealth forces were estimated as follows, though for a generation it was not statistics but memories that mattered.

Country	Strength	Killed	Missing	Wounded	Prisoners of War
United Kingdom[22]	5,896,000	264,443*	41,327	277,077	172,592
Canada	724,023	37,476	1,843	53,174	9,045
Australia	938,277†	23,265	6,030	39,803	26,363
New Zealand	205,000‡	10,033	2,129	19,314	8,453
South Africa	200,000‖	6,840	1,841	14,363	14,589
India	2,500,000	24,338	11,754	64,354	79,849
Colonies and dependencies	473,250	6,877	14,208	6,972	8,115

* There were additionally some 93,000 civilians killed
† Net full-time service figure, June 1945
‡ Includes women
‖ Approximate figure

The coming of war provoked questions of Commonwealth political organisation. How far were the lessons of the first world war relevant to the second? In particular, ought an imperial war cabinet to be reconstituted? Survivors from the earlier period, L. S. Amery among them, maintained that it should. There was debate, but it lacked something of the edge of reality. The changes of the inter-war years both in politics and in technology accounted for this. By 1939 there was a working basis for consultation among equals, of a kind that had not existed twenty years earlier. The dominions had high commissioners in London, Britain had high commissioners in dominion capitals, and the importance attached to the office in critical times was reflected in Winston Churchill's appointment of former cabinet ministers as United Kingdom high commissioners in Ottawa, Canberra and Pretoria in 1940. In London, meetings of the high commissioners, beginning informally during the period of sanctions against Italy and assuming more definite shape and greater importance in the Munich crisis, became a main factor in Commonwealth co-operation during the war years. The high commissioners often met more than once a day with the secretary of state for dominion affairs and discussed with him the great and small questions that arose from the co-operation of their countries in a common cause. The meetings were informative and frequently the debate was vigorous, covering in 1939–40 topics such as the appropriate response to Hitler's peace offer after the Nazi conquest of Poland, the need for the formulation of allied peace aims and their substance, the Finnish winter war and Commonwealth attitudes to the Soviet Union, to the desirability and possibilities of military aid for the Finns, with the consequent need for securing passage of troops through Sweden, and then, in sudden succession, all the problems that followed upon the Nazi invasions of Norway, the Low Countries and the fall of France, including the possibility of a German invasion of neutral Eire.[23] The meetings provided dominion representatives with a forum for the expression of their views and for a statement of their interests. It was of great importance to them that the secretary of state for dominion affairs should be a member of the war cabinet, so that he might transmit their opinions or conclusions to his colleagues. This was the case for most, but not for the full period, of the war.

High commissioners' meetings were reinforced by visits of individual ministers to London during the war and of British ministers to dominion capitals. There was also correspondence and communications on a scale not hitherto approached. The use of cables and the long distance telephone – Lyons had used it and got Chamberlain out of bed during the Munich crisis – meant there need be little loss of time in securing decisions at critical moments. In general, with consultation and opportunities for consultation on this scale, the case for an imperial war cabinet was sensibly weakened. But the possibility of some co-ordinating cabinet or council continued to be canvassed.

The demand for an imperial cabinet or Conference in the early years of the second world war served one constructive purpose. It elicited exposition in public of the disadvantages of the older and the advantages of the newer system of Commonwealth relations, which the public till then had had little or no opportunity of weighing. The most substantial contribution to debate was made by Mackenzie King, in whose opinion an imperial cabinet was undesirable, unnecessary and in time of war 'an impossible thing'.[24] The ground for each of these objections merits consideration.

Why was an Imperial Conference or cabinet undesirable in time of war? It was undesirable, in the opinion of the Canadian prime minister, because it meant taking prime ministers and experts away from their own countries, where in time of crisis they were most needed. Speaking to the House of Commons in Ottawa in February 1941, Mackenzie King said:

> I think I have only to ask hon. members of this House of Commons if they were, at the moment, called upon to decide whether it would be better to have the prime minister of Canada attending at the present time a council in London or to have him here in this House of Commons in immediate association with his colleagues and in a position to confer with them, not only from day to day, and hour to hour, but from moment to moment; whether they would not consider, in a situation such as exists at this time, that it is better for him to be here at the head of the government, and at the head of the country which has elected him to office.[25]

And apart from the preferences – not lightly to be disregarded – of the Canadian or other dominion Parliaments, there was the even more difficult question of authority. If a Canadian prime minister or cabinet minister were present over a long period of time in London as a member of an enlarged war cabinet, then his slightest word would probably be regarded as the opinion of Canada. It would be equally difficult and awkward for him to refer or not to refer questions to his colleagues in Ottawa. If he made a practice of consulting them, he would appear to have little authority himself; if he failed to consult them, the result would be divided responsibility and uncertainty of jurisdiction, which could hardly fail to have unfortunate results. In sum, the proper place for a dominion prime minister was at home and Mackenzie King wasted no time on his first wartime visit to London in conveying his opinion to Churchill. When, on 22 August 1941, the British government gave a luncheon at the Savoy Hotel in honour of the prime minister of Canada and when the conversation had become general Mackenzie

King turned to Churchill and said: 'I hope you and your ministers will not expect to have the prime ministers of the dominions leaving their own countries to any more extent than is necessary.'[26] For quite different reasons, this accorded well with Churchill's own views.

While such considerations made an imperial war cabinet undesirable, other factors made it (as the imperial war cabinet of 1917–8 had not been) unnecessary. Chief among them, in Mackenzie King's opinion, was the improvement of communications in the intervening years which enabled dominion governments to keep in touch with the government of the United Kingdom and one another by telegraph or telephone, by brief ministerial visits by air for particular purposes, through high commissioners posted in Commonwealth capitals and by a reasonably comprehensive exchange of written communications on matters of mutual interest or concern. As a result there was no need for one Commonwealth cabinet for there was in existence – to quote Mackenzie King again – 'the most perfect continuing conference of cabinets that any group of nations could possibly have'. 'You have already got war cabinets – five of them', he told Churchill, and in illustration of what was becoming for him a favourite theme, 'You have got a continuing conference between the lot, what more do you want?'

Churchill, to whom Mackenzie King's question was rhetorically addressed, but at whom it was not directed, wanted (contrary to the unfounded assumptions of some later commentators but as Mackenzie King already knew) no more. And the one survivor of the earlier imperial cabinet, Field Marshal Smuts, to King's 'immense satisfaction' telegraphed Churchill at this time saying,

> I was glad to see Mackenzie King's outspoken condemnation of agitation for imperial cabinet. It seems to me unwise, with vast dangers looming in Africa and Pacific, to collect all our prime ministers in London. Our Commonwealth system, by its decentralisation, is well situated for waging world war, and diffuse leadership in all parts is a blessing rather than handicap. I agree with him that our system of communications leaves little to be desired.[27]

Even though the Australians, exposed in the Pacific to dangers that threatened neither Canada nor South Africa, never came to share these views, the evidence now available makes it clear that under the extreme stress of world war predominant Commonwealth opinion was in favour of co-operation through a system of informal consultation. The debate continued, especially in 1944, but the outcome was hardly in doubt and in succeeding years the aim of most – possibly all – Commonwealth governments was that consultation should ensure the existence of something that might, without straining the ordinary use of language, be termed a continuing conference of cabinets.

Why did Mackenzie King, and Mackenzie King alone among his contemporaries, go further and speak of an Imperial War Conference or cabinet as 'impossible'? Though he did not mention it specifically, one dominant consideration was implicit in all his arguments. That consideration was power. The existence of any such central imperial body would mean that power and undivided responsibility for its exercise would, so far as Canada was concerned, no longer remain in Canada. That was why an imperial war cabinet was 'impossible'. Whether Mackenzie King gave the right answer or not, at least he asked the right question. Where would power reside? And he thought it 'impossible' that in respect of Canada it should reside in any significant measure outside Canada.

Successive Australian governments entertained very different views. They desired, if not an imperial war cabinet, dominion, and more especially, Australian representation in the British war cabinet. They felt that such representation was essential if proper attention was to be given to Australian interests and due attention paid to the problems of the Pacific. Churchill however was not forthcoming. To Arthur Fadden, who succeeded Menzies as prime minister on 29 August 1941, Churchill summarised his views in a telegram[28] that takes its place beside Mackenzie King's speech of February 1941 as an exposition of the principles at stake in all discussions on the constitution of an imperial war cabinet or Council. The tenor of Churchill's argument was that the cabinet which he had the honour to lead was responsible to parliament and held office because its members collectively enjoyed the support of a majority in the House of Commons. The presence of an Australian minister who was responsible to the legislature of the Commonwealth of Australia, as a member of that cabinet, would involve organic changes. While in practice a dominion prime minister was always invited to sit with the United Kingdom cabinet and to take full part in government deliberations during the period of his visit, that was because he was the head of the government of a sister dominion and might be presumed to be in a position to speak not only on instructions from home but with the authority of the dominion of whose government he was the head. But a dominion minister other than the prime minister would not be a principal at all but only an envoy. That deprived him of authority and made his possible contribution to the discussions of the war cabinet unequal to the disadvantage of the greater number which his presence implied. The prime ministers of Canada, South Africa and New Zealand, noted Churchill, had said that they did not desire such representation, and some of them had taken a very strongly adverse view on the ground that no one but the prime minister could speak for their government except on instructions. What might happen otherwise was that the liberty of action of dominion governments might be prejudiced by any decisions to which their minister in London became a party. From the point of view of the United Kingdom, the proposal was equally objectionable. The addition of four dominion representatives would involve the retirement from the war cabinet of an equal number of British ministers. That would destroy the basis of the coalition government, since Churchill was not prepared to increase its numbers so that they became too large for the efficient conduct of business.

Churchill suggested to Fadden, by way of compromise, the possibility of the appointment of a special envoy to discuss any particular aspect of the common war effort, but he pointed out that such an envoy would not and could not be a responsible partner in the daily work of government and, if he remained in London as a regular institution, there would be the risk of duplication of function between such an envoy and the Australian high commissioner in London. While such a risk could not be obviated, its existence should be frankly faced, especially in view of the fact that the whole system of the high commissioners, in daily contact with the secretary of state for dominion affairs, was working well.

The Australian government, with Churchill's suggestion of a special envoy before them, decided to proceed with the appointment of a ministerial representative to the British war cabinet. The choice fell on an elder statesman and former prime minister, Sir Earle Page, who was minister of commerce at the time of his appointment. Before he reached London, however, the Fadden government fell. Curtin's Labour government which replaced it invited Sir Earle Page to continue as Australia's envoy extraordinary to the war cabinet, but the authority which he could reasonably hope to command was undermined by the fact that he was now a member, not of a government, but of an opposition party. On his arrival in London, Sir Earle Page defined the nature of his mission in terms which suggested that it was partly representative and partly exploratory. His function, he said,[29] was

> to establish personal cabinet liaison between the United Kingdom and Commonwealth governments. The primary purposes of [my] mission would be the presentation of Australia's point of view on certain immediate problems of war strategy and the arrangement of the best mechanics for maintaining a system of direct cabinet representation in London.

But the nature of Australian (or other dominion) representation in the British cabinet was a matter for the British prime minister, and Churchill gave no indication of being prepared to relinquish his authority in this respect. Sir Earle Page attended the meetings of the cabinet by invitation, when matters of interest to Australia were to be discussed, but not as of right. On this Churchill stood firm. This was not what the

Australians, anxious chiefly lest preoccupation with the war in Europe should lead to a neglect of the Pacific, desired. But they had perforce to acquiesce and the story ended in 1942 with the resignation of Sir Earle Page and the appointment of Stanley Bruce to the post of Australian representative in the war cabinet over and above his existing office of high commissioner.

In the meantime the Japanese attack on Pearl Harbour in December 1941 had realised all Australia's worst fears and left her for some desperately anxious months, bereft of aircraft and with her seasoned troops far away in the middle east, as Nazi propaganda pictured her to be, 'the orphan of the Pacific'. The reaction was sharp. While there were renewed demands for a fuller voice in London, Australia's Labour government recognised that it was from the United States that succour must come and in Washington that the critical strategic decisions would be taken. The prime minister expressed his view of the political and strategic reality of Australia's position in undiplomatic but telling phrases. 'We refuse,' he wrote in a newspaper article,[30] 'to accept the dictum that the Pacific struggle must be treated as a subordinate segment of the general conflict.' What was needed was 'a concerted plan evoking the greatest strength at the democracies' disposal, determined upon hurling Japan back'. Australia, he continued,

> looks to America, free of any pangs as to our traditional links or kinship with the United Kingdom.
>
> We know the problems that the United Kingdom faces. We know the constant threat of invasion. . . . But we know too that Australia can go, and Britain can still hold on.
>
> We are therefore determined that Australia shall not go . . .

Through the Pacific war council, Australia obtained a voice in the making of strategic decisions in the Pacific war, though not as influential a one as her government hoped for, but far more important for the future. Australia was drawn decisively into the United States strategic orbit. In more senses than one it was her hour of destiny.

When it was apparent that however hard and protracted the task might prove, both Germany and Japan would suffer total defeat, Commonwealth statesmen displayed renewed interest in methods of Commonwealth co-operation in the post-war world. In September 1943 the Australian prime minister, in a well-established Australian tradition and once again with Pacific problems foremost in mind, proposed the formation of a Commonwealth consultative council to be served by a Commonwealth secretariat. Both were intended to bring about a closer co-ordination of Commonwealth, foreign and defence policies. In November 1943 Field Marshal Smuts in a speech to the Empire Parliamentary Association in London,[31] recognising that however great might be the moral prestige of the Commonwealth after the war it would necessarily emerge materially weakened, advocated a grouping of the Commonwealth countries with the like-minded democratic states of the western European seaboard so as to form in association a power equal in stature to the Soviet Union and the United States and capable of holding the balance between them. Finally in January 1944 Lord Halifax, then British ambassador in Washington, expounded in Toronto somewhat similar views. He spoke of the need for Commonwealth unity in foreign policy at least on major issues for, in his opinion, 'if we are to play our rightful part in the preservation of peace, we can only play it as a Commonwealth, united, vital, coherent'.[32] Interesting though these speculations were, more important was the response they elicited. Generally speaking it was unfavourable. Commonwealth governments did not desire formal unity in policy nor centralised machinery to bring it about. Not only did they believe that for them that would be 'a step along the road to yesterday', to quote from the comment of John Dafoe, the editor of *The Free Press*, but that in the international field it would not contribute to but might well lessen the prospect of lasting peace. It was not by the revival of a balance of power on a world scale but by the creation of an effective international organisation supported by all peace-loving states that peace could best be preserved. On this no one was more emphatic than Mackenzie King. On 31 January 1944 in the Canadian House of Commons he observed,[33] with reference to the supposed need to preserve a proper balance of power in the post-war world:

> Field Marshal Smuts thought that this might be achieved by a close association between the United Kingdom and 'the smaller democracies in western Europe' . . . Lord Halifax on the other hand declared: 'Not Great Britain only, but the British Commonwealth and Empire, must be the fourth Power in that group upon which, under Providence, the peace of the world will henceforth depend.
>
> With what is implied in the argument employed by both these eminent public men I am unable to agree.
>
> It is indeed true beyond question that the peace of the world depends on preserving on the side of peace a large superiority of power, so that those who wish to disturb the peace can have no chance of success. But I must ask whether the best way of attaining this is to seek a balance of strength between three or four Great Powers. Should we not, indeed must we not, aim at attaining the necessary superiority of power by creating an effective international system inside which the co-operation of all peace-loving countries is freely sought and given?

It was Mackenzie King's view that prevailed. The Meeting of Commonwealth prime ministers which assembled in London in the spring of 1944 discountenanced any suggestion that new machinery for the co-ordination of Commonwealth policies was required and on the contrary explicitly reaffirmed the faith of the prime ministers in the existing independence in policy, coupled with active, informal consultation. The praise which the Canadian prime minister bestowed in a speech to both Houses of Parliament upon a system which made possible 'a continuous conference of cabinets' was echoed by his Commonwealth colleagues, other than Curtin, who continued to feel that while good as far as it went the system did not go far enough. But whatever the differences, one thing was apparent. Within the Commonwealth that faith in decentralisation which had inspired General Botha more than thirty years earlier remained not merely undimmed but actually strengthened by the experiences of the second world war. In 1944 Commonwealth leaders met not in Imperial Conference, but at a Prime Ministers' Meeting, the distinguishing qualities of which were held to be a lack of formality or of fixed agenda so as to allow for intimate exchanges of view between prime ministers, uninhibited by the restraining presence of official advisers. In the communiqué[34] issued after the second of the Prime Ministers' Meetings, held in London in the spring of 1946, the talks were described as 'an informal exchange of views', and were said to have, 'contributed greatly to the elucidation of many problems' and to 'a mutual understanding of the issues involved' while 'existing methods of consultation' were said to be 'peculiarly appropriate to the character of the British Commonwealth' and 'preferable to any rigid centralised machinery'. The Commonwealth, its reputation in the aftermath of a victory memorably advanced by the sacrifices of this grouping of free peoples in free association, was at its zenith and Commonwealth leaders advanced confidently along the road to tomorrow.

CHAPTER 11

INDIA: THE TRYST WITH A DIVIDED DESTINY

The outbreak of the second world war ushered in the last phase of British rule in India. The war's impact was twofold; it intensified the Indian demand for independence and progressively weakened the British will and capacity to withhold it. The resulting possibility, or probability, of a withdrawal of the British *Raj* sooner than had hitherto been anticipated on either side, in turn and by the natural working of the laws of politics, sharpened the struggle for the succession to power within India. Where formerly the Congress and the League had stood side by side, by March 1940 at the latest, when the Muslim League at their Lahore meeting formulated a demand for separate Muslim homelands and a separate Muslim state, they stood face to face. Where once there had been a possibility of association in independence now there was, in the idiom of a later period, confrontation.

The twin pressures of the struggles for national independence and for control of the levers of power after independence were exserted within a single context, the one at every stage reacting upon the other. That context was provided at the highest political level by the policies of the British government, themselves compounded of immediate military considerations and long-term constitutional aims. First the war and then, and largely in consequence of it, the consolidation of British opinion in favour of an early transfer of power, invested those policies retrospectively with a clarity of outline that historically they did not possess. Nonetheless the record of Britain's wartime and immediately post-war advances to Indian independence on the basis of responsible government and dominion status, summarily restated, provides a necessary background to any analysis of the interrelation between constitutional advance and domestic division.

The outbreak of war underlined not so much the measure of autonomy India had so far acquired as the extent of her dependence. The viceroy, Lord Linlithgow, declared war on behalf of India without calling the leaders of the principal Indian parties, the Congress or the Muslim

League, into a consultation. Constitutionally the viceroy's action was warranted by reason of the fact that the federal provisions of the Government of India Act 1935 had not come into effect. But constitutional rectitude was no compensation for so grave a lapse in political judgment. The Congress, in particular, was deeply resentful; and Pandit Nehru contrasted the position of the dominions, including Ireland, free to decide in their several parliaments whether or not to declare war upon Nazi Germany, with that of an India committed to war without even so much as a reference to its representative political figures.[1] From this inauspicious start there was to be no sustained recovery in Anglo-Indian, or more especially in Anglo-Congress relations for the duration of the war. In this there was a certain irony in as much as British and Congress, and indeed British and Indian, opinion as a whole, far from being in conflict, coincided substantially in respect of the causes for which war was being waged.

There were differences in the attitudes of the League and the Congress to wartime co-operation, that of the League being essentially pragmatic while the Congress characteristically defined their position in conceptual terms. They professed sympathy for the Allied cause deriving from their love of liberty and the strong anti-Fascist, anti-Nazi sentiments embodied in the pre-war Congress resolutions, but maintained that despite these bonds, co-operation with Britain was precluded by India's continued dependence. India, unfree, could not fight for freedom. Such was the Congress assertion of principle. Was it reasonable to infer from it that a free India under Congress leadership would support the Allied cause in arms? The answer, and it was clearly one of potential importance in the shaping of British policy, remained debatable. In December 1939 the Congress governments in the provinces resigned rather than co-operate in a war effort directed by an alien authority. In itself and for the future this was a significant step. But it did not provide a conclusive answer about attitudes in quite different conditions. That could be founded only on less tangible and necessarily hypothetical evidence. The main body of the Congress, attentive to Jawaharlal Nehru's impassioned pre-war denunciation of militarist régimes both in Europe and Asia, would presumably have favoured the participation of a free India, provided it were unmistakably at her own choice and on her own terms, in the war on the side of the western allies. But there were also the disciples of Mahatma Gandhi, already regarded with veneration as the conscience of the Congress, who accepted without qualification his doctrines of non-violent resistance and believed them to have an absolute validity in the international, as in the domestic, field. In 1942 they were prepared with Gandhi to advocate such passive resistance to a Japanese invasion from the north-east. Nor could the British government, even assuming that it had been able to reach a conclusion reassuring to itself about the co-operation of a Congress wartime government, consider the Indian problem in its Congress setting alone. There were also the League and the princes. In terms of Britain's survival – and no less was at stake between 1940 and 1942 – was there solid advantage in conceding freedom to India, even on the assumption of thereby enlisting the aid of the Congress in the prosecution of the war, if the consequences were to be the estrangement of loyal princely allies and the opening of a struggle for power within India between the Congress and the League? Even if the answer were in the affirmative, it was at best speculative and few governments are prepared to indulge in wartime speculation so risky as this. So it was that from 1939 onwards the British government were caught in a dilemma from which, despite some facile subsequent comment, there was no escape. It may well be that the chief responsibility for the existence of such a dilemma was their own, and that in wartime Britain was paying the price of the procrastinating policies of the later 1920s and early 1930s.

It is in terms of this diminishing freedom of manœuvre and of the impact of the successive major crises of the war that British attempts to end the constitutional deadlock in India are to be viewed. On 23 October 1939 the secretary of state, Lord Zetland, reminded the war cabinet that when Parliament had 'accepted dominion status as the goal, the feeling was that the journey was a long one, but the effect of the outbreak of the war has been to bring us hard up against the implication of dominion status for India. . .'[2] The nature of British wartime proposals underlined the correctness of this analysis. The first, following closely upon the fall of France, was the so-called 'August offer', 1940. It proposed the immediate enlargement of the viceroy's council so as to include a certain number of representatives of the Indian political parties, but little otherwise. Further essays in constitution-making were firmly relegated to after the end of the war, though it was conceded that when the time came, and in accord with dominion precedent, any new constitution should be drafted in India. But even in this context, there was a restatement in uncompromising terms of Britain's obligations to the princes and of British inability to contemplate the transfer of their responsibility for the peace and welfare of India to any system of government, the authority of which was directly denied 'by large and powerful elements in India's national life'.[3] The offer concluded with the hope that, as a result of Indian co-operation in the war, a new understanding would emerge paving the way to 'the attainment by India of that free and equal partnership in the British Commonwealth which remains the proclaimed and accepted goal of the imperial Crown and of the British Parliament'.

The 'August offer', its modest attractions for the most part prospective and conditional, was spurned by the Congress and rejected, albeit with some judicious qualification, by the League. There followed a period of constitutional quiescence. It came to an end in 1942, that year of disaster to Allied arms in the east. On 11 March the prime minister announced in the House of Commons that 'the crisis in the affairs of India arising out of the Japanese advance has made us wish to rally all the forces of Indian life to guard their land from the menace of the invader'. In consequence the war cabinet had decided to send out one of their number, the lord privy seal, Sir Stafford Cripps, to India to give precision to earlier British declarations, and notably the 'August offer' 1940, about dominion status for India and to convince 'all classes, races and creeds in India of our sincere resolve' that 'the conclusions upon which we are agreed, and which we believe represent a just and final solution, will achieve their purpose'. In fact the conclusions of the war cabinet were in terms of precision, if not of principle, a decided advance upon anything hitherto formulated. At the heart of them was dominion status, with the constitution of the new Indian union to be drafted, as the Congress had consistently demanded, by an Indian Constituent Assembly in accord with dominion precedents. The new dominion was to be 'associated with the United Kingdom and the other dominions by a common allegiance to the Crown, but equal to them in every respect, in no way subordinate in any aspect of its domestic or external affairs'.[4] What was contemplated, as Sir Stafford Cripps made plain on arrival in India, was dominion status without reservation or qualification. At a press conference in New Delhi he was asked whether the new dominion would be free to secede. He replied in the affirmative. He was asked whether Canada was free to secede. He replied 'Of course'. While these answers, when reported, gave George VI some cause for uneasy reflection,[5] they gave, in so far as they were credited, a measure of reassurance in Delhi. However, the offer of dominion status which Sir Stafford Cripps thus expounded, while unconditional, remained prospective. Once again constitution-making was deferred till victory had been won. This was a major disappointment to Indian nationalist sentiment. There was the certainty of delay and, for many, no corresponding assurance about victory. Gandhi was alleged to have spoken of a postdated cheque upon a failing bank, and even if the phrase was not of his own invention – it has been attributed to K. M. Panikkar – he entertained the sentiment. Nor were Congress feelings of frustration on the constitutional front counterbalanced by the prospect of some immediate transfer of substantial administrative responsibilities to Indian hands. At the crisis of the eastern war, the British government decided on the contrary that it must retain final control of the levers of power and direct control over defence in India. Accordingly much of what it was prepared to transfer to Indian hands was of marginal relevance to government at such a time. Moreover, while these were the chief, they were not the only causes of Congress reserve. The Cripps proposals introduced a novel principle of non-accession, by which any province of British India which was not prepared to accept the constitution to be drafted after the war was to be enabled to retain its existing constitutional position unimpaired and outside the new Indian dominion. It was later added that the British government would be prepared to agree upon a new constitution giving the non-acceding provinces, collectively, if they so desired, the same status as the Indian union. The League had reason to welcome these concessions to its position, though it professed to feel that they did not go far enough. The formulation of the principle of non-accession enhanced Congress suspicions of British intentions. The final outcome was rejection of the Cripps offer, first by the Congress on the specific ground of inadequate Indian control over the defence of India but clearly also for more general reasons and then by the League. The failure to reach agreement was followed by Congress endorsement in August 1942 of a 'Quit India' resolution,[6] which resulted in rebellion and led to the imprisonment of the principal Congress leaders for the remainder of the war.

The Cripps mission did not achieve its immediate purposes but it succeeded in its long-term aims. In India, and certainly no less in London, it changed the context of discussions about Anglo-Indian relations. Churchill, who had seen Cripps, the radical, socialist friend of Nehru, depart on a highly problematic mission with mixed feelings, and who was enabled to endure its failure with fortitude, remarked to the king shortly afterwards that 'his colleagues and both, or all three parties in Parliament were quite prepared to give up India to the Indians after the war. He felt they had already been talked into giving up India.'[7] More precisely, there could be no going back on the offer of a constituent assembly and dominion status. And it was on this basis that negotiations were resumed after the war, first in conference at Simla and then, following the accession to office of the Labour government in Britain, by the sending of a cabinet mission consisting of Lord Pethick-Lawrence, the secretary of state for India, Sir Stafford Cripps, president of the Board of Trade, and A. V. Alexander, the first lord of the Admiralty, to India early in 1946. There could no longer be serious doubt about the purposes of the British government. The first was to preserve the unity of India and the second to transfer power at the earliest possible moment. These dual aims, were however, conflicting. Unity might conceivably be preserved were independence deferred;

independence might be conceded forthwith but at the price of unity. That much was made plain by the Indian response to the cabinet mission and its Report.

The mission examined but rejected the possibility of partition and proposed that there should be a union of India, embracing both British India and the princely states, with responsibility for foreign affairs, defence and communications. All other subjects and all residuary powers were to be vested in the provinces and the provinces were to be left free to form groups, with each group enabled to determine the provincial subjects to be dealt with in common.[8] This three-tier structure, with its weak centre, its potential groupings and its strongly entrenched provincial governments, was as far as the cabinet mission felt it possible to go towards satisfying minority sentiment while preserving a framework of federal unity. Their submissions, finally issued on 16 May 1946, in the form of a statement by the cabinet mission and the viceroy, were accepted initially but with reservations in respect of Pakistan by the League and subject to conditions by the Congress. Such qualified responses in themselves augured ill at this late hour for the prospects of unity, and the misgivings they inspired were fully realised with the failure of the viceroy's first attempts to obtain joint Congress-League participation in the interim government intended by the cabinet mission to prepare for the transfer of responsibility, or at any time in a constituent assembly to draft a constitution for India. In these circumstances the British government was compelled to contemplate the abandonment of one or other of its aims. Unity and an early transfer of power were self-evidently incompatible and it was arguable that communal antagonism was of such intensity that unity could not in any circumstances, or at any foreseeable time, survive the transfer of power. If this were so, the opportunities for transfer to a single successor authority were already in the past.

The last phase, from the autumn of 1946 to the summer of 1947, was marked by the formation of an interim government, in which Congress and League representatives in acrimonious association assumed responsibility for the conduct of Indian administration; by the summoning of the long-promised Constituent Assembly which, however, was boycotted by the representatives of the Muslim League; by the announcement, on 20 February 1947, of the 'definite intention' of the British government 'to take the necessary steps to effect the transference of power into responsible Indian hands by a date not later than June 1948';[9] by the arrival in March 1947 of Lord Mountbatten as the last viceroy and one who had welcomed the fact 'that his task was to end one régime and to inaugurate a new one';[10] by the succeeding weeks of intense and dramatic discussion between the new viceroy and the

Indian leaders, recorded for later generations by Alan Campbell Johnson[11] in his *Mission with Mountbatten*; by the resulting final acceptance, or acquiescence, by the leaders of the Congress and the League of the inevitability of partition; by the announcement of partition and of the transfer of power to two successor dominions by the viceroy at a press conference on 4 June, at which with unfailing assurance he answered nearly a hundred questions put to him by Indian and world correspondents; [12] by the passage through both Houses of Parliament at Westminster of the Indian Independence Act, introduced in the House of Commons by the prime minister, Clement Attlee, in a speech, which contained an apposite and moving quotation from Mountstuart Elphinstone and an allusion, deemed more felicitous then than later, to Campbell-Bannerman's parallel act of faith in restoring self-government to the defeated Boers[13] 'which bore fruit both in 1914 and in 1939'; and finally, on the midnight hour of the 14–15 August 1947, by the coming into existence of the two new dominions of India and Pakistan, with Mohammed Ali Jinnah speaking in Karachi, the new capital of a new state, of 'the fulfilment of the destiny of the Muslim nation' and with Pandit Nehru in Delhi reflecting upon the long years ago when 'we made a tryst with destiny' and of how the time had come 'when we shall redeem our pledge'.[14]

It had proved, however, to be a tryst with a divided destiny. Muslim achievement of Pakistan represented at once the frustration of Congress hopes and a defeat for British interests. The first was self-evident and the second well put in a letter from Lord Wavell to the king, in which he spoke of 'the vital necessity, not only to the British Commonwealth but to the whole world, of a united, stable and friendly India'.[15] Why then did India not remain united? That remains one of the most vexing and difficult questions of modern Commonwealth history. To seek for an answer it is necessary to leave the chronological, constitutional road and to examine the conflicts of interests, hopes and fears which produced the situation, and the psychology from which partition derived.

Contrary to what is often suggested, there is at present no evidence that the advantages and disadvantages of partition, as a solution of India's major community problems had been carefully weighed or long considered by any of those principally concerned before it took effect. It is easy to be misled by words. But dialectical exchanges about controversial proposals are not in themselves evidence that those proposals are being advanced, criticised or rejected in terms of political actualities. Certainly it was the case that after the Lahore resolution[16] of the All-India Muslim League in March 1940 – the so-called 'Pakistan Resolution' though the term Pakistan did not in fact appear in it – partition had its passionate protagonists, its outraged opponents and those who, with Mahatma Gandhi, came to acquiesce with resignation in a prospect less distasteful to them than the thought of enforced minority inclusion in a unitary state. Yet the debate was not practical and purposeful; rather was it long-range and emotive. The language used on the one side was that of Muslim homelands and a Holy War to defend them; on the other, to employ the phrase Gandhi made his own, that of the vivisection of Mother India. There is no evidence of consideration before 1947 on the part either of advocates or opponents as to what partition would mean in terms of administration, and still less, apart from generalities, in terms of frontiers, economics, social disruption, communications, distribution of assets or control of irrigation. So much indeed was understandable. The Muslim League was fighting to establish 'an impossible' aim; the Congress to defeat a stratagem which its leaders believed down to the 'Great Calcutta Killing' of August 1946 (and in some cases into 1947) to have been adopted in order to secure a strong negotiating position for the entrenchment of Muslim minority rights within an independent India. When the records of the Congress, the papers of its leaders and the files of the India Office in London are made available for study, it will be of interest to learn of the date of the first comprehensive analysis, if any, of the likely overall consequences of a partition of India.

It was not so much the complexity as the nature of relations in India on the eve of partition that made foresight difficult and discouraged realistic appraisal of future possibilities. The more important of those relations were without exception triangular. There were the three principal communities, the Hindus, the Muslims and the Sikhs, in descending order of magnitude; there were the three political groupings, the princes, the Muslim League and the Indian National Congress in ascending order of importance; and there were the three arbiters of national destiny, the British, the Congress and the League. In each triangle there was the predisposition – it is almost a law of politics – of the lesser to combine against the greatest. The League thus looked more kindly than the Congress on the pretensions of the princes; almost to the last, until in 1946 Jinnah became convinced that the viceroy, Lord Wavell, was to be regarded as 'the latest exponent of geographical unity', the League was apt to be more understanding or at least less unreceptive of British proposals than the Congress. At one time indeed, before Gandhi took up their cause, the League seemed prepared to champion the outcastes, and until early 1947 there were intermittent and still undisclosed negotiations with the Sikhs, thought to have been on the basis of possible Sikh autonomy within an undivided Punjab. The British for their part showed a preoccupation with the outcastes and with minorities generally which was thought by the Congress not to have been altogether altruistic. There was also the continuing Congress suspicion, only dispelled or partially dispelled in the period immediately before partition, of British predisposition towards Muslims. Behind allegations or assertions, difficult as they were for the most part to substantiate, lay the inconsistencies, the dissembling, and the tactical devices inseparable from triangular political situations. Purpose and reality were difficult to disentangle from stratagem and manœuvre, even at times by those engaged in employing them. In the maze of tactics the sense of direction was apt to become clouded. The existence of so many variants seemingly discouraged cool appraisal of realities – not least in one respect on the part of the Government of India and the India Office in London.

Successive British governments and viceroys, it now seems evident beyond dispute, gravely overestimated the power and authority of the Indian princes. Even the Labour government was in part the victim of such miscalculation, and as for the viceroys, only the last – perhaps because he was himself of royal blood – proved in this respect to be without illusions. Over the years this British overestimate was a complicating factor on the Indian scene. Within a few months of the transfer of power the princes were shown to be, as Gandhi had earlier claimed, at any rate not much more than 'British Officers in Indian dress'. And if *some* among a number of estimable and public spirited rulers were not shown to have been 'sinks of iniquity', as Pandit Nehru had once alleged, that may have been partly because the political adviser to the princes, Sir Conrad Corfield, to the subsequent annoyance of Mountbatten and the anger of Nehru in May 1947 ordered his subordinates in the Political Department to extract from the files confidential reports reflecting unfavourably on the public or private behaviour of the princes – 'eccentricities' was the favoured term in respect of the latter – and burn what has been calculated to have been four tons of them.[17] But earlier in that same year, 1947, there were those who conceived or cherished the hope that in an independent India, the greater at least of the states might have an autonomous existence. There were enquiries from princely officials about the nature of external association and, in Bombay businessmen discussed prospects of development in Hyderabad and Travancore on the assumption that as autonomous units they might be the most stable and solvent parts of a new India. Eighteenth-century analogies were fashionable, and if they were too artificial to carry much conviction at least they were illustrative of a trend in British-Indian thinking – and one incidentally wholly in conflict with British interests in the creation of one or if need be, two strong, stable successor states after independence. Nor was the predisposition of the British, both at the official and the unofficial level, to exaggerate the potential rôle of the princes without its lasting importance. It was the princes, not as the Congress had urged, the peoples of the states who by virtue of being empowered to sign or not to sign Instruments of Accession to either of the successor powers on the lapse of British paramountcy, who were placed in a position to determine the destiny of the states. That authority is alleged to have been given to them by the Labour government, partly to appease the Conservative opposition at Westminister. Whether this was so or not – and *prima facie* it would seem questionable – the fact of princely decision made prediction about states and accession difficult in some cases, and virtually incalculable in Hyderabad and – even apparently to princely advisers – in Kashmir.[19] Assuredly there were obligations of honour, nostalgic notions of a 'gorgeous east' and a belief in the stability of autocratic rule, but in essence continuing British reliance upon the princes sprang from long indulged preoccupations with the tactics of a triangular political situation.

In the struggle for power on the highest plane, that is to say between the British, the Congress and the League, it was the British who were familiarly cast in the rôle of the third party. In the Congress view the British in India had followed for some forty years before partition a policy of didine and rule. 'It has been the traditional policy of Britain,' complained Gandhi, after the Congress rejection of the 'August offer' of 1940[20], 'to prevent parties from uniting. "Divide and rule" has been Britain's proud motto. It is the British statesmen who are responsible for the divisions in India's ranks and the divisions will continue so long as the British sword holds India under bondage.' This was the language of politics, not history. Thoughts of 'divide and rule', however, were not absent from the minds of twentieth-century British officials and statesmen. So much is clear from files dealing with the Liberal administration of the pre-first world war years and not necessarily only in relation to India. Nor was it absent in the 1930s and 1940s. Lord Zetland, who was secretary of state for India at the outbreak of the second world war, noted, without sharing, the satisfaction which evidence of communal division gave among 'diehards', Churchill not least among them,[21] while the viceroy, Lord Linlithgow, largely because of it, thought of dominion status for India as a still distant goal.

> No one [wrote the viceroy in January 1939[22]] can, of course, say what, in some remote period of time, or in the event of international convulsions of a particular character, may be the ultimate relations of India and Great Britain . . . but that there should be any general impression . . . that public opinion at home, or His Majesty's government, seriously contemplate evacuation in any measurable period of time, seems to me astonishing.

No doubt the Congress leaders sensed that such was the viceroy's mind.

In general, the more the British government showed itself preoccupied with the position of minorities and with communal divisions, the more suspect it became to the Congress. If, as Gandhi argued, the communal problem was insoluble so long as the third party remained and if, as the British argued, they could not go until it was resolved, might that not mean they would stay forever? Or to pose the dilemma in a broader, impersonal context, how was the British view, that the resolution of the communal problem was a necessary precondition of their departure, to be reconciled with the Congress conviction that their departure was a necessary precondition of its resolution?

There was, however, an alternative analysis. It was suggested to the Round Table Conference in 1931 by a distinguished Indian Liberal. For the 'divide and rule' of Congress he substituted 'we divide and you rule'. Pushed to its logical conclusion this meant, presumably, that the divisions at root were domestic. At the Round Table Conference logic was not pressed to such extremes. Princes and Muslims were at one in proclaiming that they had no wish to create 'Ulsters in India'. But was this really so? In respect of some of the princes (and their friends) it seems questionable; in respect of the Muslims it posed the fundamental question: Were they a community, the second largest within India, or were they a separate nation? If they were the former, then the pattern of a self-protective policy might have been expected to be (as indeed it was at least down to 1940) limited cooperation with the British and the Congress in the working out of a federal structure in which the position of the Muslims, at least in Muslim majority provinces, was entrenched against a centre certain to be dominated, under any form of representative government, by representatives of the great Hindu majority in the country. But if the Muslims were not the second largest community in India but a separate nation, then any such policy of limited co-operation was precautionary and preliminary to a demand for a separate national recognition. In these matters words are not conclusive. But they are important, particularly when invested with the force which Jinnah gave them at the Lahore meeting of the League in March 1940. He castigated the British for their conception of government by parties functioning on a political plane as the best form of government for every country. He assailed *The Times* for having earlier concluded, after recognition of the differences not only of religion but also of law and culture between Hindus and Muslims, that in the course of time 'the superstitions will die out and India will be moulded into a single nation'. For Jinnah it was not a question of superstitions or of time but of fundamental beliefs and social conceptions.

Hindus and Muslims [he said] have two different religious philosophies, social customs, literatures. They neither intermarry, nor even interdine.

Indeed, they belong to two different civilisations. . . . Their views of this life and the life hereafter are different. . . . The Muslims are not a minority as the word is commonly understood. . . . Muslims are a nation according to any definition of the term, and they must have their homelands, their territory and their state.[23]

If there is substance in Jinnah's contention then it would seem to follow logically that the British must be acquitted of any final responsibility for the partition of India; or in the language of contemporary dialectics, it did not much matter in this respect whether the third party stayed or went. Had the British succeeded in imposing unity then the consequence, again accepting the fundamentals of Jinnah's analysis, might well have been, as he threatened in 1947, the bloodiest civil war in the history of Asia. For the essence of his argument was that it was the unity of India that was artificial and imposed; the division natural. And by way of epilogue it is worth noting that one of the Congress High Command, the formidable Vallabhbhai Patel, infuriated by League intransigence and possibly (in May 1947) also under the influence of Mountbatten's persuasive powers, argued with Maulana Azad, the leading Congress Muslim, in favour of partition by saying 'whether we liked it or not, there were two nations in India'.[24] If, on the other hand, Jinnah's analysis is to be questioned in its essentials, then the arguments for a more probing enquiry into the aims and purposes of British as well as Congress and League policies are conclusive. More immediately it is to be noted that while Jinnah staked his claim for Pakistan in March 1940, there was no certainty whether its dramatic presentation was a stratagem or a literal statement of his objective. Reports of some contemporary conversations he had in Lahore suggest that for all the vehemence of his language he may himself have remained undecided.[25]

Whatever the Lahore resolutions might portend for the future, they indicated at the time a shift in Muslim priorities. While the Congress continued to fight on one front against the British to secure independence, the Muslim League was engaged on two fronts against the British and against Congress; and after 1940 the second assumed even greater importance. Here was an open challenge to the claims of the Congress to represent Indian nationalist opinion. When the Congress governments in the provinces resigned in December 1939 after two and a half years of office – on the issue of non-co-operation in the war – Jinnah proclaimed Friday 22 December 1939 a Day of Deliverance from 'the tyranny, oppression and injustice' from which Muslim India had suffered under Congress rule. The source and origin of Muslim grievances is not in dispute. It lay in the fact that the Congress, after its massive victory in the 1937 provincial elections, had formed one-party governments in provinces in which the Muslim League had expected coalition governments in which they would be partners. This repudiation of the League derived fundamentally from the Congress conviction that it represented all India. There was no need accordingly for political concessions to a minority grouping or, more particularly, for recognition of a ministerial rôle for the League, which anyway had fared poorly in the elections. Muslims there would certainly be in the provincial governments – but they would be Congress Muslims or League Muslims who had renounced the League and joined the Congress as a condition of office. This general presumption was reinforced, so both Jawaharlal Nehru and Rajendra Prasad have remarked in their recorded reflections,[26] by a conviction that the conventions of British cabinet government should prevail. If there were League members of the provincial governments in, for example, the United Provinces and Orissa, what then became of notions of collective responsibility? 'Congressmen,' so Rajendra Prasad recalled,[27] 'thought it contrary to the spirit of parliamentary democracy to appoint any outsider in their ministry.' If Muslims were to serve then first claim, as party stalwarts were quick to emphasize, lay with those Muslims who were loyal members of the Congress and not with supporters of the League. Yet in retrospect, as written records suggest and personal conversations underline, most of the prominent Congress leaders remained preoccupied and even questioning as to the correctness of their 1937 conclusions. And at the time one of the Congress leaders, not surprisingly the perceptive and courageous Congress Muslim, Maulana A. K. Azad – who was to serve as president of the Congress throughout the war years – challenged and fought in vain to prevent or reverse these exclusivist decisions dictated largely by party loyalists in the provinces. What was at issue was a question of political judgment. On any reckoning the decision would seem in retrospect to have been ill-advised. Whether it was more is a matter of opinion. Sir Penderel Moon deems it to have been 'the *fons et origo malorum*' and argues that the Congress leaders 'were responsible, though quite unwittingly' for the critical change in Muslim sentiment from readiness to contemplate cooperation in an all-India federation to insistence upon separation. The Congress 'passionately desired to preserve the unity of India. They consistently acted so as to make its partition certain'.[28] But, it may reasonably be asked, did the partition of India derive from so comparatively trifling a cause? Were there not fundamental forces at work? An error or a series of errors in judgment is one thing, the source of a political event so momentous as partition ordinarily another. Or to put the issue in another way, was partition implicit in the Indian scene or not? If it were, tactics were of secondary importance and only if not, whether well- or ill-conceived, of first significance.

Before the concept of Pakistan could pass from the realm of stratagem to that of near reality, certain conditions had to be fulfilled. The first was that the imperial power should become increasingly sensitive to the claims advanced by the Muslim League. This in fact happened. It is attributed by V. P. Menon and others who have followed him[29] to Congress policies of non-co-operation and non-participation in provincial government during the war. It is an opinion to be accepted with considerable reserve in that non-cooperation during the war was almost certainly a condition of continuing Congress unity. Immoderate policies, furthermore, ensured the survival of moderate leadership during the war and its triumph thereafter. By reason of their adoption there were no significant, surviving enemies on the left; whereas wartime co-operation might well have divided and correspondingly weakened the Congress in the face of the League. But, if explanation must remain speculative, the step by step advance on the British side towards the meeting of Muslim League claims is hardly disputable. The British statement that accompanied the 'August offer' of 1940 remarked: 'it goes without saying that they [the United Kingdom government] could not contemplate transfer of their present responsibilities for the peace and welfare of India to any system of government whose authority is directly denied by large and powerful elements in India's national life.'[30] Not surprisingly, in a changed and – from the point of view of the British government – a weaker position, the Cripps mission went further in this respect than the 'August offer'. The contemplated dominion constitution was subject to 'the right of any province of British India that is not prepared to accept the new constitution to retain its present constitutional position', or should such non-acceding provinces 'so desire, His Majesty's Government will be prepared to agree upon a new constitution, giving them the same full status as the Indian Union'.[31] The introduction of 'this novel principle of non-accession' was followed, after two conferences at Simla, by the purposely vague recommendations of the cabinet mission in 1946, outlining a three-tier constitutional structure with a union government at the apex and, in an intermediate position, three groups of provinces, the one comprised of predominantly Hindu, the remaining two of predominantly Muslim provinces, dealing with all such subjects as the provinces comprising each group might desire to have dealt with in association, and, at the base, the provinces themselves dealing with all other subjects and possessing all the residuary sovereign rights.[32] Certainly this was not tantamount to Pakistan, for as has already been noted the cabinet mission had considered and deliberately rejected partition. But the Council of the Muslim League was not mistaken in considering that in these proposals there lay 'the basis and the foundation of Pakistan'.

The second condition preliminary to the achievement of Pakistan was the consolidation of Muslim opinion behind the League. Despite the difficulties inherent in the geographical distribution of the Muslim population and in the reluctance of more Muslims than may now be supposed to contemplate partition, this condition also was substantially fulfilled. To appreciate the extent to which this was so, it is necessary only to place side by side the results, in so far as the Muslim League was concerned, of the elections of 1937 and of 1946. Where at the earlier date, even in Muslim majority provinces the League had made an indifferent showing, by the later date it was polling in most if not all cases close to its maximum natural strength. This was a remarkable achievement in terms both of leadership and of organisation. One element in it was the dramatisation of issues. This was a rewarding technique but one which exacted a sometimes terrible price. The League proclaimed its day of deliverance, its days of protest, and finally on 16 August 1946, Direct Action Day, on which the black flags of the Muslim League fluttered over Muslim homes – and in Calcutta provided the occasion for what has gone down to history as the 'Great Calcutta Killing', nowhere described with more sickening realism than in the restrained pages of General Sir Francis Tuker's *While Memory Serves*.[33] Well may one ask whether Pakistan was attainable without communal violence on a scale unparalleled in all the years since the Mutiny.

There was a further condition of partition. The League had to be equated with the Congress or, as Jinnah preferred to phrase it, Pakistan and Hindustan. In numerical terms this meant the equation of minority with majority. It had happened elsewhere. It had happened in Ireland when the six counties of Northern Ireland and the twenty-six counties of Southern Ireland were given equal representation in the Council of Ireland, that 'fleshless and bloodless skeleton' as Asquith termed it, proposed in the Government of Ireland Act 1920.[34] In arithmetical terms such parity could not be defended in either case. But as Jinnah argued the debate was not about numbers nor even about communities but about nations. Nations were equal irrespective of their size. He secured his aim at the first Simla Conference in 1946, when League and Congress representation was equated, with a sharp protest by the League at the nomination by the Congress of a Muslim, Maulana Azad, as one of their representatives. It was 'a symbolic affront'. Jinnah was certainly the most formidable proponent of a two-nation theory yet to appear within the confines of the British Empire. Positively his demand was for unequivocal recognition of the separate nationality of Muslim India, which in Bengal at least was not self-evident; negatively it was for the reduction of the Congress claims to speak for all-India to a

Congress right to speak for Hindustan. Nehru was written off as a Hindu imperialist; Gandhi as a man with whom it was impossible to negotiate because by vast self-deception he had convinced himself he was a spokesman of something more than Hinduism; Maulana Azad, that prototype of Congress Muslims, denounced as a renegade or even a quisling; the idea of a secular state ridiculed as part of a design of characteristic Hindu subtlety to fasten Hindu rule upon the whole of India. Again, however, there was implicit in Jinnah's demands a price even for their formulation. The League could challenge the claims of Congress to speak for all India most effectively only by becoming ever more firmly imprisoned within the rigid concept of a future communal state.

Finally there was one last condition of partition. To the Congress demand that the British thould quit India, Muslims responded with the demand that they should divide and quit – and in that order. Here again the League were largely successful. It is true that the division for which they asked was not the division they received. The full demand was for an independent state of Pakistan comprising two areas, one in the north-west consisting of the Punjab, Sind, North-West Frontier, and British Baluchistan, the other the north-east consisting of Bengal and Assam. Accession to that demand would no doubt have created a viable state. But the demand rested upon community and as the cabinet mission concluded 'every argument that can be used in favour of Pakistan can equally, in our view, be used in favour of the exclusion of the non-Muslim areas from Pakistan'.[35] There followed the partitioning of the Punjab and Bengal and Jinnah was left with what he had once contemptuously dismissed as 'a mutilated, a moth-eaten and truncated Pakistan'.

It was on 24 August 1946 that an interim government, initially predominantly Congress in its composition, was appointed, with Lord Wavell presiding over its deliberations with a splendid, if unhelpful, soldierly reserve. It was only after it had been in existence some time that the Muslim League decided to accept the invitation to join. The Congress had then to decide on a reconstitution of the government, and in particular on the more important posts to be offered to the League. Under strong presure from Sardar Vallabhbhai Patel, understandably anxious to retain control of the Home Department and with it of relations with the princes, and against the warnings of Maulana Azad, the principal portfolio they offered was that of minister for finance. When Chaudhary Mohammed Ali heard the news in the department it is said he told Jinnah that it marked a great victory for the League. So in some respects it proved. The post was filled by Liaquat Ali Khan, and when Liaquat became the finance member (records Maulana Azad) he obtained the possession of the key to government. Every proposal of every department was subject to his scrutiny. 'Not a Chaprasi could be appointed in any department without the sanction of his department'.[36] What is more, Liaquat drafted a budget the onus of which fell, as it was intended to fall, heavily upon the wealthy supporters of the Congress. And while, to descend to trifling matters, it may be questioned whether tact mattered much at this late stage, it is still worth noting that the Congress ministers were not diplomatic in their handling of their new League colleagues. It was the practice of Congress ministers to foregather for tea before the sessions of the interim government. The invitation to the new League members to attend these gatherings came from Pandit Nehru's private secretary. They were offended.[37] They never attended. But then, of course, they might not have done so anyway.

With the statement of 20 February 1947 the British government regained the initiative. The statement[38] put an eighteen-month time limit, till June 1948, on British rule in India. For weeks it was subjected to the most careful and suspicious scrutiny in Delhi but it was found to be without trace of equivocation. The time limit enhanced the prospect of Pakistan but diminished the chances of its orderly creation and establishment. In April, Liaquat Ali Khan explained that while the statement presupposed the coming into existence of Pakistan and was therefore to be welcomed, the time limit was too short. A capital had yet to be chosen: government and administration to be organised, the inheritance of British India to be divided. Within a matter of weeks the time limit was foreshortened by nearly a year, 15 August 1947 being fixed as the date of the transfer of power. The effect was to heighten the double impact made by the statement of 20 February. Pakistan was brought that much nearer; its early administration made that much more difficult.

The initative regained by the British government was exploited by the last viceroy. His outstanding contribution, as seen from Delhi at that time, was to give a sense of purpose and direction on the British side at the moment when, with relaxing control, communal tensions might have merged into civil war and led to partial disintegration. History was being made and Lord Mountbatten brought drama to the making of it. Perhaps there was some element of illusion in the new understanding he established with the Congress leaders. Nehru, so Michael Edwardes has suggested, thought of Mountbatten as a 'straightforward English socialist', 'a sort of Philippe Egalité in naval uniform'.[39] What was important, however, was the personal rapport established with the Congress, though not with the League, leadership. Moreover, in smaller as in greater things Mountbatten sensed the time for change. He was always 'taking tea with treason', to use the diehard terminology of denunciation employed against Lord Irwin's reception of Gandhi in the early 1930s, and in the vice-chancellor's office at Delhi University Sir Maurice Gwyer, a former chief justice of India, derived wry amusement from studying the lists of those who now at long last were being entertained in the viceroy's house.

The first Mountbatten plan, sometimes irreverently known as the 'Dickie-Bird Plan' and involving the transfer of power to individual provinces, was considered by the cabinet in London but angrily rejected by Nehru as likely to lead to disintegration. Its only merit – if merit it were – was that it would have allowed opinion to be tested on the possible emergence of an independent and united Bengal. The second plan, dominion status for two successor states, was devised on his own account of it by V. P. Menon,[40] the reforms commissioner, and in substance it won acceptance. Never in all its history, it may be thought, has the Commonwealth idea made so momentous a contribution to the settlement of so complex a problem.

Two last questions remain. The first is, why did the Congress leaders at the last agree to partition? The answer, it may be suggested, was three-fold. They had ambitions for India and those ambitions could not be fulfilled without strong central government. So long as the majority of Muslims were within a united India, that meant that strong, central government was out of the question. The second, entertained by Vallabhbhai Patel but by no means universally shared by his colleagues, was the belief that Pakistan would not long endure. Patel was convinced, records Maulana Azad, who was not a friendly witness, that Pakistan was 'not viable' and would 'collapse in a short time'.[41] Nehru also, though less categoric, did not think it could last.[42] The third dominant consideration was time. The Congress leaders had struggled long for independence, they were now ageing men and they were not prepared to delay independence further. Here indeed was a root difference between Congress and the League and a source of strength to Jinnah. He was prepared to let independence wait upon division, while his opponents for the most part were not prepared to let it wait upon unity. Not all of them, however, were agreed on this count. To the last, Maulana Azad remained convinced that time was on the side of unity.[43] One, two, years' delay and the cabinet mission plan with its weak centre and its provincial groupings would prove acceptable. Patel was against him, so was Nehru and at the last Gandhi himself appeared resigned to partition. Azad, as a Congress Muslim, had his own reasons for insistence upon unity and his own grounds for misgivings about the consequences of partition. But if in this he was percipient, it may well be questioned whether he was realistic in his own recommendations.

The possible deferment of independence for one year or more in the supposed interests of unity invites certain questions. Were the resources of the Indian civil service and the British Army in India at this stage equal to the responsibilities such delay would undoubtedly involve? Were the British public at home prepared to sustain the effort that might be needed? If not, who was to govern India in the meantime? The Muslim League, Gandhi suggested, as a desperate but not an original device – Rajagopalachari had proposed it in 1940 also to avert partition. The Congress would not hear of it. Most of all, was Maulana Azad right in his presupposition that with time passions would cool? Was it not more likely that with procrastination they would in fact be further inflamed? Was it not more probable that far from diminishing the ambitions of princes, subtracting from the negatives of the League, qualifying the uncompromising attitudes of the Congress, all would be accentuated. And what of the Sikhs, who accepted partition in June 1947? Their leader, Master Tara Singh – that prophetic-looking figure, whose words so belied the benignity of his flowing beard – in late February 1947, brandishing an unsheathed sword at a mass rally in the Punjab, is alleged to have cried, 'O Hindus and Sikhs! Be ready for self-destruction. . . . I have sounded the bugle. Finish the Muslim League', and 'Death to Pakistan'.[44] It was a few years later that he enunciated his creed 'I believe in chaos.' All that was to be observed in early 1947 suggested that if the momentum of events were slowed down, the risks of chaos in central and northern India were unlikely to diminish. If there was mistiming about the settlement, it may well be that it was some ten years too late, rather than one or two years too soon. Tragedy, however, there was and no doubt within the same time-table some part of it might have been avoided. But what is apt to be overlooked and ought not to be is that once partition was to be the solution then the possibilities were not simply tragedy or no tragedy in the Punjab, but the further possibility of even greater tragedy than in fact occurred.

In the view of Britain and Pakistan there were two successor states to the British *Raj*; in the predominant Indian view there was rather a successor state and a seceding state. The distinction is more than one of semantics. If there were two successor states then each was equally entitled to division of resources and authority within the prescribed terms of reference. If however there was one successor state from which territories were carved to form a seceding state, then the presumption was that resources and authority descended to the successor state except in so far as they were specifically allocated to the seceding state. In British statute law the issue may be readily disposed of. Under the provisions of the Indian Independence Act 1947, described in its Preamble as 'An Act to make provision for the setting up in India of two independent dominions . . .', there were two successor states. Article 1(1) read: 'As from the 15th day of August, nineteen hundred and forty seven, two independent dominions shall be set up in India, to be known respectively as India and Pakistan'.[45] But could the issue be settled by reference to British statute law alone? The Indian National Congress thought not. It claimed that the Dominion of India should continue as the international personality of pre-partition India and the Indian reforms commissioner, V. P. Menon, after consulting the Legislative Department advised the viceroy that post-partition would remain identifiable with pre-partition India. 'It was our definite view,' he wrote, 'that neither variation in the extent of a state's territory, nor change in its constitution, could affect the identity of the state.'[46] In respect of international status this opinion was accepted (or in the case of Pakistan acquiesced in after protest and with reservation), with the result that India after independence remained a member of the United Nations and all international organisations whereas Pakistan, as a new state, sought such membership *ab initio*.

Psychologically the question of succession or secession was not as simple as it appeared, either in British statutory enactment or in international practice. The respective designations of the two states were in themselves significant. They were called India and Pakistan, not Hindustan and Pakistan, as Jinnah and the Muslim League deemed logical and desired. The reason was clear. Behind the name India lay the claim consistently advanced and never discarded, not even at the moment of partition, by the Indian National Congress that it was representative not of a class nor of a community but of a nation and that that nation was India. When the All-India Congress Committee met in Delhi on 14 June 1947 to approve the 3 June plan for partition, the resolution accepting partition contained these words:

> Geography and the mountains and the seas fashioned India as she is, and no human agency can change that shape or come in the way of her final destiny. . . . The picture of India we have learnt to cherish will remain in our minds and our hearts. The A.I.C.C. earnestly trusts that when the present passions have subsided, India's problems will be viewed in their proper perspective and the false doctrine of two nations in India will be discredited and discarded by all.[47]

Acharya Kripalani, the president of the Congress, issued a statement on the eve of independence, 14 August 1947, saying it was a day of sorrow and destruction for India. Kripalani was a man of Sind. But he was also the president of the Congress. His emotional reaction to partition was widely shared. It precluded neither acquiescence in the existence of Pakistan nor peaceful co-existence with her. But it rested upon considerations and derived from assumptions about partition and its meaning which neither were, nor in the nature of things could be, shared on the other side of the border.

On the subcontinent at least, the partition of India has not passed into history. It touched too painfully on sensitive nerves for that. The area of friction was progressively reduced in subsequent years – the armed forces and civil service were divided, government property and resources distributed so far as they ever would be, even the Indus Waters' dispute resolved by treaty in 1960 with the assistance of the International Bank. But reduction in the area of dispute led to no corresponding diminution in its intensity. Kashmir remained and not only Kashmir. Behind Kashmir lay wellnigh irreconcilable interpretations of what had happened in 1947.

Could the partition of India have been averted? This is a question to which no answer commanding a consensus of historical opinion has emerged or is likely to emerge for a long time. But two points may be noted in respect of the immediate context of partition. The first is that the British Labour Party, forming its first majority government in 1945, had been committed since 1920 not merely to self-government but to self-determination for India (a phrase admittedly never precisely defined and usually qualified) – in the Resolutions passed at party conferences, by an expression of hope that India would choose to remain within the Commonwealth – and that its leader Clement Attlee, prime minister in the critical years 1945–7, had a personal interest in Indian affairs, deepened by the unhappy experiences of the Simon Commission of which he was a member and well exemplified in his critical commentaries on the Government of India Bill 1935, coupled with a personal concern that the Labour Party's commitment to self-determination should be honoured by his administration.[48] No British government, therefore, was likely to give Indian affairs a higher priority, nor to seek more carefully for a solution on a basis of unity that would at once redound to the credit of its statesmanship and to the promotion of British and Commonwealth interests. If they failed, was any British government at that late stage likely to succeed? And that leads on to the second point, already underlined, namely the diminishing freedom of action of governments, parties and leaders. Partition was the product of a triangular situation which narrowed the range of options and of necessity limited the freedom of manoeuvre even of a purposeful administration or enlightened leaders. All were the prisoners of a pattern of politics which constantly pressed in upon their liberty of choice. 'There would have been no partition,' remarked Nehru in March 1958, had Mountbatten come to India as Viceroy 'a year earlier'.[49] He would have 'hustled' the British government and the speed of the transfer would have averted it. But is such a view credible?

There was contemporary awareness, even if insufficient allowance was made, for the inevitable consequences of the overall political pattern. A few months before partition the problems of India were discussed by a prominent business supporter of the Congress. He spoke, as was common at that time, about the nearly insoluble problems of the triangular relationship and of the disruptive influence of the third party. But the theme was not developed quite along accustomed lines. There was, it is true, denunciation of the third party, but somehow it did not seem to fit the third party. It was only after a while that it became clear that it was not the British who were being denounced; it was the Muslims. They, it appears, were to be regarded – and it was consistent with Congress claims to speak for all-India – as the third party in India. Could they be wished off the scene, eighty million of them, then all would be well in the new-found friendship of Britain and Congress India. Paradoxical as it may seem, this Congress spokesman was perhaps too well-grounded in British interpretations of the history of the sub-continent. He assumed, as the British are apt to assume, that the determining event in its modern history was the impact of expanding Europe.[50] But the partition of India suggested that this was not so. In the last resort it was not the British, it was the Mohammedan invaders of India, who possessed the more inflexible because more deeply grounded influence upon events. By early 1947 this was gradually coming to be realised and it helps to explain a remark by B. R. Ambedkar the leader of the Scheduled castes in the Constituent Assembly, that the war 'of which a good many people in this country seem to support the idea will not be a war on the British. It will be a war on the Muslims.'[51]

Finally there remains the question, academic in its ordinary presentation but fundamental to partition in India and elsewhere. What is a nation? How is it to be identified? Is there some criterion by which it may be judged whether or not there were two nations in the sub-continent? Or is it the case that political science does not deal in such absolutes and that only history by way of trial, error and much suffering can supply the answer?

III

THE COMMONWEALTH

'I think the chief value of this declaration and of what preceded it was that it did bring a touch of healing in our relations with certain countries. We are in no way subordinate to them and they are in no way subordinate to us. We shall go our way and they will go their way. But our way, unless something happens, will be a friendly way; at any rate attempts will be made to understand one another. And the fact that we have begun this new type of association with a touch of healing will be good for us, good for them and, I think, good for the world.'

JAWAHARLAL NEHRU IN THE INDIAN CONSTITUENT ASSEMBLY, 16 MAY 1949, ON THE COMMONWEALTH PRIME MINISTERS' DECLARATION OF APRIL 1949 ON INDIA'S REPUBLICAN MEMBERSHIP.

'The wind of change is blowing through this continent.'

THE RIGHT HON. HAROLD MACMILLAN IN AN ADDRESS TO BOTH HOUSES OF PARLIAMENT AT CAPE TOWN, 3 FEBRUARY 1960.

'L'Angleterre en effet est insulaire, maritime, liée par ses échanges, ses marchés, son ravitaillement, aux pays les plus divers et souvent les plus lointains.'

PRESIDENT DE GAULLE EXPLAINING THE EXERCISE BY THE FRENCH GOVERNMENT OF ITS RIGHT OF VETO ON BRITAIN'S ENTRY INTO THE COMMON MARKET, 14 JANUARY 1963.

CHAPTER 12

CONSTITUTIONAL TRANSFORMATION, IRISH REPUBLICAN SECESSION, INDIAN REPUBLICAN ACCESSION AND THE CHANGING POSITION OF THE CROWN

The wartime trend towards decentralisation continued with increasing momentum after the war. It was implicit in Commonwealth attitudes towards the new international organisation, and explicit in Commonwealth reconsideration of constitutional forms, more especially those of citizenship and Crown.

When the Commonwealth leaders met in London in April 1945, their most important task was the examination of the proposals prepared at the Dumbarton Oaks Conference for the Charter of the United Nations as supplemented, or modified, at Yalta. Smuts thought the resulting document too legalistic in tone, and submitted to his colleagues an eloquent declaration which, conflated with an earlier and more soberly phrased draft of Sir Charles Webster, formed in essence the preamble to the U.N. Charter. It was Smuts specifically who introduced the idea of 'fundamental human rights', later to be turned against both his own and his successors' racial policies in South Africa.[1] But essentially it was not phrases but substance that mattered to Commonwealth leaders. And substance divided them. In the subsequent debates on the provisions of the Charter at San Francisco, there was no semblance of a united Commonwealth approach. On the contrary, a feature of the San Francisco Conference was the conflict of opinion, on a number of important provisions, between the United Kingdom, as one of the Five Great Powers, and those of the dominions which were to be numbered among the foremost of the middle powers, with Australia – whose representative, Dr. H. V. Evatt, combined an expert's grasp of constitutional technicalities with formidable dialectical pugnacity – especially critical of the Great Power veto. Nor were there British Commonwealth delegations, either for the negotiating of peace treaties or for appending an overall Commonwealth signature to them. Each dominion signed in the alphabetical order, as one of the independent allied nations who had fought the war.

Developments in international relations had their counterpart in developments within the Commonwealth. The term dominion was increasingly discouraged before being finally discarded; the Dominions Office was renamed the Commonwealth Relations Office; Commonwealth citizen was approved as an acceptable alternative to British subject; and, more important, the basis of citizenship was changed. The initiative in this last instance came from Canada.

In September 1945 the Canadian government advised the United Kingdom government that it found it desirable to introduce legislation laying down the conditions of Canadian citizenship. As defined in the succeeding Canadian Citizenship Act 1946, these conditions were at variance with the traditional concepts of the status of British subjects. It had hitherto been regarded (except in the Irish Free State) as a fundamental part of the concept of Empire and Commonwealth that there should be a common nationality and that the common law rule, by which all persons born within the king's dominions were British subjects, should remain unimpaired. It is true that while the status was common, the privileges that flowed from it were particular, each self-governing member of the Commonwealth deciding for itself its own electoral and immigration laws, and while such legislation ordinarily took the fact of common status into account, it was not determined by its existence – as dominion immigration laws abundantly testified. Only in the United Kingdom was the 'open door' in terms of entry, political rights and equal opportunity a reality in law for all British subjects, whatever their country of origin. By reason of limited practical validity and in other ways, the old concept, deriving from more spacious times, no longer appeared either realistic or acceptable overseas. The Canadian legislation, taking account of the objections to it, transformed the basis of citizenship, by defining the conditions of Canadian citizenship and then providing that all Canadian citizens were British subjects. The British Nationality Act 1948 adopted this new principle. It established a local citizenship, that of the 'United Kingdom and Colonies', from which the common status of British subject or Commonwealth citizen, a term introduced for the first time, derived. The other member-states of the Commonwealth for the most part enacted legislation on the same pattern, making local citizenship the fundamental status and determining the privileges of the common status of British Subject or Commonwealth Citizen generally on a reciprocal basis – with the United Kingdom, however, continuing its open door policy on immigration until the Immigration Act 1962.[2] Reflected in these changes was recognition of the fundamental status of 'the Nations', as against 'The Commonwealth' they comprised.

More dramatic issues arose after 1945 in respect of membership. The

Balfour Report had written of common allegiance to the Crown as a conventional characteristic, tantamount to a condition, of dominion status. The language of the Report, restated in the Preamble to the Statute of Westminster, and reinforced by recollections of Lloyd George's unqualified rejection of any possibility of negotiation about an associated Irish republic, was widely though not universally[3] interpreted as exalting allegiance as the principal fact of Commonwealth life and as excluding the thought of republican membership as verging on treasonable heresy. These assumptions, under question in Irish relations with the Commonwealth since the enactment of the External Relations Act in 1936, were disturbed in the years 1948–9 by an Irish decision to end an equivocal relationship, on the assumption of the incompatibility of Irish republican and Commonwealth monarchical institutions, and by a near-simultaneous Indian request to establish republican membership, on a basis of formal recognition. Despite the overlap in time and substance in Irish republican withdrawal and Indian republican admission, the problems they presented were separately unravelled. This was not fortuitous; it was an aim of British policy to keep the two issues distinct.

Commonwealth attitudes to Irish constitutional developments were considered at the Imperial Conference 1937 on the basis of a memorandum[4] prepared by the dominions secretary, Malcolm MacDonald. In the abdication crisis of December 1936, it will be recalled, the Irish government had enacted the External Relations Act, which had empowered the Executive Council of the Irish Free State to authorise the use of the king's signature on the letters of credence to be presented to heads of foreign states by Irish diplomatic representatives, and in the following year a new constitution, republican in all but name, was submitted to the people in a plebiscite and approved by them. The British government proposed tentatively to respond to these developments, actual in the case of the External Relations Act and still prospective when the Imperial Conference met in respect of the constitution, by taking the general line that while 'not saying, of course, that the legislation makes no fundamental difference in the position', stating none the less that 'we would be prepared to treat it as not making such a fundamental alteration'. They enquired whether dominion governments would concur generally in such a view. The response was in the affirmative. MacKenzie King had no doubt of its wisdom; Hertzog, feeling that 'whatever the British government does now as regards Ireland is, in my opinion, most important for the future of the Commonwealth', thought the proposed course 'very wise' and indeed could see no reason why the Irish Free State, even if it declared itself to be a republic, should cease to be a member of the Commonwealth, so long as the king's title remained unchanged and the king continued to be recognised as the symbol of the Commonwealth; while on the Australian side there were regrets from Prime Minister Lyons at Irish developments and hopes from Stanley Bruce that 'we are not going to take this Irish question too seriously' or make an issue of it. Neville Chamberlain summed up the discussion by saying that the disadvantages of taking any decision that would have the effect of pushing the Irish Free State out when she wished to remain in, were so obvious that they could only be justified 'if they were clearly necessary to save the Commonwealth from some worse fate. We do not propose to lay down any conditions, which, if the Irish Free State were to transgress, she would put herself out of the Commonwealth.' From that position the British and the dominion governments did not depart in succeeding years.

The nature of the Irish association with the Commonwealth remained ambivalent when the war ended. The British and dominion governments for their part continued to regard Eire – to follow common practice and use the designation given to the Irish Free State after 1937 – as a member, in accord with the view formulated in 1937 that the Irish Constitution of 1937, read in conjunction with the External Relations Act of the preceding year, might be regarded as if it had effected no fundamental alteration in Irish relations with the Commonwealth, as defined in the 1921 treaty. Since common allegiance was a conventional characteristic of dominion status, this view necessarily implied Irish allegiance in some degree. The Irish government had, however, repudiated allegiance and the Irish view, as expressed by de Valera on many occasions, was that Eire could not, for that reason, be a member, but that she was, after 1937, a state outside the Commonwealth, associated externally with it, not owing allegiance to the Crown, and a republic in fact even though not specifically so described in the constitution. Irish association, therefore, continued, despite divergent and conflicting interpretations of its nature, because of mutual self-interest and on a presumably unspoken official understanding. But while it was thus the policy of governments to let sleeping dogs lie, there were others who thought it their duty to stir them up. In the Dáil, Deputies Flanagan and Dillon enquired of the Taoiseach in season and out whether the state was a republic or not, a member of the Commonwealth or not, while at Westminster, also, Labour ministers were troubled by Unionist questions, as to whether Eire was a dominion and whether, as a dominion, she had been consulted, for example, about the changes in the Royal Style and Titles, consequential upon the independence of India and Pakistan, to which the under-secretary of state, Patrick Gordon Walker, replied that she had been, as a member of the Commonwealth – a government within the Commonwealth.[5] Could the subtle, but politically fragile, ambiguities of the External Relations Act continue to serve a useful purpose, in the face of such hostile probing? De Valera, contemplating by 1947 the use of the enabling powers of the Act in other ways, so as to transfer the required formalities from the Crown to the president, by a legislative enactment, evidently entertained some misgivings. But before he had occasion to show his hand, the scene was changed by the general election of 1948 which brought about his fall from office and the formation of an inter-party administration under J. A. Costello. A more drastic solution at once became probable, the new Taoiseach having been a critic from the first of the External Relations Act and being in office with Labour and republican support. On a visit to London early in 1948, he noted without satisfaction that at an official occasion at No. 10 Downing Street, Attlee proposed the toast of 'The King' as appropriate for the country of his guests, thereby implying that on the British view Eire continued to owe allegiance to the Crown and remained a member of the British Commonwealth of Nations.[6]

The decision in principle to repeal the External Relations Act and to designate the state formally as a republic was reached unanimously, as Costello later revealed,[7] by the incoming inter-party government in the summer of 1948, but the actual announcement was made by Costello under pressure of newspaper enquiries, following unauthorised disclosure of the earlier decision of principle, while on a visit to Canada. It was the timing and not the event that was a matter for much speculation – the precise significance to be attributed to provocative gestures by the governor-general of Canada, Field-Marshal Lord Alexander of Tunis, an Ulsterman, remaining uncertain. More important were the implications of the decision. There was no dispute, as in the 1930s, about a dominion's right of secession and, therefore, on the British view, of Eire's right to secede. But in the Irish case possible ambiguity remained; did the impending repeal of the External Relations Act and the parallel decision to describe the state formally as a republic imply of necessity secession from the Commonwealth? Costello was asked that question, reputedly by a representative of the Tass agency at a press conference in Ottawa. He replied in the affirmative and so disposed of what might otherwise have been deemed an open issue. It is not known if the reply was premeditated, nor if secession was the agreed purpose of the cabinet in approving earlier the repeal in principle of the External Relations Act.

The Republic of Ireland Bill was introduced in the Dáil on 24 November 1948. The preamble stated that it was an Act to repeal the External Relations Act, to declare that the description of the state should be the republic of Ireland and to enable the president to exercise executive power or any executive function in connection with the state's external relations. This precisely described its purpose. In introducing it, the Taoiseach said that the Bill when enacted would have consequences which would mark it as a measure ending an epoch.

This bill will end [he said] and end forever, in a simple, clear and unequivocal way this country's long and tragic association with the institution of the British Crown and will make it manifest beyond equivocation or subtlety that the national and international status of this country is that of an independent republic.

The measure was not designed or conceived in any spirit of hostility to the British people or to the institution of the British Crown; on the contrary, one result of its enactment would be that Ireland's relationship with Britain would be 'put upon a better and firmer foundation than it ever has been before', and it would be 'unthinkable', Costello continued, for the Republic of Ireland to draw farther away from the nations of the Commonwealth with which 'we have had such long and, I think, such fruitful association in the past twenty-five or twenty-six years'.[8] However, that was what he was proposing the country should do.

There were two immediate practical questions to be resolved. Did Irish citizens become aliens in Britain and in the rest of the Commonwealth as a consequence of Irish secession? And did existing trade preferences come to an end? With regard to the first the key was to be found in the British Nationality Act 1948, which in effect had made British and Irish citizenship reciprocal. Citizens of Eire, under the provisions of the British Act, were no longer to be British subjects though when in Britain they would be treated as if they were. After the announcement of Irish secession the question narrowed down to whether the provisions of an Act passed in one set of circumstances would continue to apply in another. The answer by agreement of the British and Irish governments was in the affirmative and on the basis of continued reciprocity. It was arrived at on both sides in the light of their own state interests and was generally, though not universally, welcomed – George Bernard Shaw, for his part and after living in England for nearly half a century, remarking 'I shall always be a foreigner here whether I have to register as an alien or not, because I am one of the few people here who thinks objectively.' These citizenship arrangements constituted in effect the foundation of a 'special relationship' and were in accord with Costello's concept of a continuing, but henceforward informal, Irish association with the Commonwealth.

In respect of trade it was suggested that after secession there was risk that the existence of preferential duties between Britain and Ireland would be challenged as conflicting with the most favoured nation clause in commercial treaties with foreign countries and with the General

Agreement on Tariffs and Trade negotiated at Geneva in 1947. On this point however the Irish government were always and (it emerged) rightly confident. They argued that the very close and long-standing trading relations between the two countries warranted exceptional treatment and more particularly they pointed to the fact that the schedule to the Geneva Agreement listed Commonwealth countries by name and individually without any general heading implying that the preferences exchanged were conditional upon Commonwealth membership. Furthermore, in 1950 Ireland concluded a Treaty of Friendship, Commerce and Navigation with the United States, ensuring thereby among other things that the continuance of the existing trade preferences would not be questioned in Washington. Accordingly in terms of trade there was also acceptance of the idea of a 'special relationship' – which proved in immediately succeeding years of advantage to both countries but more especially to Britain's industrial exports.

What was the response to Irish secession in the wider Commonwealth setting? With the possible exception of the Canadian prime minister, Commonwealth ministers had no advance information of it. On this point the Lord Chancellor, Lord Jowitt, who made no complaint, was explicit, and to Conservative critics who maintained that Labour ministers had not done enough to persuade the Irish government to hold its hand he replied that they were not given the opportunity and furthermore that he felt that if any of them had spoken to the Irish 'with the eloquence of Demosthenes and at greater length even than Mr Gladstone, I am convinced that he would have failed – as I failed'.[9] To that extent Irish secession was deliberately settled apart from the Commonwealth. Yet despite the lack of prior consultation and the absence of Irish delegates from the meeting of Commonwealth prime ministers in October 1948, the Commonwealth did play, presumably for the last time, a rôle – it may be thought not an unhelpful one – in Irish affairs.

That Commonwealth rôle had two aspects. The first was negative. The British government considered the possibilities of a sharper reaction, *inter alia* in respect of citizenship and trade, to Irish secession than in fact they expressed – or so it would seem reasonable to infer from the lord chancellor's defence against Conservative critics of the arrangements made. Britain, he argued, should consider where her own interests lay and he made it clear that he was not prepared, out of resentment, to sponsor measures that were going to hurt Britain more than they hurt Ireland. But he then went on to explain that if the British government had taken a different line from the one they decided to take, 'we should have acted in the teeth of the advice of the representatives of Canada, Australia and New Zealand . . .'[10] Lawyers choose their words carefully. What lay behind these observations? At the time of the Commonwealth prime ministers' meeting in October there were separate discussions, first at Chequers and then at Paris, between representatives of the Irish government and representatives of the British, Canadian, Australian and New Zealand governments. It was at these discussions that there emerged – and Costello subsequently confirmed that the reasonable inference to be drawn from the lord chancellor's remarks was correct – something like a united 'old dominion' view to the effect that Irish secession should not be allowed to impair relations between Ireland and the other countries of the Commonwealth, and that in so far as this was possible the way should be left open for her return – Australia's Labour prime minister, Ben Chiffley, later making this point with some emphasis.[11] When Peter Fraser, New Zealand's prime minister, was asked what difference secession would make in New Zealand's attitude to Ireland, he replied, 'What difference could there be? There has been friendliness always', and in the New Zealand Republic of Ireland Act[12] it was expressly stated that New Zealand law should have operation in relation to the Republic of Ireland 'as it would have had if the Republic of Ireland had remained part of His Majesty's dominions'. In statutory terms friendliness could go no further than that!

But after Easter Day 1949, when the republic was proclaimed, Ireland was no longer, on any interpretation, part of His Majesty's dominions. This brought an end to constitutional ambiguity – 'the pirouetting on the point of a pin', said Costello, 'was over' – by the severance of all formal ties. That made a psychological difference. Professor J. D. B. Miller of the Australian National University has noted that

> the 1948 arrangements put paid to the whole score, with goodwill on all sides. Except for some mild scuffling between Mr Menzies's government in Australia and the Irish government about how the Australian ambassador to Eire should be designated, later relations between Eire and the old dominions have little to offer the historian.[13]

More formally, Irish representatives no longer attended prime ministers' meetings. It would be interesting to speculate about the views they might have advanced in the successive crises through which the Commonwealth passed after 1949 – African membership, the Suez affair, the Common Market, South Africa's secession, Southern Rhodesia. Two things are certain. One is that a distinctive voice, that of a European nationalism, was lost – and it may well be that the Commonwealth, especially on two of the issues mentioned – South Africa and the Common Market – was the poorer for it. The other is that twenty years later Ireland, constitutionally, would have been in a comfortable majority, republics rather than monarchies having become the norm within the

Commonwealth. It remains one of the ironies of history that Ireland seceded in the year that India as a republic became a member. How does one explain the apparent paradox? The answer is not to be found in simple constitutional contrasts but in the differences in the historic and the contemporary realities they represented. After 1916, the republic in Ireland symbolised the cause of independence whereas in India what mattered was the independence movement, with the republic incidental to it. This enabled the Indian government, as Pandit Nehru reminded the Indian Parliament at the time, to take note of Irish external association precedents which, as he explained, had shown Indians that it was possible to reconcile republicanism with Commonwealth membership but also to be flexible in respect of the monarch as symbolic head of the Commonwealth. To that extent others followed the path Ireland had pioneered, while Ireland herself elected to travel other roads. Yet history was powerfully reinforced in each case by more immediate considerations. At the moment of decision the Republic of India acceded to and the Republic of Ireland seceded from the Commonwealth because of their respective governments' interpretation of their respective state interests.

In the Irish case, those interests were interpreted increasingly in European terms. In those terms, Irish relations with Britain remained fundamental but her relations with the Commonwealth, despite ties of kinship with the old dominions which accounted in large measure for their 'friendliness', appeared an artificially imposed superstructure. The counterpart to Irish secession from the Commonwealth was accordingly her rapprochement with Europe through Irish association with the European Recovery Programme and her foundation membership of the Council of Europe in the 1940s, her negotiation in the 1960s of the Anglo-Irish Free Trade Agreement, and the Irish application, without reservation or qualification, to subscribe to the Treaty of Rome. In the broadest sense all these developments may be taken to reflect a shift of Irish interest from countries overseas, where many Irish emigrants had settled, to the geographical area of which Ireland was a part. Not for the first time might this be represented, at least when the 'off shore islands' of Gaullist phraseology become a part of the Common Market, and with certain trans-Atlantic qualifications, as a triumph of geography over recent history.

India was the counterpart to Ireland. If Indian attachment to republicanism was less deeply embedded in the national consciousness, the pull of its continental environment in the years after the war was the more pronounced. 'Strong winds are blowing all over Asia,' declared Pandit Nehru at the opening of the Inter-Asian Conference at New Delhi in March 1947[14] and there were many who attended this gathering of the leaders of a resurgent continent who believed that the ending of western imperialism should also bring to an end all formal relations with the western powers. 'Asia for the Asians' was the watchword and in that time of high emotion allied to sanguine expectation, the development of friendly associations within a continent, so long in the shadows of alien rule, was deemed to have a first or even an exclusive claim. The creation of an Asian bloc was a possibility that was accordingly widely canvassed and hopes were expressed that south-east and south Asia might become a neutralised region. Yet however attractive such proposals might seem at first sight closer analysis brought to light rivalries within Asia, as well as other factors, which cast doubt upon their practicability, apart altogether from their wisdom. Did not the maritime interests of the countries of the area in effect preclude a policy of contracting out, or of isolation from world affairs? Was it prudent, moreover, in the longer-term to dissociate Asian countries, with their large and under-nourished populations, even politically from the technologically advanced west? 'The service of India means the service of the millions who suffer',[15] declared Pandit Nehru as the day of Indian independence dawned. But was that service to be discharged without all the aid that the west might be persuaded to give? Whatever the ultimate answers, considerations such as these, and especially about some future association with the west, had their influence on Asian thinking and had perforce to be weighed by Asian leaders.

There were also, however, other countervailing factors. Two of the chief aims of Indian and of Pakistani foreign policy were proclaimed to be national freedom for colonial peoples and the ending of racial discrimination. In themselves these aims implied antagonism to European imperialisms. And clearly though a distinction was drawn between Britain's liberal policies, as applied in India, Burma and Ceylon and epitomised in Attlee's assertion that the Commonwealth desired to have no unwilling members, and the Asian policies pursued at that time by the 'reactionary imperialisms' of the Netherlands and France, it was also noted that Britain retained the greatest of the colonial empires and that its vast possessions in Africa seemed for the most part far from the goal of self-government. Furthermore it was observed, to quote from a memorandum on the Commonwealth issue drafted by eminent and independent Indians,[16] that 'in the Union of South Africa and in some of the African British colonies, racial prejudice dominates legislation and administration in regard to Indians'; and it was argued 'that we should have no link with the British Commonwealth whose policy is marred by such glaring disregard of our just rights'. Certainly the fact that South Africa, a member of the Commonwealth, enforced racial discrimination as a matter of political principle by itself, seemed to many leading Congressmen in 1947 sufficient reason why India should secede once the transitional advantages of membership had been reaped. Moreover, apart from South Africa, the older dominions were largely British and almost wholly European in origin and outlook, while Indians were never more mindful than on the morrow of independence of the fact that they were citizens of a mother country with memories and traditions that went back to prehistoric times and with a cultural influence that had at one time or another spread over much of Asia. 'At the dawn of history,' to quote from Pandit Nehru's speech of 14 August 1947 once more,[17] 'India started on her unending quest, and trackless centuries are filled with her striving and the grandeur of her success and her failures.' Could a country trailing clouds of ancient tragedies and glories find a satisfying sense of fulfilment in the membership of a Commonwealth formally united by the symbolism of another people, race and culture? Dominion status as a practical expedient, by which a threatened deadlock over the tranfer of power in 1947 might be resolved, was clearly one thing; as an enduring element in Indian life, it was another.

The problem of India's relations with the Commonwealth required both study and reflection on the part of India's leaders; for in their hands lay the freedom to decide. To some the Constituent Assembly resolution of 22 January 1947, which had declared that India would become a sovereign, independent republic, seemed to dispose of it. Even though republican sentiment in India did not possess the doctrinaire, uncompromising character of Irish republicanism after the Easter Rising of 1916, Indian leaders felt that republicanism was the only form of government appropriate to their circumstances. Monarchical institutions were associated with the British and, before them, the Mughal emperors. A republic was, moreover, the only form of government which made clear beyond question that India was an independent nation. It could be, and was argued, that dominion status too conferred full autonomy, but these arguments carried at most partial conviction. Recurring, and at times somewhat acidulous, pre-war discussions about the right of a dominion to secede or to remain neutral in a war in which the United Kingdom was engaged, had sown doubts about this which were not easy to remove. There was, however, one immediate factor which may well have been decisive. Pakistan was committed to Commonwealth membership. If India seceded, did not that, in view especially of the post-partition disputes on division of assets, evacuee property, river water and above all Kashmir, mean the likelihood of an anti-Indian Commonwealth? On 16 April 1948 Tej Bahadur Sapru, the veteran moderate who had twice been President of the National Liberal Federation, wrote to M. S. Aney, the governor of Bihar:

> There is going to be a resolution before the All-India Congress Committee asking for complete severance of all connection with England. I have no objection to India declaring herself a republic but I think it would be very unwise at least at this juncture to pass a resolution of this character. Pakistan is following a different policy. It is receiving much more support from England than Hindustan and is likely to get more support, if the Indian union completely severs its connection with England. Can you not exercise your influence and persuade your friends in the Congress not to sever connection of every kind with England?[18]

On 19 April 1948, Sapru wrote further, this time in the same terms both to Chakravarti Rajagopalachari, who in June of that year was to succeed Lord Mountbatten and serve as the last governor-general of India, and to the governor of Bombay on this theme as follows:

> I always thought that the republican form of government about which eloquent speeches were made in the Constituent Assembly was by no means inconsistent with alliance with England. If you cut off connection altogether with England and Pakistan continues to be like a dominion and if trouble arises in future between Hindustan and Pakistan, why should you blame the British if they openly render military help to Pakistan? The relations between the two dominions of Hindustan and Pakistan are by no means very pleasant at present. They may easily become worse. . . . I am, therefore, writing to you frankly that whatever form of government may be established you must not go out of the British Commonwealth of Nations at least for some time to come.

His letter was shown by the governor of Bombay to Jawaharlal Nehru, who declared himself to be in full agreement with its views, while Rajagopalachari noted that what Sapru had said 'about republican forms being not inconsistent with Commonwealth relations is quite true and now fairly well recognised'. Here the Irish precedent was important. 'I entirely agree with you,' wrote a correspondent to Sapru, 'that if the state of Ireland continues as a member of the British Commonwealth, in spite of its being a republic, there is absolutely no reason why India should walk out of it immediately, because it is going to be a republic.'[19]

The question of continued Commonwealth membership concerned two of the smaller Asian countries as well as India and Pakistan. Burma, which had been separated from India in the Government of India Act 1935, had experienced the full rigours of war and of enemy occupation between 1941 and 1945. But Japanese propaganda on the theme of 'Asia for the Asiatics' had made an impact little qualified by the harshness of their military rule, and with the return of peace-time conditions younger men impatient of the old order, with Aung San outstanding among them, came to power. They demanded independence and they were met more than half-way by the British government, which expressly declared that it had no wish to stand in the way of Burma's freedom, nor to limit in any way Burma's freedom of choice thereafter in leaving or remaining within the Commonwealth. In January 1947 a Burmese delegation led by Aung San came to London to make arrangements for the transfer of power. Examination of the possibility of the association of a Burmese republic with the Commonwealth on the Irish model was discouraged as being at once impractical and undesirable in view of inpending and larger decisions still to be taken in respect of Indian independence and membership. The positive outcome of the discussions with the United Kingdom government was an agreement for the Commonwealth issue to be left in continuing suspense, for a constituent assembly in Burma (for which elections were in fact held in April that year) to be called, and for the process of the transfer of power to be completed within a year.

The elections resulted in an overwhelming victory of the Anti-Fascist People's Freedom League, the party of Aung San, and on 16 June Aung San moved a resolution in the Assembly declaring that the constitution should be that of 'an Independent, Sovereign Republic to be known as the Union of Burma'. It was to be outside the Commonwealth. Aung San's assassination, with eight others in the executive council a month later, did not modify the attitude of the Constituent Assembly towards Commonwealth membership, and when the draft constitution was approved in September all that remained to complete the process of separation was the enactment of the necessary legislation by the United Kingdom Parliament.[20] Was this not a step that India too was bound to take? The Burmese leaders at least entertained no doubt when they acted, that it was. They were mistaken.

The secession of Burma was counterbalanced by the progress of another Asian country, Ceylon, towards dominion status. Since 1931 the island had enjoyed representative though not responsible cabinet government. During the war its strategic importance was great and its people, influenced by the rising tide of nationalism in Asia, were accordingly well placed to press for self-government. The response in London, at first somewhat hesitant, became more forthcoming by 1945 and the United Kingdom government then declared its willingness to co-operate with the Ceylonese in establishing it. They were much influenced in their policy by the argument of the colonial secretary, Arthur Creech-Jones, that what was being conceded to Indian nationalism after Congress policies of non-cooperation in the war could not properly be withheld from the Ceylonese after their co-operation. Under the Soulbury Constitution of 1946, which was based largely on the recommendations of a commission of which Lord Soulbury had been chairman, the island attained self-government in all matters of internal administration. In June 1947 the colonial secretary stated in the House of Commons that the United Kingdom government was preparing to negotiate with the government of Ceylon for the amendment of the constitution so as to give to Ceylon full self-government in external as well as in internal affairs. In November 1947 the Ceylon Independence Bill was introduced in Parliament and it came into force on 4 February 1948. It was supplemented by agreements on defence and external affairs which were signed on 11 November 1947. The first was short-lived, being terminated in 1956 at the request of the Ceylon government, while under the second the government of Ceylon undertook to adopt and follow the resolutions of past imperial conferences and to observe the accepted principles and practice of Commonwealth consultation. For its part the United Kingdom government undertook to support Ceylon's application for membership of the United Nations, which was not in fact secured, owing to Russian objections, till 1956.[21]

Ceylon's advance from colonial to dominion status was 'the first occasion in our history', as Lord Addison, the lord privy seal and a former dominions secretary, remarked, in introducing the second reading of the Ceylon Independence Bill in the House of Lords on 4 December 1947,[22] 'upon which a colony, developing this system of self-government of its own accord, has deliberately sought to become a dominion state in our Commonwealth . . . but we hope and expect it will not be the last.' Encouraging however though the implications of Ceylonese membership might be thought to be in London, in terms of the appeal of Commonwealth and non-European peoples it was on the decision of India and Pakistan that the prospect of a Commonwealth in Asia ultimately depended. Would they follow the precedent set by Burma or the example of Ceylon?

The Meeting of Commonwealth prime ministers in London in October 1948 was notable in the history of the Commonwealth because it was the first time at which the three new dominions of Asia were represented at such a gathering. But if the presence of their prime ministers was the outward sign of a new phase in Commonwealth relations, a phase in which non-British and non-European peoples were to take part as equals in Commonwealth deliberations, the form of their membership or relationship was not discussed in full session at all. On the contrary, the Meeting concerned itself with questions of defence, security and economic development, and though the consequence of the Irish repeal of the external relations had to be considered coincidentally, a prior understanding that constitutional questions affecting the Asian dominions should be left on one side was adhered to. The purpose of these characteristically Attleean tactics was to enable the prime ministers of the Asian dominions to gain some first-hand experience of how the Commonwealth worked before formulating their conclusions about their countries' future relationship with it.

Since India, Pakistan and Ceylon 'have come into the Commonwealth', said Liaquat Ali Khan, the prime minister of Pakistan after the meeting, 'its complexion has changed – now it is a Commonwealth of free nations who believe in the same way of life and in the same democracy. To my mind, these ideas are even stronger than racial ties'. His words suggested a feeling on the part at least of one of the Asian leaders that there might be sufficient community of spirit for Asian dominions to find an enduring place in the Commonwealth. There was also evidence of second thoughts in India. In judicious phrases the Congress meeting on 18 December 1948 at Jaipur resolved that

> in view of the attainment of complete independence and the establishment of a Republic of India which will symbolise that independence and give to India a status among the nations of the world that is her rightful due, her present association with the United Kingdom and the Commonwealth of Nations will necessarily have to change. India, however, desires to maintain all such links with other countries as do not come in the way of her freedom of action and independence, and the Congress would welcome her free association with independent nations of the Commonwealth for their common welfare and the promotion of world peace.

The Jaipur Resolution however, in reflecting a more accomodating Congress attitude to Commonwealth membership, implicitly posed the problem with which Commonwealth statesmen were squarely confronted in April 1949. It was a republican India that contemplated continued association with the Commonwealth. There was no suggestion from any quarter that India would or should renounce republicanism for membership. The question was, could the two be reconciled? The problem was similar in principle to that posed by the Irish in 1921 though in practice there was a distinction, inasmuch as India was already a dominion as Ireland had not been. Undoubtedly this in itself strengthened the Indian bargaining position. It was an existing partner that intended to adopt a republican constitution and expressed a wish to continue thereafter as a full member of the Commonwealth. But even so the Indian desire to reconcile republicanism with full membership could be met only by a modification, even if for her case alone, of one of the conventional characteristics of membership, namely allegiance to the Crown, as set out in the Balfour Report and restated in the Preamble to the Statute of Westminster.

The question of India's republican membership was raised at a time when the form and structure of the Commonwealth was already under review in London. The British prime minister was chairman of a cabinet Committee on Commonwealth Relations, appointed in 1947 with the task of finding a formula to 'enable the greatest number of independent units to adhere to the Commonwealth without excessive uniformity in their internal constitutions'. Until March 1948 all action was concentrated, so King George VI's biographer records,[23] on attempts to devise some form of relationship through the Crown, but thereafter other possibilities, less restrictive, including the setting up of a 'Commonwealth' of 'British and Associated States', were examined. In January 1949, after there had been considerable public discussion, and some months after the Republic of Ireland Bill had been introduced in the Dáil, the Committee on Commonwealth Relations produced a memorandum which was read, as well it might be, with deep interest by the king. His private secretary, Sir Alan Lascelles, summarised the point for decision in these terms:

> . . . we are at a fork in the road. If we follow one arm, we tell India that, unless she agrees to pay allegiance to the Crown, she must go. She will then go – with the consequence which anybody can foresee.
>
> If we follow the other arm, we agree to the principle of 'inner and outer' membership of the Commonwealth: we admit that the Balfour declaration must be revised; that the 'common allegiance to the Crown' is no longer the *sine qua non* of membership; that it is possible for membership, with all its political and economic privileges, to be enjoyed by states that do not recognise the Crown – in other words, by republics. . . .[24]

Phrased in these terms republican membership no doubt seemed somewhat alarming. But Lascelles also reminded the king of a warning of Mackenzie King's to the effect that any attempt to find a 'link' between republican India and the Crown would 'inevitably tend to make the position and functions of the sovereign the subject of violent political discussion, not only in India itself but all over the world'. On 17 February 1949, after considering 'Ten Points' and 'Eight Points' memoranda from the Indian prime minister, Attlee himself submitted a paper to the king in which he allowed that he had always found it difficult to discover any satisfactory nexus for the Commonwealth other than allegiance to the Crown and in consequence to see 'how a republic can be included'. He was at the same time impressed with India's desire to remain a member and with the strong expressions of view, especially from Australia and New Zealand, that she should be enabled to do so. Moreover, were India's request to be rejected, the likelihood was that she would become the leader of an anti-European Asiatic movement whereas if she remained 'there is a great possibility of building up in south-east Asia something analogous to Western

Union'. As for the constitutional issue, the prime minister thought it an open question whether the admission of a republic would lead to the spread of republicanism or whether insistence on allegiance, as an essential nexus, might not lead to the secession of other Commonwealth states. Only a Commonwealth Conference, he concluded, could decide and it was impossible to forecast 'what conclusion will be reached by the Conference members'. But a few days later the prime minister had himself decided that the political advantages of Indian membership were so great as to justify adapting the Commonwealth to include a republican state, owing no allegiance to the Crown. The cabinet agreed with this conclusion on 3 March.[25]

The Commonwealth prime ministers, including those of the three new dominions in Asia, met again in London in April 1949 to determine the issue. Attlee, with his long-standing interest in India and his faith in the future of the Commonwealth, had arranged for detailed preliminary consultation on both a personal and a written basis before the prime ministers' meeting, and as a result of his foresight and preparation agreement was reached in the short period of six days. The text of the communiqué issued at the conclusion of the Meeting explained the nature of it:

During the past week the prime ministers of the United Kingdom, Australia, New Zealand, South Africa, India, Pakistan and Ceylon, and the Canadian secretary of state for external affairs have met in London to exchange views upon the important constitutional issues arising from India's decision to adopt a republican form of constitution and her desire to continue her membership of the Commonwealth.

The discussions have been concerned with the effects of such a development upon the existing structure of the Commonwealth and the constitutional relations between its members. They have been conducted in an atmosphere of goodwill and mutual understanding, and have had as their historical background the traditional capacity of the Commonwealth to strengthen its unity of purpose, while adapting its organisation and procedures to changing circumstances.

After full discussion the representatives of the government of all the Commonwealth countries have agreed that the conclusions reached should be placed on record in the following declaration:

> The Governments of the United Kingdom, Canada, Australia, New Zealand, South Africa, India, Pakistan, and Ceylon, whose countries are united as members of the British Commonwealth of Nations and owe a common allegiance to the Crown, which is also the symbol of their free association, have considered the impending consitutional changes in India.
>
> The Government of India have informed the other governments of the Commonwealth of the intention of the Indian people that under the new

> constitution which is about to be adopted India shall become a sovereign independent republic. The Government of India have, however, declared and affirmed India's desire to continue her full membership of the Commonwealth of Nations and her acceptance of The King as the symbol of the free association of its independent member nations, and as such the Head of the Commonwealth.
>
> The governments of the other countries of the Commonwealth, the basis of whose membership of the Commonwealth is not hereby changed, accept and recognise India's continuing membership in accordance with the terms of this declaration.
>
> Accordingly the United Kingdom, Canada, Australia, New Zealand, South Africa, India, Pakistan and Ceylon hereby declare that they remain united as free and equal members of the Commonwealth of Nations, freely co-operating in the pursuit of peace, liberty and progress.

These constitutional questions have been the sole subject of discussion at the full meetings of prime ministers.

The settlement reached, it will be noted, was specific, not general, in application. There was no decision that a republic as such could be a full member of the Commonwealth. The Conference simply recorded that when India, under her new constitution, became a sovereign, independent republic, in accordance with her own wishes she would remain a full member of the Commonwealth and would acknowledge the king as a symbol of the free association of its independent member-nations, and, as such, the head of the Commonwealth. The Indian republic, therefore, owed no allegiance to the Crown and the king had no place in its government. It was in this respect that the settlement involved a break with the doctrine enshrined in the Preamble to the Statute of Westminster in which the members of the Commonwealth were declared to be 'united by a common allegiance to the Crown'. Republicanism, in the past synonymous with secession, was now accepted as compatible with full membership. It has been maintained that this compatibility extended only to the case of India and that one exception did not constitute a category and did not modify the general conditions of Commonwealth membership. In 1955 and 1956 it was, however, agreed that Paskistan and Ceylon should continue their membership on the same basis and thereafter the majority of African Commonwealth states opted to follow the same course.

The Indian constitutional settlement was important not because of its metaphysical refinements but because it went far to reconcile constitutional forms with political realities. In the dominions, and particularly in the older dominions which were predominantly British in extraction, loyalty to the Crown had been a strong unifying force. For them all the constitutional position remained unchanged. But the different traditions, the very different history, of India required that she should have another symbolism, which, with the agreement of all her partners, was accepted in April 1949 as compatible with membership of the Commonwealth.

In Delhi, the Constituent Assembly endorsed the settlement reached in London with only one dissentient voice. This did not fairly reflect the balance of opinion within India, for the settlement was criticised by Socialists as well as by Communists both then and later when India's first general election was held in 1951–2. Yet the general satisfaction with the solution reached was unmistakable. Pandit Nehru's carefully balanced language did something to explain it.

We join the Commonwealth [he told the Constituent Assembly] obviously because we think it is beneficial to us and to certain causes in the world that we wish to advance. The other countries of the Commonwealth want us to remain, because they think it is beneficial to them. . . . In the world today where there are so many disruptive forces at work, where we are often at the verge of war, I think it is not a safe thing to encourage the breaking up of any association that one has . . . it is better to keep a co-operative association going which may do good in this world rather than break it'. He allowed that he was 'a bad bargainer', that he was not used 'to the ways of the market place' and that he had thought it, in London, 'far more precious to come to a decision in friendship and goodwill than to gain a word here or there at the cost of ill will'.[26]

There were mutual and substantial interests in making a settlement, on the British side of trade, investment and security, and on the Indian of stability, aid and as a counterpoise to Pakistan. But given the existence of those interests, there was also, and additionally, magnanimity on the Indian side, to which the prime ministers of the Commonwealth responded with imaginative understanding. It was to two men – Jawaharlal Nehru and Clement Attlee – that chief credit for the settlement belonged. There followed in the early 1950s, despite differences in the attitudes of newer and older members to world politics, some brief and, retrospectively, golden years of hope in a multi-racial Commonwealth and in its potential contribution to human understanding.

The 1949 settlement modified the position of the Crown in the Commonwealth. The period of potentially self-destructive rigidity on this issue was ended, though it may still be questioned, in the light of Burmese and Irish secession and the critical debate on Indian republican membership, whether there had been lack of foresight in not considering earlier the bearing of the central position accorded to the Crown in the Statute of Westminster Commonwealth, upon prospective post-war problems and not least those related to possible non-European

Commonwealth membership. In any event after 1949 the Crown could no longer be spoken of in Baldwin's phrase as the 'only link'. There was no longer common allegiance, as a condition of membership, but only, so to speak, as an option. The result of free constitutional choice was a variety of constitutional relationships, reflected in 1953 in the variety of titles, with which Queen Elizabeth II was invested at her coronation. It was the newest, 'Head of the Commonwealth', that alone was common to all. In time, for the majority of Commonwealth states, it became the only formal acknowledgement of the position of Crown. This was chiefly because a direct relationship, in terms of allegiance, appeared inappropriate to independent states with non-British populations, but also because the monarchical system on the British model presupposed an executive reponsible to Parliament. Since, in subsequent years, the practice continued in Africa and elsewhere of transferring power at the outset, as in India, to a successor authority, monarchical in form, independence was apt to be followed after the lapse of a year or more by the declaration of a republic remaining, with the explicit consent of Commonwealth prime ministers, within the framework of Commonwealth. This provided a second occasion for national celebrations, but was hardly conducive to the enhancement of the dignity of the Crown in the Commonwealth.

One African example may suffice to illustrate the process and to suggest some of the factors that lay behind it. In March 1961 the Tanganyika government reaffirmed its intention to apply for membership, and this was subsequently agreed by existing members of the Commonwealth. Tanganyika's membership at the outset was monarchical in form. On reconsideration it was decided however that the country should become a republic one year after independence, namely on 9 December 1962. The reasons were set out in a White Paper, understood to have been drafted by Julius Nyerere, the leader of the dominant national party. It read:

> On 9th December 1961 we became – suddenly – a monarchy. By deciding to remain within the Commonwealth, without making immediate provision for introducing a republican form of government at independence, we automatically followed the precedent set by the other non-republican countries of the Commonwealth. The Queen, who is Head of the Commonwealth and Sovereign of its several member countries, became our Sovereign. . . .
>
> This direct association of Tanganyika and the British monarchy was something quite new; for, until the 9th December, their association was only indirect. When the British government assumed responsibility for the administration of Tanganyika at the end of the first world war it was not as a colony or a protectorate but by virtue of a mandate conferred on Britain

by the League of Nations. So long as the mandate and Trusteeship system continued, Tanganyika was not part of Her Majesty's dominions, and the relationship between the people of Tanganyika and the Crown was an indirect relationship depending on the position of the Monarch as Head of State in the country charged with the duty of administering the territory. For Tanganyika, therefore, the British monarchy has always been a foreign institution.[27]

Independence, the White Paper proceeded, had increased the sense of alienation. Tanganyika therefore should have an indigenous, republican form of government. This was consistent with membership of the Commonwealth and that, according to the prime minister, Kawawa, was a link 'it is very important to maintain'. Why? Because 'whether we like it or not, we have something in common and we understand each other'. And also because the Commonwealth helped better understanding in the world. 'If we dissolve a means of understanding, I think, we are doing a disservice to the world.'[28] The Indian precedent, therefore, was followed in republican membership of the Commonwealth. But as distinct from India there was in Tanganyika more in the change than the discarding of an alien and the adoption of an indigenous symbolism of nationhood. The substance as well as the form of government was at issue. That also was made clear in the White Paper.

Broadly speaking [it read] there are two types of republic. There are republics where the Head of State occupies the same constitutional position as that occupied by a Constitutional Monarch: his position is largely a ceremonial and formal one. This is the 'Westminster Model'. Except in very unusual circumstances he acts only on the advice of the prime minister, or the cabinet, who are the real government. This division between formal authority and real authority can be understood in countries where it has come about as a result of historical changes. . . . Such a division, however, is entirely foreign to our tradition. The honour and respect accorded to a Chief, or a King, or, under a republic, to a President, are forces indistinguishable from the power that he wields.

The other type of republic is that in which the President of the Republic is both Head of State and Head of the Government. He is called an Executive President. This is the type the Government is proposing.

The preference for the American presidential, as distinct from the Westminster parliamentary, model might therefore, as in the case of Tanganyika, have a bearing upon the relationship to be established with the Crown and on the form of Commonwealth membership. But essentially this was a secondary factor. It was as a symbol of indisputable indigenous national sovereignty that a republican constitution appealed to African and to Asian people.

CHAPTER 13

THE CLIMAX OF COMMONWEALTH AND THE DAWN OF DISENCHANTMENT

The final stages in the transformation of the British Empire into a Commonwealth of Nations was the product partly of conviction, partly of experience and perhaps, most of all, of circumstances. Britain and the dominions stood side by side in both world wars from their outbreak to their victorious close. Their overall participation in them was longer than that of any other country on either side.[1] The dominions had entered the second world war by their own free choice. For a year, in the (not quite exact) Churchillian phrase, they had 'stood alone' and they had made their contributions in every theatre of war from the Mediterranean and western Europe to south-east Asia and the Pacific. To the peoples of Britain and the dominions it seemed as if their experiment in free and equal association had been memorably vindicated. But it was far otherwise with the Colonial Empire. It emerged from the second world war, despite the evidence of a greater sense of social responsibility on the part of the metropolitan power, implicit in the Colonial Development and Welfare Acts (notably that imaginatively enacted in the summer of 1940), with its image tarnished and itself discredited. This was due immediately to the collapse of south-east Asia before the Japanese, and most of all to the fall of Singapore, one of the great humiliations of British arms in modern times. In beleaguered, wartime Britain the disintegration of western colonialism in Asia was interpreted, not in terms of mistaken strategy, inadequate military preparation, insufficient allocation of military and desperately needed air resources, but rather viewed against a backdrop of easy living, gin drinking, demoralised colonialists drawn from the novels of Somerset Maugham or of the ridiculous pomposities of Noel Coward's 'Mad dogs and Englishmen'. On the longer view, it may be accepted, as A. J. P. Taylor remarks at the end of his *English History 1914–1945*, that in the war 'traditional values lost much of their force. Other values took their place. Imperial greatness was on the way out; the welfare state was on the way in.'[2] But it was 'Empire' in its limited sense that was out. It was the diminished reputation of the dependent Empire and the enhanced reputation of the free dominions that combined at one and the same time to destroy an old faith in Empire and to produce a new faith in Commonwealth.

To a widely shared conviction and wartime experience were to be added the circumstances of the post-war world. That world was dominated by two great Powers, both of which were anti-colonial. The psychology and concepts behind Russian and American anti-colonialism were very different. But what mattered after 1945 was their common antipathy to colonial rule. This at once encouraged the anti-colonialism of subject peoples, and diminished the capacity and possibly also the will of the western metropolitan powers, Britain included, to resist what had the appearance of the march of history. But here again, at least in the United States, a distinction was increasingly drawn between the British Commonwealth and the British Empire. After all, the northern neighbour of the United States was the oldest of the dominions and a founder member with Britain of the Commonwealth of Nations. No sensible American (admittedly not all Americans qualified on this topic) any longer supposed that Canada, which had played so notable a part in the war and which under Mackenzie King's leadership had so firmly yet judiciously underlined its autonomy, was a political dependency of Britain. Even in the Soviet Union, and indeed later in China, note was taken of the phenomenon of Commonwealth as something distinct from a relic of empire. In the abstract, therefore, the external circumstances deriving from the new balance of world power tended to encourage the advance of Commonwealth, in much the same measure as they pressed for the dissolution of empire. What remained to be tested was the opinion of hitherto subject peoples. That they were anti-imperialist was no longer seriously doubted. But were they prepared themselves to distinguish between Empire and Commonwealth and to contemplate membership of a society of states, which had grown historically out of empire, or would memories of conquest or sense of past exploitation, reinforced by the tide of Asian and African nationalism, carry them to an independence beyond its confines?

Indian independence and Commonwealth membership, reinforced by that of Pakistan and Ceylon, provided the critically important first formulation of an answer from the most prestigious of sources. The image of Commonwealth was thereby embellished in the eyes both of Asian, African and other colonial nationalist leaders and also in those of hitherto unenthusiastic or, more usually, sceptical left-wing progressives in Britain and the old dominions. The age of Smuts and King was ending and in their place there was emerging Jawaharlal Nehru as a representative figure with views that were compulsively attractive to an unusually wide conspectus of opinion in a new multi-racial society of nations. But more than personal appeal, or new-found enthusiasm for multi-racial association, was required to ensure effective existence or even survival. The newly enlarged Commonwealth, Eurasian in its membership for the decade 1947–57, had first to demonstrate its capacity to hold together, despite the conflicting pulls and pressures of an external world upon its membership, even as its member states were seeking to come to terms with the realities of their own relationship. Time was what was needed most to ease national sensitivities and to work out an acceptable pattern of association founded on equality and recognising interdependence. And of time, in the post-war world, there was short measure.

The Commonwealth was in no sense self-sufficing; its member-states being able neither to disregard nor to defer their own post-war problems pending the emergence of a Commonwealth consensus upon them. Britain and Canada had to determine their relations with Europe and the emerging Atlantic Community; Australia and New Zealand to decide, in the light of their wartime experiences, upon the future of their relationship with the United States; Asian members had to formulate for the first time regional and international policies, acceptable to the nationalist anti-colonialist sentiments of their peoples, and at the same time consistent with their national political and more especially economic interests. The pursuit of such varied and at times conflicting purposes within the framework of Commonwealth was evidence of the flexibility of its decentralised system of co-operation through consultation. By this much store was set by governments and their officials. What was apt to be overlooked, however, in the earlier years of this new Commonwealth experiment, was the fact that there was bound to be a limit in practice, even if it were not susceptible of theoretic definition, to such flexibility, beyond which meaningful Commonwealth existence ceased for its member-states. That frontier between reality and nothingness was approached in international and racial policies in the two post-war decades in which, paradoxically as it may seem, the Commonwealth idea acquired content and substance in respect of social, economic and educational cooperation, such as it had never hitherto possessed.

In the immediate post-war years Commonwealth thinking was dominated by problems of regional security, international alliances and the Cold War. As early as 1943 Smuts had outlined ideas of how the Commonwealth, through association with the free peoples of the western European seaboard, might contribute to European and world stability.[3] In the form in which he presented them, these ideas were not realised. Smuts foreshadowed an association of like-minded western European and Commonwealth states which would together form a third great

Power, balancing between the Soviet Union in the east and the United States in the west, whereas the grouping that eventually emerged was regional, thereby automatically excluding the overseas members of the Commonwealth from membership of it and diminishing its potential in the scales of power. Yet in the early and largely defensive stages in the evolution of western European union, overseas Commonwealth members were, as they were bound to be in the light of recent history, concerned with its purposes and composition, and most of all with Britain's rôle in it.

The strategic commitments into which the United Kingdom entered in western Europe after the war, notably the Five Power Brussels Pact of March 1948, were generally welcome to the governments of the old dominions on grounds of a common interest in the military security of the treaty area. In an established tradition, the treaty itself was not subscribed to by any of the dominions, but there were indications of a significant departure from pre-war precedents in Canadian readiness to participate as a member in the work of the permanent military committee set up in London under the terms of the treaty. It was indeed on the political, not on the military or still less the economic side, that there were signs of dominion misgivings about the possible and progressive absorption of the United Kingdom in a purely European grouping. In Australia and New Zealand especially, it was felt, even at this early date, that the closer Britain drew to Europe, the further it must necessarily draw away from the Commonwealth, with the consequence that it would not have a sufficient margin of resources to sustain its position in the world overseas, and particularly east of Suez. It was to allay these misgivings that Attlee emphasised in May 1948 that, in respect of every development in western Europe the United Kingdom government had kept

> in the closest touch with the other Commonwealth countries . . . and we take very full account of their views . . . I was disturbed with the suggestion . . . that we might somehow get closer to Europe than to our Commonwealth. The Commonwealth nations are our closest friends. While I want to get as close as we can with the other nations, we have to bear in mind that we are not solely a European Power but a member of a great Commonwealth and Empire . . .[4]

For the Commonwealth overseas these were reassuring words and at the meeting of Commonwealth foreign ministers in Colombo in 1950 it was formally accepted that 'there need be no inconsistency between the policy followed by the U.K. government in relation to western Europe and the maintenance of the traditional links between the U.K. and the rest of the Commonwealth . . .'.[5] Larger, and for the Commonwealth more divisive questions were posed, however, by the extension of military alliances outside Europe.

Anglo-American accord on the broad issues of foreign policy had long been recognised as a principal objective of Canadian policy. It received formal fulfilment in the North Atlantic Treaty 1949, to which the United States, Britain and Canada were all signatories. The treaty marked the opening of a new phase in Canadian and, as it was to prove, in Commonwealth foreign policies. The active Canadian rôle in the negotiation of the treaty and the subsequent Canadian signature of it indicated a dramatic departure from the Canadian, and indeed general dominion reluctance to assume specific commitments, which had been so pronounced a feature of their policies in the inter-war years. Two things, in the Canadian case, prompted this radical break with the past. The first, already mentioned, was the joint Anglo-American sponsorship. The second was experience. 'We must', said Louis St Laurent, the secretary of state for external affairs in 1948, 'at all costs avoid the fatal repetition of the history of the pre-war years when the nazi aggressor picked off its victims one by one. Such a process does not end at the Atlantic.'[6]

It did not end at the Pacific either. Australia and New Zealand, with a lively recollection of how United States naval power had ended the threat of Japanese invasion, with decisive victories at Midway and in the Coral Sea, followed the Canadian precedent in 1951 by signing a Pacific Security Agreement with the United States. It was the first treaty signed by the two Pacific dominions with a foreign country, and since Britain, to Churchill's chagrin, was not a party to it, the treaty signified in effect the future military dependence of those two Commonwealth members upon the United States, in the same way as the North Atlantic Treaty had indicated the dependence of Canada and of Britain itself on American power. For Australians, and more especially for New Zealanders, far out at the end of the line, it represented a triumph of strategic realism over deep, sentimental attachment. It led on directly to Australian and New Zealand association with United States policies in the Far East and south-east Asia, and in 1967 reached a temporary culmination in Australian participation at divisional strength in the war in Vietnam at the side of the United States, while Britain and the other members of the Commonwealth apart from New Zealand remained non-belligerent and for the most part critically aloof.

In 1954 the growing network of regional alliances was more controversially extended to south-east Asia, with the creation of the South-East Asian Treaty Organisation under the terms of the Manila Pact. This treaty underlined not Commonwealth unity but Commonwealth disunity. Britain, Australia and New Zealand were signatories; so also was

Pakistan, but India and Ceylon were not. Nehru was angered by it. His principal cause of complaint was that major decisions about Asia were being taken without the agreement of the principal Asian states in the area concerned. 'Asian problems, Asian security and Asian peace', he complained in September 1954, 'are not only discussed but actions are taken and treaties are made in regard to them chiefly by non-Asian countries.' 'Our Hon. Members may remember the old days . . .' he told the Lok Sabha a little later,

> when Great Powers had spheres of influence in Asia and elsewhere – of course, the countries of Asia were too weak to do anything. The quarrel was between the Big Powers and they, therefore, sometimes, came to an agreement about dividing the countries in spheres of influence. It seems to me, this particular Manila Treaty is looking dangerously in this direction of spheres of influence to be exercised by powerful countries . . .[7]

Apart from the fact that Pakistan was a signatory to the treaty, the critical Indian reaction was to be attributed to two principal reasons. The chief aim of Indian foreign policy was to preserve south and south-east Asia as an area of no war, and it was thought that military alliances extending to the area would prejudice the prospect of its fulfilment. The other which often received emotional expression during the Korean war, was a suspicion that the western world, of which the United States was conceived of as a part, was almost as insensitive to the sufferings as they had been to the subjection of ancient Asian peoples. The response, therefore, to the treaty alignments of the older Commonwealth countries, reinforced in 1954 by Pakistan, was renewed insistence in Delhi upon the virtues of the policy of non-alignment, to which India had subscribed since independence and which was held, not without reason, to have contributed significantly to the ending of the war in Korea. Some aspects of that policy, as well as the attitude behind it, were given formal expression in the Preamble to the 1954 Indo-Chinese Treaty on Tibet where the *PANCH SHILA* or *FIVE PRINCIPLES* summed up in familiar phrases – mutual co-existence, co-operation and non-interference in the domestic affairs of friendly countries – were enunciated. Thereafter non-alignment assumed the character of a dogma in the conduct of Indian foreign policy, receiving widespread acclaim among the non-committed nations, not least among African countries that were soon to become independent.

Alignment and non-alignment dividing the older from the newer members of the Commonwealth – Pakistan always excepted – imposed strain upon Commonwealth co-operation and the system of consultation, which was its foundation. Where the member states could not agree on major issues of international policy, were they still prepared to consult and confer about them? The answer would seem to have been broadly in the affirmative down to 1954, a year which, with the SEATO Pact and an agreement on American military aid to Pakistan, deeply resented in India, marked a parting of the ways. Before that date on some issues, for example the recognition of the Chinese People's Republic and the ending of the war in Korea, consultation was close, continuous and productive, even where there was no consensus as in the case of recognition, of positive action on the part of some governments. There was also a succession of ministerial and prime ministerial meetings; and the attendance at them, with almost unfailing regularity, of men carrying great domestic and, in some instances world responsibilities, was an impressive tribute to the vitality and vigour of the refashioned Commonwealth. Yet satisfaction was less apt than in earlier years to be untempered by judgment. The conference of cabinets continued; it was the principal means whereby an experiment in co-operation between nations, of a kind to which history afforded no exact parallel, was not unsuccessfully attempted; it brought and kept together, as perhaps nothing else could have done, men of influence from all continents. Yet, despite these achievements, praise for the system became more muted, faith in it more qualified as the years went by. Where there was no agreement on defence policies, there could be little fruitful discussion on defence. Was this also to be true of the wide range of issues dominating world politics in the Cold War Years?

In 1947 Ceylon, it will be recalled, in a formal document,[8] agreed generally to observe the principles and practice of Commonwealth consultation in regard to external affairs. In no later instance was this formula repeated. It belonged to earlier, less questioning, years. In the speech from the throne at the opening of Parliament at Westminster in 1955 the Queen stated: 'My government will maintain and strengthen consultation within the Commonwealth for the fulfilment of our common aims and purposes'.[9] That was not repeated in comprehensive form either. It proved the prologue to the failure of the British government to consult or inform its Commonwealth partners in advance about the joint Anglo-French intervention at Suez the following year, consequent upon President Nasser's nationalisation of the Suez Canal. Of their neglect in this respect the first thing that needs to be said is implicit in the words of Greville's famous judgment on Sir Robert Peel's sudden and surprising conversion to Catholic emancipation: 'I do not see how he can be acquitted of insincerity save at the expense of his sagacity and foresight'.

The second thing to be remarked is that for a Commonwealth accustomed to thinking of consultation, or when time did not allow of it of the prompt communication of information about immediate intentions, as the foundation of its informal system of inter-state co-operation, the deliberate failure to consult by the senior partner marked a departure from principle and a breach in practice which signalised lack of confidence on the part of the British government in its power to persuade its Commonwealth partners even to acquiesce in the enterprise on which it was resolved to embark, and added to the sense of outrage with which many of them first received news of it. Of course consultation or no consultation, there would have been open and undisguised conflict of opinion within the Commonwealth, but with consultation something of the dangerous edge of acrimony might well have been blunted. It is true that even as things were the tone of most of the correspondents, disposed to disapprove of the Anglo-French action at Suez in the Canadian press, more critical generally than that of any other in the old dominions, was said to be one of pain and sorrow rather than anger, 'almost tearful', as the correspondent of *The Economist* observed 'like finding a beloved uncle arrested for rape'.[10] But in initial Asian reactions, surprise and regret little softened the sharpness of judgment. The prime minister of India 'after fairly considerable experience in foreign affairs' could not think 'of a grosser case of naked aggression' and felt that in the middle of the twentieth century 'we are going back to the predatory method of the eighteenth and nineteenth centuries'.[11] The government of India dispatched a formal protest to London; Rajagopalachari, that most respected of elder statesmen, recommended that India should leave the Commonwealth;[12] while to Lester Pearson, the Canadian secretary of state for external affairs, as to many others less well informed, it seemed in the first days of the fighting as if the Commonwealth had been brought to 'the verge of dissolution'.[13] Nor did feeling all run one way. It is difficult for governments, as for individuals, to accept rebuke without resentment, even when its expression is deemed sincere and the scales of judgment evenly balanced. In one respect the Indian condemnation seemed, even to those predisposed to concur in it, somewhat partial and Sir Anthony Eden retrospectively laid emphasis upon this apparent defect. 'The Indian reaction', he wrote,[14] 'was remarkable. Mr Nehru declared in a speech that whereas in Egypt "every single thing that had happened was as clear as daylight", he could not follow "the very confusing situation" in Hungary.' The Indian prime minister's studied restraint in judgment upon the Soviet action in Hungary, which might be regarded as a part of the price of the Suez diversion, in fact supplied retaliatory ammunition for its protagonists. A campaign of recrimination, with the Rhodesian crisis a decade later as the only near parallel in Commonwealth history, was opened; how and when would it close?

If the British advance to Suez was precipitate, the retreat was masterly. It was eased by the re-emergence of a near-consensus of Commonwealth views. 'Britain's action, I personally say – and I will say it if I am the only one left to say it – was brave and correct.'[15] So the Australian prime minister, Robert Menzies expressed himself as early as 12 November 1956 – and his choice of words betrayed his isolation. Apart from Sir Anthony Eden, soon to withdraw from public life, Menzies was left alone among leading Commonwealth statesmen to say it. For the rest, whether initially supporters or critics, two broad considerations prompted restraint and calmer reappraisal. On the one hand, the prospect of possible dissolution enhanced appreciation of the value of the Commonwealth, and on the other there was recognition that the Suez adventure was not only out of character with the pattern of recent British policy overseas but out of line with the realities of her power position. In conjunction the two encouraged Commonwealth policies outwardly restoring the *status quo ante*, but inwardly marking a readjustment in intra-Commonwealth relations. For the Commonwealth overseas Britain remained the principal and predominant partner, but with a leadership less likely than hitherto to secure backing, or at the least acquiescence, in doubtful or disputed issues; while in Britain itself, and especially within the ranks of the ruling Conservative party, the traditional assumption that the Commonwealth was an asset for the first time came in for questioning that was often distressing but none the less persistent. There was a link in psychological terms between the traumatic experiences of 1956 and the manner of the British application for membership of the Common Market six years later, even if the latter was dictated chiefly by economic considerations.

One lesson of Suez was not to be overlooked. In Commonwealth relations, as in other matters, it is not conventional procedures but substance and purpose that matter. At the time over-much weight was paid to the one and too little to the others. The Commonwealth Relations Office made a practice of publishing the number of telegrams sent to their missions in other Commonwealth countries – twenty thousand it may be or thirty thousand, or even thirty-five thousand – in a year.[16] From the context in which these figures appeared it seemed that the public was expected to infer from them that the increase denoted a growing intimacy – to use a deplorable phrase firmly embedded in the Commonwealth vocabulary – in relations between Commonwealth governments. But it could also have meant – and this in retrospect appears the more likely – differences that were getting harder to resolve, coupled no doubt with a fashionable depreciation in Commonwealth cable currency.

The Suez crisis in its Commonwealth context was the reflection rather than the cause of changing concepts of Commonwealth. Sir

Winston Churchill, presiding in 1955 over the last Prime Ministers' Meeting he was to attend, had spoken of it in terms of 'a fraternal association'.[17] This was a description that came readily to the lips of those who had worked together closely over the years, as representatives of a comparatively small group of sovereign states, all governed in accord with the principles of the British parliamentary system. It was perhaps peculiarly appropriate in the brief years of exclusively Eur-Asian membership, when mother-daughter analogies were outdated[18] and there existed a fresh and lively sense of an experiment in equal relations between peoples and governments of different races. A decade later the use of 'fraternal association' would have seemed forced and an Australian commentator, Professor J. D. B. Miller, came nearer to reflecting the spirit of that later time when he wrote of the Commonwealth as 'a concert of convenience'[19] with the pull of sentiment, notably in the United Kingdom itself, much diminished and survival conditional, therefore, upon calculations of national advantage on the part of all the member-states. This was made self-evident, even in traditionalist circles where the time-lag between reality and reputation was most pronounced, with the expansion of Commonwealth into Africa. But it was antecedent to African, or indeed to Asian membership and may be thought implicit in the notion of free association.

The political transformation of the continent of Africa dominated Commonwealth, and indeed world affairs in the decade 1957–67. That an African revolution should succeed to the greater Asian revolution was not in itself surprising. This is not to suggest that independence in British Africa came as a byproduct of the ending of colonialism in Asia, though unquestionably the Indian struggle for independence eased the way for independence in Africa without protracted struggle in many cases and without struggle at all in some. Even in the age of late Victorian imperialism, British expansion in Africa was largely determined by British preoccupation with the stability and security of the Indian Empire[20] and the premise, therefore, that policy in Africa should be conditional upon developments in South Asia was well grounded in British thinking. What requires explanation is not, therefore, the fact of change so much as the pace of it and the outcome in terms of Commonwealth membership.

Ghana became the first African member of the Commonwealth, on achieving independence in 1957, evidently not discouraged by the Suez crisis of the preceding year. Nigeria followed after a three year interlude in 1960 and then in quickening succession came Sierra Leone and Tanganyika in 1961, Uganda in 1962, Kenya, and Zanzibar (later to form with Tanganyika the Union of Tanzania) in 1963, Nyasaland (renamed Malawi) and Northern Rhodesia (renamed Zambia) in

1964 the Gambia in 1965 and two of the high commission territories in southern Africa, Basutoland as Lesotho and Bechuanaland as Botswana, in 1966, with Swaziland following in 1968. The transformation seems the more remarkable when stated in broader terms. On 1 January 1957 the British Colonial Empire in Africa remained at its fullest extent: on 31 December 1967 nothing remained of it in fact, and in name only Swaziland shortly to become independent, and sanction-beleaguered, rebel-administered Southern Rhodesia. Or, in more positive Commonwealth terms, where on 1 January 1957 there had been no African member-state, by the close of 1967 there were no less than twelve,[21] all of whom had freely opted for membership and none of whom by that time, even under the strains of the Rhodesian question, had renounced membership.

Why was the process not more protracted? Two reasons may be offered. One, the more obvious, was the nationalism of many of these African states, varying in intensity and still in most instances awaiting systematic historical analysis, reinforced by the pressures of anti-colonial powers at the United Nations and anti-colonial opinion in the world at large. What was less evident, but no less real in the later phase, was the resolve first of a British Conservative government, and then of its Labour successor, to end British colonial responsibilities, not only in Africa, but in the West Indies, where Jamaica, and Trinidad and Tobago became independent states in 1962 with Barbados and mainland Guyana following in 1966; in south-east Asia, with Malaysian independence dating from 1957 and that of secessionist Singapore from 1965; in the Mediterranean, with independence for Cyprus after a four year state of emergency in 1960 and for Malta in 1967; and elsewhere, ultimately even in islands such as Mauritius, scattered around the oceans, irrespective of whether or not there was any strong indigenous pressure for that sovereign status.

The trend of British thinking was first publicly indicated in an address by the British prime minister in Cape Town in 1960 towards the conclusion of a tour of Commonwealth and British Colonial Africa. On 3 February that year Harold Macmillan, speaking 'very frankly' told a joint session of the South African Houses of Parliament that:

> what governments and Parliaments in the United Kingdom *have* done since the last war in according independence to India, Pakistan, Ceylon, Malaya and Ghana and what they *will* do for Nigeria and other countries now nearing independence – all this, though we must and do take full responsibility for it, we do in the belief that it is the only way to establish the future of the Commonwealth and of the free world on sound foundations.
>
> All this, of course, is of deep and close concern to you. For nothing we do in this small world can be done in a corner and remain hidden. What *we* do

today in West, Central and East Africa becomes known to everyone in the Union whatever his language, colour or traditions. . . .

. . . in our own areas of responsibility we must each do what we think right. What we British think right derives from a long experience both of failure and success in the management of these affairs. We have tried to learn and apply the lessons of both. . . . This experience of ours explains why it has been our aim, in the countries for which we have borne responsibility, not only to raise material standards of life, but to create a society which respects the rights of individuals – a society in which men are given the opportunity to grow to their full stature, and that must in our view include the opportunity of an increasing share in political power and responsibility; a society finally in which individual merit, and individual merit alone, is the criterion, for a man's advancement, whether political or economic.

The impact of the British prime minister's unexpectedly explicit challenge was heightened by the use of phrases earlier in the speech which became the current coin of African commentaries. The most striking of all the impressions he had formed on his African travels was, he said, 'of the strength of this African national consciousness. In different places it may take different forms. But it is happening everywhere. The wind of change is blowing through this continent.'[22] It was true. It was also true, and almost as important, that there was a change of wind in Downing Street. This was something on which Macmillan understandably preferred not to dwell. But British settlers in Kenya and the Rhodesias were soon to feel the breath of anti-colonialism from London, as well as from indigenous Africa, in what one of them later termed *So Rough a Wind*.[23]

Conservatives are well placed under the British party system to carry through radical measures, as Parnell well understood, when he sought first a Conservative alliance to carry Home Rule for Ireland in 1885. It was accordingly without serious domestic opposition that a Conservative government was able to wind up British colonial responsibilities in Africa, south-east Asia, the West Indies and elsewhere at a pace, which had not been contemplated by the leading colonial experts in Britain, which surprised the majority and shocked a minority of their own supporters, and incidentally outdistanced many of their critics – neutralist anti-colonialists, communists, the U.N. special Committee on Colonialism and even trans-Atlantic academics, one of whom in 1960 was still admonishing the British for 'a failure in historical insight and a certain moral blindness at the human level' in their colonial policies, while evidently remaining oblivious of the fact that the British government's concern, by that time, was how to grant independence to its remaining colonial possessions, whether in Africa or elsewhere, in the shortest possible time.[24] In Tanganyika power was transferred some years before the date first demanded by the principal nationalist party or that recommended by a visiting U.N. Mission. At the Malta Independence Conference held in London in July, 1963 the secretary of state for the colonies, Duncan Sandys, found it necessary to reassure Maltese delegates by saying 'We in Britain have no desire to hustle Malta into independence . . .', while at the British Guiana Conference later in the year he spoke with every sign of mounting irritation about the need to settle domestic differences so as not to delay the plans of Her Majesty's government for an early transfer of power.[25] For the Tacitean 'divide and rule' of Empire, there was thus substituted an injunction more appropriate to Commonwealth – 'unite and abdicate'. The secretary of state for the colonies in the Labour government, formed in October 1964, Anthony Greenwood, declared that his main purpose at the Colonial Office was 'to do himself out of a job' and by 1966 he had succeeded. The Colonial Office was no more.

The virtual completion of the policy of transforming an Empire into a Commonwealth accounted for a new assurance, even an occasional asperity, in British reactions at the United Nations to anti-colonial critics. In a debate on colonialism in the United Nations General Assembly on 1 October 1963, the British foreign secretary, the Earl of Home, after alluding 'to the vicious attack on us' by Indonesia, following the establishment of the Federation of Malaysia and the rupture in diplomatic relations between Somalia and the United Kingdom because of the disputed Kenya frontier, went on to say that these events 'seem to us to be strange byproducts of the grant of independence which is urged upon us as a policy by every Asian and African country'. For Britain the only issue was not *whether* any country should become independent, but only *when*.

> The only check on the transfer of power from the United Kingdom to the government of the country concerned is that we want to be sure that, when independence is granted, the country will be able to make both ends meet economically and that it was accepting a constitution, from the day of independence, which will work for the well-being of every section of society. . . .

He hoped Britain could

> go along with the majority of the United Nations in these colonial matters since it accepted the principles of unqualified self-determination, majority rule and safeguards for minorities.[26]

Lord Home's contribution to the United Nations deserves attention for three reasons. There is always a time-lag in reputation and the conviction that a western imperial power was deliberately divesting itself of the remnants of empire was too unexpected to strike quick roots. The anti-colonialists continued to campaign, slow to understand that the campaign in respect of Britain was concluded. The second reason why Lord Home's speech merits attention flows from the first. In the years following Indian independence it was widely maintained, not least in the United States, that a Commonwealth divided between colonialists and anti-colonialists could not endure. This view, which *inter alia* discounted the strength of anti-colonial, pro-Commonwealth sentiment within Britain, and especially within the then dominant Labour party, was evidently without substance. All were anti-colonialists, as all were socialists in Harcourt's day. This meant there were some strange figures in the ranks, looking for their chance to break away, but the solid mass of opinion kept them more or less in formation. Nor was there reason to doubt that in bringing about this new measure of agreement on a potentially divisive issue, the influence of Asian membership of the Commonwealth over a period of years was pronounced. In that sense, as Professor Rajan maintained,[27] it proved to be a Commonwealth new in character that came into existence in 1947.

Finally Lord Home's assertion that the issue for Britain was not *whether* but *when* any country should become independent, may serve as a touchstone by which to review British policy at this time. Certainly it had not been universally true, even a few years earlier. On 28 July 1954, the minister of state for colonial affairs, Mr Hopkinson, told the House of Commons that Her Majesty's government had decided that the time had come to take 'a fresh initiative' in the development of self-governing institutions for Cyprus, but it emerged under questioning that this development was not intended to lead to self-government. On the contrary, in the words of the minister, 'there are certain territories in the Commonwealth which, owing to their particular circumstances, can never expect to be fully independent'.[28] As Louis Napoleon once observed: '*en politique on ne doit jamais dire "jamais"*' and neglect of such elementary political prudence on this occasion exacted its harsh price in British involvement in years of island strife. Elsewhere there was no parallel to such a policy of negation, nor indeed to a situation of such complexity and elsewhere, with the qualified exceptions of Ghana and Kenya, there was no organised national revolt against British colonial rule.

In the earlier years of African, as of Asian decolonisation, there was a disposition to transfer power by stages – internal self-government with certain powers reserved, full domestic self-government, the chief minister becoming prime minister with a cabinet responsible to an elected Assembly, consideration of administrative needs and internal security, enquiry into the position of minorities – the Willink Commission report on Nigeria, despite the civil war *dénouement* of later years, being the classic document of the period in this field – [29] the holding of a constitutional conference preparatory to agreement on a constitution and the inclusion in it of any necessary entrenchment, as in the Nigerian Constitution of 1960[30] or that of Trinidad and Tobago in 1962, of fundamental freedoms or human and minority rights, then independence embodied in an Independence Act of the British Parliament, with all the governments of the Commonwealth being invited to concur in Commonwealth membership. Time was allowed for each advance to be tested and for misgivings, notably on the part of minorities, to be expressed and this was coupled with mistrust of a timetable defining and committing the British government in advance. Subsequently this phased transfer of power, with either implied or stated conditions for each further advance, gave way to transfer with time as the first priority. Symptomatic of it, noted one contemporary observer,[31] was 'an increasing readiness to see the preparations for independence as a paper exercise of Lancaster House conferences, a challenge to chairmanship rather than a duty to find a constitutional framework genuinely acceptable to the people of the country concerned and relevant to their needs and conditions.' And some confirmation of this may be seen in the perceptible decline in the substance and quality of British ministerial speeches introducing independence acts in the House of Commons. What had once been a venture in statesmanship, essayed with deliberation, was now reduced to little more than the application of a formula. While this reflected chiefly the change, if not in outlook at least in temper on the part of the metropolitan power, it was also, it is proper to add, in part also the product of growing experience. In the twenty years after the second world war, the Commonwealth collectively probably produced the largest number of written constitutions ever composed in so short a period. The many devices of federalism, the varying balances between executive and legislature, the machinery of judicial control, were all there to be copied or exploited as occasion demanded. One thing that was lacking – and it was soon to be in some demand – was a blue-print to serve as the prototype for the creation of a one party state.

In the process of decolonisation the British government encouraged the creation of federations in the West Indies, Malaysia and in Central Africa, but none of them in fact survived intact. In the case of the West Indies the causes of failure lay on the one hand in the strength of regional loyalties, which stood in the way of comprehensive membership – British Honduras, observed the federal prime minister, Sir Grantley Adams, 'having no more intention of joining the federation than I have of going aloft in a Sputnik!' – and strengthened psychological resistance even to the idea of federation, and on the other, in economic inequalities, which rendered impossible the negotiation of a generally acceptable apportionment of fiscal burdens. The Federation of Malaysia, it is true, survived, but with the secession of the Chinese-dominated port of Singapore. Both remained within the area of Commonwealth, and especially of Anglo-Australian-New Zealand defence interests, with Malaysia receiving significant support in her confrontation with Indonesia and the base at Singapore being made available, while use for it remained, by the government of Singapore to Britain, as a strategic centre east of Suez. It was, however, significant that it was increasingly the Australians who wished to maintain and the British, under economic pressure, who desired to diminish to vanishing point, Britain's historic east of Suez rôle. The third of the federations – that of the Rhodesias and Nyasaland – posed fundamental issues and in so doing confronted Britain and the Commonwealth with its last major problem of decolonisation.

Given the will, the liquidation of colonialism, in the sense of imperial rule over other peoples, presented issues which were in character partly technical and partly political, that is to say, it had to be decided in each case to whom power should be transferred and how it should be transferred. Both could ordinarily be decided by the imperial power with a certain impartiality and detachment. But the liquidation of imperial rule in territories where there were colonists in the Greco-Roman sense, while posing the same technical problems was apt to raise the political question in a form so acute as to be virtually different in kind. Popular emotions, notably in the territory concerned but also in the metropolitan country, were likely to be stirred and to sway the judgment and the actions of governments. Ireland between 1886 and 1921 had provided a classic example of this. In South, Central and East Africa British colonists had settled, with the encouragement of their fellow-countrymen in most instances, and had become in varying degrees privileged, influential or ruling minorities, differing in cultural background and above all in race from the indigenous majorities. Usually, but not invariably, well intentioned spokesmen encouraged thoughts of partnership, but while this commended itself warmly to liberal opinion, the principal protagonists, mindful of the impending withdrawal of imperial government, were more preoccupied with the succession of power. It was at root that preoccupation which accounted for the collapse of the long-considered, but at the last somewhat hastily improvised, federal experiment in Central Africa.

The federation came into being in 1953 and comprised Southern Rhodesia, which exercised responsible self-government, dominated by a European settler minority, on a restricted but not a rigid colour franchise; Northern Rhodesia, with a white community on the copper-belt but with an administration controlled by the Colonial Office in London;

and Nyasaland, also under Colonial Office jurisdiction, without white settlement, poor in resources, but with an African population educationally comparatively advanced through the work of Mission schools. Theoretically, at least, the federation was conceived in terms of ultimate partnership between European minority and African majority and to this end its constitution contained built-in safeguards for the Africans.

The attractions of federation in terms of administration, communications and development of resources were not in serious dispute. It possessed economic advantages for all its component parts, but most of all for Nyasaland, the poorest of the three. But politics were in conflict with economics, and politics in these circumstances and at this juncture in time, were bound to prevail. The Federation of the Rhodesias and Nyasaland was not so much misconceived as conceived out of time and place. It belonged to an age when there was if not acceptance then acquiescence by Africans in European control. That age was passing at the very moment the federation was formulated. To politically self-conscious Africans in all three territories, federation consequently appeared to be essentially a device for extending the period of colonialism and of economic exploitation for the advantage of the European settlers. In 1959 the Report of a Commission of Enquiry under the chairmanship of Mr Justice Devlin into disorders in Nyasaland, noted the resolve of the African majority that federation should be liquidated and enquired why it was so strongly entertained. The answer was as follows: 'Federation means the domination of Southern Rhodesia: the domination of Southern Rhodesia means the domination of the settler: the domination of the settler means the perpetuation of racial inferiority . . .'.[32] A year later the commission appointed to review the working of the Constitution of Rhodesia and Nyasaland under Lord Monckton's chairmanship elaborated the same point. They reported:

> It is inevitable and natural that the prospect of independence, seven years ago unthinkably remote, should now appear to many Africans to be a right from which they should be no longer debarred: and racial feeling, far from having merged into a sense of multi-racial nationhood, has grown sharper and stronger. It now appears to many Africans that only the presence of the European community politically entrenched behind the federal constitution stands between them and the form of freedom already granted to their fellow Africans in most other parts of the continent.[33]

The British government decided to dismantle the federation. The process was painful – how painful may best be judged by reading the account of the federal prime minister, Sir Roy Welensky[34] – there were allegations of misleading assurances given by British ministers and even of broken pledges, and a mistrust between the British settlers in Rhodesia and the British government was sown which later developed into open antagonism. Yet as early as 1954, at a Commonwealth Conference in Lahore, a British spokesman had remarked, to the dismay ironically enough of British Conservative delegates, that if at any time Britain was compelled to choose between the white settlers, practising racial discrimination in Africa and 'Gold Coast democracy' she would be bound in her own self-interest and in the interests of Commonwealth unity, to come down on the African side.[35] That is precisely what happened in Central Africa nine years later. On 31 December 1963 the federation was dissolved and in Nyasaland and North Rhodesia, as already in Kenya, the privileges and the power of the colonists were ended. But in Southern Rhodesia the colonists, whose privileged minority position the British government deemed politically expendable and the African majority desired to see politically expended, were more numerous and prepared to be recalcitrant. For a multi-racial Commonwealth their resistance to the winds of change was in due course to present delicate issues, touching on sensitive racial chords.

One result of the African, following upon the Asian, transfers of power was the elevation of race equality, or multi-racialism, as a basic principle, shared by the Commonwealth community of states. In an earlier period allegiance to the Crown had been made, and after 1949 the practice of responsible parliamentary government was generally considered to be a condition of membership. But by the mid 1960s not only did the number of republican exceed the number of monarchical member-states, but furthermore about one-third of the members no longer practised parliamentary government on the Westminster model and it was accepted, though not in some instances without misgiving, that this also was a matter of domestic concern. But in respect of the ordering of race relations such a plea was conclusively rejected. South Africa provided, as had been long foreshadowed, the test case, for as the Commonwealth was moving towards equality and multi-racialism, the government of the Union was enforcing within South Africa its theory of racial separation. First known as apartheid and then in the face of world-wide criticism, reformulated with more sophistication as differential development, it was little distinguishable in its earlier application from racial discrimination, though it had as its professed goal the separation of African and European into racially homogeneous states within a South African Commonwealth. The test, as it happened, came in such a way as to associate newer and now dominant racial with older constitutional issues.

The background was provided by developments in South Africa. In 1960 the Pan-African Congress planned a number of demonstrations to protest against the pass laws, and on 21 March many thousands of

Africans marched on the police station at Sharpeville, near Vereeniging. Their leaders maintained that they had gathered to make a peaceful protest; the police, discounting this, opened fire with rifles and automatic weapons and sixty-seven Africans were killed and about 180 injured. The massacre, with pictures of it circulated round the world, caused a wave of horror. A week later on 31 March some thirty thousand non-Europeans marched on Cape Town, and were halted not far short of the centre of the city. While the racial question in South Africa thus apparently neared a violent climax, the Nationalist government decided the time had come at last for the declaration of a republic. The question was submitted, as had been consistently promised, to a referendum (in which voting was restricted to Europeans) and approved. A republican constitution, substituting a state president for the governor-general, was given a first reading in January 1961 and later enacted by the South African Parliament.

When the prime ministers of the Commonwealth met in London on 8–17 March 1961, they had, like the rest of the world, every reason to 'remember Sharpeville', and they had before them an application from the government of the Union for South Africa's continued membership of the Commonwealth. Commonwealth precedent in respect of India, Pakistan, Ceylon and Ghana suggested that a request couched in conventional form for continued republican membership would be acceded to if constitutional considerations alone were at issue. But while the desirability of distinguishing the constitutional from broader political considerations was recognised by most of the Commonwealth prime ministers,[36] John Diefenbaker of Canada being, however, a notable exception, South Africa's application was made the occasion, as public opinion in many Commonwealth countries demanded, of a general debate upon South Africa's racial policies. This debate, as the brief communiqué issued on 15 March recorded,[37] took place with the consent of the South African prime minister, Dr Verwoerd. There followed an open attack upon South Africa led not, as might have been expected, by an African or an Asian leader, but by the Canadian prime minister who, according to Menzies (who was not a friendly critic), 'came armed with a resolution of his parliament and presented his views with immense emotion', not even 'some side-queries to him about the Red Indians and Eskimos in Canada' deflecting him from his course.[38] The Canadian initiative, significant in itself of the Commonwealth-wide revulsion against South Africa's racial laws – Menzies disapproved of the policies, while not approving of Commonwealth debate upon them – contributed to the Commonwealth consensus that emerged.

Subsequent accounts given by prime ministers to their individual parliaments revealed something of the fluctuating course of the prime minister's discussions and dramatic conclusion.[39] At the heart of it lay the simple fact that Dr Verwoerd was prepared to make neither apology nor concession. Apartheid, in his view, was not a matter of convenience or expediency: it was an expression of the right view of race relations and as such had to be defended with the uncompromising zeal of a religious conviction. There would be no change in practice or direction and his Commonwealth colleagues, thus faced with the prospect of acquiescence and the threatened price of division among them, or of pressing home their criticisms, adopted the latter course. Dr Verwoerd thereupon foreshortened debate by announcing the withdrawal of South Africa's application, thereby fixing 31 May, the fifty-first anniversary of the Act of Union, and the date already determined for the inauguration of the republic, as the date when South Africa's membership of the Commonwealth would lapse.

Dr Verwoerd subsequently stated that he took this step with 'great regret'. South Africa's request had been made in the expectation that it would have been willingly granted, 'as was done also on behalf of South Africa in the previous cases of India, Pakistan, Ceylon, Ghana . . . in spite of our great differences with them', but he had been amazed at, and shocked by, the spirit of hostility and even vindictiveness shown towards his country. This had made it clear that South Africa's continued membership would no longer be welcomed. He believed it marked 'the beginning of the disintegration of the Commonwealth'. The comments of his fellow prime ministers, other than Sir Robert Menzies, who confessed himself because of Commonwealth debate upon the management by a member-state of its own affairs, 'deeply troubled' by what had happened, were regretful, but also in varying degree indicated their relief at South Africa's departure. The president of Pakistan thought that as a result the Commonwealth would emerge as a stronger organisation; Diefenbaker that South Africa's withdrawal was unavoidable because discrimination in respect of race or colour could not continue if the Commonwealth was to be 'a force for good'; Mrs Bandaranaike of Ceylon saw in it 'a dramatic vindication of the equality and human dignity for which the Commonwealth stands'; Nehru though he wondered (and it would seem not without cause) whether the decision would in any way benefit non-Europeans in the Union, had little doubt the effect 'will be to strengthen the Commonwealth', and Macmillan, for whom the outcome represented the frustration of initial aims, spoke more simply of regrets that circumstances had made the breach inevitable. Implicit in all that was said was the conviction that a turning-point in Commonwealth history had been passed and hope predominated over anxiety as to what it might portend. It was widely noted that this was the first occasion on which the views of a United Kingdom government had not prevailed in a matter of major importance in Commonwealth internal policy. Virtually unnoted was the fact that the issue was decided by the prime ministers themselves in a tense atmosphere in London, apparently without continuing consultation with their own cabinets and after a protracted debate, the course of which was seemingly not uninfluenced by an inspired article by Dr Julius Nyerere, then prime minister of Tanganyika and later, president of Tanzania, published in *The Observer*, of Sunday 21 March. In it, Nyerere gave notice that Tanganyika, which was not to become independent till 9 December that year, could not 'join any "association of friends" which includes a state deliberately and ruthlessly pursuing a racialist policy'.[40] The strength of Pan-African sentiment was beginning to make itself felt in Commonwealth councils, with the president of Ghana, Dr Nkrumah, its most formidable protagonist.

The South African government by its decision to withdraw from the Commonwealth indicated a resolve not to be blown off course by the winds of change, but to withstand them. They had confidence in their ability to do so and on the short term assessed more justly than the majority of their critics the actual as distinct from the apparent balance of power in Africa. The Europeans in South Africa were long established, their society rested upon resources of wealth and economic experience without parallel in the continent and capable, as was to be strikingly evidenced in the years of economic growth that followed secession, of development at a rate that placed the republic among the world's leaders. But there was also another European community, recently settled, without comparable economic resources, that decided also to seek to resist the winds of change. They were the whites of Southern Rhodesia, numbering less than two hundred thousand in a population of nearly four million Africans.

When the Federation of the Rhodesias and Nyasaland was dismantled, Northern Rhodesia as Zambia, and Nyasaland as Malawi, became independent member-states of the Commonwealth. Southern Rhodesia did not. For nearly twenty years the prime ministers of Southern Rhodesia and of the federation had successively attended Prime Ministers' Meetings by courtesy, though not as of right. But it had been widely assumed, certainly in Britain and Rhodesia, that in one capacity or another the right would follow with an independence that, as a matter of policy, would not precede but shortly succeed upon the acquisition of independent member-status by an African state. That status was attained by Ghana in 1957; Nigeria and East and Central African states followed, but far from there being signs of early Rhodesian advancement, there was evidence of a change in the climate of British official thinking, critical of the settlers and their claims. Independence and Commonwealth membership were to be made conditional upon assurances of majority African rule in some foreseeable future. The settlers, their experience of the dismantling of federation fresh in their minds, decided if need be to go down fighting rather than concede by stages, as seemed otherwise inevitable, their position of predominance. As it became increasingly apparent that they could not secure independence on their terms by constitutional means, they threatened to seize it unconstitutionally and by unilateral declaration of the independence of Rhodesia. 'There should be no delusions in Rhodesia', they were warned by Britain's Labour prime minister, Harold Wilson, 'about the ability and determination of the British government to deal with the utmost firmness with any act of rebellion; or about the effects of the mass of international condemnation to which Rhodesia would expose herself.' But the white Rhodesians, led by Ian Smith, were not to be deflected. On 11 November 1965 they declared independence unilaterally, the first settler revolt against British imperial authority since the American War of Independence. U.D.I. was interpreted in Africa as a challenge to the new Africanism, a test of British and Commonwealth good faith, and an expression of settler intention to disregard fundamental African rights. It was greeted in turn with loud protests, with limited trade sanctions imposed by Britain and other Commonwealth states and then by United Nations sanctions, but not by force. Britain, which alone could apply it, was not prepared to do so; while the African states, who had not themselves the military resources, sought passionately to persuade Britain to use it. One result was that the Commonwealth in Africa came near to foundering on the suspicions and antagonisms aroused by the Rhodesian settler régime's existence and still more its survival. Another was that for the first time, the Commonwealth collectively sought and secured an active rôle in a matter which in principle lay between the British government in London and a colony in Africa under its jurisdiction and within its sphere of responsibility. How that rôle was played affords an insight into the structure and the tensions within a multi-racial Commonwealth.

There was substantial consistency in the approach of successive British governments on the conditions on which independence might be conceded to Southern Rhodesia, once the federation had been dissolved. They were formulated first by the Conservative administration as five principles, which were restated by the succeeding Labour government on 21 September 1965, and then extended in January 1966, with the addition of a sixth. These principles were as follows: 1. The principle and intention of unimpeded progress to majority rule, already enshrined in the territory's 1961 constitution, would have to be maintained and guaranteed. 2. There would also have to be guarantees, against retrogressive amendment of the constitution. 3. There would have to be immediate improvement in the political status of the African population. 4. There would have to be progress towards the ending of racial discrimination. 5. The British government would need to be satisfied that any basis proposed for independence would be acceptable to the people of Rhodesia as a whole. 6. It would be necessary to ensure that, regardless of race, there was no oppression of majority by minority or of minority by majority.

These principles envisaged no immediate transfer of control from Europeans to Africans, which indeed was considered unrealistic in London in view of Rhodesian African divisions and the quality of African leadership in the colony, but they sought, with earlier South African experience very much in mind, to ensure that power would be progressively transferred beyond possibility of retraction over a period of years. It was, however, precisely this prospect of steady erosion of their position, which the settlers, or the great majority of them, had sought to avert by their unilateral declaration of independence. Would economic restrictions suffice to persuade them to retrace their steps, return in effect to the *status quo ante*, accept the six principles, and so open the way to African majority rule within a reasonable period of years? The British government, in a position to use force only at the price of dividing opinion at home, and risking confrontation with South Africa, professed their confidence in an affirmative answer.

On 10 December 1965, the British prime minister told the House of Commons that the economic measures Britain had undertaken to bring Rhodesia at the earliest possible moment back to constitutional government were harsh and would cause hardship, but the government considered that 'quick and effective measures will involve less suffering than a long drawn out agony'. The prime minister's confidence, however, was not shared by the majority of African states, clamorous for war against Rhodesia, even if it were to involve the risk of South African involvement.

It was in an attempt to remove growing African mistrust of Britain's resolution and even of her good faith, and so to preserve the threatened unity of the Commonwealth that two meetings of Commonwealth heads of government – a designation embracing both presidents and prime ministers – were held in 1966, one in Lagos in January, at the invitation of Sir Abubakar Tafawa Balewa, the prime minister of the Federation of Nigeria, the other in London in September. The Lagos meeting was notable, as the first held outside Britain and also as the first to be organised by the Commonwealth secretariat established a year earlier (the two things not being unrelated, in that the existence of the secretariat facilitated the organisation of conferences in capitals other than London). One consequence was that it was not the British prime minister, as heretofore, but the prime minister of the host-country, the Federation of Nigeria who presided. This was of some moment since the Lagos Conference had been called on Nigerian initiative to discuss a single topic – Rhodesia. Two member-states, Ghana and Tanzania, which had already broken off relations with Britain on the Rhodesian issue, were not represented, while Australia sent an observer indicating, so Sir Robert Menzies explained, the concern of his government lest other Commonwealth countries should interfere in what was properly a British responsibility, and by pressing for the use of force in Rhodesia should strain the structure of the Commonwealth. The final communiqué in fact reaffirmed that the authority and responsibility for guiding Rhodesia to independence rested with Britain. But it also acknowledged that the problem was one of wider concern to Africa and the Commonwealth leaders expressed their sense of the danger to all multi-racial communities, particularly in East and Central Africa, and to the future of the multi-racial Commonwealth itself, if the situation in Rhodesia were to continue. But while all were agreed that the rebellion should be brought to an end, some expressed concern that the steps taken so far had not ended it. The use of military force was discussed and it was accepted that it could not be excluded. On the other hand, the British prime minister stated that on the expert advice available to him the cumulative effects of the economic and financial sanctions might well bring the rebellion to an end within a matter of weeks rather than months. The forecast was received with general, and as it was to prove, justified scepticism. The Conference decided accordingly and by way of reinsurance to appoint two continuing committees, composed of representatives of all Commonwealth countries, and assisted by the Commonwealth secretariat to meet with the secretary general in London, one of them to review regularly the effect of sanctions and the other to co-ordinate a special Commonwealth programme of assistance in training Rhodesian Africans for future responsibilities. The heads of government left it open to the sanctions committee to recommend the reconvening of their Conference when it was judged to be necessary, and in any event decided they would meet again in July if the rebellion had not been ended before then.[41] The Commonwealth over whose destinies Britain had once presided, was in effect to act as a watch dog upon Britain. This was accepted but not relished in Whitehall.

The Rhodesian rebellion was not in fact ended in July, nor yet in September when, somewhat behind their self-appointed timetable, the prime ministers met again in London. Between the two Conferences there were informal talks between British officials and members of the

Rhodesian administration. They were talks on the British side directed to finding out whether a basis for negotiation existed: they were, as the phrase went, talks about talks and without commitment. They served, however, despite British protestations, to heighten African suspicions of British intentions. As the talks continued intermittently, with rumoured breakdown followed by resumption, these suspicions continued the more to flourish. They dominated the September Conference.

The September Meeting was attended by the heads of government of Australia, Britain, Canada, Cyprus, Gambia, Guyana, Malawi, Malaysia, Malta, New Zealand, Sierra Leone, Singapore and Uganda; by the acting prime minister of Jamaica and by ministerial and governmental representatives of Ghana, Trinidad and Tobago, India, Pakistan, Zambia, Ceylon and Nigeria. Tanzania alone did not send a delegation. Nine of the eleven days' Meeting were devoted to Rhodesia. Most of the heads of government expressed their firm opinion that force was the only sure means of bringing down the illegal régime in Rhodesia. The British government, not altogether isolated however, stood firm in its objections to force as a means of imposing a constitutional settlement. There was also very strong pressure upon the prime minister that Britain should make a categorical declaration to the effect that independence would not be granted before majority rule, on the basis of universal adult suffrage. Here the prime minister conceded much without conceding all. He agreed that any settlement must be, and be seen to be, acceptable to the people of Rhodesia as a whole and that this implied that there would be no independence before majority rule, unless the people of Rhodesia as a whole were shown to be in favour of it. There was less optimism than in January about the impact of sanctions. The illegal régime was, therefore, to be presented with an ultimatum by the British government. It was to the effect that, unless the initial and indispensable steps were taken to end the rebellion and to vest executive authority in the governor before the end of the year, the British government would in the first place withdraw all previous proposals for a constitutional settlement and in particular would not thereafter be prepared to submit to Parliament any settlement which involved independence before majority rule, and in the second place they would be prepared to join in sponsoring in the Security Council a resolution, providing for selective mandatory economic sanctions against Rhodesia.[42]

The time limit, reinforced with the threat of international action, implied an intensification of the struggle and a prospective widening of the area of it. But its acceptance neither stilled doubts nor silenced criticism in the African Commonwealth. The Zambian foreign minister, who left before the Meeting was over, commented that Zambia had got nothing at the Conference – President Kaunda had been the principal and consistent protagonist of the use of force by the British to end the Rhodesian rebellion – but the vice-president of Kenya was more temperate, remarking that while the African, Asian and Caribbean delegations had not achieved all they had hoped for, the very dangerous situation of independence before majority rule had been avoided. As for Harold Wilson, under the extremes of Commonwealth pressures, in a situation which allowed him little freedom of manœuvre, given the Portuguese and South African gaps in the sanctions ring, he felt that

> We are getting a little tired of carrying the can internationally for a régime that has no regard for international opinions. We have had to pay a very heavy price for carrying that can in the last ten days. We have faced very serious dangers of the break-up of the Commonwealth, because of the actions of a small group of men.

The ultimatum, with its end of year time limit encouraged further talks between the British government and the Smith régime with the governor, an isolated figure, with his telephone wires cut in his residence in Salisbury, continuing to serve as an intermediary and an insistent advocate of negotiations. In November there was a visit by the commonwealth secretary to Rhodesia, and on 1 December, the prime minister having 'reason to think we were within hailing distance of a solution', gave the dramatic news to the House of Commons that he was flying out that evening for a 'sea-summit' with Ian Smith off Gibraltar on board *H.M.S. Tiger*. The talks lasted two days. A working document for a constitutional settlement was drafted and the Rhodesian leader given the opportunity of discussion with his colleagues in Salisbury before accepting or rejecting it as a whole. They rejected it. The document, subsequently published,[43] set out the basis of a long term constitutional settlement within the framework of the six principles; and also the procedure by which an immediate return to legality might be made and the acceptability of the new independent constitutional proposals to the Rhodesian people as a whole ascertained. While professedly prepared to accept the constitutional proposals, the Rhodesian régime stated that the procedure outlined for a return to legality was objectionable, and that, in view of its nature, the Rhodesian government, so Ian Smith maintained, 'would be extremely foolish were they to abandon the substance of their present constitution for the shadow of a mythical constitution yet to be evolved'.[44] Rejection was followed forthwith by British application to the United Nations for the imposition of selective mandatory sanctions, extended under Commonwealth African pressure to include oil and a declaration that all previous offers made by the

British government were invalidated and that in consequence there would be no independence before majority rule [NIBMAR].

In the earlier phases of the Rhodesian crisis, and again when talks were resumed off Gibraltar in October, 1968 the British government emphasised the binding character of the six principles and of the commitments into which they had entered in subscribing to the Commonwealth communiqués at Lagos and London. In no previous phase in the process of decolonisation had Commonwealth participation in the shaping of British policy been so pronounced, nor British freedom of manœuvre become so narrowly constricted, nor the limits of British authority been so painfully and so publicly demonstrated over a long period of time. For the short term, the political price of Commonwealth in Africa was seen to be high. Disillusion spread and it was deepened by African disorder. The Lagos Conference was followed within a matter of days by an army revolt in Nigeria, hitherto the most stable as well as the most populous of Commonwealth states in Africa, in which the premiers of the Northern and Western Regions were murdered and the prime minister of the federation, who had presided over the conference with quiet distinction, kidnapped and subsequently found dead. In less than a month President Nkrumah, while on a state visit to Peking, was ejected from power, also by an army revolt in neighbouring Ghana. These things played their part in hardening an existing and already pronounced predisposition on the part of parties and people in Britain to look in hope not to Africa, nor to other parts of the Commonwealth overseas but nearer home – to Europe.

It was not long after South Africa's withdrawal from the Commonwealth that positive steps towards effecting a change in the direction of British policy were taken. On 13 June 1961, Harold Macmillan announced that three senior ministers were to visit Commonwealth capitals to consult with Commonwealth governments about Britain's relations with the European Economic Community. The announcement was rightly interpreted as indicating a major shift in British policy. The three emissaries, however, and for that reason, proved more successful in eliciting misgivings about the effects, political as well as economic, for the Commonwealth overseas of Britain's membership of the EEC, than in persuading overseas Commonwealth governments of its desirability. While the economic and political strengthening of western Europe was recognised to be a general Commonwealth interest and while it was explicitly conceded in communiqués[45] issued after the talks that Britain's membership of the EEC was a matter for decision by the British government, Australian ministers, to take a not unrepresentative example and to quote the communiqué issued on 11 July, expressed their concern at 'the weakening effect they believed this development would have on the Commonwealth relationship' and while they 'did not feel entitled to object to the opening of negotiations by the British government', they made it clear that 'the absence of objection should in the circumstances not be taken as implying approval'. When the question was considered collectively by Commonwealth ministers attending the meeting of the Commonwealth Economic Consultative Council at Accra, 12–14 September that year, such strong language was used by the Canadian delegates as to suggest that the Canadian government considered that Britain had to make a choice between the Commonwealth and the EEC. The official communiqué[46] itself spoke of 'the grave apprehension and concern' of all overseas Commonwealth representatives regarding 'the possible results of the initiative taken by the United Kingdom'.

The Accra communiqué represented a position more extreme than was in evidence in subsequent negotiations or at the Commonwealth Prime Ministers' Meeting in September 1962. The difficulties of Britain's economic position and the lack of any convincing Commonwealth alternative to membership of the EEC were becoming increasingly apparent. In the crucial export field, United Kingdom exports to the Commonwealth between 1955 and 1963 remained nearly static, her exports to the United States and the EEC more than doubled. It is true that exports to Commonwealth countries in 1962 remained greater in value than those to the United States and the EEC put together, and more immediately relevant, that exports to the Commonwealth that year amounted to £1,032 million as against £720 million to the Six. Commonwealth trade, in other words, remained immensely valuable, accounting for about one-third of Britain's total trade. But it was also either stagnant or in slow decline, holding out, so it seemed to most economists, little possibility of growth. Yet there remained many in the Commonwealth overseas, even where so much was conceded, especially in the old dominions, who accepted the truth of some things that were said by General de Gaulle on 14 January 1963,[48] when he used his country's right of veto to terminate negotiations on Britain's entry into Europe. They were disposed to agree that Britain was in fact insular, maritime, bound by its history, its political, financial and trading systems to many and distant countries. While they had become generally reconciled to the thought of Britain's membership of the Common Market, with hardly negotiated safeguards and with reservations of their special interest, her complete absorption in the European community, which the general professed to consider then and later a necessary condition of membership, was something which other member-states of the Commonwealth were apt to view with dismay. Resentment, therefore, at the brusqueness and the lateness – after months of thought and bargaining in which all Commonwealth governments had been in some measure involved – of the president's pronouncement was not wholly dissociated from a sense of temporary relief. There was now time to make new dispositions. The course of British policy had been checked, but its direction was not changed. Where Macmillan left off, Wilson resumed four years later. By then debate within the Commonwealth, aside from some outspoken Australian protests, was over, new dispositions where possible were made or being made – in 1967 Australian trade with Japan for the first time exceeded her trade with Britain – and the consequences for Commonwealth were awaited with resignation. In the middle of the nineteenth century Great Britain, carrying through her own commercial revolution, 'in effect had broken away from her own empire';[49] and overseas it was assumed that, in the later twentieth century, she would likewise break away, under compulsion of economic circumstance, from a Commonwealth over whose destinies, as chief among equals, she had long presided.

CHAPTER 14

MEN OF COMMONWEALTH: SMUTS, MACKENZIE KING AND NEHRU

History and circumstance permitted, even it may be predicated the emergence of Commonwealth in some form. But they did not determine, still less predetermine, the pattern of it. That is to be traced to the influence of individuals and, in some measure, the collective will of peoples. The latter, at all times hard to assess, is in this case chiefly to be inferred from response to challenge, and in less exacting days from participation or at the least acquiescence in the activities necessary to meaningful Commonwealth existence. The former, the place of personality, at times seemingly defined with deceptive ease in records which appear to offer convincing and on occasion even conclusive interpretations in personal terms of the developments they describe, affords with certain cautionary reservations more fruitful ground for reflection. The emergence or existence of a Commonwealth of Nations gave to many men in official or unofficial capacities opportunities for influencing or seeking to influence a segment of international relations which otherwise they would not have enjoyed. Chamberlain and Milner; Botha and Campbell-Bannerman; Laurier and Deakin, Borden and Hughes; Balfour, Hertzog and O'Higgins; Montagu, Amery, Irwin, Mountbatten; Mackenzie King, Curtin, Fraser, Menzies, Attlee; Liaquat Ali Khan, Louis St. Laurent, Macmillan, the Bandaranaikes, Abubakar Tafawa Balewa, Julius Nyerere, Lester Pearson, Jomo Kenyatta among statesmen with many more besides; and Jebb, Lionel Curtis, Geoffrey Dawson and the Round Tablers, J. W. Dafoe and Canadian liberal-radicals, K. M. Panikkar, among exponents or prophets, and, if little known to a wider public, by no means least many distinguished administrators – all left a mark on the politics, the concept or the working of this association of nations and, outside their own countries, are remembered chiefly or largely for their impact upon it. There are others, cast in a larger mould, whose influence is to be thought of in a more spacious context, J. A. Hobson among writers, Smuts, Churchill, Gandhi, Nehru, Jinnah, de Valera and Nkrumah, among national leaders, but whose impress upon the Commonwealth was, in some instances at least, no less pronounced than that of those to whom its development in whole or in part was a principal preoccupation.

It would no doubt be possible to write the history of the Commonwealth in biographical terms, and in many respects it would be illuminating. But historically the attempt would be almost as misconceived, though no doubt a good deal more entertaining, as the constitutional straitjacket into which the story was for so long forced to fit. It would be misconceived because it would rest upon a false equation of man and circumstances. It was the latter, in the first instance brought into play by British expansion and settlement overseas, which made possible and conditioned the experiment of Commonwealth. What remained, and it was much, for individuals was to impart where they could present meaning and a sense of future purpose to political, cultural and human connections, which they had as a result inherited. The system was important but so also were the men who worked or developed it. What sort of men were they? What were their dominant interests and purposes? Francis Bacon concluded his essay upon the Greatness of Kingdoms with the reflection that while 'no man can, by care-taking (as the Scripture saith) add a cubit to his stature, in this little model of a man's body; . . . in the great frame of kingdoms and commonwealth, it is in the power of princes, or estates, to add amplitude and greatness to their kingdoms'. The age of princes is past, but even in a century of scientific discovery, technological revolution and the common man, individuals in positions of power or symbolic significance may still enhance or diminish the reputations of states or societies and either enrich or impoverish that historical tradition which, by illuminating the way a country or community has come, may serve to cast light on some parts of the road ahead.

General J. C. Smuts: He was defeated.

In May, 1902, when the Boers debated the issue of peace or war at Vereeniging, Smuts maintained that peace must be made. His presentation of the case was factual and formidable, though the suppressed emotion comes through in the climax. 'Brothers, we resolved to stand to the bitter end; let us admit like men that the end has come for us – has come in a more bitter form than we had ever thought possible'.[1] He was thirty-one. He was defeated. His biographer has termed it 'strange defeat'.[2] It provides, however, a clue to an understanding of the strangest of all Commonwealth careers.

His biographer, Professor Hancock, has shown Smuts on both sides of the hill. In Smuts' lifetime, the far – the Boer – side remained unfamiliar to the great body of Smuts' English and Commonwealth admirers. But to Smuts it was home. It was there, brilliant and intense, that he went to school, taking no part in the games of 'the puerile element', and with no reason to pay any special regard to that slow, persistent plodder, D. F. Malan, three years his junior. Stellenbosch and then Cambridge followed with firsts and prizes all the way. But at Cambridge they did not compensate for being away from home. In his first year he was 'utterly desolate'. Yet Cambridge and England left their mark. 'An anglicised Afrikaner is as disgusting a creature as an anglicised Scotchman', his benefactor and early mentor, Professor Marais, felt reason to warn him.[3] The events of succeeding years might seem to have made the warning superfluous.

Misplaced faith in Rhodes, shattered by the Raid, was followed by Smuts' migration to the Transvaal, where he became Kruger's state attorney and the leading personality in the republic after the president. He negotiated with Milner who thought him high-minded, recognised his outstanding ability, but doubted his staying power and political insight. For his part, Smuts, though tempted to dismiss Milner with 'the academic nobodies who fancy themselves great imperial statesmen', finally realised that Milner was resolved to confront the republic with total capitulation or total war. The second was chosen. Smuts campaigned. He found that 'military life agrees wonderfully with me'.[4] It equipped him, moreover, at the outset of the century, for what was to be the dominant international factor of his lifetime – preparation for war and war. But in 1902, after the exhilaration of commando raids there came the end, not merely in the form of defeat but defeat in a war which Smuts believed to have been unjustly forced upon his people. 'Perhaps it is the fate of our little race', he reflected to his wife in the first letter which she received from him for over a year, a year in which their son died, 'to be sacrificed on the altar of the world's ideals; perhaps we are destined to be a martyr race.'[5]

Defeat, and especially defeat in such circumstances, usually prompts either despair or an uphill climb by paths that are often devious. It is the vanquished, not the victors, who have need to be 'slim'. 'Mr Smuts', wrote a Colonial Office official of him, at the time of his visit to London early in 1906, 'is a Boer and a lawyer. His memorandum . . . exhibits all the cunning of his race and calling'.[6] There was some truth in this. Smuts was concerned not with means but with the long uphill climb from defeat. The most notable step on it was his famous meeting on the evening of Wednesday, 7th February 1906, with Campbell-Bannerman. That meeting was 'the creative encounter'[7] of his political life. With advancing years, Smuts's recollection of it became more vivid, though the Colonial Office files indicate that it had not quite the significance he attributed to it. But his instinct was sound. A man who has been defeated is apt to be a good judge of the political magnanimity that opens the way to recovery from defeat. There followed the day, 4 March 1907, on which Smuts was sworn in as a member of His Majesty's Government in the Transvaal. He wrote of it to Merriman:

One is apt to look upon an event such as this as a matter of course . . . but after all, viewed from a larger standpoint, it is really most remarkable. My mind went back to Vereeniging – separated from the present by only six brief years – and the determination to win finally which buoyed me up even there in that darkest hour of our history.[8]

And one step still further on in the upward climb, at the National Convention 1909, Patrick Duncan noted how

the fertile mind of Smuts busies itself in producing compromises on . . . contentious issues. He does not care much what he gives away as regards constitutional principles or power, and still less as regards material interests so long as he thinks the thing will go through in a form not too tightly tied up for him to pull it about afterwards as a member of a strong government with a docile Parliament. . .'[9]

Smuts was sanguine enough to believe that the contagion of magnanimity would spread. But in one respect he himself had ensured that it should not. The original draft of the relevant provisions of the Treaty of Vereeniging stated that the franchise would not be given to natives until after the introduction of self-government. It was Smuts, so Professor Hancock revealed, who re-wrote the article completely so that it read: 'The question of granting the franchise to natives will not be decided until after the introduction of self-government'.[10] For the clear implication that the natives at a later date would enjoy the franchise, there was thereby substituted a franchise at the discretion of those who had stated their unqualified objection to granting it. Here is, according to the point of view, a classic example of Smuts's skill as a draftsman or of his 'slimness'. Of course the final responsibility for accepting the amended draft rested with the British government. But Smuts got what he and his people wanted. In 1902, it can reasonably be argued, it was his duty, the more bounden upon him because he was a Transvaaler only by adoption, to salvage what he could from defeat. But the views he expressed in the formative period of union indicate that there was for him a frontier beyond which the contagion of magnanimity did not spread. The natives, he continued to think, were better out of politics and he helped through his subsequent long years of power to keep them in the position in which he had found them.

What mattered to Smuts was the reconciliation of Boer and Briton and the Union which symbolised its achievement. In the pursuit of the first, he moved far and fast – too far and too fast for the majority of his fellow Afrikaners. Even as early as the Convention, Patrick Duncan remarked upon the feeling that Botha and Smuts

> are losing the true national spirit, and have been contaminated by the Anglicising influence of the Transvaal. Botha's liking for bridge seriously disturbed some of them, especially since he was found playing one Sunday evening. It is one of those small things which strike the imagination of the staid Boer as a sign of a falling away from . . . the ideals of the people.[11]

In the deeper sense Smuts never 'fell away'. But at times he did become dangerously insensitive to some of the innermost aspirations of his own people. He neglected language, he was unwise, if even more unlucky, in his reaction to the 1914 rebellion and, preoccupied with Commonwealth and world affairs in London, he so lost touch with the source of his own being as to regret that he had not stood in 1918 as a candidate for the British House of Commons. Was the price of increasing absorption in the idea and the possibilities of Commonwealth to be detachment from his own Afrikaner people? That was a suspicion, and far more than a suspicion, on the part of many, who found no satisfaction in the spectacle of a Boer general finding fulfilment as a 'handy-man of Empire'.

The price of detachment, however, was something to be paid in the future. In the London of the concluding war years it may well have been a positive advantage. Smuts had a range of experience and of gifts to which few of his contemporaries could aspire. Professional soldiers, it is true, were apt to be critical of his strategy, professional philosophers to discourage his philosophising,[12] while politicians felt that in dealing with problems of intermediate range Smuts's judgment was not altogether reliable. Yet when so much has been said, his qualities, supported by an almost terrifying industry, remained. No one can read the concluding chapters of the first volume of Professor Hancock's biography, telling of Smuts's contribution to the creation of the Royal Air Force, to the transformation of Empire, to planning for a future international order and to thinking about war and peace, without enlarging his understanding of the history of those years, without sensing in Smuts the quality, albeit fallible, of greatness and without recognising how much even one man of vision and political stature might do to give meaning to the new idea of Commonwealth.

Behind the Commonwealth and international statesman, there remained the man conditioned by his experiences. During the Boer war Smuts knew enough to know that there was an England other than the country of Rhodes, Chamberlain and late nineteenth century imperialists. Even if it is hard to believe that intimations of John Bright played quite so large a part as Professor Hancock suggests, there was the importunate, impossible, meddlesome 'messenger sent from Heaven' when 'our race seemed doomed to extermination', Emily Hobhouse, who had first brought home to the British public and to Campbell-Bannerman the evils of the War Office concentration camps in the South African war. With her, with Quakers, anti-imperialists and pacifists who worked and pleaded for South Africa in her hour of need – Smuts's association was lasting. Years later when he was a member of the war cabinet, his biographer tells us how Smuts spent his weekends, not with Lloyd George at Churt, nor with other political colleagues, but more congenially with those who mistrusted empire and detested war. Emily Hobhouse, seeing his name in big print in *The Times*, 'that mighty organ that emulates Divinity for it putteth down one and setteth up another', hoped that something of the old 'Oom Jannie' remained; enough to enjoy association with the 'pacifist and anti-imperialist I am prouder than ever to be'. It did. Friendships dating from the days of defeat were still cherished. Away from the citadels of power which so strongly attracted him, Smuts relaxed with those who scorned them. This may be held up as an example of 'slimness'; it might equally well be regarded as a healthy antidote to the corruption of power.

When Smuts's intellect and his emotion were harnessed, as they were in peacemaking, then the man in his full stature appeared. General Botha who in the eyes of Smuts and of many others bore with Campbell-Bannerman the stamp of magnanimity, wrote on his agenda papers after he had signed the Treaty of Versailles on 28 June 1919, 'Today I recall 31 May 1902 (Vereeniging).' For a year or more that thought had been constantly in Smuts's mind. In 1900–2 Milner had striven for total victory and unconditional surrender; in 1917–8 Smuts argued for limited objectives, early peace and above all magnanimity in victory. The spirit of magnanimity did not, however, pervade Versailles. His pleas rejected, Smuts resolved, in turmoil of heart and mind, not to sign the treaty. Yet in the end, a man without illusions, one sinner, as he said, with the rest, he signed.[13] It was loyalty to South Africa and to Louis Botha, whose faithful friend he was in calm and storm, that decided him; it may be at the expense of those larger claims of suffering humanity which he at least had the vision to comprehend. But rarely indeed, can a political decision have been more hardly reached. Smuts's whole attitude to peacemaking was ambivalent and it was his experience that made it so. He sat with the victors at Versailles but his heart was more often with the vanquished. He too, had been defeated.

For Smuts it was not only '*The Sanguine Years*' of the first volume of Professor Hancock's biography that had drawn to a close by 1919; it was also that his range of freedom was henceforward to be restricted. With Botha dead, Smuts became, and remained for the rest of his days, in office or out of it, imprisoned within the South African political system. From shipboard in July 1919, he wrote of feeling like Ulysses coming home at last and of wondering 'what will Ulysses do in his little Ithaca?'[14] Given Smuts's immediate past it was understandable speculation; given his national background it was no less understandable that his South African critics should denounce his known indulgence in such reflections. Either way not much harm would have been done had his Ithaca been little. But it was not, either in the obvious geographical sense, or – far more important – in deeper political reality. On the contrary it comprehended most of the problems that trouble the twentieth century and some of them in their most acute form. The returning Ulysses, superbly endowed by intellect and breadth of experience, lacked one of the qualities required to deal with them – the predisposition to give them, consistently and over the years, the priority they demanded.

In his earlier years Smuts had understood the full gravity of the long-term implications of the native question and had reflected that beside the ultimate realities of relations between black and white differences between Boer and Briton would appear superficial and prove transient. But throughout his political life, and never more conclusively than in the Fusion ministry of the 1930s he subordinated the first to the second. Anglo-Afrikaner co-operation remained, as at Union, his first priority. This may have been mistaken but it was a deliberate choice consistently adhered to. 'South Africa', he wrote in intensity of feeling on 6 September 1939, 'has a divided soul, but if we are faithful to the vision of forty years ago that soul will be one yet. Time is a causal factor and there has not yet been enough time'. The soul once more so deeply divided by war was a European soul. It was that division which he sought to heal and his attitude to the native question was conditioned by that overriding purpose. 'Let them develop', remained his philosophy of race relations – if it may be so described – and only in his last years of office, did he come to sense that they were developing far and fast. 'Colour queers my poor pitch everywhere', he complained in November 1946.[15] By then it was true. In part he was paying the price of easy acquiescence in compromise during the 1930s, but still more of political longevity. The order of priorities was changing and he was too old to change with it.

For his failures in insight and comprehension in respect of colour Smuts has been forgiven neither by white racial supremacists nor by liberal humanitarians nor yet by the leaders of a new Africa. 'It has always seemed to me a pity', wrote Chief Luthuli, 'that a man as gifted as Smuts should have gone into eclipse, not because of adherence to any principle, but because of obtuseness. Yet, since he did not at home ever stand on principle, perhaps that was just'. And Chief Luthuli, thence proceeded to the crushing judgment: 'It did not seem to us of much importance whether the whites gave us more [in 1948] of Smuts or switched to Malan'.[16]

Smuts' reputation as a statesman was also served indifferently by his frequent commentaries on world affairs. His experiences at Versailles conditioned his thinking and accounted for many of his insights as well as his fallibility as a guide in the inter-war years. It had not been a magnanimous peace; in his view it should have been. The difference accounted for much; but not quite so much as Smuts supposed between 1935 and 1938. As a result the pronouncements on European affairs which he felt called upon to make and which he made without being shown the secret information from London which was sent to General Hertzog as a dominion prime minister, were apt to reflect surprisingly many of the misconceptions of the times. He could also be memorably mistaken as when in 1943, outlining a possible future Western European Commonwealth association, he spoke of France as having gone as a Great Power and continued, 'We may talk about her as a Great Power, but talking will not help her much. We are dealing with one of the greatest and most far-reaching catastrophes in history, the like of which I have not read of . . . France has gone and will be gone in our day, and perhaps for many a day'.[17] These were words neither overlooked nor forgotten in later-day Paris!

Whatever Smuts' misconceptions about Europe he responded heroically to the challenge of a second German war. Largely by force of his own personality and conviction he brought South Africa in on the allied side in September 1939. Few will be disposed to quarrel with his biographer's assessment of the significance of his action at that time or of the consequences which flowed from it. From 1939 to 1943, notes Professor Hancock, Smuts' achievement was immense.

If Hitler's image was not to be stamped upon this planet his country was geopolitically necessary and he was politically necessary. The Cape of Good Hope lived up to its name and assumed once again its historic primacy in oceanic strategy. Without the Cape route, the Commonwealth could hardly have survived the war; without the Commonwealth, the Russians and Americans could hardly have won it. But the victory in Africa changed all that. Henceforward the Mediterranean was open again and the Cape route, although still useful, was no longer indispensable.

It was the irony of fate that Smuts and his country should find themselves so much diminished by victories they had done so much to win.[18]

There was a deeper irony in store. If South Africa dissociated herself from her friends in the British Commonwealth, Smuts had argued in September 1939, the day would come when she would find herself isolated in a dangerous world. She did not dissociate herself but the day none the less came when she found herself isolated. But by then Smuts's world was in ruins.

Not only in Africa, but throughout the Commonwealth, that sequel, coupled with recollections of Smuts' own passivity in matters of racial policy, shadowed his later reputation. Yet however large race relations may loom in the mind of a succeeding generation they should not be allowed to obscure foresight or achievements in other fields, at least as immediate in their importance and as challenging in their nature, in earlier times. Union itself, a memorable part in two world wars, an unrivalled perception of the principles that determined the transformation of Empire into Commonwealth – these were things in their own day of counterbalancing weight. In the perspective of history, after all, it was not colour but war, peace and their consequences that dominated the years of Smuts' political maturity from 1897 down to 1945 and what the times immediately demanded Smuts supremely gave. It may be that he owed more than is commonly allowed to others, before and during the first world war to Botha, a man of wiser counsel though not of comparable intellectual attainments and during the second world war to J. H. Hofmeyr, the 'boy prodigy' of earlier years, who assumed responsibility for three or more departments of state as well as serving as deputy prime minister while Smuts played his part on a wider stage and with whom Smuts' relationship remained strangely tentative and by no means uniformly to his credit.[19] Yet the crowds that acclaimed Smuts in Johannesburg on triumphal tour when the second world war had finally ended with the surrender of Japan were not mistaken in their tremendous tribute to one who at decisive moments throughout a long life had shown supreme gifts of leadership.

Down the years, at least until 1945, Smuts's faith in the Commonwealth was not diminished but enhanced. For him it was the continuing basis of Anglo-Afrikaner reconciliation at home and the chief hope of peace abroad. 'I am a firm believer', he wrote in January 1940, 'in the Commonwealth, not only for its own sake and that of South Africa, but as the first tentative beginnings of great things for the future of the World'. The source of that faith, embellished though it was by philosophy, may be traced to his experience. And in that experience there were two decisive events – defeat and reconciliation. The second had reality because of the first, and it was the man who had been defeated who sensed more truly than any of his contemporaries the meaning with which the phrase, 'Commonwealth of Nations' might be invested and the beckoning vision which it might offer of equal brotherhood of those who had ruled with those who had been ruled. De Valera recalled many years later, that if any man could have convinced him of the advantages of dominion status for Ireland, it was Smuts, who on a secret visit to Dublin on 5 July 1921, under the improbable pseudonym of Mr Smith, expounded its characteristics with a force and logic beside which Lloyd George's later explanations appeared shallow and counterfeit.[20] Smuts, the man who in his younger days had written of 'a century of wrong', who deemed that he had himself experienced its climax, late in life spoke in clipped part-foreign accent to the people who had perpetrated the 'wrong', as partners in friendly and equal association with his own in a Commonwealth of Nations, which he thought of even in the darkest days of the second world war as the proudest political monument of time. Whether inspired or mistaken, it was a judgment few men were better qualified by their own experiences to make.

W. L. Mackenzie King: Prime Ministers' Prime Minister.

As Edmund Spenser is traditionally spoken of as the poets' poet and Gustave Flaubert often thought of as the writers' writer, so Mackenzie King may be thought of as the prime ministers' prime minister. In each instance the appeal is less to the public than to the professional – be he poet, writer, or politician. What is common is a mastery of technique of a kind likely to be appreciated, in all its refinements, only by those who practise the self-same art. William Lyon Mackenzie King was not a man of profound intellect, he possessed power without popularity, he abhorred the spectacular, he had an intriguing but not a commanding personality, and there would be little reason for him to be remembered were it not for his supreme mastery of the techniques of politics.

Memoirs and biographies, especially of nineteenth-century English statesmen, were Mackenzie King's favourite reading. No doubt he perused them, as he did most things, more for the possible political profit than for the pleasure to be derived therefrom, but whatever the motive the fact renders the more fitting the biographical monument on a more than Victorian scale (even if somewhat lacking in the reticences then conventional) that is being fashioned in six volumes (including two based on the diary entries of his later years) and by several hands to preserve the memory of his doings.[21] The subtitle of the second volume of the biography, 'The Lonely Heights', has an overall appropriateness – so long as it does not elicit misplaced sympathy for the subject of it. King was single-minded in his resolve to reach and to stay on the heights, and he liked being alone. Even when his closest friends left his country home at Kingsmere after the briefest of sojourns, his diary usually recorded his satisfaction at being alone once more, free to walk the fields with his dog at his side. Whether he was solitary because he was single-minded or single-minded because he was solitary may remain a matter for speculation. But that he was single-minded in the pursuit and the exercise of power is not to be doubted. This indeed was the abiding source of strength for one who lacked, as he was himself well aware, many of the superficial gifts of leadership.

Mackenzie King's attention to detail – that hallmark of the professional in all human activities – became proverbial. He always wished to have things, and above all, words, exactly right. He delivered few speeches without complaining afterwards that there had not been enough time for their preparation. He was almost boyishly pleased when a speech went well and there were no limits to his satisfaction when words of his succeeded in discomforting his Tory opponents. Late in life, with the example of Roosevelt and Churchill before him, he was encouraged to speak more often impromptu, and the later pages of *The Record* contain many expressions of regret that he had not done so more frequently in earlier years. Yet if in this he had missed opportunities he had also avoided risks. In the long run his care in the choice of words repaid him well. Those anxious and exacting days of preparation, for his secretaries as well as for himself, represented not wasted time but time spent in the consolidation of his political position. He also derived from them a heightened awareness of the meaning of words and the implication of phrases, and he was from time to time able to use this with devastating effect against careless or ill-considered assertions by political opponents. It also enabled him at Imperial or Commonwealth Meetings to seize upon small but significant points of drafting, the implications of which might otherwise have been overlooked. Such unremitting attention to detail was not only part of the man but an important factor in his political survival.

Mackenzie King, writes Dr Neatby, 'was no crusader, eager to ride a white charger to oblivion'. This was certainly true. But while lacking a self-sacrificing sense of dedication, Mackenzie King had a cause. That cause, to which he sacrificed both friends and principles when he deemed occasion demanded it, was the unity of Canada. No other leader, and no party other than the Liberal, the only truly national party as he thought of it, was really equipped to serve that cause. But a condition of such service both for himself and the Liberal party was the consistent maintenance of a moderate, central, national position on all issues. In all the difficult situations which politics present, so King argued, 'there must be a point somewhere at which a proper balancing can be effected'. With fixity of purpose, he sought for it. The very phrase – a proper balancing – epitomised the temper of his approach to politics. And this appreciation of the importance of balance made him correspondingly mistrustful of extremes. 'The extreme man', he once observed to a friend, 'is always more or less dangerous, but nowhere more so than in politics. In a country like ours it is particularly true that the art of government is largely one of seeking to reconcile rather than to exaggerate differences – to come as near as may be possible to the happy mean'. This was because the difficulty, as King observed on another occasion, 'of maintaining unity in Canada is very great indeed'.[22]

Mackenzie King approached imperial-commonwealth relations from the standpoint of his abiding preoccupation with national unity significantly reinforced by a temperamental mistrust of imperialists and their manifold machinations. Where Empire would certainly divide, Commonwealth would equally certainly help to unite Canada. He wished, therefore, to dispose of the remnants of centralised Empire and to substitute for them only such links as were consistent with decentralised Commonwealth. But while he saw his goal with something of the deceptive clarity of the single-minded, the successive British administrations with which King had to deal, appeared to him to be confused about Commonwealth goals and in the 1920s double-minded in many of their ways. The chilling indignation with which he damped Lloyd George's imperial impetuosity at Chanak is a matter of history, while as for Ramsay MacDonald, King's only doubt (and one evidently shared by his biographer) was whether Britain's first Labour prime minister was stupid, or untrustworthy, or both. Mackenzie King accordingly, with 'wary vigilance and stubborn insistence at every turn' persisted in his attempts to bring enlightenment about the nature of dominion status and to defeat the stratagems of the outdated and recalcitrant in Downing Street. 'Bourbons', his biographer calls them, and comments with appreciation on how 'amazingly patient' the Canadian prime minister was in trying to get them to understand, amid the intricacies of conference representation and treaty-making, the essentials of dominion autonomy. But Ramsay MacDonald, it is clear, remained either uncomprehending or resolute in his refusal to comprehend. 'On the basic concept of future Empire relations', concludes Dr Neatby bluntly of these years 'Mackenzie King was right and Downing Street was wrong'.[23] If by this is meant that Mackenzie King had correctly diagnosed the forces at work and foreseen the outcome for Commonwealth relations in, so to speak, the middle distance, the judgment seems warranted.

In terms of political and personal drama, the refinements of Commonwealth were overshadowed in King's early years of office by the controversies and confrontations of domestic politics carrying overtones of Empire. Of none was this more true than of the tangled, triangular relationship of King, Meighen, Byng, which bore so closely upon Canadian attitudes at the 1926 Imperial Conference. While Dr Neatby does not share King's own belief that the constitutional issue decided the general election of 1926, called, it will be remembered, when the governor-general conceded to Meighen the dissolution he had refused to King – considering rather that it was the fervour of King's convictions that won him votes[24] – he is clear that because this opinion came to be generally accepted, electoral victory also gained for King an enviable reputation for political infallibility. That reputation, by reason of the imperial issues involved, extended beyond Canada. It was not altogether unmerited. In the fluctuations of fortune, which make the King-Byng incident at once remarkable and memorable, King, it is true, had luck – but also a reliability of judgment and a grasp of essentials to which Meighen, a rival whose debating qualities he feared, could not pretend. But equally it was not an episode calculated to win esteem for King, for all the political expertise he displayed. Indeed the strongest feeling may be one of sympathy for Lord Byng, the soldier, who was misled at the outset by notions of fair play altogether alien to politics; who showed more foresight than is often allowed; who perhaps unwisely but not unpardonably excused himself from studying the constitutional works of Berriedale Keith and Kenneth Pickthorn, which Mackenzie King had thoughtfully brought along to Government House, on the ground 'that the situation was different to anything that had arisen at any time' and who, despite a telegram of birthday greetings from Mackenzie King during the election campaign (the dispatch of which was duly recorded in King's diary with expressions of self-congratulation upon his observation of the constitutional proprieties even at a time of tension) did not respond, as King later had occasion to note without gratification, with a card for Christmas 1926. No doubt the time had come when the soldier felt, 'enough is enough.'

Mackenzie King came to the Imperial Conference 1926 with his decisive constitutional victory already won. He was by reason of this the better placed to adopt the mediatory rôle that was most congenial to him. Vincent Massey later wrote of King as having made 'the greatest contribution towards conciliation' at the Conference and recalls Amery's speaking of him as 'the great constructive figure among the dominion statesmen' there. But all that emerges conclusively is that Mackenzie King, well grounded in the implications of the root principle of equality as the touchstone of future Commonwealth relations, was unusually well placed to help to find a balance. If, further, it be accepted that as his biographer suggests Mackenzie King was the only prime minister who believed that the Commonwealth had been strengthened by the Conference,[25] that is illustrative first of a more positive faith in the idea than is customarily attributed to him and secondly of his belief that Canadian national unity would be strengthened by Canada's free and equal association within the reconstituted Commonwealth.

The pinnacle of Mackenzie King's political good fortune was attained when he was defeated in the general election 1930, and in consequence out of office during the years of the Great Depression. He was inexperienced as an opposition leader and more than usually anxious about the responsibilities thrust upon him, but characteristically he never weakened in his resolve to regain power. On one of the three occasions on which he spoke in the House for more than four hours his purpose was to place on record all the promises that R. B. Bennett had made during the election campaign. Taking the long view this was a telling tactic, but only a leader subordinating all else to considerations of power would have ventured to inflict upon the House the colossal tedium of this confessedly formless compilation. Later his speech on the budget, again of more than four hours and without any planned ending, came to a stop only when Bennett laughed at an ill-judged moment and King, commenting 'The prime minister laughs', sat down to the enthusiastic applause of his followers.[26] He allowed himself to think the acclaim was tribute to the effectiveness of his improvised conclusion; but with due respect to the known resilience of Canadian parliamentarians it may equally well have been prompted by relief that the speech, like Swinburne's river, had found its way somewhere safe to sea. But King was not out of office in the 1930s and his support for the policy of appeasement (already related) remains, less fortunately for him, a part of Commonwealth history. Unlike others, he never saw reason to repent of it. And there was his visit to Hitler in 1937 at which the German chancellor impressed him as a man of deep sincerity and a genuine patriot, who despite some observations of expansionist purport about eastern Europe, was not contemplating war against France or Britain. It is clear, and it remains surprising, that Mackenzie King was not so much deceived – there is no evidence that Hitler was planning a war against the west in 1937 – as duped.[27] But it is not clear that this had significant political consequences – essentially it was the situation in Canada, not the situation in Europe that determined his approach.

Mackenzie King was superficially as ill-equipped for survival as a wartime prime minister as Asquith or Neville Chamberlain. But, unlike them, he survived. How he did so may be studied in *The Mackenzie King Record*[28] based on extracts from the diary which he had kept since boyhood. It is an illuminating if not always an inspiring story. In war as in peace Mackenzie King's conception of leadership was not, it need hardly be said, in the romantic Churchillian tradition. Far from it. 'I really believe', he wrote on 26 September 1940, 'my greatest service is in many unwise steps I prevent'.[29] A leader, he explained later to the leader of the Progressive Conservative party, could guide 'so long as he kept to the right lines. I did not think it was a mark of leadership to try to make the people do what one wanted them to do . . .'.[30] He regarded himself essentially as the representative of the people of Canada. His power derived from them and he believed that 'the people had a true instinct in most matters of government when left alone'. They were not swayed, as especially favoured individuals were apt to be, by personal interest but rather 'by a sense of what best served the common good'. When in August 1941 Beaverbrook asked him in London how he gauged public opinion so accurately, Mackenzie King replied that he did the thing he thought was right and held to 'a responsible self-government and the supremacy of Parliament in everything'. The people, he continued, understood common sense; they believed 'in one's integrity to one's word'. He attributed his success to these things; above all to the fact that he had been close to the people as a source of government.

Mackenzie King was at once affronted and dismayed by criticism of his wartime leadership. He was disposed to regard it, and for most of the period not wholly without cause, as criticism of a professional in the art of government by amateurs. He was also, in the manner of English Conservatives, in times of crisis apt to conclude that such criticism was in essence 'factious'. It was something that he, like Laurier before him, was called upon to suffer – in political extremity he was deplorably disposed to make allusion to the Garden of Gethsemane – and rarely indeed did he attribute creditable motives to those who assailed him. Under stress of war also the Gladstonian overtones in many of his utterances became more pronounced. He had the same sense of Providence guiding his actions and (as critics of both would allege) the same capacity for deceiving himself and others with high-sounding moral platitudes. King felt proud that he had declared in Parliament that the Bible was the foundation of his beliefs, and he always hoped 'that the day might come when, in the Canadian Parliament, I might stand for the kind of thing that Gladstone stood for in the public life of England in the matter of political action being based on religious convictions and the latter known and boldly stated'. These convictions sustained him in the responsibilities of wartime office but they blunted neither the resolution with which he acted nor the ruthlessness of his actions when he deemed that the interests of his party or his country – and he did not always distinguish very carefully between the two – demanded it. In 1940, in an election which he had timed with his customary sureness of political instinct, he noted of his own final national broadcast that he was 'particularly happy about its references to the tone of public life', and after the sweeping Liberal victory he felt that his own name and that of Lapointe would be linked together in the history of the country as 'a not uncertain example to those who may follow us in the administration of its public affairs'.[31]

While Mackenzie King's emphasis on precept and example was wholly Gladstonian, his dislike of crusading was not. There is no Midlothian campaign by which he will be remembered; he weighed the consequences too nicely ever to champion uncertain, far away causes. Had he been confronted with Turkish massacres in Bulgaria, he might possibly have felt – to judge by some of his comments on the dress of the Moderator of the General Assembly whom he heard preach during his stay in Balmoral in August 1941 – as did some Free Churchmen of the time, a rather lukewarm sympathy for the idolatrous 'Wafer Worshippers' of the Orthodox Church who were being massacred. But this should not obscure the fact that Mackenzie King, despite his un-Gladstonian repudiation of the spectacular in word or deed, had at the very fibre of his being a Gladstonian feel for 'the politics of virtuous passion'.[32] The 'virtuous passion' which he felt was not for massacred Bulgarians and against the unspeakable Turk; it was for Canada and against imperialism. If there was no campaign it was because the imperialists, unlike the Turks, gave no occasion for one. But no one could doubt that the smouldering fires of self-righteous passion were there. As late as 1944, Lord Halifax, by talking in his innocence in Toronto of a post-war common foreign policy fanned them into flame.

Mackenzie King's instinctive fear of imperialist machinations was, if anything, heightened under stress of war. Asquith once remarked of John Bright: 'There is the only man in public life who has risen to eminence without being corrupted by London society.' King to the last accepted the implication of that comment. Society was corrupting, London society peculiarly so, and worst of all by subtle influences likely to wean Canadians from the loyalty they owed to Canada first and all the time. 'It required a lot of courage, if I say it myself, to hold firmly to the line I felt would be right, and not be influenced by . . . hospitality.'[33] So he wrote one evening in London during the Commonwealth Prime Ministers' Meeting in the Spring of 1944 when his prestige in Canada and in the Commonwealth was at its zenith.

> The more I think [he wrote a few days later][34] of the high pressure methods that have been used, the more indignant I feel. It makes me tremble to think of what Canada might be let in for if a different type of person were in office. Where would we have been had Bennett been in office at this time? What annoys me is the social devices and other attentions paid with a view to getting some things done, to influence one's mind even against one's better judgment. I think I have gone through this battle without wavering.

His fears were not groundless but it is astonishing that they should be so vividly entertained at this time. His friendship with Churchill was firmly established and his views on the future of the Commonwealth had been accepted. History, more particularly family history, is usually taken to account for them. Certainly memories of his rebel maternal grandfather were easily stirred to life. But at root lay his belief that as eternal vigilance was the price of continuing power, so uncompromising restatement was the condition of successful achievement of aims. In this he was not mistaken.

Mackenzie King's dislike of centralised empire was matched by his increased attachment, even occasional enthusiasm for the idea of Commonwealth. Both were derivative. At the heart lay Canada. It was his country's interests and her place in the society of states that moved him. 'My first duty is to Canada.' That was something he rarely forgot. He had hard words for those who were seemingly prepared to sacrifice Canada to the interests of crown or empire or of North American solidarity. 'My view', he wrote in 1941, 'is that the only real position for Canada to take is that of a nation wholly on her own vis-à-vis both Britain and the United States'. Only by taking such a line would Canada secure recognition of her national identity.[35] It was because Commonwealth membership with full equality of status furthered this aim that he valued Commonwealth membership. He referred in December 1942 to

> the efforts that would be made by the Americans to control developments in our country after the war, and to bring Canada out of the orbit of the British Commonwealth of Nations into their own orbit. I am strongly opposed to anything of the kind. I want to see Canada continue to develop as a nation to be, in time, as our country certainly will, the greatest of nations of the British Commonwealth.[36]

Mackenzie King's conception of Canadian interests, coupled with his belief in parliamentary government determined – one might say predetermined – his attitude towards Commonwealth wartime developments. There is an account in *The Record* of how Mackenzie King first came to fashion the telling phrase 'a continuing conference of cabinets' and of how much thought generally he devoted to the question of reconciling full parliamentary responsibility with some effective means of Commonwealth co-operation. He appears to have at least partially convinced Menzies of the impracticability of an imperial war cabinet in 1941, and the enunciation of his objections to its reconstitution and his reaffirmation of faith in existing methods of consultation on his first wartime visit to London elicited a personal message of warm-hearted agreement from General Smuts.[37] In Commonwealth affairs he remained concerned with the meaning of words. In 1944, he asked first Cranborne and later Churchill the meaning of the then fashionable phrase 'Empire and Commonwealth', and he got very different answers! He was careful to ensure that not the singular 'policy' but the plural 'policies' should appear in communiqués. He elaborated on the distinction between a prime ministers' meeting and an Imperial Conference to Churchill and other members of the war cabinet, who (perhaps not altogether surprisingly) found some difficulty in grasping all the niceties of the distinction by which King set such store. With characteristic attention to detail and by a constant reiteration of the main lines of his thought Mackenzie King exercised the decisive influence on the Commonwealth of the later war and early post-war years. This is an impressive tribute to the cumulative effect of his carefully assembled arguments in an international context when one recalls that Churchill, Smuts and Curtin were among those with whom he had to deal.

Mackenzie King's Commonwealth contribution reflected, however, the weakness as well as the strength of his professional approach. His industry, his power of political penetration, his appreciation of Canada's long-term Commonwealth interests – all were there. But good judgment cannot dispense with the need for popular appeal. Mackenzie King thought in terms of government, but if the refashioned Commonwealth was to play the part that he hoped then it would have to appeal also to peoples. Here his distaste for the spectacular stood in the way of comprehension. He failed to understand, as Churchill and Roosevelt both understood so well, the need for a dramatic element in democratic leadership, especially in wartime. A message was received from Churchill through the British high commissioner, Malcolm MacDonald, on 6 August 1941, expressing the hope that Mackenzie King would approve of Churchill's Atlantic Meeting with President Roosevelt. But Mackenzie King did not approve. He wrote in his diary that evening:

> I feel that it is taking a gambler's risk, with large stakes, appalling losses, even to that of an Empire, should some disaster overtake the gamble. To me, it is the apotheosis of the craze for publicity and show. At the bottom, it is a matter of vanity. There is no need for any meeting of the kind. Everything essential can be done even better by cable communications, supplemented by conferences between officials themselves. Neither the prime minister of Britain nor the president of the United States should leave their respective countries at this time.[38]

He was wrong. It was a meeting that gave hope to beleaguered Britain and encouragement to defeated but not subdued European peoples. With better reason, but on the same grounds, he dismissed all idea of an early wartime Imperial Conference. The unobtrusive, businesslike behind-the-scenes approach he judged right for others irrespective of occasion he practised himself. With quiet persistence he pressed for recognition of Canada's part in the war but he refrained, even when he felt that the occasion might demand it, from all dramatic protest.

Within two weeks of the American entry into the war, he told a cabinet meeting in Ottawa of the problems that were likely to arise. He pointed out that

it might be necessary for Canada to realise Churchill's difficulties in not showing preference as between dominions. Also in making allowances for a certain aggressiveness on the part of America and her probable effort at a monopoly of control. Also a certain forgetfulness on the part of Britain and the United States combined of Canada's part in the struggle.[39]

This showed astonishing foresight. Here, in these few sentences, are the dominant themes of Professor Trotter and C. C. Lingard's volume covering the years 1941–4 in the *Canada in World Affairs* series.[40] As the editor (J. W. Pickersgill) of *The Record*, pointed out, Mackenzie King was to complain of all the things that he had foreseen before the war was over. Vehement public protest on some well-chosen issue might well have been more effective than the series of pained reproaches privately communicated now to Whitehall and now to Washington. But it was not in character. Nor was it in accord with the chief aim of his wartime policy, the bringing together of Britain and the United States in a great alliance of the English-speaking peoples. Part of the price he paid was popular underestimate of his very considerable achievement and part popular misconception of his aims.

Mackenzie King found a continuing and human satisfaction in reflections on the changes which time had brought in Empire and Commonwealth, and he was apt to moralise about them. When the governor-general, the Earl of Athlone with his wife, Princess Alice, stayed in the farmhouse at Kingsmere for the period of the first wartime Conference in Quebec, King reflected:

Little could my grandfather have seen when he was in prison and in exile, or my father and mother when they were making their sacrifices for the children's education, that some day one of their name would be entertaining the president of the United States and the prime minister of Britain at the Citadel of Quebec (where my father's father's remains lie) at a time of world war, and that, in the same week, the granddaughter of Queen Victoria would be finding her moment of rest and quiet and peace in the home of one of their own.[41]

However the moment there was a suggestion that the governor-general might be given a more prominent place than Canada's prime minister on this international occasion, the realist came brusquely into his own again.

With the progressive publication of biographical volumes and especially of *The Record*, Mackenzie King became a more knowable Canadian. He was, like the superstitious John Aubrey some three centuries earlier, 'a little inclinable to credit strange relations'. He indulged in North American neo-Gothic fantasies by assembling ruins at Kingsmere. Much importance is likely to continue to be attributed to his eccentricities since the New World expects greater conformity among its public figures than the Old. But it is not as a perplexing personality but as a professional of outstanding quality in the art of politics that Mackenzie King will be remembered in Canada and in the Commonwealth. He was a wholetime and a calculating politician. Perhaps he was something more. He may even, in time, come to be accepted as one of those rare beings – a statesman masquerading as a politician. In years when Canadian unity was not threatened and the western world was not engulfed in war his qualities of judgment and restraint came to be discounted, just as the merits of Attlee's matter-of-fact administration of affairs were more widely appreciated in Britain after indulgence in a spectacular Suez adventure. But whatever the changes in reputation that time may bring to Mackenzie King, the carefully recorded reflections and actions of a prime minister's prime minister will surely continue to be read and pondered by all whose eyes are drawn by interest or ambition to Parliament Hill in Ottawa. And so long as there remains a Commonwealth of Nations, predominantly parliamentary in their form of government, recollections of this prickly, prudent, unspectacular and solitary man will remain to guide, to counsel and to warn.

Jawaharlal Nehru: The Spokesman of Liberal-Internationalism.

'He could hardly at this time be described as a politician at all. He was a revolutionary. Whenever there appeared some tenuous hope of settlement, he was always at hand to urge extreme courses, and his efforts were reinforced by a beautiful appearance and a glowing eloquence.' . . . 'He was at this time an agitator who thrived on tumultuous meetings where motions subversive of British rule were passed amid wild excitement. He was one of the foremost agents of the new "propaganda of war" which, indifferent to truth, organised hatred with ice-cold logic.'[42] The period was the later 1920s; the man Jawaharlal Nehru, most gifted son of a distinguished father; the writer, Lord Birkenhead in his biography of Lord Halifax, who as Lord Irwin had served as viceroy, looking forward with well-intentioned, liberal-imperial gaze to a dominion status for India which would concede autonomy within the British Empire, but not the complete independence which the younger Nehru demanded. With the passage of time and the evolution of Commonwealth the distinction wore thin, but even a generation later Englishmen of conservative temper found it hard to efface earlier impressions of the handsome young Indian with his English schooling and his imperial friends[43], who left his affluent home in Allahabad to challenge the British Raj with weapons forged in the armoury of English liberal thought and sharpened with an edge of Marxist dialectic. To Smuts, who had fought against the British, all might be forgiven and more than forgiven, but against Nehru, even when an elder statesman of the Commonwealth, much was remembered. Both were intellectuals, both graduates of Cambridge, the one in Law, the other in Natural Sciences, both were at once nationalist and internationalist, both were leaders, as Mackenzie King so emphatically was not, of charismatic appeal. But where Smuts – and herein perhaps from the point of view of continuing British sensitivities lay the crucial difference – was a traditionalist in social as in racial policies, Nehru was at once a national and a social revolutionary, deeply influenced by Marxism though certainly in later life highly critical of its rigid conceptual framework and hostile to its dialectical certitudes. This difference was reflected in practical affairs. Where Smuts devoted his gifts to immediate and definable purposes – the winning of war, the refashioning of Commonwealth, the creation of a new world order – Nehru, in pursuit of aims that might appear equally commendable, advocated means and employed arguments which were in many cases not only revolutionary in much of the thought that lay behind them but abstract in their conception or presentation. Non-alignment, the Panch Shila or Five Principles, areas of 'no-war', coupled with pained rebuke and admonition to those who sought security in alliances and built up strength against possible aggression – all these were attitudes or policies or, and perhaps most of all, language which many in Britain found it hard to stomach. In the past it had been the British who had lectured others on the folly of their ways – they found it in consequence doubly difficult to bear with equanimity the admonitions of another couched in intellectual-moral terms. They noted inconsistencies, or detected them where none existed. They were apt to associate and to confuse Nehru's with Gandhi's views on non-violence, and having done so, to point an accusing finger at Nehru's policy in Kashmir or Indian absorption of Goa by the use or threat of force. Nehru's immediate and unqualified condemnation of the Suez adventure, coupled with delayed and qualified denunciation of Russia's rigorous suppression of the contemporary Hungarian revolt – in itself an error of judgment, indicating a political imbalance deriving from over-sensitivity to the type of imperialism against which he had struggled and insufficient sensitivity to manifestations of one with which he was unfamilar – rankled, in many minds besides that of Sir Anthony Eden. On many occasions Pandit Nehru gave hostages to political fortune by his practice of relating international affairs to first principles and expressing his opinion on how they ought to be conducted. To conservative pragmatists the first was an irrelevance and the second, when actions of theirs had fallen short of the prescribed standard hard to forgive.

Many of the things that made Jawaharlal Nehru suspect to the right served to enhance his standing with liberal-internationalists of the left. Over Smuts there hung the shadow of native policy (or lack of one), and while liberals and nationalists alike welcomed Smuts' insistence upon a Commonwealth decentralised to the limit, he remained for them an enigmatic figure, enlightened in his concepts of a world order, but the protagonist of a white sub-imperialism in Africa; too preoccupied with preserving intact the domestic jurisdiction of national states to be the authentic herald of a new international society concerned to uphold and to advance human rights; over-much occupied with power politics to give sufficient attention to the claims of the weak or the downtrodden. In Nehru they found their ideal. Eloquent and sensitive, he possessed at once personal magnetism and the gift of effortless leadership. His credentials as an opponent not only of imperialism, but in the 1930s of Nazism, Fascism and Japanese militarism, were impeccable. On his European travels he had scorned the advances of Mussolini, sensed the deeper significance of the civil war in Spain, looked down with critical regard from the Gallery of the House of Commons upon Neville Chamberlain speaking in the dramatic debate which preceded his flight to Munich and felt that there was a man in whose countenance there seemed to be 'no nobility', who looked 'too much like a business man', who was very evidently 'not a man of destiny but a man of the earth, earthy'.[44] He had warned his contemporaries, in the language of a Churchillian internationalist, of the awful consequences of the rise of militarism in Europe and Asia, and he recalled, when on trial for sedition at Gorakhpur in 1940, that there were few Englishmen who had denounced Fascism or Nazism with the same consistency and outspokenness as he had done. Having seen 'with pain and anguish how country after country was betrayed in the name of this appeasement and how the lamps of liberty were being put out', had he not the more reason for resentment that 'the hundreds of millions of India' should be thrust in 1939 'without any reference to them or their representatives into a mighty war' fought 'in the name of freedom and self-determination'?[45] When eight years later the hour came for him, as prime minister of an independent India, to tread the stage of history he showed his ability, as was noted at the time, to rise to great responsibilities. 'He has developed', wrote Rajagopalachari to Sapru in April 1948, 'in a most remarkable way. . . . You must have seen this about Jawaharlalji with natural pleasure and gratification'.[46] While Nehru always lacked capacity for sustained and purposeful administration, few could match his sense of style or occasion. From the midnight hour on 14–15 August 1947, when the Congress kept 'its tryst with destiny', to that memorably moving broadcast six months later on 30 January 1948 which told India and the world of Gandhi's assassination – 'the light is gone out of our lives, and there is darkness everywhere' for 'our beloved leader, Bapu, as we called him, the Father of the Nation, is no more'; from crowded demonstrations in the capitals of Asia, from Prime Ministers' Meetings in London, at which his attendance was unfailing, to the dramatic symbolism of Delhi's Republic Day celebrations on 26 January each year, to the receptions of potentates and presidents, prime ministers and revolutionary leaders from all over the world, at dusk in the Red Fort where, presiding over the ceremony, immaculate in Gandhi cap and white achkan, with a red carnation in his buttonhole, he rarely failed to leave upon his hearers the impress of his personality and his pervasive sense of the movement of history.

Jawaharlal Nehru was a fluent speaker and prolific writer, with autobiographical fragments in almost every work. The breadth of his appeal lay in his ability to reflect the aspirations of his time, as much as of his own people and to speak in their own terms, both to the villagers of India in their millions and to the new political élites of the cities. He was enabled to do so because he spoke quietly and directly, a microphone always with him, in a personal way – as though he were among close friends, obviously happy to communicate his thoughts to them – and also because, as has been truly said, both as a man and in his style of speaking he 'transcended sophistication with a certain natural simplicity'.[47] Secularist and humanist, Nehru was the spokesman of a liberal-reformist approach at once to the divisions of community and caste at home, and to questions of peace and war abroad. He never wavered in his faith in the parliamentary process in India and, deploring the long-range abusive, propagandist dialectic of the Great Powers in the Cold War, urged quiet discussion in conference even of the most intractable issues. There was a transcendent quality in his appeal to the intellectuals, to the sometimes self-consciously enlightened, to younger generations weighed down by the menace of nuclear annihilation and finding neither psychological satisfaction nor congenial refuge in the alliances of the cold war years. The new, more sanguine, more meaningful, more idealistic and, be it added, simpler approach to the complexities of international relations which they looked for, they found, as nowhere else, in the utterances of India's prime minister. The aristocratic, westernised high-caste Kashmiri Brahmin thus became the mouthpiece of the new, classless societies of the mid-twentieth century. He hated war, and denounced the armaments and alliances he believed would lead once more to it; he was outraged by the pretensions of racialists whether in Asia or in Africa; he was the sworn and proven enemy of imperialism; he was the angry champion of the underprivileged, and most of all he desired to harness the twentieth-century technological revolution to the service of the overpopulated and undernourished areas of the former colonial world. If Jawaharlal Nehru loomed so large in the world and the Commonwealth of the 1950s that was because he expressed with vision, superb command of a language not his own, and rare gifts of leadership, so much of the aspirations of his time.

While Nehru's appeal was world-wide, his heart came to beat with the continent and the people to whom he belonged. There was, it is true, an earlier time when with his westernised education he felt that he had 'become a queer mixture of the east and west, out of place everywhere, at home nowhere . . . I am a stranger and alien in the west. I cannot be of it. But in my own country also, sometimes, I have an exile's feeling'.[48] But in maturity, and under Gandhi's influence, his roots struck deep in his native land. Constantly, as prime minister of India, he returned to the theme of the awakening of Asia and of India after a long sleep; of the attention after long neglect the west must pay to Asian interests and Asian opinions; of the 'torment in the spirit of Asia', 'the tremendous ferment of change' in a continent whose growth had been arrested for some two centuries.[49] While there was much that dismayed or distressed him in this stormy resurrection of a continent, he did not doubt that with national freedom and the ending of the 'dire poverty' of so many of her people, Asia would become 'a powerful factor for stability and peace'. 'The philosophy of Asia', he said, 'has been and is the philosophy of peace'. 'India', he said at another time, 'may be new to world politics and her military strength insignificant in comparison with that of the giants of our epoch. But India is old in thought and experience and has travelled through trackless centuries in the adventure of life. Throughout her long history she had stood for peace and every prayer that an Indian raises, ends with an invocation to peace'.[50] The sceptics remained unconvinced, but for a time at least a Gandhian image was partially superimposed not merely upon a nation, but a continent. It was tarnished by Indian intransigence in Kashmir and Indian action in Goa, and destroyed by the Chinese attacks upon the Indian frontier. In each case Nehru's reputation was damaged, and these events must now be commented on.

The Maharajah of Kashmir acceded to India. The circumstances were debatable, but the Indian title rested upon the legality and the finality of that accession. Nehru, the liberal, offered a plebiscite. There was no obligation upon him to do so. Nehru, the Kashmiri and nationalist, found a succession of reasons, some convincing, others unconvincing, for ensuring that, in circumstances that had admittedly changed, the offer was not given effect. For his own reputation it would have been better had he rested his case throughout upon the signature by the Maharajah of an Instrument of Accession in the form approved by the India Independence Act 1947. But Nehru desired, over and above the sanction of law, the approval of the people of Kashmir. This, in a sense satisfying to world opinion, he did not secure. Likewise Nehru desired to gain possession of Goa by persuasion; in the end, confronted with Portuguese intransigence and under political pressure at home, he was persuaded to sanction force. To the nationalist in him the acquisition of Goa represented the fulfilment of the national movement for independence and, in this instance again, Nehru's nationalism proved stronger than his sense of an internationalism that conceived of change only by peaceful means. On his own nationalist argument, little weighed by critics in the west, his error may well have been in delaying so long. In the late 1940s the take-over by a newly independent India of the small Portuguese enclaves in the subcontinent might well have been accepted by the world at large as a further and inevitable step in the liquidation of western colonialism in Asia. But once decision was deferred to a point in time when the national movement had lost its initial momentum, and an air of stability had been recreated, the liquidation even of so minor an outpost of European colonialism by forceful means was received in the west not with resigned acquiescence but with a storm of protest. There remained the liberal image of a pacific Asia, to be brutally shattered by the Chinese invasions across the Indian border in October-November 1962. Many had forewarned Nehru, not least Acharya Kripalani in the Lok Sabha,[51] but lost in illusions of Sino-Indian friendship he had not taken their words to heart. It was, therefore, bitter disillusionment that drew from him the confession 'we were getting out of touch with reality in the modern world'.[52]

Therein was reflected the tragedy of more than a man, or even a country. It was the hopes of the new independent Asia that had been shattered.

Nehru reinterpreted the idea of Commonwealth to fit his own philosophy of international relations. The Commonwealth was an association of governments and peoples brought together by history which – and this to him was of first importance – gave to India, as to other Asian members of it, equal standing with members of European origin and afforded to Asian governments opportunities, not otherwise open to them in quite the same way, of influencing world politics, particularly in respect of Asia. The Commonwealth was a means, more generally, of associating in fruitful partnership the technological achievements of the west and the age-old wisdom of the east. It was a bridge between peoples and continents. It must be made, at the deepest level, multi-racial. It was, also, something of an example to the world of Gandhian principles applied to relations between states in circumstances that might ordinarily be expected to lead to estrangement or lasting hostility. Mahatma Gandhi, remarked Nehru, 'taught us a technique of action that was peaceful: yet it was effective and yielded results that led us not only to freedom but to friendship with those with whom we were, till yesterday, in conflict'.[53] And later, addressing the Canadian Parliament, Nehru returned to the same theme.

I am convinced [he said] that this development [India's republican membership] in the history of the Commonwealth, without parallel elsewhere or at any other time, is a significant step towards peace and co-operation in the world.

Of even greater significance is the manner of its achievement. Only a few years ago, Indian nationalism was in conflict with British imperialism and that conflict brought in its train ill-will, suspicion and bitterness, although because of the teaching of our great leader Mahatma Gandhi, there was far less ill-will than in any other nationalist struggle against foreign domination. Who would have thought then that suspicion and bitterness would largely fade away so rapidly, giving place to friendly cooperation between free and equal nations? That is an achievement for which all those who are concerned with it can take legitimate credit. It is an outstanding example of the peaceful solution of difficult problems and a solution that is a real one because it does not create other problems. The rest of the world might well pay heed to this example.[54]

Pandit Nehru was apt to dwell more positively on the nature of the initial achievement of Indian membership in freedom and equality than on subsequent practice. This was partly because he wished to define beyond doubt or dispute the limits of Commonwealth action or co-operation. 'Presumably', he said in 1950, 'some people imagine that our association with the Commonwealth imposes some kind of restricting or limiting factor upon our activities. . . . That impression is completely unfounded. . . . We may carry out any policy we like regardless of whether we are in the Commonwealth or not.[55] He underlined, against Pakistan, the principle of non-intervention in domestic affairs, and India's objection to any Commonwealth tribunal or any Commonwealth mediatory responsibilities in intra-Commonwealth disputes. And against the aligned members of the older Commonwealth (and Pakistan after 1954) he emphasised India's non-participation in common war or defence policies. 'We have never discussed', he stated categorically to the Lok Sabha in June 1952, 'defence policies in the Commonwealth, either jointly or separately.' He was equally explicit about India's political and constitutional independence. 'The Republic of India', he said, 'has nothing to do with England constitutionally or legally.' Indeed the attraction of the Commonwealth was its freedom from the notions of obligation or commitment. 'Our association with the Commonwealth is remarkable in that it does not bind us down in any way whatsoever . . .'.[56]

Was Indian membership then to be thought of only in terms of negation? The answer to that in part is that it was often expressed in terms of negation not to concede advantage to its critics. But on essentials Nehru did not retreat from his initial constructive approach. He, more than any other man, had brought India into the Commonwealth and he stood unyielding by his action. He believed he had good reasons for so doing. They were not, however, reasons that by their very nature allowed of public exposition. 'We do hardly anything', he said in December 1950, 'without consulting the countries of the Commonwealth.' He believed such consultations to be useful in themselves and valuable for the opportunities they presented. To those who wanted India to leave because of South African racial policies Nehru replied in 1952 that in principle this was one of the reasons why he thought India should remain. And why? Because by remaining 'we have better chances of being able to influence the larger policies of the Commonwealth than we otherwise would. Being in the Commonwealth means a meeting once or twice a year and occasional consultations and references. Surely, that is not too great a price to pay for the advantages we get.' He never doubted that those advantages were substantial, not least among them being that as India was open to other influences so also there was 'the possibility that we may also greatly influence others in the right direction'.[57] That right direction was greater world understanding of Indian and Asian problems, of the strength of anti-colonialist, anti-racialist sentiment and the concern of mankind for peace. And the measure to which the Commonwealth was moved along it is recorded in many of its collective conclusions and sometimes in phrases or sentiments in official communiqués which bear unmistakably the impress of Nehru's thoughts and use of language. If the sense of developing partnership never recaptured its earlier part-emotional appeal after the Suez crisis of 1956, it had not wholly departed. 'I wish I could paint to the House', said Harold Macmillan on his return from a Commonwealth tour in 1958, 'a picture of the thousands of people gathered in Shah Jehan's great courtyard in the Red Fort. Here there was something more than the traditional courtesy of the Indian people. I felt both then and in the meetings I had with the Indian prime minister . . . and his colleagues, a real sense of partnership in the truest sense of the word.'[58] If, on the Indian side, it was Gandhi who had laid the foundations of partnership, it was Jawaharlal Nehru who had built upon them. Even if it should prove that his service was chiefly to his own generation, it remains an honourable one, reflecting largeness of mind.

Nehru will be remembered for failures of judgment no less than for his insights into the minds of men – in pre-partition days his share of responsibility for the rejection of proffered Muslim League co-operation in Indian Provincial governments in 1937, for the opportunities given to the Muslim League to strengthen its position during the war, for the Congress failure to sense the reality of the Muslim threat to partition India until it was imminent, remains to be precisely assessed but was certainly considerable. After 1947 as prime minister of an independent state Nehru is open to the charge of mistaking the enunciation of high-sounding principles for foreign policy, of disregarding the likely price of non-alignment in terms of isolation, of blindness to the threat of Chinese aggression in the 1950s, of alternating resolution and irresolution in Kashmir. The indictment is formidable, yet in essence it is so because Nehru was a natural leader with ideas, themselves inconstant, at times irreconcilable, often pursued with insufficient regard for the realities of India's power or his own position, but for all that often stimulating, original, and uplifting in their purposes and beneficial in their consequences. One of those ideas was India's membership of a multi-national, multi-racial Commonwealth. It was in his lifetime amazingly fruitful. But for him, India almost certainly would not have become the first republican member-state of the Commonwealth, and but for Indian membership almost certainly nationalists elsewhere in Asia and, still more, in Africa would not in their turn have opted also for membership. In the consequent addition of anti-imperialist Asian and African states to a Commonwealth which had grown out of an Empire, by procedures that became so conventional as to cease to cause remark, an idea achieved its most spectacular triumph. Not Smuts, not Mackenzie King but Nehru was the architect of that achievement. In the short term nothing can detract from it; on the longer run its endurance will depend upon the reality of those virtues – the touch of healing, the equal association of races, the readiness and the capacity of the richer Commonwealth states to assist the poorer – which in his more sanguine moments Nehru believed the Commonwealth to possess.

'Jawaharlal is my political heir. He may differ from me while I am living. But when I am gone he will begin speaking my language.' So Gandhi had foretold to the All-Indian Congress Committee Meeting at Wardha in 1942. His forecast proved to be substantially true. In national and international affairs Nehru used the language and echoed the thought of the Mahatma. But behind the words the differences in political temper and philosophy remained. Nehru's approach to human affairs was at once less limiting and more sanguine than Gandhi's.[59] The India that Nehru dreamed of would not confine itself to self-realisation and self-control but would play a leading rôle in the political, social and scientific revolutions of the age. He spoke of the dynamic outlook and the spirit of adventure which had distinguished India in past ages and reflected that 'old as we are, with memories stretching back to the early dawn of human history and endeavour, we have to grow young again, in tune with our present time . . .'.[60] It was on the foundation of Gandhian teaching on reconciliation, supplemented by his own expansive, hopeful, humanist interpretation of India's place in world affairs that Nehru thought of India's Commonwealth membership. He was 'un homme considérable dont il y a tant à dire', and his conception of India's relations with the Commonwealth was one of many things, not necessarily to him of the highest importance, that still deserves to be spoken of. There were many others – some of them of necessity left undone. In his last year, Nehru had beside him lines he had copied from Robert Frost:[61]

> The woods are lovely and dark and deep,
> But I have promises to keep,
> And miles to go before I sleep,
> And miles to go before I sleep.

He had, however, travelled his miles along the Commonwealth road, and the impress of his footprints was left clear upon it.

CHAPTER 15

THE HISTORICAL EXPERIENCE

'Here I sit and govern it with my pen: I write and it is done: and by a clerk of the council I govern Scotland now, which others could not do by the sword.'[1] Such may be thought the British ideal of imperial government – trouble-free; economical, with a clerk of the council sufficing as the agent of imperial authority; and pacific. But while King James I of England and VI of Scotland could boast in these words of having achieved it in his northern kingdom, no nineteenth-century British statesman, plagued by the 'small wars of empire' and their expense, could even aspire to so happy a state. By then the Empire was too large, too variously composed and too expensive to allow of the direct, economical exercise of authority or of a reasonable prospect of general peace. On the contrary by Victorian times its administration had come to be popularly, and not unreasonably, associated with troubles, expense and wars. That association meant that the argument of Empire was rarely stilled. But by 1870 one outcome of the argument at least was clear. It was, as Lord John Russell contended in the sentences reprinted on the title page of this book, that there could be no going back. '*Tu regere imperio populos, Romane, memento.*'* The British Empire was the nineteenth-century heir to the Roman; it had its colonies of settlement and conquered peoples of other races under its sway and while it had, as the Roman Empire had not had, the rivalry of European Empires with which to contend, it out-distanced them all in extent and, so most nineteenth-century Englishmen would have alleged (or more probably simply assumed) in the enlightenment of its imperial administration. And the prospect before that Empire, as sketched for example in

* Virgil *Aeneid* vi, 851. Because of the varied implications of *imperium* the passage is not easy to translate. A. G. Lee, who has helped me with it, suggests 'Roman, remember to rule the nations with might and right.' Cecil Day Lewis' translation reads: 'But, Romans, never forget that government is your medium.' And Jackson Knight's: 'But you, Roman, must remember that you have to guide the nations by your authority.' Some elements of all three would seem to have been implicit in Russell's thought.

Sir John Seeley's by no means uncritically expansionist lectures in 1881, was of still further territorial acquisitions and an apogee of greatness yet to be attained. Well might the later nineteenth century be retrospectively regarded, and not only in India, as the Augustan age of the British Empire.

Unlike Scotland under King James that Empire was not to be governed by a pen. In the last resort it was, one category excepted, governed if not by the sword then in knowledge of the existence of the sword. That exception, at times subject to some qualification, was provided by the colonies of British settlement overseas. They were not held by force; they were tied to Britain by kinship. She was their mother country; they were her children. Surely, it might be thought, that they at least, even more than the Scotland of King James, might be governed by the pen. But it proved otherwise. They were far away, their peoples were at once of independent mind and accustomed to a share in government; and the dispatches through which authority was perforce expressed still, as in Burke's day, might take months to come and go across the oceans. Overmuch reliance upon the imperial pen, indeed, was more likely than anything else to necessitate recourse to the imperial sword. For that reason, considerations of self-interest combined with good sense prompted the transfer of responsibility for the domestic government of these colonies of settlement to their own peoples. That was the step that marked the foundation of Commonwealth. It was not taken with any such end in view. It was taken to avoid further, unnecessary dissension and in a way that was consistent with the Victorians' sense of responsibility, economy – defence, it is always to be remembered, was expensive and the Gladstonian dictum that self-government begets self-defence always relevant – and their belief in the aptitude of British people, wherever they might be, to govern themselves.

The first and critical step in the colonial self-government that led to Commonwealth was taken in British North America. It was followed, sometimes on the initiative, as with Cape Colony, of the imperial authority, but more usually under pressure from the colonists, with the result that, at the end of the century, it was generally accepted, and specifically by the colonial secretary, Joseph Chamberlain, that in respect of the ordering of their domestic affairs, the will of the colonists in all ordinary circumstances should prevail. 'The mother of Parliaments', to quote again the assertion made by J. B. Haldane in the debate on the Commonwealth of Australia Bill, 'does not coerce her children'.[2] By then it was true. But it invited a question. Who were her children? Were they to be thought of literally as being only those of British descent? The Irish member who interrupted Haldane to say, 'We do not accept that statement', presumably did not interpret the phrase so narrowly. Nor did the leaders of the defeated Boer republics brought by force within the confines of Empire, nor yet the moderates of the Indian National Congress, who in the earlier years of the century proclaimed self-government on the colonial-dominion model to be the goal of their political endeavours, consider that there should be a frontier fixed by kinship to non-coercion or to constitutional autonomy.

The breaking down of that frontier and with it successively of the barriers of culture and race was an important part of the cumulative experience of Commonwealth. It had happened in respect of culture with the French in Canada, but then they had obtained self-government within the reassuring confines of a majority English-speaking confederation. The more significant breakthrough occurred two generations later when the Boers in South Africa, destined to comprise the majority European community in the Union, had self-government restored to them. The Irish Free State followed, after attempted coercion which left scars that did not heal, but the barrier in respect of race was not broken until India obtained her independence eighty years after the making of the first dominion. This was an event of critical importance in Commonwealth history.

Until 1947 the emphasis within the self-governing Commonwealth had been upon the status of the dominions and their equality in all respects with Britain, not upon extending the frontiers of national freedom to non-British dependencies. In the later nineteenth and earlier twentieth century Canada outside Quebec, Australia and New Zealand, and English-speaking South Africa had shown themselves predisposed to lend moral or as need arose material support to British imperial rule or expansion. In 1889 Canada and Australia had sent troops to fight in the Sudan; Canadian, Australian and New Zealand contingents had fought in the South African war, the Australians being criticised by Irish nationalist members during the passage of the Commonwealth of Australia bill for being a people prepared to assist in the suppression of the liberties of others while engaged in securing their own; and collectively the dominions had shown themselves to be concerned to ensure and perpetuate their own regional predominance. Australia and New Zealand were intent before 1914 in establishing an Anglo-Saxon hegemony in the Pacific, and in keeping the foreigner out, and in 1919 Australia's prime minister flatly rejected notions of race equality, while in South Africa Briton and Boer were at one chiefly in their resolve to consolidate minority European rule, over an African majority. The peace treaties in 1919 transferring responsibility for former German colonies in the Pacific and in south-west Africa to Australia and New Zealand in the first instance and to South Africa in the second, albeit under trust, on balance probably strengthened for a brief period the 'imperial' element in the old dominion tradition.

An anti-imperialist bias at national level was introduced into the Commonwealth in 1921 with the addition of the Irish Free State to the number of the dominions. In its concepual origin, however, Irish anti-imperialism derived from European rather than extra-European sources, and partly for that reason, but also because of pressing Irish preoccupations at home, did not extend to a theoretic assertion of the right of non-European colonial peoples to be freed from imperial rule. But with the accession of India and Pakistan in 1947 the position was transformed. The voice of non-European anti-colonialism was henceforward to be heard in the innermost councils of the Commonwealth, both persistently and powerfully. It was that, rather than events in Africa itself, important as the 1949 Gold Coast riots and the Mau Mau rebellion in Kenya unquestionably were, which predisposed British and other Commonwealth statesmen to rethink their attitudes to the dependent Empire. It was not chance but rather the product of a developing experience that within two decades of Indian independence, the Mother of Parliaments had not merely ceased (with the unwished-for exception of Rhodesia) to coerce or seek to coerce any of the territories formerly under her jurisdiction, but had abandoned or was in process of abandoning even her power of coercion. There was, apart from some few small scattered outposts or islands, nothing left of the Empire on which the sun never set and no more occasion for the witticism that it did not do so, because even God Almighty could not trust it in the dark.

The ending of Empire broadly viewed and including southern Asia as well as the colonial Empire is apt increasingly to be interpreted in terms of resistance of subject peoples and changing patterns of world power. Both were very important elements in it, but they were not all-sufficient. Had they been so, there would have been in 1968 no succeeding Commonwealth in existence at the will of more than twenty-five independent states. There was a further factor – it was the British imperial response to such pressures. It was individual and it was conditioned by ideas and by history. 'No western peoples', Professor Plamenatz has remarked,[3] 'have cared more for freedom than the British and the French, or have done so much to elucidate it and to elaborate the rules and institutions needed to establish it. They have also created the largest empires in Asia and Africa.' That regard for liberty continuing side by side with Empire was one factor, as the lessons drawn from past history were another, in determining the British reaction. It was the past that suggested, first in a limited and mainly British colonial context, that in the face of quasi-nationalist or nationalist demands for autonomy, there was a possibility other than counter-resistance or abdication. That possibility was association, ultimately to be interpreted in terms of equality. Once the idea of forceful subjection was abandoned – and this happened at different times in relation to different peoples and places – such association offered, in place of the bleak prospect of abdication, with a final severance of all ties, the possibility of a new and, after the first world war, of a tried relationship, on the basis of co-operation, progressively between equals. The extent to which there was an element of illusion on the British side about what was taking place, remains debatable. But even conceding that there was apt to be an over-sanguine interpretation of what the Commonwealth that superseded Empire would mean in terms of continuing British influence, that fictional ingredient served only to reinforce fact in easing psychologically, and in a way that would otherwise have been inconceivable, the concluding stages of British decolonisation.

In Corneille's *Cinna*, from which the second extract on the title page is taken, Maxime, a republican conspirator, seeks to persuade the Emperor Augustus to abdicate and so become famous among later generations, less for having conquered than for having despised and abdicated Empire. Cinna made reply to Maxime:

> On ne renonce point aux grandeurs légitimes;
> On garde sans remords ce qu'on acquiert sans crimes;
> Et plus le bien qu'on quitte est noble, grand, exquis,
> Plus qui l'ose quitter le juge mal acquis.

Not surprisingly it was the arguments of Cinna, not those of Maxime, to which Augustus Caesar paid heed; for whatever may be the glory with posterity, neither emperors nor empires are easily persuaded to abandon their dominion. It is true that in Britain between the wars, and more especially during and after the second world war, there was evidence of a revulsion – scorn remains too strong a word – against Empire which more widely though probably less justly than at any time hitherto, had come to be associated with the class structure, with exploitation overseas which underpinned the foundations of capitalist society at home, and with war. But while reconsideration of Empire in consequence appeared to much left-wing opinion as a fitting and necessary counterpart to the coming of the welfare state and of peace, renunciation was bound to cause deep division in a country with so long a tradition of imperial greatness, and heart-searching even among professed anti-imperialists. It did both in the early post-war phase, but thereafter it came to be accepted by stages as a national policy. Two things in particular helped to bring this about – positively, the prospect of Commonwealth membership which softened the sharp edge of finality, and negatively, earlier Commonwealth experience which warned of the hazards of attempted repression. Without either prospect to encourage or experience to warn, there might have been, despite the anti-colonialist tide of opinion at home, in the British case also, as Bacon presumed there would always be, the wars associated with 'the shivering' of great empires.

There remained a price to be paid. While the existence and experience of Commonwealth made easier the ending of Empire, the earlier existence of Empire, coupled with its increasingly rapid foreclose, made the more difficult the life of Commonwealth. There was little time for readjustment; ideas did not keep pace with actualities; the imperial past bore in oppressively upon the Commonwealth present; attitudes appropriate to Empire were carried over into Commonwealth and what had been associated with the former survived to trouble the latter.

The psychological carry-over from Empire to Commonwealth, inevitable under any circumstances, was the more pronounced because of British concentration on one element in the evolutionary process. That process, of its nature, comprises both continuity and change, but the British emphasis was consistently upon the first. It is true that no one in the revolutionary situation in Ireland in 1921 and the near-revolutionary prospect in India in 1947 could doubt that a momentous change was taking place, with the respective transfers of power to indigenous successor authorities. But subsequent transfers of power in south-east Asia, Africa, the West Indies and elsewhere, in accordance with precedents and procedures that were becoming increasingly familiar, and leading without sign of serious debate in almost every case to Commonwealth membership, made a delayed rather than an immediate impact upon British opinion. It was some time before possessive imperial attitudes, expressed for example in references to 'our Commonwealth', disappeared. Britain forgot, complained Mrs Pandit after seven years as Indian high commissioner in London, 'that you cannot run a Commonwealth as you run an Empire'.[4] In a sense the actual process of transformation encouraged Britain to do so. True, in the territories that had themselves passed from a state of imperial dependency to sovereign independence there was no possibility of such forgetfulness. No one in Dar-es-Salaam after 9 December 1961 could doubt that political authority resided with Julius Nyerere and the dominant party of which he was the leader, or in Nairobi after 12 December 1963 that it rested with Jomo Kenyatta (destined in old age to assume the mantle of the elder statesman of Commonwealth Africa), or listen to the prime minister of Malta, Dr Borg Olivier, welcome Queen Elizabeth II in the presence of Commonwealth high commissioners and diplomatic representatives of some twenty nations, in November 1967, in the sixteenth-century Palace which had been for more than two centuries the residence of the Grand Masters of the Knights Hospitallers, as Queen of Malta and as such a 'visible sign' of the Island's nationhood and of its three year old independence,[5] without having borne in upon him the reality of change. But in Britain itself and in the world outside nothing so diminished regard for the Commonwealth's rôle in assisting such change as the ease with which it was in most instances effected and the air of continuity with which it was deliberately invested.

In one instance only was that continuity broken. In the case of Cyprus there was an interval in time between the ending of British rule and the accession of the Island Republic, under the presidency of its autocephalous archbishop, to the Commonwealth, by and with the consent of Greek and Turkish representatives – in the former case for a trial period – and also of the Communists on the unusual ground that in the conditions created by a 'long period of colonial servitude' there remained no immediate alternative to Commonwealth membership.[6] This Cypriot break between imperial ending and Commonwealth beginning, not only held the balance evenly between change and continuity but underlined that the element of continuity was at the will of the representatives of an independent people. In the post–1945 era this was so in every case, but nowhere else was it expressly indicated *after* a transfer of power had been effected.

The evolutionary process of the transformation of Empire into Commonwealth had a further, overall consequence. It meant that there was no dividing line between Empire and Commonwealth but instead a protracted process of transition during which the two existed side by side, together appearing (as Palmerston forthrightly complained of the 'semi-Byzantine design' first proposed by Sir Giles Gilbert Scott for the block of buildings in Whitehall in which for a period both the Dominions and Colonial Offices were to be housed) as 'neither one thing nor t'other – a regular mongrel affair',[7] neither Empire nor Commonwealth. But while Palmerston could decree, despite 'the terrible state of mental perturbation' caused to the architect, that the building should be in the Italianate style, the processes of peaceful political transition, whatever the price that time exacts, were not to be thus peremptorily foreshortened. Indeed in respect of individual territories in the later phases, the period may well have been less rather than more than that demanded by local circumstances. But even if and when this was so, it did not diminish the problem for a Commonwealth, entangled with a still continuing Empire, and suffering in popular comprehension and often esteem from the association.

The continuing association of Commonwealth with Empire was the product of time and unfolding circumstances and not of an overall conception. Empire meant the government of men by a superior authority, Commonwealth interpreted, notably by Lionel Curtis, in idealistic terms as the government of men by themselves, at the least rested minimally upon the foundation of government of peoples by themselves. On any reckoning, and with whatever qualifications, Empire and Commonwealth represented incompatible and antithetical concepts comprehended for half a century or more within one polity.

The government of men by themselves, that was the ideal and in many instances the distinguishing characteristic of Commonwealth throughout the greater part of its history, was expressed institutionally in the adoption and where necessary the adaptation of the British system of parliamentary government to conditions overseas. This meant, whatever the variations or qualifications, that there was brought into being a common pattern of politics and administration, which in its turn provided a community of experience which was a strong, perhaps the strongest, bond of Commonwealth.

The Westminster model, transplanted to other environments and to other societies, was apt, especially in the eye of a critical foreign beholder, to be chiefly remarkable for the air of artificiality or even incongruity with which its proceedings were invested. 'The opening and closing of the session', wrote André Siegfried of what he had seen of them in Ottawa,

> are carried out just as they are in London, with an antiquated ceremony somewhat out of keeping with the simplicity of this colonial milieu, but to which Canadians of all races and classes are tenaciously attached. As to the debates, they partake of that curious mixture of discipline and *laisser-aller* which characterises all English gatherings from which the women are excluded. Members wear their hats while seated, the lounging attitudes are allowed – are even considered to be a sign of elegant nonchalance. Members refer to each other not by their own names, but by that of the constituency represented. This often produces a quaintly exotic effect in the French Canadian language, such as the following exordium: 'Monsieur l'orateur, l'honorable membre pour Québec a dit . . .'. Approbation is signified by sonorous guttural cries of 'Hear, Hear!' The whole impression is thoroughly British.

But M. Siegfried further observed, and he was well qualified to do so, that the French Canadians were very proud of being affiliated in some way to the venerable *Mater Parliamentorum*.[8] The ambition to become associated and that pride in affiliation with Westminster was widely shared by non-British as well as by British peoples. As late as 1954 the common practice of parliamentary self-government and a common faith in democracy were recognised, at a Commonwealth Conference,[9] to be the foundation of the Commonwealth relationship, even if not in themselves sufficient to preserve it. Historically that was of great importance.

Initial overseas attachment to parliamentary government was not of itself surprising. Peoples of British descent had inherited it; peoples of non-British extraction had learned in dependence to desire it. Few notions are more erroneous or more persistent than that Britain thrust parliamentary institutions upon reluctant dependencies. This was no more true of Africa in the 1930s than it had been of southern Asia in earlier decades. In 1937 the British approach to government in African colonial territories, conveniently summarised in a memorandum circulated for the information of dominion delegations to the Imperial Conference, indicated that almost the precise opposite was the case.[10] Reliance, the memorandum stated, was placed not upon the development of parliamentary institutions in African dependent territories but upon indirect rule through native institutions. The aim was to make 'the native a good African' and that aim 'cannot be achieved if we destroy all the institutions, all the traditions and all the habits of the people, superimposing upon them what we consider to be better administrative methods and better principles but destroying everything that can make the administration really in touch with the thoughts and customs of the people'. For this reason alone direct rule was not possible since it meant 'the imposition of British ideas through the intermediary of a bureaucracy of half-educated native clerks' whereas the policy of indirect rule by contrast aimed to establish a delegated machinery of government 'by maintaining and supporting native rule and native institutions'. For this reason the Colonial Office thought that it was most important to check 'the disintegrating influences which are impairing the authority of the chiefs over their peoples, as, if that authority is undermined and completely disappears, the only foundation on which it is possible to build has been destroyed'. They looked forward indeed to the days of literate and progressive chiefs just at a time when the urban African élites were beginning to see the future in terms of political parties and popular representation. It was accordingly not the Colonial Office but the indigenous leaders of African (and other) dependencies that came to demand responsible government on the Westminster model, the principal qualification being the reservations of minorities, by no means least of European minorities, about the consequences for them of the majority rule ultimately implicit in the British system. It was the British who changed their approach and responded at last to these overseas demands.

Nowhere was the true position more succinctly set out than in some paragraphs of the 1945 Soulbury Report on Constitutional Reform in Ceylon. They read:[11]

The constitution we recommend for Ceylon reproduces in large measure the form of the British constitution, its usages and conventions, and may on that account invite the criticism so often and so legitimately levelled against attempts to frame a government for an eastern people on the pattern of western democracy.

We are well aware that self-government of the British parliamentary type, carried on by means of a technique which it has taken centuries to develop, may not be suitable or practicable for another country, and that where the history, traditions and culture of that country are foreign to those of Great Britain, the prospect of transplanting British institutions with success may appear remote. But it does not follow that the invention of modifications or variations of the British form of government to meet different conditions elsewhere will be any more successful. It is easier to propound new constitutional devices and fresh constructive solutions than to foresee the difficulties and disadvantages which they may develop. At all events, in recommending for Ceylon a constitution on the British pattern, we are recommending a method of government we know something about, a method which is the result of very long experience, which has been tested by trial and error and which works, and, on the whole, works well.

But be that as it may, the majority – the politically conscious majority of the people of Ceylon – favour a constitution on British lines. Such a constitution is their own desire and is not being imposed upon them. It is true that, if in our opinion it were manifestly unsuitable for Ceylon, our duty, notwithstanding the demands of the Ceylonese, would be so to report. We could not recommend a constitution of the British type and then, when its failure had become apparent, merely retort – 'Vous l'avez voulu, Georges Dandin.'

But we think Ceylon is well qualified for a constitution on the British model . . .

No man's knowledge, observed John Locke, goes beyond his experience; or to quote a medieval but equally relevant maxim *Nemo dat quod non habet* – no one gives what he has not got. Both conditioned the British response. They had experience of parliamentary government and their political knowledge in any deeper sense did not go beyond that experience. Parliamentary government was the one thing they could at least hope to give. But equally, and this was the other side of the transfer of power equation, the one thing the British had got, was what dependent peoples at the outset wanted. Even where, as in Pakistan, Ghana, Nigeria or elsewhere, that form of government was soon to be superseded or suspended, its initial adoption was important, if only in easing first the transition from dependence to Commonwealth and then the early phase of the new Commonwealth relationship. And remarkable to the point of paradox was the fact that the politics of race in South Africa and Southern Rhodesia, while in themselves, and especially in Rhodesia, a cause of estrangement, helped to deepen the sense of Commonwealth commitment to a traditional, liberal, representative, responsible parliamentary solution, even on the part of those states that had themselves discarded parliamentarianism.

The parliamentary system of government predetermined the Commonwealth system of co-operation through consultation, from the time of the first Colonial Conference in 1887, through Imperial Conferences to Meetings of Prime Ministers and Heads of State. It presumed that ultimate authority would reside in cabinets responsible to individual parliaments or, when circumstances required, with a head of state and his advisers. In the two world wars, which played so great a part in earlier Commonwealth experience, there was no significant departure from parliamentary practices and the imperial war cabinet of the first world war and the continuing conference of cabinets that developed in the second both demonstrated anew and, in time of peril, the attachment of the older Commonwealth to the parliamentary system. That attachment, that pattern of co-operation, was carried over into the period of Asian and of early African membership. Deriving from parliamentary government, it was the second conditioning element in the Commonwealth experience. It also possessed its characteristic virtues and limitations.

The system of co-operation meant that at all levels the Commonwealth operated, at least until the creation of a Commonwealth secretariat in 1965, not through a formal administrative organisation but by means of discussion and consultation as seemed natural to parliamentarians. If indeed discussion be deemed, as A. D. Lindsay argued in *The Essentials of Democracy* that it should be, the great essential of democracy, then the Commonwealth was democratic in its consultative processes. But discussion, with decisions left to be taken by individual governments in the light of that discussion, was not easily communicated or publicised to a wider audience. To the prudent reticences of governments was added thereby a problem of communication inherent in the system. 'Take the pen, Matucewic', said Talleyrand to the Russian Pole, who drafted the reports of many European congresses after 1815, 'You who know all the neutral words'.[12] Commonwealth conferences were, indeed, well served by officials who knew 'all the neutral words'. But even had this not been so the process of association through discussion, by its very nature, was bound to be lacking in dramatic quality or popular appeal. It was sensible, it was liberal, it was democratic and it was dull.

The near-attainment of one set of Commonwealth purposes in the independence and free association of all former subject peoples presented problems pressing upon the frontiers of earlier Commonwealth experience. Between 1940 and 1968 the total sovereign membership of the Commonwealth increased from six to twenty-eight. Even had all else remained equal, it was clearly more difficult to maintain co-operation by traditional means of Imperial Conference or continuing conference of cabinets among twenty-eight than among six. To the problem of arithmetic was added the problem of interest, or more precisely, of range of interest. The Commonwealth at the outbreak of the second world war was dominated by the United Kingdom. Canada, the senior dominion, was diplomatically represented at that time in three foreign capitals; in 1968 in fifty-five. In the Commonwealth in earlier times there was only one state with the inclination and the resources to pursue interests which were world-wide, namely the United Kingdom. In the latter day Commonwealth there were seven or eight states with interests, actively pursued, which if not world-wide at least were more than regional or continental. By contrast, however, there were at this later period other states whose interests were narrowly restricted. Their resources, political, economic and administrative were strained even to support their recently acquired independent statehood. Inevitably as both numbers and range of interest increased, the system, and more especially the character, of Commonwealth meetings, which were its focal point, perceptibly changed.

To outward seeming a gathering of twenty-five or more prime ministers and heads of state, was an impressive, as it was apt to be a lively occasion. But it did not allow of the easy exchange of view or of the confidences by which such store was set in earlier days. On the contrary, with the larger audience there developed a tendency towards the statement and re-statement of national interests or policies at the expense of discussion, and by no means always with regard for the realities of power or of the resources available for any particular course of action. As a result the Commonwealth by enlargement of membership was brought face to face for the first time with difficulties, earlier encountered by the United Nations, the League of Nations and nineteenth-century European congresses, of seeking to relate the representation of states, unequal in size and resources, to the facts of political and economic life. At the European congresses of the post-Napoleonic period it was the practice for representatives of lesser as well as of greater powers to be present, and for all alike to attend the sessions of general interest, but it was the prerogative of the greater alone to attend all sessions. Such a precedent, though considered in modified form, did not commend itself to the Commonwealth, one, and in itself sufficient, reason being that among the lesser were also without exception to be found the newer member-states, the representatives of which were disposed in consequence to react sharply to any suggestion that distinctions in terms of political stature unfavourable, as it would appear, to their independent status, might be drawn. On more general grounds, moreover, it could be and was argued that any such distinction, even if required at international conferences by the exigencies of power politics, was alien to the concept of a fraternal, Commonwealth, relationship. On all these grounds the Commonwealth perforce had to adapt itself to its new numbers, with members resorting to informal arrangements for limited consultation when they deemed that circumstances so demanded.

The increase in Commonwealth membership coincided roughly in time with, but was not solely responsible for, a perceptible shift in dominant Commonwealth preoccupations in the decade that followed Suez. Negatively the cleavages in Commonwealth opinion on many of the larger issues of international politics discouraged thoughts of seeking to use it for diplomatic or defence purposes, while positively there was pressure for the pursuit of new ends. Liberalism and its expanding frontiers were of the past; development, economic growth and welfare conceived to be of the future. Any contribution which the Commonwealth could make to their advancement was understood to be of necessity limited and partial. Its members collectively might initiate or supplement; they could not ordinarily assume a full responsibility. It was realistic accordingly to think not in terms of Commonwealth solutions but, more modestly, in terms of Commonwealth contributions. So much, indeed, was predicated by the unfavourable ratio within the Commonwealth, as between developed and underdeveloped countries and their respective populations. Yet within the limits thus imposed by Commonwealth resources in relation to Commonwealth needs, and with awareness of them, there was a significant shift in Commonwealth interests represented by a concerted endeavour to further agreed economic and social purposes. Among these were the organisation of intra-Commonwealth aid for welfare and development: new co-operative ventures in technical and university education, following upon the Report of a Conference held in Oxford in 1959: collaboration between professional organisations and interchange of many kinds; and collective endeavours to contribute to the raising of living standards, first under the aegis of the Colombo Plan, a decade of whose working was completed in 1960[13] in south and south-east Asia and later by adaptations of it in Africa. It was these new purposes and the possibility of their further advancement that had been responsible for the creation, at African instigation, of the Commonwealth secretariat in 1965, intended chiefly to stimulate an increase in the flow of aid for development and welfare, by providing a necessary means for the co-ordination and direction of planning and by encouraging governments to give effect to policies, the application of which might have been collectively approved at Commonwealth Prime Ministers' Meetings, but which required subsequent individual state action for their implementation. No machinery, however, could be more than marginally useful. What mattered was the availability of resources and the will of the governments who controlled them to give priority to expenditure for such purposes.

In the earlier days of multi-racial membership, Commonwealth statesmen delighted, as in the third quotation on the title page, to extol this great experiment in co-operation between peoples and nations from every continent; to speak of the Commonwealth as a bridge between east and west; between developed and underdeveloped societies; between European, Asian and African; to emphasise its unique character and to think of it as a model of what the whole world might one day become. And even in later and less sanguine years, was there not some continuing cause for gratification and for hope in the fact that the governments of so many peoples should have sought or retained Commonwealth membership? From India with a population approaching 400 million to Lesotho with a population of three-quarters of a million, from the heady pan-Africanism of Kwame Nkrumah's Ghana to the social conservatism of Tunku Abdul Rahman's Malaysia, from thinly settled New Zealand where, as Pacific rollers broke on the wooded coastline by Kiakoura, it could be felt that there was the end of the world, as surely as ever it was by the 'sad sea-sounding wastes of Lyonesse'[14] to West Indian islands, too widely scattered to compose one polity, too close historically to feel altogether apart, countries and peoples had decided to share in the bond of Commonwealth. That bond was described by a Maltese delegate to the Commonwealth Parliamentary Conference at Kampala 1967, as a symbol of community in independence and he added that 'coming to Uganda as a member of Parliament of a free and sovereign nation of the Commonwealth' was 'an object of pride in the judgment of history'.[15]

The phrase was apt. The pride in the judgment of history lay in the working out of a political pattern which had widened the frontiers of national, if not always of personal, freedom. That was what many Commonwealth leaders had themselves experienced and about which they had reason, in many instances, to feel emotionally. They rarely doubted, even when as in many parts of Africa independence was followed by turmoil, by military *coups d'état* or even, as in Nigeria, by civil war, that expanding the frontiers of freedom had been and must continue to be the concern of Commonwealth. It had been first conceived in terms of a liberal-nationalist philosophy of politics and government; it was developed and interpreted within that framework of ideas and even when their power of attraction was in decline the Commonwealth remained, by reason of experience reinforced by the nature of the relationships it had established, in essence so bound to them that it was hard to conceive of a future in other terms.

By the middle 1960s there was, however, diminishing confidence in that future in most parts of the Commonwealth. The shift in emphasis from international politics to co-operative endeavour in policies of development and welfare while it served to give to the Commonwealth a more contemporary and a more human appeal also underlined Commonwealth insufficiencies in economic resources. In the past there had been reliance in all fields upon Britain, and in fact the presumption of British power and preeminence in the Commonwealth outlived the reality. But after the retreat from the Suez adventure in 1956, rebuff in Europe, defiance by Rhodesian rebels whose walls did not fall even at the third blast on the sanctions trumpet, unexpansive trade, a succession of balance of payments crises (and the largely consequential withdrawal of a British military presence East of Suez) the decline in Britain's position, both in the Commonwealth and in the world was progressively, even cruelly, driven home. Neither militarily, economically nor even perhaps politically could she any longer provide, as in earlier years, the solid, material basis of Commonwealth or retain, in consequence, her earlier predominant influence in the shaping of policies. What then was to be her attitude towards it?

In the later nineteenth century Sir John Seeley, reflecting upon past British expansion and contemplating Britain's 'prodigious' future greatness, had remarked that some countries such as Holland and Sweden 'might pardonably regard their history as in a manner being wound up', its one practical lesson for them being one 'of resignation'. Had that lesson its ironic relevance for a latter-day Britain? If so, there was reluctance to accept it, in its bleak finality. Debate about Britain's rôle continued, the range of choice admittedly much contracted, but with some overtones from more spacious days still to be heard. 'The issue is not a mean one', Disraeli had told his Crystal Palace audience in 1872. 'It is whether you will be content to be a comfortable England, modelled and moulded upon continental policies, or whether you will be a great country, an imperial country . . .' And Gladstone, it will be remembered, had retorted that Empire was not the source of British power, which derived not from far flung possessions but from the people and the wealth of 'these islands'. A century later the issue was still thought to be 'not a mean one'. But it was widely concluded that a sufficient foundation for a future, conceived in a spirit of hope rather than resignation, lay either in Britain itself, externally associated perhaps with other European or Atlantic powers or alternatively in unreserved British participation in a wider European, or conceivably North Atlantic, community. On either view there was no place for the Commonwealth that had superseded Disraelian empire. And for that reason it was asked with increasing insistence, how far were British interests still served by membership of a scattered community of states, in which Britain's pre-eminence was no longer tacitly acknowledged? '*Il a voulu que la France soit à la tête de l'Europe*', remarked Paul Reynaud in criticism of General de Gaulle, '*et il n'a pas voulu l'Europe*'. That also had been the underlying British attitude to Commonwealth, her governments desiring leadership, but lacking consistency of purpose in willing a Commonwealth. With leadership to be earned, not conceded, what attitude was to be taken? Even the posing of such questions, whatever might be the answers to them, indicated that for Britain the age of faith in Commonwealth had drawn to its close.

Sir Robert Menzies, who was prime minister of Australia 1939–41, and continuously from 1952–66, had a vision of Empire and Commonwealth, which belonged to the days when it was British in name, in loyalties, largely in composition and in its united purposes. To him it meant, as he once recalled,

> King George and Queen Mary coming to their Jubilee in Westminster Hall . . . at Chequers Winston Churchill, courage and confidence radiating from him . . . Australian boys in tired but triumphant groups at Tobruk and Benghazi . . . at Canberra, at Wellington, at Ottawa, at Pretoria, the men of Parliament meeting as those who met at Westminster seven hundred years ago; at Melbourne the lawyers practising the Common Law first forged at Westminster . . . [and also] Hammond at Sydney and Bradman at Lords and McCabe at Trent Bridge, with the ghosts of Grace and Trumble looking on . . .'[16]

By 1968, for most people, it was likely to mean something rather less, Smith and sanctions perhaps, with the ghosts of Rhodes and Lobengula looking on. A Conservative critic in *The Times* had written of it a few years earlier as 'a gigantic farce'.[17] '*Le Figaro*',[18] with satisfaction, dismissed it as 'naguère qu'une chimère' on the morrow of Britain's second application to join the Common Market and – a last irony – former imperialists, 'praisers of gone times' because now they had 'none of their own', cherished it as the offspring of Empire. But if it had been, or was being, reduced to all or any of these things, it also retained its own unquestioned place in the longer perspective of time. There it was to be viewed as the product and the embodiment of an experience, familiarly charted by famous constitutional landmarks, yet to be thought of not in the constricting context of constitutional documentation nor of 'what one clerk said to another' but in terms of a historical process which had affected the lives of millions, and which had culminated in the national freedom and the association in partnership – at the least during critical years of transition – of the majority of the peoples whose destinies were formerly determined by the greatest of European empires. It may be that in the accomplishment of this end, the Commonwealth lost its *raison d'être*; or alternatively that it still had other causes to advance. But the interpretation of the past is neither to be subjected to 'the tyranny of the contemporary'[19] nor yet to be influenced by uncertain speculation on the future. It is an end sufficient in itself.

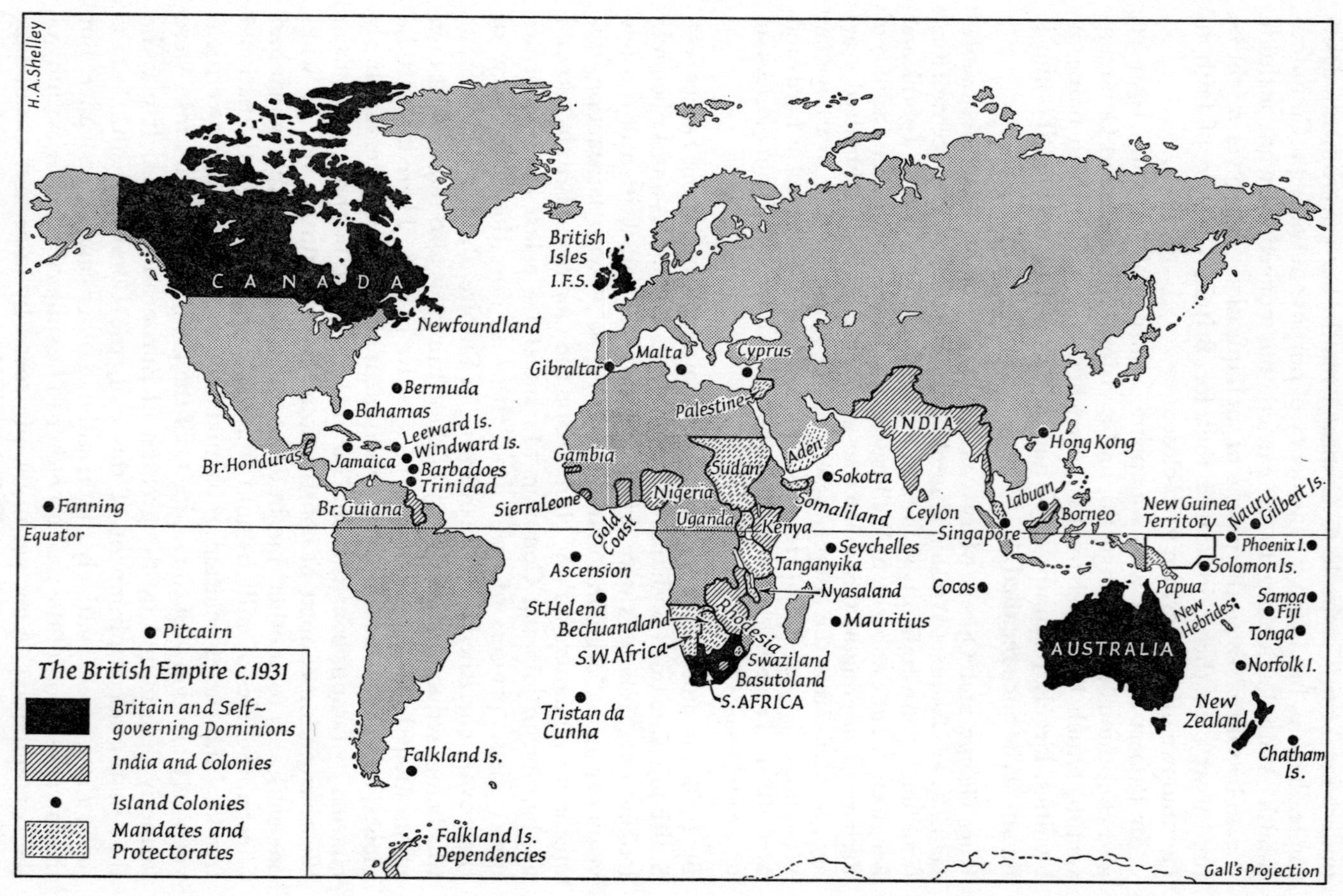
H.A.Shelley
The British Empire c.1931
Britain and Self-governing Dominions
India and Colonies
Island Colonies
Mandates and Protectorates
CANADA
Newfoundland
Bermuda
Bahamas
Leeward Is.
Windward Is.
Jamaica
Barbadoes
Trinidad
Br. Honduras
Br. Guiana
Fanning
Pitcairn
Equator
Falkland Is.
Falkland Is. Dependencies
British Isles
I.F.S.
Gibraltar
Malta
Cyprus
Palestine
Gambia
Sierra Leone
Gold Coast
Nigeria
Sudan
Aden
Uganda
Kenya
Tanganyika
Nyasaland
Rhodesia
Bechuanaland
S.W. Africa
Swaziland
Basutoland
S. AFRICA
Ascension
St.Helena
Tristan da Cunha
Sokotra
Somaliland
Seychelles
Mauritius
INDIA
Ceylon
Cocos
Singapore
Labuan
Borneo
Hong Kong
New Guinea Territory
Nauru
Gilbert Is.
Phoenix I.
Solomon Is.
Papua
New Hebrides
Samoa
Fiji
Tonga
Norfolk I.
AUSTRALIA
New Zealand
Chatham Is.
Gall's Projection

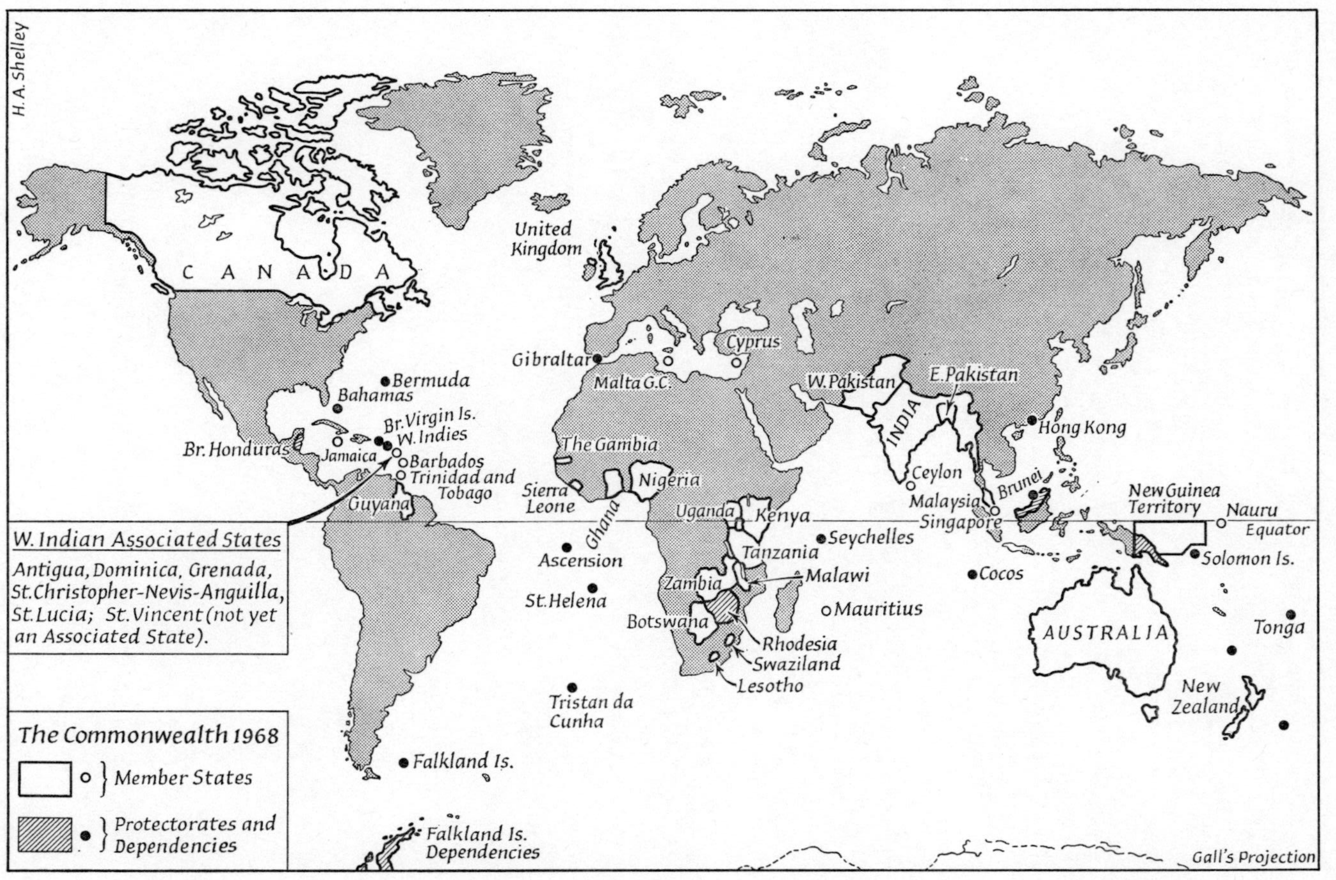
H. A. Shelley
CANADA
United Kingdom
Gibraltar
Malta G.C.
Cyprus
Bermuda
Bahamas
Br. Virgin Is.
W. Indies
Br. Honduras
Jamaica
Barbados
Trinidad and Tobago
Guyana
The Gambia
Sierra Leone
Ghana
Nigeria
Uganda
Kenya
Tanzania
Malawi
Zambia
Botswana
Rhodesia
Swaziland
Lesotho
Ascension
St. Helena
Tristan da Cunha
Seychelles
Mauritius
W. Pakistan
E. Pakistan
INDIA
Ceylon
Malaysia
Singapore
Brunei
Hong Kong
Cocos
New Guinea Territory
Nauru
Equator
Solomon Is.
AUSTRALIA
Tonga
New Zealand
Falkland Is.
Falkland Is. Dependencies
Gall's Projection
W. Indian Associated States
Antigua, Dominica, Grenada, St. Christopher-Nevis-Anguilla, St. Lucia; St. Vincent (not yet an Associated State).
The Commonwealth 1968
Member States
Protectorates and Dependencies

NOTES

CHAPTER I

1 W. S. Churchill, *My African Journey*, London, 1908 (as reprinted 1962), pp. 3 and 144.
2 George Bennett, *The Concept of Empire, Burke to Attlee* 1774–1947 (2nd ed.), London, 1962, is a notably well and evenly balanced selection to which the criticisms that follow in no way apply.
3 Hansard, *Parliamentary Debates* (Commons), Third Series, vol. xix, col. 536.
4 Earl of Ronaldshay, *The Life of Lord Curzon* (3 vols), London, 1928, vol. 2, p. 230; Philip Woodruff, *The Men Who Ruled India* (2 vols), London, 1953–4, vol. 2, p. 199, also alludes to the incident. The quotation which follows is from a speech at Birmingham on 11 December 1907, reprinted in Bennett, *The Concept of Empire*, pp. 354–7.
5 W. F. Monypenny and G. E. Buckle, *The Life of Disraeli* (6 vols), London, 1910–29, vol. 5, pp. 194–6; and Hansard, *Parl. Deb.* (Lords), vol. ccxxxix, col. 777.
6 *The Annual Register* 1886, p. 181.
7 Merriman Papers, Cape Town Public Library.
8 As stated in the records in Rhodes's cottage at Muizenberg.
9 E.g. F. H. Underhill in his admirable *The British Commonwealth*, Durham, North Carolina, 1956, covering the period from the Durham Report onward never mentioned Rhodes.
10 See however an interesting and speculative consideration of it by D. A. Low, 'Lion Rampant', *Journal of Commonwealth Political Studies* (1964), vol. ii, no. 3, pp. 235–50.
11 A. P. Newton, *A Hundred Years of the British Empire*, London, 1940, pp. 240–1.
12 Sir Kenneth Roberts-Wray, *Commonwealth and Colonial Law*, London, 1966, pp. 98–116, provides an authoritative analysis of the acquisition of colonies; J. M. Ward, *Empire in the Antipodes, The British in Australasia* 1840–1860, London, 1966, pp. 53–4, summarises the facts on New Zealand.
13 *The Cambridge History of the British Empire* (2nd ed.), Cambridge, 1963, vol. 8, p. 516.
14 S. G. Millin, *Rhodes* (new and revised ed.), London, 1952, p. 229; see also Low, 'Lion Rampant', p. 244.
15 Monica Hunter, *Reaction to Conquest* (2nd ed.), London, 1961, p. 8.

16 Prakash Tandon, *Punjabi Century, 1857–1947*, London, 1961, pp. 12–3.
17 Low, 'Lion Rampant', p. 237; see J. G. Lockhart and The Hon. C. M. Woodhouse, *Rhodes*, London, 1963, p. 479, for an account of the incident.
18 J. D. Kestell, *Through Shot and Flame*, London, 1903, p. 285; Kestell was chaplain to President Steyn and a joint secretary to the two republican governments.
19 A. G. Gardiner, *The Life of Sir William Harcourt* (2 vols), London, 1923, vol. 1, p. 497.
20 Quoted in S. R. Mehrotra, *India and the Commonwealth*, 1885–1929, London, 1965, p. 47.
21 Sir Michael O'Dwyer, *India as I Knew It, 1885–1925*, London, 1925, chapters 17 and 18, gives an account of what happened and of his reasons as lieutenant-governor of the Punjab for backing Dyer's action, while disapproving of some of his subsequent measures.
22 Jawaharlal Nehru, *An Autobiography*, London, 1936, pp. 43–4 and 190.
23 Jawaharlal Nehru, *The Discovery of India*, Calcutta, 1946, p. 281.
24 The Marquess of Crewe, *Lord Rosebery*, (2 vols), London, 1931, vol. 1, pp. 185–6.
25 Lord Rosebery, *Oliver Cromwell: A Eulogy and an Appreciation*, London, 1900.
26 Quoted by S. R. Mehrotra in 'On the Use of the Term Commonwealth', *Journal of Commonwealth Political Studies*, vol. 2, no. 1 (November 1963), p. 9.
27 *Fabianism and the Empire*, A Manifesto by the Fabian Society, London, 1900; quotations from p. 1, pp. 8 and 32, pp. 15 and 23, pp. 49–50 note 1.
28 Dr Mehrotra has discovered and recorded many of them in his article.
29 Richard Jebb, *Studies in Colonial Nationalism*, London, 1905, p. 1.
30 Merriman Papers, 24 June 1909.
31 See W. K. Hancock, *Survey of British Commonwealth Affairs* (2 vols), London, 1937, vol. 1, p. 53 note 2.
32 *Minutes of Proceedings of Imperial War Conference*, 1917, Cd. 8566, p. 5.
33 *Ibid.*, p. 40–1.
34 *Ibid.*, p. 47; also J. C. Smuts, *War-Time Speeches*, London, 1917, pp. 13–9.
35 As reprinted in W. K. Hancock and Jean van der Poel, *Selections from the Smuts Papers* (4 vols), Cambridge, 1966, vol. 3, pp. 510–1; see also Smuts, *War-Time Speeches*, pp. 25–38, for an amended version.
36 *Minutes Imp. War Conf.*, Cd. 9177, p. 18.
37 Hancock and Van der Poel, *Selections from the Smuts Papers*, vol. 3, p. 518.
38 Gladstone Papers, Ms. 44632, ff. 36–45 and 111–3. I am indebted to Dr D. G. Hoskin for first drawing this fact to my attention. Gladstone also had before him extracts from the constitution of the United States.
39 Campbell-Bannerman Papers, B.M., Ms. 41243, f. 62.
40 Hancock and Van der Poel, *Selections from the Smuts Papers*, vol. 2, p. 374, letter dated 8 January 1908, and pp. 417–8, letter dated (?) March 1908; and Merriman Papers, 26 October 1908 for constitutional commentaries.
41 See speech by the Rt. Hon. C. R. Attlee reprinted in N. Mansergh, *Documents and Speeches on British Commonwealth Affairs* 1931–1952, (2 vols), London, 1953, vol. 2, p. 685.

42 Quoted by S. R. Mehrotra, 'Imperial Federation and India, 1868–1917', *Journal of Commonwealth Political Studies*, vol. 1, no. 1 (November 1961), p. 33.
43 N. H. Carrier and J. R. Jeffery, *External Migration: A Study of the Available Statistics, 1815–1950*, HMSO, London, 1953, p. 33. For Irish emigration see O. MacDonagh, 'Irish Emigration to the United States of America and the British Colonies During the Famine', in R. Dudley Edwards and T. Desmond Williams, *The Great Famine*, Dublin, 1956, especially appendix, p. 388.
44 CAB. 32. E-6. The paper was prepared for the Imperial Conference, 1921.
45 L. S. Amery, *My Political Life* (3 vols), London, 1953, vol. 2, pp. 385 and 389–90.
46 Hancock, *Survey*, vol. 1, pp. 60–1.
47 Roberts-Wray, *Commonwealth and Colonial Law*, p. 9; see generally pp. 7–14 for a discussion of this and other precedents.
48 *Parl. Deb.* (Commons), 1949, vol. 464, col. 643–4.

CHAPTER 2

1 J. S. Mill, *Representative Government*, first published London, 1861; reprinted London Everyman Edition, 1910, in *Utilitarianism, Liberty and Representative Government*, p. 377.
2 Sir Charles Lucas (ed.), *Lord Durham's Report on the Affairs of British North America* (3 vols), Oxford, 1912; in abridgement, Sir R. Coupland, *The Durham Report*, Oxford, 1945.
3 Cf. Chester New, *Lord Durham's Mission to Canada*, Ottawa, 1963; The Carleton Library no. 8, pp. 53–8 and 161.
4 Sir H. Maxwell (ed.), *The Creevey Papers*, London, 1905, p. 374.
5 It is often spoken of as unique but this is not so. On the other side of the St Lawrence (to go no further) there is also a common memorial to General Murray and the Marquis de Lévis.
6 G. W. Pierson, *Tocqueville and Beaumont in America*, New York, 1938, pp. 319–24; the sketch of the obelisk faces p. 320.
7 Hansard, *Parl. Deb.* (Commons), 16 January 1838, vol. xl, col. 41.
8 *Ibid.*, col. 309–10. A representative selection of extracts from this debate is reprinted in George Bennett, *The Concept of Empire* (2nd ed.), London, 1962, pp. 115–24.
9 The flavour of Mackenzie's thinking is best recaptured in his own speeches and writings, full as they were of anger, protest and indignation against what he deemed injustice. They are reprinted in Margaret Fairley's collection of his *Selected Writings 1824–1837*, Toronto, 1960. Mackenzie also wrote his own narrative of *The late rebellion – exhibiting the only true account of what took place at the memorable seige of Toronto, in the month of December* 1837, Toronto, 1937.
10 Helen Taft Manning, *The Revolt of French Canada, 1800–1835*, London 1962, supplies the background to the revolt and an account of Papineau's earlier ideas and career. For a more general analysis see D. G. Creighton, *Dominion of the North*, Cambridge, Mass., 1944, chapter 5.

11 Pierson, *Tocqueville and Beaumont in America*, pp. 319–24.
12 Lucas (ed.), *Lord Durham's Report*, vol. 2, p. 16.
13 *Ibid.*, p. 70.
14 *Ibid.*, pp. 77–8.
15 *Ibid.*, pp. 72–3.
16 The phrase had been in current use among reformers in Upper Canada for some time before Lord Durham's mission but it had lacked definition and any accepted meaning; see Chester New, *Lord Durham's Mission to Canada*, pp. 28–41.
17 Lucas (ed.), *Lord Durham's Report*, vol. 2, pp. 279–80.
18 *Ibid.*, p. 282.
19 *Cambridge History of the British Empire* (2nd ed.), Cambridge, 1963, vol. 2, chapter 10: J. R. M. Butler, 'Colonial Self-Government, 1838–1852,' pp. 342–3.
20 Charles Buller, *Sketch of Lord Durham's Mission to Canada in 1838*, reprinted in Lucas (ed.), *Lord Durham's Report*, vol 3, p. 340; see also Chester New, *Lord Durham's Mission to Canada*, p. 50.
21 Lucas (ed.), *Lord Durham's Report*, vol. 2, p. 288.
22 J. M. de Moine, *Quebec Past and Present*, pp. 277–80.
23 Only one wing of the château had survived and as it was too small to accommodate the high commissioner and his retinue he took up residence in the Quebec Parliament Buildings which were themselves burned down in 1854. Lord Durham '*en fit raser les ruines*' of the château; see Literary and Historical Society of Quebec, *Transactions 1880–1*, Quebec, 1881. *Notes sur le Château St Louis*. Préparées par E. Gagnon.
24 Charles Buller, *Sketch of Lord Durham's Mission to Canada in 1838;* Lucas (ed.), *Lord Durham's Report*, vol. 3, p. 370.
25 *The Union Act, 1840*, 3 and 4 Vict. C. 35; and see also Creighton, *Dominion of the North*, p. 250.
26 Quoted in C. A. Bodelsen, *Studies in Mid-Victorian Imperialism*, New York, 1935, p. 18 note 1.
27 *Selections from the speeches of John, First Earl Russell 1817 to 1841 and from Dispatches 1859 to 1865* (2 vols), London, 1870, vol. 2, pp. 66–9; reprinted in A. B. Keith, *Selected Speeches and Documents on British Colonial Policy 1763–1917*, (2 vols), vol. 1, pp. 173–8.
28 *Cf.* Bodelsen, *Studies in Mid-Victorian Imperialism*, chapter 1.
29 Douglas Pike, *Paradise of Dissent, South Australia 1829–57*, London, 1957, examines critically Wakefield's actual rôle in the founding of the colony.
30 *Responsible Government for Colonies*, London, 1840; reprinted in E. M. Wrong, *Charles Buller and Responsible Government*, Oxford, 1926. See also Paul Knaplund in *James Stephen and the British Colonial System, 1813–1847*, Madison, 1953. for a critical reappraisal of Buller's indictment of Stephen.
31 Hansard, *Parl. Deb.* (Commons), 23 January 1838, vol. xl, coll. 384–6.
32 R. B. Pugh, 'The Colonial Office', *The Cambridge History of the British Empire*, vol. 3, chapter 19, p. 723.
33 *Parl. Deb.* (Commons), 6 March 1838, vol. xli, coll. 476–83.

34 Sir Arthur G. Doughty, *The Elgin-Grey Papers, 1846–1852* (4 vols.), Ottawa, 1937, vol. I, pp. 351–2.
35 Quoted *The Cambridge History of the British Empire*, vol. 2, p. 680.
36 D. G. Creighton, 'The Victorians and the Empire', *The Canadian Historical Review* (1938), vol. xix, p. 144.
37 Bodelsen, *Studies in Mid-Victorian Imperialism*, p. 59.
38 'Agenda for the Study of British Imperial Economy, 1850–1950' *Journal of Economic History* (1953), vol. xiii, no. 3, p. 257.
39 Creighton, 'The Victorians and the Empire', p. 141.
40 Doughty, *Elgin-Grey Papers*, vol. i, p. 448.
41 Creighton, *Dominion of the North*, pp. 256–7.
42 Creighton, 'The Victorians and the Empire', p. 144.
43 John Gallagher and Ronald Robinson, 'The Imperialism of Free Trade', *Economic History Review* (1953), vol. vi, no. 1, pp. 1–15; see also vol. xiv (April 1962) for a critique by O. G. Macdonagh, 'The Anti-Imperialism of Free Trade'. The phrase 'informal empire' to describe the expansion of Britain's financial and commercial power and indirect control beyond the limits of imperial sovereignty is said to have been first used by Professor C. R. Fay in *Imperial Economy and its Place in the Foundation of Economic Doctrine 1600–1932*, Oxford, 1934; see R. W. Winks, *The Historiography of the British Empire-Commonwealth*, Duke, 1966, p. 58.
44 Earl Grey, *The Colonial Policy of Lord John Russell's Administration* (2 vols), London, 1853, vol. 1, pp. 17–8.
45 G. S. Graham, 'A Canadian Declaration of Independence', *The Listener*, 5 November 1959.
46 The Memorial and the dispatches are reprinted in Keith, *Selected Speeches and Documents*, vol. 2, pp. 51–83.
47 See A. R. M. Lower, *Colony to Nation* (4th ed. revised), Toronto, 1964, pp. 281–9 and 379–80.
48 Quoted in Donald Creighton, *The Road to Confederation*, Toronto, 1964, p. 37.
49 *Ibid.*, pp. 136–40.
50 Public Archives of Canada, Series G, vol. 221A, 7 September 1866. Quoted in W. Menzies Whitelaw, 'Reconstructing the Quebec Conference', *The Canadian Historical Review* (1938), vol. xix, p. 137.
51 *The Quebec Resolutions* are reprinted in Keith, *Selected Speeches and Documents*, vol. 1, pp. 245–63.
52 P. B. Waite (ed.), *The Confederation Debates in the Province of Canada, 1865*, The Carleton Library, no. 2, Ottawa 1963, p. 57.
53 *Le Monde*, 26 July 1967, p. 6, col. 1.
54 Quoted Pierson, *Tocqueville and Beaumont in America*, pp. 343–4.
55 Waite (ed.), *The Confederation Debates*, p. 49.
56 Quoted by Alexander Brady in *The Transfer of Institutions*, W. B. Hamilton (ed.), Duke, 1964, chapter 3, 'Canada and the Model of Westminster,' p. 68. Professor Brady's analysis, pp. 59–80, is concise and illuminating.
57 André Siegfried, *The Race Question in Canada*, London, 1907, p. 133.
58 Keith, *Selected Speeches and Documents*, vol. 1, p. 292. The reference is given

to Keith on grounds of convenience. Macdonald's speeches are however also and more extensively reproduced in Waite (ed.), *The Confederation Debates*, pp. 39–48, 130–1, 134–5, 139–46 and 155–7.

59 Keith, *Selected Speeches and Documents*, vol. 1, p. 292.

60 On this point see A. Brady's *Democracy in the Dominions* (3rd ed.), Toronto, 1958, pp. 44–9.

61 *Cf*. K. C. Wheare, *Federal Government* (3rd ed.), London, 1953, pp. 19–21.

62 Borden Papers: The papers of Sir Robert Laird Borden in the National Archives, Ottawa.

63 30 and 31 Vict. c. 3.

64 Creighton, *Macdonald*, vol. 1, p. 464.

65 Hansard, *Parl. Deb.* (Commons), 28 February 1867, vol. clxxxv, col. 1184.

66 Creighton, *The Road to Confederation*, pp. 421–2.

67 *Ibid*., pp. 423–4.

68 Creighton, *Dominion of the North*, pp. 312–3.

CHAPTER 3

1 W. K. Hancock, *Smuts. The Sanguine Years 1870–1919*, Cambridge, 1962, pp. 108–10; see also Alan Paton, *Hofmeyr*, Cape Town, 1964, p. 73.

2 *Cf*. C. W. de Kiewiet, *British Colonial Policy and the South African Republics, 1848–1872*, London, 1929, pp. 2–3, on concepts of South African history, and the same author's *A History of South Africa, Social and Economic*, Oxford, 1941, pp. 47–8 on the nature of its problems.

3 W. K. Hancock and Jean van der Poel, *Selections from the Smuts Papers* (4 vols), Cambridge, 1966, vol. 1, p. 117.

4 James Bryce, *Impressions of South Africa*, London, 1897, p. 571.

5 A. F. Hattersley, 'Slavery at the Cape', *The Cambridge History of the British Empire*, vol. 8, pp. 272–7.

6 G. McC. Theal, *History of South Africa South of the Zambesi, 1843–54*, Cape Town, 1926–7, pp. 90–115; *The Cambridge History of the British Empire*, pp. 324–6, and E. A. Walker, *The Great Trek*, London, 1934.

7 The routes of the Voortrekkers were graphically set out in an exhibition at the Cape Archives in 1964.

8 See J. S. Galbraith, *Reluctant Empire: British Policy on the South African Frontier, 1843–54*, California, 1963, and also a review of it by E. A. Walker in *The Historical Journal*, vol. viii, no. 1 (1965), pp. 145–7.

9 I am indebted to Dr Ernst Kohl of the Deutsche Afrika-Gesellschaft for drawing my attention to this point. The original text is reproduced in G. W. Eybers, *Select Constitutional Documents illustrating South African History, 1795–1910*, London, 1918, p. 364.

10 For what is claimed to be the only authentic record of the discovery given by Jacobs in his old age, see Eric Rosenthal, *River of Diamonds*, Cape Town, 1957, pp. 10–2.

11 Hedley A. Chilvers, *The Story of de Beers*, London, 1939, pp. 6–7.

12 Two important studies have been made of British policy in South Africa at this time. The first was C. W. de Kiewiet, *The Imperial Factor in South*

Africa, Cambridge, 1937, and the second Dr C. F. Goodfellow's *The Policy of South African Confederation, 1870–1881*, Cape Town, 1967. Dr Goodfellow's study also includes (in chapter 2) an account of Earl Grey's embryonic scheme in the 1850s and an appraisal of its bearing on Carnarvon's later proposals.

13 G. McC. Theal, *History of South Africa, 1873–1884* (2 vols), London, 1919, vol 1, p. 271.

14 It was the subject of a study by Sir R. Coupland, *Zulu Battle Piece: Isandhlwana*, London, 1948.

15 Hansard, *Parl. Deb.* (Lords), vol. cclxxxvi, coll. 7–8.

16 James Bryce, *Impressions of South Africa* (new ed.), London, 1899, pp. xxi–xxiii.

17 J. S. Marais. *The Fall of Kruger's Republic*, Oxford, 1961, p. 1.

18 *Cf.* Alan Paton, *Hofmeyr*, Cape Town, 1964, pp. 7 and 158; 'Onze Jan' was a cousin of J. H. Hofmeyr, the subject of Paton's biography.

19 H. Marshall Hole, *The Making of Rhodesia*, London, 1926, p. 17–8.

20 A. G. Gardiner, *Pillars of Society*, London, 1913, pp. 12–5.

21 *German Diplomatic Documents, 1871–1914* (4 vols), selected and translated by E. T. S. Dugdale, London, 1928, vol. 3, p. 114.

22 There is uncertainty about when and how Rhodes' substantial contribution was paid; see C. C. O'Brien, *Parnell and his Party*, Oxford, 1957, p. 266 note 4.

23 Marais, *The Fall of Kruger's Republic*, p. 88.

24 A memorial volume, with photographs of the president, commemorating the first journey on the Delagoa Bay line, is preserved in Kruger's home, now a museum, in Pretoria.

25 John Buchan, *Memory Hold-the-Door*, London, 1940, p. 99.

26 Marais, *The Fall of Kruger's Republic*, p. 89.

27 J. L. Garvin, *The Life of Joseph Chamberlain* (3 vols), London, 1932–4, vol. 3, pp. 71–2.

28 The history of it has been written by Jean van der Poel, *The Jameson Raid*, Cape Town, 1951, and Elizabeth Pakenham, *Jameson's Raid*, London, 1960; see also Ethel Drus, 'A Report on the Papers of Joseph Chamberlain relating to the Jameson Raid and the Inquiry', *Bulletin of the Institute of Historical Research*, vol. xxv (1952), and 'The Question of Imperial Complicity in the Jameson Raid', *English Historical Review*, vol. lxviii (Oct. 1953).

29 Alfred Austin, *Jameson's Ride*; understandably this poem was not reprinted in later volumes of Austin's collected poems.

30 Garvin, *The Life of Joseph Chamberlain*, vol. 3, p. 78.

31 Pakenham in *Jameson's Raid* presents the case for Chamberlain; Van der Poel in *The Jameson Raid* and Marais in *The Fall of Kruger's Republic* the case against him. Professor Marais', indictment set out in chapter 4 is summarised pp. 94–5; it appears, given the lack of evidence on certain points, as conclusive as may be.

32 N. Rich and M. H. Fisher (eds), *The Holstein Papers* (4 vols), Cambridge, 1955–63, vol. 1, pp. 162–3.

33 A photograph in the museum at Dar es Salaam, where the colonel commanded German forces during 1893–5, makes the description plausible.
34 Dugdale, *German Diplomatic Documents 1871–1914*, vol. 2, p. 287.
35 Pakenham, *Jameson's Raid*, p. 96.
36 R. C. K. Ensor, *England 1870–1914*, Oxford, 1936, p. 246, and Marais, *The Fall of Kruger's Republic*, pp. 210–2.
37 See C. Headlam (ed.), *The Milner Papers, South Africa 1897–1899* (2 vols), London, 1931–3, vol. 1, p. 212, and also Marais, *The Fall of Kruger's Republic*, pp. 200–2, for an account of the electoral campaign.
38 Quoted by Marais, *The Fall of Kruger's Republic*, p. 196.
39 Headlam (ed.), *The Milner Papers*, vol. 1, pp. 221–2.
40 Marais, *The Fall of Kruger's Republic*, p. 298 note 1.
41 Headlam (ed.), *The Milner Papers*, vol. 1, pp. 349–53.
42 Ensor, *England 1870–1914*, p. 250–1.
43 For an account, especially of Smuts's rôle before and during the Bloemfontein conference see W. K. Hancock, *Smuts. The Sanguine Years*, Cambridge, 1962, chapter 5.
44 *Ibid.*, p. 99.
45 Headlam (ed.), *The Milner Papers*, vol. 1, pp. 407–15; for an account of the conference see chapter 15.
46 *Fabianism and the Empire*, London, 1900, p. 13.
47 This is the title of the first chapter of Professor G. H. Le May's *British Supremacy in South Africa, 1899–1907*, Oxford, 1965. The quotations that follow are from p. 36.
48 Quoted *ibid.*, p. 89 and see generally chapters 3 and 4.
49 The record is set out in *The Peace Negotiations*, Rev. J. D. Kestell (secretary to the Orange Free State government) and D. E. Van Velden (secretary to the government of the South African republic), London, 1912.
50 *Ibid.*, p. 59.
51 *Ibid.*, pp. 76–7.
52 *Ibid.*, pp. 79–87.
53 *Ibid.*, p. 91.
54 Merriman Papers, Cape Town Public Library.
55 The argument set out in the following pages is more fully developed in N. Mansergh, *South Africa 1906–1961: The Price of Magnanimity*, London, 1962.
56 Lord Riddell, *More Pages from My Dairy, 1908–1914*, London, 1934, p. 144; see also Randolph Churchill, *Churchill*, London, 1967, vol. 2, pp. 144–56, and R. Hyam, *Elgin and Churchill at the Colonial Office, 1905–1908*, London, 1968, pp. 103–36, for a detailed analysis of the circumstances surrounding the decision to restore self-government.
57 Hansard, *Parl. Deb.* (Commons), 1906, vol. clxii, col. 84.
58 This emerges *inter alia* from notes in the Campbell-Bannerman Papers at the British Museum.
59 J. A. Spender, *The Life of Sir Henry Campbell-Bannerman* (2 vols), London, 1923, vol. 2, pp. 237–8.

60 W. K. Hancock *Smuts* (2 vols), Cambridge, 1962 and 1968, vol. 2, p. 518.
61 Meriman Papers.
62 The first letter is in the Merriman Papers, Smuts to Merriman, 28 Nov. 1906, the second dated 1 August 1907, in Hancock and Van der Poel, *Selections from the Smuts Papers*, vol. 2, p. 355.
63 *Ibid.*
64 *Ibid.*
65 The authoritative account is L. M. Thompson, *The Unification of South Africa, 1902–10*, Oxford, 1960.
66 Quoted in Thompson, *The Unification of South Africa*, p. 169.
67 C.O. 417/351 ff. 392–3.
68 Le May, *British Supremacy in South Africa*, p. 177.
69 C.O. 291/112.
70 Merriman Papers
71 *Ibid.*, letter dated 13 March 1906; also reprinted in Hancock and Van der Poel, *Selections from the Smuts Papers*, vol. 2, p. 242.
72 *Ibid.*, vol. 2, p. 526; letter to Merriman dated 2 October 1908.
73 *Ibid.*, pp. 440–2; Smuts to Hobson, 13 July 1908.
74 *Ibid.*, pp. 530–2; letter dated 16 December 1908.
75 *Ibid.*, pp. 446–8; letter dated 19 July 1908.
76 Hansard, *Parl. Deb.* (Lords), 1909, vol. 2, col. 767.
77 Headlam (ed.), *The Milner Papers*, vol. 1, p. 178, and Le May, *British Supremacy in South Africa*, pp. 11–2, where the whole passage is quoted.

CHAPTER 4

1 J. A. Froude, *Oceana, or England and Her Colonies*, London, 1886, p. 82.
2 James Bryce, *Impressions of South Africa*, London, 1899, p. 589.
3 Froude, *Oceana, or England and Her Colonies*, p. 103.
4 André Siegfried, *Democracy in New Zealand*, London, 1914, p. 63.
5 *Ibid.*, pp. 48 and 90.
6 Alan Moorehead, *Cooper's Creek*, London, 1963, Chapter 1.
7 Edward Gibbon Wakefield, *A Letter from Sydney, the Principal Town of Australasia, Together with the Outline of a System of Colonisation*, London, 1829, pp. 201–2.
8 C. W. Dilke, *Greater Britain*, London, 1885, p. 391.
9 N. H. Carrier and J. R. Jeffrey, *External Migration, 1815–1950*, H.M.S.O., 1953, p. 95.
10 Elie Halévy, *A History of the English People in the Nineteenth Century* (new ed., 6 vols), London, 1961, vol. 3, *The Triumph of Reform*, pp. 230–3; A. G. L. Shaw, *Convicts and the Colonies. A Study of Penal Transportation from Great Britain and Ireland to Australia and other parts of the British Empire*, London, 1966, gives in an appendix (pp. 363–8) statistical details about the numbers of convicts, their countries of origin and their Australian destinations on the basis of available records.
11 *A Letter from Sydney* (see note 7 above).
12 *Ibid.*, pp. 169–70.

13 *Cf.* Keith Sinclair, *A History of New Zealand*, London, 1961, p. 52.
14 Carrier and Jeffrey, *External Migration*, p. 95.
15 In 1951 a department store in Christchurch erected a panoramic representation of the landing of a Victorian family; top-hatted, frock-coated father, mother with bonnet and bustle, followed by a boy and a girl and solid Victorian furniture coming ashore, in celebration of the centenary of the arrival of the Canterbury settlers 1851. In response to protests that the mother was wearing no wedding ring, an outsize ring was painted in!
16 Quoted in Harold Miller, *New Zealand*, London, 1950, p. 143.
17 F. W. Eggleston, *Reflections of an Australian Liberal*, Melbourne, 1953, chapter 3 and Shaw, *Convicts and the Colonies*, p. 358.
18 E. H. Hargraves, *Australia and its Gold Fields*, London, 1855, pp. 114–6; see also C. M. H. Clark, *Select Documents in Australian History 1851–1900*, Sydney, 1955, pp. 3–4.
19 Quoted in *ibid.*, pp. 5–8.
20 Miller, *New Zealand*, pp. 75–6.
21 Quoted in Clark, *Select Documents*, p. 473.
22 Governor Grey to Earl Grey 3 May 1847, quoted in W. K. Jackson and G. A. Wood, *New Zealand Parliament and Maori Representation*, Institute of Commonwealth studies, Reprint series no. 22. The article is a valuable concise summary of the question.
23 Keith Sinclair, *The Origins of the Maori Wars*, Wellington, 1957, pp. 85–110.
24 Miller, *New Zealand*, p. 53, and see chapter 5 *passim.*
25 Jackson and Wood, *New Zealand Parliament and Maori Representation*, pp. 387–94.
26 Siegfried, *Democracy in New Zealand*, pp. 350–1.
27 Angus Ross, *New Zealand Aspirations in the Pacific in the Nineteenth Century*, Oxford, 1964, pp. 112–3 and chapter 16 *passim.*
28 *Ibid.*, p. 290.
29 Keith Sinclair, *A History of New Zealand* (2nd ed.), London, 1961, p. 165.
30 F. L. W. Wood, *Understanding New Zealand*, New York, 1944, pp. 61–3.
31 Siegfried, *Democracy in New Zealand*, pp. 50–6.
32 *Ibid.*, p. 61.
33 James Bryce, *Modern Democracies* (2 vols), London, 1921, vol. 2, *New Zealand*, pp. 300–2, and W. P. Reeves, *The Long White Cloud* (4th ed.), London, 1950, pp. 302–3; see also Siegfried, *Democracy in New Zealand*, pp. x–xi, on Seddon.
34 Siegfried, *Democracy in New Zealand*, pp. 97–9.
35 Keith Sinclair's *William Pember Reeves, New Zealand Fabian*, Oxford, 1965, provides a biographical study.
36 Clark, *Select Documents*, pp. 477–8.
37 Dilke, *Greater Britain*, pp. 285–6.
38 Quoted in M. Clark, *Sources of Australian History* (new ed.), Oxford, 1963, p. 433.
39 Clark, *Select Documents*, p. 475.
40 *Ibid.*, p. 474–6.

41 J. A. La Nauze, *Alfred Deakin. A Biography* (2 vols), Melbourne, 1965, vol. 1, pp. 158 and 167; chapter 8 contains much important evidence on Deakin's rôle and on the movement to federation.
42 Quoted in A. B. Keith, *Selected Speeches and Documents on British Colonial Policy, 1763–1917* (2 vols), vol. 1, p. 344.
43 L. F. Crisp, *The Parliamentary Government of the Commonwealth of Australia*, London, 1949, pp. 1–2.
44 A. Deakin, *The Federal Story* (2nd edition, edited by J. A. La Nauze), Melbourne, 1963; see also La Nauze, *Deakin*, vol. 1, p. 171 and chapter 8 *passim*.
45 Keith, *Selected Speeches and Documents*, vol. 1, p. 347.
46 *Ibid.*, p. 351.
47 *Ibid.*, p. 361.
48 63 and 64 Vict. c. 12.
49 La Nauze, *Deakin*, vol. 1, p. 190 and chapter 9 *passim.*
50 *Cf.* K. C. Wheare, *The Constitutional Structure of the Commonwealth*, Oxford, 1960, pp. 50–2.
51 Crisp, *The Parliamentary Government of the Commonwealth of Australia*, pp. 224–6.
52 *Ibid.*, p. 236.
53 Geoffrey Sawer, *Australian Government Today* (new and revised ed.), Melbourne, 1964, pp. 26–7.
54 Bryce, *Modern Democracies*, vol. 2, p. 181.
55 *Ibid.*, p. 178.

CHAPTER 5

1 J. R. Seeley, *The Expansion of England*, London, 1883, p. 2.
2 *Ibid.*, p. 8.
3 *Ibid.*, p. 14.
4 *Ibid.*, p. 13.
5 *Ibid.*, p. 11.
6 *Ibid.*, p. 16.
7 *Ibid.*, p. 300.
8 *Ibid.*, p. 293.
9 *Ibid.*, p. 46.
10 *Ibid.*, pp. 302–4 and 196.
11 *Ibid.*, p. 16.
12 W. F. Monypenny and G. E. Buckle, *The Life of Disraeli* (6 vols), London, 1910–29, vol. 5, p. 194; also quoted in George Bennett, *The Concept of Empire* (2nd ed.), London, 1962, p. 257; see above, p. 5.
13 Philip Magnus, *Gladstone* (new ed.), London, 1963, p. 264.
14 Seeley, *The Expansion of England*, pp. 11–2.
15 W. C. B. Tunstall, *The Cambridge History of the British Empire*, vol. 2, *Imperial Defence, 1815–1870*, p. 806; C. P. Stacey, *Canada and the British Army, 1846–1871*, Toronto, 1936, p. 43; also quoted in R. A. Preston, *Canada and 'Imperial Defense,'* Durham N.C., 1967, p. 23.

16 Hansard, *Parl. Deb.* (Commons), vol. cc, col. 1900–3. Reprinted in Bennett, *The Concept of Empire*, pp. 254–5 for Gladstone, and Hansard, *Parl. Deb.* (Commons), vol. clxv, col. 1060, for the Resolution on the Mills Committee.
17 Monypenny and Buckle, *The Life of Disraeli*, vol. 5, p. 193.
18 See D. C. Gordon, *The Dominion Partnership in Imperial Defense, 1870–1914*, Johns Hopkins, 1965, chapter 2 *passim*, and Preston, *Canada and 'Imperial Defense'*, chapter 1. For later developments see *The Cambridge History of the British Empire*, vol. 3, chapter 5 by R. E. Robinson and chapter 7 by W. C. B. Tunstall, *Imperial Defence 1870–1897*.
19 C. W. Dilke, *Greater Britain* (2 vols), London, 1868, vol. 2, p. 151.
20 H. W. Lucy, *A Diary of Two Parliaments* (2 vols), London, 1885–6, vol. 1, p. 419.
21 Magnus, *Gladstone*, p. 261.
22 See Gordon, *The Dominion Partnership*, pp. 62–7, and Preston, *Canada and 'Imperial Defense'*, pp. 91–3 and 131–6, for recent accounts of its work based on the use of the original papers.
23 *Cambridge History of the British Empire*, vol. 3, pp. 220–1.
24 A. Tilney Bassett (ed.), *Gladstone's Speeches*, London, 1916, p. 570.
25 A. J. P. Taylor, *Germany's First Bid for Colonies 1884–1885*, London, 1938, p. 4.
26 See above, p. 42.
27 Reprinted in Bennett, *The Concept of Empire*, p. 262.
28 S. R. Mehrotra, 'Imperial Federation and India, 1868–1917', *Journal of Commonwealth Political Studies*, vol. 1, no. 1.
29 *Proceedings of the Colonial Conference, 1887*, vol. 1 (C. 5091), p. 5. H.C. (1887), lvi., p. 19.
30 Gordon, *The Dominion Partnership*, pp. 91–2; Preston, *Canada and 'Imperial Defense'*, pp. 102–5.
31 C. 7553. *Report by the Right Hon. the Earl of Jersey on the Colonial Conference at Ottawa, with the Proceedings of the Conference and certain Correspondence*, London, August 1894.
32 J. Schull, *Laurier, The First Canadian*, Toronto, 1965, pp. 346–55, gives a graphic account of the celebrations and their impact on Laurier who became both a privy councillor and a knight.
33 C. 8596. *Proceedings of a Conference between the Secretary of State for the Colonies and the Premiers of the Self-Governing Colonies at the Colonial Office*, London, June and July 1897, pp. 5–6.
34 Borden Papers, 35345, and see also Schull, *Laurier, The First Canadian*, p. 356.
35 C. 8596, pp. 7–8 for Chamberlain's speech and pp. 15–18 for the subsequent naval debate.
36 Lady Violet Bonham Carter, *Winston Churchill As I knew Him*, London, 1965, pp. 50–2.
37 Maurice Ollivier (ed.), *The Colonial and Imperial Conferences from 1887 to 1937* (3 vols), Ottawa, 1954, vol. 1, p. 153 and Cd. 1299, p. 4. No report of the 1902 Conference Proceedings was published in London. Papers relating to the Conference were, however, published there in Cd. 1299 and correspondence relating

to the proposed publication of the Report of the Proceedings in Cd. 1723.

38 *The Poems of Matthew Arnold 1840–1867*, London, 1913, p. 429, 'Heine's Grave'.

39 Ollivier, *Colonial and Imperial Conferences*, vol. 1, pp. 154–5. Cd. 1299, p. 5.

40 Reprinted in A. B. Keith, *Speeches and Documents on British Colonial Policy 1763–1917* (2 vols), Oxford, 1948, vol. 2, p. 238. See also Gordon, *The Dominion Partnership*, pp. 147–8, for an account of the discussions preceding the drafting of the memorandum.

41 Ollivier, *Colonial and Imperial Conferences*, vol. 1, p. 155.

42 The speeches of Selborne, Laurier and Barton are reprinted in Ollivier, *Colonial and Imperial Conferences*, vol. 1, pp. 161–8 see; also Gordon, *The Dominion Partnership*, chapters 7–9, and R. A. Preston, *Canada and 'Imperial Defense'*, pp. 287–307.

43 Canada, *Parliamentary Debates* (Commons), vol. li, col. 72 (5 Feb. 1900).

44 *Ibid.*, vol. lvii, col. 4726 (12 May 1902).

45 Julian Amery, *The Life of Joseph Chamberlain* (4 vols), London, 1951, vol. 4, p. 423. The first three volumes of the biography were written by J. L. Garvin.

46 Ollivier, *Colonial and Imperial Conferences*, vol. 1, p. 156; see generally pp. 155–7.

47 *Survey of British Commonwealth Affairs*, vol. 2, part 1, p. 85.

48 *Ibid.*

49 *Cf.* Amery, *The Life of Joseph Chamberlain*, vol. 4, p. 525, for Chamberlain's letter on this point to the Duke of Devonshire; see also pp. 400–7 for circumstances in which the duty on corn was imposed, and for Commonwealth Imperial Preference generally see chapter 47.

50 For a recent political analysis see Alfred Gollin, *Balfour's Burden: Arthur Balfour and Imperial Preferences*, London, 1965.

51 Richard Jebb, *Studies in Colonial Nationalism*, London, 1905; see especially the Preface and chapters 6 and 7 on 'The South African War' and 'The Colonial Conference, 1902', respectively.

52 Amery, *The Life of Joseph Chamberlain*, vol. 4, p. 435.

53 *Correspondence relating to the Future Organisation of Colonial Conferences*, 1905, Cd. 2785.

54 Cd. 3523. There was an illuminating discussion on the substitution of the term 'dominion' for 'colony', *ibid.*, pp. 78–83.

55 J. A. La Nauze, *Alfred Deakin: A Biography* (2 vols), Melbourne, 1965, vol. 2, p. 500.

56 Cd. 3523, pp. 71–2; see also Deakin's earlier comments pp. 8–10, 26–9, 41–4, 63–5; La Nauze, *Alfred Deakin*, vol. 2, chapter 22, for background; and J. A. Cross, 'Whitehall and the Commonwealth', *Journal of Commonwealth Political Studies*, vol. 2, no. 3, pp. 190–1.

57 Cd. 3523, p. 35.

58 *Ibid.*, pp. 37–42.

59 See generally J. A. Cross, *Whitehall and the Commonwealth: British Departmental Organisation for Commonwealth Relations 1900–1966*, London, 1967; for the 1907 reforms see chapter 3.

60 India Office Library. Morley Papers MSS. Eur.D. 573/2; Schull, *Laurier*, p. 348, and La Nauze, *Deakin*, vol. 1, p. 203.
61 Cd. 3523, p. vii.
62 C.I.D. Paper 161B. *Committee of Imperial Defence: Constitution and Functions*, 27 August 1912 (Cab. 4/5).
63 L. S. Amery, *Thoughts on the Constitution*, Oxford, 1953, p. 146; and Maurice Hankey, *The Supreme Command 1914–1918* (2 vols), London, 1961, vol. 1, pp. 43 and 125.
64 Cd. 3523, pp. 97–9.
65 Cd. 3524, p. 19.
66 *Memorandum on Sea Power and the Principles involved in it*, presented to the Colonial Conference 1902, Cd. 1299, and in amended version Cd. 1597, 1903.
67 Hansard, *Parl. Deb.* (Commons), 17 March 1914; reprinted in Keith, *Speeches and Documents*, p. 354.
68 *Cf.* R. C. K. Ensor, *England 1870–1914*, Oxford, 1936, pp. 412–13, Gordon, *The Dominion Partnership*, chapter 10, and Preston, *Canada and 'Imperial Defense'*, chapter 13, for a detailed account of the 1909 naval crisis and U.K.–dominion discussions.
69 For Canadian views and generally see Borden Papers, 66441–5 for notes on the Liberals and a fleet unit; also 35352–4 for notes on Imperial Defence and for Australian views. See also Hankey, *The Supreme Command*, vol. 1, pp. 125–7, and see Gordon, *The Dominion Partnership*, pp. 237–9.
70 Cd. 5741, p. 84.
71 *War Memoirs of David Lloyd George* (new ed., 2 vols), London, 1938, vol. 1, p. 28, and Hankey, *The Supreme Command*, vol. 1, pp. 128–9.
72 Cd. 5745. Also reprinted in Keith, *Speeches and Documents*, vol. 2, pp. 304–7.
73 Keith, *Speeches and Documents*, vol. 2, pp. 308–38.
74 *Ibid.*, p. 353.
75 C.I.D. Paper 81–C. The Representation of the Dominions on the Committee of Imperial Defence, 18 May 1911; also Harcourt's despatch of 10 December 1912 to Governors-General of the dominions in Borden Papers 66218–20, and Hankey, *The Supreme Command*, vol. 1, pp. 130–2.
76 The relevant memoranda and other particulars as circulated are *inter alia* to be seen in the Laurier Papers, 1907 and 1911, vols 742–44, the Union Archives, Pretoria, and Harcourt's despatch (no. 30) of 20 January 1911 to Viscount Gladstone, governor-general of South Africa.
77 CAB. 37/106 1911, no. 52.
78 Cd. 5745. *Minutes of Proceedings of the Imperial Conference, 1911*, pp. 194–6 in respect of Civil Service exchanges. New Zealand had advanced more limited proposals in 1907, relating only to the staff of the Colonial Office. Elgin had argued that it would serve no useful purpose and indeed that the proposal might be founded on a misapprehension since the C.O. had nothing to do with local administration in the dominions and dealt with business which depended more on principles than local characteristics. Cd. 3523, p. 619 and also Cd. 5746, p. 214 (XII) for summary on 'Interchange of Civil Servants'.

79 *Ibid.*, pp. 55–6.
80 Keith Sinclair, *Imperial Federation. A Study of New Zealand Policy and Opinion 1880–1914*, London, 1955, p. 41–4.
81 Cd. 5745, p. 70.
82 *Smuts Papers*, vol. 3, p. 36.
83 Hankey, *The Supreme Command*, p. 130 and chapter 13 *passim.*
84 Cd. 5745, p. 22 and also reprinted in Keith, *Speeches and Documents*, vol. 2, p. 243–4.
85 C.I.D. Minutes of 119th Meeting, 1 August 1912 (885 B).
86 The Laurier Papers in the National Archives, Ottawa, and more especially the Memoranda on Colonial and Imperial Conferences and on proposals for an Imperial Council in the Borden Papers, National Archives, Ottawa, which provide a valuable retrospective summary in terms of Canadian interests, have been consulted in the writing of this chapter (35344–54 and 65924). The National Archives in Pretoria have also been consulted, especially the correspondence and other records relating to the Imperial Conference, 1911.

CHAPTER 6

1 C. S. Goldman (ed.), *The Empire and the Century*, London, 1905.
2 C. Headlam, *The Milner Papers* (*South Africa*) *1897–1905* (2 vols), London, 1931–3, vol. 2, p. 561. The letter was dated 27 February 1906.
3 S. Gopal, *British Policy in India 1858–1905*, Cambridge, 1965, pp. 180 and 303–4.
4 The story is told in Sir Almeric Fitzroy, *Memoirs* (2 vols), London N.D., vol. 1, p. 348.
5 R. Hyam, 'Smuts and the Decision of the Liberal Government to Grant Responsible Government to the Transvaal, January and February 1906', in *The Historical Journal*, vol. viii, no. 3 (1965), p. 380–98, emphasises Elgin's rôle in this issue. His valuable book, *Elgin and Churchill at the Colonial Office 1905–1908*, argues on the basis of a full scale examination of the evidence for a reassessment of Elgin's rôle.
6 See R. R. James, *Rosebery*, London, 1963, chapter 9, *passim.*
7 See Asquith Papers, Dep. 11. Churchill to Asquith, 14 March 1908.
8 Asquith Papers, Bodleian Library. Box 11, letter dated 14 March 1908.
9 India Office Library, Morley Papers, MSS. Eur. D. 573/2.
10 *Ibid.*, MSS. Eur. D. 573/2 and 573/11.
11 Roy Jenkins, *Asquith*, London, 1964.
12 *List of Cabinet Papers*, P.R.O., H.M.S.O., London, 1964. Copies are in the Asquith Papers. Photo copies of the full set 1868–1916 are on Cab. 41., P.R.O.
13 See above p. 132.
14 E. T. S. Dugdale (ed.), *German Diplomatic Documents, 1871–1914* (4 vols), London, 1928, vol. 1, pp. 177–8.
15 Maurice Hankey, *The Supreme Command 1914–1918* (2 vols), London, 1961, vol. 1, p. 130.

16 *Ibid.*, pp. 134–5.
17 Dugdale, *German Diplomatic Documents*, vol. 4, pp. 359–60.
18 R. A. Preston, *Canada and 'Imperial Defence'*, Durham N.C., 1967, pp. 462–3.
19 For an account of 'The Empire at War, 1914–1918, see *The Cambridge History of the British Empire*, chapter 16, from which the statistics are taken.
20 W. K. Hancock, *Smuts* (2 vols), Cambridge, 1962 and 1968, vol. 1, pp. 379 and 390.
21 *C.H.B.E.*, vol. 3, p. 634.
22 O. D. Skelton, *Life and Letters of Sir Wilfrid Laurier* (2 vols), Toronto, 1921, vol. 2, p. 437.
23 A. R. M. Lower, *Colony to Nation* (4th ed)., Toronto, 1964, p. 466.
24 *C.H.B.E.*, vol. 3, p. 634.
25 Borden Papers, letter of 3 November 1915.
26 Borden Papers, letter of 4 January 1916 to Sir George Perley.
27 W. M. Hughes, *The Splendid Adventure*, London, 1929, chapters 2–4 (see especially pp. 40–1).
28 Hansard, *Parliamentary Debates* (Commons), vol. lxxxviii, col. 1355.
29 L. S. Amery, *My Political Life* (2 vols), London, 1953–4, vol. 2, p. 91. See also Lord Long, *Memories*, London, 1923, p. 237, for improvements in communication effected by him as colonial secretary at this time.
30 Cd. 9005, p. 6.
31 Hankey, *The Supreme Command*, vol. 2, p. 660.
32 Records of the imperial war cabinet were handled by the war cabinet office in the same way as those of the war cabinet and its minutes are classified in a separate series – Imperial War Cabinet Minutes in Cab. 23; *Cf. The Records of the Cabinet Office to 1922*, London, P.R.O., 1966, pp. 4–5, and also Hankey, *The Supreme Command*, vol. 2, pp. 658–9.
33 Hankey, *The Supreme Command*, vol. 2, p. 658.
34 *Ibid.*, p. 816, and *The Records of the Cabinet Office*, p. 5.
35 Amery, *My Political Life*, vol. 2, pp. 105–7.
36 *Ibid.*, p. 108.
37 Hankey, *The Supreme Command*, vol. 2, p. 816 and Preston, *Canada and 'Imperial Defence'*, pp. 519–22.
38 L. S. Amery, *Thoughts on the Constitution* (2nd ed.), London, 1953, p. 120.
39 Borden Papers.
40 *Ibid.*
41 *Ibid.* On Hughes' role see L. F. Fitzhardinge, *Canadian Historical Review*, June 1968, vol. xlix, 2, pp. 160–9.
42 L. C. Christie, *Notes on the Development at the Paris Peace Conference of the Status of Canada as an International Person*, July 1 1919, Borden Papers.
43 Amery, *My Political Life*, vol. 2, pp. 177–8.
44 *Official History of Australia in the War of 1914–18*; Ernest Scott, *Australia During the War*, vol. 2, pp. 787 and 796.
45 See Hancock, *Smuts*, chapter 21 and below p. 374.
46 *Cf.* K. C. Wheare's comment in *C.H.B.E.*, vol. 3, p. 664.
47 *Minutes of Proceedings of the Imperial Conference*, 1917, Cd. 8566.

48 C. O. 886/10. For an account of the circumstances in which the memorandum came to be written, as well as an analysis and appraisal of its content, see Hancock, *Smuts*, vol. 2, pp. 38–49. Cf. also C. M. van den Heever, *General J. B. M. Hertzog*, Johannesburg, 1946, p. 212; O. Pirow, *Hertzog*, Cape Town, 1957, p. 103; and H. Duncan Hall, *The American Political Science Review*, December 1953, pp. 1005–6.
49 Cmd. 1474.
50 *Ibid.*
51 Hancock, *Smuts*, vol. 2, p. 49.
52 Cmd. 1474.

CHAPTER 7

1 The Anglo-Irish background to the Treaty Settlement is examined in N. Mansergh, *The Irish Question 1840–1921*, London, 1965, and in longer perspective in J. C. Beckett, *The Making of Modern Ireland, 1603–1923*, London, 1966.
2 Philip Guedalla, *The Queen and Mr. Gladstone* (2 vols), London, 1933, vol. 2, p. 177.
3 The Redmond Papers are in the National Library, Dublin.
4 A. P. Thornton, *The Habit of Authority*, London, 1966, p. 291.
5 Sir Henry Lucy, *A Diary of Two Parliaments, 1880–1885*, London, 1886, pp. 84–5.
6 Quoted in Kenneth Young, *Arthur James Balfour*, London, 1963, p. 100.
7 Sir Henry Lucy, *Memories of Eight Parliaments*, London, 1908, pp. 155–7.
8 Quoted in L. P. Curtis, *Coercion and Conciliation in Ireland 1880–1892. A Study in Conservative Unionism*, Princeton, 1963, p. 179. This book provides the authoritative account of A. J. Balfour's Irish administration and the ideas behind it.
9 John Biggs-Davison, *George Wyndham: A Study in Toryism*, London, 1951, p. 236.
10 See Young, *Arthur James Balfour*, p. 139, for a strange forecast of Wyndham's early death.
11 Biggs-Davison, *George Wyndham: A Study in Toryism*, p. 132.
12 *Ibid.*, pp. 152–3.
13 Stephen Gwynn (ed.), *The Anvil of War: Letters between F. S. Oliver and his Brother, 1914–1918*, London, 1936, p. 23.
14 Robert Blake, *The Unknown Prime Minister*, London, 1955, p. 531. The author believed that until the war Ulster was one of the two things Bonar Law really cared about. The other was tariff reform.
15 A. M. Gollin, *Proconsul in Politics: A Study of Lord Milner in opposition and in power*, London, 1964, pp. 45–6 and 193. See generally pp. 184–94.
16 Hansard, *Parl. Deb.* (Commons), lxxxiii, coll. 801–2.
17 Arthur Griffith, *The Resurrection of Hungary: A Parallel for Ireland* (3rd ed.), Dublin, 1918, pp. 89–91.
18 It is reprinted in Dorothy Macardle, *The Irish Republic* (new ed.), New York, 1965, pp. 135–7.

19 W. S. Churchill, *The World Crisis; The Aftermath*, London, 1929, p. 281.
20 Macardle, *The Irish Republic*, chapter 27 and T. D. Williams (ed.), *The Irish Struggle*, London, 1966, chapter 3, 'Sinn Féin Policy and Practice (1916–26)' by Desmond Ryan.
21 W. B. Yeats, *Collected Poems*, London, 1934, p. 205. W. K. Hancock, *Survey of British Commonwealth Affairs* (2 vols), London, 1937–42, vol. 1, p. 99, and D. MacDonagh's essay on 'Plunkett and MacDonagh' in F. X. Martin (ed.), *Leaders and Men of the Easter Rising: Dublin 1916*, London, 1967, pp. 166–7.
22 Churchill, *The World Crisis; The Aftermath*, p. 290.
23 Harold Nicolson, *King George V*, London, 1952, pp. 346–9.
24 *The Round Table*, vol. xi, no. 43 (June 1921), p. 505.
25 Churchill, *The World Crisis; The Aftermath*, p. 290.
26 The arrangements for the meeting are recorded in extracts from Miss Stevenson's diary reprinted in Lord Beaverbrook, *The Decline and Fall of Lloyd George*, London, 1963, pp. 85–6; the account of the interview, at which Miss Stevenson was not present, is as recollected by President de Valera. The differences are only in respect of detail.
27 Cmd. 1470, p. 1.
28 Tom Jones, *Lloyd George*, London, 1951, p. 188–9.
29 Hansard, *Parl. Deb.* (Commons), vol. cxxvii, col. 1125.
30 See Nicolson, *King George V*, pp. 349–51, and Hancock, *Smuts*, vol. 2, pp. 51–9, for accounts of this episode.
31 Sir Charles Petrie, *The Life and Letters of the Right Hon. Sir Austen Chamberlain* (2 vols), London, 1939, vol. 2, pp. 166–7.
32 Cmd. 1474, p. 23.
33 Dáil Éireann: Debate on the Treaty between Great Britain and Ireland; Session December 1921 – January 1922, p. 34.
34 *Ibid.*, pp. 45–6.
35 *Ibid.*, p. 27.
36 *Ibid.*, pp. 24–6.

CHAPTER 8

1 A. B. Keith, *The Constitution, Administration and Laws of the Empire*, London, 1924, pp. 21–34, examines the continuing limitations on dominion sovereignty in this period. See also the same author's *The Dominions as Sovereign States*, London, 1938, chapter I, for an historical appraisal of developments in their status. There is a brief but cogent unpublished analysis in the Government of India, Home Department Special File No. 94/29 on the Constitutional Growth and International Position of the Dominions, prepared for the information of the viceroy in 1929, which has also been consulted by permission of the Indian National Archives, New Delhi.
2 Cf. India Home Department 94/29 and Keith, *The Dominions as Sovereign States*, p. 16.
3 Vincent Massey, *What's Past is Prologue*, Toronto, 1963, p. 109. Massey

was appointed first Canadian minister at Washington by Mackenzie King in 1926.

4 Keith, *The Dominions as Sovereign States*, p. 8.
5 *Ibid.*, pp. 15–16.
6 Cab., 23 E–6.
7 A. B. Keith, *Speeches and Documents on the British Dominions*, pp. 46 and 86.
8 R. MacGregor Dawson, *William Lyon Mackenzie King 1874–1923*, London, 1958, pp. 404–16, contains the most informative account of the incident as seen through the eyes of the prime minister who made it important in Commonwealth history. For a general account see W. K. Hancock, *Survey of British Commonwealth Affairs*, vol. 1, pp. 251–2.
9 Canada, *Parl. Deb.* (Commons), 1 Feb. 1923, vol. 1, p. 33.
10 Dawson, *William Lyon Mackenzie King*, pp. 432–5.
11 *Ibid.*, p. 425.
12 *Ibid.*, p. 423.
13 *Ibid.*, p. 438.
14 Quoted *ibid.*, p. 420.
15 Marchioness Curzon of Kedleston, *Reminiscences*, London, 1955, p. 181.
16 Dawson, *William Lyon Mackenzie King*, pp. 467–8.
17 Keith, *Speeches and Documents*, p. 318; Dawson, *William Lyon Mackenzie King*, pp. 477–8.
18 *Ibid.*, pp. 479–80.
19 Massey, *What's Past is Prologue*, p. 135, and F. H. Soward, *Some Aspects of Canadian Foreign Policy in the Last Quarter Century*, Transactions of the Royal Society of Canada, 4th series, vol. iv, section iii (1966), p. 139.
20 L. S. Amery, *My Political Life* (2 vols), London, 1955, vol. 2, pp. 335–6.
21 H. Duncan Hall, 'The Genesis of the Balfour Declaration of 1926', *Journal of Commonwealth Political Studies*, vol. 1, no. 3, pp. 171–8.
22 See Hansard, *Parl. Deb.* (Commons), vol. 188, coll. 520–1 for Chamberlain's speech quoted above, and for discussions at the Imperial Conference see CAB. 32/56 E(I.R.–26).
23 O. Pirow, *J. B. M. Hertzog*, Cape Town, 1957, p. 105.
24 Harold Nicolson, *King George V*, London, 1952, pp. 476–7.
25 L.J.R. 95 P.C.C. 114. Reprinted in Frederick Madden, *Imperial Constitutional Documents, 1765–1952*, Oxford, 1953, pp. 47–54.
26 On the Irish position see especially CAB. 32/56 E(I.R.–26) 3, and for comment on it E(I.R.–26) 31B, and also M. McInerney, 'Mr John A. Costello Remembers' in *The Irish Times*, 4 September 1967. For Canada see H. Blair Neatby, *William Lyon Mackenzie King, 1924–1932*, Toronto, 1963, p. 182, and CAB. 32/56 E(I.R.–26) 6th meeting.
27 Neatby, *Mackenzie King*, p. 183.
28 CAB. 32/56 E(I.R.–26). See also C. M. Van den Heever, *General J. B. M. Hertzog*, Johannesburg, 1946, pp. 213–17.
29 T. de V. White, *Kevin O'Higgins*, London, 1948, p. 221.
30 CAB. 32/56 E(I.R.–26) 3 reproduced the Irish memorandum on existing anomalies; CAB. 32/47, E115 that on Privy Council appeals.

31 The drafts are reproduced in CAB. 32/56. For comments see De V. White, *Kevin O'Higgins*, p. 222.

32 Imperial Conference 1926; Summary of Proceedings, Cmd. 2768, contains the Report of the Committee. It is reprinted in Keith, *Speeches and Documents*, pp. 161–70. See also Amery, *My Political Life*, vol. 2, pp. 379–98.

33 Blanche E. C. Dugdale, *Arthur James Balfour* (2 vols), London, 1936, vol. 2, pp. 281–2, and personal information.

34 This is very questionable. The belief that Britain retained control is implicit for example in the published German Foreign Office Documents on the origins of the second world war.

35 See Nicholas Mansergh, *Survey of British Commonwealth Affairs: Problems of External Policy 1931–1939*, London, 1952, pp. 73–9, 429–32, for some assessment of this.

36 Hancock, *Survey*, vol. 1, p. 263.

37 K. C. Wheare, *The Statute of Westminster and Dominion Status* (4th ed.), London, 1949, pp. 28–9.

38 See *ibid.*, p. 79.

39 Cmd. 3479.

40 Cmd. 3717 and 3718.

41 See Nicolson, *King George V*, pp. 483–4.

42 Cmd. 3717.

43 Nicolson, *King George V*, pp. 477–82.

44 Cmd. 3479, sec. 60; reprinted in Keith, *Speeches and Documents*, p. 189.

45 22 Geo. 5, c. 4.

46 The text of the statute and source material on dominion reactions to it are to be found in Nicholas Mansergh, *Documents and Speeches on British Commonwealth Affairs, 1931–1952* (2 vols), London, 1953, vol. 1, secs. 1 and 2.

47 *Ibid.*, pp. 21–7.

48 Reprinted *ibid.*, pp. 4–6.

49 The statement of 22 March 1932, here summarised and the subsequent exchanges referred to below were reprinted in a British White Paper, Cmd. 4056 and an Irish White Paper, P. No. 650. See also Hancock, *Survey*, vol. 1, chapter 6.

50 The Judgment, *Moore and Others versus the Attorney General for the Irish Free State* is reproduced in Mansergh, *Documents and Speeches*, vol. 1, pp. 305–14.

51 Lord Beaverbrook, when he learned of the procedure adopted, commented to the king, 'Sir, you have put your head on the execution block. All that Baldwin has to do now is to swing the axe.' *A King's Story. The Memoirs of H.R.H. the Duke of Windsor*, London, 1951, pp. 346–7.

52 The relevant legislation and speeches on the abdication are reprinted in Mansergh, *Documents and Speeches*, vol. 1, sec. 5.

53 Wheare, *The Statute of Westminster*, pp. 288–9. See generally chapter 11.

54 Hancock, *Survey*, vol. 2, part 1, p. 233. Chapter 1 contains the classic analysis of intra-Commonwealth trade in these years.

55 J. B. Brebner, *North Atlantic Triangle*, New Haven, 1945, p. 309.

56 Hancock, *Survey*, vol. 2, part 1, pp. 245–51.

CHAPTER 9

1 And not only on the lips of South African politicians. In the debate in 1906 on self-government for the Transvaal, the under secretary of state for the colonies, Winston Churchill, the leader of the opposition, A. J. Balfour, and a young Labour member, J. Ramsay MacDonald, used it in this sense. The 'native question' was the phrase applied to relations between the peoples of European and African race. See Hansard, *Parl. Deb.* (Commons), 4th series 1906, vol. 162, coll. 776–804.
2 See his speech of March 1954 at the opening of the Fifth (unofficial) Commonwealth Relations Conference at Lahore as reprinted in N. Mansergh, *The Multi-Racial Commonwealth*, London, 1955, p. 144.
3 J. A. Hobson, *Imperialism: A Study* (3rd ed.), London, 1938, p. 51.
4 S. Gopal, *British Policy in India 1858–1905*, Cambridge, 1965, p. 261.
5 Hansard, *Parl. Deb.* (Commons), Third series, vol. cccxlii (1890), col. 93.
6 See Government of India Reforms Office File 142/30–R, where extracts from the dispatches are reprinted in a paper on 'The Interpretation of the term Responsible Government' prepared by W. H. Lewis, dated 12 June 1930.
7 Hansard, *Parl. Deb.* (Lords), 4th series, vol. 198, col. 1985. See also John, Viscount Morley, *Recollections* (2 vols), London, 1917, vol. 2, pp. 172–3.
8 *Report of the Indian Statutory Commission*, Cmd. 3569 (1930), *vol. 2, Recommendations*, pp. 6–7.
9 Government of India Act 1858, 21 and 22 Vict., c. 106.
10 The Indian Councils Act 1861, 24 and 25 Vict., c. 67, reprinted C. H. Philips, *The Evolution of India and Pakistan 1858–1947: Select Documents*, London, 1962, pp. 35–8.
11 *Cf.* R. B. McDowell, *The Irish Administration*, London, 1964, p. 61, and chapter 2 generally.
12 Philips, *The Evolution of India and Pakistan*, p. 3.
13 Parl. Papers, vol. 56, no. 102, col. 1515, reprinted in Philips, *The Evolution of India and Pakistan*, p. 13.
14 The dispatches are reprinted in Philips, *The Evolution of India and Pakistan*, pp. 19–23.
15 Quoted in Gopal, *British Policy in India*, p. 249.
16 Philip Woodruff, *The Men Who Ruled India* (2 vols), London, 1954, vol. 1, *The Founders*; vol. 2, *The Guardians*.
17 H. A. L. Fisher, *James Bryce* (2 vols), London, 1927, vol. 1, pp. 259–60. The letter was to his mother and dated 20 November 1888.
18 Curzon to Hamilton, 4 June 1903. Quoted in Philips, *The Evolution of India and Pakistan*, p. 73.
19 K. M. Panikkar, *Asia and Western Dominance*, London, 1953, p. 16.
20 Gopal, *British Policy in India*, pp. 224–5.
21 Reprinted in Government of India Home Department Special No. 94/29.
22 Indian Round Table Conference (Second Session) (7 Sept. – 1 Dec. 1931), Cmd. 3997 (1932), pp. 389–90.

23 Earl of Ronaldshay, *The Life of Lord Curzon* (3 vols), London, 1928, vol. 2, pp. 320–1.
24 *Cf.* Gopal, *British Policy in India*, p. 298.
25 Ronaldshay, *The Life of Lord Curzon*, vol. 2, p. 151.
26 Report on Indian Constitutional Reforms (1918), Cd. 9109, para. 6.
27 Government of India Home Department 94/29.
28 *Ibid.*
29 Reprinted in Sir M. Gwyer and A. Appadorai, *Speeches and Documents on the Indian Constitution 1921–47* (2 vols), Bombay, 1957, vol. 1, p. 220.
30 *Cf. ibid.*, pp. 221–2.
31 The Earl of Halifax, *Fulness of Days*, London, 1957, pp. 114–23.
32 Government of India File No. 29/37 – G (D) 1937 Lewis to Laithwaite and extract from a private letter of 21 June 1937 from the secretary of state to the viceroy.
33 *Ibid.* Home Department 9/M.A./39 letter of Ewart to Thorne 17 February 1939 in which the Muslim League outlook on elections is described as 'typically unbusinesslike and opportunist'.
34 Personal conversation with the secretariat of the Indian National Congress, 1958.

CHAPTER 10

1 Quoted A. B. Keith, *Speeches and Documents on the British Dominions 1918–1931*, Oxford, 1932, p. 275.
2 *Ibid.*
3 James Eayrs, *In Defence of Canada: Appeasement and Rearmament*, Toronto, 1965, pp. 16–27, provides a lively and authoritative account of the 'Riddell incident'.
4 G. P. de T. Glazebrook, *A History of Canadian External Relations*, Toronto, 1950, p. 411.
5 Quoted in Eayrs, *In Defence of Canada*, p. 26.
6 Canada, *Parl. Deb.* (Commons), 1936, vol. 1, p. 98. See also N. Mansergh, *Survey of British Commonwealth Affairs 1931–1939*, London, 1952, pp. 116–7.
7 *Ibid.*, p. 232, and generally. Also Gwendolen Carter, *The British Commonwealth and International Security*, Toronto, 1947, p. 243.
8 Lord Halifax, *Fulness of Days*, London, 1957, p. 197.
9 *Daily Telegraph*, 23 March 1936. See also Mansergh, *Survey of British Commonwealth Affairs*, p. 234.
10 CAB. 32/130 (1937) records the discussions on foreign policy. For the published report see Imperial Conference 1937. *Summary of Proceedings.* Cmd. 5482.
11 J. Shepherd, *Australia's Interests and Policies in the Far East*, New York, 1940, p. 73.
12 Mackenzie King's account of his conversation is reprinted in Eayrs, *In Defence of Canada*, pp. 226–31, document 3.
13 Reprinted in F. H. Soward *et al*, *Canada in World Affairs: The Pre-War Years*, Toronto, 1941, pp. 270–1.

14 C. M. van den Heever, *Hertzog*, Johannesburg, 1946, p. 271.

15 Vincent Massey, *What's Past is Prologue*, Toronto, 1963, pp. 259–62.

16 Quoted in Alan Watt, *The Evolution of Australian Foreign Policy 1938–1965*, Cambridge, 1967, p. 4.

17 D. C. Watt, *Personalities and Policies*, London, 1965, essay 8, on the Commonwealth and the Munich crisis, provides an interesting reappraisal. On Canadian policies at Munich see Eayrs *In Defence of Canada*, pp. 67–72.

18 For Lord Templewood, see 'The Lesson of Munich' in *The Listener*, 9 December 1948 and for Lord Halifax, see Halifax, *Fulness of Days*, pp. 197–8.

19 E. L. Woodward and Rohan Butler (eds), *Documents on British Foreign Policy, 1919–1939* (10 vols), 3rd Series, London, 1949–61, vol. 1, p. 602 and vol. 2, p. 252; and Watt, *Personalities and Policies*, p. 169.

20 W. S. Churchill, *The Second World War* (6 vols), London, 1950, vol. 1, p. 271; and W. K. Hancock, *Smuts* (2 vols), Cambridge, 1962 and 1968, vol. 2, p. 311.

21 G. Heaton Nicholls in *South Africa in My Time*, London, 1961, has a movingly candid account of the episode, pp. 339–44.

22 *Cmd. 6832* (1946), gives United Kingdom figures.

23 Viscount Bruce of Melbourne kept a record of the proceedings at these meetings throughout the war years and through his courtesy the author has had an opportunity of reading them. The range and liveliness of the discussions that took place was not widely appreciated because of their private and informal character.

24 J. W. Pickersgill, *The Mackenzie King Record* (2 vols), vol. 1, Toronto, 1960, p. 241.

25 Canada, *Parl. Deb.* (Commons), 17 February 1941, reprinted N. Mansergh, *Documents and Speeches on British Commonwealth Affairs, 1931–52* (2 vols), London, 1954, vol. 1, pp. 530–1.

26 Pickersgill, *The Mackenzie King Record*, p. 241.

27 *Ibid.*, p. 247.

28 See his telegram to Sir Arthur Fadden August 1941 in Churchill, *The Second World War*, vol. 3, pp. 758–60, reprinted in Mansergh, *Documents and Speeches on British Commonwealth Affairs, 1931–1952*, vol. 1, pp. 540–2.

29 *The Times*, 8 September 1941, quoted in N. Mansergh, *Survey of British Commonwealth Affairs, Problems of Wartime Cooperation and Post-War Change 1939–1952*, London, 1958, p. 114.

30 *The Melbourne Herald*, 28 December 1941, reprinted in Mansergh, *Documents and Speeches on British Commonwealth Affairs 1931–1952*, vol. 1, pp. 549–50.

31 Reprinted in Mansergh, *ibid.*, pp. 568–75.

32 Ibid., pp. 575–9.

33 Canada, *Parl. Deb.* (Commons), 1944, vol. 1, pp. 41–2; reprinted in Mansergh, *Documents and Speeches on British Commonwealth Affairs, 1931–1952*, vol. 1, pp. 583–4.

34 *Ibid.*, pp. 595–6.

CHAPTER II

1 Jawaharlal Nehru, *The Unity of India*, London, 1948, p. 307.
2 Quoted by K. Veerathappa, *Britain and the Indian Problem (September 1939–May 1940)* in *International Studies* (Bombay), vol. 7, no. 4, p. 546. Also see article generally, pp. 537–67.
3 N. Mansergh, *Documents and Speeches on British Commonwealth Affairs, 1931–1952* (2 vols), London, 1954, vol. 2, pp. 612–14.
4 Hansard, *Parl. Deb.* (Commons), vol. 378, coll. 1069–70, reprinted in Mansergh, *Documents and Speeches on British Commonwealth Affairs, 1931–1952*, vol. 2, pp. 614–15; see also pp. 616–17 and, for Indian reactions, pp. 617–25.
5 J. W. Wheeler-Bennett, *King George VI, His Life and Reign*, London, 1958, p. 697.
6 Reprinted in Mansergh, *Documents and Speeches, 1931–1952*, vol. 2, pp. 633–5.
7 Wheeler-Bennett, *King George VI*, p. 703.
8 Cmd. 6821. Reprinted in N. Mansergh, *Documents and Speeches, 1931–1952* vol. 2, pp. 644–52.
9 Cmd. 7047. Reprinted *ibid.*, pp. 659–61.
10 Wheeler-Bennett, *King George VI*, p. 711.
11 Alan Campbell-Johnson, *Mission with Mountbatten*, London, 1951, p. 38–114.
12 *Ibid.*, pp. 108–10, and for record see Earl Mountbatten of Burma, *Time Only to Look Forward*, London, 1949, pp. 26–47.
13 10 & 11 Geo. 6, Ch. 30, reprinted in Mansergh, *Documents and Speeches, 1931–1952*, vol. 2, pp. 669–85.
14 *Ibid.*, pp. 700–2.
15 Wheeler-Bennett, *King George VI*, p. 702.
16 Reprinted in Cmd. 6196, *India and the War*, and in Sir Maurice Gwyer and A. Appadorai, *Speeches and Documents on the Indian Constitution 1921–47* (2 vols), Bombay, 1957, vol. 2, pp. 443–4, and Mansergh, *Documents and Speeches, 1931–1952*, vol. 2, pp. 608–9.
17 Leonard Mosley, *The Last Days of the British Raj*, London, 1961, pp. 162–5 tells the story and on p. 163 assesses the weight of the material destroyed. In the Preface he states that he put questions to Sir Conrad Corfield amongst others without their being responsible for what he subsequently wrote. The incident is also recorded in Michael Edwardes, *The Last Years of British India*, London, 1963, pp. 186–9.
18 E.g. The Resolution of the Congress at the Ramgarh Session, 20 March 1940: 'The Congress cannot admit the right of the rulers of India states . . . to come in the way of Indian freedom. Sovereignty in India must rest with the people, whether in the states or the provinces. . ..' Cmd. 6196 and reprinted in Mansergh, *Documents and Speeches*, vol. 2, pp. 606–8.
19 *Cf.* Wilfrid Russell, *Indian Summer*, Bombay, 1951, pp. 102–5.
20 D. G. Tendulkar, *Mahatma: Life of Mohandas Karamchand Gandhi* (8 vols), Bombay, 1951–4, vol. 6, p. 11.
21 Marquess of Zetland, *'Essayez': the Memoirs of Lawrence, Second Marquess of Zetland*, London, 1956, p. 292.

22 *Ibid.*, p. 265.
23 Reprinted in Gwyer and Appadorai, *Speeches and Documents*, vol. 2, pp. 440–2, and in Mansergh, *Documents and Speeches, 1931–1952*, vol. 2, pp. 609–12.
24 Maulana A. K. Azad, *India Wins Freedom*, Calcutta, 1959, p. 185.
25 Personal information.
26 Jawaharlal Nehru, *The Discovery of India*, Calcutta, 1946, pp. 320–2, and Rajendra Prasad, *Autobiography*, Bombay, 1957, pp. 444–8, and personal conversations with both.
27 Prasad, *Autobiography*, p. 446.
28 Azad, *India Wins Freedom*, pp. 160–2, and Penderel Moon, *Divide and Quit*, London, 1961, p. 14.
29 V. P. Menon, *The Transfer of Power in India*, Bombay, 1957, p. 97, and cf. also Percival Spear, *India*, Michigan, 1961, pp. 404–5, on the Congress rejection of the Cripps offer 1942.
30 *Statement of 8 August 1940*. Reprinted in Mansergh, *Documents and Speeches, 1931–1952*, vol. 2, pp. 612–4, and see above p. 297.
31 Cmd. 6350. Reprinted *ibid.*, vol. 2, pp. 616–17.
32 Cmd. 6821. Reprinted *ibid.*, vol. 2, pp. 644–52.
33 Sir Francis Tuker, *While Memory Serves*, London, 1950, chapter 12, 'The Great Calcutta Killing'.
34 Hansard, *Parl. Deb.* (Commons), vol. 127, col. 1112.
35 Cmd. 6821.
36 Azad, *India Wins Freedom*, p. 167.
37 *Ibid.*, p. 168. But Pandit Nehru mentioned to the author on 6 April 1954 and therefore long before Azad's work was published that at the morning session of the cabinet the Muslim League members had been invited to tea and had declined.
38 Cmd. 7047, reprinted in Mansergh, *Documents and Speeches, 1931–1952*, vol. 2, pp. 659–61.
39 Michael Edwardes, *The Last Years of British India*, p. 95.
40 Menon, *The Transfer of Power in India*, pp. 358–65. See also Campbell-Johnson, *Mission with Mountbatten*, pp. 62, 88–90.
41 Azad, *India Wins Freedom*, p. 207.
42 Michael Brecher, *Nehru, A Political Biography*, London, 1959, pp. 376–7. Nehru, he notes, did not believe Pakistan was a viable state and took the view that 'sooner or later the areas which had seceded would be compelled by force of circumstances to return to the fold'.
43 *Ibid.*, pp. 206–27.
44 Quoted in Brecher *Nehru*, p. 338; Moon, *Divide and Quit*, p. 77. See also Ian Stephens, *Pakistan*, London, 1963, pp. 131–6, 143 and 182 *et seq.*, where there is an understanding account of the Sikh predicament and the Sikh reaction to it.
45 Indian Independence Act, 1947 (10 & 11 Geo. 6 Ch. 30).
46 Menon, *The Transfer of Power in India*, p. 404. See generally, pp. 404–7.
47 Quoted *ibid.*, p. 384.
48 Georges Fischer in *Le Parti Travailliste et la Décolonization de l'Inde*, Paris, 1966, has written a detailed analysis of the Indian policies of the Labour

Party: on self-determination see especially pp. 123–33; C. R. Attlee, a terse account of the policy of the Labour government in *As It Happened*, London, 1954, pp. 179–86, and some further comments are recorded by Lord Francis-Williams in *A Prime Minister Remembers*, London, 1961, pp. 202–19.

49 To the author in Delhi on 4 March 1958.

50 Personal conversation in Bombay, April 1947.

51 Legislative Assembly Debates (1947), vol. 1, p. 101.

CHAPTER 12

1 W. K. Hancock, *Smuts* (2 vols), Cambridge, 1967, vol. 2, pp. 431–3.

2 The text of the legislation on nationality and citizenship in all parts of the Commonwealth is grouped with comment upon its purposes in N. Mansergh, *Documents and Speeches on British Commonwealth Affairs, 1931–1952* (2 vols), London, 1954, vol. 2, section xix and the Commonwealth Immigrants Act, 1962 (10 and 11 Eliz. 2, c. 21) is reprinted in N. Mansergh, *Documents and Speeches on Commonwealth Affairs, 1952–62*, London, 1963, pp. 741–7.

3 This proposition was questioned in Britain by Professor A. B. Keith as early as 1922, and in Ireland by Professor James Hogan of University College, Cork, who conceived of an Irish republican dominion.

4 Cab 32/130. E.37 No. 12.

5 E.g. *Dáil Deb.* 29 November 1944, vol. 95, coll. 1024–5; *ibid.*, 19 June 1946, vol. 101, coll. 2181–2; *ibid.*, 24 June 1947, vol. 107, col. 87 and Hansard, *Parl. Deb.* (Commons), 22 April 1948, vol. 449, col. 1975.

6 Michael McInerney, 'Mr John A. Costello Remembers', in *The Irish Times*, 8 September 1967.

7 *Ibid.*

8 The Republic of Ireland Act 1948 (No. 22 of 1948), and Mr Costello's speech, *Dáil Deb.*, vol. 113, coll. 347–87, introducing the bill are reprinted in Mansergh, *Documents and Speeches, 1931–1952*, vol. 2, pp. 802–9.

9 Hansard, *Parl. Deb.* (Lords), 15 December 1948, vol. 159, coll. 1051–93; reprinted in Mansergh, *Documents and Speeches, 1931–1952*, vol. 2, pp. 811–21.

10 *Ibid.*

11 McInerney, 'Mr John A. Costello Remembers', and Australia, *House of Representatives Deb.*, 26 November 1948, vol. 200, pp. 3583–4; reprinted in Mansergh, *Documents and Speeches, 1931–1952*, vol. 2, pp. 809–11.

12 New Zealand. Republic of Ireland Act (No. 13 of 1950); reprinted in Mansergh, *Documents and Speeches, 1931–1952*, vol. 2, p. 837.

13 J. D. B. Miller, *Britain and the Old Dominions*, London, 1966, p. 147.

14 A Report of the proceedings of the conference was published under the title *Asian Relations*, Delhi, 1948. The author was one of the United Kingdom observers at the conference.

15 India, Constituent Assembly Deb., vol. 5, pp. 4–5, reprinted in Mansergh, *Documents and Speeches, 1931–1952*, vol. 2, p. 701.

16 Sapru Correspondence. Government of India, National Library, Calcutta, P. 381. Enclosed with letter from Sir Jagdish Prasad.
17 *Indian Constituent Assembly Deb.*, vol. 5, pp. 4–5.
18 Sapru Correspondence A–68.
19 *Ibid.*, R.42, R.43, S.253 and S.361, letter dated 24 April 1948 from S. Sinha.
20 H. Tinker, *The Union of Burma* (4th ed.), London, 1967, pp. 22–7. The relevant documents are reprinted in Mansergh, *Documents and Speeches, 1931–1952*, vol. 2, pp. 760–93.
21 The papers relating to the independence of Ceylon are reprinted *ibid.*, section xii.
22 Hansard, *Parl. Deb.* (Lords), Deb., vol. 152, col. 1205.
23 J. W. Wheeler-Bennett, *King George VI*, London, 1958, p. 721–3.
24 *Ibid.*, p. 722.
25 *Ibid.*, pp. 723–6.
26 Reprinted in Mansergh, *Documents and Speeches, 1931–1952*, vol. 2, pp. 847–57. See section xv generally for dominion comment and reactions.
27 Reprinted in Mansergh, *Documents and Speeches on Commonwealth Affairs, 1952–1962*, London, 1963, pp. 304–6.
28 *Ibid.*

CHAPTER 13

1 The point is made in A. J. P. Taylor, *English History 1914–1945*, Oxford, 1965, p. 600 note 1.
2 *Ibid.*, p. 600.
3 See above pp. 292–3.
4 *Parl. Deb.* (Commons), vol. 450, coll. 1315–9, reprinted in N. Mansergh, *Documents and Speeches on British Commonwealth Affairs, 1931–1952*, London, 1953, vol. 2, pp. 1131–3.
5 Mansergh *ibid.*, p. 1138.
6 Canada, *Parl. Deb.* (Commons), 1948, vol. 4, pp. 3441–50; reprinted in Mansergh, *ibid.*, pp. 1128–9.
7 *Lok Sabha Deb.*, 1954, pt. 2, vol. vii, coll. 3675–85, reprinted in N. Mansergh, *Documents and Speeches on Commonwealth Affairs, 1952–1962*, London, 1963, p. 463, and see *The Times of India*, 10 September 1954, for report of Speech to Delhi Press Association.
8 Cmd. 7257. See above p. 332.
9 *Parl. Deb.* (Commons), 19 June 1955, vol. 542, col. 42.
10 Quoted in James Eayrs, *Canada in World Affairs, October 1955 to June 1957*, Toronto, 1959, pp. 187–8, from *The Economist*, 10 November 1956.
11 Quoted in James Eayrs, *The Commonwealth and Suez: A Documentary Survey*, London, 1964, p. 194. This work provides a lively connecting commentary linking the documentary records.
12 In a statement issued in Madras on 4 November 1956, and reprinted in Mansergh, *Documents and Speeches, 1952–1962*, p. 521, and in Eayrs, *The Commonwealth and Suez*, p. 256.
13 Canada, *Parl. Deb.* (Commons), 27 November 1956, 4th (spec) sess. pp. 52–

5, reprinted in Mansergh, *Documents and Speeches, 1952–1962*, p. 515.

14 *Full Circle: The Memoirs of the Right Hon. Sir Anthony Eden*, Cambridge, Mass. 1960, p. 610.

15 Quoted in Eayrs, *The Commonwealth and Suez*, p. 168. For an account of Menzies' own role in the Suez crisis see Sir Robert Menzies, *Afternoon Light: Some Memoirs of Men and Events*, London, 1967, chapter 8.

16 Duncan Sandys, *The Modern Commonwealth*, London, H.M.S.O., 1962, pp. 9–10.

17 *The Annual Register, 1955*, p. 74.

18 *Report of the Committee on Representational Services Overseas appointed by the Prime Minister under the Chairmanship of Lord Plowden, 1962–3*, Cmnd 2276 (1964) observed that 'before the war the relationship of Britain to other Commonwealth countries was still largely a maternal one in the sense that British ambassadors in foreign countries normally looked after the interests of the dominions as well', pp. 3–7.

19 J. D. B. Miller, *The Commonwealth in the World*, London, 1958, p. 275.

20 This is a principal theme of R. E. Robinson's and J. Gallagher's *Africa and the Victorians*, London, 1961.

21 One former colonial territory, British Somaliland, on independence became part of the larger independent state of Somalia, which united British with Italian Somaliland in the Somali Republic, a state outside the Commonwealth.

22 Mansergh, *Documents and Speeches, 1952–1962*, p. 347. Professor Rajan drew the author's attention to the fact that Mr Macmillan used the self-same phrase – 'wind of change' – in Accra at the outset of his tour of Africa but it had attracted no particular attention.

23 The title Sir Michael Blundell chose for his autobiography (London, 1964).

24 S. C. Easton, *The Twilight of European Colonialism*, New York, 1960, p. 519 and generally.

25 Held in London in July and November 1963 respectively. See Cmnd 2121, Annex A and Cmnd 2203, Annex A.

26 *Commonwealth Survey* (London), 22 October 1963, vol. 9, no. 22, pp. 885–8.

27 M. S. Rajan, *The Post-War Transformation of the Commonwealth*, Delhi, 1963.

28 *Parl. Deb.* (Commons), vol. 531, coll. 504–5. Reprinted in Mansergh, *Documents and Speeches, 1952–1962*, pp. 213–18.

29 *Nigeria, Report of the Commission appointed to inquire into the fears of minorities and the means of allaying them*, Cmnd 505. See Mansergh *ibid.*, pp. 57–66.

30 Nigeria (Constitution) Order in Council S.1. No. 1652, 1960.

31 W. P. Kirkman, *Unscrambling an Empire*, London, 1966, p. 13. For the text of the reports of Colonial Constitutional Conferences, draft constitutions and speeches on Independence Bills in the House of Commons, see Mansergh, *Documents and Speeches, 1952–1962*, pp. 35–290.

32 *Report of the Nyasaland (Devlin) Commission of Enquiry 1959*, Cmnd 814. See Mansergh, *ibid.*, pp. 133–40.

33 *The Advisory (Monckton) Commission on the Review of the Constitution of Rhodesia and Nyasaland*, 1960, Cmnd 1148. See Mansergh, *ibid.*, pp. 141–52.

34 Sir Roy Welensky, *Welensky's 4000 Days. The Life and Death of the Federation of Rhodesia and Nyasaland*, London, 1964. See especially chapters 11–14.
35 *The Multi-Racial Commonwealth, Proceedings of the Fifth Unofficial Commonwealth Relations Conference, Held at Lahore, Pakistan, 17–27 March 1954. A Report by* N. Mansergh, London, 1955, p. 114.
36 Sir Robert Menzies thought the departure from 'sound procedure fatal', *Afternoon Light*, p. 213.
37 *Cf. The Annual Register 1961*, pp. 63–4 for a contemporary record written by the author on which this account is based. See also the South African articles in *The Annual Register* 1961 and also 1960.
38 Menzies, *Afternoon Light*, p. 213.
39 The speeches are reprinted in Mansergh, *Speeches and Documents, 1952–1963*, pp. 365–400.
40 Reprinted in part, *ibid.*, p. 370 note 1.
41 For Final Communiqué see Cmnd. 2890. Earlier *Documents relating to the negotiations between the United Kingdom and Southern Rhodesian Governments* November 1963–November 1965 are in Cmnd. 2807.
42 For Final Communiqué see Cmnd. 3115.
43 Cmnd. 3171.
44 Prime Minister's Department, Salisbury CSR 49–1966.
45 Cmnd. 1449 and reprinted in Mansergh, *Documents and Speeches, 1952–1962*, pp. 634–45.
46 Mansergh, *ibid.*, pp. 650–1.
47 *The Commonwealth and the Sterling Area* Statistical Abstract No. 84, 1963 provides the essential figures. For as convincing an argument as could be made for Commonwealth trade expansion and its importance to Britain see the Editorial in *The Round Table*, July 1967, entitled *Saving Commonwealth Trade*. For the statistical trend see B. R. Mitchell with Phyllis Deane, *Abstract of British Historical Statistics*, Cambridge, 1962.
48 *Ibid.*, p. 667. For an official record see Commonwealth Relations Office List 1964, London H.M.S.O.
49 D. G. Creighton, *Dominion of the North*, Cambridge, Mass., 1944, p. 256.

CHAPTER 14

1 See above p. 83.
2 W. K. Hancock, *Smuts* (2 vols), vol. 1, *The Sanguine Years, 1870–1919*, Cambridge, 1962, chapter 10.
3 *Ibid.*, p. 37.
4 W. K. Hancock and J. van der Poel, *Selections from the Smuts papers* (4 vols), Cambridge, 1966, vol. 1, part 3 include Smuts's correspondence during the Anglo-Boer War and his unfinished and heretofore unpublished Memoirs of it. For the quotation see his letter to his wife dated 2 June 1901 from Standerton, pp. 392–4.
5 *Ibid.*
6 *African*, 837a. The writer was Frederick Graham. See also above p. 84.
7 Hancock, *Smuts*, vol. 1, p. 215, and generally.

8 Merriman Papers.
9 The Papers of the Right Hon. Sir Patrick Duncan. Letter to Lady Selborne from the South African National Convention, Cape Town, 28 January 1909.
10 Hancock, *Smuts*, vol. 1, p. 159.
11 Duncan Papers.
12 Hancock, *Smuts*, vol. 1, p. 301.
13 *Ibid.*, chapter 21.
14 Hancock, *Smuts*, vol. 2, pp. 10 and 324.
15 *Ibid.*, p. 473.
16 Albert Luthuli, *Let My People Go*, London, 1962, p. 197.
17 Speech to the Empire Parliamentary Association, 25 November 1943, reprinted N. Mansergh, *Documents and Speeches on British Commonwealth Affairs, 1931–1952*, London, 1953, vol. 1, p. 569.
18 Hancock, *Smuts*, vol. 2, p. 412.
19 Alan Paton, *Hofmeyr*, Cape Town, 1964, chapters 29–40 *passim*.
20 President de Valera's judgment was the more telling, because he felt he had also been a victim of Smuts' 'slimness.' Professor Hancock's account in *Smuts*, vol. 2, pp. 56–61, makes clear the limits of Smuts' understanding of Irish nationalist sentiments. For quotation above see *ibid.* p. 325.
21 The two volumes of the biography so far published are R. MacGregor Dawson's *William Lyon Mackenzie King, vol. 1, 1874–1923*, Toronto, 1958, and H. B. Neatby's *William Lyon Mackenzie King, 1924–1932*, Toronto, 1963.
22 Neatby, *William Lyon Mackenzie King, 1924–1932*, pp. 355–6. For earlier quotations see pp. 29 and 207.
23 *Ibid.*, p. 44 and see generally chapter 3, entitled 'Educating Downing Street'.
24 *Ibid.*, chapter 9.
25 *What's Past Is Prologue, The Memoirs of the Right Hon. Vincent Massey, C.H.*, Toronto, 1963, p. 112 and Neatby, *William Lyon Mackenzie King, 1924–1932*, pp. 190–1.
26 Neatby, *William Lyon Mackenzie King, 1924–1932*, p. 363.
27 See above, pp. 276–7, and James Eayrs, *In Defence of Canada: Appeasement and Rearmament*, Toronto, 1965, p. 63, and document 3 in appendices. For Eden's subsequent comments see N. Mansergh, *Survey of British Commonwealth Affairs, 1931–1939*, Oxford, 1952, pp. 124–5.
28 J. W. Pickersgill, *The Mackenzie King Record* (2 vols), vol. 1, Toronto, 1960, alone published.
29 *Ibid.*, p. 150.
30 *Ibid.*, p. 301.
31 *Ibid.*, pp. 72–3.
32 *Cf.* R. T. Shannon, *Gladstone and the Bulgarian Agitation, 1876*, London, 1963, chapter 1.
33 Pickersgill, *The Mackenzie King Record*, vol. 1, p. 681.
34 *Ibid.*, p. 687.

35 *Ibid.*, p. 234.
36 *Ibid.*, p. 436.
37 *Ibid.*, p. 247.
38 *Ibid.*, pp. 233–4.
39 *Ibid.*, p. 318.
40 C. C. Lingard and R. G. Trotter, *Canada In World Affairs, 1941–1944*, Toronto, 1950.
41 Pickersgill, *The Mackenzie King Record*, vol. 1, pp. 530–1.
42 The Earl of Birkenhead, *Halifax: The Life of Lord Halifax*, London, 1965, pp. 220 and 243.
43 The Rt. Hon. Lord Butler, *Jawaharlal Nehru: The Struggle for Independence*, Cambridge, 1966, pp. 8–11.
44 Jawaharlal Nehru, *The Unity of India*, London, 1941, pp. 290–3, and Mansergh, *Survey of British Commonwealth Affairs 1931–39*, pp. 359–60.
45 Jawaharlal Nehru, *The Unity of India*, p. 397.
46 Sapru Papers, Letter dated 22 April 1948.
47 Pandit Nehru told the author in 1947 that he never went on any speaking tour without a second microphone by way of reinsurance. The quotations are from Marie Seton, *Panditji. A Portrait of Jawaharlal Nehru*, London, 1967, p. 174.
48 Jawaharlal Nehru, *An Autobiography*, London, 1936, pp. 597–8.
49 *Jawaharlal Nehru's Speeches, 1949–1953* (2nd imp.), Ministry of Information and Broadcasting, Delhi, 1957, pp. 159, 189 and generally 158–60, 179–93.
50 *Ibid.*, pp. 127 and 124.
51 India, *Lok Sabha Debates*, 2nd ser., 1959, pt. 2, vol. xxxiv, coll. 8006–12, and reprinted N. Mansergh, *Documents and Speeches on Commonwealth Affairs, 1952–62*, pp. 590–4.
52 *Annual Register*, 1962, p. 66.
53 *Nehru's Speeches*, p. 124.
54 *Ibid.*, p. 126.
55 *Ibid.*, p. 272.
56 *Ibid.*, pp. 223–5.
57 *Ibid.*, pp. 225 and 272–3.
58 Mansergh, *Documents and Speeches, 1952–62*, pp. 762–4.
59 S. Abid Husain, *The Way of Gandhi and Nehru*, Bombay, 1959, chapters 8 and 9.
60 *Ibid.*, p. 156.
61 Seton, *Panditji; A Portrait of Jawaharlal Nehru*, p. 454.

CHAPTER 15

1 Quoted in C. V. Wedgewood, *Truth and Opinion*, London, 1960, p. 157.
2 *Parl. Deb.* (Commons), 14 May 1900, vol. lxxxiii, col. 102.
3 J. P. Plamenatz, *On Alien Rule and Self-Government*, London, 1960, p. 17.
4 India, *Lok Sabha Deb.* 3rd series, vol. xlvi–no. 29 (24 Sept. 1965), col. 7528.

5 *The Times of Malta*, 15 November 1967.
6 Reprinted in N. Mansergh, *Documents and Speeches on Commonwealth Affairs, 1952–1962*, London, 1963, pp. 276–8.
7 Sir George Gilbert Scott, *Personal and Professional Recollections*, London, 1879, chapter 4.
8 André Siegfried, *The Race Question in Canada*, London, 1907, pp. 178–9.
9 N. Mansergh, *The Multi-Racial Commonwealth*, London, 1955, pp. 132 and 142.
10 CAB. 32. E. 37. No. 12 paras 40–2.
11 Cmd. 6677. Reprinted in N. Mansergh, *Documents and Speeches on British Commonwealth Affairs, 1931–1952* (2 vols), Oxford, 1954, vol. 2, pp. 718–19.
12 Quoted in Sir Charles Webster, *The Art and Practice of Diplomacy*, London, 1961.
13 For the relevant Reports see Mansergh, *Documents and Speeches, 1952–1962*, pp. 692–9 and 702–14.
14 Seeley, pp. 1–2.
15 *The Sunday Times of Malta*, 12 November 1967. The delegate was Dr Guildo de Marco, Nationalist Member of the House of Representatives.
16 Sir R. Menzies, *The British Commonwealth of Nations in International Affairs.* A Lecture (Adelaide, 1950).
17 *The Times*, 2 April 1964.
18 *Le Figaro*, 5 November 1967.
19 The phrase was used by Dr Ramsay, Archbishop of Canterbury, preaching at the University Church of Great St Mary's, Cambridge.

BIBLIOGRAPHY

The subject and the literature upon it are so vast that even a selective bibliography must necessarily run into many pages. There is furthermore the problem of the frontiers, on the one side dividing Commonwealth from imperial history and on the other side from the national histories of the member-states. Bibliographies tend to fall into two principal categories – the comprehensive Empire-Commonwealth and the more specifically Commonwealth. In the first category two recent and valuable bibliographies are *The Historiography of the British Empire-Commonwealth*, Durham N.C., 1966, edited by Robin W. Winks and Professor J. E. Flint's *Books on the British Empire and Commonwealth*, London, 1968, and two of continuing usefulness are Professor V. T. Harlow's *The Historiography of the British Empire and Commonwealth since 1945* submitted to *XIth Congrès International des Sciences Historiques* at Stockholm, 1960, and published in *Rapport V. Histoire Contemporaine*, Uppsala, 1960, and, in great detail but for an earlier period only, *The Cambridge History of the British Empire*, vol. 3, *The Empire-Commonwealth, 1870–1919*, pp. 769–907. For a general historiographical essay on both Empire and Commonwealth there is Philip Curtin's 'The British Empire and Commonwealth in Recent Historiography', *American Historical Review*, vol. lxv, October 1959. The Historical Association's pamphlet, *Notes on the Teaching of Empire and Commonwealth History*, London 1967, by G. M. D. Howat, offers a useful commentary with a book list. The second more specifically Commonwealth category is the less well served. The bibliography at the end of Frank H. Underhill's *The British Commonwealth. An Experiment in Co-operation among Nations*, Durham N.C., 1956, is valuable while A. R. Hewitt's *Guide to Resources for Commonwealth Studies*, London, 1957, admirably fulfils its mainly research purposes. There are also more general guides in A. J. Horne, *The Commonwealth Today*, Library Association, 1965, and *Commonwealth History*, National Book League, 1965.

General histories are also apt to fall into the same two categories – those which are primarily histories of the British Empire, carrying over in some cases into the Commonwealth period but with their emphasis and perspective predominantly imperial; and those which focus their attention chiefly on Commonwealth. On Empire C. E. Carrington's lively *The British Overseas: Exploits of a Nation of Shopkeepers*, Cambridge, 1950, and D. K. Fieldhouse, *The Colonial Empires, a Comparative Survey from the Eighteenth Century*, London, 1966, provide general and, in the second case, comparative overall studies. Among more specialised works, chief place in respect of comprehensiveness is to be given to *The Cambridge History of the British Empire* in eight volumes. The first three, published over a wide spread of years, with the second appearing in 1940 and the third in 1959, relate the general history of British overseas expansion and imperial policy and the remaining five deal with the history of British India (2 vols), Canada and Newfoundland, Australia and New Zealand, and South Africa (2nd ed. 1963). Some of the regional volumes, however, are now so dated as to rank as works chiefly of historiographical interest. In the predominantly imperial category are also to be included Lord Elton, *Imperial Commonwealth*, London, 1945; some mainly narrative histories, of which Professor E. A. Walker's *The British Empire: Its Structure and Spirit* (2nd ed.), Cambridge, 1953; Paul Knaplund, *The British Empire 1815–1939*, London, 1942; A. P. Newton, *A Hundred Years of the British Empire*, London, 1940, are to be mentioned, and also works devoted to analysis of ideas notably Sir Ernest Barker, *Ideas and Ideals of the British Empire*, Cambridge, 1951; John Strachey's *End of Empire*, London, 1959; A. P. Thornton's *The Imperial Idea and its Enemies* (2nd ed.), London, 1966; R. Koebner and H. D. Schmidt's *Imperialism, The Story and Significance of a Political Word, 1840–1960*, Cambridge, 1964, a study in semantics not limited to 'Empire' in British history; C. A. Bodelsen's *Studies in Mid-Victorian Imperialism*, Copenhagen, 1924; and B. Porter, *Critics of Empire*, London, 1968. To these may be added four articles, D. G. Creighton, 'The Victorians and the Empire' in *The Canadian Historical Review*, vol. xix (1938); John Gallagher and Ronald Robinson, 'The Imperialism of Free Trade' in *The Economic History Review*, vol. vi, no. 1 (1953); W. K. Hancock, 'Agenda for the Study of British Imperial Economy 1850–1950' in *The Journal of Economic History*, vol. xiii no. 3 (1953); and D. K. Fieldhouse, ' "Imperialism": An Historiographical Revision' in *The Economic History Review*, vol. xiv (1961).

In the second, and more immediately relevant Commonwealth category, there is Professor F. H. Underhill's brief but incisive lecture review in the already mentioned *The British Commonwealth*. No full-scale interpretation of Commonwealth, as distinct from Empire, from its nineteenth-century origins to the present day appears to have been published. In respect of earlier, formative years there are works of historical and historiographical significance which, in whole or more often in part, throw light upon the developments which ultimately led to the emergence by name of a British Commonwealth of Nations. Among the more important of these, taking Sir C. P. Lucas (ed.), *Lord Durham's Report on the Affairs of British North America* (3 vols), Oxford, 1912, or Sir R. Coupland, *The Durham Report*, Oxford, 1945, as a starting-point, were Charles Buller, *Responsible Government for Colonies*, London, 1840; E. G. Wakefield, *A View of the Art of Colonization*, London, 1849; Goldwin Smith, *The Empire: A Series of Letters 1862–3*, London, 1863; J. R. Seeley, *The Expansion of England*, London, 1883; J. A. Froude, *Oceana: Or, England and Her Colonies*, London, 1886; C. W. Dilke, *Problems of Greater Britain*, London, 1890; J. A. Hobson, *Imperialism: A Study*, London, 1902 (5th imp. 1954); R. Jebb, *Studies in Colonial Nationalism*, London, 1905; L. C. Curtis, *The Problem of Commonwealth*, London, 1916; H. Bourassa, *Independence or Imperial Partnership? A Study of the 'Problems of the Commonwealth'*, Montreal, 1916. Of later date, but still relevant to the earlier formative period, H. Duncan Hall, *The British Commonwealth of Nations*, London, 1920; and A. Zimmern, *The Third British Empire*, London, 1926.

The Commonwealth as such has been studied historically mainly since 1918, with the publication of Professor W. K. Hancock's *Survey of British Commonwealth Affairs, Vol. 1, Problems of Nationality, 1918–1936*, Oxford, 1937, heralding a new phase in Commonwealth historiography. It was followed by the same author's *Survey*, vol. 2 (in two parts), Oxford, 1942, on *Problems of Economic Policy*. The series was continued after the war with N. Mansergh's *Survey of British Commonwealth Affairs: Problems of External Policy 1931–1939*, Oxford, 1952, and his *Problems of Wartime Cooperation and Post-War Change 1939–1952*, Oxford, 1958. In more recent years there has been evidence of appraisal and reappraisal on an extensive scale, with the emphasis shifting from comprehensive to regional, national and local studies, for which, however, the Commonwealth has continued to provide the setting. A selection of these works may be conveniently listed later under their regional or national headings.

The principal printed source material for the study of the history of the Commonwealth is to be found in the Reports of Colonial and Imperial Conferences and of Meetings of Commonwealth Prime Ministers and Heads of State; in the Parliamentary Debates and State Papers of Commonwealth member-states and in the Reports of particular Constitutional Conferences. Unpublished sources are rich and varied. On the British side are the official records of the relevant departments of state:– the Colonial Office, the India Office, the Dominions Office, later renamed the Commonwealth Relations and the Commonwealth Office and by 1966, responsible for relations with all member-states or territories of the Commonwealth, the Minutes of the Committee of Imperial Defence from its inception and Cabinet Papers and Minutes relating to Commonwealth issues. To these should be added Minutes of Imperial Conferences and, for the period 1917–9, those of the Imperial War Cabinet and British Empire Delegation to Paris. *The Records of the Cabinet Office to 1922*, Public Record Office Handbooks, no. 11, London, H.M.S.O., 1966, provides a valuable guide to Cabinet, Imperial War Cabinet, Imperial Conference and C.I.D. papers. The records of the inter-war Imperial Conferences down to and including those of the 1937 Conference have been consulted on important issues in the writing of this book, and are listed with the Cabinet Papers in the Public Record Office in London. These British official records, now available for inspection after thirty years, have their counterpart in the records of the dominions, of the Government of India down to 1947 and of member states of the Commonwealth. There is no uniformity in respect of the 'closed' period. Dominion records on Commonwealth relations in the earlier period are usually on the files of Prime Ministers' Offices, since even after the creation of departments of external affairs, the more important or delicate issues of Commonwealth policy remained under prime ministerial control. This unpublished official material is supplemented by collections of Private Papers, published or unpublished, among those consulted in the writing of this book being the papers of Sir Wilfrid Laurier, Sir Robert Borden and W. L. Mackenzie King (down to 1922), together with the published *The Mackenzie King Record 1939–1944*, Toronto, 1960, edited by J. W. Pickersgill and based on Mackenzie King's diary entries, in Canada; those of J. X. Merriman, J. C. Smuts down to 1919, as edited by W. K. Hancock and J. van der Poel and published in *Selections from the Smuts Papers* (4 vols), Cambridge, 1966, and Sir Patrick Duncan in South Africa; of the Viscount Bruce of Melbourne, for the years 1939–45 and of Sir Tej Bahadur Sapru, on particular points; on the British side, those of W. E. Gladstone and Sir Henry Campbell-Bannerman. There are many others.

Especially welcome in comparatively recent years has been the publication of autobiographies and biographies of outstanding Commonwealth interest. Among the former may be mentioned W. M. Hughes, *The Splendid Adventure*, London, 1929; Jawaharlal Nehru, *Autobiography*, London, 1936; Maulana Azad, *India Wins Freedom*, Bombay, 1959; Vincent Massey, *What's Past is Prologue*, Toronto, 1963, with its account, by no means uncritical, of diplomatic service under Mackenzie King's suspicious eye; Sir Robert Menzies, *Afternoon Light*, London, 1967; L. S. Amery, *My Political Life* (2 vols), vol. 2, *War and Peace*, London, 1953; and, from a distinctive standpoint, Sir Roy Welensky, *Welensky's 4000 Days*, London, 1964. Among the biographies should be listed D. G. Creighton, *John A. Macdonald* (2 vols), Toronto, 1952 and 1955; J. A. La Nauze, *Alfred Deakin* (2 vols), Melbourne, 1965; J. Schull, *Laurier*,

Toronto, 1965; C. M. van den Heever, *General J. B. M. Hertzog*, Johannesburg, 1946; T. de V. White, *Kevin O'Higgins*, London, 1948; W. K. Hancock, *Smuts* (2 vols), Cambridge, 1962 and 1968; Alan Paton, *Hofmeyr*, Cape Town, 1964, movingly illustrative of the problems of a liberal in a racially divided society; R. MacGregor Dawson and H. B. Neatby, *William Lyon Mackenzie King* (2 vols), Toronto, 1958 and 1963, Dawson's volume covering the years 1874–1923, Neatby's 1924–32, with succeeding volumes to come and already mentioned, J. W. Pickersgill, *The Mackenzie King Record 1939–1944*, vol. 1, which, being on the borderline of biography and personal record, is also deserving a place here; S. Gopal, *The Viceroyalty of Lord Irwin 1926–1931*, Oxford, 1957; M. Brecher, *Nehru, A Political Biography*, London, 1959; M. A. H. Ispahani, *Qaid-E-Azam Jinnah, As I Knew Him* (2nd ed.), Karachi, 1967; and in a rather different category with the Commonwealth seen, so to speak, from its symbolic apex, Harold Nicolson's *King George V*, London, 1952, especially chapters 21, 28 and 29, and Sir John Wheeler-Bennett's *King George VI*, London, 1958, especially chapter 11. Autobiographies, or biographies, of leading British statesmen, Churchill very much included with them, usually contain material of Commonwealth interest.

There are two periodicals devoted mainly or wholly to Commonwealth affairs – *The Round Table* and *The Journal of Commonwealth Political Studies*. The *Annual Register* year by year provides a near-contemporary record of Commonwealth developments.

Selections of the more important documents and speeches of general Commonwealth interest have been published in a number of volumes. G. Bennett, *The Concept of Empire, From Burke to Attlee* (2nd ed.), London, 1962, provides with convenient compactness an historical documentary background to changing ideas. The more important texts of Commonwealth interest are to be found in:—

K. N. Bell and W. P. Morrell, *Select Documents on British Colonial Policy, 1830–1860*, Oxford, 1953.

A. B. Keith, *Speeches and Documents on British Colonial Policy 1763–1917*, Oxford, 1948.

A. B. Keith, *Speeches and Documents on the British Dominions 1918–31*, Oxford, 1932.

A. F. Madden, *Imperial Constitutional Documents 1756–1952. A Supplement*, Oxford, 1953.

M. Ollivier, *The Colonial and Imperial Conferences from 1887–1937* (3 vols), H.M.S.O., Ottawa, 1954.

N. Mansergh, *Speeches and Documents on British Commonwealth Affairs 1931–1952* (2 vols), Oxford, 1953, and *Speeches and Documents on Commonwealth Affairs 1952–62*, Oxford, 1963.

J. Eayrs, *The Commonwealth and Suez*, Oxford, 1964.

There are also two collections of particular relevance relating to India, namely:

C. H. Philips, *The Evolution of India and Pakistan 1858–1945, Select Documents*, London, 1962.

Sir M. Gwyer and A. Appadorai, *Speeches and Documents on the Indian Constitution 1921–47*, (2 vols), Bombay, 1957.

The constitutional development of the Commonwealth has attracted the interest both of constitutional historians and of lawyers. There is much useful information to be found in the annual official publication known successively, in accord with changes in departmental nomenclature, as *The Dominions Office List*, *The Commonwealth Relations Office Year Book*, and from 1967, with the absorption of the Colonial Office, *The Commonwealth Office Year Book*, recent and much expanded issues being especially valuable. H. J. Harvey, *Consultation and Co-operation*, London, 1951, is useful for reference. J. A. Cross, *Whitehall and the Commonwealth*, London, 1967, sets out concisely the history of departmental responsibility in London for relations with the Commonwealth overseas, while R. Hyam in *Elgin and Churchill at the Colonial Office 1905–8: The Watershed of Empire-Commonwealth*, London, 1968, provides a study (which the present author had seen in typescript) in depth of the outlook and working of the Colonial Office in some critical years. J. E. Kendle has made a recent study of *The Colonial and Imperial Conferences 1887–1911*, London, 1967. Professor A. B. Keith, whose Minutes, as a Colonial Office official, on the restoration of self-government to the former Boer republics and on other constitutional questions may be read with difficulty but studied with profit, later made a formidable contribution to the study of dominion constitutional development in a number of books, his *Responsible Government in the Dominions* (2nd ed., 2 vols), London, 1928, being the standard work of the period. Also useful is R. MacG. Dawson (ed.), *The Development of Dominion Status 1900–1936*, London, 1937, a constitutional history in the form of a commentary upon documents reprinted in the second half of the book. For the later period the authoritative study is K. C. Wheare's *The Statute of Westminster and Dominion Status* (5th ed.), Oxford, 1953. The same author's *The Constitutional Structure of the Commonwealth*, Oxford, 1960, treats of developments in the post-Statute of Westminster period, as does S. A. de Smith's *The New Commonwealth and its Constitutions*, London, 1964, in the more particular context indicated by the title. W. I. Jennings and C. M. Young, *Constitutional Laws of the Commonwealth* (3rd ed.), London, 1957, vol. 1, *The Monarchies* (vol. 2, on *The Republics* has not been published) provides commentary and essential texts, while G. Marshall, *Parliamentary Sovereignty and the Commonwealth*, Oxford, 1957, uses South Africa as a test case, in a legal-constitutional enquiry into the effects of the enactment of the Statute of Westminster on the authority of the British and dominion parliaments. There is further G. W. Keeton's (ed.), *The British Commonwealth, The Development of its Laws and Constitutions*, London, 1951–, of which ten volumes have been published and which was intended as a series, to be comprehensive on a national basis – an intention which in view of the rapid constitutional changes, or transformations, in some member-states must seem more difficult of satisfactory fulfilment now than when first adopted. *Commonwealth and Colonial Law*, London, 1966, by Sir Kenneth Roberts-Wray, the former legal adviser to the Commonwealth Relations and Colonial Offices pronounces, with the authority of experience, on many matters at once complex and important. Of continuing interest is the last chapter in L. S. Amery's *Thoughts on the Constitution*, Oxford, 1953.

Government in the Commonwealth has produced many comparative studies. Outstanding among them are Alexander Brady's *Democracy in the Dominions* (3rd ed.), Toronto, 1958; and K. C. Wheare's *Federal Government* (3rd ed.), Oxford, 1956, which, while treating of federalism in general, pays much attention to federations within the Commonwealth. To these should be added A. H. Birch, *Federalism, Finance and Social Legislation in Canada, Australia and the United States*, Oxford, 1955; and W. S. Livingston's cogently argued *Federalism and Constitutional Change*, Oxford, 1956. Finally reference is to be made to two works by Sir Ivor Jennings, *The Commonwealth in Asia*, Oxford, 1951, and *The Dominion of Ceylon – The Development of its Laws and Constitution*, Oxford, 1952, compiled from the vantage point of the vice-chancellor's residence in Colombo and with personal knowledge of Ceylon's advance to independence.

War and international relations have much preoccupied the Commonwealth since the coming of the first world war and have received due attention from its historians. In respect of defence policies three general works may be mentioned: D. C. Gordon, *The Dominion Partnership in Imperial Defence 1870–1914*, Johns Hopkins, 1965; F. A. Johnson, *Defence by Committee*, London, 1960; and R. A. Preston, *Canada and 'Imperial Defense'*, Durham N.C., 1967; with Lord Hankey's *The Supreme Command 1914–18* (2 vols), London, 1961, written with authority but also, alas, with great discretion. Like the United Kingdom, both Australia and New Zealand have published official histories, both civil and military, of the second world war. The Australian Civil Series comprised five volumes, with one of broad historical interest by Paul Hasluck on *The Government and the People 1939–41*, Canberra, 1952, and a second to follow. F. L. W. Wood in *The New Zealand People at War: Political and External Affairs*, Wellington, 1958, provided the New Zealand counterpart to Hasluck's volume. Both authors wrote with unrestricted access to official records, including War Cabinet papers. Even more extensive are the publications on Commonwealth and international affairs. G. M. Carter's *The British Commonwealth and International Security*, Toronto, 1947, dealt with dominion attitudes to the League in the inter-war years, while of a more recent period Professor J. D. B. Miller's *The Commonwealth in the World* (2nd ed.), London, 1965, which provides a readable, general conspectus, may be supplemented by reference to individual national series, pioneered by the Canadian Institute of International Affairs, with their biennial reviews of *Canada in World Affairs*, and creating a precedent that has been followed with profit by the Australian Institute and by the Indian Council of World Affairs. These series reflect the expanding rôle of the Commonwealth states, other than Britain, in international affairs after the second world war. In *Commonwealth D'Abord*, Paris, 1955, Y. G. Brissonnière considered British Commonwealth relations with Europe from a continental standpoint and with attention to the possibility of association as distinct from membership.

The transfer of power in India and in the Colonial Empire attracted much attention, possibly overmuch in respect of its technical and ephemeral aspects, and apart from works of regional interest, some books may be mentioned as providing contemporary or near-contemporary background: H. V. Hodson, *Twentieth Century Empire*, London, 1948; R. Hinden, *Empire and After*, London, 1949; N. Mansergh, *The Commonwealth and the Nations*, London, 1948; Sir Ivor Jennings, *The Approach to Self-Government*, Cambridge, 1956; Sir Charles Jeffries, *Transfer of Power*, London, 1960; and W. B. Hamilton (ed.), *The Transfer of Institutions*, Duke, 1964. In respect of India, on British party attitudes there is Georges Fischer's *Le Parti travailliste et la décolonization de l'Inde*, Paris, 1966, and the as yet unpublished dissertation of K. Veerathappa on *The Attitude of the British Conservative Party to India's Demand for Independence*, unpublished dissertation, Indian School of International Studies, New Delhi, 1967. On the I.C.S. there is Philip Mason, *The Men who ruled India* (2 vols), London, 1953–54, especially vol. 2. On the conditions and circumstances of the transfer there is Sir Penderel Moon, *Divide and Quit*, London, 1962; I. M. Stephens, *Monsoon Morning*, London, 1966; A. Campbell-Johnson, *Mission with Mountbatten*, London, 1951; V. P. Menon (at the time Reforms Commissioner of the Government of India), *The Transfer of Power in India*, London, 1957; and E. W. R. Lumby, *The Transfer of Power in India*, London, 1954, all written in the light of personal experience and knowledge. The government and administration of former Colonial territories lies outside the scope of this bibliography, but useful for background to self-government and independence. M. Wight, *The Development of the Legislative Council, 1606–1945*, London, 1946, and *British Colonial Constitutions*, Oxford, 1952; Kenneth Robinson, *The Dilemmas of Trusteeship*, London, 1965 (a highly compressed and valuable review); R. Heussler, *Yesterday's Rulers*, Oxford, 1963; Margery Perham, *The Colonial Reckoning*, London, 1961; and, for the first-hand impressions of the last phase as seen by *The Times* correspondent in Africa, W. P. Kirkman's, *Unscrambling an Empire*, London, 1966.

There have been some general works on the period subsequent to the transfer of power in India. Here a notable place is to be given to *The Commonwealth*, London, 1962, by Patrick Gordon Walker, a former Labour Secretary of State for Commonwealth Relations and a commited supporter of the Commonwealth connection. A popular exposition is to be found in Sir Kenneth Bradley, *The Living Commonwealth*, London, 1961. There are also two collections of specialised studies by divers hands from the Commonwealth Studies Center at Duke University: N. Mansergh *et al*, *Commonwealth Perspectives*, Durham N.C., 1959; and W. B. Hamilton, K. Robinson and C. D. W. Goodwin (eds), *A Decade of the Commonwealth, 1955–64*, Durham N.C., 1966. The Proceedings of the Fourth Unofficial Commonwealth Relations Conference at Bigwin Inn, Ontario, 1949, provide the material for F. H. Soward's *The Changing Commonwealth*, Oxford, 1950, and the Fifth, held at Lahore in 1954, for N. Mansergh's *The Multi-Racial Commonwealth*, London, 1955. J. D. B. Miller has contributed a study of *Britain and the Old Dominions*, London, 1966, in the period of decolonisation and consequent Commonwealth expansion, and H. V. Wiseman one of *Britain and the Commonwealth*, London, 1967.

Finally a small selection from works of regional or national interest may be listed as providing an all-important counterbalance to more widely ranging over-all Commonwealth studies and also as an indication of the contemporary and often remarkable growth of historical studies in many parts of the Commonwealth overseas. Each list is prefaced by one or two general works and some include studies read by the author, but not yet published. Other books which have been consulted are listed in the footnotes to each chapter.

CANADA

G. E. Graham, *Canada*, London, 1950.
J. M. S. Careless, *Canada. A Story of Challenge*, Cambridge, 1953.
D. G. Creighton, *Dominion of the North* (2nd ed.), Toronto, 1965.
A. R. M. Lower, *Colony to Nation* (4th ed.), Toronto, 1964.

Chester New, *Lord Durham's Mission to Canada*, Oxford, 1929 rpt. Toronto, 1963.

D. G. Creighton, *The Road to Confederation 1863–67*, Toronto, 1964.

P. B. Waites (ed.), *The Confederation Debates on the Province of Canada 1865*, Toronto, 1863.

D. M. L. Farr, *The Colonial Office and Canada, 1867–1887*, Toronto, 1956.

G. P. de T. Glazebrook, *A History of Canadian External Relations*, Toronto, 1950.

James Eayrs, *In Defense of Canada* (2 vols), Toronto, 1964; vol. 2, especially throws light on Commonwealth international policies in the period of appeasement.

F. M. Wade, *The French Canadians, 1760–1945*, Toronto, 1956.

AUSTRALIA AND NEW ZEALAND

C. M. H. Clark (ed.), *Select Documents in Australian History* (2 vols), Sydney, 1950 and 1955.

J. M. Ward, *Empire in the Antipodes*, London, 1966.

A. G. L. Shaw, *Convicts and the Colonies*, London, 1966.

G. Greenwood (ed.), *Australia: A Social and Political History*, Sydney, 1955.

T. R. Reese, *Australia in the Twentieth Century*, London, 1964.

D. Pike, *Australia: The Quiet Continent*, Cambridge, 1962.

Alfred Deakin, *The Federal Story* (revised ed. by J. A. La Nauze), Melbourne, 1963.

L. F. Crisp, *The Parliamentary Government of the Commonwealth of Australia* (rev. ed.), London, 1961.

J. D. B. Miller, *Australian Government and Politics* (2nd ed.), London, 1965.

G. Sawer, *Australian Government Today* (rev. ed.), Melbourne, 1964.

J. C. Beaglehole, *New Zealand*, London, 1936.

W. P. Reeves, *The Long White Cloud*, London, 1898.

F. L. W. Wood, *Understanding New Zealand*, New York, 1949.

H. Miller, *New Zealand*, London, 1950.

K. Sinclair, *A History of New Zealand* (2nd ed.), London, 1961.

K. Sinclair, *The Origins of the Maori Wars*, Wellington, 1957, and *Imperial Federation. A Study of New Zealand Policy and Opinion 1880–1914*, London, 1955.

Angus Ross, *New Zealand Aspirations in the Pacific in the Nineteenth-Century*, Oxford, 1964.

A. Siegfried, *Democracy in New Zealand*, London, 1914.

C. G. F. Simkin, *The Instability of a Dependent Economy 1840–1914*, Oxford, 1951.

AFRICA

J. Gallagher and R. E. Robinson, *Africa and the Victorians*, London, 1961.
C.W. de Kiewiet, *A History of South Africa: Social and Economic*, Oxford, 1946.
E. A. Walker, *A History of Southern Africa* (3rd ed.), London, 1957.
J. S. Galbraith, *Reluctant Empire: British Policy on the South African Frontier, 1834–1854*, Berkeley, 1963.
F. A. van Jaarsveld, *The Awakening of Afrikaner Nationalism 1868–1881*, Cape Town, 1961.
C. W. de Kiewiet, *The Imperial Factor in South Africa*, Cambridge, 1937.
G. H. Le May, *British Supremacy in South Africa, 1899–1907*, Oxford, 1965.
C. F. Goodfellow, *Great Britain and South African Confederation*, Cape Town, 1966.
*Jean van der Poel, *The Jameson Raid*, Cape Town, 1951.
*Elizabeth Pakenham, *Jameson's Raid*, London, 1960.
G. B. Pyrah, *Imperial Policy and South Africa, 1902–1910*, Oxford, 1955.
J. S. Marais, *The Fall of Kruger's Republic*, Oxford, 1961.
N. Mansergh, *South Africa 1906–1961; The Price of Magnanimity*, London, 1962.
L. M. Thompson, *The Unification of South Africa 1902–1910*, Oxford, 1960.
G. M. Carter, *The Politics of Inequality*, New York, 1958.
D. W. Krüger, *South African Parties and Policies, 1910–1960*, Cape Town, 1960.
Albert Luthuli, *Let my People Go*, London, 1962.
Dennis Austin, *Britain and South Africa*, London, 1966.
A. J. Hanna, *The Beginnings of Nyasaland and North-Eastern Rhodesia 1859–95*, Oxford, 1956.
P. Mason, *Birth of a Dilemma*, London, 1958.
Colin Leys, *European Politics in Southern Rhodesia*, Oxford, 1959.
L. H. Gann, *The Birth of a Plural Society*, Manchester, 1958.
C. Palley, *The Constitutional History and Law of Southern Rhodesia*, Oxford, 1966.
J. D. Fage, *An Introduction to the History of West Africa* (3rd ed.), Cambridge, 1962.
J. E. Flint, *Nigeria and Ghana*, New York, 1966.
C. W. Newbury, *The West African Commonwealth*, Duke, N.C., 1964.
Dennis Austin, *Politics in Ghana, 1946–1960*, London, 1964.

---

* To these two books should be added Dr Ethel M. Drus' articles in the Bulletin of the Institute of Historical Research 1952, vol. xxv and in the E.H.R. October 1953 vol. lxviii, *A Report on the Papers of Joseph Chamberlain, relating to the Jameson Raid, and the Inquiry* and *The Question of Imperial Complicity in the Jameson Raid* respectively. It is a curious fact that the Jameson raid, which on any reckoning was an altogether manly affair should have attracted so much attention from women historians.

IRELAND

J. C. Beckett, *The Making of Modern Ireland 1603–1923*, London, 1966.
N. Mansergh, *The Irish Question, 1840–1921*, London, 1965.
F. A. Pakenham, *Peace by Ordeal*, London, 1935.
D. Williams (ed.), *The Irish Struggle 1916–1922*, London, 1966.
D. Harkness, *The Irish Free State and the British Commonwealth of Nations, 1921–32*, London, 1968.
H. Harrison, *Ireland and the British Empire, 1937: Conflict or Collaboration?* London, 1937.

SOUTH AND SOUTH-EAST ASIA

C. H. Philips, *India*, London, 1949.
T. G. P. Spear, *India*, Michigan, 1961.
K. M. Panikkar, *Asia and Western Dominance*, London, 1953.
E. Stokes, *The English Utilitarians and India*, Oxford, 1959.
S. Gopal, *British Policy in India 1858–1905*, Cambridge, 1965.
R. J. Moore, *Liberalism and Indian Politics 1872–1922*, London, 1966.
Sir R. Coupland, *India: A Restatement*, Oxford, 1945.
Sir P. Griffith, *The British Impact on India*, London, 1952.
J. Nehru, *The Discovery of India*, London, 1946.
M. Edwardes, *The Last Years of British India*, London, 1963.
H. Tinker, *Experiment with Freedom: India and Pakistan 1947*, London, 1967.
W. H. Morris Jones, *Parliament in India* (2nd ed.), London, 1965.
R. Symonds, *The Making of Pakistan* (3rd ed.), London, 1951.
G. W. Choudhury, *Pakistan's Relations with India 1947–1966*, London, 1968.
I. M. Stephens, *Pakistan*, London, 1963.
S. R. Mehrotra, *India and the Commonwealth, 1885–1929*, London, 1965.
B. H. Farmer, *Ceylon: A Divided Nation*, London, 1963.
H. Tinker, *The Union of Burma* (4th ed.), Oxford, 1967.

UNPUBLISHED CAMBRIDGE UNIVERSITY PH.D DISSERTATIONS

D. G. Hoskin, *The Genesis and Significance of the 1886 Home Rule Split in the Liberal Party*.
D. J. N. Denoon, *Reconstruction in the Transvaal 1900–1905*.
M. N. Lettice, *Anglo-Australian Relations 1901–1914. A Study at the Official Level*.
M. Hasan, *The Transfer of Power to Pakistan and its Consequences*.

INDEX